PENGUIN BOOKS

A HISTORY OF WALES

John Davies is a native of the Rhondda. He was educated at schools in Treorci, Bwlch-llan and Tregaron and at University College, Cardiff, and Trinity College, Cambridge. His wife comes from Blaenau Gwent, and they have two daughters and two sons. Until recently he was a member of the Department of Welsh History at the University of Wales, Aberystwyth, and Warden of Neuadd Pantycelyn. He now lives in Cardiff. His other publications include *Cardiff and the Marquesses of Bute*, *Broadcasting and the BBC in Wales* and *The Making of Wales*.

This volume, first published in Welsh as *Hanes Cymru* in 1991 won the Welsh Arts Council Book Prize for Non-fiction for that year.

JOHN DAVIES

———

A HISTORY OF WALES

PENGUIN BOOKS

For
A. E. H.

PENGUIN BOOKS

Published by the Penguin Group
Penguin Books Ltd, 27 Wrights Lane, London W8 5TZ, England
Penguin Putnam Inc., 375 Hudson Street, New York, New York 10014, USA
Penguin Books Australia Ltd, Ringwood, Victoria, Australia
Penguin Books Canada Ltd, 10 Alcorn Avenue, Toronto, Ontario, Canada M4V 3B2
Penguin Books (NZ) Ltd, 182–190 Wairau Road, Auckland 10, New Zealand

Penguin Books Ltd, Registered Offices: Harmondsworth, Middlesex, England

First published in Welsh, under the title *Hanes Cymru*,
by Allen Lane The Penguin Press 1990
First published in English by Allen Lane 1993
First published in Penguin 1994
7 9 10 8 6

Printed in England by Clays Ltd, St Ives plc

Contents

===

List of Maps and Diagrams

===

Preface to the Original (Welsh) Edition

━━━

Over the years, Penguin Books, through its Pelican series, has been building up a library of volumes on the history of the nations. When Peter Carson, Penguin's Editor in Chief, considered adding Wales to the list, he decided to commission a volume in Welsh, an unexpected but highly commendable decision by one of the most distinguished publishing houses of the English-speaking world. In agreeing to accept the commission, I seized the opportunity to write a lengthy volume spanning the whole course of the history of Wales and the Welsh. When I had finished, I had a typescript which was almost three times larger than the original commission. Penguin Books was so gracious as to accept the typescript in its entirety and decided to publish it as a hardback volume under the Allen Lane imprint rather than as a paperback in the Pelican series.

In recent years, Welsh historians have been remarkably lively and productive. While this volume was in the press a number of excellent studies appeared, among them the comprehensive contributions of Professors R. R. Davies, Glanmor Williams and Geraint H. Jenkins to the series on the history of Wales published jointly by the Clarendon Press and the University of Wales Press. I had hoped to provide an account of the history of Wales which would take the story up to the present day. But the essence of history is constant change and, while printing was in progress, there were important developments which have not been fully discussed in the book. Among the most significant of them was the increasing concern about the environment and the transformation of many Welsh communities in the wake of the huge momentum in the housing market.

A great deal of this book was written away from home. The University College of Wales kindly allowed me sabbatical leave, a splendid opportunity to take myself off and write without interruption. The first three chapters were written while I was in contact with the European University in Florence and I am much indebted to that excellent institution. The fourth was written in various hotels in Italy, Greece and Germany, and I thank the many hoteliers who eased the way for me. The fifth and sixth were written while I was a fellow of the Institute of Advanced Studies at Edinburgh University, and the kindness I received at Edinburgh was a memorable experience. The remaining chapters were written in Neuadd Pantycelyn, and I am grateful to the civilized community residing there for allowing me the leisure and providing me with the inspiration to carry on with the task.

I amassed many obligations while preparing this book. My first debt is to my friend Dr Harri Pritchard-Jones, who set me on my way. My colleagues in the Department of Welsh History and my fellow-wardens at Neuadd Pantycelyn were particularly obliging. In particular, I wish to thank Mrs Tegwen Owen, the bursar of Neuadd Pantycelyn, for her ready cooperation over the years. I received every assistance from Penguin Books, especially from Peter Carson, Stephen Davies, Jonathan Riley and Karen Mitchell. Various chapters of the book were read by Professor Ellis Evans, Professor Beverley Smith, Dr Llinos Smith, Professor Glanmor Williams, Professor Ieuan Gwynedd Jones and Dr Deian Hopkin and I benefited enormously from their comments. Dr John Rowlands was particularly kind to me; he corrected the entire typescript, thus vastly improving it in terms of grammar and clarity of expression. The text was edited by Robert Jones and Richard Owen, who proved to be impressively thorough. I also thank Glenys Howells for assisting with the proofs. I wish to acknowledge the many kindnesses I received from librarians, particularly those of the library of the University College of Wales, the National Library of Wales, the National Library of Scotland and the library of the European University. I am grateful for the assistance I received from the David Hughes-Parry Fund. Most of the typing was done by Linda Healy and Delyth Fletcher, to whom I am much indebted. I also thank Raymond Turvey for turning my crude drawings into attractive maps and charts.

My chief debt, however, is to the commote of Ystrad Yw in Brecknock. Ystrad Yw is Carnhuanawc country, and I would be delighted if it were considered that this volume is in his tradition. It is also the native district of my wife, Janet Mackenzie Davies, and had I not known that I would receive her assistance I would not have undertaken this task. I have been singularly fortunate in the females in my life – all six of them. This book is dedicated to the first of them.

Department of Welsh History   John Davies
University College of Wales   Neuadd Pantycelyn
Aberystwyth   Aberystwyth
                                                                        2 October 1987

Preface to the Translation

This book was written in Welsh, with a Welsh-speaking readership in mind. If it had been originally written in English, it would have been a different book. I did consider rewriting it, with an English-speaking readership in mind, but as there seemed to be a demand among English-speakers to read what was already available to Welsh-speakers, I decided to do no more than translate the original. Once more, I am vastly indebted to my wife, Janet Mackenzie Davies. Penguin Books has again treated me with great kindness and patience and I am particularly grateful to David Duguid for his thoroughness and perspicacity.

Hanes Cymru, and its translated version, bring the story up to the late 1980s. Since then, the march of history has continued. Mining under the auspices of the National Coal Board has almost been consigned to oblivion, as, apparently, has the Board itself. Hopes that the south Wales coalfield would be revitalized through the Valleys Initiative have not as yet been fulfilled. The vast momentum in the housing market, referred to in the original preface, has been succeeded by a property slump. Unemployment, which had fallen to 6.3 per cent in April 1990, stood at 10 per cent in October 1992.

The general election of 1992 showed that the trend apparent in 1987 – the recovery of the Labour Party from its nadir in 1983 – was continuing. Its share of the popular vote rose to 49.5 per cent and it won twenty-seven of the thirty-eight Welsh constituencies. The election also confirmed that the Conservative advance which manifested itself in 1979 and 1983 has ebbed. The party now has six seats in comparison with fourteen in 1983. The Liberals (now the Liberal Democrats), who won thirty-one of the thirty-four seats in Wales in the general election of 1892, held only one a century later. In 1992, Plaid Cymru added Ceredigion and Pembroke North to the three seats it already held, and it is now possible to travel from Fishguard to Holyhead without leaving Plaid Cymru-held territory.

The growth of Welsh institutions has continued apace with the establishment of organizations as diverse as the Curriculum Council for Wales and the Countryside Council for Wales. At the Welsh Office, Peter Walker has come and gone, yielding his place to David Hunt. A number of factors, the increasing prominence of the European dimension in particular, have caused the devolution issue to return to the political agenda, and several of the anti-devolutionists of 1979 have publicly expressed contrition. From 1911 to 1981 the number of Welsh speakers declined census by census. In 1991, however, those claiming a knowledge of the language were marginally more numerous than had been the case in 1981, and the increase among the younger age groups was especially remarkable. Thus the sentiments expressed in the last paragraph of this volume are increasingly valid; indeed, it is more stimulating to be a member of the Welsh nation in the last decade of the twentieth century than it has ever been before.

John Davies
Pontcanna
Cardiff
October 1992

Further Reading

As I was writing this book, I noted the sources of quotations, together with a vast number of references to books and articles, but it soon became apparent that the publication of the notes would double the size of the book.

Those who wish to read extensively in the field should consult Philip Henry Jones, *A Bibliography of the History of Wales* (third edition, microfiche, 1988). *The Local Historian* (volume 17, numbers 5 and 6) contains an article entitled 'What to read on the history of Wales', and there are lively notes on books and articles in Gwyn A. Williams, *When Was Wales?* (1988). So far, four volumes have appeared in the series on the history of Wales published jointly by the Clarendon Press and the University of Wales Press and there are valuable bibliographies in each one of them. See R. R. Davies, *Conquest, Coexistence and Change, Wales, 1063–1415* (1986), Glanmor Williams, *Recovery, Reorientation and Reformation, Wales, c.1415–1642* (1987), Geraint H. Jenkins, *The Foundations of Modern Wales, 1642–1760* (1987) and Kenneth O. Morgan, *Rebirth of a Nation, Wales, 1880–1980* (1981). On the period before 1063, there are useful lists in H. N. Savoury and others, *Ancient Monuments in Wales* (1976), and in Wendy Davies, *Wales in the Early Middle Ages* (1982). For the earlier part of the period 1760–1880, there is a bibliographical essay by Gwyn A. Williams in David Smith (ed.), *A People and a Proletariat* (1980); for the later period see Ieuan Gwynedd Jones, *Explorations and Explanations* (1981).

CHAPTER ONE

The Beginnings: Paviland, Tinkinswood
and Llyn Cerrig Bach

Once upon a time, the Welsh knew when their history began. It began about 1170 BC. That was when the Ark of the Covenant was captured by the Philistines and when Brutus, a descendant of the Trojans, landed on the shores of Britain. Apart from a few giants, the island had no inhabitants. Brutus and his companions were the first of the Britons and the ancestors of the Welsh. This was Geoffrey of Monmouth's account of the early history of Britain, written in AD 1136, an account which would be central to the consciousness of the Welsh for many centuries.

Such precision about the beginnings of Wales and the Welsh has long ceased to be tenable. It is possible to suggest a number of dates as the starting-point of the history of Wales: it appears that Wales as a territory having a coast-line similar to that of today came into existence around 6000 BC; Wales, or part of it, tiptoes into the historical record for the first time with Tacitus's description of the Roman attack in AD 48 upon the Deceangli, a tribe living between the rivers Clwyd and Dee; the royal houses of Wales traced their origins to the generation before AD 400; it is likely that the name *Cymry* was adopted around AD 580; the territory of Wales was defined with some exactness about AD 790 with the building of Offa's Dyke. There are valid arguments for beginning the story with any one of these dates. Yet it would be better to begin in the beginning with the earliest evidence of the presence of human beings in that part of the world which was eventually to be known as Wales. But what kind of evidence? If it is assumed that the task of the historian is to offer an interpretation of the past based upon written evidence, then the story must begin in AD 48. But if history is a study of the past based upon the widest possible variety of sources, then the story begins not two thousand but more than two hundred thousand years ago.

Although the techniques of the archaeologist are very different from those of the historian, both are involved in the same task – that of analysing change and development in human society. To begin with 'history' and to ignore 'prehistory' is to lose sight of the basic fact that, when the people of Wales first appeared upon the stage of history, almost every development of importance had already taken place. That people could create and control fire, cook food, cultivate the land, rear stock, build dwellings, make metal, brew beer, theorize about the world to come, produce fine art, cure sickness, practise literature, maintain political structures and kill and oppress their fellow-creatures. That is, they had all the cultural, spiritual and social attributes of humanity. Furthermore, the technical knowledge which would maintain the economic foundations of society, at least for the following eighteen centuries, was almost all already known to them. The main difference between them and the people of the centuries to come was the inability of anyone among them to produce written material, and that was hardly a great difference when it is considered how scarce and fragmentary such material would be for at least another thousand years.

By AD 48, communities of human beings had been in existence in Wales, in unbroken sequence, for ten thousand years and more, but there is evidence of their temporary presence hundreds of centuries earlier. Some fifteen or twenty million years have passed since the earliest hominids developed characteristics not shared by other species of apes, and over the succeeding thousands of millennia they progressed to or achieved or were granted humanity. These develop-ments occurred in the warmer parts of the Earth, and it is only in the last half a million years that *homo sapiens* has spread over the greater part of the world. This happened in the later period of the Pleistocene Era (the most recent of the geological ages), an era of great fluctuations in climate and environment. There were lengthy periods when the whole of Wales was covered with ice, but there were others when the temperature was as least as high as it is today. The level of the sea varied from about 150 metres below the present level to eight metres above. The flora changed with the climate from tundra vegetation to a lush covering of hazel, oak and beech.

The earliest evidence of the presence of man in Britain comes from Eartham in Sussex, where the artefacts discovered have been dated to around 350,000 BC. They were produced by people of the culture of the Lower Palaeolithic Age, the earliest period of the Old Stone Age. Of the Lower Palaeolithic objects to have been found in Britain, 97 per cent come from the south-eastern parts of the island – although in that period it was only occasionally that it was an island. These are the parts defined by Cyril Fox as the Lowland Zone of Britain. Fox's theory concerning the 'personality' of Britain, with its emphasis upon the differences between the lowland south and east and the highland north and west – although it has been revised over the years – has strongly influenced the study of the varied communities of the island. Wales belongs to the Highland Zone, one of the factors which has given the country a measure of identity throughout the ages. It would be wrong, of course, to suggest that the culture of the prehistoric inhabitants of Wales had an identity not shared by inhabitants of other parts of Britain. Nevertheless, some of the elements which have nurtured the distinctiveness of Wales over the last two thousand years existed five and ten thousand years earlier. Geography and geology have given Wales a form and a shape. In consequence, the personality of Wales and the culture of its people over many millennia are valid subjects of study, as the work of archaeologists of the greatest distinction amply testifies.

The only evidence of the presence in Wales of people of the Lower Palaeolithic cultures comes from caves. The most exciting evidence is that from Pontnewydd cave in the Elwy valley in Clwyd. It is a human tooth whose owner lived about 250,000 years ago. Despite the jocular suggestion of the editor of *Antiquity* that the tooth had been in the mouth of the 'first Welshman', it would be misleading to suggest that its owner was among the ancestors of the present inhabitants of Wales. It would also probably be mistaken to think of him as a native of Wales, for in the climate of his time even a small population group would have needed a territory larger than Wales from which to draw its sustenance. It may be supposed that the tooth's owner was a member of a tribe of a few hundred roaming vast expanses extending from Wales to the Netherlands. The hand axe found at Pen-y-lan near Cardiff belongs roughly to the same period, and that too probably belonged to a visitor rather than to a permanent resident. Subsequently, as the cold intensified, there were tens of thousands of years when Wales was wholly uninhabited. Human beings may have returned between 125,000 and 70,000 BC, an era during which there were comparatively mild periods, and it is believed that they left evidence in the caves of Coygan and Laugharne in Dyfed. Then, about 70,000 BC, the latest of the Ice Ages began. It was interrupted by periods of greater warmth around 59,000 and 37,000 BC, when caves at Pontnewydd and Ffynnon Beuno in Clwyd, Coygan in Dyfed and Paviland in Gower may have been occupied by people of the Mousterian culture.

There was an improvement in the quality of artefacts from about 35,000 BC. This marked the beginning of the Upper Palaeolithic Age, which lasted until about 8500 BC. In France, it was characterized by a succession of cultures – the Aurignacian around 28,000, the Gravettian around 20,000 and the Magdalenian around 10,000 BC. The people of those cultures produced knives, chisels and needles as well as hand axes. They had some form of religion and they possessed striking artistic talents, as the paintings in the caves of the Dordogne valley bear witness. Hunters and gatherers rather than producers of food, they dwelt, according to the brilliant archaeologist Gordon Childe, in 'palaeolithic savagery', although they showed a rich understanding of their environment and a sophisticated ability to profit from flocks and herds and shoals. In Britain, about forty sites have yielded evidence of the earlier period of the Upper Palaeolithic Age. A quarter are in Wales, among them Paviland and Ffynnon Beuno, where tools dated to around 26,000 BC have been discovered. Some sixty sites belonging to the later period have been identified, ten of which are in Wales. Of all the Upper Palaeolithic remains, the most famous is the 'Red Lady of Paviland', a skeleton which William Buckland, who discovered it in 1823, considered to be that of a young woman of the Roman era. Earlier in this century, it was believed that the bones were those of a young man who lived about 16,000 BC, a time when the climate was exceptionally severe. However, the skeleton has now been dated to about 24,000 BC, when the temperature was rather higher. The care taken in interring the bones and the red ochre with which they were coloured suggest that they received a ritual burial, with the soul of the 'Red Lady' being entrusted to the gods (or more likely the goddesses) of his people.

The ice began its final retreat around 10,000 BC. By 8300 BC Wales was free of glaciers, and the temperature continued to rise until 3000 BC, when northern Europe was some 2.5° C warmer than it is today. The change had a revolutionary impact upon the environment. As the glaciers melted, vast quantities of water were released, causing

Britain to become an island. The Severn Sea came into existence and a sea rather than a strait came to separate Wales from Ireland. The story of the drowning of Cantre'r Gwaelod and the assertion in the *Mabinogi* that the waters between Wales and Ireland had once been narrower and shallower may represent very ancient folk memories of these changes. With the higher temperatures, the land was clothed with trees – birch first and then pine, hazel, alder and oak. By 5500 BC, the whole of Wales with the exception of the sand dunes and the high places over 750 metres was covered by a thick canopy of forest. The reindeer, the bison and the mammoth vanished and their place was taken by the red deer, the boar and the ox. This led to the destruction of the Palaeolithic economy, based as it was upon a symbiotic relationship between man and the wild herds. The new fauna was less gregarious than the old and because of the density of the woodland there was a dearth of open grassland.

These changes took place with considerable rapidity, although the pace of change was not so great that man was unable to demonstrate his ability to adapt himself to his environment and to begin to adapt the environment to his own needs. In the Near East, where the rise in temperature led to aridity and the expansion of the desert, the inhabitants reacted by inventing agriculture. One of the great revelations which have come in the wake of the Carbon 14 dating method – a discovery which has revolutionized archaeology – is the antiquity of this development. There were villages of farmers in Iraq by 9000 BC, at least two thousand years earlier than was supposed a generation ago. The invention of agriculture lay at the heart of what Gordon Childe called the 'Neolithic Revolution'. Of all the crucial steps taken by mankind, claimed Childe, this was the most momentous. It was the mainspring of progress: agriculture made possible the rise of settled, populous communities and all that developed from that – permanent buildings, cities, political structures. The growing of crops – grain in particular – meant that food could be stored. A community could therefore produce and amass goods in excess of its basic needs; that is, it had a surplus, it created capital. The existence of a surplus allows some members of the community to be released from the task of ensuring an adequate supply of food, enabling them to develop other skills; this was the beginning of the division of labour and of social stratification. A community owning a surplus can become the object of the envy of other communities, motivating them to arm themselves to take possession, not so much of the land of the farmers as of the farmers themselves, and to turn them into slaves or serfs to serve their conquerors.

This interpretation of the 'Neolithic Revolution' has been severely criticized: 'a tired concept' says Piggott; 'simplistic and superficial' says Ellis Evans. It implies too definite a gulf between the hunter/gatherer on the one hand and the agriculturalist on the other. The portrayal by Gordon Childe and his followers of the ascent from the savage huntsman to the barbaric farmer and on to the urban and literate civilization of the empires of antiquity suggests a crude evolutionism, and it can be little more than a weapon to justify imperialism. The life of a hunter is not necessarily more savage than that of an agriculturalist; it can be less tyrannous and implicit in it is a profound understanding of the relationship between man and his fellow-creatures. Yet although there is substance to the criticism of the 'Revolution', it is difficult to deny that the coming of agriculture represents a fundamental turning-point. The older generation of archaeologists were, perhaps, too ready to assume that all change represents progress, but they were wholly correct in their emphasis upon the degree to which change accelerated as man won an increasing measure of mastery over his environment. After the hundreds of thousands of years of minimal change in the pre-agricultural era, there are only some eleven thousand years between the first farm and the atomic bomb and the computer. As man's material capital increased, man himself could multiply, and there has been no more dynamic factor in the history of the human species than the numbers of its members.

Wales was a long way from these developments, although it was to be drawn into them eventually. In Wales, as in the rest of north-western Europe, the new environment created by the retreat of the ice prompted a different reaction. In the Mesolithic Age, which lasted in Britain from about 8500 to about 4500 BC, man learnt to hunt the small animals of the forest, to exploit the food offered by the warmer seas and lakes, and to develop equipment – microlithic arrows, nets and boats – to catch his prey. It is quite possible that he did more than that. There is some evidence that he used fire to destroy forests in order to create glades in which animals could be penned, and dogs had been tamed to help with the work by about 8000 BC. It is likely also that he (or rather she – it appears that it was the women who were the gatherers) sought to protect particularly productive plants and trees. Thus the Mesolithic peoples developed into quasi-pastoralists and quasi-agriculturalists before the coming of a fully fledged agriculture. Such an agriculture could not have been independently developed by the inhabitants of north-western Europe, for its essentials – grain to plant and ruminants suitable for domestication – were not indigenous to their part of the world.

Tools and some evidence of the dwelling-places of the Mesolithic inhabitants of Wales have been discovered in about half a dozen sites, among them Prestatyn, Aberystwyth, Burry Holmes (Gower) and Nab Head (Pembroke). The site of Starr Car in Yorkshire has been thoroughly excavated and the results of the excavation are probably broadly relevant to the sparse Mesolithic population of Wales. In about 7600 BC, a community of some two hundred and fifty people dwelt at Starr Car. Their chief source of food was the meat of the red deer; they used hunting dogs and they sought their sustenance over a territory of twenty-five kilometres square. The Mesolithic remains discovered in Wales lack the distinction found in more advanced Mesolithic cultures such as the Azilian culture of France and the Maglemosian culture of Denmark. Nevertheless, they prove that man in Wales had responded successfully to the challenge of a new environment and that his species was rather more numerous there than it had been in the previous age.

Until the 1960s, it was believed that there were no agriculturalists in Britain until the years around 2000 BC, and the Neolithic Age, the age of farmers lacking metal, was considered to have lasted for about four hundred years. Another of the revelations of Carbon 14 is that there were fairly numerous communities of agriculturalists in Britain by 4000 BC, and that the Neolithic Age came to an end around about the period when previously it was thought to have begun. The first of the farmers of Wales were colonists from mainland Europe who brought with them their grain and stock. There is a conflict of views concerning the relationship between the Neolithic incomers and the Mesolithic natives. According to one interpretation, the scanty Mesolithic population was swept aside, although ethnographers once believed that something of their characteristics could be found among the population of mid-Wales. The inhabitants of the Pumlumon region were much surprised when H. J. Fleure, in seeking to substantiate the theory, set about measuring their heads. According to another

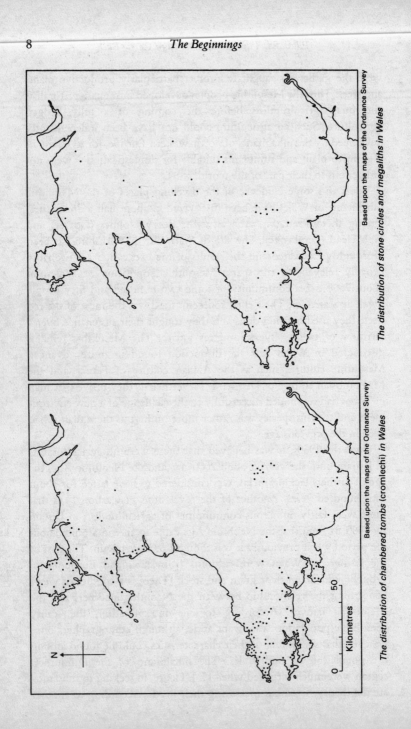

The distribution of chambered tombs (cromlechi) in Wales

Based upon the maps of the Ordnance Survey

The distribution of stone circles and megaliths in Wales

Based upon the maps of the Ordnance Survey

Kilometres

0   50

N

interpretation, the relationship was highly creative, for it was in precisely those areas where the intrusive farmers met the indigenous population that architecture was born. The western extremities of Europe – Spain, Brittany, Britain and Ireland – are dotted with the megalithic structures usually known as *cromlechi*, although it should be remembered that to the archaeologist the *cromlech* is only one version of such structures. It used to be assumed that the inspiration to build the *cromlechi* came from the Near East, but through another of the revelations of Carbon 14 it has been proved that they are the first substantial, permanent constructions of man and that the earliest of them are nearly fifteen hundred years older than the first of the pyramids of Egypt.

There are about a hundred and fifty *cromlechi* in Wales. The first generations of farmers lacked the resources to build them but, as the agriculturalists won increasing mastery over their environment, flourishing communities developed. In order to create arable and grazing land, forests had to be destroyed, and by 3500 BC the task of transforming the landscape was under way in districts such as the Vale of Glamorgan, Pembroke, Anglesey and the Usk valley. This was the period of *cromlech* building; the Gwernvale *cromlech* in the Usk valley was closed about 3500 BC and there was major work afoot at Barclodiad y Gawres, Anglesey, around 3200 BC. The ability to build *cromlechi* indicates the existence of communities far more populous than those of previous ages. In the Vale of Glamorgan, for example, the labour of at least two hundred men would have been needed to crown the Tinkinswood *cromlech* with its capstone. They are also proof of the wide-ranging connections of the inhabitants of Neolithic Wales: Barclodiad y Gawres is in the tradition of the rich culture of the Boyne valley in Ireland, while the *cromlechi* of Glamorgan and Breconshire, and also that of Capel Garmon in the Conwy valley, belong to the Severn–Cotswolds group which was heavily influenced by the culture of Brittany. The distribution of the *cromlechi* has an obvious bias to the west, suggesting that they were the work of a people familiar with the western sea-routes. This is an aspect of the 'personality' of Wales which can be overlooked if the country is seen as no more than part of the Highland Zone of Britain. Eastwards, Wales faces the lowlands of England, but it also faces the western waters, with their network of sea-routes. People and influences came from the one direction and the other, and the interplay between what came by land and what came by sea is one of the most fascinating of the themes of the early history of Wales.

To the archaeologist, the *cromlech* is a chambered tomb, although as Alwyn D. Rees once remarked, doubtless the same term would be applied to Westminster Abbey if that building were to be excavated. Bodies were certainly placed in them, but as they were the centres of the ritual of the community they were more than mere burial-places. Where they exist in groups – in Ardudwy and in the Nyfer valley, for example – they offer a key to an understanding of the nature of the communities which constructed them. It is believed that they were the work of fairly egalitarian clans and that a *cromlech* was the focus for the life of a community of a few dozen, although it would have been built through the joint effort of several such communities. The community owned the land around the *cromlech* – two hectares (five acres) of arable land per head, perhaps – and its members moved their dwellings from place to place within their territory as they exhausted the fertility of the soil. Although farmers, they were not husbandmen, for they did not manure the land. Their only permanent building was the *cromlech* and they gathered in it to perform rituals in the presence of their ancestors. Little is known of the food of the Neolithic people of Wales but, if the evidence of about 3700 BC from Windmill Hill, Wiltshire, is relevant, beef would have loomed large; mutton, pork and goat's meat was also eaten but game was almost wholly absent. At Windmill Hill, emmer wheat represented 90 per cent of the grain consumed, and it is possible that the inhabitants had some means of ploughing. The evidence for grain in Wales in the Neolithic period is slight; it was probably grown but it is likely that the emphasis was upon the raising of stock, as it would be in subsequent ages.

In addition to the *cromlechi*, the inhabitants of Wales felt the need for more extensive meeting-places. That need was answered by the henge, a circular area surrounded by a dyke and a ditch which served as a place of assembly, trade and ritual for the inhabitants of a wide area. There are about seventy henges in Britain, including a fine example at Llandygái near Bangor, an important location at the conjunction of land-routes and sea-routes. Llandygái is among the earliest of henges, for remains found within it have been dated to the period 3650–3390 BC. Not far from Llandygái stands Penmaen-mawr Mountain, with its deposits of ignaceous rock, a material well suited to axe-making. To Neolithic peoples, the axe was wholly essential as the tool for felling trees and for cutting and shaping wood, their most important raw material; every one of the early ages was more of an age of wood than it was an age of stone or bronze or iron, a fact lost sight of because of the obliteration of the evidence. Graig Lwyd on Penmaen-mawr Mountain was extensively quarried in the centuries after 3000 BC and axes made from the rock have been found in many parts of Britain. The activities of Gwynedd's first quarrymen suggest a degree of division of labour, and the distribution of the axes proves that Neolithic peoples had the ability to engage in trade over great distances. The same conclusion may be drawn from the distribution of pottery, the archaeologist's favourite artefact. Unadorned vessels of the Early Neolithic Age have been found in Anglesey and Pembroke; it is likely that these were of local manufacture, but the more refined pottery of the Later Neolithic Age was probably imported into Wales.

It is accepted that Neolithic agriculturalists were more or less sedentary – more so indeed than the peoples of later ages – but very little evidence of their dwellings has been recovered. Most of what is known about them comes from their ritual rather than from their daily labours. This is so throughout prehistory, at least until the Iron Age. It could almost be claimed that a people lacking religion leave no trace of their existence; they would also have had no art, nor, if Alwyn D. Rees was correct in claiming that ritual rather than necessity is the mother of invention, any motive for inventiveness either. Apart from Skara Brae in the Orkney Islands, no Neolithic settlement larger than a single dwelling has been discovered in Britain. The evidence is sadly incomplete, for less than one hundredth of the known sites have as yet been excavated. In Wales, there has been digging at Clegyr-Boia near St David's, at Cefn Mabwnws, Breconshire, and at Mount Pleasant, Glamorgan, where excavations revealed an oblong stone house 5.7 metres by 3.3, together with the holes for the poles which held up a roof of straw or reeds.

If the Neolithic Age is defined as the era of communities of farmers using stone tools, then it did not totally come to an end in Wales until about 1400 BC, when some metal tools were probably within reach of the entire population. But there were metal objects in Wales from about 2500 BC onwards – objects of copper initially and later, as it was realized that copper is hardened by the addition of tin, objects of bronze. It was once assumed that the coming of metal was a crucial turning-point, but it is now considered that, as the supply was so limited in the Early Bronze Age, it did not immediately lead to wholesale innovation. Indeed, the current tendency is to deprecate the notion of abrupt change and to emphasize the continuance and development of the existing society. Until about 1400 BC, the temperature was rather higher than it is today. As more than half of Wales is over two hundred metres above sea level, this was of great significance, for in the uplands a variation of 1° C can determine the success or failure of crops. Tools became more sophisticated, cloth was woven, the wheel was adopted and oxen were harnessed; above all, the principles of manuring were mastered and thus farmers became husbandmen, a development essential to the growth of settled communities.

The evidence for most of these developments is sparse and difficult to interpret. Evidence for burial practices is more plentiful and in these there was a marked change. By about 2000 BC, the dead were buried in individual graves which contained vessels richer in their decoration than any previous pottery. The graves were those of the Beaker Folk, a people who migrated to Britain from the estuaries of the river Rhine but whose culture contained elements which may have originated in the steppes of southern Russia. It was once assumed that there was a distinct break between the Beaker Folk with their round heads and the Neolithic people with their long heads, but there is now a tendency to consider that the migration was not large; although the newcomers probably imposed themselves as a ruling class over the natives, it appears that the one group was enriched by the experience and the culture of the other.

The Beaker Folk were more warlike than the Neolithic people; they had battle-axes, bronze knives and daggers and bows and arrows; they craved gold and they knew the secret of brewing beer. In those parts of Britain which produced a significant surplus – the Downs of Wessex in particular – a powerful aristocracy (or possibly a priesthood) arose which had the ability to create vast structures. The most prominent of these is Silbury Hill in Wiltshire. That was raised about 2200 BC and represents the full-time work of five hundred men for fifteen years. So great was the power of those who constructed Silbury Hill that it was felt far beyond the Downs, and the influence of

Wessex culture may be discerned in objects discovered in Wales. There may be a more specific connection between Wales and Stonehenge, the great stone circle which stands about thirty kilometres from Silbury Hill and which was probably the product of the same political system. Stonehenge is one of the wonders of Europe. It is believed that there were three periods of construction, ranging from 2800 to 1400 BC. The second period saw the erection of a circle of some eighty blue stones, each of them weighing around four tons. They are generally considered to have been quarried from the rock of the Preseli Mountains, although there are supporters of the view that such stone could have been carried to the Downs through glacial action. Proponents of the Preseli origins of the blue stones have offered fascinating theories to explain how such heavy objects were transported over such a long distance. They have also theorized about the motives for the transportation. Preseli was the most prominent landmark for those sailing from Ireland to the Severn Sea and it may therefore have been considered a holy mountain. If so, there was magic on the hills of Dyfed from very early times.

Until fairly recently, the dominant feature of the prehistory of Britain was considered to be a sequence of invasions, and the influx of the Beaker Folk was seen as one in a series of migrations. It was believed that changes in material culture could be explained only in terms of a succession of migrants who brought to the inhabitants of the far west something of the culture and the technology of the civilized east. As Egypt was seen as the inspiration of the *cromlech* builders, so the culture of Wessex was believed to be an echo of the glories of Crete and Mycenae. By now, with the abandonment of the theory of diffusion, it is realized that the invasion theory was an offspring of the imperialist mentality of the nineteenth century. The indigenous people of Britain had the ability to change and develop. They received ideas and techniques from mainland Europe, but these could have come through trade or through the example of wandering craftsmen. It is not necessary to postulate a series of migrations and there is very little evidence to support such a supposition. It would probably be more correct to assume that Wales had received the bulk of its original stock of people by about 2000 BC. The economy which those people created would be the basis of life for thousands of years, until, indeed, the material circumstances of the Welsh people were transformed in the last two hundred years.

Evidence of that economy has been discovered at Penmon in Anglesey, where there are traces of fields, ninety metres by forty, formed to grow wheat, barley and flax, and on Penmaen-mawr Mountain, where it is possible to detect the piles of stones heaped up when the fields were originally created. On Penmaen-mawr Mountain there are also traces of the banks and lynchets produced by the early plough – the light ard which ripped the soil rather than turning the sod. In Glamorgan and Pembroke, similar evidence has been found, but it is sadly incomplete and there is a pressing need for further field studies. Many sites where meat was boiled have been identified, but so far Wales has not yielded a single dwelling belonging to the Early Bronze Age (2400–1400 BC), which may indicate that the prevalent way of life was that of nomadic pastoralism. This assumption is perhaps confirmed by the numerous remains – graves and stone circles in particular – which are located in the mountains. The favourable climate of the time permitted extensive use of the high land. Of the burials in Caernarfonshire belonging to the Early Bronze Age, a third are situated over four hundred metres above sea level and there are notable stone circles in such places as Ysbyty Cynfyn in the upper reaches of the Rheidol valley and St Harmon in the hills of Radnorshire. Wales has about fifty stone circles, but graves are by far the most common remains of the Bronze Age; there are four hundred in Glamorgan alone. On the basis of burial evidence, valiant and entertaining efforts have been made to estimate the size of the population, the estimates varying from a few thousand to a figure similar to the number dwelling in Britain around AD 1100. The basis of the discussion is flimsy, for it is impossible to know what proportion of the population received a ritual burial. So far, very few of the graves have been dated with any degree of certainty, but 1650 BC has been suggested as the date of the burial at Ysgwennant, Denbighshire, and 1500 BC as the date for the ashes in Bedd Branwen, Anglesey. The objects found in the graves of Wales are meagre compared with those found in the graves of the Wessex aristocracy, but in so far as they can be classified they suggest that the culture of Bronze Age Wales had a high degree of unity and that the country was the meeting-place of influences from Ireland and from southern England, almost as if those two territories were contending for cultural hegemony over Wales.

The climate deteriorated in the centuries following 1400 BC and the uplands could no longer sustain a substantial population. Agriculture was abandoned there, but nature failed to restore the uplands to the condition in which they had been before the interference of man. Today, the mountains of Wales are considered to be of unspoilt beauty, but they are in truth a derelict landscape with their natural condition destroyed. As the circumstances of life in the Highland Zone became harsher, the differences between it and the Lowland Zone intensified, and up to the Roman invasion and beyond there was a marked contrast between the material culture of the one zone and the other. Archaeologists are struck in particular by the relative absence of pottery among the Highland Zone communities in the last thousand years of prehistory, a scarcity which deprives them of convenient artefacts to classify and categorize. Doubtless the scarcity is in part the result of poverty; it may also be the consequence of the semi-nomadic nature of society, for to nomadic communities vessels of wood, metal or leather are more convenient than crockery. In the centuries after 1400 BC, distinct regional patterns emerged and the distribution of material remains suggests that the tribal groupings which existed in Britain on the eve of the Roman invasion were in the process of formation by about 1000 BC.

In the Later Bronze Age (1400 to 600 BC), the beakers, burial cairns and stone circles characteristic of the earlier period are less in evidence. More prominent are collections of bronze tools, weapons and ornaments, together with an occasional object made of gold. The mining of copper expanded greatly in the years around 1000 BC. The chief centre was the eastern Alps, although mining and smelting were also on the increase in Britain and Ireland, and the standard of the artefacts produced is proof of the advancing skills of the smiths of Europe. Among the notable objects discovered in Wales are the gold *lunula* of Llanllyfni, the Moel Siabod shield and the Nannau bucket. These were probably imports, but there were also talented smiths at work in Wales; their bronze axes, in particular, indicate the existence of regional schools of skilful craftsmen. Most of the collections were hoards, probably deliberately hidden by travelling salesmen; such hoards, together with the prominence of weapons among the objects discovered, suggest that society in the centuries after 1000 BC was increasingly warlike and unstable.

This assumption would seem to be confirmed by the hill-forts, the most prominent remains of the last centuries of the prehistory of Wales. A generation ago, they were considered to be the work of Iron Age invaders and were therefore ascribed to the centuries after 600 BC. As it is now believed that Wales, or for that matter Britain, did not receive any great numbers of migrants in the Iron Age, the present tendency is to consider that the hill-forts were essentially an indigenous development. The earliest ramparts at Dinorben have been dated to around 1000 BC; they are therefore contemporary with the Jerusalem of King David. It is claimed that the need for such fortifications arose not, as was once believed, as a result of the turmoil created by the coming of iron, but because of the competition for land which was the consequence of the rise in population and the contraction in agricultural land which stemmed from the deterioration in the climate.

There are almost six hundred hill-forts in Wales, if it is accepted that the term embraces a host of small enclosures as well as forts of six hectares or more. The two hundred or so which extend over less than half a hectare were probably individual fortified farms. The middle-sized structures are considered to be folds for animals, sacred enclosures, centres for seasonal agricultural activities, occasional refuges or the strongholds of petty chieftains. There are twenty-two which exceed six hectares, and these provided protection for the homes of a substantial number of people, proof that the economy in the last centuries of prehistory, in some parts of Wales at least, was capable of sustaining quasi-urban communities.

The hill-forts are the earliest constructions in Wales to have clear military implications; their existence suggests the growth of the territorial principle and the need or the desire to defend that principle. They also suggest that the population was less nomadic in the centuries after 1000 BC than it is believed to have been in the Bronze Age. On the basis of the remains discovered in the few hill-forts that have been excavated, it can be assumed that mixed, settled farming was the basis of the economy. Querns (handmills) have been found in the forts of Dinorben and Mynydd Conwy, an indication that grain was grown; nevertheless, the heaps of bones discovered at Coygan and Pendinas (Aberystwyth) indicate that stock-raising was the chief activity. The hill-forts, in particular the most elaborate, are proof that their designers had skills of a high order, although too much should not be claimed for them in view of the fact that the Parthenon at Athens, which was begun in 477 BC, is earlier than most of them. They are also proof of the existence of a hierarchical society in which a ruling class had the power to force others to undertake back-breaking toil, and few tasks can have been more exhausting than the building of forts such as Llanymynech, Caer Goch or Pendinas.

The hill-forts of Wales were constructed over a period of a thousand years. They vary in their nature and distribution from one area to another, a fact which throws light upon the social and political order in the different regions of Wales. They are at their most numerous in the south-west, where there are more than a hundred and fifty fortlets of under half a hectare. Many of these consist merely of a dyke and a ditch across a promontory above the sea – cliff castles similar to those which dot the coasts of Cornwall. Walesland, one of the raths which are so common in western Dyfed, has been thoroughly excavated. Within its unmortared stone walls are the remains of six round huts which were built and rebuilt over the period 250 BC to AD 250. From later evidence, it is known that south-west Wales was the territory of the Demetae. The multiplicity of small forts and the scarcity of larger fortifications among them suggests that the Demetae were organized in family groups and that they lacked any substantial central authority.

There are cliff castles along the coasts of Gwynedd also. In addition, Gwynedd has one of the most remarkable prehistoric sites in Britain – the settlement of Tre'r Ceiri on the slopes of Yr Eifl. It is surrounded by a stone wall which in places is still as much as four metres in height, and within the walls are the ruins of about a hundred and fifty stone huts. There is evidence that the village was occupied in the Roman period, but it appears that its beginnings belong to the years around 200 BC. The huts, with their thick walls and turf roofs, were no doubt quite snug, but it is reasonable to assume – as Tre'r Ceiri is over four hundred metres above sea-level – that the huts were the habitation of summer shepherds whose winter dwellings in the lowlands have long since been obliterated. In other parts of Gwynedd – on Mynydd Conwy, for example and on Garn Fadrun and Garn Boduan – there are numerous stone huts, but it is not always possible to know whether they are prehistoric. If they are, they doubtless belonged to the Ordovices, as did the fort at Dinorwig which commemorates the name of the tribe.

The northern marches of Wales contain some of the most

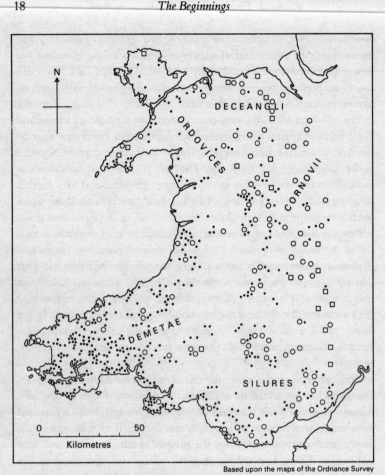

Based upon the maps of the Ordnance Survey

□ Hill-fort of more than six hectares (15 acres)

○ Hill-fort of between one and six hectares (2.5–15 acres)

• Hill-fort of less than one hectare (2.5 acres)

The distribution of hill-forts in Wales

magnificent hill-forts in Britain. The hill-fort at Llanymynech extends over fifty-seven hectares and its magnitude is probably explained by the copper mines in its vicinity. Llanymynech, Breiddin, Ffridd Faldwyn and Oswestry Old Fort – the most impressive of the hill-forts of the marches – are located in the district where the uplands of Wales obtrude upon the lowlands of Shropshire and they may be interpreted either as the eastern outworks of the Ordovices or as the defences of the Cornovii, the tribe which inhabited the rich lands of the middle Severn valley. It was a thickly populated district and excavations at Ffridd Faldwyn have yielded the foundations of entire streets of houses. Initially, the forts would have had single-ditch defences, but around 200 BC a second ditch was added to forts such as Dinorben and Penycorddyn-mawr, possibly as a reaction to the increasing use of the javelin. About 100 BC, with south-eastern England under the control of the aggressive kings of the Belgae, tribes on the periphery of their attacks seem to have felt the need for further fortifications, and towers, guard-chambers and complex entrances were built in the chief hill-forts.

In south-east Wales there is nothing similar to the great hill-forts of the northern marches. Along the coast of Glamorgan, there are cliff castles similar to those of Dyfed and Cornwall, although one of them, that of Dunraven, contains the foundations of twenty-one houses. On the other hand, the forts at Sudbrook and Llanmelin are closer in plan to those of Wessex. South-east Wales was the home of the Silures, a tribe which had a high degree of political cohesion, as is proven by its stubborn resistance to the power of Rome.

It was the territory of the Silures that yielded the oldest iron artefact yet discovered in Britain. Part of a sword dating from 600 BC, it was discovered at Llyn Fawr above the Rhondda in 1908. The coming of iron was highly significant; iron is the most common of the metals of the earth and although it is more complicated to produce than copper, the process, once discovered, makes possible an almost inexhaustible supply of material for the making of tools, weapons and equipment. To Gordon Childe, iron was the 'democratic metal' and so great is its usefulness that the Iron Age has lasted until today. Those knowing the secret of iron-making represented a threat to those ignorant of the secret; there is an echo of that threat in the story of the Lady of Llyn y Fan Fach in which the Lady, a symbol of the old order with her magic and her white cattle, returned to her own world on being struck thrice with iron.

Although iron would not become common in Britain for at least two centuries after 600 BC – centuries which saw the craft of the copper-smith reaching its apogee – it is the sword from Llyn Fawr which raises the curtain upon the British Iron Age. Archaeologists have been remarkably industrious in categorizing the evidence of that age. Its alphabet – cultures A, B and C – has been the subject of earnest debates, but the debates have little immediate relevance to the inhabitants of Wales, for pottery, the main evidence involved, was rare among them. As in the Later Bronze Age, so also in the Iron Age, objects of metal were more important than earthenware as indications of the influences upon the population of Wales. The Llyn Fawr sword belongs to the Hallstatt Culture, the dominant culture of central Europe around 700 BC. Hallstatt is a village near Salzburg in Austria whose fame arises from the fact that the salt mined there pickled and preserved the remains of human bodies and artefacts. The Hallstatt Culture developed from a culture which had flourished on the borders of Bavaria and Bohemia five hundred years earlier, that of a people who created extensive cemeteries in which to bury urns containing the ashes of their dead. The people of the Urnfield Culture were associated with the development of the copper resources of the Alps and with a marked mastery of the art of horsemanship. So great was their energy and their wealth that their influence was felt over wide areas of Europe; excavations in Wales have yielded objects characteristic of them, such as the bronze pins found at the forts of Breiddin and Dinorben.

In addition to the sword, Llyn Fawr also yielded a razor in the Hallstatt style, and a harness in the same style has been found at Parc y Meirch near Dinorben. The people of the Hallstatt Culture expanded into west and south-west Europe and, in so doing, they came into contact with the civilizations of the shores of the Mediterranean; as a result, they developed a taste for the products of those civilizations, wine in particular, a taste which gave rise to extensive trade. They were also in contact with the Scythians of southern Russia, and by about 500 BC the heirs of the Hallstatt Culture had succeeded in absorbing the influences which came to them from the south and the east, thereby creating an artistic synthesis which is among the most exquisite of the creations of mankind. This was the La Tène style, named after a village on the banks of Lake Neuchâtel in Switzerland. It is characterized by a delight in symbol and pattern rather than in pictorialism and naturalism; La Tène art, with its subtlety and its ambiguity, its confidence and its tension, contains intimations of the divine and the infinite.

Among the earliest objects in the La Tène style found in Wales is the Cerrigydrudion hanging-bowl, which dates from about 400 BC.

Many examples of La Tène art were imported into Britain, among them the Merthyr Mawr brooch and the Coygan bracelet, but it is believed that the style struck roots within Britain itself, giving rise to regional schools of talented metal-workers. South-eastern England was the most productive area; it was there, around 100 BC, that objects such as the Trawsfynydd tankard and the Capel Garmon fire-dogs were made. Wales also had craftsmen working in the highest traditions of La Tène; the beautiful plaques found at Tal-y-llyn, for example, were made of metal smelted from ore mined at Nantyrarian near Aberystwyth. Over half the examples of La Tène art found in Wales were discovered in Anglesey; there, in 1942, almost a hundred metal objects belonging to the most developed period of the style came to light at Llyn Cerrig Bach. A large number of them are associated with the art of horsemanship, but they also include plaques adorned with the characteristic motifs of La Tène. The sources of the collection are varied; they include the work of the craftsmen of Ireland, Yorkshire and south-eastern England, proof of the presence in Anglesey in the years between 150 BC and AD 50 of men of far-reaching influence, thus confirming documentary evidence that the island was the chief centre in Britain of the druidical religion.

The objects from Llyn Cerrig Bach date from the threshold of the historical period, for there is some written evidence relating to Britain in the century before the Roman invasion of AD 43. The evidence shows that by then a Celtic language – Brittonic – was spoken by the ruling classes of southern Britain. Hitherto, the use of the words Celt and Celtic has been avoided. In its essence, the term Celt refers to a group of languages, and archaeological evidence found in Wales cannot be linked with a branch of the Indo-European or any other family of languages. Nevertheless, among those who first used the term – and they were Greeks of around 500 BC – it meant something more than a linguistic group: it referred to a people or peoples possessing a material and spiritual culture which, according to the classical authors and to the archaeological record, dominated large areas of Iron Age Europe. And that culture, as well as the language, was present in Britain when the island first appeared upon the platform of history.

How did this come about, in view of the supposition that there was no major influx of population into the island during the Iron Age, nor for that matter during a thousand years and more before the Iron

Age? This is one of the considerations which caused Myles Dillon to argue that it was the Beaker Folk, around 2000 BC, who brought the Celtic language or languages to Britain. He asserted that the Celts carried the Indo-European inheritance westwards from the heartland of Indo-Europa in southern Russia at much the same time as the Aryans carried it eastwards, to India. This theory helps to explain the survival of some of the earliest elements of that inheritance among its most westerly legatees – the Celts – and among its most easterly ones – the Aryans. The theory also helps, argued Dillon, to explain the substantial differences which developed between the British version (P-Celtic) and the Irish version (Q-Celtic) of the original Celtic tongue. Assuming that both islands received the same Celtic language in the Early Bronze Age, enough time would have elapsed by the beginning of the historical period to enable such differences to develop. Dillon's arguments have considerable appeal: it would no doubt be a matter of satisfaction to Welsh-speakers of today to be able to believe that their language and the ancestors of their language have been present in their land for four thousand years.

But this is a complex matter, and those who are not experts in the field must tread warily. Few scholars accept Dillon's theory in its entirety, although there is some readiness to believe in the possibility that the Beaker Folk spoke an Indo-European language and that there were Proto-Celts (whatever they may be) in Britain from a very early age. Nevertheless, the current orthodox view is that the Celtic language and the essentials of Celtic culture were brought to Britain in the centuries after 600 BC by small groups of migrants who were not large enough to change the basic racial composition of society but who were powerful and confident enough to be culturally dominant. Other parts of the world provide wholly reliable evidence of the ability of small groups of invaders to change some of the chief features of the societies which come under their control. In AD 642, Egypt had a population of some four million, which was Christian in religion and Egyptian in language; the country probably did not receive more than a few tens of thousands of Arabic-speaking Islamic invaders, but within a fairly short time the language and the religion of the new-comers were taking hold of the majority. Nevertheless, the society and the economy continued to be based upon the practices which the *fellahin* had developed over several millennia. In the same way, it may be imagined that a small class, Celtic in language, seized power in

Britain in the last centuries of prehistory and that the culture of that class permeated society to so great an extent as to cause the archaeological and documentary evidence to suggest that their culture was that of the totality of the inhabitants. Yet the economy undoubtedly continued to be based upon the pattern of activity which had been developed by the multitude of generations that had dwelt in Britain and in Wales before the coming of the Celts. Indeed, it is possible that some of the features considered to be specifically Celtic – the respect for women, for example, or the rituals of the druids (and, possibly, elements of the syntax of the Brittonic and Welsh languages) – should be attributed, not to the Celts, but to their predecessors.

Nevertheless, while the enduring elements in the society of Wales should be stressed and while it should be emphasized that the blood of the men of Hallstatt scarcely courses through the veins of the present inhabitants of Wales, these are not arguments for belittling the achievements of the Celts or for disparaging their formative contribution to the history of Wales. Theirs was the first culture of true splendour to develop in Europe north of the Alps. That culture had a striking unity, as museums from Lisbon to Ankara bear witness; it was essentially the same among the Galatians of Anatolia as it was in Spain or northern Italy or Bohemia. The history of the Celts became interwoven with that of the Romans and the Greeks; they mounted an attack upon Rome in 390 BC and upon Delphi in 278 and they joined in battle at Thermopylae. Their descendants in Galatia received a letter from Paul; Jerome knew of them at Trier, as did Martin at Tours. They left a deep mark upon the toponymy of Europe. The names of the rivers Rhone, Rhine and Danube are Celtic, as are those of the cities of London, Paris and Vienna; Gallipoli is the city of the Celts or the Gauls, and the town of Bala was built on the banks of a lake in Anatolia centuries before the building of Bala, Penllyn.

Their culture had a tenacious longevity. The characteristics of the Celts, as described by the classical authors, can be clearly discerned a millennium later in the laws and the myths of the Irish; half a millennium later still the same characteristics may be seen in the society portrayed in the *Mabinogi*, and in centuries yet later still there is more than an echo of them in the social order praised by the Welsh poets. They were the characteristics of a heroic, hierarchical society. There is evidence of kings of divine descent in the more traditional communities, but it would appear that the usual pattern of government was rule by an aristocracy. Only two classes, the priests and the warriors, enjoyed the full rights of free men. The rest lived in some measure of servitude and the evidence concerning them is very slight, although archaeologists are developing techniques which may throw light upon their laborious lives. It is the warriors who attracted the attention of the commentators of the ancient world and it is their possessions which loom largest in the archaeological record. The classical authors stress their pride and their readiness to defend their honour. Archaeology provides evidence of the standard of their weapons; they were, says Strabo, infatuated with war. Feasting played a central role in their lives; they craved wine, says Plato, and Diodorus Siculus describes them drinking through their thick moustaches with the 'liquid flowing as through a sieve'. They took great pride in their ancestry and ties of kinship were of central importance among them. Their standard of horsemanship was high, the gear of their horses was refined and they held the stallion in high regard.

The classical authors also have much to say about the priesthood of the Celts, and excavation has yielded some of the objects used in their rituals. The leading figures in the priesthood were the druids, but the order also included the poets and the *vates* or seers; linked with them were the lawyers, the doctors, the musicians and the artists. Most of the evidence concerning the Celtic priesthood comes from Gaul, but the portrayal of the classical authors is confirmed by the ancient, pre-Christian traditions of the Irish. That portrayal was doubtless also relevant to Wales although, as Wales has virtually no surviving traditions dating from the period before the adoption of Christianity, it is only suggestions here and there in its early literature which confirm that the Celtic priesthood was once dominant in its society also. The function of the priesthood was to propitiate the omnipresent magical powers and to organize the rituals which governed the activities of the community – that is, it was the priesthood which maintained and safeguarded the culture of the Celts. Much of the power of the druids arose from their control over the calendar, and the Coligny Calendar, one of the most remarkable of the relics of Gaul, is proof of their knowledge of astronomy. The magical powers were propitiated by ritual in which the figure three had an occult significance and the human head a key role. (Compare the story of Bendigeidfran in the *Mabinogi*.) To the Celts, everything was holy, but a particular sanctity belonged to glades and lakes; the objects found in Llyn Cerrig Bach were in all probability gifts to the gods. The names of over four thousand Celtic gods have been recorded, but it is likely that most of them were local variants of prominent gods such as Mabon, Lleu, Taran and Nudd. It has been argued that the Celts lacked an organized pantheon, but there are suggestions that they possessed a notion of a single divine spirit and that, despite the cruelty of some of their rituals, their moral comprehension was well developed.

Around the year 300 BC, the Celts were the most powerful people in Europe, with a territory which extended from Ireland to Anatolia. They possessed energy, talent and pride. In some aspects of the fine arts and of technology, their achievements were equal to those of the classical world, and the lands under their control were potentially wealthier than those of the shores of the Mediterranean. But they had not developed the discipline of civic society and the ability to maintain a cohesive centralized state. Strenuous battles were fought before the Celts yielded to more organized enemies, but yield they did. Galatia was conquered by Pergamon in 232 BC and Pergamon was swallowed by Rome in 130 BC. The Celts of northern Italy came under the authority of Rome in 222 BC and the Celtiberians of Spain had been wholly overcome by 179 BC. Then, with the campaigns of Julius Caesar, came the turn of Gaul, and following the wars of 58 to 55 BC it was subjected to Roman power. The independence of the Celts of mainland Europe came to an end with the failure of Vercingetorix's heroic stand at Alesia in 52 BC. And the time was approaching when Wales also would be subjected to the power and would experience the appeal of the strongest of the empires of the ancient world.

CHAPTER TWO

===

Wales and Rome: Caer-went, Whitton and Segontium

In August 55 BC, Julius Caesar with ten thousand soldiers landed on the coast of Kent. He was in the middle of his conquest of Gaul, and according to him the purpose of his expedition was to punish the Belgae of Britain for the assistance that they had given to their cousins, the Gauls, although it is probable that it had more to do with his own ambitions. He returned to Gaul after a campaign of less than a week during which he had hardly left the coast. He returned the following year and again his visit was short. He wrote an account of these incursions in his *De Bello Gallico*. His portrayal of the inhabitants of Britain in their colourful nudity was to be a major obstacle to a true understanding of the inhabitants of Britain before the coming of the Romans, in particular because his account was for centuries a student text and thus that portrayal became deeply embedded in the consciousness of many generations.

Thereafter, a century elapsed before a serious attempt was made to invade Britain, although Caligula played with the notion in AD 39. During that century, the Belgae consolidated their hold over the south-eastern parts of the island. By about AD 30, Cunobelinus (the Cynfelyn of Welsh tradition) of the tribe of the Catuvellauni had brought the area from Essex to Surrey under his control. His kingdom, with its coinage, its wheel pottery, its lively trade, its prosperous agriculture and its suggestion of the beginnings of literacy, was highly developed. In an arc around Cunobelinus's kingdom lived the Iceni, the Coritani and the Dubonni, tribes which had not been conquered by the Belgae but which had adopted some of their innovations, in particular coinage and wheel pottery. Beyond them dwelt the tribes of Wales – the Silures, the Demetae, the Ordovices and Deceangli; although elements of the culture of the Belgae were rare among them, they also felt the effects of the new power in south-eastern

Britain, as the strengthened fortifications of their hill-forts bear witness.

Cunobelinus died about A D 40 and his kingdom was inherited by his sons, Caratacus and Togodumnus. Their brother, Amminius, had been exiled by Cunobelinus, and he appealed to Rome to help him gain a share of his father's territories. Amminius's appeal, along with the complaints of the tribes which had suffered from the attacks of the Belgae, provided the Romans with an excuse to invade the island, although their real motive was their desire to seize the fertile lowlands. These, with their surplus of corn, appeared rich to those used to the poor coastlands of the Mediterranean. But if only the lowlands were seized – and this appears to have been the original intention – another border would be created, and the Empire already had more than enough borders; indeed, the Emperor Augustus, shortly before his death in A D 14, had declared that Rome already had as many borders as it could effectively defend. A generation after the death of Augustus, greed triumphed over prudence, although it may be doubted whether Britain was ever a profitable addition to the Empire. For centuries, one tenth of the legions were stationed there, although the area of the province was less than one thirtieth of that of the territories of Rome. Nevertheless, the planting of the eagles across the sea, in the further ends of the world – and that was how the Romans viewed Britain – was a matter of pride, as the verses of the poets and the speeches of the rhetoricians testify.

In May A D 43, Aulus Plautius sailed across the Channel with four legions and a host of auxiliary soldiers – forty thousand men in all. Within three months, it was considered that Rome's hold upon south-eastern Britain was secure enough to allow the Emperor Claudius, the most inoffensive member of the complex Julio-Claudian family, to visit the new province and to make a ceremonial entry into Camulodunum (Colchester), the capital of the Catuvellauni, on an elephant. By A D 47, at the end of his period as governor, Aulus Plautius had fulfilled the purpose of the invasion: south-eastern Britain was part of the Empire and the Fosse Way, which ran from Lincoln to Exeter, had been established as the frontier of the conquered territory. The power of the Catuvellauni had been broken, much to the satisfaction of tribes such as the Iceni of Norfolk and the Regni of Sussex, who viewed the Romans not as conquerors but as deliverers.

The Fosse Way was an unstable frontier. Roman power came

under attack from the independent tribes living beyond it. Chief among them were the Silures of south-east Wales. They attacked the new province in AD 47 and 48 at the behest of Caratacus (the Caradog of Welsh tradition), who had fled to the territory of the Silures following the defeat of the Catuvellauni. The Romans were also concerned about the attitude of the Brigantes, a federation of tribes whose territory extended across northern England and who were, formally at least, allies of the Romans. Anti-Roman sentiment among the Brigantes was probably fomented by druidical influences emanating from Anglesey. The Romans rapidly came to grasp a fundamental fact about the geography of Britain – that the Highland Zone, unlike the Lowland, is not a compact unity. In the lower valley of the Dee – the Cheshire Gap – a tongue of lowland afforded the Romans an opportunity to thrust a wedge between the Brigantes and the tribes of Wales; in the same way, those tribes could be separated from the Dumnonii, the inhabitants of the uplands of Devon and Cornwall, by establishing a centre of Roman power in the plains of the lower Severn valley. This was done. Ostorius Scapula, the successor of Aulus Plautius, reached the banks of the Dee in AD 48 and there he received the submission of the Deceangli. The event is noted by Tacitus, the chronicler of the invasion and one of the world's greatest historians, and that reference is the first in writing to a territory in Wales. In AD 49, a fort was erected for the Twentieth Legion near the place where the city of Gloucester would later be founded and it was linked with smaller forts at Usk, Clyro and other places, with the intention of putting pressure on the Silures. Caratacus continued his resistance among the Ordovices and it was in their territory, near Caersŵs perhaps, that he was defeated and his wife and children were captured in AD 51. Caratacus himself fled to the Brigantes, but he was yielded up to the Romans by their queen, Cartimandua. He was taken to Rome and there, according to Tacitus, he made a speech which has resounded down the ages.

The resistance of the tribes of Wales did not come to an end with the capture of Caratacus. In AD 52, a legion – probably the Twentieth – was defeated by the Silures. Around the year AD 57, the Emperor Nero authorized a determined campaign to bring the entire island under Roman control, and in AD 60 Anglesey, the chief centre of anti-Roman sentiment, came under attack. Tacitus provides a dramatic description of the anguish of the Roman soldiers as they saw across the Menai Straits the druids in awesome panoply. But they soon cast aside their fear and their clothes; they swam the straits, killed the druids and destroyed the sacred groves. The Romans were prevented from consolidating their hold upon north-west Wales because the Iceni, embittered by the treatment meted out to them by Roman officials, rose in revolt under their valiant queen Boudicca (or Buddug, to give her the name coined by Theophilus Evans). The revolt was ferocious. Thousands of Romans and their allies were slaughtered; London, which was already becoming the *de facto* capital of the province, was burnt so thoroughly that a layer of ash was excavated there almost two thousand years later. The revenge of the Romans was even more ferocious. Tens of thousands of Britons were killed and Norfolk was left desolate for generations.

Rome itself was in upheaval at the end of the sixties with the extinction of the line of the Julio-Claudians. In A D 69, a new dynasty, the Flavians, was established by Vespasian, a man who had served in Britain under Aulus Plautius. Under the Flavians, the forward movement continued. Julius Frontinus gave priority to the subjugation of the Silures and the Ordovices, and during his governorship (A D 74–8) the headquarters of three of the four legions campaigning in Britain were located in the borderlands of Wales. From A D 67 to 84, the Twentieth Legion was at Viroconium (Wroxeter) near Shrewsbury, and in about A D 75 fortresses were established for the Second Legion (Adiutrix) on the banks of the Dee at Deva (Chester) and for the Second Legion (Augusta) on the banks of the Usk at Isca (Caerleon). The Silures had been defeated by A D 75; Julius Frontinus wore down the Ordovices, but it was his successor, Julius Agricola (A D 78–84), who subjugated them, a subjugation accompanied by much slaughter. Agricola sought to extend Roman power to the further reaches of Scotland and to Ireland, 'so that the arms of Rome,' wrote Tacitus, 'should be everywhere and there would be no sight of freedom'. Nothing came of the notion of conquering Ireland and the fact that Roman soldiers never trod Irish soil is a basic element in the history of the island. Agricola won a great victory at Mons Graupius in the heart of Scotland, a victory which according to Tacitus allowed King Calgacus to say biting things about the aggressiveness of Rome. Nevertheless, the Empire's intention of conquering the whole of northern Britain was not fulfilled. In consequence, the Romans were obliged to maintain a troublesome border between their province,

Britannia, and the independent peoples living to its north; buffer-states were encouraged to develop along the border, a policy of significance in the history of Scotland and of Wales.

The task of subduing Wales proved long and costly. There were at least thirteen campaigns in Wales and its borders between A D 48 and 79. They needed careful planning. Grain, the staple food of the legionaries, was scarce in Wales and the guerrilla methods of the men of the mountains were unfamiliar to the invaders. With such tactics, a small group of men could pin down large forces, and during the seventies perhaps as many as thirty thousand of the soldiers of the Empire were campaigning in Wales. While campaigning, the Romans built temporary camps and at least twenty of these have been identified in Wales. Similar camps were erected on the plains of England, but on the plains the Romans did not feel the need to build permanent fortifications. There is not a single permanent fort in those areas defined by Cyril Fox as the Lowland Zone. In the Highland Zone, the invaders could not feel as confident that their authority would be accepted. Legionary fortresses were built at Deva and Isca (the legionary fortress at Viroconium was abandoned after A D 84), and were linked to a network of smaller camps. Archaeologists have identified thirty-five auxiliary camps in Wales and its borderlands. The territory of the Silures was dotted with them; in central Wales, every eastern-facing valley had its fort, and in the north-west the Menai Straits were defended by Segontium (Caernarfon), a fort linked to others in the Conwy valley and in Snowdonia. On the other hand, in the south-west, the territory of the Demetae, a tribe which has left no evidence of resistance to Rome, there are very few structures of military significance; that is also true of the territory of the Deceangli. The network of forts was clearly a cohesive system. The forts were linked by straight roads and were situated a day's march – twenty kilometres on average – apart from each other. The pattern of fortifications devised by Julius Frontinus seems to have represented a development of importance in Roman thinking on defence, for versions of it were adopted in other parts of the Empire.

The map of the 'Roman Frontier in Wales' is very familiar – the neat quadrilateral with its corners at Chester, Caerleon, Carmarthen and Caernarfon. Yet it is misleading, for it presents too static a picture. There was no necessity to retain the system in its totality for

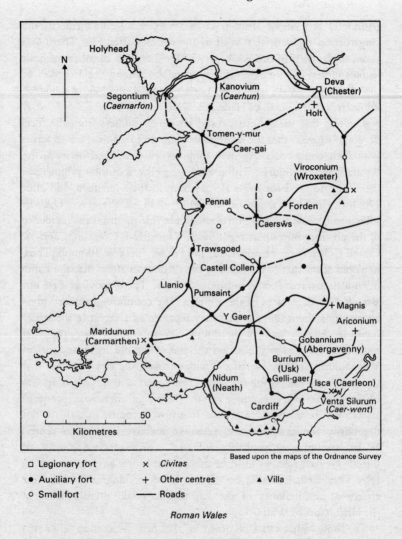

Based upon the maps of the Ordnance Survey

□ Legionary fort   × *Civitas*

● Auxiliary fort   + Other centres   ▲ Villa

○ Small fort   — Roads

Roman Wales

three hundred years, with each fort having its full quota of soldiers. The legionary fortresses were used for two centuries and more, but Chester and Caerleon did not house complete legions of 5,300 men throughout those years. It is possible that the Second Legion (Augusta) was never in Caerleon in its entirety after 117. It is known that the Twentieth Legion (which took the place of the Second Legion

(Adiutrix) at Chester around AD 87) played a leading role in the construction of Hadrian's Wall in the decades after 120. There was room in the forts of the Wall for 9,500 soldiers and members of both legions served in its garrisons; they were also among the defenders of the Antonine Wall, the new border created in 143, a hundred kilometres to the north of Hadrian's Wall.

The fact that the Romans could withdraw soldiers from the forts of Wales suggests that the inhabitants were prepared to come to terms with their conquerors. An increasing accord developed between the Romans and the Silures; within a few generations of their subjugation there was no need for full-scale garrisons in their territory, and after 170 little use was made of the forts south of the river Usk. In subsequent years, the only forts which provide unmistakable evidence of the presence of soldiers are those of Caernarfon, Caerhun, Caersŵs, Castell Collen (near Llandrindod) and Forden (near Welshpool). Thus, it would seem that it was among the Ordovices alone that the flame of enmity towards Rome continued to burn. The Ordovices were not attracted by the graces of the Empire. The continuing military presence among them suggests that they represented a threat to the settlements in the rich lands of the middle Severn valley. There, the chief settlement was the city built on the site of the old legionary fort of Viroconium, and the scarcity of villas around the city indicates that the area was not wholly secure. There was a time when it was believed that every example of the repair of forts was proof of attacks by the enemies of Rome. It is now accepted that this is not necessarily the case, but the extensive military activity in central Wales around 200 probably indicates a considerable degree of unrest. Nevertheless, as most of the auxiliary forts have not yet been fully excavated, it would be unwise to be too dogmatic about the ability or the inability of the Romans to retain the allegiance of the inhabitants of Wales.

To those inhabitants, Rome, in the first generation after the conquest, meant the army; indeed, for the people living in the uplands, this would be so throughout the centuries of the Empire. It was the army of Rome rather than an army of Romans, for the legionaries and the auxiliaries were more likely to hail from the valleys of the Rhine and the Danube than from the valley of the Tiber. The army represented wealth on a wholly unprecedented scale. In Caerleon, a legion of 5,300 men with money to spend was a magnetic attraction.

Outside the walls of the fort, a *vicus* developed – a township where people from far and near settled in order to profit from the money of the soldiers. By about AD 100, the *vicus* at Caerleon had a population of around two thousand; the reduction in the size of the garrison was a crushing blow to its inhabitants, particularly to the women who had borne children to the soldiers. Smaller *vici* arose on the outskirts of the auxiliary forts – at Caernarfon, for example, and at Caersŵs and Y Gaer (Brecon) – and there is evidence of some form of *vicus* even at Tomen-y-mur near Trawsfynydd. In addition, townships arose in conjunction with the industrial activities of the Romans: Holt on the banks of the Dee, the centre of tile-making for the Twentieth Legion, has yielded evidence of a considerable settlement; the gold-mines of Dolaucothi with their two thousand metres of tunnels provided employment for a substantial workforce; Ariconium, in the forests of the Wye valley, grew to be a sizeable township based upon a flourishing iron industry.

In addition, the Empire sought to encourage more formal urban settlements, for the Romans considered that the city was the key to civilized life. The city of Viroconium was the *civitas* of the Cornovii. The *civitas* was a privilege extended to a tribe of whose allegiance the Romans could be confident, the privilege of building a city which was ruled by the elders of the tribe and which served as the centre of its territory. By 200, Viroconium was the fourth in size of the cities of Britannia, and it was probably the setting for many wild nights as the soldiers from Castell Collen or Caersŵs came for rest and recreation. The same privilege was extended to the Silures. Their *civitas* was the city of Caer-went. There, the earliest Roman remains have been dated to around AD 75, the time of the final subjugation of the Silures. However, in view of their dogged resistance, it is unlikely that Caer-went was a *civitas* from its inception. It is more probable that the Silures were granted the privilege during the reign of Hadrian (117–38), as a result of the reorganization carried out in south-east Wales following the departure of soldiers to Hadrian's Wall. But if there is uncertainty about the date, there is no uncertainty about the status of Caer-went, for a stone was discovered there bearing the words *ex decretio ordinis respub[lica] civit[atis] Silurum* (through the command of the republic of the city of the Silures). In about 260, Caer-went was surrounded by stone walls, sections of which up to seven metres high still exist. The designers of the walls were over-ambitious: eighteen hectares were enclosed, a considerably larger area than was needed, for within the walls there are hectares of land upon which there is no evidence that buildings were ever erected. It is estimated that Caer-went in its heyday had a population of three thousand, much less than the ten thousand in Viroconium or the thirty thousand in London; yet for fifteen hundred years to come there would be no other town in Wales with so substantial a population. Caer-went had all the features of a Roman city – a basilica, a forum, bath-houses, a forty-room hotel, at least three temples and about two dozen gentry houses with murals, mosaic floors and central heating. In accordance with the Roman predilection for oligarchy, the administration of Caer-went, like that of the other *civitates* of Britannia (about twenty in all), was in the hands of a hundred *decuriones*. They provided the magistrates of the city and the delegates which were sent to the Provincial Council of Britannia. The *decuriones* were presumably chosen from the ranks of the aristocracy of the Silures and thus something of the organization of the tribe probably persisted throughout the years of the Roman occupation.

Until recently, Caer-went was believed to be the sole *civitas* in Wales, partly on the grounds that the lowlands of the south-east were believed to be the only part of Wales where a *civitas* was likely to be established. But the excavations conducted at Carmarthen since 1968 have proved the existence of the civic settlement of Maridunum, and it has been suggested that the town was the *civitas* of the Demetae. Maridunum has not yielded an inscription which would place the matter beyond doubt, but it is believed that by about 150 the fort created there had been replaced by a town of about six hectares. The town walls were rebuilt in stone between 200 and 230 and an amphitheatre was erected large enough to serve as a place of assembly for the Demetae.

The theory that Carmarthen was a *civitas* is strengthened by the existence in its vicinity of dwellings which bordered upon the status of villas, for it was only in the 'safe' civil areas of the province that villas were built. The villa was the centre of a large farm or estate, a house or a mansion that was Roman in its style and comfort. It was the chief feature of the economy in those parts of the Empire which had been thoroughly Romanized. They were numerous in regions such as Provence and Tuscany where the peasantry had become the serfs or the slaves of the owners, but although the remains of almost seven hundred villas have been discovered in Britain, they represent a rather exotic development there. The majority of them are located in the south-east of the island, although there is a striking group in the Cotswolds around the Roman towns of Gloucester, Bath and Cirencester. Villas played an important role in the economy of Britannia. Their owners were the pioneers of a more progressive agriculture: they introduced capitalist farming, a development assisted by the army's demand for grain. They encouraged the use of the heavy plough and were responsible for the introduction of new species of plants. It is possible that oats and apples were unknown in Britain before the conquest, and it is fairly certain that it was the Romans who brought carrots, turnips, parsnips, leeks, cherries, vines, walnuts and sweet chestnuts to the island.

The villa at Abercyfar near Carmarthen was the most westerly in Britain. About a dozen others have been identified in Wales. The most famous is the villa at Llantwit Major. In 1888, excavation there revealed a block of buildings, eighty-five metres by sixty, including a bath-house and rooms with mosaic floors. A tenuous thread links the villa at Llantwit Major – wholly Roman in the style of its buildings and in the life of its inhabitants – with the dwelling at Corsygedol, Meirionnydd, where signs of the existence of the Empire are very scanty indeed. Yet all the habitations which existed in Wales during the centuries of Roman rule can be placed somewhere along that thread. It appears that the buildings at Llantwit Major were Roman from the beginning, but not far away, at Whitton near St Nicholas, an Iron Age farmhouse was transformed step by step into a Roman villa. There is evidence of a less thorough transformation at Cwm-brwyn near Llanddowror and at Llanfrynach in the Usk valley. In north and central Wales, virtually no indigenous dwellings which show the influence of Roman building methods have been discovered. Tacitus declared that Agricola had exterminated the Ordovíces; it is hardly likely that this was literally true, yet evidence of the presence of anyone other than Roman soldiers is rare in their territory in the generation immediately after the conquest. In the hill-forts of Castell Odo and Breiddin there are signs of the destruction of fortifications, perhaps representing an attempt by the Romans to render such places ineffective as strongholds for their enemies. In the later centuries of the Empire, hill-forts such as Dinorben and Breiddin were reoccupied. Their inhabitants had an Iron Age culture, but the few coins and pieces of pottery discovered within them are proof of some contact with the Roman world. Similar discoveries have been made in the stone huts which dot the hills of Gwynedd – at Tre'r Ceiri, for example, and at Braich y Ddinas; it was probably through the *vicus* at Caernarfon that their inhabitants came into contact with the products of the Empire, but such contacts were clearly rare and intermittent.

The same pattern – full Romanization, degrees of Romanization and the continuance of the old order – can be seen in art and in religion. With the conquest, the ruling classes abandoned the La Tène style in favour of the Roman provincial style, the rather uninspired medium of a large number of sculptures, such as the memorial at Caerleon to poor Julia Iberna, who died at the age of sixteen. Unlike in Ireland, where there was an unbroken development of the La Tène style and where it had aristocratic patrons, only a vestige of the tradition continued in Wales, largely in the craft of tinkers under peasant patronage; those vestiges may be seen in some of the objects made of Anglesey copper, in the adornments of hanging-bowls and on the handles of buckets.

In religious matters, the Empire permitted a variety of faiths as long as they lacked anti-Roman implications (as druidism did not). In the legionary and auxiliary forts, the official rites of Rome were celebrated before the image of the emperor, but on the outskirts a range of mystery religions flourished, most of which had their origins in the Near East – the cult of Mithras, for example, which had followers at Caernarfon and Caerleon. Despite the suppression of druidism, the religion of Britain had its place even in the centres of Roman power, as the stone head of around 300 found at Caerleon testifies. There was an attempt to identify Celtic gods with those of the Roman pantheon, as with the temple to Mars-Oculus at Caer-went. The most striking of the temples to Celtic gods was that built about 367 at Lydney, across the Wye from Caer-went. It was a temple to Nodens, the god of healing; Lydney was a sort of Celtic Lourdes, with its chapels, its baths, its hotels and its sacred enclosures.

When the temple of Nodens was built, the age of the Celtic gods was rapidly coming to a close; a generation or two after 367, there would be no evidence of any religion apart from Christianity among the ruling classes of the Britons. It is likely that the lower classes continued for some time to worship Nodens and his kind and the memory of them continued for centuries; the characters of the

Mabinogi are the old gods transformed into heroes. Christianity spread quite rapidly through the eastern parts of the Empire in the generations immediately after Pentecost, and it was probably merchants and officials (and the wives of officials) from those parts who first introduced the religion to the west. Despite (or perhaps because of) periods of persecution – including the martyrdom of Julius and Aaron at Caerleon – Christianity had by 300 pulled ahead of the other mystery religions which were competing with it, at least in the more populous cities. Christians were allowed to worship without restriction in 313; the Emperor Constantine was baptized on his death-bed in 337 and all other religions had been outlawed throughout the Empire by 400.

Christianity was the religion of the urban Roman world and the bishop in the city was the pivot of its organization; the countryside, the *pagus*, was the habitat of pagans. When the Empire of the West collapsed, a version of it survived in the Church; the Church became the guardian of Latin culture and it used the structures of Rome for its own purposes. As in the rest of the Empire, early British Christianity was Roman and urban. Three bishops from Britain were present at the Council of Arles in 313 and there were three others at Rimini in 359. The poverty of the bishops – a fund had to be raised to pay the expenses of their journey home from Rimini – suggests that the Church in Britain in 359 was rather feeble, but it is possible that by then all twenty of the *civitates* had a bishop. The archaeological evidence is slight, although as Christian rites were often held in ordinary rooms such usage would not have left much in the way of evidence. A church was built at Silchester (Hampshire) about 350 and it has been argued that an apsed building erected at Caer-went in about 400 was a church, although archaeologists are not unanimous on the matter. Caer-went has yielded a pewter bowl bearing a Christian monogram, part of a collection, perhaps, of sacred vessels. Some of the villas of England have mosaic floors featuring Christian symbols; nothing similar has been found in Wales, although it has been suggested that graves near the villa at Llantwit Major are aligned in a Christian fashion.

The documentary evidence is more affirmative. In the generation after 350, the Church in the West had a handful of talented and energetic leaders, among them Martin of Tours, who successfully evangelized in Gaul between 370 and 400. He had links with the Christians of Britain and it appears that the Faith spread rapidly in the island in the age of Martin. The theologian and heresiarch Pelagius left Britain about 360 after receiving a thorough grounding in Christian theology. Patrick, the saint of the Irish, was born about 390 – near Carlisle, perhaps – and, as his Confession testifies, he was brought up in a Christian community.

Although Patrick's Christianity was Roman in its ritual and its organization, he states that Latin was not his mother tongue, a remark which is consistent with the belief that Romanization did not penetrate into the very marrow of the population of Britain (and even less so that of Wales) as it did in the greater part of the Western Empire. Latin was learnt and, as the graffiti at Caer-went and elsewhere prove, knowledge of it and literacy in it were common in the cities. But Kenneth Jackson in his *Language and History in Early Britain* (a study which is not universally accepted) argues that an effort had to be made to learn Latin and that it did not replace Brittonic as the mother tongue of the broad mass of the population. The cities of Britannia were bilingual communities, although doubtless Latin was more audible, for in every age the imperial language has its own peculiar pitch and its own peculiar stridency. It was in this bilingual context that Latin words were absorbed by Brittonic. Apart from a few eccentric borrowings – *pysg* (fish), for example, and *braich* (arm) – they were words for things foreign to the Britons before the coming of the Romans. They therefore throw light upon the material and cultural as well as the lexical debt of the Britons to Rome. In the military arts, the words *cleddyf* (sword) and *gwayw* (javelin) come from Brittonic, but the words *caer* (fort) and *ffos* (ditch) come from Latin. In the field of literature, the words *bardd* (bard), *prydydd* (poet) and *telyn* (harp) are native, but the words *llyfr* (book), *ysgrif* (essay) and *awdur* (author) are borrowings. In domestic matters, the words *tŷ* (house), *drws* (door) and *aelwyd* (hearth) are of pre-Roman origin, but the words *ffenestr* (window), *pared* (partition) and *ystafell* (room) came with the Romans. Welsh inherited few legal terms from Latin, proof of the tenacity of the Celtic legal tradition, and the number of Latin personal names which won long-term popularity was not great, although some remained fashionable for a period after the fall of the Empire.

Although Brittonic held its own – remarkably so when its history is compared with Gaulish and the various old languages of Spain and Italy – the loan-words show that Rome had no mere superficial impact upon the culture of Britannia, at least upon the culture of its urban and upper classes. The term Romano-British has been coined to denote that culture and the people who embraced it. Yet in the first hundred and fifty years after the conquest, very few of those people were full members of the Empire, for in its early centuries citizenship was a rare honour. In 214, however, the Emperor Caracalla extended citizenship to every freeman throughout the Empire. It is not known what proportion of the population was affected by this edict but, to that proportion, the distinction between Romans and Britons was meaningless after 214. The Britons (at least those of the upper classes) were Romans; Rome was their country and the memory of that fact remained for generations after its substance had vanished.

It was probably in the reign of Caracalla, also, that the system of government in Britannia was reorganized. It was originally a single province under the authority of the *prefectus dioecesis* of Gaul, but around 213 (or perhaps a decade earlier) it was divided into two – Britannia Inferior and Britannia Superior. The boundary between the two provinces is not known in detail, but it is believed that Wales was part of Britannia Superior. The reorganization may have been a reaction to the upheavals caused by the attempt of the army in Britain in 196 to elevate Albinus, the governor of Britannia, to the purple. Such upheavals were to become increasingly common in the history of Rome: in the forty years between 244 and 284 the legions elevated fifty-five emperors. The Empire was divided between 259 and 274, a period when the *dioecesis* of Gaul was ruled by the usurper, Postumus. From 286 to 296, Britannia had its own emperors – Carausius (the Carawn of Welsh tradition) and then Allectus – although they sought not an independent Britannia but dominion over the Empire in its entirety. In 296, Allectus was overthrown by Constantius. He was the *Caesar* of the West, an office created by Diocletian (284–305), who ruled as *Augustus* in the East and who believed that the Empire was too great a burden for one man. It was Constantius also, it is believed, who turned the two provinces of Britannia into four; Wales was probably part of Britannia Prima, with its capital at Cirencester.

Diocletian's reorganization of the government of the Empire was a reflection of the differences between the Latin West and the Hellenistic East. The superiority of the East in terms of wealth, population and defensibility was underlined in 330 when the new city of

Constantinople was recognized as the equal of Rome and as the main administrative centre of the Empire. This was done by Constantius's son, Constantine (the Cystennin of Welsh tradition), who was proclaimed *Augustus* by the legions at York in 324 – the only successful attempt by the army in Britain to raise an emperor. Constantine's decision proved percipient – his city would be the capital of the Eastern Empire for 1123 years – but at the time his new Rome was founded there was less than a century of meaningful existence remaining to the Western Empire. The Western Empire was weakened by social and economic problems and its lengthy frontiers were threatened by the Germanic tribes living beyond them. As early as 275, strong walls were built around Rome, proof that Italy itself was no longer safe from invasion. The borders of Gaul was overwhelmed by Germans in 350, attacks which were accompanied by much slaughter and destruction. Some of the invaders were allowed to settle within the confines of the Empire and their recruitment to the legions grew to such an extent that the imperial forces became armies of Germans employed to defend the Empire from other Germans. It was Gaul which suffered the greatest ravages. In Britain, despite the upheavals caused by usurpers, the century 250 to 350 was fairly prosperous. The economy of the villas flourished and in 361 the *Caesar* Julian could still depend upon the island's corn surplus. Outside pressures were increasing, but the Empire proved skilful in dealing with them. The Picts of northern Britain coveted the wealth of Britannia. The Antonine Wall, erected to keep them out, was abandoned in about 211; instead, peace beyond Hadrian's Wall depended upon the cooperation of peoples dwelling between the rivers Tyne and Forth, in particular the Votadini or the Gododdin, a tribe which had been consistently friendly towards Rome. Hadrian's Wall continued to be garrisoned, but there was an awareness of the need for more flexible forces as well. Such a force was established about 300; it was a mobile army based at York under the command of a new officer, the *Dux Britanniarum* (duke or leader of Britain).

In the west, Britannia was threatened by the Irish. The waters between Britain and Ireland have been called the Celtic Mediterranean, and ever since the Neolithic Age they had been the scene of much to-ing and fro-ing. This did not wholly come to an end with the Roman conquest, for there was lively trade between the two islands, as the large numbers of Roman objects found in Ireland testify. The Empire sought to curb the activities of pirates and looters and to restrain the Irish from colonizing the western peninsulas of Britannia. Some time after 300, the defences of Wales were reorganized so as to make them more effective against attacks from the sea. A fleet was established in the Severn Sea, forts were built at the mouth of the harbour at Holyhead and on the banks of the Taff at Cardiff and parts of the fortifications at Caernarfon were rebuilt. These measures were not wholly successful, for it appears that the Romans were obliged to permit considerable numbers of Irish colonists to settle in north-west and south-west Wales.

In eastern Britannia the threat came from the Germans inhabiting the coasts across the North Sea. The Empire extended to the estuaries of the river Rhine. To the north and east dwelt Frisians, Saxons and Franks, who were attracted by the wealthy lands ruled by Rome and who suffered from a chain of pressures which extended from the depths of Asia to the banks of the Rhine, pressures which were to explode in the *Völkerwanderung* (wandering of peoples) which would escort the Western Empire to its grave. Through the army, a substantial number of Germans had found their way to Britain and it is likely that the Roman authorities had allowed Saxons and Frisians to settle in eastern Britain as they had allowed Irish to settle in the west. Yet, as in the west, attempts were made to prevent looting and uncontrolled migration. In about 324, the office of *Comes Litus Saxonicum* (count of the Saxon Shore) was established, and the *comes* was provided with a fleet and a chain of coastal stations.

These activities prove that Rome reacted with vigour to the threat from beyond its boundaries. Up to 400 and beyond, there is no lack of examples of dedicated officials concerned to defend the Empire. None of its citizens sought its demise, but it was increasingly paralysed by the ambition of generals who conspired to rule it. In 350, Magnentius, a German from Gaul, made an attempt upon the throne, crossing to mainland Europe with a portion of the garrison of Britannia. Soldiers from Britain also played a part in the successful campaign launched in Paris in 361 to elevate Julian, *Caesar* of the West, to supreme power, a campaign which gave rise to one of the most remarkable reigns in the history of the Empire. Then in 367 came the *Barbarica Conspiratio* (the Conspiracy of the Barbarians), when Britannia was attacked from the north, the east and the west. It was once believed that this was the final disaster, but the authorities succeeded in reasserting control and in the years after 369 Count Theodosius was energetically strengthening the defences of the island. There is evidence of his work at Caernarfon and at Forden, and it is possible that he gave formal recognition to the role of the rulers of Strathclyde, and the Votadini in the defence of the northern frontier of Britannia.

But by 369 the stability of the Empire was under increasing threat. In 383, Magnus Maximus (the Macsen Wledig of Welsh tradition – a man who will need further consideration), who may have been the *Dux Britanniarum*, began his campaign to dethrone Gratian, the ruler of the West. He had some success: Gratian was killed and Magnus ruled the greater part of the Western Empire until he in turn was killed by the Emperor Theodosius at Aquileia in north-western Italy on 28 July 388. Magnus crossed the Channel with a large proportion of what remained of the garrison of Britannia. The *Notitia Dignitatum*, a document which records the location of the forces of Rome, seems to suggest that there were no imperial troops in Wales by 390 and this appears to be confirmed by the work of archaeologists. The *Notitia* records that the *Seguntiensis*, a regiment undoubtedly raised at Caernarfon, was in Illyricum, to the south-east of Aquileia.

The increasing instability was a heavy blow to the economy. By 383 there is little evidence that Roman style and comfort still prevailed in the villas. It was once believed that their inhabitants were slaughtered by invaders and evidence found at Llantwit Major can be interpreted to support that belief. It is more likely, however, that the villas declined because the economy that had sustained them collapsed as a result of the general insecurity and the disappearance of the market represented by the legions. The fact that buildings in which grain could be dried were erected inside city walls may be a sign of such insecurity, for their existence suggests that the harvest could not be left in the fields to ripen. The 'barbarians' hardly ever succeeded in capturing a fortified city, and it would appear that the walls of Caerwent were strengthened in about 369. But although people continued to live in the cities, that is not the same as the continuance of civic life. In the decades after 350, evidence for civic life becomes increasingly rare; at Viroconium, for example, it seems that the basilica ceased to be used after that year.

The fragile unity of the Empire vanished in 395 when Honorius, the son of Theodosius, was recognized as independent Emperor in the West. It was his government which organized the last attempt to consolidate Roman control over Britannia, a task undertaken by Stilicho from 396 onwards. Stilicho was a faithful servant of the Empire, although he belonged to the tribe of the Vandals, the epitome of the barbarians. By 401, however, with Italy itself in danger, he in turn was sending troops from Britain to defend the heartland of the Empire. In 405, the western coasts were plundered by the Irish chieftain, Nial (Nial of the Nine Hostages of Irish tradition), and it seems likely that further Irish colonists settled in Gwynedd and Dyfed. Over the next two years, attempts were made to elevate three of the generals of Britain to the purple, campaigns which denuded the island of the remaining forces which could be considered part of the armies of Rome. Honorius was obliged to recognize Constantinus, the last of them, as the ruler of Britain and Gaul but, when Constantinus sought to add Italy to his dominions, he was killed in 411. Honorius repossessed Gaul but he lacked the resources to restore Britain to the Empire. It would appear that the Romano-British, deprived of the protection of Roman troops, seized power from Honorius's officials in 408. In 410, Honorius recognized their action and advised them to make arrangements for defending themselves.

Honorius's message is as good a conclusion as any to the rule of Rome in Britain. It was not an orderly conclusion: it should not be imagined that the legions went to their ships with bands playing, in the presence of the ministers of a recognized independent government; no member of Honorius's family came to Britain to pull down the imperial flag, returning to Rome in the company of the last of the Roman officials. Indeed, when Honorius was writing his message, Rome itself was falling into the hands of the Gothic forces of Alaric. Some success was achieved in reviving the power of the Western Empire; it did not formally come to an end until 476, and doubtless it was hoped that Britain would be reunited with it. It has been argued that steps in this direction were taken between 416 and 419, but this notion is now discounted. Britain slipped from the hold of Rome and became estranged from its organization and its culture. The estrangement was a long process: it took a century and more, and during those years the nation of the Welsh was born.

CHAPTER THREE

===

400–800: Dinas Powys, Catraeth and Llantwit Major

The demise of the Roman Empire has been mourned to excess. Its essence was violence and its accomplishments were fundamentally second-rate. Its achievements in the world of science and technology were few; what need was there for new inventions in a society which had an abundance of slaves? Its literature and fine arts were a pale reflection of the splendours of classical Athens. As Mortimer Wheeler, among the most distinguished of the interpreters of the Empire, put it: 'I suffered from a surfeit of things Roman. I felt disgusted by the mechanistic quality of their art and by the nearness of their civilization at all times to cruelty and corruption.'

Yet those who delight in empire see the collapse of Roman power in the west as ushering in the 'Dark Ages' – in Britain and in Wales more than anywhere. With the vast contraction in the number of archaeological sites and artefacts, it appeared that civilization had yielded to barbarism. With the evidence of the classical authors ceasing, historians were deprived of a coherent chronicle of events. With the long sunset came an age of myth and fantasy almost devoid of historical certainties. There has been a healthy reaction against the more extreme assertions concerning the darkness of the 'Dark Ages' and the time has come to abandon the term. Nevertheless, it cannot be denied that western Europe experienced great changes in the centuries following the collapse of Roman power. It is believed that the economy which had developed under the Empire survived to a considerable extent for a century or more after its collapse, but by 650, partly because of the sweeping victories of Islam, that economy was stone-dead and the trade, the industries, the cities and the extensive literacy which had been dependent upon it had vanished. With them vanished the ethos which had sprung from the Greeks and which had been spread by the Romans. That ethos was resuscitated during the Renaissance and became the basis of the culture of modern Europe; in consequence, the Roman period can appear less alien than does the period which followed it, and some of the vilification suffered by that period is the result of an inability to understand and appreciate it.

The years 400–600 are wholly central to the history of Wales and Britain. That was the era when Britain came to be divided into a Brythonic west, a Teutonic east and a Gaelic north, and when the nations of the Welsh, the English and the Scots crystallized. It was the era which saw the establishment of the dynasties of the main kingdoms of Wales and the transformation of Brittonic into a language which can be recognized as Welsh. It was also the age when Christianity so pervaded Wales that most of its parishes came to bear the names of the glorious army of the saints. Unfortunately, these seminal changes are cloaked in the deepest obscurity. In this generation, valiant attempts have been made to penetrate the obscurity, and studies have been published which prove the ability of historians and archaeologists to coax meaning out of the most intractable evidence. And it is its intractability rather than its scarcity which is the main feature of the evidence. Although not plentiful, there is more written material relating directly to Wales in the two hundred years from 400 to 600 than there is for the previous two centuries or, indeed, for the following two centuries. But because the period 400–600 is so central, the desire to come to grips with it is greater than the desire to come to grips with the earlier and the later periods; greater too is the opportunity to offer varying interpretations of it and to debate them incessantly. Indeed, the years 400–600 have become a tournament for scholars, with each successive contributor to the debate eager to unhorse his predecessor.

It is impossible to appreciate these debates without grasping the nature of the evidence. The most influential document is *De Excidio Britanniae* (Concerning the Fall of Britain), which was written by the monk Gildas in about 540. There are some 25,000 words in the *De Excidio* and, had Gildas written in the manner of the classical historians, his book would have been a source of magnificent import. But Gildas is a splendid example of the irate cleric and what he offers is a sermon reviling his contemporaries, the kings of Britain, rather than a chronicle of his age. His Latin is characterized by a verbose opaqueness and he writes in a cryptic style with a host of biblical quotations. The traditional story of the coming of the Saxons is that of Gildas: he interpreted their success as the vengeance of God upon the Britons for their sins, and this interpretation, which was repeated by Bede, became an influential weapon in justifying the power of the English.

Apart from the work of Gildas, other contemporary writings having a bearing upon events in Britain in the period 400–600 include a few Frankish chronicles, some of the lives of the Irish saints, and *The Life of St Samson*, the only example of Welsh hagiography written in the 'Age of Saints'. In addition, there is the earliest Welsh literature, the poems of Taliesin and Aneirin; the oldest extant copies of the poems date from the generation after 1250, but Ifor Williams's theory that the core of their work was composed around 600 is broadly accepted. Inscribed stones form the most important element in the non-documentary material; there are in Wales 139 stones bearing inscriptions carved in the quarter millennium after the fall of the Empire. Of the few sites occupied in that period that have been excavated, Dinas Powys and Dinas Emrys have yielded exciting finds. There is nothing in Wales comparable with the rich objects found in the Saxon graves of southern and eastern England, where the bodies are those of pagans and are accompanied by objects intended to comfort the deceased in the afterworld. Archaeologists have cause to bemoan the Christianity of the Welsh.

This is almost the totality of the evidence which has survived from the period 400 to 600, but in succeeding centuries further documentary evidence was produced. About 730 Bede wrote his *Ecclesiastical History of the English*, a magnificent work, far-reaching in its influence but marred by a deep prejudice against the Welsh. In about 890, the original version of *The Anglo-Saxon Chronicle* was compiled; it was based upon annals written from 635 onwards and it provides a narrative of the beginnings of the English kingdoms. Some time around 960, a collection was made – probably at St David's – of a variety of documents, pedigrees and annals. It is believed that the pedigrees were drawn up at the request of Owain ap Hywel Dda and they are central to an understanding of the early history of the Welsh kingdoms. The annals contain brief notes on 151 of the years between 447 and 954 and include about twenty-five sentences dealing with the period 447–600. These are the *Annales Cambriae*; they were based on various sources, including the chronicles of the Irish and the notes occasionally

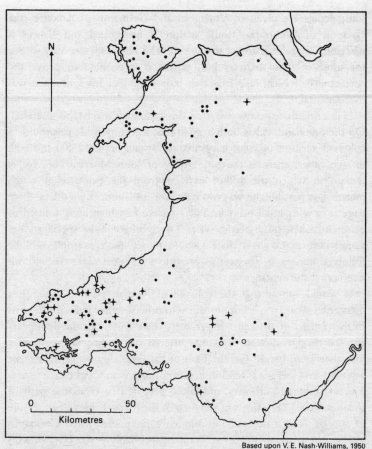

Based upon V. E. Nash-Williams, 1950

+ Stone bearing a bilingual inscription – Latin and Ogam

o Stone bearing an Ogam inscription

• Stone bearing a Latin inscription

The distribution of inscribed stones of the period 400 to 700

written on the Pascal Tables of the monastery of St David's. Bound with the pedigrees and the annals is a version of the jumble of stories to which the title *Historia Brittonum* (History of the Britons) was given in around 1150. At that time they were ascribed to Nennius, and it is believed that the kernel of the material was gathered together in about 830. Nennius's work contains the story of Cunedda and his sons; details are given of Vortigern and Germanus of Auxerre (the Garmon of Welsh tradition); Arthur is mentioned and Brutus is described as the ancestor of the Welsh. The *Historia* is the only source for most of these matters but, where it is possible to prove the correctness of Nennius's material, it is clear that his ignorance was monumental.

It is difficult to know what to do with such intractable material. On the one hand, it has been argued that it is impossible to provide a coherent account of what happened in Britain between 400 and 600; on the other, there is the bold study of John Morris, *The Age of Arthur*, in which the author extracts from the evidence as much meaning as possible; he was rewarded for his labours by a thirty-three page review in small print in *Studia Celtica* in which he is accused of being mistaken on a heroic scale. The work of most specialists lies somewhere in between these two extremes; their example will be followed here in an attempt to provide a plausible narrative without overtaxing the evidence.

It would appear that the collapse of Roman power, although a disaster to some, was an opportunity to others. Among the inhabitants of the *civitates* of Britannia, there were those to whom the disappearance of the jurisdiction of Rome offered the chance to take power into their own hands. On the basis of the fragile evidence, it may be assumed that there was tension between those who sought the restoration of imperial authority and those prepared to tread the path of independence. The efforts of the men of the *civitates* enjoyed a measure of success. The cities did not suddenly disappear: when Germanus visited one of them in 429 – Verulam, probably – the civic officers were still attending to their duties. But in seizing power it is unlikely that the leaders of the *civitates* were undertaking a role that was wholly congenial to them. They had long since been imbued with the notion that sovereignty belonged elsewhere, and as the Romans, within regions where their authority was undisputed, had prohibited civilians from bearing arms, military traditions had withered among the men of south-eastern Britain. The inhabitants of the less Romanized regions – those of Wales and the northern marches of Britannia – were less hesitant and within a few decades of the demise of the Empire it would appear that authority had been seized by the men of the periphery.

Among them was Vortigern (the Gwrtheyrn of Welsh tradition). It would seem that Vortigern was a native of the borders of Wales and he appears in the genealogies as an ancestor of the kings of Powys. Nennius has a considerable amount to say about him but he is not mentioned by Gildas. If the core of the traditions concerning Vortigern is accepted – including the story that it was he who yielded land to German mercenary soldiers in return for help against the Picts – it is reasonable to assume that he had a measure of authority throughout Britannia some time between the years 420 and 450. Vortigern's agreement with the Germans was consistent with Roman practice, and it was successful, for after the period of his presumed rule nothing is heard of the threat of the Picts. Nevertheless, to later generations of Britons, Vortigern was considered to be the personifica- tion of folly and perfidy, and so great was the antipathy towards him that there is some suggestion that attempts were made to write him out of the pedigree of the kings of Powys. His vilification arose from the conviction that it was his action that had caused the Britons to be deprived of their inheritance. The Romans left a vacuum of authority; but equally importantly, they had created an image of authority – the image of Britannia under a single government, the image of the Crown of the Kingdom. There was so much embellishment of this theme following the publication of Geoffrey of Monmouth's *History of the Kings of Britain* in 1136 that it is now difficult to appreciate the strength of its appeal in the centuries before Geoffrey. Yet Gildas, around 540, and the author of *Armes Prydein*, around 929, display a deep sense of loss. The natural inheritors of the power of Rome over Britannia were the Romano-British, particularly in view of the fact that the ruling class in Britain considered themselves to be Roman. By the age of Gildas, much of Britannia had been lost by the Britons and had been appropriated by the pagan Saxons. This was at the root of their anguish, anguish which would become the motive force of much of Welsh mythology.

Bede attributed that appropriation to one sudden incursion. Accord- ing to him, it happened in 446; in that year, wrote Bede, the kingdoms of the Saxons, the Angles and the Jutes were established. It is now believed that there was no such sudden incursion and that the greater part of Britannia remained in the hands of the Britons for at least a century after the fall of the Empire. Nora Chadwick described that century as one during which it was possible to travel from Edinburgh to Cornwall in the assurance that Brittonic would be understood along the whole of the journey, and as a period when Brythonic kingdoms were paramount in the island.

Those kingdoms varied in their origins, but the genealogical lists compiled about 960 suggest that most of them could claim some degree of association with the Roman order. It should be remembered that it is only the pedigrees of successful royal houses that have survived. The inscribed stones bear the names of a number of men who had probably been powerful in their localities, but they cannot be recognized in any king-lists. It is probable that numerous small kingdoms emerged in the wake of the collapse of the Empire. This may be reflected in the *cantrefi* (hundreds), the units of local government of later times. Although there is no definite information relating to the boundaries of the *cantrefi* of Wales for at least seven hundred years after 400, they may well date from the immediate post-Roman period. The *Mabinogi* begins with a reference to the seven *cantrefi* of Dyfed and the Laws of Wales mention the seven bishops' houses of Dyfed. In Ireland, the early kingdom – the *tuath* – was very small; there were ninety-seven in all and every *tuath* had its bishop. It would be unwise to rely heavily upon evidence from Ireland; as the island was never part of the Roman Empire, there was no break in the development of its native institutions as there was in Wales. The old Celtic system, with its semi-divine ruler, the *ri* (Welsh *rhi*), survived in Ireland, but the Welsh adopted the word *brenin* to denote their less archaic form of kingship. Nevertheless, the extent of the territory of the first kings of Wales was probably broadly comparable with that of the *tuath*, and it is likely that the earliest kingdoms known to history were a combination of a number of such territories. It may be assumed that the stronger kings annexed the territories of their weaker neighbours and that the lineages of the victors are the only lineages to have survived.

Of these lineages, the most powerful by 540 was that of Maglocunus, a ruler portrayed by Gildas as a man of impressive sinfulness. Maglocunus was the Maelgwn Fawr or Maelgwn Gwynedd of Welsh tradition. The pedigrees state that he was a descendant of Cunedda who, according to Nennius, came to Gwynedd from among the Men of the North – the inhabitants of southern Scotland. Cunedda is not mentioned by Gildas and the first surviving reference to him is four hundred years later than his alleged lifetime. The story of Cunedda may be a myth invented in about 800 when Merfyn ap

Gwriad, also of the lineage of the Men of the North, became king of Gwynedd. Nevertheless, the Welsh treasured traditions relating to the northern kingdoms, in particular the kingdom of the Votadini (Gododdin) on the banks of the river Forth. Aneirin, the poet of the Votadini, claimed that men from Gwynedd joined the army of the king of the Votadini in its attack upon Catterick around 600, and a brooch in the same style as the brooches of the Forth valley has been discovered at Pant-y-saer in Anglesey. These are considerations which make it difficult not to give some credence to Nennius's account. He states that Cunedda, the *atavus* of Maelgwn Gwynedd, came with eight sons and one grandson from Manaw Gododdin and drove the Irish out of Gwynedd, an event which occurred 146 years before the reign of Maelgwn.

Historians have derived much innocent pleasure from the 146 years and the word *atavus*. One possible interpretation is that Cunedda came to Gwynedd between 380 and 400; if so, it would be reasonable to link his coming with the vacuum of authority created when Magnus Maximus denuded Segontium of its garrison in 383. The present tendency, however, is to favour a year around 440 as the date of the migration, and it has been argued that it occurred under the aegis of Vortigern. According to the pedigrees, Cunedda's grandfather was Padarn Beisrudd (Paternus of the red cloak), an epithet which suggests that he had worn the cloak of a Roman officer. If Cunedda were a contemporary of Vortigern, his grandfather would have been in his prime around 383, and it is possible that he had been invested with his cloak as part of the efforts of Magnus Maximus to secure the borders of Britannia before departing with his army. Cunedda would certainly have been accompanied by a band of warriors, but it is unlikely that the story of his sons – Ceredig, Edern and the others – and the kingdoms they founded – Ceredigion, Edeirnion and so on – is trustworthy. Early Welsh literature contains a wealth of stories seeking to explain place-names, and doubtless the story is propaganda aimed at justifying the right of Cunedda's descendants to territories beyond the borders of the original kingdom of Gwynedd. That kingdom probably consisted of the two banks of the Menai Straits and the coast over towards the estuary of the river Conwy, the foundations upon which Cunedda's descendants created a more extensive realm. There is evidence besides that of Nennius concerning the success of the campaign against the invaders from Ireland. It is possible that colonies of Irish continued to exist in Gwynedd up to the time of Maelgwn Fawr – a memory of them remains in place-names such as Llŷn and Dinllaen – but there is a determinedly Brythonic, and indeed Roman, air to early Gwynedd.

It was quite otherwise in south-west Wales, for the kingdom of Dyfed was of Irish origin. There are in Dyfed twenty inscribed stones bearing letters in ogam, the script of the Irish. This is one of the factors which led John Rhys to argue that it was the Q-Celts who were the first to colonize Britain and that the western peninsulas were not Brittonicized (or P-Celticized) until about A D 500. This theory is no longer accepted, but the ogam stones are an indication of considerable Irish colonization in Dyfed in the last decades of the Empire and in the immediate post-Roman period. One of the legends of the Irish mentions the coming of the tribe of the Deisi to Wales, an event which can probably be dated to the years between 350 and 400. In Castelldwyran near Narberth there is a stone bearing the name Voteporix (Gwrthefyr) in both Latin and ogam; it is a memorial to the man described by Gildas in his least offensive vein as *tyrannus Demetarum*. On his stone he is given the title *Protictoris*, which suggests that one of his ancestors was a member of the retinue of an emperor and that the title had become hereditary. The name of Magnus Maximus occurs in his pedigree; it is possible that it was Magnus who permitted the migration of the Deisi to Dyfed and that one of Voteporix's forefathers had been in his service. Traditions relating to Brychan, the eponymous founder of the kingdom of Brycheiniog, also have an Irish context. There are six ogam stones in Brycheiniog, part of the large body of evidence relating to the ancient routes linking west Wales with the Usk valley.

The name 'Powys' probably comes from the word 'pagus'; both therefore are cognate with the word 'pagan'. It is believed that the nucleus of the kingdom of Powys was the *pagus* or the hinterland of the territory of the Cornovii and that Powys expanded to include not only that territory – the rich lands of the middle Severn valley – but also the lands between the upper reaches of the rivers Wye and Dee. According to tradition, Vortigern was the founder of the royal house of Gwrtheyrnion in southern Powys, but the column erected near Llangollen about 825 in memory of King Eliseg states that Gwrtheyrn was also the founder of the main line and that his wife was the daughter of Magnus Maximus.

In the south-east, the most Romanized area of Wales, the kingdoms developed from a combination of the Roman settlements and the old traditions of the Silures. Caer-went, which had come to an end as an urban settlement by 500, gave its name to Gwent, as Ariconium gave its name to Erging (Archenfield). The pedigrees state that Caradog Freichfras was the founder of the royal house of Gwent and it has been claimed that his name is evidence of a desire to commemorate a man who had been a hero among the Silures. It is probable that Caradog Freichfras arose from among the *decuriones* of Caer-went; he may therefore have been a descendant of the aristocracy which had existed among the Silures four hundred years earlier. Gwent was the district between the rivers Usk and Wye. To the north-east lay the kingdom of Erging; according to the charters copied by the compilers of *The Book of Llandaf* around 1130, it would appear that the kings of Erging, the descendants of Erb, were the leading figures in south-east Wales in the period 500–600. To the west of Gwent lay the kingdom of Glywysing; by 600 its king was Meurig ap Tewdrig, the ancestor of a line of kings which would rule in the south-east for over five hundred years. Material in *The Book of Llandaf* provides ground for believing that Meurig and his descendants extended their power over Erging and Gwent as well as over Glywysing. It was they who created the kingdom of Morgannwg (Glamorgan), which may have been named after Morgan ab Athrwys who died about 665, although some specialists attribute the name to Morgan ab Owain who died in 974. There is little definite evidence concerning the origins of the kings of Glywysing, although it is claimed that Magnus Maximus lurks somewhere in their pedigree.

In the history or the mythology of the beginnings of the kingdoms of Wales, Magnus is a ubiquitous lurker. He also figures in stories of the saints; he appears in the early literature of Cornwall and in the traditions of the Men of the North and it is he who is the hero of the story *Breuddwyd Macsen*. So great was his appeal to the Welsh imagination and so substantial was his alleged contribution to the establishment of the early Welsh kingdoms that A. W. Wade-Evans and Martin Charlesworth suggested that he could be considered to be the father of the Welsh nation. This view is supported by Gwynfor Evans, who argues that Magnus, in acknowledging the role of the leaders of the Britons in 383, opened the way for independent political organizations to develop among the Welsh earlier than they did among most of the other nations of Europe. It is also supported by Gwyn A. Williams, perhaps because of his desire to give a neat symmetry to his interpretation of the history of Wales – that the nation came into existence during the death-throes of one empire and went out of existence during the death-throes of another. If it is accepted that a nation has an organic nature similar to that of a human being – a concept full of difficulties – then perhaps it is not over-fanciful to consider 383 as the year of the conception of the Welsh nation and to accept Magnus Maximus as the father of that nation.

And it was the conception rather than the birth of the nation which occurred in 383, for the word *Cymry* had not been adopted as the name of the nation and Wales was not its only territory. The kingdoms of southern Scotland were of the same nature as those of Wales: Strathclyde with its centre at Dunbarton Rock (Dun Breatann) in the river Clyde, Rheged with its centre possibly at Carlisle and the land of the Votadini with its centre at Edinburgh. These kingdoms have an important place in the history of Wales, for among their inhabitants were the authors of the earliest surviving examples of literature in the Welsh language. To the south of Rheged lay the kingdom of Elfed, which extended across the Pennines, while Devon and Cornwall constituted the kingdom of Dumnonia reigned over by King Constantine, towards whom Gildas was so impolite. There were doubtless other Brythonic kingdoms in southern and eastern Britain. *The Anglo-Saxon Chronicle* mentions King Nantleod, who met his death in 508, and the kings Conmael, Condidan and Farinmail, who were killed at Dyrham near Bath in 577, and the scale of the fortifications at Cadbury in Somerset prove that a powerful Brythonic ruler lived there around 550. Virtually nothing is known about these rulers; unlike the rulers of the Men of the North, they do not seem to have had close ties with the kings of Wales; thus, after their kingdoms had been overwhelmed by the English, no one in later generations had any motive for remembering them.

The most substantial evidence relating to the nature of the early Brythonic kingdoms comes from Gwynedd. Gwynedd had sufficient cohesion as a kingdom for its inhabitants to be consciously Venedotian; on the memorial stone of Cantiorix, raised at Penmachno in about 500, he is described as *Venedotis Cives* (citizen of Gwynedd). There is evidence in Gwynedd of a desire to cling to the Roman world; on the stone commemorating Melus at Llangian in Anglesey, it is noted that he is a *medicus* (doctor), and Cantiorix's stone records that he was the cousin of Maglos, the *magistratus*. The inscribed stones, together with the work of the archaeologists, prove that Wales in the centuries after the fall of the Empire was not without contact with the culture of the other regions which had been under the sway of Rome. The traditional notion that Saxon colonization in south-eastern Britain created a wedge which prevented contact between Wales and mainland Europe is a mistaken one. In prehistory, the greater part of such contact had occurred via the western sea-routes. With the collapse of the Empire, voyages along those western routes revived; indeed, it could be argued that the period of Roman rule was an unusual episode in the experience of Wales, a time when it was pulled away from its natural westerly axis. The memorial to the son of Avitorius at Penmachno states that the stone was raised during the consulate of Justinus, a man who is known to have been appointed consul in 540 by the remnant of Roman power still existing in the West. The epitaph carved for King Cadfan following his death in about 625 shows that an artist in Gwynedd was aware of the most recent fashion in lettering, and the format of inscriptions provides evidence of links with France, northern Africa and the eastern shores of the Mediterranean. The fort at Degannwy, the seat of Maelgwn Fawr, has yielded fragments of glass and pottery from the Black Sea, Athens and Bordeaux, as has Dinas Emrys, a site associated with Vortigern.

Evidence from the other Welsh kingdoms is less plentiful, although excavations at Dinas Powys in Glamorgan have proved that around 500 the fort was occupied by a chieftain who had pottery and glass at least as varied in their origins as those of Maelgwn Fawr. Similar objects have been found in about half a dozen sites known to have been occupied in the centuries immediately following the fall of the Empire. Their style indicates that the trade extended over several generations, although the sum of what has been discovered would suggest that cargoes did not arrive more than once every decade or two. The pottery and glass were probably exchanged for leather or skins, for coinage virtually vanished from Britain within a few years of the end of Roman rule. Indeed, on the basis of the archaeological evidence, it would seem that society was poorer in material terms after the fall of the Empire than it had been before the coming of the Romans. Metal-working continued, as the smithy at Dinas Powys testifies, but there is no suggestion that masterpieces similar to those of the La Tène era were created. Furthermore, no attempt was made to build anything remotely comparable with the hill-forts of the Iron Age; only half a hectare was enclosed at Dinas Powys, and at Garn Boduan, where the pre-Roman fort extends over six hectares, a fortification of about a quarter of a hectare was built within it, perhaps around 500.

It is likely therefore that in AD 500 the population of Wales was smaller than it had been in 100 BC. It has been suggested that on the eve of the Roman occupation Wales had a population of about 250,000, but as the evidence is so slight it would be unwise to make too much of the figure. Evidence relating to the economy of Wales and to the nature of the life of its inhabitants is equally slight. The portrait of the chroniclers and the poets is that of a 'heroic' society, although it should be borne in mind that the only members of that 'heroic' society were the highest class of the inhabitants – the king and his retinue. Because of the nature of the evidence, there is a tendency to give excessive prominence to the king when considering society in early Wales. A number of factors gave cohesion to that society; the king was among those factors but there were others of equal or greater importance. The 'heroic' society of the age of Maelgwn Fawr would persist in its essentials for at least half a millennium, and a fuller discussion of its characteristics will be deferred until the narrative approaches the time of the composition of documents which can throw some light upon the society which maintained the king and the 'heroes'. It is reasonable to believe that those documents – the Welsh law-books in particular – include material which is relevant to the age of Maelgwn. They contain elements which date back to the age before the Brythonic kingdoms in England and Scotland were overwhelmed by the English.

The overwhelming of the Brythonic kingdoms is the central fact in the history of Britain in the period 400–800; it was a relatively slow process and even in 700 the English were not in secure possession of the entire territory which would eventually constitute England. It is likely that German soldiers came to Britain with Aulus Plautius in AD 43; the practice of recruiting among the Germans increased markedly in the later years of the Empire and a substantial number of the legionary veterans settled permanently in the districts in which they had served. By about 300, a Germano-Roman culture was developing in Britain, considerable evidence of which has been found in the

German cemeteries situated in the vicinity of the Roman cities of eastern England. Of the various German tribes, it was the Frisians and Saxons who dwelt between the estuaries of the rivers Elbe and Rhine who provided Britain with the greater part of its migrants. Probably little attention should be given to Bede's attempt to distinguish between Angles, Saxons and Jutes. To the Britons who wrote in Latin, the migrants were *Saxones*; in Welsh, they were *Saeson*.

Although Germans were numerous in Britain before the fall of the Empire, the traditions of the English maintain that it was later invaders who established the English kingdoms of the south-east of the island. Those traditions date the beginnings of the royal house of Kent to around 450, that of Sussex to around 480 and that of Wessex to around 495. These dates can be harmonized with Nennius's story of Vortigern granting the Isle of Thanet in Kent to the English in 428, although if Gildas's account is preferred it would be necessary to suggest rather later dates. It is likely that the mercenaries cast off the sovereignty of Vortigern and that they invited more of their compatriots to join them. There is an entry in the Frankish annals which states that by the 440s Britain was in the possession of the Saxons, but that comment was probably only relevant to the extreme south-east of the island. From their footholds in south-eastern Britain, the Saxons were well placed to plunder their British neighbours and it was probably these raids which caused the Britons to appeal to the Empire in 446 (or perhaps between 457 and 462). The appeal was ignored and in the decades after 450 the Saxons grasped the opportunity to plant small kingdoms in south-eastern Britain. Their territories were not extensive – London was not in their possession – and their attempts to extend them were frustrated by the campaigns associated with the name of Ambrosius (the Emrys Wledig of Welsh tradition). There are suggestions of rivalry between Ambrosius and Vortigern; it would appear that Ambrosius came from a more Romanized background than his rival, and his campaigns may have represented the last stand of the *civitates*.

Over the greater part of Britain the small footholds of the English may not have been seen as much of a threat. This would seem to be confirmed by the readiness of the Britons in about 469 to send soldiers to Gaul to assist the Emperor Anthemius, a magnanimous gesture to an empire on its death-bed. Up to about 480, the threat from Ireland was probably at least as great as that from mainland Europe; it has been argued that it was Irish raids upon Devon and Cornwall which caused the first wave of migration to Brittany between about 460 and 480, for the language introduced into Brittany was the Brittonic of south-western Britain rather than that of the regions threatened by the English.

The archaeological record suggests that by about 490 substantial English communities had been established, particularly in the middle Thames valley, the later nucleus of the kingdom of Wessex; it also suggests that between 500 and 550 those communities stagnated or even contracted. Excavations in the Low Countries have yielded evidence of Saxon migration from Britain in that period, archaeological evidence which accords with statements by Frankish chroniclers. This reverse migration is consistent with Gildas's reference to a great victory won by the Britons at Mons Badonicus, a battle which was fought, wrote Gildas, in the year of his birth. He was approaching his forty-fourth birthday when he wrote the *De Excidio* and thus the date of the battle hinges upon the date of Gildas's work. Mons Badonicus could have been fought at any time between 490 and 518, but there is a tendency to favour a year around 496. The fame of the battle arises from the fact that Nennius attributed the victory to Arthur. Centuries after Nennius's lifetime, Arthur was elevated to be one of the great heroes of Europe and, for an entire continent, his court was seen as the fount of chivalry. Geoffrey of Monmouth in his *History of the Kings of Britain* portrays Arthur as a glorious hero, but the only references to him which survive from the centuries before the publication of Geoffrey's work in 1136 are Nennius's comment, together with a few other slight allusions. Although some historians doubt whether Arthur was a historical figure at all, it is reasonable to believe that a man of that name did exist and that he was the leader of Brythonic forces, perhaps on the pattern of the *Dux Britanniarum* of the previous century. It is credible also that his forces won a victory of importance in about 496 and that he was killed – or that he vanished – in about 515, following the battle of Camlan. To say more than that would be inadmissible, and the fame of Arthur remains one of the mysteries of the history of Wales, Britain and Europe – although it may represent a desire to pay tribute to the last of the heirs of Rome to make a successful stand against the 'barbarians'.

There have been lengthy debates about the location of Mons Badonicus. It may be Badbury Rings, in which case it would represent a victory over the Saxons of Sussex; it may be near Bath, which would probably mean that it was a victory over a campaign launched by the colonists of the mid-Thames valley. Nennius states that Mons Badonicus was one of Arthur's many victories and the list of battles in the *Historia* offers a basis for believing that Arthur campaigned against all the emerging English kingdoms. Such campaigns would be consistent with the notion that he was the leader of mobile cavalrymen and would also accord with the existence of Arthurian traditions in widely separated parts of Britain. Gildas states that in his day the English were not waging war upon the Britons. Nevertheless, according to tradition, it was during his lifetime that the two kingdoms which would represent the greatest threat to the Britons came into existence. In the years between 495 and 530, Cerdic, the founder of the house of Wessex, won authority over southern Hampshire, and in 547 Ida created the nucleus of the kingdom of Bernicia (Brynaich) by building the fort of Bamburgh on the coast of Northumbria. Yet these were small footholds, and it is likely that most of Britain remained under the authority of Brythonic kings at least until the death of Maelgwn Fawr in 549. On the basis of his study of river-names, Kenneth Jackson argued that it was only those areas in which there are virtually no Celtic names that were in the hands of the English by 550. Those are the areas east of a line from Scarborough to Southampton. If his argument is correct (it should be noted that not all experts accept it), the English in 550 were still a considerable distance away from those keys to mastery over southern Britain – the two stretches of lowland which extend to the estuaries of the rivers Dee and Severn and which divide the Highland Zone into three.

The time of decision was the century 550 to 650. Those were the years when the English won supremacy over the greater part of southern Britain. It would appear that the Britons offered only a feeble resistance to the campaigns of the rulers of Wessex which started about 550. *The Anglo-Saxon Chronicle* notes a series of their victories, including the capture of Salisbury in 552 and of Aylesbury in 571, victories which (such was the rapacity of the descendants of Cerdic) included triumphs over their fellow-English as well as over the Britons. Among their victories was that of 577 at Dyrham, twelve kilometres from Bristol, a battle in which they killed three kings and captured Bath, Cirencester and Gloucester. Thus the men of Wessex had reached the coast of the Severn Sea, although it is doubtful

whether that coast was colonized by the English in the immediate
wake of their victory. Somerset did not firmly come into their pos-
sesion until after 650 and there was a Brythonic king in Devon until
710. Cornwall retained a measure of independence for at least another
two hundred years and the last reference to a Cornish king does not
occur until 878. Cornwall had been absorbed into the kingdom of
Wessex by 950, but it remained essentially Celtic in speech and in
culture for centuries to come, and the consciousness of that inheritance
remains significant to this day. The victories of the English were
probably a stimulus for further Brythonic migration to Brittany. The
migrants almost certainly hailed from the borders of Wessex, although
there are suggestions that their leaders came from Wales. The second
wave of migration began about 530; it reached its peak in the years
550–80 but it did not come to an end until about 700. By then the
language and the traditions of the Britons were dominant throughout
western Brittany and the cultural life of Lesser Britain developed on
the basis of influences which sprang in the main from Wales, although
the historian Fleuriot argues that the Celtic culture of Brittany also
includes elements inherited from Gaul.

As they had captured Gloucester, it would be reasonable to assume
that the men of Wessex would seek to take possession of the northern
as well as the southern coast of the Severn Sea. Despite the formidable
obstacle represented by the gorge of the lower Wye, the coastlands of
south-east Wales are essentially a tongue of the Lowland Zone. According to tradition, the men of Gwent defeated the English in about 630,
a victory which thwarted English attempts to gain control of the
northern coastlands of the Severn Sea. Their victory was among the
most important events in the history of Wales, for it was this success
in defending the Wye border which saved Gwent and Glywysing for
Wales.

While the Britons of south-western Britain were yielding to
Wessex, those further north were seeking to dislodge the English
colonies in their midst. It is possible that it was in 577, the year of
Dyrham, that Urien, king of Rheged, attacked Lindisfarne (Ynys
Medgawdd), besieging Deodric, the king of Bernicia. Nennius notes
that three other kings fought alongside Urien, but that one of them,
Morgan, jealous of the fame of Urien – the fame which is the main
theme of the poems of Taliesin – brought about his death during the

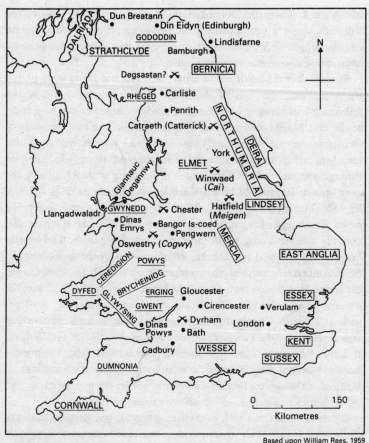

Based upon William Rees, 1959

<u>GLYWYSING</u> : British kingdom

MERCIA : English kingdom

✕ Battle

Britons and English, 500–700

siege. About twenty years later – in 595 possibly – the Men of the North attacked Deira (Deifr), a kingdom which had perhaps developed from the German colony at York. If Ifor Williams's argument is correct, the heroes of this attack are the subject of Aneirin's great poem *Y Gododdin*. Its object was to capture the old Roman fort of Catterick (Catraeth), and Mynyddog Mwynfawr, the king of the Votadini, spent a year planning his campaign. It was a total failure and the words of Aneirin can be interpreted to mean that he alone of Mynyddog's men escaped with his life.

Shortly after the battle of Catterick, Bernicia and Deira were united by Aethelfrith, the first of the kings of Northumbria, and in the following half century Northumbria absorbed most of the kingdoms of the Old North. Aedan, king of Scots, was defeated in the battle of Degsastan in 603; Ceredig, king of Elfed, was driven from his kingdom in about 617; Rheged was annexed about 635, perhaps through the marriage of Oswy of Northumbria with Rhianfellt, the great-grand-daughter of Urien. Carlisle was securely in English hands by 685. The kingdom of the Votadini came to an end about 638 when Edinburgh was captured by Oswy. By then, Strathclyde was the only one remaining of the Brythonic kingdoms of the Old North. Strathclyde survived for another four hundred years; indeed, when Northumbria succumbed to pressure from the Danes, Strathclyde expanded to include much of the old kingdom of Rheged. There, for a century and more after 900, Brythonic influences revived, as names such as Penrith, Caerdunog and Lanercost bear witness. Strathclyde was absorbed by the kingdom of the Scots in about 1018, but William II, king of England, seized its southern parts in 1092. Thus the present border between England and Scotland cuts across the kingdom of Rheged, although on neither side of the border do memories survive of the heroes and kingdoms which once flourished there.

It was in Wales that such memories survived, and after the battle of Catterick it is only Wales that provides continued evidence of Brythonic resistance. Although Northumbria did not extend from sea to sea until at least 650, Aethelfrith (593–616) conducted several campaigns in the direction of the western sea. One such campaign resulted in the battle of Chester in about 616 when Selyf, king of Powys, was defeated and when Aethelfrith, a pagan, ordered the slaughter of the monks of Bangor Is-coed – twelve hundred of them according to Bede – because they had fought against him with their prayers. Westward campaigns were continued by Edwin, Aethelfrith's successor and the first English king to be called *Bretwalda* – the overlord of the whole of Britain. Bede states that Edwin invaded Anglesey and an entry in the *Annales Cambriae* notes that he besieged Catguollaun on Ynys Glannauc (Puffin Island) in 629.

Catguollaun was Cadwallon of the line of Maelgwn Fawr, a man who was himself not without claims to the status of *Bretwalda*. His father Cadfan, who died about 625, was certainly considered worthy of the title, to judge from his epitaph in Llangadwaladr, Anglesey: *Catamanus Rex sapientissimus opinatissimus omnium regum* (King Cadfan, the wisest and the most renowned of all kings). Edwin's success was short-lived: in 632, he was killed by Cadwallon in the battle of Meigen (Hatfield near Doncaster). In 633, Cadwallon killed Edwin's successors, Osric of Deira and Eanfrith of Bernicia, and Bede declared that it was Cadwallon's intention to exterminate the English race. That may have been a feasible proposition in 633, but in the following year Cadwallon in his turn was killed by Oswald, the brother of Eanfrith. The year 634 denotes the extinction of the possibility of restoring Brythonic supremacy in Britain. Centuries later, the author of *Brut y Tywysogyon* felt the need to emphasize that extinction when noting the death of Cadwaladr, the son of Cadwallon, in 682 (or possibly 664), a note which undoubtedly reflects the influence of Geoffrey of Monmouth. To the bald entry of the *Annales Cambriae*, the author of the *Brut* added: 'And from that time onwards the Britons lost the crown of the kingdom and the Saxons won it.'

In the battles of 632–3, Cadwallon's ally was Penda, king of Mercia. After Cadwallon's death, Penda resumed the struggle with Northumbria; Oswald was killed in the battle of Cogwy (Oswestry) in 641, and Penda was killed by Oswy, the brother of Oswald, in the battle of Cai (Winwaed) in 654. Mercia – midland England – was the last of the kingdoms of the English to come into existence. From 640 to 800, Mercia was the most important of those kingdoms and it was the Mercian kings who laid the foundations of the unity of England. The inhabitants of Wales had dealt from afar with the kingdoms of Wessex and Northumbria, but as Mercia expanded into the valleys of the Dee, the Wye and the Severn the Saxons came to the periphery of Wales, and it would be the western border of Mercia which would determine the border of Wales. That border was defined at the expense of Powys. The territory of the Cornovii continued to be part of Powys at least until 600, but thereafter the region was infiltrated by Saxon colonists; in about 610, Beuno heard the English language – the language of paganism – being spoken on the further bank of the river Severn, an experience which caused him to migrate to Gwynedd. It appears that Viroconium, the capital of the Cornovii, had been abandoned by about 550 and that the court of Powys had moved to Pengwern, a more defensible site. Pengwern has been identified with Shrewsbury in the loop of the Severn, but a more likely locality is The Berth in the marshes and mosslands to the north of Baschurch. There is no contemporary evidence relating to the conquest of the middle Severn valley by Mercia, but two hundred years later, when Powys was again in anguish, poems were written which commemorate the conquest. They express the desolation of Princess Heledd on seeing the destruction of Pengwern and on hearing of the death of her brother, Cynddylan – events which probably belong to the years around 642. They are magnificent poems and in the dignity of her mourning Heledd gives the defeat of Powys a universal significance.

With the capture of Pengwern, the Saxon settlers had reached the fringes of the uplands of Wales. In doing so they severed the links, central to the pattern of agriculture, which had existed between highland and lowland. Such a border was inherently unstable: the men of the hills were bound to seek to repossess the plains, and there is evidence of efforts to do so in 655, 705–7 and 722. Mercia reacted by building Wat's Dyke, which extends from the Severn valley northwards towards the estuary of the Dee. The dyke marks the edge of the lowlands, and according to Cyril Fox it was the work of Aethelbald, king of Mercia from 716 to 757. It appears that Powys revived after his reign. There is a reference to a battle at Hereford in 760, and the Eliseg Pillar states that King Eliseg, who was in his prime around 750, freed Powys from the power of the English. By about 780, however, Offa, king of Mercia, was at the height of his authority; it is recorded that he attacked Wales in 778 and 784, and there is no reason to reject the tradition that it was during his reign (757–96) that the dyke associated with his name was constructed.

Offa's Dyke is one of the most remarkable structures in Britain. Offa's intention was to provide Mercia with a well–defined boundary from Prestatyn to Chepstow, a distance of 240 kilometres. Natural barriers were utilized where that was practicable; where it was not, an earth embankment was built which in places still stands to a height of two and a half metres and which is, with its ditch, up to twenty metres wide. A total of 130 kilometres of dyke was constructed, assuming that all the sections of the earthwork associated with the name of Offa can be considered part of the same project. It is unbroken from Treuddyn in Flintshire to the river Arrow in Radnorshire, but around Llanymynech the opportunity was seized of using the river Severn as the boundary. To the south of the river Arrow, there are seventy-five kilometres in which there are only occasional signs of the dyke, probably because the thick forests of the Wye valley acted as a sufficient barrier. Between Monmouth and the Severn Sea it reappears, although with gaps, and it terminates on the coast in the Beachley peninsula. In the north, there is no evidence of the dyke over twenty-five of the forty kilometres between Treuddyn and the sea, a fact which suggests that it was unfinished when Offa was killed in the battle of Rhuddlan in 796.

The labour of thousands of men was needed to build the dyke, proof that the kingdom of Mercia possessed a high degree of cohesion; in places it is absolutely straight for kilometres, proof of the technical skills of its designers. It is twelve kilometres longer than Hadrian's Wall but, unlike Hadrian's barrier, that of Offa is an earth not a stone construction and it was never garrisoned. Its purpose was to denote rather than to defend the frontier. Where both lie side by side, Wat's Dyke is up to seven metres to the east of Offa's Dyke; the one gives Oswestry to Wales, the other to England. Wat's Dyke marked the boundary of the lowlands, but parts of Offa's Dyke are located as much as four hundred metres above sea level. The intention, no doubt, was to give to Mercia command of the approaches to the lowlands as well as of the lowlands themselves, an interpretation confirmed by the attempts of its designers to locate it in places which provide an extensive view to the west. It is hardly likely that the dyke marked the precise boundary between the two peoples; during the age of Offa, there were English communities to the west of it and Welsh communities to the east. If the intention was to create such a boundary, it was a failure, for the Welsh in later centuries repossessed large areas beyond it, particularly in the north-east.

In Cyril Fox's study of Offa's Dyke, his most interesting conclusion is that it was not the *diktat* of an English king which decided the location of every kilometre of it. In planning it, there was a degree of consultation with the kings of Powys and Gwent. On the Long Mountain near Trelystan, the dyke veers to the east, leaving the fertile slopes in the hands of the Welsh; near Rhiwabon, it was designed so as to ensure that Cadell ap Brochwel ab Eliseg, king of Powys, retained possession of the fortress of Penygardden. Even more remarkable was the respect shown to the interests of the kingdom of Gwent. There is no more obvious boundary in the whole of Britain than the gorge of the lower Wye, but – assuming that the dyke in that region is part of Offa's project – his men went to the trouble of building the dyke on the crest to the east of the gorge, clearly with the intention of recognizing that the river Wye and its traffic belonged to the kingdom of Gwent; this recognition was underlined by continuing the dyke across the Beachley peninsula, where there was probably a harbour serving the trade of Gwent. During the years 750 to 800, the kings of Gwent – and probably of the whole of Glamorgan – were the sons and grandsons of Morgan ab Athrwys. It is clear that their kingdom wielded considerable influence, and on the basis of her study of the *Book of Llandaf* Wendy Davies has shown that it had a high degree of social stability.

When Offa's Dyke was being constructed, it was only in Wales, Strathclyde and Cornwall that Brythonic kingdoms still survived. In other parts of Britain, however, Britons survived in very considerable numbers, for the traditional belief that the Saxons killed or swept away the entire population of the territories overrun by them is wholly mistaken. In their desire to stress the essential Teutonism of the English nation, nineteenth-century historians such as Freeman and Green gave wide currency to that belief, and they could turn to Gildas and Bede for support. The central myth of British imperialism was the racial superiority of the English. The characteristics of the English were their emotional stability, their political maturity, their courage and their enlightened judgement, characteristics not shared by the Celts, the inhabitants of Ireland above all. Thus there could be no blood connection between the English and the Celts. Indeed, there were some English scholars who were reluctant to accept that the Irish and the Welsh were even Celts, for if they were they would be 'members', as were the Teutons, of the Indo-European 'family'. It is this reluctance which explains the popularity of terms such as 'Milesian' and 'Iberian'. Some of the historians of Wales and Ireland sought to refute such notions, but it is the voice of racist imperialism which reached the schools and it is only recently, in the wake of the collapse of racist–cultural theories as a result of the appalling calamities they have caused, that descriptions of the Welsh and the Irish as remnant peoples have disappeared from the text-books.

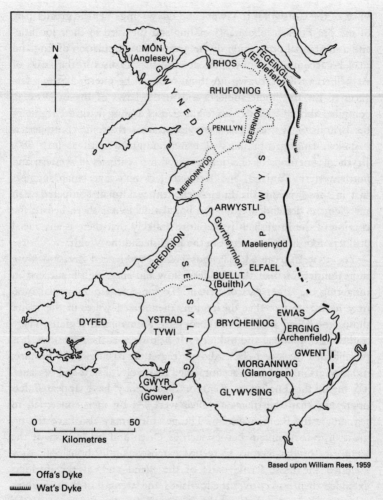

Based upon William Rees, 1959

▬▬▬ Offa's Dyke
ᴜᴜᴜᴜ Wat's Dyke

The early kingdoms

It is likely that there was slaughter, occasionally on a scale bordering upon genocide but, to judge from the comments of Bede on Cadwallon, it was not the monopoly of the English. It is likely too that people fled before the invaders, some to Brittany and others to Wales, including perhaps an exodus of the descendants of the owners of the rich villas of the Cotswolds to Gwent and Glywysing. Yet the greater part of the pre-English inhabitants of England survived in their localities and a substantial proportion of the present-day population of England may be accounted among their descendants. Clauses in the Laws of Aethelbert of Kent, drawn up about 602, can be interpreted as references to his Brythonic subjects and in the Laws of Ina of Wessex, compiled about 690, there are eight clauses dealing with the rights of the Britons of Wessex. There is evidence that Brittonic continued as a spoken language in parts of eastern England until at least 700. Brythonic methods of taxation survived for centuries in western and north-western England, and Kenneth Jackson's river map suggests that in those regions the English element was small compared with the element descended from the population living there before the coming of the English. It is therefore unlikely that there is any racial distinction of substance between the English and the Welsh.

Yet, if it is accepted that those who experienced invasion were more numerous than the invaders, how did the English succeed in mastering the larger part of Britain? To some degree the explanation may lie in the fact that the regions they seized were, in the main, those which had been most thoroughly Romanized, regions where traditions of political and military self-help were at their weakest. It is possible that the lower classes did not regret the passing of the Empire; its last years in Gaul were accompanied by revolts of serfs and peasants. To them, the English in Kent or Sussex may have appeared less oppressive than the *civitates*, which were led by men concerned to perpetuate the Roman system. The peasantry may also have felt no great urge to maintain heroes such as Urien and his fellows. If the territories of the Saxons were not extensive until about 550, they included the most fertile parts of the island and, as the invaders extended their power over the lowlands, the strength of their strategical position increased. It has been argued that the resistance of the Britons was undermined by their internecine strife; Arthur was killed in a battle with his fellow Britons and one of Taliesin's poems commemorates the battle of Argoed Llwyfain fought between Urien and Flamddwyn. Too much should not be made of this argument, for such struggles were not a monopoly of the Britons; *The Anglo-Saxon Chronicle* is studded with stories of wars between the English. The success of the English after 550 may have resulted in part from the inability of the Britons to resist them because they had been enfeebled by the plague. The plague originated in Egypt in 541; it had reached western Britain by 549, when it carried off Maelgwn Fawr. It would appear that it did not attack the English, perhaps because they, unlike the Britons, lacked contacts with the shores of the Mediterranean. The plague of 549 is believed to have been as devastating as the more famous plague of 1349, and there is some evidence of an almost equally deadly pestilence a century earlier. Both scourges seem to have been particularly inimicable to what was left of the Roman order. If there is truth in the assertion that the English avoided the old Roman cities, the explanation may lie in fear of the plague.

Yet, in comparison with the rest of the Western Roman Empire, it is not the success of the English which is striking but rather the length of time they took to achieve that success and the tenacity of the resistance of their opponents. In France, Spain and Italy, the 'barbarians' were rapidly victorious; by 486 almost the whole of Gaul was in the hands of the Franks, a people of an ancestry similar to that of the Saxons. The Gallo-Romans offered only feeble resistance, but within a few generations their culture had been adopted by their conquerors and the Latin of Gaul, proto-French, had become the language of the entire community. In the territories seized by the English the structures inherited from Rome disappeared, structures which in any case were not as firmly rooted as they were in the rest of the Western Empire. The invaders did not adopt the language of the natives; instead, the generations of struggle served to deepen ethnic and racial consciousness on the one side and the other. The undefeated peoples adhered to their Celtic language, while the language of the English spread over those parts of the island which came into their possession. At the same time, western Scotland was colonized by the Scots, migrants from Ireland; they planted in Dalriada, their kingdom in Argyll, a version of the Irish language, although it is likely that there were speakers of Q-Celtic in Scotland already. From Dalriada, the Irish or the Gaelic of the Scots spread to become, at least for a time, the language of most of the communities of Scotland. Thus the languages of Britain, unlike those of most of western Europe, are not descendants of colloquial Latin.

In 400, the inhabitants of Wales spoke Brittonic; in 700, they spoke Welsh. The evidence available for studying this linguistic change is scarce and complex; no complete sentence of Brittonic has survived and the first surviving words in Welsh are those inscribed around 700 on the famous stone in the church at Tywyn. Brittonic was cognate with Latin and, like Latin, its nouns had different forms in the nominative, the accusative and so on, together with the termination *-os* (comparable with the Latin *-us*) and a number of other terminations. In changing into Welsh, these terminations disappeared and a name like Maglocunus became Maelgwn. P-Celtic lost many of its old formations in the century 450–550; although it is now doubted whether the change was as sudden as it was once believed to be, it is claimed that Vortigern (*c.*430) would not have understood Aneirin (*c.*595), although Gildas (*c.*540) would have understood both.

Early Welsh was the medium of Taliesin and Aneirin and, if it is accepted that the nuclei of their poems were written around 600, they prove that this 'new' language had the ability to be the medium of great literature. That ability was based upon centuries of composition in Brittonic, a tradition of praising rulers and heroes, of celebrating courage and generosity and of upholding the consciousness of the community, the function of the Brittonic poet and his Welsh successor for at least two thousand years. That tradition and the society which sustained it probably continued in a more unbroken form in the Old North, beyond Hadrian's Wall, than it did in Wales, although it is known that Maelgwn Fawr had his poets and that Taliesin sang in the court of Powys as well as in that of Rheged. The poems were composed to be chanted during the feasts of the court, for heroes enjoyed hearing about heroes, and part of the training of an apprentice poet was the commitment to memory of thousands of lines of the work of the masters – a practice noted by Julius Caesar among the Celts of Gaul. But at some stage, perhaps as early as 600, Welsh began to be written down. This was a bold act for, throughout the territories that had been part of the Western Empire, the Latin of Rome was the sole written medium, and hardly any attempts were made to write Latin's daughter-languages, French, Spanish and Italian, until after 1000. It is unlikely that there were many early Welsh manuscripts; paper had disappeared from western Europe by about 650 and parchment was expensive (most early writing in Welsh survives as marginalia); nevertheless, they were numerous enough for there to have been a cell in which to keep them at the fort of Dinbych Penfro (Tenby) in about 880. Alas, nothing remains of what might have been in that cell; all the early Welsh literature that has survived consists of later copies providentially preserved.

It is possible that the earliest poems in Welsh were composed before the adoption of the word *Cymry*. The heroes of Aneirin and Taliesin were *Brythoniaid* (Britons), but a praise poem to Cadwallon probably written about 633 contains the line: *'Ar wynep Kymry Cadwallawn was'*. The poet was referring to the country rather than the people – the words *Cymru* (Wales) and *Cymry* (the Welsh people) were both spelled *Cymry* or *Kymry* until about 1560. Initially, the word undoubtedly referred to the Old North as well as to Wales, for it survives today in Cumbria, the heart of the old kingdom of Rheged. There is no evidence that it was in use among the Britons of south-western Britain, which may indicate that it was not current in the period before the battle of Dyrham (577). The word *Cymry* evolved from the Brittonic word *Combrogi* (fellow-countryman), and its adoption suggests a deepening self-awareness among the Britons. Although the author of *Armes Prydein* (*c.* 930) used the word *Cymry* or *Cymro* fifteen times, it only gradually came to oust the word *Brython*. That was the favourite word of the author of *Brut y Tywysogyon*; his entry for 1116 is the first to mention the *Cymry* and it was not until the years after 1100 that *Cymry* became as usual as *Brythoniaid* in the work of the poets.

To Nennius, his compatriots were *cives*, citizens – Romans, therefore – and there is also an echo of Romanization in the word used by the Saxons to denote the Britons. It is often claimed that the word 'Welsh' is a contemptuous word used by Germanic-speaking peoples to describe foreigners. Yet a glance at a dictionary of any of the Teutonic languages will show that that is not its only meaning. 'Welsh' was not used by Germanic speakers to describe peoples living to the east of them; to the English, *wealh-stod* meant an interpreter, but they had a different word for a translator from Danish. It would appear that 'Welsh' meant not so much foreigners as peoples who had been Romanized; other versions of the word may be found along the borders of the Empire – the Walloons of Belgium, the Welsch of the Italian Tyrol and the Vlachs of Romania – and the *Welsch-nuss*, the walnut, was the nut of the Roman lands.

This recognition of the persistence of the Roman tradition is striking, particularly when it is placed alongside the continuance of the Brittonic language and its successor. It is often claimed that Wales is the sole country among those which were once a part of the Western Roman Empire in which a version of the language spoken by the inhabitants before the coming of the Romans is still in use. That is among the factors which have given rise to the belief that Wales is unique among the territories of the Western Empire in being the only part not conquered after the fall of the Empire by peoples from beyond its borders. These are attractive theories but they need some revision. From the point of view of language, the same claim could be made for the Basques of Euskalherria or the Berbers of the Maghreb. As far as external conquest is concerned, authority was seized in Gwynedd and Dyfed by dynasties from beyond the borders of the Empire, and it can be doubted whether mid-Wales was ever within the Empire; the Romans of today do not believe that it was, as the maps on the walls of the Forum testify. Gwent, Erging and Glywysing, the most Romanized areas of Wales, are the only regions for which there is no evidence that they were overwhelmed by invaders from outside the Empire.

The uniqueness of south-east Wales in this respect may explain the key importance of those regions as the cradle of the Celtic Church and the starting point of a movement which was to revitalize Europe. The history of the Celtic Church has a great fascination, but so scarce is the contemporary evidence and so abundant the stories invented in later centuries – usually with an ulterior motive – that it is now difficult to distinguish between the true and the false. Perhaps the very term 'Celtic Church' gives rise to confusion, for it was in fact an integral part of the universal Church; the idea that it was proto-Protestant is a mistaken notion of reformers a thousand years later. Indeed, it would be better to describe it as the Church among the speakers of Celtic languages. Although it had its own distinct features, there has been an excessive tendency to discover within it the exceptional and the abnormal. If the Pope had virtually no authority over it, it should be borne in mind that in the period 400–800 the authority of the Pope over the Church as a whole was small in comparison with what it would become. Indeed, in those years Christendom had very little uniformity either in ritual or in organization.

It has been argued that the Church of Dyfrig, Illtud and David owed nothing to the Christianity that had existed in Britain at the time of the Roman Empire. It has been claimed that that Christianity perished in Wales as it did in England and that the Celtic Church originated from the work of missionaries sailing the western sea-routes. The present tendency, however, is to believe that it originated from a variety of influences and that it was in south-east Wales, above all, that those influences came together. The context of the life of Dyfrig (Dubricius), the first of the 'saints' of the Celtic Church, was essentially Roman. Although traditions relating to him were contorted in later centuries as a result of the ambitions of the bishops of Llandaf, it would be reasonable to consider that he was a bishop in Erging and that he presided over a Roman form of organization, perhaps from his bishop's seat at Ariconium. The dates of the 'saints' are highly uncertain, but it has been suggested that Dyfrig lived from 425 to 505, dates which would not be inconsistent with the tradition that he was a disciple of Germanus of Auxerre (died 445) and that he was therefore heir to the orthodoxy preached by Germanus in Britain in 429 and 442. Perhaps there is significance in the story that a daughter of the king of Erging was married to Magnus Maximus. Magnus was zealously orthodox, the patron of Martin of Tours, and there are suggestions that some of the churches of Erging were dedicated to him.

Dyfrig's successor as the leading figure among the Christians of Wales was Illtud, a man who can be discussed with a greater degree of certainty, for he is mentioned in *The Life of St Samson* which was written in Brittany in about 610. Illtud was an abbot rather than a bishop, an indication that the monastic tradition established by Anthony in Egypt before 310 and upheld at Tours by Martin and at Lerrins near Marseille by Honorius had struck root in Wales. That tradition had severely ascetic elements, but it was also characterized by devotion to scholarship, and Lerrins has been described as the first Christian university in western Europe. It is the scholarship of Illtud which is stressed. He was the 'renowned master of the Britons, learned in the teachings of the Church, in the culture of the Latins and in the traditions of his own people'. A later generation of monks would seek the desolate places, but the monastery of Llanilltud Fawr (Llantwit Major) was in no sense desolate. Not far from it stood the villa of Llantwit, almost certainly a ruin in Illtud's day although it would not be unreasonable to believe that Illtud was of the same lineage as its owners. Eighteen kilometres away stood the settlement of Dinas Powys, perhaps the seat of the kings of Glywysing; in Illtud's lifetime, it was a place where objects from Bordeaux, Athens and Alexandria were in use – and if pottery could be carried to the Vale of Glamorgan

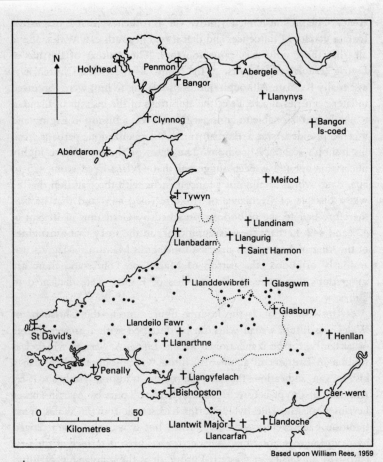

Based upon William Rees, 1959

†   Mother church

•   Church dedicated to David (Dewi) by about 1250

·········· The boundary of Deheubarth

The Celtic Church

so also could ideas, books and students. Llantwit Major can be considered to be the axis of the Christianity of the Celtic-speaking peoples. Samson was a student there, leaving for Dol about 520 to become the father of Breton monasticism. Samson's fellow students included Paul Aurelian, a leading figure in the traditions of Cornwall; they also included Gildas, who was considered by the

Irish to be the leading authority on ritual and discipline. Indeed, almost all the leaders of early Irish monasticism had been trained in Wales.

The mood changed in the years after 500. It is no longer possible to recognize a figure like Dyfrig, a bishop in an essentially Roman environment, probably because that environment vanished when the economy which had sustained it collapsed. Asceticism gained ground at the expense of more worldly and scholarly values and there was a great increase in the desire to retreat to remote and desolate places. By 550 – perhaps as a result of the plague – the appeal of ascetic monasticism was almost irresistible. This was the true 'Age of the Saints', the years when Christianity consolidated its hold upon the inhabitants of Wales and when the *llan* became central to the country's toponymy. The first need of a community of Christians was a consecrated enclosure in which to bury their dead; the enclosure was the *llan*, and probably many centuries went by before most of the *llannau* were graced by places of worship.

The majority of the 'saints' commemorated in the *llannau* of Wales have only a very local fame; in many cases they were probably the donors of the land on which the enclosure was located and it is likely that they would have been forgotten had not local pride woven legends about them over the centuries. Yet there must be sound foundations for the wide recognition gained by men such as David (Dewi), Padarn, Teilo and Deiniol. There is virtually no contemporary evidence relating to them, and so far archaeology has yielded disappointingly little – a few huts at Penmon and Ynys Seiriol, the foundations of a chapel at Clynnog and virtually nothing else. Attempts have been made to interpret the range of the activities of the 'saints' on the basis of the churches dedicated to them, but as it is not known whether the dedications were contemporary or whether they reflect a later cult, there is now a tendency not to give too much weight to such studies. Nevertheless, there must be significance in the fact that, in the region between Pembroke and Hereford, there were by about 1200 more than sixty churches dedicated to David. (This is more than any other of the 'saints'; Teilo, with about twenty-five, ranks second.) It cannot be claimed that the dedications denote the extent of the region which directly experienced David's ministry. Yet, from about 900 onwards, there is increasing evidence of the fame of David and his church and it is reasonable to assume that such fame was based on traditions of a man wholly exceptional in influence and sanctity.

The Life of St David, written by Rhygyfarch (Ricemarch) of Llanbadarn in about 1090, is the earliest of the lives of the Welsh 'saints', and further details were provided by Giraldus Cambrensis around 1200 and by the anchorite of Llanddewibrefi in about 1346. Despite the lateness of these works and despite the incredible nature of much of the material they contain, some of their contents appears plausible. It is credible that David was of the royal house of Ceredigion and his emphasis upon hard work, vegetarianism and temperance shows that he belonged to the most ascetic branch of the monastic tradition. It is also likely that in his day he was the most respected leader of the Christians of Wales. It was that respect, no doubt, rather than any hierarchical office he held which allowed him to preside over ecclesiastical synods such as that at Llanddewibrefi, held some time around 570. That was the occasion of his most famous miracle when the hill rose beneath his feet – although in view of the nature of the landscape of Ceredigion it would be difficult to conceive of any miracle more superfluous.

There is no certainty about the dates of David's lifetime, but the years 530–89 are a likely approximation. Teilo, Padarn and Deiniol belong to broadly the same period. They were abbots and, according to the fuller evidence of Ireland, they ruled monasteries or *clasau* containing a number of small churches in addition to the huts of the monks. Although Bede can have hardly been strictly correct when he states there were at least 2,100 monks at Bangor Is-coed in about 616, the *clasau* could be substantial. A stone raised at Aberdaron around 550 carries the inscription that Senacus was lying among his host of brothers; Llandeilo and Meifod were described as ecclesiastical cities and the word *civitas* was used by the Irish to denote a monastery. Nora Chadwick wrote an enchanting description of the life of these monasteries and she claimed that never did Europe have a Christianity more captivating in its appeal. The greater part of the evidence she used came from Ireland, but although Irish monasticism was the child of Welsh monasticism it cannot be accepted that what is true of the one is also true of the other. Ireland is more fertile than Wales and it had not been impoverished by the struggle against the Saxon invader; its material culture was therefore richer and the artistic heritage of its monasteries was far more magnificent. Ireland had never been under the rule of Rome, and the Roman Christianity, episcopal in its organization, planted there by Patrick between 432 and 461, proved short-lived; it was overwhelmed within a generation or two by the monastic system, and in Ireland the abbot replaced the bishop to a far greater extent than in Wales.

One of the outstanding features of Irish Christianity was its missionary zeal. In 563, Columba went to Iona to evangelize among the Scots and in 634 Aidan went from Iona to Lindisfarne to win the English to the Faith. The mission spread to mainland Europe: from 610, when the monastery of Luxeuil was established in Burgundy by Columbanus, until 1090, when a group of Irish monks set out for Regensburg on the river Danube, the Christianity of Europe would be heavily indebted to the zeal of the Irish. Bede claimed that the Welsh made no effort to convert the English; although his statement is not free of prejudice, the reference of Aldhelm (who died in 709) to the Welsh purifying the dishes used by the English and the story of Beuno on the banks of the Severn suggest that the Christians of Wales were not anxious to have contact with the pagan English. If they had to have enemies, it was preferable for those enemies to be pagans; they would not then reach heaven as well as Pengwern. Yet it is difficult to accept Bede's statement in its entirety. Nennius's comment that Rhun, the son of Urien of Rheged, baptized the people of Northumbria is plausible; some of the most famous of the monasteries of Wessex may have had Brythonic origins and the Christianity of western Mercia must have been indebted to the Welsh. But the most zealous efforts of the Welsh were directed towards their fellow-Celts; they included missions not only to Ireland, Cornwall and Brittany but also to a community of *Brittones* dwelling in Galicia on the north-western coast of Spain.

Aidan's mission to Lindisfarne was the result of an invitation from Edwin, king of Northumbria. Aidan is the true apostle of the English. In later centuries, his contribution was played down in order to give the most prominent place to Augustine, whose mission to England in 597 was initiated by Pope Gregory the Great. Augustine established his chief church at Canterbury, the seat of Aethelbert, king of Kent, a man who had won overlordship over most of the English kingdoms. Gregory gave Augustine authority over all the Christians of Britain but, when Augustine rather arrogantly sought to give substance to that authority in 603, he was rebuffed by the Welsh bishops, Beuno perhaps among them. It was not fully accepted at the time that the Pope had the power to determine who was subject to whom, and there was very little reason for the long-established Christianity of Wales to accept the superiority of an archbishopric which had been in existence for less than a decade. Furthermore, there were political dangers in submitting to the authority of a religious leader who would of necessity be heavily under the influence of the policy of an English king. Thus began the sad saga of the relationship between Wales and Canterbury, a saga which lasted for over thirteen centuries.

Augustine had a measure of success in Kent, but Canterbury's missions to Essex and Northumbria proved short-lived; it was from the efforts of Aidan and his followers that the Christianity of most of northern and midland England sprang. There were differences in organization and ritual between the tradition of Aidan and that of Augustine. The most important was the disagreement over the date of Easter: the Celtic Church adhered to a system devised by the Western Church in 314, while Rome followed a system adopted there in 457. It was the desire to abide by the traditions of the fathers, rather than ignorance of the change, which is the most satisfactory explanation for the conservatism of the Celts; as has been seen, they did not, between 457 and 603, lack contact with the shores of the Mediterranean. The date of Easter was no negligible matter – twenty thousand Russians met their death in a struggle over a similar issue between 1682 and 1690 – and the Easter of the Celts was elevated to be a symbol of freedom from the interference of Augustine and his successors.

It was the Celts who were the furthest away from Canterbury, and therefore the least likely to suffer from such interference, who were the first to conform. The Christians of the south of Ireland accepted the Roman Easter in 630. The matter was discussed in the Synod of Whitby in 664 and, when faced by the argument that it was Peter not Aidan who held the keys to the Kingdom of Heaven, the Northumbrians accepted the Roman dating. Northumbria was followed by Strathclyde in 688, by the north of Ireland in about 697 and by the Church of Iona in 716. When Bede was writing his history, Wales was the most substantial of the territories which was resisting Rome, a fact which helps to explain his anti-Welsh sentiments, including his approval of the slaughter of the monks of Bangor Is-coed. The Welsh retained the old system until 768, when the date of Easter was changed among them by Elfoddw, *archiepiscopus Guenedotae regione*, as the *Annales Cambriae* described him. While the Welsh stood out against Rome, there seems to have been hardly any contact between their Church and the rest of Christendom; their isolation must have weakened them, for there is very little sign of activity in the Welsh Church in the century up to 768.

Indeed, there is very little evidence relating to any aspect of life in Wales in that century. It was the period when the economy of Europe reached its lowest ebb and when the heartlands of the continent almost fell into the hands of the victorious warriors of Islam. Light shone in a few places – in Ireland and Northumbria, for example, where Celtic and Roman traditions were interwoven into a rich synthesis – but there is little evidence of a similar synthesis in Wales. The Welsh had been weakened by their long struggle against the invaders and they reacted by adopting sterile isolationism – a response that characterizes them on occasion. The classical scholarship and the refined Latin which had once been treasured in places like Llantwit Major decayed. The Latin of Nennius, about 830, is uncouth compared with that of Gildas, about 540. After 642 there is no further evidence of contact between the Welsh and the Men of the North, and Yvi, about 720, was the last known link between Wales and Brittany. The importation of fine pottery ceased and the practice of commemorating the dead with stone inscriptions came to an end. The nation of the Welsh was conceived on the death-bed of the Roman Empire; it was born in the excitement of the 'Age of Saints' but its infancy was meagre and lonely. Yet, as shall be seen, it would have an exhilarating adolescence.

CHAPTER FOUR

800–1282: Aberffraw, Dinefwr and Mathrafal

The Early Middle Ages, the half a millennium after 800, were years of ferment and promise in Wales. Attempts were made to create political unity and each successive attempt had greater organizational force than its predecessor. The consolidation of states was a feature of the age throughout Europe, and in economic and social matters too the Welsh experience was in accord with that of Europe as a whole. At the beginning of the period, western Europe was impoverished and beleaguered, but from about 1050 onwards there was a marked advance: the population increased, rural settlement intensified, town life expanded and local and international trade multiplied. Wales partook of all these developments but, as the country was situated on the edge of Europe, its experience of them was not as thorough-going as was that of the more central countries of the continent. New relationships were created between Wales and Europe and those relationships were by no means one-way; legends emanating from Wales captured the imagination of Europe and Arthur and his knights became the epitome of chivalry. New architectural styles were introduced to Wales; the literary tradition of Wales was enriched and the Welsh came face to face with the glories and the arrogance of the Latin Church.

The existence of Offa's Dyke may well have deepened the self-awareness of the Welsh people, for, in the generation following its construction, kingdom was linked with kingdom with the result that the greater part of the inhabitants of Wales became the subjects of a single ruler. If the genealogies, almost the sole evidence for these developments, are reliable, it appears that it was through marriage rather than through conquest that the kingdoms of Wales were united. The heir of one kingdom married the heiress of another, although it is probable that there would have been fewer heiresses had there not been considerable slaughter among their male relations. A chain of marriages begins around 800 when Gwriad, of the lineage of the Men of the North, married Esyllt of the line of Maelgwn Fawr; their son, Merfyn, became king of Gwynedd in 825 on the death of Esyllt's uncle, Hywel ap Rhodri. Merfyn married Nest of the house of Powys, and their son, Rhodri, married Angharad of the house of Seisyllwg (Ceredigion and Ystrad Tywi). Rhodri became ruler of Gwynedd in 844 on the death of his father, of Powys in 855 on the death of his uncle, Cyngen, and of Seisyllwg in 871 on the death of his brother-in-law, Gwgon; he died in 877, king of a realm extending from Anglesey to Gower.

A later generation of chroniclers hailed Rhodri ap Merfyn as Rhodri Mawr (Rhodri the Great), a distinction bestowed upon two other rulers in the same century – Charles the Great (Charlemagne, died 814) and Alfred the Great (died 899). The three tributes are of a similar nature – recognition of the achievements of men who contributed significantly to the growth of statehood among the nations of the Welsh, the Franks and the English. Unfortunately, the entire evidence relating to the life of Rhodri consists of a few sentences; yet he must have made a deep impression upon the Welsh, for in later centuries being of the line of Rhodri was a primary qualification for their rulers.

Rhodri's fame sprang from his success as a warrior. That success was noted by *The Ulster Chronicle* and by Sedulius Scottus, an Irish scholar at the court of the Emperor Charles the Bald at Liège. It was his victory over the Northmen in 856 which brought him international acclaim. The first attack by the Northmen upon western Europe was recorded in 789, when they ravaged the coasts of England. Their favourite targets were rich and defenceless coastal monasteries and as they were pagans they felt no compunction at desecrating the holy places. But they were not mere plunderers: they planted towns, they revived trade and it was their activities which caused coinage to circulate again in Wales. There were political and demographic factors forcing them to migrate from Scandinavia and they sought new lands to colonize. By 800 there were numerous communities of Northmen in the Scottish islands, and around 830 they began to plant colonies in Ireland, of which Dublin would become the most important. The Danes settled in northern and eastern England from 865 onwards, and in 911 a large part of northern France came into the possession of the

400–500	KINGS OF CEREDIGION AND YSTRAD TYWI	KINGS OF GWYNEDD

Esyllt = Gwriad

Gwgon ap Meurig

THE HOUSE OF GWYNEDD

Anarawd

Idwal

Meurig

Idwal

Iago

Cynan

GRUFFUDD

OWAIN GWYNEDD

Iorwerth   Cynan

LLYWELYN
THE GREAT

Gruffudd   DAFYDD

LLYWELYN DAFYDD Rhodri

GWENLLIAN   Thomas

OWAIN
LAWGOCH

THE HOUSE
OF DEUBARTH

Einon

Cadell

Tewdwr

RHYS

GWENLLIAN = Gruffudd

THE LORD RHYS

Gruffudd Rhys Gryg Maelgwn

Maredudd   Owain   Maredudd Maelgwn

Llywelyn   Maredudd   RHYS   Rhys

Maredudd   Owain   Rhys

Llywelyn   Llywelyn   MAELGWN

MADOG   Thomas

The royal houses of Wales, 400–1400

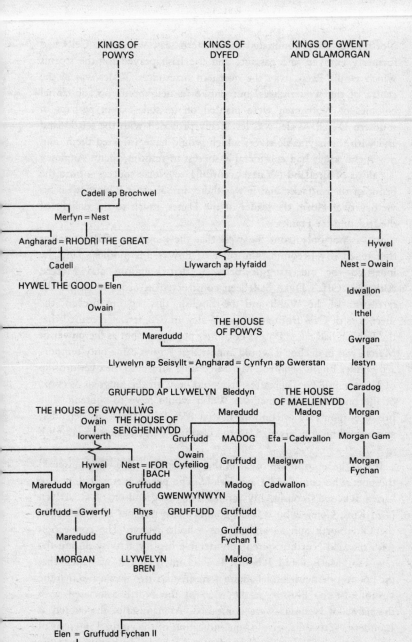

Northmen. They dominated the western seas, where the Celts had formerly enjoyed safe passage, and the Irish prayed for the storms which would keep away the northern marauders. Wales was in the centre of the western seas, but unlike its neighbours no substantial colonies of Northmen were planted on its soil, except perhaps in southern Dyfed. Wales was less richly provided with the fertile land and with the navigable rivers which would have attracted them, and the Welsh kings had considerable success in resisting them. Anglesey – a third of Bretland (Wales) according to Norse sources – bore the brunt of their attacks, and it was there, in 856, that Rhodri won his victory over Horn, the leader of the Danes, much to the delight of the Irish and the Franks.

It was not only from the west that the kingdom of Rhodri was threatened. By becoming the ruler of Powys, his mother's land, he inherited the old struggle between that kingdom and Mercia. Although Offa's Dyke had been constructed in order to define the territories of the Welsh and the English, this did not prevent the successors of Offa from attacking Wales. In 822, it was recorded that the English had taken Powys into their possession, but as the power of Mercia was in decline it would appear that Powys came only temporarily under English control. Mercia became subject to the overlordship of Wessex in 829. Thereafter, it would be with the kings of Wessex, of the line of Cerdic, that the Welsh would have to contend. The pressure upon Powys continued; after 855, Rhodri was its defender, and he and his son, Gwriad, were killed in a battle against the English in 877.

It was the anguish of Powys in the years around 850 which inspired the poet who composed *Canu Heledd*. The poems were attributed to Urien Rheged's cousin, Llywarch Hen, the grandson of Coel Hen (Old King Cole), who was the founder of a number of dynasties in the Old North and an ancestor of Rhodri Mawr. The connection with the Old North inspired considerable literary activity during the reigns of Merfyn and Rhodri. It is claimed that it was then that the poems of Aneirin and Taliesin were first written down and that the versions of the history of the Men of the North associated with the name of Nennius were composed. A manuscript discovered at Bamberg, Franconia, gives some indication of the cultural interests of the members of the court of Merfyn and Rhodri: Irish visitors to the court were presented with a cryptogram which could only be solved by transposing the letters from Latin into Greek. It was not only the territories acknowledging the authority of Rhodri which experienced cultural revival. The memorial at Llantwit Major to Rhys, king of Glamorgan, who died in 860, is proof of an ability to carve stone with skill and imagination, and the fact that Asser was summoned from St David's to Wessex in about 880 to help Alfred to civilize his kingdom suggests that there was respect for the scholarship of the Church of David beyond the boundaries of Dyfed.

Asser's *Life of Alfred* – if the convincing arguments that it is not a fake are accepted – throws light upon the situation in Wales following the death of Rhodri in 877. According to Asser, the rulers of Dyfed and Brycheiniog feared the power of the sons of Rhodri, while the rulers of Gwent and Glywysing were threatened by Aethelred, earl of Mercia. When Alfred came to the throne in 871, the whole of England, apart from the southern rim of Wessex, was in the hands of the Danes but, as a result of his successes against them, Alfred came to enjoy great power and renown. Asser states that the smaller rulers of Wales asked him for his patronage and that Anarawd ap Rhodri, king of Gwynedd and Powys, followed their example, abandoning his alliance with the Danish kingdom of York. It is likely that his brother Cadell, ruler of Seisyllwg, did the same, and thus the king of Wessex became overlord of the whole of Wales. The precise nature of that overlordship is not known, but it provided a basis for the more extensive suzerainty of Alfred's successors. The recognition by Welsh rulers that the king of England had claims upon them would be a central fact in the subsequent political history of Wales. There was an attempt to portray the submission as the result of a desire for unity among Christian rulers against the pagan Danes and as a tribute to the greatness of Alfred. Nevertheless, it undoubtedly contained an element of coercion, as is demonstrated by the fate of Idwal ab Anarawd, who raised the standard of revolt and who was killed by the English in 942.

If the intention of the rulers of Dyfed and Brycheiniog in seeking the patronage of Alfred was to remain free from the clutches of the house of Rhodri, they failed. About 904, Llywarch ap Hyfaidd, king of Dyfed, died; his kingdom came into the possession of Hywel ap Cadell ap Rhodri, the ruler of Seisyllwg and the husband of Elen, Llywarch's sister. It would appear that Hywel also took possession of Brycheiniog, for its royal line ends with Tewdwr ap Giffri, who died

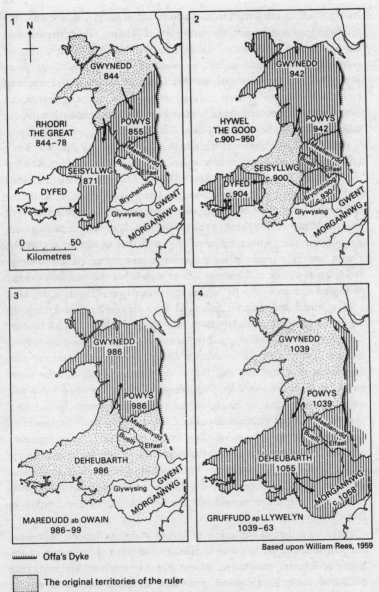

Based upon William Rees, 1959

━━━━━━ Offa's Dyke

The original territories of the ruler

The additional territories brought under his rule

The uniting of Wales, 844–1063

about 930. The enlarged kingdom came to be known as Deheubarth, a unit of central importance in the history of Wales during the following four centuries. Deheubarth was united with the territories of Idwal ab Anarawd ap Rhodri – Gwynedd and Powys – in 942, and Hywel died in 950 the ruler of a kingdom which extended from Prestatyn to Pembroke. Glamorgan was not part of Hywel's realm, a fact which is sometimes cited in support of the theory that it was outside the main stream of Welsh history in the Early Middle Ages. The theory has very little substance. Glywysing was subject to the men of the west around 600 and again around 1000, and there were times when Glamorgan extended its power over the lands between the rivers Tawe and Tywi. Although its kings were not fully linked with the leading royal house of Wales, they were descendants of Rhodri Mawr through his daughter, Nest, and efforts were made to trace their ancestry back to Cunedda and Coel Hen. The social and legal system of Glamorgan was similar to that of the rest of Wales, and some of the formative elements in Welsh religion and mythology originated there.

Like Rhodri, his grandfather, Hywel was given an epithet by a later generation. He became known as Hywel Dda (Hywel the Good), although it would be wrong to consider that goodness to be innocent and unblemished. In the age of Hywel, the essential attribute of a state builder was ruthlessness, an attribute which Hywel possessed, if it is true that it was he who ordered the killing of his brother-in-law, Llywarch of Dyfed. Yet in order to have won his epithet, he must have been responsible for some act of virtue. Although contemporary evidence is lacking, there is no reason to reject the tradition that this act was the consolidation of the Law of Wales. Among Hywel's contemporaries there were rulers who won fame as law-givers. He almost certainly knew of them; he was a regular visitor to the English court and in 928, when in the flower of his manhood, he went on pilgrimage to Rome; he was there, it must be admitted, when the Papacy was at its most degraded – he may have been in the city when John X was strangled. In later centuries it was claimed that he took copies of his laws to Rome, where they were blessed by the Pope. Tradition also provides details of the circumstances under which the laws were compiled and promulgated. The further the author is from the events he describes the more detailed his story becomes and the role of the Church increases from version to version. Most of these stories are inventions created in an attempt to disprove claims that the Law of Wales was non-Christian. Nevertheless, it is not necessary to reject them all. It is plausible that the meeting to consolidate the Law was attended by men of substance and learning from all parts of Wales and that it was held at Whitland, a place close to the border between Dyfed and Seisyllwg.

The Law is among the most splendid creations of the culture of the Welsh. For centuries it was a powerful symbol of their unity and identity, as powerful indeed as their language, for – like the literary language – the Law was the same in its essence in all parts of Wales. The Law of Hywel was not a body of law created *de novo*; it was the systematization of the legal customs which had developed in Wales over the centuries. The Law of Wales, therefore, was folk law rather than state law and its emphasis was upon ensuring reconciliation between kinship groups rather than upon keeping order through punishment. It was not concerned with the enforcement of criminal law through the apparatus of the state; because of that, distinguished historians – Maitland, for example – have claimed that it was primitive and that as society became more complex it would inevitably have become defunct. It is now realized that its ability to evolve has been mistakenly disparaged, and Dafydd Jenkins, the most talented and untiring of its interpreters, has shown that it contained elements of mercy, common sense and respect for women and children which would be lacking in the Law of England until very recently.

Its ability to evolve lies at the root of the problems facing the historian of the Law of Wales, for, if it had fossilized as did the Law of Ireland, it could be claimed that the law-books are a record of the Law promulgated at Whitland in about 930. A total of forty-two copies have survived from the period when the Law was still at least in partial use. Of these, thirty-six are in Welsh and six in Latin; the Latin versions are adaptations, for Welsh was the language of the Law. The earliest surviving manuscript is in Latin; it is a copy, written about 1230, of a text compiled in about 1175. Its contents are not the Law as promulgated by Hywel at Whitland, but neither are they a record of the Law administered in the courts of Wales in 1175. The Law evolved so as to answer the needs of society in 1175, but clauses no longer in force were not deleted from the law-books. A lawyer would add to the original Law of Hywel, would note an explanation in the margin, would quote the result of a case and would change one clause and augment another. Text, amendments and marginalia would all be copied without distinguishing between the ancient and the contemporary. As a result, each version of the Law contains sections which were old in the age of Hywel and sections which were brand new when the manuscript was compiled.

It is wholly appropriate therefore that specialists on the Law of Wales stress that the law-books cannot in their entirety be considered to furnish evidence of the nature of society in the age of Hywel. Nevertheless, they acknowledge that sections of them do contain material that is very ancient. On the basis of that material and on the basis of the other scant sources, a portrayal of society in Wales in the age of Hywel may be attempted. It was a wholly rural society, for there would be no town in Wales for five hundred years and more after the demise of Caer-went. It was once believed that the agriculture of early Wales was very primitive. It has been claimed that hardly any grain was grown, that settled dwellings were rare and that the population consisted in the main of nomadic shepherds. These notions have now been abandoned. It is recognized that there was a nomadic element in society, for the mountain and the plain were united in a single coherent economy and a proportion of the population moved from the *hendref* (the winter home) to the *hafod* (the summer home) at the beginning of the summer. Gildas refers to this practice of transhumance, and the shape of the *cantrefi* (hundreds) – in Glamorgan, for example – indicates the essential unity of highland and lowland. Yet a society which practises transhumance is not necessarily a nomadic society. It may have settled roots in the lowlands and it is increasingly accepted that such was the case in Wales.

Although pastoral agriculture was of central importance, there is considerable evidence of the role of arable farming in early Wales. The querns found at Dinas Powys, Dinas Emrys and Dinorben prove that grain was an integral part of the diet, and arable fields cultivated around 600 have been discovered at Pant-y-saer and elsewhere. The poems attributed to Llywarch Hen refer to stubble and furrows; the law-books mention the need to protect crops from animals and they provide details of the amount of grain to be paid to the king by his subjects. Furthermore, it is impossible to reconcile the theory that society was nomadic with the recognition that land had its owners. This was a principle with deep roots in Wales, as the Law of *priodolder* and the grants recorded in *The Book of St Chad* and *The Book of Llandaf* testify.

It was the landholding system which gave the society of early Wales its equilibrium, for despite the often erratic behaviour of its kings that society had a marked stability. A man's right to land depended upon his status, for all men were not equal in the sight of the Law of Wales, any more than they were in the sight of the other law systems of early Europe. In law, the most basic division was that between the free and the unfree. Those of free status were the king and his relations, along with the *bonheddwyr* – those who had *bon* or ancestry (compare *gens* in gentleman). Those of unfree status included the *taeogion* (villeins), who had rights protected by law, and also the *caethion* (slaves), who were wholly lacking in rights. In addition, the Law recognized the existence of the *alltud* – the incomer from beyond the boundaries of Wales. Surveys prepared around 1300 showed that at that time over half the inhabitants of Wales were of free status; in Meirionnydd, for example, three quarters of the males listed in the surveys were of the status of *bonheddwr*. Pride has been expressed in the fact that the majority of the Welsh enjoyed free status in an age when the greater part of the population of Europe lived in some degree of bondage. It is now believed that the high proportion enjoying free status in Wales in 1300 was a fairly recent phenomenon and that it was the result of the great upheavals which occurred in the generations after 1100. Leslie Alcock found difficulty in discovering any substantial free element among the Britons of the age of Arthur; the over-neat analysis of the commote provided by the law-books assumes an unfree majority, and this is confirmed by the note in *Domesday Book* on the *cantref* of Tegeingl in 1086.

There were basic differences between the settlements of the free and the unfree. There is very little evidence concerning the location of the one or the other for at least three centuries after the age of Hywel, but there is growing support for the arguments of Glanville Jones that from very early times the compact villages of the *taeogion* were the chief settlements in the most fertile areas. According to the law-books, each commote had its *maerdref*, where the *taeogion* laboured under the direction of *maer y biswail* (the mayor of the dunghill) to supply the needs of the king and his court. It is believed that there were *maerdrefi* under the shadow of the forts of Dinas Powys and Dinorben, and it is probable that at Aberffraw, the chief seat of the kings of Gwynedd, there was a fort, a church, a court and a *maerdref* perhaps as early as the age of Maelgwn Fawr. The *maerdref* was not the only *taeogdref*. *The Book of Iorwerth*, compiled in about 1240, provides a description of the *maenor* or manor which consisted of a group of villein townships (*taeogdrefi*). The *maenor* was undoubtedly an ancient institution, for in the margin of *The Book of St Chad*, compiled about 740, there is a description of the *maenor* of Medd-yfnych, which was broadly equivalent to the modern parish of Llandybïe. Every adult male *taeog* had a right to a share of the land of the *taeogdref* and the duty of apportioning the land fell to the *maer*; his office had ancient roots – it was also recorded in the Old North. This was the system of the *tir cyfrif*, commendable in many respects, although the *taeog* was fated to be owned by the land rather than to be the owner of it, for he was barred from the few routes which would free him from the bonds of the soil – the callings of the priest, the poet and the smith.

The *taeogdrefi* were unfree, compact, 'manorial' settlements, with the emphasis upon crop-raising. The sources portray the settlements of the *bonheddwyr* as free, scattered and 'tribal', with the emphasis upon stock-raising. From the surveys drawn up between 1300 and 1500, it can be seen that it is land called *tir gwelyog* which corresponds among the *bonheddwyr* to the *tir cyfrif* of the *taeogion*. The *taeog* received his land as a member of a community; the *bonheddwr* received his as a member of a *ceneдl* – *cenedl* in the sense of kindred. The members of a kindred group or a *gwely* established themselves around the *hendref* – the original settlement of their ancestor. The sons of a *priodor* (a full member of the *gwely*) had equal claims upon the arable land, the meadows, the woodlands and the grazing land of their father, and they could divide the land between them or work it jointly. But a man without sons did not lack heirs; his brother, then his cousin and then his second cousin had their rights, for the *gwely* was an agnatic group extending over four generations. The settlement pattern which resulted from the *gwely* system was a scattered one, the holdings of its members consisting of a strip here and a parcel there. T. Jones Pierce, the great pioneer of these complex studies, showed that the men who were considered to be the founders of the *gwelyau* belonged to the generations around 1150; consequently, he argued that it was in that period that the *gwely* became established. It is recognized, however, that the agnatic group which was central to it had deep roots in Celtic society and it is now believed that landholding among the *bonheddwyr* was based upon the *gwely* system from very early times.

Those sections of the Law dealing with *galanas* are also ancient, for that is another word which survived in the Old North. The *galanas* of a man was the fine which had to be paid to his kindred (or, in the case of a slave, to his owner) if he were killed. It represented an attempt, similar to that found in other early societies, to tame the desire to shed blood in avenging a wrong. The amount of a man's *galanas* depended upon his status; that was largely determined by his ancestry, although sometimes a man could enjoy a higher status through holding office. The law-books note that the *galanas* was paid in money, but in the age of Hywel it was probably paid in cattle. Even if it is accepted that silver pennies were minted for him, there is no evidence that coinage was used on any scale in Wales before the age of his grandson, Maredudd ab Owain. The law-books provide fascinating details of the payers and the receivers of the *galanas*; indeed, they record such a complex system of kin obligations that it is difficult to comprehend how, in an age which lacked computers, it was decided exactly what sums were due from the various relations.

A daughter had half the *galanas* of her brother, and a wife had a third of the *galanas* of her husband. Furthermore, a woman could neither own land nor transfer rights to land to her children. Thus the status of the two sexes was fundamentally unequal. Nevertheless, the status of women under the Law of Wales was in many ways higher than it was under others of the legal systems of Europe. The daughter (and the son) was not wholly without rights in the face of the authority of the father as was the case in those countries which had inherited the Law of Rome, and the husband did not gain unrestricted control over his wife's property as he did under the Law of England. The wife had some degree of compensation if her husband were unfaithful to her; if she in turn were unfaithful, her fate was less appalling than it was in most of the countries of Europe.

The attitude of the Law of Wales towards these matters stemmed from the assumption that the union of a man and a woman was a contract rather than a sacrament; as Dafydd Jenkins put it, the Law kept the Church in its place. It recognized, as Canon Law did not, that a union could come to an end, and the law-books provide detailed guidance as to how the family property and the responsibility for the children were to be shared if that should happen. Nine forms of union are discussed and, although it is suggested that a church marriage had a special status, the others were not invalid. As a result, the chasm between legitimate and illegitimate children was foreign to the Law of Wales. It was not the nature of the union between the father and the mother, but rather the father's readiness to acknowledge his son which gave the son the rights which stemmed from his ancestry; thus, a bastard could inherit the property and the status of his father, much to the consternation of the upholders of Canon Law. In the age of Hywel, the canon lawyers were legislating upon what degree of consanguinity should constitute a barrier to marriage. They laid down so many restrictions that by 1051 there was hardly a princess in Europe whom the king of France could marry. These rules were ignored in Wales, where marriages between cousins were frequent occurrences. Three hundred years after the age of Hywel, Canon Law would be at the apogee of its influence. Because of the reluctance of the Law of Wales to conform, either to the canon lawyers' view of marriage or to their enthusiasm for Old-Testament-type punishments, it would be condemned as the work of the devil.

The readiness to marry close relations reflected the central role of the bonds of kinship in early Wales. In the age of Hywel Dda, it was a man's standing in a network of kindred rather than his standing as the citizen of a state which determined his social status, his economic rights and his legal obligations. Yet the role of the king should not be underestimated. It was he who gave coherence to a territory wider than that of the local community; although the Law of Hywel was folk law, it was the king or his deputy who called together the court of the *cantref*, where the law was administered in the presence of and with the consent of the *bonheddwyr*. The law of *galanas* stressed that murder was a crime against the kindred, but it was also developing into a crime against the state. It has been argued that the first step towards public law has been taken when the state insists upon at least a portion of the fine. That step had been taken in Wales within about a century of the death of Hywel, for the note on Erging in *Domesday Book* in 1086 states that a third of the *galanas* belonged to the king. Furthermore, it was the king who had the first claim upon whatever surplus the community produced. As well as the produce of the *maerdref*, the king received the *dawnbwyd* (the food rent paid by villeins) produced by his other *taeogdrefi*. The *taeogion* were also obliged to house his officials on their travels, to carve out paths for him through the forests, to feed his hunting dogs and to erect the buildings of his court. The duties of the *bonheddwyr* were more dignified; through the *gwestfa* (the food rent paid by freemen), they yielded to the king some of the fruits of their labour, but the payment was made as a recognition of lordship rather than as rent. They contributed to the *cylch* (the journey of the king's war-band) but, apart from the periods of military service expected of them, they were not obliged to offer him their labour.

The law-books stress the rights of the king, for the consolidation of royal power was one of the main aims of those who compiled them. Every version of the text begins with the king and his officials. Chief among them was his *penteulu*, the leader of the *teulu* or the war-band which was constantly in the king's company and which constituted the basis of his power and the heart of his kingdom. It is to the war-band that the *bardd teulu* sang, although the *pencerdd* was the chief poet of the kingdom. Order at court was kept by the *ynad*; the king's spiritual health was cared for by the priest and his physical health by the doctor; the *distain* looked after his food and the *gwas ystafell* took care of his clothes, and in addition he enjoyed the services of a number of lesser officials. In some of the texts there is a suggestion that the chief officials had wider responsibilities – that they were, so to speak, the 'cabinet' of the king. Throughout Europe, the administrators of kingdoms sprang from the personal servants of the sovereign and it is possible that some such development was afoot at the court of Hywel; as he had united a number of different territories under his rule he needed more elaborate administrative structures than those of his predecessors.

It was probably the need to give cohesion to those different territories that prompted Hywel to codify the law. He was also successful in defending his territories, for there is no record that they were ravaged by the Northmen during his reign. Neither were they attacked by the English. Hywel adhered to the close relationship with England initiated by his father-in-law, Hyfaidd of Dyfed; indeed, it has been claimed that he based his policy upon anglophilia. Yet it is unlikely that he relished the diminution in status and the heavy demands for tribute which resulted from his association with the kingdom of England; rather was he recognizing the facts of power – the power which in his lifetime extinguished the Brythonic kingdom of Cornwall and which brought about the death of his cousin, Idwal of Gwynedd.

The power of the kingdom of England was particularly evident during the reign of Alfred's grandson, Aethelstan (924–39). Aethelstan was addressed as 'Basileus of the English and in like manner the ruler of the whole orb of Britain' and he was determined to give substance to the title. *The Anglo-Saxon Chronicle* notes that in 929 he imposed a heavy tax upon Wales, including twenty pounds of gold and 25,000 oxen. Between 928 and 935, when the kings of the Scots and the Northmen – rulers who were also subject to Aethelstan's overlordship – were increasingly restive, it would seem that Hywel was frequently invited to the English court, for in those years he was witness to English royal charters on seven occasions. The unrest among the Scots and Northmen exploded in 937. They were thoroughly beaten by Aethelstan at the battle of Brunanburh and his victory was lauded in one of the most remarkable of Old English poems.

About the same time, one of the most remarkable of Welsh poems was composed and it offers a very different interpretation of the troubles of the time. The poem is *Armes Prydein*, which according to Ifor Williams was composed about 930, possibly in St David's. In it the poet expresses his contempt for the English, 'so lacking in lineage'; he calls upon the Welsh to unite with the Irish and the men of Dublin (the Northmen) and Cornwall and Strathclyde to defeat them, and he longs to see the 'Foreigners [Saxons] setting out into exile'. The author was almost certainly one of Hywel's subjects and his poem is proof that the king's pragmatism could appear to a contemporary as cowardly compromise. The earnest appeal of the poet of St David's was ignored and the Welsh kept away from the troubles which led to the battle of Brunanburh. Hywel attended the coronation of Eadred, Aethelstan's brother, in 946 when he was described, not as *subregulus* as in previous charters, but as *regulus*, the title he was given in the two charters of Eadred which he witnessed a year before his death in 950.

Hywel's creation, the kingdom of Deheubarth, survived his death. In 950 it passed to his son Owain, a man of historical interests, for it would appear that the genealogies and the *Annales Cambriae* were compiled at his request. Gwynedd and Powys returned to the line of Idwal ab Anarawd while Glamorgan continued to be subject to its own kings. Although the union between Gwynedd/Powys and Deheubarth was broken, Wales had only three kingdoms after 950, compared with over twice that number two centuries earlier. It is impossible to reconcile this process of consolidation with the notion that the territory of a Welsh king was divided after his death among all his sons. In the four hundred years separating Rhodri from his ancestor, Maelgwn Fawr, there were about a dozen generations. If Maelgwn had had two sons – a conservative estimate if illegitimate sons were to be included – and if they had had two sons apiece, and so on over twelve generations, and if every one of them had received part of Maelgwn's original kingdom, by the age of Rhodri there would have been 2,048 kings in Gwynedd; they would have been fortunate to be sovereigns of smallholdings. Such foolishness is implicit in the idea that the Welsh had no concept of the unity of a kingdom and that they lacked the political instinct which characterized others of the nations of Europe.

The truth of the matter is that there was nothing particularly exceptional about the pattern of succession in early Wales. No kingdom in Europe had a wholly cast-iron rule for determining who was the king's heir. If a man of exceptional personality succeeded in extending his authority over a cluster of territories, there was a strong tendency for his creation to fall apart after his death, and examples of this may be found in the history of France, England, Castile and Denmark as well as in that of Wales. Nevertheless, there were some units which were not divided. They included the 'basic' kingdoms of Wales such as Gwynedd and Dyfed; there is in their early history no more evidence of a desire to divide them than there is in the early history of Wessex or Mercia. Sometimes brothers ruled as joint sovereigns or an appanage might be created which would be the responsibility of a relation of the king, but neither of these arrangements implied the destruction of the unity of the kingdom. It was not usual anywhere for the king to be succeeded by his eldest son. If such succession were to be the rule, an infant could become king – an unrealistic situation, as the king was above all a war leader. A ruler sought to appoint his successor, but there was usually a struggle for the kingdom after his death. The right to kingship belonged to a wide kindred rather than to a narrow lineage, and any man related up to the fourth generation to a previous king could claim the throne. Thus in Wessex in 685, Centwine was succeeded by the great-great-grandson of the brother of his great-grandfather, and similar examples may be found in the history of Mercia and Northumbria. It was the most energetic and most ruthless member of the royal kindred who won a kingdom in the Europe of the Early Middle Ages. This was an unstable and a bloody system and, as kingdoms developed structures which were less dependent upon the personality of the king, there was a contraction in the lineage considered to be royal and examples of the succession of the eldest son multiplied. Such succession became deeply rooted among the Capetians of France from 996 onwards, but it had not become wholly established in the Old English Kingdom when that kingdom was seized by William I in 1066. Wales was also moving in the same direction: by the age of Hywel, the principle of primogeniture was gaining recognition and the Law of the Court gave a prominent position to the *edling*, the king's heir.

Nevertheless, the Welsh did not succeed in creating a united enduring state. As a result, their experience was very different from that of the English, for by 1066 the unity of England had struck deep roots and the numerous kingdoms characteristic of its early history had disappeared. But the unity and cohesion of the Old English Kingdom were exceptional; it should not be considered that the English pattern is the measuring rod of normality and that Wales is abnormal when it does not conform to that pattern. England was united under very remarkable circumstances: all her kingdoms other than that of Wessex were conquered by the Danes, and it was a crusade under the leadership of the house of Cerdic which brought all the English under the rule of a single king. The kingdom of England was created by *conquistadores* campaigning to restore their country to their race and their faith, an experience which fostered an imperial spirit among them as it did in not wholly dissimilar circumstances among the men of Castile centuries later.

It was that spirit, rather than any basic weakness in the political instincts of the Welsh, which frustrated the growth of a united Welsh state and which prevented the principle of primogeniture from striking deep roots in Wales. After Rhodri had succeeded in uniting most of Wales, he was killed by the English before his creation won full recognition, and a similar fate awaited Gruffudd ap Llywelyn. The lesser kings, in their natural desire not to be dispossessed by a strong Welsh ruler, could look to England for help in their resistance, as could the younger sons of a Welsh king when they opposed the consolidation of power in the hands of their eldest brother. But the failure to create a united Welsh kingdom cannot wholly be explained in terms of the ability of elements in Wales to depend upon English interference. Geography played its part. The problem was not so much too many mountains as too many plains. The kingdom of

Scotland grew around the lowlands watered by the rivers Tay and Forth, a region without equal throughout the country in terms of wealth and population. In Wales there were at least four fairly fertile regions capable of being the nucleus of a kingdom – Anglesey for Gwynedd, the Severn valley for Powys, the Vale for Glamorgan and the Tywi valley for Deheubarth – but not one of them had an indubitable superiority over all the others in terms of wealth and population. In ancient kingdoms such as Fife and Moray, there was a deep sense of separatism, but the kingdom of Scotland had sufficient power to bind such regions to it. Gwynedd was the nucleus of Welsh consolidation in the age of Rhodri, and Deheubarth in the age of Hywel, but they were too equal; neither of the two territories had the resources or the structures necessary to bind the other kingdoms to it permanently.

Centuries after the age of Hywel, some of his descendants would seek to create structures to that end, but in the half century or so after his death the political history of Wales was depressing in the extreme. From 986 to 999 Maredudd, the grandson of Hywel, succeeded in re-creating the kingdom of his grandfather, but the years of his supremacy were troubled ones. The attacks of the Northmen recommenced; it was probably in that period that Scandinavian names – which were later adopted in English – were given to islands and coastal locations such as Anglesey, Bardsey, Caldey, Fishguard and Swansea. There is some evidence that the Northmen established small trading-stations in Cardiff, Swansea and Haverfordwest, and studies based upon blood-groups suggest that a substantial number of them settled in the *cantref* of Penfro. From their strongholds in Dublin and the Isle of Man, they mercilessly ravaged the coasts of Wales. Once again, it was Anglesey which suffered worst, and it was recorded in 987 that two thousand of the men of the island were seized and sold as slaves. In 988 the Northmen plundered Llanbadarn, St Dogmael's, Llancarfan and Llantwit Major and in the following year Maredudd ab Owain was obliged to raise a penny poll-tax to bribe them to stay away. They attacked Anglesey again in 993; in 997 they came in a host to the banks of the Severn and in 999 they attacked St David's, killing Morgenau, the bishop.

In so calamitous an age, the leadership of members of ancient royal houses seemed inadequate, and in England, France, Ireland and Germany power passed into the hands of rulers from 'new' lines. In

Wales also the house of Rhodri was abandoned on occasion. Virtually nothing is known of the ancestry of Llywelyn ap Seisyll, who ruled in Gwynedd from 1018 to 1023, nor of that of Rhydderch ap Iestyn, who was king of Deheubarth from 1023 to 1033, and the origins of Edwin ap Gwriad, who seized authority over Gwent in about 1015, are even more obscure. By far the most important source of information for this period and for centuries to come is *Brut y Tywysogyon* (The Chronicle of the Princes). It exists in three Welsh versions; they are translations of a lost Latin chronicle which for the years from about 900 to 1100 is an expansion of annals compiled at St David's. The contents of the *Brut* in the years 950 to 1150 are harrowing; it records twenty-eight murders and four blindings. As it contains little beyond these horrors, historians have been mesmerized by the heinousness of the chronicler's account and have thus portrayed the decades around the year 1000 as the most savage and fruitless in the history of Wales.

Other sources show that violence was not the totality of the experience of the Welsh in those years. While the chronicler at St David's was reporting carnage and mayhem, a craftsman at Penally was carving an elaborate cross in memory of Maredudd ab Edwin, the man who restored the line of Rhodri to the throne of Deheubarth in 1033. Sculptors were also active in Glamorgan; there was a school of them at Margam and Llantwit Major, and although the design of the Welsh crosses is inferior to that of the high crosses of Ireland the execution of the work is often superior. Not far from Llantwit Major lies Llancarfan, the birthplace in about 1020 of Herewald, bishop of Glamorgan from 1056 to 1104. He trained a number of learned men to serve the bishopric, among them his sons, Lifris, the author of *The Life of St Cadog*, and Steffan, the author of *The Life of St Teilo*. Even more learned was the family of Sulien of Llanbadarn. Between 1030 and 1050, Sulien slaked his thirst for knowledge by means of a saga of journeys. He became bishop of St David's in 1073 and he raised his sons to serve the Church of David; one of them was Rhygyfarch (Ricemarch), an accomplished Latin stylist and the author of *The Life of St David*; another was Ieuan, a skilful calligrapher and the copyist of the works of Augustine of Hippo. A scholar of a rather earlier generation than that of Sulien was the author of the manuscript known as *The Computus Fragment*; it is a study of the stars and it testifies to the ability of a Welshman of about 940 to discuss complex matters in his mother tongue.

Among Sulien's contemporaries was someone who may without exaggeration be placed among the great literary figures of the Middle Ages, if it is accepted that *Pedair Cainc y Mabinogi* was composed about 1060. The splendours of the *Pedair Cainc* testify not only to the gifts of the author but also to the richness of the Welsh language as a literary medium. The stories of Pwyll, Pryderi, Branwen, Manawydan and the rest survived virtually by accident. If *The White Book of Rhydderch* and *The Red Book of Hergest* had disappeared, there would hardly be a suggestion that they had ever existed. Doubtless many similar stories have disappeared; keys to this vanished literature have been kept in the *Triads* – pithy sayings, a stimulus to the memory, rather like the heads of sermons of later generations; the numerousness of the *Triads* are proof of the magnitude of the loss.

It is not only stories that have been lost. Nothing has survived of the praise poems to Rhodri Mawr, to Hywel Dda, to Maredudd ab Owain and to Maredudd's grandson, Gruffudd ap Llywelyn. Such poetry must have been composed, and nothing would have inspired the poets so much as the achievements of such men, particularly those of Gruffudd ap Llywelyn, the only Welsh king ever to rule over the entire territory of Wales. Gruffudd was the son of Llywelyn ap Seisyll, the man who seized the throne of Gwynedd in 1018, and of Angharad, the daughter of Maredudd ab Owain. In 1039, Gwynedd and Powys came into his possession after he had killed Iago ab Idwal, the great-grandson of Idwal ab Anarawd. He then sought to seize Deheubarth but his ambition was thwarted by another Gruffudd, the son of Rhydderch ap Iestyn, who had been king of Deheubarth between 1023 and 1033. Deheubarth did not come firmly into his possession until 1055, when he encompassed the death of Gruffudd ap Rhydderch. A year or two later Gruffudd ap Llywelyn seized Glamorgan, driving out its ruler, Cadwgan ap Meurig of the line of Hywel ap Rhys. Thus, from about 1057 until his death in 1063, the whole of Wales recognized the kingship of Gruffudd ap Llywelyn. For about seven brief years, Wales was one, under one ruler, a feat with neither precedent nor successor.

Gruffudd ap Llywelyn's method of uniting the nation was brutal. He was taunted with his readiness to kill his opponents, and Walter Map, the garrulous story-teller from Hereford, reported that he replied: 'Talk not of killing. I only blunt the horns of the progeny of Wales lest they should wound their dam.' His activities aroused the enmity of other branches of the house of Rhodri. They also created concern in England, for Gruffudd ap Llywelyn was the first Welsh ruler since Cadwallon who had the power to interfere in the affairs of England. There, in 1042, the line of Cerdic was restored to the throne in the person of Edward the Confessor, the son of Aethelred the Unready. Edward's leadership was ineffective; the provincial earls enjoyed great power and were involved in bitter rivalry. England's weakness was Wales's opportunity. Gruffudd coveted the rich lands beyond Offa's Dyke which had been in the possession of English settlers for three hundred years and more. In 1039, he defeated the forces of Leofric, earl of Mercia, at Rhyd-y-groes near Welshpool. In 1055 he allied with Leofric's son, Aelfgar, who had been exiled from England through the machinations of the sons of Godwine, earl of Wessex; the allies burned Hereford and Gruffudd expelled a large proportion of the population of the borderland. Thus did the Welsh repossess Whitford and Hope, Bangor Is-coed and Chirk, Presteigne and Radnor. The revenge of the kingdom of England came in 1063 when Harold, Godwine's son and successor as earl of Wessex, led forces over land and sea to defeat Gruffudd. Gruffudd was pursued from place to place, and he was killed somewhere in Snowdonia on 5 August 1063. The *Brut* states that he was killed by his own men, an entry which J. E. Lloyd interprets as meaning that he met his death through treason; *The Ulster Chronicle*, however, states that he was killed by Cynan ap Iago, whose father, Iago ab Idwal, had been put to death by Gruffudd in 1039; if so, his death may be attributed to filial loyalty.

Three years after his victory over Gruffudd ap Llywelyn, and in part because of that victory, Harold was elected king of England. No consideration was given to the claims of the heir of Edward the Confessor (his great-nephew, Edward the Aethling) or to the far vaguer claims of William, duke of Normandy. Harold married Gruffudd ap Llywelyn's widow, Ealdgyth, the daughter of Aelfgar; thus she was in turn queen of Wales and queen of England – her grandmother was Lady Godiva. Harold did not annex any part of Wales in the wake of his victory, except parts of the lowlands of Gwent perhaps; his aim was to prevent unity and he was prepared to allow the Welsh to rule in Wales as long as they were disunited. It appears that Cynan, the senior representative of the house of Gwynedd, had been killed in the battles of 1063; his heir was

Gruffudd, a boy of eight who lived in Ireland with his mother, the daughter of the Norse king of Dublin. Gwynedd and Powys came into the possession of Bleddyn and Rhiwallon, the half-brothers of Gruffudd ap Llywelyn, and Deheubarth passed to Maredudd ab Owain of the line of Hywel Dda. Caradog, the son of Gruffudd ap Rhydderch, seized Gwent and Gwynllŵg, while the rest of Glamorgan returned to the rule of Cadwgan ap Meurig.

This was the political situation in Wales on 14 October 1066, the day of William of Normandy's victory at Senlac Hill. That victory has been elevated to be the one universally known date in English history. The date also has significance in the history of Wales. The Normans were colonists of genius. They were colonists from the beginning, for they originated as Scandinavians from whom the king of France bought peace in 911 by allowing them to settle in the Seine valley. Within a century, they had created the powerful duchy of Normandy. Before another century had passed, they had had experience of colonization in southern Italy, Greece, Palestine, England, Ireland and Wales. An imperial people, their poets, in comparing their capital, Rouen, with Rome, were not indulging in mere bombast. Northern France in the years of their supremacy was the most vigorous region of Europe; it was there that the Gothic style of architecture was developed, a style which would sweep through the countries of the Latin Church; the region was the well-head of the ideas which were to be the basis of the cultural and ecclesiastical renaissance which characterized the decades after 1100; it was there that the social, military, legal and economic structure known as feudalism grew to its full stature; northern France was the home of the great fairs which were the main centres of trade between northern and southern Europe. It was the Normans who connected Wales with these developments, although, had the Normans never left Normandy, the Welsh would have come into contact with the main stream of European development; it would have happened more slowly, no doubt, but the process would have been far less painful.

After an eight-hour battle near Hastings, the kingdom of England was seized by William; further campaigns would be needed, particularly in northern England and in East Anglia, but by 1070 the entire realm was under his control. So secure was the grip of the Conqueror over his new territory that he was able in 1086 to carry out a detailed inquiry into its resources, the basis of that extraordinary document, *Domesday Book*. Henceforth, the English would be second-class citizens in England. Their language was no longer the language of law and government, and almost three centuries would elapse before the throne of England would again be occupied by a man fluent in English. Upper-class patronage for English literature came to an end and the powerful flow of that literature became a feeble rivulet. The English aristocratic families were dispossessed of their estates; by 1086 almost all the landowners of England were Norman, almost half the country being in the hands of the king, his relations and about twenty of his leading followers. The Normans came to despise the people they had conquered; by the age of Giraldus Cambrensis (1146–1220), the English were considered to be lazy, dirty, servile and drunk.

This was not the fate of the Welsh, at least not yet. When the literature of the English was suffering eclipse, that of the Welsh was entering one of its most flourishing periods, and when English was being exiled from court and council, Welsh was developing increasing suppleness as a medium of law and government. For generations after 1066, Welsh and Norman aristocrats would meet as equals; although there would be enmity between them, there would also be inter-marriage and each would be enriched by the traditions of the other.

As king of England, William could claim a degree of suzerainty over the kings of Wales and Scotland. His suzerainty over both countries was essentially the same, but the attitude of the Normans to the rulers of Scotland was not the same as their attitude to the rulers of Wales. In 1092, Cumbria was taken from the kingdom of Scotland, but thereafter the frontiers of that kingdom were not violated. Many Normans settled there, but they came at the invitation of the kings of Scotland. To the Normans, Scotland appeared to be a kingdom deserving recognition, with rights and borders that could be respected, although it should be borne in mind that they had problems in northern England which it would have been unwise to complicate through excessive involvement in Scotland.

The attitude of the Normans to the men ruling in Wales following the downfall of Gruffudd ap Llywelyn was very different, and it must be acknowledged that those rulers did not project an image which was likely to command respect. The power of Bleddyn and Rhiwallon was challenged by the sons of Gruffudd ap Llywelyn; they, along with Rhiwallon, were killed in a skirmish in 1070. In 1072, Maredudd

ab Owain of Deheubarth was killed by Caradog ap Gruffudd of
Gwynllŵg, and in 1074 Caradog drove Cadwgan ap Meurig from
Glamorgan and seized his kingdom. In 1075, Bleddyn was killed by
Rhys, the brother of Maredudd ab Owain, and Rhys in turn was
killed in 1078 by Caradog ap Gruffudd. Bleddyn's kingdom passed to
his cousin, Trahaearn ap Caradog, but Trahaearn was killed, along
with Caradog ap Gruffudd, in the battle of Mynydd Carn in 1081.
With that battle, the carnage was halted. The victors were Gruffudd
ap Cynan of the senior branch of the royal house of Gwynedd and
Rhys ap Tewdwr of the senior branch of the royal house of
Deheubarth, branches to which the two kingdoms would henceforth
remain loyal.

By 1081, however, it seemed as if none of the kingdoms of Wales
had much future. William had no intention of annexing Wales.
Nevertheless, with the memory of Gruffudd ap Llywelyn's incursions
over the border still fresh, and with rulers such as Bleddyn ap Cynfyn
showing a readiness to ally with anti-Norman elements in England,
ensuring a secure frontier was a matter of importance to him. Often,
the simplest way of ensuring such a frontier is to move it further
away. William gave lands along the border to some of his most
faithful followers – Hereford to his kinsman William Fitzosbern,
Shrewsbury to Roger Montgomery and Chester to Hugh the Fat of
Avranches – and even if he did not encourage them to overrun the
territories of the Welsh he certainly did not forbid them to do so. The
border barons were hard men from the frontiers of Normandy, ready
to seize every opportunity to add to their power and their lands. The
castle and the knight were the keys to their success. The earliest castles
were of earth and timber; some five hundred of these motte-and-
bailey structures were built in Wales and its borderlands, but by 1110
solid castles of stone were being erected in places such as Chepstow.
There had been mounted warriors among the Welsh from a very
early time, but the arms, armour and horses of the Normans were of
a higher standard; central to their feudalism was the knight's fee,
each about the size of a small parish, which the Normans established
in order to provide for the maintenance of their knights.

Domesday Book provides details of the degree of success achieved by
the first wave of Norman invaders. By 1086, they had castles at
Chepstow, Monmouth and Caerleon, and the Welsh kingdom of
Gwent had been extinguished after an existence of almost seven

hundred years. William Fitzosbern, the author of its destruction, died in 1071 and his son was imprisoned for treason in 1075. He had no successor as earl of Hereford and thus the pressure upon south-east Wales slackened. In the absence of a dominant overlord, lands on the border were amassed by lesser lords such as Ralph Mortimer of Wigmore, Roger de Lacy of Weobley, Ralph de Toeni of Clifford, Osbern Fitzrichard of Richard's Castle and his son-in-law Bernard of Neufmarché, founders of families which would loom large in the history of Wales. Glamorgan and Deheubarth had not yet suffered invasion. When William I visited St David's in 1081 – to pay his respects to the shrine of David according to Welsh sources; to display his power to the Welsh, according to English ones – he recognized Rhys ap Tewdwr's position as the ruler of Deheubarth, and *Domesday Book* recorded that Rhys was paying an annual tribute of £40 to the king of England.

The Normans were not so considerate towards the rights of Gruff-udd ap Cynan, Rhys's fellow victor in the battle of Mynydd Carn. Shortly after that victory, he was captured by the men of Hugh the Fat, earl of Chester, and the earl kept him imprisoned for at least twelve years. In 1086, it would appear that *Domesday Book* considered north-east Wales up to the river Clwyd to be part of the earldom of Chester. For the lands to the west of the river, Robert, the cousin of Hugh the Fat, paid £40 a year to the king of England, a suggestion that Robert's status in Gwynedd was similar to that of Rhys ap Tewdwr in Deheubarth. In view of the strength of its natural defences, it is strange that it was Gwynedd, in 1086, that seemed to be the most likely of the major kingdoms of Wales to fall victim to the invaders.

The threat to Powys was almost as dire. By 1086, Roger, earl of Shrewsbury, had built a castle to guard the major Severn ford of Rhydwhiman; it was named Montgomery after Roger's home in Normandy. The Normans claimed the *cantrefi* of Iâl, Cynllaith, Edeirnion and Nanheudwy; they pushed forward towards Ceri, Cedewain and Arwystli, and there was every sign that the whole of the kingdom of Powys would shortly be under the control of the earl of Shrewsbury and his followers.

William I died in 1087 and his territories were divided among his sons – his eldest, Robert, became duke of Normandy and his second son, William Rufus, became king of England. William II was less masterful than his father and less able to maintain the patronage which Rhys ap Tewdwr had received from William I. In 1088, Bernard of Neufmarché attacked Deheubarth; he captured Brycheiniog and began to build a castle at the confluence of the rivers Usk and Honddu (Aberhonddu – Brecon). In 1093, in seeking to resist him, Rhys ap Tewdwr was killed. There was no longer any constraint upon the attacks of the Normans. A few months after the death of Rhys, the forces of Roger, earl of Shrewsbury, surged from Powys into Ceredigion; they built a castle on the estuary of the river Teifi (Aberteifi – Cardigan) and they continued their way towards the fertile lands of southern Dyfed. There, Roger's son Arnulf seized the *cantref* of Penfro, where he built Pembroke Castle, one of the greatest of the strongholds of the Normans in Wales. Hywel, Rhys's youngest son, was imprisoned by Arnulf, and Gruffudd, the eldest, was taken to Ireland for refuge. It is hardly surprising that chroniclers in Wales and in England saw the killing of Rhys ap Tewdwr as marking the end of kingship in Wales.

At much the same time as the seizure of Brycheiniog and Penfro, the kingdom of Glamorgan also fell to the invaders. The last of its kings was Iestyn ap Gwrgant, third cousin of Cadwgan ap Meurig, into whose possession it had probably come following the death of Caradog ap Gruffudd in 1081. The leader of the attack upon Glamorgan was Robert Fitzhammo, a landowner in Gloucestershire, but so many legends have gathered around the conquest that it is difficult to distinguish between truth and fable. The fate of Glamorgan was a smaller-scale version of the fate of Wales as a whole; the lowlands between the Ogwr and the Usk were seized in the first stage of the conquest, but the power of the lord of Glamorgan in the uplands remained slight for generations, and long campaigns and costly castle-building were to be necessary before the district came firmly under the authority of the lord at Cardiff.

The Normans won England after barely four years of campaigning; by 1090, it seemed that the whole of Wales would be subject to them after barely a quarter of a century of campaigning. But that did not happen. Although they had erected numerous castles, it was only in a few regions of Wales that the Norman grasp was firm. Internecine struggles among the Welsh had been so intense that the invaders must have felt that vigorous resistance was unlikely. But the Welsh still had territories outside Norman control from which counter-attacks could

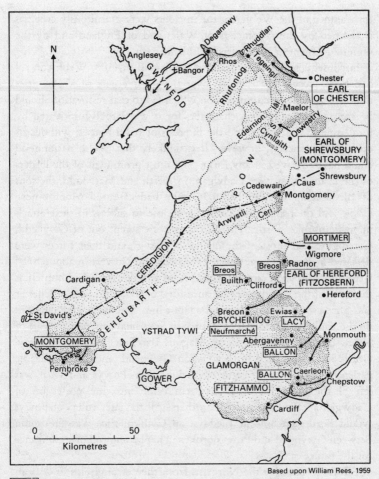

Based upon William Rees, 1959

BREOS : Marcher Lords

The Norman assaults upon Wales, 1067–99

be launched and, unlike the ruling class of the Old English Kingdom, they were allowed time to understand the nature of the Norman threat and to devise answers to it. There were limits to the power of the border lords, especially if the king of England did not support them with the resources of his kingdom. There were limits also to the forbearance of the Welsh, for the invaders were gratuitously cruel, as is testified by the chroniclers of Wales and of England and by the dignified lament of Rhygyfarch of Llanbadarn.

In consequence, by the death of William II in 1100, Welsh control had been successfully restored over the greater part of Wales. It is doubtful whether the insurrection which led to that restoration should be considered national in character, for it was largely motivated by local issues, racial anger and the interests of royal houses; without its comparative success, however, it is unlikely that Welsh nationhood could have survived in any form. The most prominent of the leaders of the insurrection were Cadwgan, Iorwerth and Maredudd, the sons of Bleddyn ap Cynfin. By 1096, they had captured Montgomery Castle and their allies had come very close to success in their attack upon Pembroke Castle. The Normans were swept out of Gwynedd, Ceredigion and most of the *cantrefi* of Powys, and their forces were defeated in Brycheiniog, Gwent, Cydweli and Gower. In about 1094, Gruffudd ap Cynan escaped from prison and re-established himself as the ruler of the kingdom of his ancestors. In 1098, the earls of Chester and Shrewsbury led a campaign against him, but they were defeated on the banks of the Menai by a force of Scandinavians, and the earl of Shrewsbury was shot dead by Magnus Barefoot, king of Norway. Gruffudd consolidated his hold upon Gwynedd, and for decades he patiently rebuilt the strength of his kingdom. Powys and what was left of the kingdom of Deheubarth came into the possession of Cadwgan ap Bleddyn and his brothers. All the later rulers of Powys would be descendants of Bleddyn ap Cynfyn; thus was the union between Gwynedd and Powys broken, a happening full of significance for the future of Wales.

Efforts to dislodge the Normans from their strongholds in Gwent, Glamorgan, Brecon, southern Dyfed and the borders of Powys were not successful. If the Welsh leaders had been faced only with the forces of the border lords, it is likely that they would have restored the whole of Wales to their rule. But the king of England was not prepared to tolerate that; it was difficult for him to allow some of his leading vassals to be defeated, and the existence of a *cordon sanitaire* of Norman lordships between his kingdom and the territories of the Welsh rulers was advantageous to him. As a result, the king of England was increasingly drawn into the troubles of Wales. Within a few decades of their commencement, the campaigns of the Normans in Wales had ceased to be mere private baronial ventures. In 1095 and again in 1097, William II sent royal forces to Wales, and the involvement of his brother and successor, Henry I, would be substantially greater. This interference was sufficient to ensure the survival of the Norman lordships, but it was insufficient to uproot Welsh rule in the greater part of Wales. Thus it would be for over two hundred years. The king of England lacked the resources – or he did not choose to expend the resources – which would have been needed if Wales were to be thoroughly subjugated, but he expended enough to ensure that Norman power would not be extinguished there and that Wales would not be united under Welsh rule.

These were the conditions which gave rise to the March, a central element in the history of Wales for four hundred years and more. By the early years of the reign of Henry I (1100–1135), the boundary between the territories of the Marcher Lords and the territories which would remain under Welsh rule – between *Marchia Wallie* and *Pura Wallia* – had been more or less established. The boundary would move on occasion, in the one direction and in the other, but for the greater part of the period during which Welsh rule endured, the boundary line that had come into existence by 1105 would be the boundary of *Pura Wallia*. Beyond it (to use the old county names) were the fringes of Flintshire and Montgomeryshire, most of Radnorshire, Breconshire and Glamorgan, Monmouthshire almost in its entirety, along with southern Carmarthenshire and virtually the whole of Pembrokeshire. But the situation was more complex than that, for several of the lordships of the March had their own *Purae Walliae* – the Welshries: in Glamorgan, Brecon, Radnor and elsewhere there were districts which were as Welsh in their culture and social structure as were the heartlands of Gwynedd. As the boundary between the two *Walliae* was fairly stable, it has been argued that it represents a divide with deep roots in the history of Wales; there are advocates of the view that, in interpreting the experience of the Welsh people, greater significance should be attached to the division between inner and outer Wales than to the more traditional division between northern and southern Wales. Furthermore, on the basis of the boundaries of the Welshries, it has been claimed that the Normans seized the land up to two hundred metres above sea level and that those dwelling above that contour were left undisturbed. These theories are interesting and valuable, although it is possible to stray too far along the road of geographical determinism.

The fact that they were subjects of the king of England was wholly central to the position of the Lords of the March. Nevertheless, the March was not part of England and it was not answerable to the English system of government. As has been seen, the cohesion of the Old English Kingdom was exceptional; it was further strengthened by William I, by his son, Henry I, and particularly by Henry's grandson, Henry II. By 1200, England was a feudal kingdom of a strongly centralized character with its Common Law and its writs and its royal courts of law. That was not true of the March, where the Common Law was not administered and where the king's writ did not run. While centripetal forces were at work in England, centrifugal forces were at work in Wales. The Marcher Lords were lords of men as well as of land. In England, the crown was increasingly successful in its efforts to insist that all cases of importance should be heard in the royal courts, but the Marcher Lords had their own courts as extensive in their authority as the courts of the king. The law they administered was the Law of the March – Welsh Law as seen through Norman eyes, to quote one definition of it. While there were restrictions upon the freedom of the barons of England to build fortifications and to indulge in private warfare, there were no restrictions upon the right of the Marcher Lords to erect castles and to wage war against their neighbours.

These were exceptional powers. They were far greater than the powers of the Anglo-Norman baronage which later developed in Ireland, and their origins have been much discussed. It has been suggested that the king acquiesced in them in order to encourage the Marcher Lords to subjugate the Welsh. Goronwy Edwards argued that the powers the Marcher Lords exercised were those of their predecessors, the Welsh kings. He claimed that the unit of sovereignty in Wales was the commote; by taking possession of a commote, a Norman lord became invested with sovereignty over it. Not all historians accept this view in its entirety. The framework of the commote was not universally respected and it is unlikely that the invaders made a close study of the rights of their predecessors. It is difficult to accept Goronwy Edwards's argument that sovereignty in Wales was so fragmented that it was possible to tear a piece of it away like tearing a sheet of stamps. It is easier to believe in the situation which is implicit in *Domesday Book*'s reference to the position of Osbern Fitzrichard on the borders of Powys: 'He has what he can

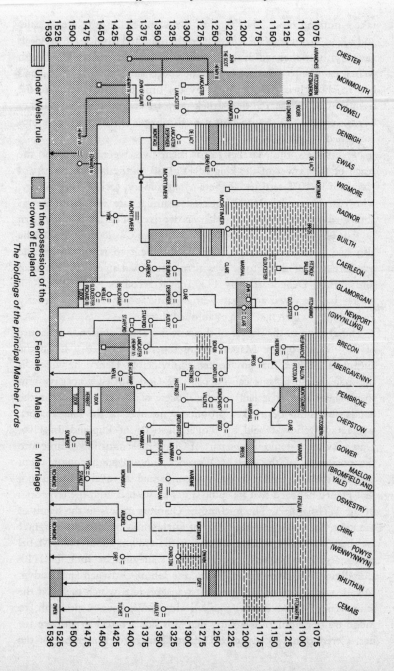

The holdings of the principal Marcher Lords

take – nothing more.' The right of the Marcher Lords to erect castles and to engage in warfare was not a right inherited from some previous sovereignty; rather was it the condition of their existence. The Welsh March came into existence before the courts and the writs of England had reached their full maturity; by the time they had done so, the traditions of the March had struck deep roots and thus the Marcher Lords, unlike the Anglo-Norman baronage of Ireland, were not enmeshed by those courts and writs.

Nevertheless, the Marcher Lords themselves were not beyond the reach of the power of the king of England, as the fate of the earl of Hereford in 1075 testifies. Robert Montgomery, earl of Shrewsbury, who rose in revolt in 1102, suffered a similar fate. His earldom was abolished and his brother, Arnulf, was deprived of his lands in southern Dyfed. Henry I took possession of Pembroke Castle and by 1109 he also had a castle at Carmarthen. From the two royal castles, the overlordship of the crown was firmly imposed upon the Norman lordships of Deheubarth; by 1130, royal accounts – the Pipe Roll which has survived for that year – provide proof of the orderly government which had been established there.

The growth of the power of the crown was the outstanding feature of the history of the March during the reign of Henry I. To the author of the *Brut*, that power seemed invincible. Henry, he wrote, 'is the man whom no one can oppose save God himself who gave him so much power'. The lands of the diocese of St David's were in the hands of Bishop Bernard, a prominent member of the king's court, while Cydweli was held by Roger, Justiciar of England. In 1106, Gower (which would not be part of Glamorgan until 1536) came into the possession of the earl of Warwick, not through conquest but through the king's gift; the gift was confirmed by royal charter, proof that Henry believed that he could do as he wished with the territories of the Welsh rulers. The lordship of Glamorgan was in the hands of the king, for following the death of Fitzhammo in 1105 his daughter and heiress, Mabel, became a ward of the crown; about 1120, Mabel was married to Robert, one of Henry's illegitimate sons. In 1110, Ceredigion was taken from Owain, the son of Cadwgan ap Bleddyn. Owain was guilty of a number of transgressions which included the seduction of Nest, the wife of Gerald of Windsor – although, to judge by her numerous affairs, that was not a novel experience for her. Ceredigion was given to Gilbert Fitzrichard, a member of the house of Clare, a family which would be prominent in the history of Wales for two hundred years. A branch of the same family held Gwent Is Coed (Chepstow or Striguil), while the lords of Gwent Uwch Coed (Abergavenny) and of Brecon were men wholly loyal to the king. On the fringes of Powys, the void caused by the downfall of the house of Montgomery was filled by the king's representative, Payne Fitzjohn, who encouraged or acquiesced in the attacks of Philip de Breos upon Radnor and Builth and the campaigns of Hugh Mortimer in Elfael and Maelienydd.

The leading Marcher Lords were among the most powerful of the barons of England. Their holdings in the March were often append-ages of even vaster estates in England; they were closely involved in high politics and they probably did not spend a great deal of time in their castles in the March. It was the lesser men, permanently settled there, who created that synthesis of Norman, English and Welsh elements which would become part of the heritage of the Welsh nation. They included men such as Gerald of Windsor, the castellan of Pembroke; he married Nest, the daughter of Rhys ap Tewdwr, because (to quote his grandson, Giraldus Cambrensis) of his desire to strike roots in that part of the country. Gerald was one of the host of Normans, English, Bretons and Flemings who came to Wales in the wake of the Marcher Lords. The colonists included the retinue of knights accompanying the lord and they expected their share of the lands won through their endeavours. That share could be large. The lord of Glamorgan received less than a tenth of the income produced by the lands of the lordship; the rest went to his knights, men like de Londres, le Sor and de Humfreville, the owners of estates which provided for the maintenance of twenty-four knights. They were responsible for guarding the lord's castle and were answerable to his court at Cardiff, the centre of the *comitatus* or county of Glamorgan.

The knights' fees were organized on a manorial basis, a system which may not have differed greatly from that of the *maenor* which had existed in parts of Wales before the coming of the Normans. The earliest records concerning the knights' fees are two hundred years later than the reign of Henry I; they show that most of the tenants of the manors in the Vale of Glamorgan bore English names, and they contain no suggestion that the tenants were recent incomers. It is clear therefore that English peasants as well as Norman knights had migrated to Wales, not only to the Vale of Glamorgan but also to the

Gower peninsula, Pembroke and Gwent Is Coed; as the history of Ireland amply proves, a dense settlement of peasants is always a more effective way of consolidating conquest than a thin layer of gentry. The ethnic nature of the most fertile areas of the southern fringes of Wales was changed by immigrants whom the Welsh were unable fully to assimilate. Of these colonizations, the only one referred to in contemporary sources is that mentioned by *Brut y Tywysogyon* in its entry for 1105. The *Brut* states that in that year Henry I allowed a colony of Flemings to settle in the *cantrefi* of Rhos and Daugleddau in southern Dyfed. According to Giraldus Cambrensis, they received the special patronage of the crown and although the Welsh sought on several occasions to expel them, the character of the region settled by them was transformed to such an extent that only seven of the almost fifty parishes of the two *cantrefi* bear Welsh names. The Flemish and English languages were fairly similar at the time of the coloniza-tion, and it would seem that Flemish had become extinct in Dyfed by about 1350; nevertheless, two hundred years later the word *malus* was used to describe the English spoken by the inhabitants of Haverfordwest.

Rural colonization was not the only means whereby the conquest was consolidated. Urban settlement was also a weapon of the Normans, as it was of their contemporaries, the Germans, who were intent upon colonizing the Slav lands of eastern Europe. Between 1070 and 1300, about eighty towns were established in Wales, some twenty of which had come into existence before 1135. As Wales's urban potential was not great, these figures are surprisingly high. The towns of Wales were small. At the peak of their prosperity in the High Middle Ages, Cardiff was the largest; it had perhaps two thousand five hundred inhabitants at a time when there were in western Europe dozens of towns with populations in excess of twenty thousand. The multiplicity of small towns in Wales can probably be explained by transport difficulties, by the existence of a considerable number of pockets of fairly fertile land and by the fragmented nature of the political structure of the March. They were built under the shadow of the more substantial of the castles in order to satisfy the garrison's need for food, relaxation and religious services and in order to create centres from which the local economy could be controlled. Their earliest inhabitants were incomers wholly dependent upon the patronage of the invaders. The location of the towns was largely determined by military factors and when those factors became less important the towns which failed to assume other functions fell into rapid decline.

William Fitzosbern, earl of Hereford, was the first Norman to plant towns in Wales. He gave to their inhabitants the privileges of the burgesses of Hereford, privileges which were based upon the charter of Breteuil, his home in Normandy; in terms of their charters, almost all the towns of Wales would be daughters and grand-daughters of Hereford and Breteuil. As most of the towns of Wales are alien in origin, there developed a belief (which still has its advocates) that the Welsh are an intrinsically non-urban people and that their values and way of life can flourish only in a rural environ-ment. The basis of the belief is flimsy. Apart from exceptional places such as Amalfi and Venice, the economy of western Europe was incapable for at least four centuries after 600 of producing much in the way of a surplus; without a surplus, it lacked trade and therefore it lacked towns. With the greater stability which characterized the years after about 1050, towns sprang up like mushrooms across the length and breadth of the continent. Towns would have come into existence in places like Cardiff, Carmarthen and Haverfordwest had the Normans never ventured to Wales; the logic of the economy of the age demanded them. As the most 'urbanizable' regions of Wales were in alien hands when the time was ripe for the rebirth of towns, that rebirth occurred under alien auspices. But a similar ripening can also be traced in those parts of Wales which were not in alien hands, a development which their rulers would be eager to encourage.

During the reign of Henry I, those regions were Gwynedd, the greater part of Powys, a few of the *cantrefi* of Deheubarth and the uplands of some of the Marcher Lordships, Glamorgan in particular. In the uplands of Glamorgan, Afan, Miskin and Glynrhondda were ruled by descendants of Iestyn ap Gwrgant, Gwynllŵg by descendants of Caradog ap Gruffudd and Senghennydd by Ifor ap Meurig, and the bonds which tied them to the lord at Cardiff were slight ones. In the lands between the rivers Wye and Severn – the southern part of Powys but a region detached from that kingdom under circumstances which are difficult to interpret – lay the *cantrefi* of Elfael, Gwrtheyrnion and Maelienydd; they were ruled by the descendants of Elstan Glodrydd, the founder of one of the five lineages which later antiquarians would delight in calling the five royal tribes of

Wales. In Powys itself, after much bloodshed among the unruly members of the house of Mathrafal, the descendants of Bleddyn ap Cynfyn, the kingdom came into the possession of Maredudd ap Bleddyn. Maredudd died in 1132 and was succeeded by his son, Madog ap Maredudd. In Deheubarth, Gruffudd, the son of Rhys ap Tewdwr and head of the house of Dinefwr, had by about 1125 gained some degree of authority in the upper reaches of Ystrad Tywi. There, in the commote of Caeo, he awaited the opportunity to restore the authority of his family.

In Gwynedd, Gruffudd ap Cynan of the house of Aberffraw was intent upon rebuilding his shattered kingdom. The borders of the realm which he had regained in 1098 were the river Mawddach to the south and the river Conwy to the east. For twenty years, he did not venture beyond those borders, seeking rather to give his subjects the peace which would allow them to plant their crops in full confidence that they would be able to harvest them. Then, from about 1118 onwards, taking advantage of the endemic troubles of the rulers of Powys, he seized commotes which had previously been in their possession. Rhos and Rhufoniog were annexed in 1118 and Dyffryn Clwyd in 1124, three of the four *cantrefi* of the Perfeddwlad (the Middle Country – Tegeingl was the fourth). Gruffudd's successors would be resolute in maintaining their hold over the Perfeddwlad, a region they knew as Gwynedd Is Conwy (Gwynedd below the Conwy). In 1123, Gruffudd seized the *cantref* of Merionnydd, the district between the rivers Dyfi and Mawddach, and in 1137, shortly before his death, Ceredigion also came into the hands of the house of Aberffraw.

It is possible to go into considerable detail about the career of Gruffudd ap Cynan, as a biography of him was written about twenty years after his death. It was written in Latin, for it was intended for a readership outside Wales, but the Welsh translation is the only version to have survived. The biography is a manifesto, a declaration of Gruffudd's right to Gwynedd – an absolute right through descent, not a qualified right based upon the favour of the king of England – and a declaration also of Gwynedd's primacy among the kingdoms of Wales. The biographer belittles the rulers of Powys and claims that Rhys ap Tewdwr had hailed Gruffudd as king of the kings of Wales and had offered him half the kingdom of Deheubarth. The efforts of Gruffudd's successors to give substance to these declarations would be central to the history of Wales over the following century and a half.

Gruffudd's biographer states that harpists and poets had accompanied Gruffudd from Ireland to Gwynedd, and a tradition
developed that he had reformed the orders of the poets and the
musicians. Doubt has been cast upon the emphasis on Ireland implicit
in this tradition, but it is striking that, while there is only intermittent
evidence of the work of the poets before the age of Gruffudd,
thereafter that evidence is unbroken. The work of the poets – mainly
from Deheubarth – which is preserved in *The Black Book of Carmarthen*,
together with that of Meilyr, who sang to Gruffudd, are the earliest
surviving examples of the poetry of the court poets or the *Gogynfeirdd*.
Yet Meilyr and his fellows would hardly have considered themselves
to be the founders of a new literary tradition. They were inheritors
rather than innovators; conscious of the ties which bound them to
Aneirin and Taliesin, their work is characterized by the use of archaic
words and expressions. Yet, the literature of Wales in both Welsh and
Latin developed increasing vigour and a sense of commitment as the
Welsh successfully withstood the Normans and as new ideas reached
Wales in the wake of the invaders. Contact with the great world
which used the French of the Normans sharpened Welsh pride, and
Cymraeg hardd (beautiful Welsh) and *Cymraeg coeth* (refined Welsh)
were praised in a poem composed in about 1130 by (or perhaps to)
Cuhelyn of Cemais, one of the ancestors of Dafydd ap Gwilym.

These words were copied on one of the pages of *The Black Book*,
probably at Carmarthen Priory, possibly around 1200, when the
priory was in the hands of the Welsh, although specialists now favour
a date around 1250. Carmarthen Priory was one of the religious
houses established as part of the campaign of the Normans to reorganize the Welsh Church and to use it to consolidate their hold upon
Wales. The reform movement in the Church associated with the
name of Pope Gregory VII was at its height at the time of the
Norman incursions. Gregory sought the triumph of justice, and
Rome's method of achieving justice was to seek uniformity in
organization, ritual and discipline throughout Christendom. The
Normans were godly in their way, faithful to the Papacy which had
blessed their venture in England. They used the Church as a weapon
to subdue the Welsh, but they were also prepared to promote the
interests of Rome and to make Wales a full member of the community
of Latin Europe.

Although the Welsh had accepted the Roman Easter in 768, in

almost all other matters they had remained faithful to the practices of their forefathers. To enthusiastic reformers, the eccentricities of the Welsh Church were abhorrent, although they were trifles in the main and it would not have been difficult to discover examples of the sins which were specifically attributed to it in other parts of Christendom. It lacked stone churches – this, perhaps, was the root cause of the contempt of the Normans – and there were in Wales no monasteries following the Rule of St Benedict, the most powerful of the influences giving unity to Latin Europe. One of the first acts of the Norman invaders was to introduce Benedictine monasticism. There were Benedictines in Chepstow by 1071 and by 1150 they had seventeen houses in Wales. Their houses were cells and priories dependent upon some of the chief monasteries of France and England; Chepstow, for example, belonged to the abbey of Cormeilles and Brecon belonged to the abbey of Battle. Many new monastic orders came into existence in the wake of the revival of the Latin Church; by 1135, the orders of Cluny, Tiron, Savigny and Cîteaux had houses in Wales, all of them under the patronage of the Normans.

Priests, as well as monks, desired to live a regular life and the Rule of St Augustine was devised for them. The priory at Carmarthen was an Augustinian house; there was another at Haverfordwest and yet another at Llanddewi Nant Hodni (Llanthony), an enchanting place, renowned for its sanctity. The Augustinian houses were not so very different from the *clasau* of the Celtic Church; when the *clasau* of Penmon, Beddgelert and Aberdaron felt the need to become an integral part of Latin monasticism, it was the Rule of St Augustine that they adopted. Other *clasau* were not so fortunate. To the Normans, the *clas*, with its wooden huts, its married abbots and its hereditary offices, was a barbaric institution. Most of them became ordinary parish churches and their income was transferred to monasteries, mainly in England. At the time of the invasion, many Welsh churches came to be owned by religious houses; the monastery at Gloucester, for example, won possession of Llancarfan and the monastery at Tewkesbury became the owner of Llantwit Major. Thus monasteries which were already wealthy became wealthier, and dioceses which were already impoverished became poorer.

The chief aim of the Normans in their dealings with the Welsh Church was to gain control of the dioceses. The precise nature of the bishoprics of Wales before the coming of the Normans has been a matter of extensive debate. There may well have been bishops in places such as Llanbadarn Fawr, Llandeilo Fawr, Clynnog Fawr, Meifod and Holyhead, and seven bishops' houses were recorded in Dyfed. Every one of the early kingdoms probably had its bishop, but when kingdom was united with kingdom most of the bishoprics probably languished and became extinct. By the time of the Norman invasions, it would appear that there were only three bishops in Wales. The bishop of Deheubarth certainly had his *cathedra* at St David's, and the bishop of Gwynedd, at least since 800, had his at Bangor, but the location of that of the bishop of Glamorgan is a matter of debate. There is no fully authentic record linking him with Llandaf until 1119, and it has therefore been claimed that the church at Llandaf was not elevated to the status of a cathedral until that year. Wendy Davies, however, has argued that *The Book of Llandaf*, if correctly interpreted, offers evidence that a bishopric which could claim succession from the labours of Dyfrig in Erging had been established at Llandaf by about 950. The functions of a Welsh bishop were essentially of the same nature as those of his fellows throughout Europe, but in comparison with the bishops of the European heartland the organization of his cathedral was irregular, the borders of his diocese were indeterminate and the hierarchy to which he belonged was vague.

The irregularities of the Welsh Church were abolished as the result of the efforts of its bishops – some of them foreigners but a number of them Welshmen or men with Welsh connections – to make it subject to the authority of the Canon Law of the Latin Church and to incorporate it within the archdiocese of Canterbury. Several Welsh bishops had been consecrated by the archbishop of Canterbury before the coming of the Normans, but it appears that that did not necessarily mean that the bishops of Wales were then subject to the authority of Canterbury. The first of the bishops of Wales to swear an oath of allegiance to the archbishop of Canterbury was Urban, the bishop of Glamorgan from 1107 to 1134. He probably welcomed the association with Canterbury, for he needed a powerful patron to assist him in his attempts to keep Church property out of the hands of the rapacious Norman knights. Urban organized his diocese along the pattern of the Latin Church; he appointed a dean and divided the Vale of Glamorgan into small parishes. About 1115, he began to turn the meagre church at Llandaf into a building which would be worthy of his diocese. Llandaf Cathedral would suffer

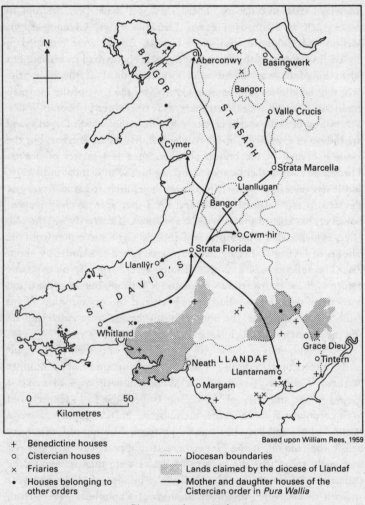

+   Benedictine houses
○   Cistercian houses
×   Friaries
●   Houses belonging to
    other orders

Based upon William Rees, 1959

········· Diocesan boundaries

▓   Lands claimed by the diocese of Llandaf

⟶   Mother and daughter houses of the
     Cistercian order in *Pura Wallia*

Dioceses and monasteries

many indignities, but some of Urban's work may still be seen there, including a fine arch which is – along with the churches of Chepstow and Ewenni – among the earliest examples in Wales of Romanesque architecture.

The diocese of Llandaf was based upon the kingdom of Glamorgan. As there had been occasions when the rulers of Glamorgan had extended their power over Erging and over parts of Deheubarth, Urban claimed that his bishopric extended from the river Tywi to the river Wye. He asserted that it was the inheritor of the labours of Dyfrig and Teilo and that it could therefore claim all the churches dedicated to them. The bones of Dyfrig were transferred from Bardsey Island to Llandaf in 1120 (Llandaf already had one of the three alleged bodies of Teilo). In furthering his aims, Urban enjoyed the enthusiastic support of the members of the family of Llancarfan, the descendants of Herewald. It is probably they, around 1125, who were responsible for that remarkable document, *The Book of Llandaf* – a collection of biographies, charters and records compiled to prove that Llandaf had been a diocese, extensive in area and substantial in property, for at least six hundred years. Medieval churchmen, in Rome and in Canterbury as well as in Llandaf, were prone to fake their evidence; the efforts of the men of Llancarfan were of a high standard and, where it is possible to separate the true from the false, the information recorded by them is of great value. Nevertheless, they were unsuccessful; the ambitions of the bishop of Llandaf aroused the enmity of the bishops of St David's and Hereford, and Urban and his associates failed in their attempt to extend the boundaries of the diocese of Llandaf beyond the confines of the old kingdoms of Gwent and Glywysing.

Bernard, a Norman appointed bishop of St David's in 1115, was the man most responsible for foiling Llandaf's ambitions. He was the first of the bishops of St David's to swear an oath of allegiance to Canterbury and to do homage to the king of England for the lands of the diocese. An able and energetic man, he was chaplain to Henry I's wife, Matilda, the daughter of Margaret, queen of Scots, a determined opponent of Celtic ecclesiastical particularism. The *clas*, or traditional Celtic monastery, of St David's was dissolved and Bernard established a chapter of canons in its place; he erected a Romanesque cathedral, supported Latin monasticism and attended the assemblies of the English Church as regularly as any of the bishops of England. During his episcopate, much was made of the cult of David. The saint became an object of pride among the Normans as well as among the Welsh; the region from Cardigan Bay to Herefordshire became studded with churches dedicated to him and there is some evidence that he was canonized by Rome around 1123.

In St David's, a demand arose that the diocese should be elevated into an archbishopric with authority over the other dioceses of Wales, and it was suggested that David himself had been an archbishop, although there is no reliable evidence that the Celtic Church ever recognized such an office. This campaign was afoot in St David's at a time when the idea was taking root at Rome that every nation should have at least one archbishopric. Four archbishops were consecrated in Ireland in 1151, and by 1200 Denmark, Sweden, Norway, Bohemia and Poland all had their archbishops. The struggle to elevate St David's – and to elevate himself – fought by Bernard in the last twenty years of his life (he died in 1148) was therefore wholly consistent with the tendencies of the age. In his letters to the Pope, he stressed that the Welsh had their own language, their own law and their own customs – that they were a *natio*. In 1147, the Pope announced that Bernard could not become an archbishop because he had sworn an oath of allegiance to the archbishop of Canterbury. Nothing was decided concerning the status of St David's itself; the issue was raised again in 1176 and 1179, and at the end of the century Giraldus Cambrensis campaigned heroically to elevate the status of the Church of David.

In Bangor, Hervé, a Breton and one of the chaplains of William II, was thrust upon the diocese in 1092; he was driven out in 1098 and was to have no successor until 1120, when David was appointed bishop. Although known as David the Scot, it appears that he was in fact a Welshman. Despite the opposition of Gruffudd ap Cynan – who may have intended to have him consecrated in Ireland – David also was obliged to swear an oath of allegiance to Canterbury. By 1120, therefore, the three dioceses of Wales had been incorporated into the archdiocese of Canterbury, and when a fourth was added its fate would be similar. The fourth was St Asaph, created in 1143. The tradition that St Asaph had been the centre of a diocese in the 'Age of the Saints' is very doubtful, but there had probably been a bishop in Powys, possibly at Meifod, before Powys had become subject to the kings of Gwynedd in 855. The new cathedral was located close to the Norman stronghold of Rhuddlan and its first bishop was a Norman called Gilbert. The region administered by him was torn by war and there is no evidence that his successor ever visited his diocese.

The second bishop of St Asaph was Geoffrey of Monmouth, a man deserving close attention, for his book, *Historia Regum Britanniae* (The

History of the Kings of Britain), which he wrote around 1136, is one of the most influential of the writings of the Middle Ages. Geoffrey wrote in the manner of the historians of the period and he provided details of his sources; all attempts to discover those sources have failed and it appears that most of the *Historia* is the product of his own imagination. He claimed that he was giving an account of the history of Britain from its first colonization by human beings to the coming of the English. His theme is Britain under Brythonic rule, and it was natural therefore that it should be of absorbing interest to the Welsh. It was frequently translated into Welsh; there are in existence about eighty manuscripts of *Brut y Brenhinedd* (The Chronicle of the Kings) – the name given to the Welsh version of Geoffrey's work – and *Brut y Tywysogyon* was planned as its sequel. Geoffrey states that the earliest of the Britons was Brutus, who fled from Troy after the Greeks had captured the city; thus the Britons shared their origins with the Romans, for it was claimed that Rome had been founded by Aeneas, who was also a Trojan. Brutus had three sons, Locrinus, Camber and Albanactus, and it is they who created the kingdoms of Lloegr (England), Cymru (Wales) and Alba (Scotland). The golden age of the Britons was the reign of Arthur and almost a third of the book is devoted to a description of its glories. A whole continent was bewitched by Geoffrey's portrait of Arthur and, within twenty years of the publication of the *Historia*, *Rex Arturus* was immortalized in the mosaics of the floor of the cathedral at Otranto, on the furthest fringes of Latin Europe.

Although the Welsh embraced Geoffrey's book and accepted it as a faithful record of their early history, its message to them was ambiguous. Geoffrey emphasized that the whole of Britain once belonged to the Britons and that they – and he, for Geoffrey was a Breton – had a noble ancestry, but he declared that they had been unworthy of their inheritance and that as a result of the multiplicity of their sins the inheritance had passed into the hands of others. The essence of Geoffrey's message was the unity of Britain under the Crown of London, and he devoted the first three chapters of his book to a description of the disasters which could occur if that principle were denied. He stressed that Locrinus was the eldest son, a statement which would be a stumbling-block to the Scots in their struggle for independence. Although his work has been described as a remarkable example of nationalistic history, it was the hegemony of London that it sought to promote and it eased the way for those Welshmen who hoped to find a place for themselves within that hegemony.

Geoffrey's patron was Robert, earl of Gloucester, the lord of Glamorgan and the illegitimate son of Henry I. After Henry's death in 1135, Robert was the most dedicated defender of the right of his half-sister, Matilda, to succeed her father; he and his fellow Marcher Lords refused to acknowledge the authority of Stephen, Henry's nephew and the anointed king of England. The reign of Stephen were the years of the 'Anarchy' and England lacked firm government until his death in 1154, when he was succeeded by Matilda's son, Henry II. The 'Anarchy' provided a golden opportunity for the Marcher Lords to augment their freedom from the interference of the English crown. The reign of Stephen is considered a key period in the growth of their privileges, not only in Wales but also in places such as Clun, which had once been in Shropshire but which was drawn into the March because of the decline of the power of the crown.

Yet despite their readiness to take advantage of the absence of a powerful king in England, the Marcher Lords soon came to realize how vulnerable they were in the face of the revival of the power of the Welsh rulers when they were deprived of a sovereign capable of defending them. The Norman hold upon Deheubarth was especially fragile. There, Gruffudd ap Rhys ap Tewdwr and his wife Gwenllian were killed in an attack upon the invaders, but by about 1150 their sons had succeeded in seizing almost the whole of Ystrad Tywi and much of Dyfed. In 1153, they also took possession of Ceredigion where the power of the house of Clare had been extinguished in 1136 by the sons of Gruffudd ap Cynan. Owain ap Gruffudd – Owain Gwynedd, the ruler of Gwynedd from 1137 until his death in 1170 – was the most prominent of the sons of Gruffudd. He also took advantage of the 'Anarchy', largely at the expense of the earldom of Chester and the kingdom of Powys. When Henry II came to the throne, Rhuddlan, Ystrad Alun, Iâl and Tegeingl had fallen to Owain, and his realm extended almost to the walls of Chester. Although Powys lost some of its northernmost commotes to Gwynedd, the 'Anarchy' gave its ruler the opportunity to capture the lordship of Oswestry. At the same time, the lordship of Usk became part of the territories of the descendants of Caradog ap Gruffudd, lords of Caerleon.

The situation changed in 1154 with the accession to the throne of

Henry II, the first English king of the house of Plantagenet. His territories and resources were far greater than those of any of his predecessors, for before the end of his reign he was claiming authority from the borders of Spain to the furthest reaches of Scotland. Impressed by his power, Madog ap Maredudd of Powys yielded to Henry in 1156 in order to seek his support in the struggle to protect Powys against the ambitions of Gwynedd. In 1157, when Henry led an army into Wales, he received the assistance of Madog. This was one of the numerous examples of the readiness of the rulers of Powys, in their conflict with Gwynedd, to turn to the king of England, a readiness which a later generation portrayed as treachery to the national cause. If the aspirations of the Welsh in 1157 were already centred upon Gwynedd, there is perhaps substance to the accusation, but if the loyalties of the Welsh were still essentially local and dynastic, then the charge is meaningless. Owain Gwynedd yielded to Henry following the campaign of 1157, but he succeeded in keeping all his gains apart from Tegeingl. In Deheubarth, the resistance of Rhys ap Gruffudd, the only surviving son of Gruffudd and Gwenllian, was more dogged. With the assistance of the king, most of Deheubarth was repossessed by the Marcher Lords and attempts were made to confine Rhys to the upper reaches of the Tywi. He was unwilling to accept the loss of his ancestral lands, and on several occasions between 1158 and 1163 there were campaigns against him by the forces of the English crown.

The authority of Henry II was gravely weakened from 1163 onwards as a result of his quarrel with Archbishop Becket. The decline in his authority gave the Welsh rulers an opportunity to seek to regain the territories they had held before Henry had assumed the throne. They were successful. Under the leadership of Owain Gwynedd, they stood united; although Henry II brought the full force of his army against them in 1165, his hopes were drowned in the mud and mire of the Berwyn Mountains. Owain recaptured Tegeingl, destroying the royal castle at Rhuddlan. Henry's hands were tied by the Becket troubles – Becket was murdered in 1170 – and by difficulties in his French possessions. Owain sought to gain advantage from the one problem and the other; as the archbishop of Canterbury was in exile, he sent Arthur, his appointee as bishop of Bangor, to Ireland to be consecrated; as Louis VII, king of France, was in conflict with Henry II, Owain wrote to Louis in 1168 offering to assist him – an act which indicates that the horizons of Welsh rulers were widening and which suggests that the Welsh could well have developed a relationship with France similar to that of the Scots.

In Deheubarth, Rhys ap Gruffudd succeeded in capturing Ceredigion, Emlyn and Cantref Bychan, and so great was his pressure upon the Norman lordships of Dyfed that their lords were anxious to find other lands to colonize, a desire which Rhys was eager to see fulfilled. He released Robert Fitzstephen, the former castellan of Cardigan, from imprisonment on condition that Robert would lead a force to Ireland, where King Dermot was seeking assistance to repossess the throne of Leinster. Fitzstephen and his companions sailed to Ireland in 1169 and were followed there in 1170 by Richard, earl of Pembroke (Strongbow); the kingdom of Leinster was invaded and, following the death of Dermot in 1171, Richard became its king. Henry II was not prepared to permit one of his subjects to enjoy such power. He claimed for himself the overlordship of Ireland, a claim which received the blessing of Pope Adrian IV, the only Englishman ever to have occupied the chair of St Peter. In 1175, Henry received an oath of allegiance from the native Irish rulers. At the same time, he was determined to restrict the powers of the Norman aristocrats who were carving out estates for themselves in Ireland, for he did not wish them to enjoy the privileges of the Marcher Lords of Wales. Thus, the sorrowful history of English involvement in Ireland has Welsh roots. The invasion sprang from the situation in Dyfed; its leaders were partly Welsh – they included various descendants of Nest, the daughter of Rhys ap Tewdwr, the 'queen-bee of the Cambro-Norman swarm' – and their battle cry was 'Sein Daui'. The relationship between Wales and Ireland was an ambiguous one. There was much fruitful contact in the 'Age of Saints' but the *Mabinogi* does not offer a portrait of two countries in close Celtic embrace. In 1110, Madog ap Rhirid of Powys was glad to return to Wales because he 'could not bear the godless morals of the Irish'; nevertheless, to him and his like, Ireland offered a refuge. As a result of the invasion, and particularly following the development of Dublin as a centre of English power, the king of England was able to threaten the Welsh rulers from the west as well as from the east; the success of the venture of the Cambro-Normans would therefore be a factor in the ultimate subjugation of Wales.

But this development belonged to the future. The venture benefited

Rhys ap Gruffudd, for it led to the removal of some of his most energetic opponents. Furthermore, Henry II became aware of his need for a deputy in Wales as a counterpoise to the power of the great lords of Ireland. Although he had often challenged the authority of the king of England, Rhys was the only possible candidate for such an office. In 1172, he was appointed justice of south Wales, and his right to the territories he had brought under his rule was recognized. It appears that the title meant that the Welsh rulers of Gwrtheyrnion, Maelienydd, Elfael and the upland lordships of Glamorgan, Gwent and Brycheiniog (men whom Rhys had already bound to him through a series of marriages) were answerable to the king of England through Rhys. From 1172 onwards, therefore, Rhys enjoyed in the south of *Pura Wallia* the substance of the position which Llywelyn II won over the entire *Pura Wallia* a century later.

Rhys's primacy among the Welsh rulers was underlined by the eisteddfod which he held in his castle of 'stone and mortar' at Cardigan in 1176. That primacy was assisted by the fact that there were at that time no men of comparable stature in Gwynedd and Powys. Madog ap Maredudd died in 1160 and Owain Gwynedd in 1170, and in both kingdoms there was a struggle for the succession. In Powys, Madog had granted Cyfeiliog to his nephews, Owain and Meurig, in 1149, not with any intention of separating the commote from the rest of his kingdom, but in order that it should be ruled as an appanage in accordance with the custom of the age. Owain Cyfeiliog was a poet of distinction and he had powerful friends in England, where he was respected for his wit. He succeeded in withholding Cyfeiliog from the senior line of the house of Powys. He added to it others of the commotes and *cantrefi* of Powys and, when he died in 1197, his son, Gwenwynwyn, inherited almost the whole of what would later be the county of Montgomery, a territory which became known as Powys Wenwynwyn. Gruffudd, the son of Madog, had to be content with northern Powys – the valley of the Dee from Edeirnion to Maelor – and after his son, Madog, inherited that region in 1191, it became known as Powys Fadog. Although both the one Powys and the other would have roles to play in the history of Wales, the division meant that the house of Mathrafal could no longer be considered to be the equal of the houses of Aberffraw and Dinefwr.

In Gwynedd, Iorwerth, the eldest of Owain Gwynedd's legitimate sons to outlive him, was his father's heir, but his nickname (*trwyndwn*) suggests that he may have suffered from some disability; kings had to be without blemish – that was the motive for the blindings and the castrations. An entry in *Brut y Tywysogyon* suggests that, after the death of Owain Gwynedd in 1170, Gwynedd was divided between his various descendants, but the English sources show that the authorities in England considered that the ruler of Gwynedd was Dafydd, the son of Owain by his second wife (and cousin), Cristin. Conflict with his kinsmen caused Dafydd's position to be weaker than that of his father. Nevertheless, in the great ceremony arranged by Henry II in 1177, it was he alone from Gwynedd who swore an oath of allegiance to the king of England. By then, he was Henry's brother-in-law, for in 1174 he had married Emma, the illegitimate daughter of Henry's father, Geoffrey of Anjou, receiving as dowry the valuable manor of Ellesmere in Shropshire.

The marriage suggests that the English crown's relationship with the chief Welsh rulers was similar to its relationship with the king of the Scots: Alexander I had married the illegitimate daughter of Henry I and when Henry II received oaths of allegiance from Rhys ap Gruffudd and Owain Gwynedd in 1163 an oath was also sworn by Malcolm IV, Alexander's nephew. All three were kings. On more than one occasion, Owain Gwynedd referred to himself as *rex* and in denoting Welsh rulers English chroniclers would continue to use the word up until about 1200. But in referring to the leading rulers of Wales, there was an increasing tendency to use *princeps* (prince) rather than *rex* (king). In his later years, Owain Gwynedd used the title *princeps Wallensium* (the prince of the Welsh), almost certainly an expression of Owain's claim to be recognized as the leader of the entire nation. As he had led forces from all parts of *Pura Wallia* to victory on the Berwyn Mountains, his claim had substance. It appears that Dafydd ab Owain favoured the title *princeps Norwalliae* (the prince of north Wales), while Rhys ap Gruffudd was referred to on occasion as *proprietarius princeps Sudwallie* (the proprietory prince of south Wales).

These titles are important, for they provide virtually the only evidence of the way in which the Welsh rulers viewed themselves and of the way in which their status was interpreted by the outside world. The change from king to prince did not necessarily mean a diminution in status. There had been a time when there were many kings in Wales. There would only be two princes – one in Gwynedd and one in Deheubarth; the other rulers had to be content with the title lord, much to the chagrin of Gwenwynwyn of Powys. The principality was indivisible and after Deheubarth was partitioned there would no longer be any princes there. The new title is evidence of a desire to define the position of the Welsh rulers within the empire which exercised lordship over them. Although they had ceased to be kings, they enjoyed a higher status than that of the barons of England. They swore an oath of allegiance to the king of England, but Henry II and his predecessors did not attempt to exercise the detailed rights of a feudal overlord in the territories of their Welsh vassals. Henry's successors would seek to draw *Pura Wallia* increasingly into the feudal system, but that policy was a two-edged sword, for the Welsh rulers in turn could use feudalism to strengthen their power, as the activities of Llywelyn I and Llywelyn II would amply prove.

Latin monasticism was also a two-edged sword. It could further the interests of the invader, but it could also strengthen the identity of the Welsh. This is what happened. The Benedictine Order had been used as a means of securing Norman control over the property of the Welsh Church and the Normans were also the patrons of the second wave of Latin monasticism to reach Wales. The third wave coincided with the climax of the authority of Rhys ap Gruffudd, and the Welsh cherished the religious houses which were established in its wake. Those houses belonged in the main to the Order of Cîteaux. The Cistercians sought the lonely and desolate places and it has been claimed that their monasteries seemed to be re-embodiments of the *clasau* of the Celtic Church. The order was a supranational institution and every one of its houses was answerable to the head abbot. He dwelt in Cîteaux in Burgundy and was thus not directly subject to the power of the king of England – an additional reason, perhaps, for the appeal of the Cistercians to the Welsh. It was Norman patronage which led in 1140 to the foundation of Whitland, the mother monastery of the Cistercianism of *Pura Wallia*, and also to the foundation in 1164 of Strata Florida, the first of its daughters. But when the greater part of Deheubarth had come under the authority of Rhys ap Gruffudd, the two monasteries were drawn into the mainstream of the life of *Pura Wallia*. Soon, every Welsh ruler sought to establish within his territory a house of White Monks, monasteries which were daughters and grand-daughters of Whitland. Strata Marcella was founded in Powys Wenwynwyn in 1170, Cwm-hir in Maelienydd in 1176, Llantarnam near Caerleon in 1179, Aberconwy in Gwynedd in 1186, Cymer in Merionnydd in 1198 and Valle Crucis in Powys Fadog in 1202. (There was already some connection between the Welsh of upland Glamorgan and the Cistercian monastery of Margam.)

Before the foundation of Whitland and its daughters, the Welsh had had few opportunities to experience Latin monasticism, for there was little welcome for them – except in Margam perhaps – in the houses of the Normans. The proliferation of Cistercian houses proves how eager they were to have that experience and how dependent was their opportunity upon the existence of Welsh political power. By 1202, there were several hundred Cistercian monks in *Pura Wallia*; they were mainly drawn from among the sons of the *bonheddwyr* (freemen) and the priests and they were served by less privileged men – the lay-brothers who cultivated the lands of the monasteries. Those lands were extensive, for the monks were granted thousands of hectares of grazing land, where they pioneered the Welsh woollen industry; there is very little evidence that sheep were important in the Welsh economy before the coming of the Cistercians. They also had need of estates in the lowlands to grow crops and to winter their flocks, and such was their greed for land that their neighbours lived in terror of them. It was the wealth of their estates that allowed them to erect buildings which are proof of the existence of a Welsh interpretation of Romanesque and Gothic architecture. Many Welsh manuscripts were copied and preserved in those buildings, and but for the existence of stone abbeys – those of the Cistercians in particular – most of the early literature of Wales, together with the annals of its early history, would either have been lost or would never have come into being. Naturally enough, the monks of *Pura Wallia* enthusiastically supported the interests of their patrons, the Welsh rulers; they gave them a home in their old age and provided a resting place for their bodies, and so great was their readiness to support their policies that in 1212 King John declared his intention of destroying the monastery of Strata Florida because it 'harboured our enemies'.

The welcome given to the Cistercians is only one example of the readiness of the Welsh in the age of Rhys ap Gruffudd to draw closer to Latin Europe. Latin Europe was becoming increasingly confident, as is evident from the launching of the Crusade, a venture in which a number of Welshmen, Rhys among them, expressed a desire to take part. By this time, foreign war was no new experience for the Welsh;

Owain ap Cadwgan, who had been in Henry I's army in Normandy in 1114, was probably the first of the long succession of Welshmen to serve the kings of England in France. Rhys was undoubtedly fluent in French as well as Welsh, although it is unlikely that he knew English. Giraldus Cambrensis records an anecdote in which Rhys mingles with the relations of the house of Clare as if he were a full member of the *Francigenae* – the French-speaking aristocracy which formed the ruling class from Jerusalem to Dublin, from Sicily to Hungary.

Yet in the heartland of Europe there was deep suspicion of the peoples of the periphery such as the Celts, the Slavs and the Scandinavians. 'The Welsh are Christian in name only,' wrote the archbishop of Canterbury to the Pope in 1159; 'they are barbarians, as can be seen from the fact that Owain, their prince, has taken his uncle's daughter as his wife.' 'The Welsh,' wrote Henry II to the Byzantine emperor, 'are a wild people who cannot be tamed.' Similar comments may be found in the voluminous writings of Giraldus Cambrensis, works which offer a portrayal of Welsh society and of the character of the Welsh people. As Giraldus was so fervent an advocate of the rights of St David's, there is a tendency to consider him to be an outstanding Welsh patriot, but his attitude to Wales was complex to say the least.

He was born at Manorbier, a wild and desolate place according to the biographer of Virginia Woolf, although in fact it lies in the middle of the arable land of southern Dyfed. He took pride in his Welsh descent – he was the grandson of Nest, the daughter of Rhys ap Tewdwr – but he complained that he was too much of a Norman for the Welsh and too much of a Welshman for the Normans. In many respects he was the first non-Welsh-speaking Welshman, and he gave vent to frustrations which would not be wholly irrelevant three quarters of a millennium after his time. Giraldus was, above all, the eulogist of the exploits of the Marcher Lords and of the power of the Church. Trained in Canon Law at Paris, he was determined to bestow its blessings upon the Welsh people. Canon Law was an imperialist ideology and its advocates were prepared to argue that peoples who disregarded it should be swept away. Giraldus suggested that that would be a fitting fate for the Welsh, and in his portrayal of them he emphasized the chasm which divided him from them: he was the disciplinarian of the universal Church, eager for the patronage of the sovereign of a centralized kingdom and a native of fertile lowlands where corn was grown and bread was eaten; they were heedless of the rules of the Church, anarchic in their attitude to the law, lacking in any understanding of centralized power and wholly dependent for their diet upon the products of pastoral agriculture. Through the work of T. Jones Pierce and others, it has been shown that this portrayal is highly misleading. Yet Giraldus's writings have many virtues. He was a pioneer of applied anthropology and his perceptions were undoubtedly sharpened by his experience of living in a divided society. He was an admirable story-teller too; his works are the only source for some of the most famous of the stories of the Welsh people, such as Ifor Bach's attack upon Cardiff Castle, the refusal of the birds of Llangors Lake to sing to anyone save their true lord and the declaration which expresses the confidence and the fears of the old man of Pencader.

The same ambiguity may be seen in Giraldus's efforts to elevate St David's to the status of an archbishopric. In his autobiography he states that he had always been a staunch defender of the rights of the Church of David, conveniently forgetting his travels in 1188 in the company of Baldwin, archbishop of Canterbury, who used the journey to emphasize his authority over the four cathedrals of Wales. Consistency was not one of Giraldus's virtues. Yet between 1199 and 1204, his devotion to the cause of St David's was heroic. He made four journeys to Rome; he was tenacious in seeking the attention of Innocent III, the most powerful of the Popes; he was eloquent in arousing support in Wales; he was courageous in challenging kings and archbishops; he was dignified in expressing the anguish felt by the Welsh when spiritual as well as military weapons were deployed against them. Although the Pope recognized that Wales was no mere province of England, in the last resort he accepted the standpoint of Hubert Walter, justiciar of England and archbishop of Canterbury, who argued that the ambitions of the Welsh 'barbarians' should not be fulfilled at the expense of the interests of the kingdom of England. Thus the Church of David was not granted equality with Trondheim, Lund and Esztergom.

In his campaign in favour of St David's, Giraldus stressed, as had Bernard before him, that the distinctiveness of the Welsh in terms of culture and customs was justification for granting them an archbishopric. The writings of Giraldus offer proof that the Welsh in his age were acknowledged to be, and were fully aware that they were, a community of people living in a defined territory, claiming a common ancestry and seeking to defend their identity; thus Giraldus, in his discussions of the Welsh, offers an early definition of the essence of nationhood. That essence was racial, cultural and social, but from the age of Giraldus onwards there is evidence of the growth of a desire to give it a political dimension as well. Among the intellectuals of Europe – those of France in particular – the theory of the *patria* of the kingdom was replacing the yearning to restore the unity symbolized by the Roman Empire, and T. Jones Pierce suggested that the Cistercians, with their close French connections, fostered in Wales the notion of the people of the *patria* united in allegiance to a single prince. Throughout Europe, the champions of such ideas were the secular lawyers. In Wales, successive versions of the Law provide evidence of the efforts of lawyers to promote the interests of the prince and to undermine the *cenedl* in the sense of a kinship group and to strengthen the *cenedl* in the sense of the *natio*. The poets' loyalty was to lineage and locality – the love of locality so characteristic of the Welsh finds its finest expression in the poetry of Hywel ab Owain Gwynedd, the most readable of the *Gogynfeirdd* – but in the generation after 1200 there is at least a suggestion that they also were seeking to foster wider allegiances. They showed an increasing tendency to use the word *Cymro* (Welshman) rather than *Brython* (Briton), and similar trends may be observed in *Brut y Tywysogyon*, especially in the author's striking entry on the death of Rhys ap Gruffudd.

The consciousness of being Welsh rather than Brythonic was further encouraged by the metamorphosis which overtook the Arthurian legend. The monks of Glastonbury discovered the grave of Arthur in 1180; he was therefore a mortal man and was not sleeping in his cave awaiting the opportunity to rid Britain of the English. Furthermore, he was transformed from being the hero of the Britons into the glorious forerunner of the kings of England; the step-daughter of Henry II was the patron of Chrétien de Troyes, a key figure in the development of the Arthurian legend; Edward I celebrated his victory over the Welsh by holding an Arthurian 'Round Table', and *König von England* is the title given to Arthur on Maximilian I's cenotaph at Innsbruck. Arthur was received into the Valhalla of his enemies. So great was the power of the kingdom of England that the hope of restoring Brythonic sovereignty over Britain faded. There had been very little substance to that hope since at least the time of *Armes*

Prydein, although its shadow survived for centuries in the *canu brud* (prophetic verse). In the century after 1200, *canu brud* declined in popularity; Wales offered hopes of realistic political advances, for it was, as Giraldus put it, the home of a people who 'if they would be inseparable, they would be insuperable'.

When Giraldus wrote these words in about 1194, division was rife in Wales. In Gwynedd, so intense was the rivalry between the descendants of Owain Gwynedd that Dafydd was able to exercise authority only over the Perfeddwlad. In Deheubarth, Rhys ap Gruffudd was troubled by the waywardness of his sons, and the agreement between Rhys and the king of England came to an end when Henry II was succeeded by his son, Richard I, in 1189. Rhys died in 1197. His heir was his eldest son, Gruffudd, whom the *Chronica de Wallia* referred to in 1200 as prince, the last of the rulers of Deheubarth to be given that title. Gruffudd was challenged by his brothers, Maelgwn and Rhys Gryg in particular, and following his death in 1201 the authority of his son, Rhys Ieuanc, was restricted to Cantref Mawr, the region between the rivers Tywi and Teifi. In the struggles in Deheubarth, Maelgwn received the support of John, who became king of England on the death of his brother, Richard, in 1199. John had direct interests in Wales, for, through his marriage with the heiress of Glamorgan, he was lord of the greatest of the Marcher Lordships. In 1199, John bestowed Ceredigion and Emlyn on Maelgwn through royal grant and, much to the disgust of the author of the *Brut*, Maelgwn yielded to the king all rights over Cardigan Castle, his father's favourite residence and the 'key and stay of the whole of Wales'. The conflict between Rhys ap Gruffudd's sons was a fatal blow to Deheubarth unity; after his death, the rulers of Deheubarth would be mere pawns in the struggle between the prince of Gwynedd and the king of England.

With division in Gwynedd and Deheubarth, Powys Wenwynwyn was the most united of the territories of the Welsh rulers. Gwenwynwyn yearned for recognition as a prince and considered himself to be the leader who would, as the author of the *Brut* put it, restore to the Welsh 'their ancient rights and their old boundaries'. He saw himself as fulfilling the role once undertaken by Rhys ap Gruffudd – that of defending the power of the Welsh rulers of the region between the rivers Wye and Severn. There, the Mortimer and de Breos families were seeking to uproot the authority of the descendants of Elstan Glodrydd with a ferocity unparalleled in the bloody chronicle of the March. Gwenwynwyn lacked the resources needed to fulfil the role. The Marcher Lords received the assistance of the justiciar of England, and in 1198 Gwenwynwyn was defeated with great slaughter near Painscastle. As a result, his hopes of leading the Welsh were dashed, but he was reluctant to see that task being undertaken by another of the Welsh rulers.

That other ruler was Llywelyn, the son of Iorwerth Drwyndwn, and – according to the rules of primogeniture – the true heir of Owain Gwynedd. In 1194, when he was twenty-two years old, he defeated his uncle, Dafydd, near the estuary of the Conwy. Dafydd retired to his manor at Ellesmere and Llywelyn took possession of the Perfeddwlad. He became ruler of the rest of Gwynedd on the death of his cousin, Gruffudd, in 1200, and in England it was considered judicious to come to terms with him as a counter-weight to the ambitions of Gwenwynwyn. He swore an oath of allegiance to John in 1201 and married Joan, the king's illegitimate daughter, in 1205. John was a man of unstable character. Although recent research shows that he was not the monster of the traditional portrayal, he had a genius for making enemies. He attracted the anger of Innocent III, who in 1207 imposed an interdict upon religious services in John's dominions, Wales among them. His barons came to feel such antagonism towards him that they forced him in 1215 to accede to the *Magna Carta*. In his dealings with France, he gave King Philip Augustus the opportunity to deprive him of the French territories which he had inherited from his father, although he retained his hold upon Bordeaux and Gascony, the territories he had inherited from his mother. As a result of the loss of Normandy, the English Channel became a frontier, a fact which greatly assisted the tendency of the *Francigenae* to consider themselves to be Englishmen, a development not without significance in the history of Wales.

John's relationship with William de Breos, the lord of Brecon, Builth, Radnor and Abergavenny, provides an example of his inconstancy. In 1200 he had granted William a licence to seize as much as he could of the territories of the Welsh rulers, but in 1208 he stripped him of his entire possessions. Gwenwynwyn sought to take advantage of William's disgrace and thereby attracted the king's enmity. Llywelyn seized the opportunity to take possession of Powys Wenwynwyn and at the same time he drove Maelgwn, Gwenwynwyn's ally, from northern Ceredigion. This was a bold demonstration of the determination of the ruler of Gwynedd to be master of *Pura Wallia*. Yet it was not without precedent, for Llywelyn could appeal to the story of the sons of Cunedda, to the fame of Maelgwn Fawr, to his position as the heir of the senior branch of the line of Rhodri and to *The Life of Gruffudd ap Cynan*. Owain Gwynedd had absorbed commotes on the borders of Powys, Ceredigion had been temporarily under his control and his forces had crossed the Teifi and had captured Gwyddgrug Castle, but Llywelyn's dealings with Gwenwynwyn and Maelgwn prove that he was prepared to be considerably more forceful than his grandfather.

In extending his authority, Llywelyn was careful not to antagonize John, his overlord and father-in-law. He accompanied the king on his invasion of Scotland in 1209; this was the repayment of an old debt, for Alexander I had joined Henry I in his attack upon Gruffudd ap Cynan in 1114. Nevertheless, by 1211, John had come to the conclusion that Llywelyn was among the most dangerous of his enemies; he invaded Gwynedd and for the first time for a century the forces of the king of England were encamped upon the banks of the Menai. Llywelyn had no choice but to yield; his authority was restricted to Gwynedd Uwch Conwy and he was obliged to recognize the king as his heir should his marriage to Joan not produce a son. The lesser Welsh rulers abandoned Llywelyn. This is a story which will have to be repeated *ad nauseam*. If they were obliged to have an overlord, the lesser rulers preferred one who was a long way away, a suzerain who would be unlikely constantly to interfere with their rights. Naturally, therefore, they opted for what they hoped would be the unobtrusive overlordship of the king of England rather than what they knew would be the thrustful paramountcy of the prince of Gwynedd.

The situation changed when it became evident that John was intent upon intrusive overlordship. He erected a castle near the estuary of the river Ystwyth (Aberystwyth Castle, near the estuary of the Rheidol, is a later construction), and in Powys and the Perfeddwlad he showed that he was resolved upon the subjugation of the Welsh. In 1212, his policies produced a reaction. In his entry for that year, the author of *Cronica de Wallia* – who was probably writing at Whitland – recorded that the Welsh had conspired against the king and had 'chosen for themselves one leader who was Llywelyn, the prince of Gwynedd'. The castle near the estuary of the Ystwyth was burned, the Perfeddwlad was regained by Gwynedd and attacks were made upon the Marcher Lordships. As John was an enemy of the Church, Innocent III gave his blessing to the Welsh revolt and it is possible that he freed *Pura Wallia* from the interdict. It was probably Innocent also who urged Philip Augustus to make contact with Llywelyn. Philip's letter has not survived, but Llywelyn's reply is preserved in the French national archive. It shows that the prince felt pride and some degree of reverential awe on being invited to ally with so powerful a sovereign. Because of the Welsh revolt, John had to postpone his attack upon Philip and, faced with the discontent of his barons, he was unable to lead an army to Wales to impede the growth of Llywelyn's power. In his frustration, he hanged a number of Welsh hostages, Maelgwn's seven-year-old son among them; he offered a shilling apiece for the heads of the Welsh insurgents and the king's accounts for 1212 record a payment of six shillings for the heads of the men of Cadwallon ab Ifor Bach of Senghennydd.

John yielded to the Pope in 1213 and thereby gained a powerful ally. But his attempt to reconquer Normandy ended in disaster; as a result, the anger of his barons intensified. Llywelyn was eager to exploit the divisions within the English kingdom, and the barons were anxious for his support. Llywelyn's contribution to their campaign – in particular his seizure of Shrewsbury in May 1215 – was one of the factors which persuaded John to seal the *Magna Carta* in June 1215. A time would come when that document in its entirety would be of relevance to the Welsh people, for four hundred years after the reign of John it would be considered to be a fundamental statement of the rights of the subjects of the crown. At the time, only three clauses were directly of concern to them. It was agreed that neither the Welsh nor the English should remain in possession of lands unjustly seized, and it was acknowledged that the right to land in *Pura Wallia* should be decided according to the Law of Wales and in *Marchia Wallie* according to the Law of the March – the first clear reference to that hybrid. Conflict did not cease with the sealing of the Charter and the ensuing civil war offered Llywelyn a golden opportunity. Between 1215 and 1218, he and his allies captured a number of castles, Carmarthen and Cardigan among them; they threatened such long-established centres of Marcher power as Haverfordwest, Swansea and Brecon, and the author of the *Brut* expressed his delight on hearing of the 'French' in flight.

Llywelyn aimed at a status superior to that of mere war leader and he used the structures of feudalism to strengthen his authority. It appears that Gwenwynwyn had sworn him an oath of allegiance and had done homage to him, and, when he broke his oath in 1216, Powys Wenwynwyn was seized by Llywelyn in accordance with the rights of a feudal overlord. Llywelyn also received the homage of the rulers of Deheubarth and Powys Fadog, and he extended his patronage to the Welsh rulers of Gwent, Glamorgan and the region between the rivers Wye and Severn. In 1216, he presided over an assembly at which Deheubarth was shared among the descendants of Rhys ap Gruffudd. The assembly was held at Aberdyfi, probably a conscious choice, for according to tradition it was at Aberdyfi that the suzerainty of Maelgwn Fawr had been recognized seven hundred years earlier. At Aberdyfi, the lesser Welsh rulers formally affirmed their homage and their allegiance to Llywelyn. To quote Beverley Smith: 'Henceforth, the leader would be lord, and the allies would be subjects.'

John died in 1216 and the coalition ranged against him collapsed. He was succeeded by his nine-year-old son, Henry III, and as the royal government was insecure the young king's advisers, in particular Guala, the Papal Legate, urged that a settlement should be made with Llywelyn. In 1218, through the Treaty of Worcester, the English crown recognized his pre-eminence in Wales. Although he was not permitted to retain the homage of the lords of Deheubarth and Powys, he was allowed to keep the castles of Carmarthen and Cardigan until the king came of age, and as Gwenwynwyn had died in 1216 it was agreed that Llywelyn should hold Powys Wenwynwyn until Gruffudd ap Gwenwynwyn reached manhood.

Within five years of the Treaty, the officials of the English crown again sought to restrict Llywelyn to Gwynedd. In 1223, the castles of Carmarthen and Cardigan were seized by William, earl of Pembroke and *rector* of the kingdom of England. At the same time, Hubert de Burgh, justiciar of England, ordered a castle to be built at Montgomery on a site more defensible than that of the old castle of the Montgomery family. But when Hubert sought to extend his authority over the commotes of Powys, he was utterly trounced by Llywelyn at Ceri in 1228. Hubert won control of a number of Marcher Lordships. Llywelyn reacted in 1231 with a campaign in which he led his forces to regions where a Welsh army had not been seen for a century or more. The army burned Brecon, marched through Glamorgan and destroyed Neath. Henry III was seriously concerned and appealed to Ireland for help, offering Anglo-Irish knights the right to own any lands they won in Wales. His efforts proved ineffective; ineffectiveness was his main characteristic – Dante placed him in that part of purgatory reserved for simpletons. Hubert de Burgh was dismissed in 1232 and opposition arose among the barons to the favouritism and incompetence of Henry's rule. Llywelyn allied with the barons, and when the conflict came to an end in 1234 he succeeded through the Peace of Middle in regaining the position he had won during the reign of John. He continued to rule Powys Wenwynwyn; he subjected the lords of Powys Fadog and Deheubarth to his authority through bonds of allegiance and he obtained possession of Gwrtheyrnion, Builth and Maelienydd. Perhaps in order to stress that he was not merely ruler of Gwynedd, he adopted the title of Prince of Aberffraw and Lord of Snowdonia, a style which emphasized his unique position among the rulers of Wales.

Although Llywelyn had won his position through conflict with the king of England, his relationship with Henry III was not one of continuous contention. During the greater part of the period 1218 to 1240, there was amity between the king and the prince who were, after all, brothers-in-law. In 1220, Henry supported Llywelyn in his efforts to ensure that his son by Joan, Henry's nephew Dafydd, should be heir to Gwynedd. That dispensation involved disinheriting Llywelyn's eldest son, Gruffudd, who had been born to Tangwystl before the marriage with Joan. In 1222, the arrangement was granted the blessing of the Pope. In 1226, Dafydd received oaths of allegiance from the 'great men of Wales', and the Pope freed Joan from the stigma of illegitimacy. In 1229, Dafydd went to London to do homage for the lands and rights he would inherit, and in the same year he married Isabella, the daughter of William de Breos.

That was one of a series of marriages between Llywelyn's offspring and members of the great families of the March, for apart from Gruffudd, who married Senana, a descendant of Rhodri ab Owain Gwynedd, all Llywelyn's progeny married into the *Francigenae*. So great was the desire of the de Breos family to ally with the prince that the uncle, the brother and the daughter of William de Breos married members of the house of Aberffraw. Yet the relationship between the two families did not prevent Llywelyn from hanging William de Breos in 1230 for excessive familiarity with Joan. The hanging was an

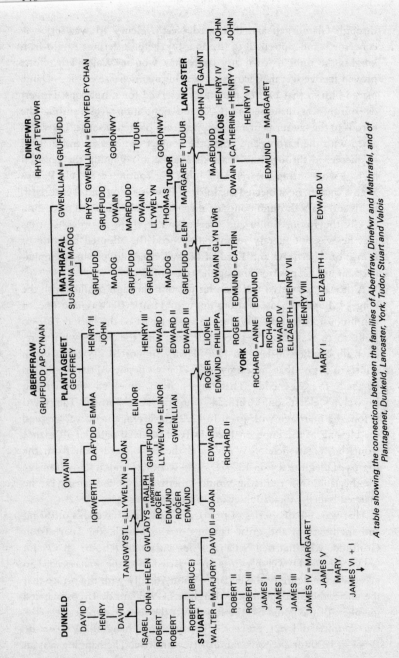

A table showing the connections between the families of Aberffraw, Dinefwr and Mathrafal, and of Plantagenet, Dunkeld, Lancaster, York, Tudor, Stuart and Valois

audacious act and the lack of reaction to it is proof of the power of Llywelyn and of the intensity of the desire of William's sons-in-law to obtain their share of his possessions, for William was the last of his branch of the de Breoses. The male line died out remarkably frequently among the families of the Marcher Lords and the marriages of co-heiresses played a key role in the dismemberment of the empires of their fathers.

In the wake of the dismemberment of the de Breos empire, the Bohun and Cantelupe families joined the ranks of the leading Marcher Lords and the Mortimer family strengthened its position in the borderlands of central Wales. The Mortimers also intermarried with the house of Aberffraw; Ralph Mortimer's wife was Llywelyn's daughter, Gwladus Ddu, and their descendants would include Edward IV and his daughter Elizabeth, the wife of Henry VII, a fact which led David Powel in 1584 to claim that Henry VIII had inherited England from his father and Wales from his mother. During the age of Llywelyn, the most powerful of the Marcher Lords was Rannulf, earl of Chester, and the constant friendship between the prince and the earl was a central factor in the stability of the Gwynedd's eastern border. John – nephew and heir to Rannulf and great-grandson of David, king of Scots – married Llywelyn's daughter, Helen, but the marriage was childless, a misfortune of importance in the history of Wales and of Scotland. When John died in 1237, his territories passed to the crown, and Edward I's campaigns in Wales would be greatly facilitated by the fact that he held the earldom of Chester.

It is sometimes claimed that these marriages and others are proof that the ruling families of Wales were being assimilated into the *Francigenae*, and that in consequence French was the language of the court of Aberffraw. There is very little evidence to prove or disprove the claim. Doubtless knowledge of French was fairly common among the members of the upper classes of *Pura Wallia* during the age of Llywelyn I; 107 words were absorbed into Welsh earlier than they were into English, and French influence is obvious in romances such as *Peredur* and *Geraint*. Nevertheless, it is highly likely that Joan, Isabella and the others learned Welsh. Welsh certainly enjoyed a more central role in the court of Gwynedd than did English in the court of England, and Dafydd Jenkins has argued that the strength of Welsh in the law courts more than compensated for any leanings towards French in the prince's court.

By the age of Llywelyn, both courts were very different from the portrayal offered by the earliest sections of the law-books. Llywelyn's archive has disappeared, but a few of his letters have survived. Most of them have been preserved in the archive of the kingdom of England, a body of evidence which increases significantly after about 1200, and they prove the ability of the prince's chancery to produce documents of high quality. T. Jones Pierce showed that *Pura Wallia* in the age of Llywelyn I was developing all the requisites of a cohesive state, with the *distain* as 'prime minister', the chamberlain as 'treasurer' and the prince's clerks as 'chancellors'. At their head was Llywelyn, and as in England or France the ruler's decisions were executed under the authority of his great and privy seals. The autonomy of the local community and the importance of the bonds of kinship declined under the pressure of the prince's power. Although the *galanas* (blood-fine) unit did not cease to exist – it had other functions – murder was an offence against the state rather than against the kindred by the age of Llywelyn I, and in Gwynedd, if not in Deheubarth, it was the prince's judge who passed sentence in the commote court.

Llywelyn's ability to augment his economic and military resources was central to his success. This was the motive for ensuring that as much as possible of his territories was subject to his direct rule, sometimes – as in Meirionnydd – at the expense of the local dynasty. The same motive caused him to be determined to retain control of Tegeingl and Powys Wenwynwyn, the one a source of lead and the other of cavalry horses, both necessities for a war leader. *The Book of Iorwerth*, compiled about 1240, shows that the prince's authority over his *taeogion* (villeins) was greater than it had been in 1175, the period of the compilation of the Latin A version of the Law of Wales. *The Book of Iorwerth* refers to payments in money, and T. Jones Pierce claimed that by the age of Llywelyn I the contribution of the *bonheddwyr* to the maintenance of the prince was changing from produce (the *gwestfa*) to cash (the *twnc*) at least in the more fertile of the commotes of Gwynedd. Thus money must have been in circulation, a development which postulates the existence of trade. It appears that Llywelyn fostered the growth of quasi-urban settlements as centres of trade, settlements which would be further encouraged by his grandson, Llywelyn II.

Trade gave rise to new social classes outside the simple division of *bonheddwr* and *taeog*. This was also the consequence of the king's need for men with a greater obligation to serve him than had the *bon-heddwyr*. The obligation of the *bonheddwr* to serve for specific periods in the prince's forces was the consequence of his rank rather than of the land he held, but Llywelyn granted land to some of his more prominent subjects in return for more extensive service. Among them was Ednyfed Fychan, the *distain* of Gwynedd from 1216 to 1246 and the ancestor of the Tudors of Anglesey. Such grants were the essence of feudalism and Llywelyn's emphasis upon castles also belonged to the feudal world. He built a chain of them from Tegeingl to Meirion-nydd; the king of England built a parallel chain from Cardigan to Montgomery, and central to the prince's strategy was the breaking of its links. Equally consistent with feudal tradition was the ceremony held at Strata Florida in 1238, in which Llywelyn's vassals swore an oath of allegiance to his heir, Dafydd, emulating an act which had deep roots in Capetian France.

Llywelyn died on 11 April 1240. Gwynedd passed to Dafydd without difficulty, but Henry III soon showed that he would not permit the son to enjoy the status of the father. Six weeks after Llywelyn's death, Dafydd and Henry met at Gloucester, where Dafydd was confirmed in possession of the territories which his father had held *de jure*. Henry insisted that the allegiance of the lesser Welsh rulers belonged exclusively to the English crown. The way was opened for Gruffudd ap Gwenwynwyn to repossess Powys Wenwynwyn and for Ralph Mortimer to revive his claim to Maelienydd and Gwrtheyrnion, while through the royal castles of Cardigan and Carmarthen the lords of Deheubarth were drawn into the web of the king's authority. In 1241, Henry laid down that Gwynedd should pass to the king of England if Dafydd should die without an heir. In the same year Henry compelled Dafydd to hand over his elder brother, Gruffudd, a man who could be used to undermine the unity of Gwynedd. Gruffudd was imprisoned in London's White Tower and he fell to his death on St David's Day, 1244, while lowering himself from his prison on a rope of sheets. As Dafydd no longer had a competitor, he re-created the alliance with the men of the south which had been so important to his father. He did so, it would appear, with the support of Gruffudd's second son, Llywelyn, a young man who wielded considerable influence in the Perfeddwlad. Henry retaliated, attacking Gwynedd in a campaign of remarkable ferocity. In his adversity, Dafydd wrote to the Pope, Innocent IV, offering to hold his principality as a Papal vassal, citing the fact that Rome had, in 1222, acknowledged his rights as heir to Gwynedd. His offer had numerous precedents: by 1244 about a dozen European rulers had become direct vassals of the Papacy, and the Pope had proved his ability to make and to unmake kingdoms. In writing to the Pope, Dafydd's intention was to free himself from the overlordship of the king of England, and the essence of his offer was an attempt to assert the independence of his principality. It was no longer the principality of Gwynedd for, while awaiting the Pope's reply, Dafydd had begun to style himself prince of Wales. The title was more challenging, in so far as it was more territorial, than the title prince of the Welsh which had sometimes been employed by his predecessors. To the Pope, gaining Dafydd as vassal was less important than receiving the income which was due to him from the kingdom of England; having been assured that the money would be paid, Innocent announced in January 1245 that he would not accept Dafydd as vassal.

A year later, Dafydd died. His marriage with Isabella had been childless; thus, in accordance with the agreement of 1241, the king could claim his nephew's territories. Yet, although able to attack Gwynedd, Henry seems to have doubted that he had the ability wholly to uproot Welsh rule in north-west Wales. The men of Gwynedd accepted Llywelyn ap Gruffudd and his eldest brother, Owain, as their rulers. Their authority was circumscribed. With Gwynedd suffering under the hammer of the king's armies and with its population starving after three years of plunder, the brothers obtained an armistice and in April 1247 they appeared before the king at Woodstock. They were confirmed as lords of Gwynedd Uwch Conwy in exchange for the services of twenty-four knights and one hundred foot soldiers. As Beverley Smith put it, the purpose of the Treaty of Woodstock was to 'demote the status of Gwynedd so that that lordship would conform in all matters to the status of one of the ordinary lordships of the kingdom of England'. In 1247, the chronicler Matthew Paris recorded that 'Wales had been pulled down to nothing'. During the following decade, Henry III made strenuous efforts to strengthen his hold upon Wales, efforts upon which Edward I would build twenty years later.

Nevertheless, there were limits to the power of the king in Wales. He could not depend upon the support of the Marcher Lords, suspicious as they were of the increase in the authority of the crown.

Walter de Clifford, lord of Llandovery, was so incensed when he received a summons from Henry III that he forced the royal messenger to eat it, seal and all. In the lands seized by the crown – lands which were held from 1254 onwards by Edward, Henry's son and heir – heavy burdens were placed upon the inhabitants. They longed for a deliverer. There was one to hand. In 1255 disputes arose between the three joint rulers of Gwynedd (another brother, Dafydd, had received a share of the inheritance in 1252). Llywelyn defeated and imprisoned his two brothers; he made himself sole ruler of Gwynedd Uwch Conwy and in 1256 he added the Perfeddwlad to his territories at the request of its oppressed inhabitants.

In the following two years, Llywelyn swept through Wales. He seized Meirionnydd and established his authority over Builth and Gwrtheyrnion. Gruffudd ap Gwenwynwyn was driven out of Powys Wenwynwyn and Llywelyn's allies among the descendants of Rhys ap Gruffudd gained possession of Ceredigion and Ystrad Tywi. In 1257, the men of Deheubarth won a victory over royal forces in the battle of Y Cymerau near Llandeilo. In the same year, Henry III led an attack upon Gwynedd, but as the campaign was mismanaged the king was unable to impede Llywelyn's progress. Henry's failure induced Gruffudd ap Madog of Powys Fadog to abandon his attachment to the crown and to promise Llywelyn his allegiance. In 1258, it appears that representatives of the ruling houses of Powys, Deheubarth and Glamorgan acknowledged Llywelyn, not only as their leader but also as their lord, proof, argues Beverley Smith, that 'the Welsh were resolved upon nationhood'. At the same time, Llywelyn made contact with those elements in Scotland who were opposing Henry III's hegemony. In his letter to the Scots, he referred to himself as prince of Wales, thus demonstrating that he intended to use the allegiance of the Welsh lords as the basis of a new polity in Wales.

From 1258 to 1262, Llywelyn refrained from any further campaigns. His main purpose during those years was to secure what he had won by obtaining the king's recognition of his position and title. Through a series of truces, peace was ensured year by year, but Henry III proved unwilling to come to an agreement with Llywelyn. From 1258 onwards, the authority of the king was undermined by the baronial revolt led by Simon de Montfort. It is often argued that the Barons' War was a major cause of Llywelyn's success. Yet he had achieved most of his successes before the kingdom of England was torn by conflict, and the undermining of the authority of the crown was among the factors which prevented Henry from holding meaningful discussions with Llywelyn.

In 1262, with the truce crumbling, Llywelyn attacked Maelienydd, a lordship claimed by his cousin, Roger Mortimer, and in 1263 his forces marched into the lordships of Brecon and Abergavenny. Although they were defeated at the foot of the Blorenge Mountain, it was recorded that a large number of the inhabitants of the March – men *de lingua Wallensica* – voluntarily accepted the suzerainty of Llywelyn. In April 1262, the prince received a heavy blow when his brother, Dafydd, deserted him, but in December he won an important addition to his ranks when Gruffudd ap Gwenwynwyn made homage to him. Early in 1264, Llywelyn allied with Simon de Montfort, a few months before the king and the government of the realm came into the hands of Simon as a result of the battle of Lewes (May 1264). In June 1265, at Pipton near Glasbury, Simon, in the name of the crown, recognized Llywelyn as prince of Wales and as the overlord of the *magnates Wallie* (the great men of Wales). Llywelyn was to hold his principality as a vassal of the king of England and was to pay the king the sum of £20,000.

Llywelyn was probably aware that the Pipton Agreement would not give him the security he craved, for by June 1265 Simon de Montfort's power was in decline. Indeed, within six weeks of sealing the agreement, he had been defeated and killed at the battle of Evesham. Two years elapsed before Henry III came to terms with Llywelyn, and when he did so it was at the urging of Ottobuono, the Papal Legate. In 1267, through the Treaty of Montgomery, Llywelyn succeeded in obtaining from the king confirmation of the substance of what he had won through the Pipton Agreement, confirmation for which he was obliged to pay 25,000 marks (£16,666). It was acknowledged that he was prince of Wales and that he had the right to the homage of all the Welsh lords with the exception of Maredudd ap Rhys of Dryslwyn. (He bought the right to Maredudd's homage in 1270.) He was allowed to retain Builth, Gwrtheyrnion and Brecon and was given leave to prove his right to other Marcher Lordships, although his gains in the March were at the expense of Mortimer and Bohun, the staunchest of the supporters of the crown. Llywelyn acknowledged that he was a vassal of the king of England; he promised land to his brother, Dafydd, and yielded some of the lands he had seized on the borders of Cheshire and Shropshire.

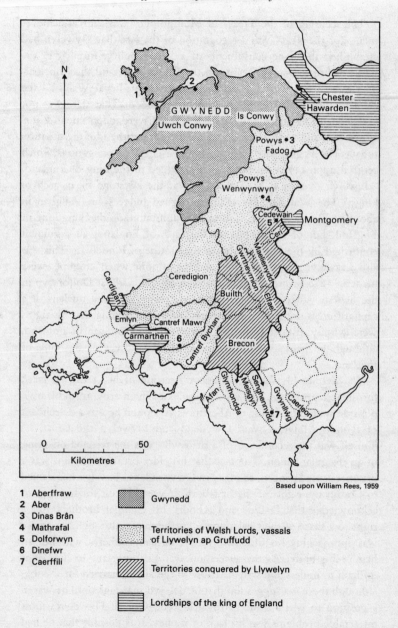

Based upon William Rees, 1959

1 Aberffraw
2 Aber
3 Dinas Brân
4 Mathrafal
5 Dolforwyn
6 Dinefwr
7 Caerffili

Gwynedd

Territories of Welsh Lords, vassals of Llywelyn ap Gruffudd

Territories conquered by Llywelyn

Lordships of the king of England

Wales in 1267: The Treaty of Montgomery

The securing of the Treaty of Montgomery was a great achievement, for the treaty was a recognition of the fact that Llywelyn had established the basic constituents of a Welsh polity. Implicit in the status of prince was the territory, the Principality, and the Principality's existence was proof that there were in medieval Wales all the elements necessary for the growth of statehood. That state was not independent; in the Middle Ages, few states were independent *de jure* although many were independent *de facto*, the antithesis of the situation today. The Principality existed within a chain of obligations which centred upon Llywelyn but which extended to the king of England. 'Llywelyn,' wrote F. M. Powicke, 'was the keystone in an arch of kings.' The Wales of Llywelyn II, argued Judge John Vaughan in about 1670, was a part, not of the dominion of the kingdom of England, but of the empire of the king of England, an argument confirmed by the introduction to the Statute of Rhuddlan. This was also Llywelyn's interpretation of his position; when attempts were made in 1273 to prevent him from erecting a castle at Dolforwyn in the Severn valley – a castle intended, perhaps, as the nucleus of a capital for his domains – he disregarded them, arguing that his rights were wholly distinct from the powers of the kingdom of England, although he held his Principality under the power of the king of England.

Yet, despite Llywelyn's confident assertion of his status, he faced formidable problems. The most complex of them arose from his own position within the house of Aberffraw. Although he was a descendant of Rhodri Mawr, Owain Gwynedd and Llywelyn the Great, he himself was the second son of a man who was the rejected offspring of an irregular union. The fact that his elder brother, Owain, was a prisoner caused concern to many in Gwynedd; as Llywelyn had denied to Owain the rights of the first-born, it was difficult for him not to acknowledge that Dafydd and Rhodri, his younger brothers, had a right to a share of their patrimony. Furthermore, although the prince was approaching his fiftieth birthday, he had neither a wife nor an heir of his body. As the succession was so important to him, it is difficult to understand why he chose to remain unmarried for so long, although there is a suggestion that he delayed marriage until he was in a position to win a bride of royal descent. One of Llywelyn's most intractable problems was his lack of money. It is possible that he had an annual income of between £5,000 and £6,000, far more than the income of any previous Welsh ruler, but far less than his needs. As he was obliged to pay substantial sums to the king of England, and as he needed to finance his many campaigns, he had to press heavily upon his people; as a result, his rule could appear rapacious and oppressive, as the complaints of some of his leading subjects testify. In creating his Principality, Llywelyn had aroused the enmity of powerful men in both Wales and England. Gruffudd ap Gwenwynwyn had accepted Llywelyn's overlordship with the greatest reluctance and the allegiance of Maredudd ap Rhys of Dryslwyn and his son, Rhys ap Maredudd, was equally shallow. By enlarging his territories to include lordships beyond the borders of *Pura Wallia*, Llywelyn had antagonized those mighty barons, Mortimer and Bohun, both of whom were intent upon undermining his authority. But despite the problems, the prospects of Llywelyn's Principality were bright, for the Principality had come into existence not only through military success but also because there was in Wales a determination 'to resolve upon nation-hood'.

Llywelyn's emphasis upon retaining his conquests in the March shows that he gave priority to securing his hold upon a chain of lordships along the eastern border of *Pura Wallia*, perhaps at the expense of easier victories in the west. Between 1267 and 1271, he became involved in northern Glamorgan, causing Gilbert de Clare, lord of Glamorgan and the richest of the subjects of the king of England, to join the ranks of his enemies. As the Treaty of Montgomery had granted to the prince of Wales the homage of the Welsh lords, Llywelyn believed that he had the right to the allegiance of those Welshmen who retained a measure of authority in the com-motes of northern Glamorgan. Hywel ap Maredudd of Miskin had been one of his earliest allies; in 1269, Edward, the king's heir, recognized Llywelyn's claim to the homage of Maredudd ap Gruff-udd, lord of Machen, and the attempts to secure the allegiance of Gruffudd ap Rhys of Senghennydd were a central part of the prince's policy in the south-east. Indeed, it is possible that Llywelyn was seeking to create an eastern border which would reach the Severn Sea, a border which would enclose the royal and baronial lordships of the south-west and which would provide him with much-needed income from the fertile lowlands of the south-east. This ambition was not a fantasy, for one of the most remarkable buildings of the Middle Ages was constructed in order to frustrate it. That building was

Caerffili Castle, a symbol of the pride of the house of Clare and an
abiding reminder of the strength of Llywelyn's appeal to the Welsh of
northern Glamorgan. Although a native of north-west Wales, it was
in the south-east that Llywelyn was at his most challenging; it is
fitting therefore that it was inhabitants of northern Glamorgan, in
1882, who began the tradition of honouring him at the place where
he met his end.

The year 1271, when he attacked Caerffili Castle in the company of
Dafydd and Gruffudd ap Gwenwynwyn, marks the apogee of
Llywelyn's power. His authority extended from Anglesey to Machen,
from the outskirts of Chester to the outskirts of Cydweli. He was lord
of about three quarters of the surface area of Wales and of a somewhat
lower proportion of its inhabitants. He had perhaps two hundred
thousand subjects. By his age it is possible to offer an estimate of the
population of Wales, although the evidence is highly debatable.
Giraldus Cambrensis claimed that the Welsh should pay the Pope 200
marks (32,000 pence) in St Peter's Pence. The tax was a penny per
household; if households contained five persons on average, Giraldus's
comment suggests that in the 1190s Wales had 160,000 inhabitants.
The population increased rapidly during the following century, and
on the basis of the records of the tax imposed upon Wales in 1292–3 it
would seem that the country had about three hundred thousand
inhabitants by the 1290s. In consequence, it has been argued that
Wales -- which like the rest of Europe would soon be experiencing a
demographic crisis – was more populous in the generation around
1300 than it would be for another three hundred years.

The growth in population is the key to many of the developments
of the age of Llywelyn II. It allowed the prince to lead substantial
forces, although it is unlikely that his soldiers were ever as numerous
as the thirty thousand attributed to him in 1262. It also caused the
gwelyau (clan lands) of the *bonheddwyr* (freemen) to multiply to such
an extent that their members were obliged to carve out holdings in
the waste ten miles and more from the original *hendref* of their *cenedl*
(kindred group). By 1334, the *gwely* of Edryd ap Marchudd, which
originated in Abergele, had fifteen settlements extending from Betws-
y-coed to Bodelwyddan. Alongside the increase in rural settlement,
there was growth in the urban population. By the age of Llywelyn II,
perhaps as many as 10 per cent of the inhabitants of Wales were
town-dwellers. This development was most pronounced in the

southern Marches, but it was also encouraged in Gwynedd, at places such as Llan-faes, Nefyn and Pwllheli. As in the rest of Europe, population growth in Wales was the result of a number of factors – more stable social and political conditions, for example, and a more favourable climate: the average temperature was a degree or two higher than it is today, a crucial bonus for arable agriculture in a country like Wales. Importance should also be attached to new sources of energy – the windmill, the fulling-mill and the horse collar (which doubled the efficiency of horse-power) – and to the enrichment which resulted from the development of trade.

Before about 1300, there is very little evidence of trade in Wales, and Giraldus Cambrensis asserted that the Welsh had no interest in buying and selling. Yet there must have been some trade throughout the centuries, for the country was not self-sufficient. It did not produce salt and wine, and not enough wheat was grown and iron smelted to satisfy the needs of the inhabitants. The richer among them sought luxuries from London and Paris, and the monks wanted to build churches from carvable stone from quarries in England. The imports were exchanged for the primary products of Wales – cattle, skins, cheese, timber, horses, wax, dogs, hawks and fleeces – although, with the growth of the fulling-mills, flannel was becoming second only to cattle among the exports of Wales. The country's need for products from beyond its borders was a weapon in the hands of its enemies. In 1223, Henry III allowed unrestricted trade between England and Wales as long as his concord with Llywelyn I lasted, and in 1277 attempts were made to prevent salt, wheat and iron from reaching the Welsh enemies of the king of England.

As the economy diversified, the structure of society became more complex. In the Gwynedd of Llywelyn II, that structure was shaped like a decanter rather than a pyramid, to quote the perceptive comment of Keith Williams-Jones. The bottom layer, the *taeogion* (slaves as a class had long disappeared), was narrower than the layer above it, the *bonheddwyr*, while the richer layer was very narrow and was far above the other two. In other parts of Wales, particularly in the southern March, the unfree were still substantial; indeed, in the lordship of Chepstow they were hardly less numerous than they were in the most manorialized regions of England. The Marcher Lords needed them, for the years around 1300 saw the climax of their efforts to farm the demesne lands of their lordships. On the other hand, over the greater part of Wales – a wide arc from the Perfeddwlad to Cantref Mawr – there was no sign of absolute villeinage by the age of Llywelyn II, and T. Jones Pierce argued that the *taeogion* had vanished as a result of the frequent conquest and reconquest suffered by the inhabitants of those regions.

Outside the more manorialized and anglicized areas, therefore, the Welsh *bonheddwyr* constituted the majority of the population. According to Rees Davies, the rank of *bonheddwr* was essentially the same in all parts of Wales. Yet not all *bonheddwyr* were equal. The tax records of 1292–3 show that differences in wealth were beginning to undermine the unity of the rank – that social division based upon legal rank was yielding to social division based upon property, and that in Wales there were signs of the incipient growth of a squirearchy. In 1293, one third of the property in the lordship of Abergavenny was owned by one thirtieth of the households. The distribution of wealth was more equitable in the west; nevertheless, while 85 per cent of the heads of households of Meirionnydd had movable property worth less than five pounds, every neighbourhood had a handful of families who owned property worth ten pounds and more. The tax records also reveal the existence of substantial groups who were not directly dependent upon the land, among them fishermen, administrators, professional men and craftsmen. A total of thirty-seven different trades were followed in Meirionnydd, where there were eight goldsmiths, four poets and twenty-six shoemakers. There was a doctor in Cynwyd and a hotel-keeper in Maentwrog, and the twenty-six parishes of Meirionnydd were served by twenty-eight priests. Two of the priests were graduates; by 1250, there were about a dozen universities in Europe and Welshmen were drawn to a number of them, Oxford above all.

Recent research has shown that Wales in the age of Llywelyn II had a larger population, a more developed economy, a more complex society and people of greater sophistication than was previously realized. These are further considerations to support the belief that the prospects of Llywelyn's Principality were bright. Goronwy Edwards argued that time was its chief need – time to allow it to become an undisputed political fact. This is precisely what was not vouchsafed to it, for it received a severe blow in 1277 and was entirely destroyed in 1282–3. Yet, after being in existence for hardly a decade, the king of England's campaign against it in 1277 cost him heavily in money, time and energy, and the campaign of 1282–3 was even more burden-some. Edward I, the most powerful of the medieval kings of England, was obliged to devote the entire resources of his kingdom to the task at a time when that kingdom was united under his authority. If the Principality had survived his reign, it is difficult to believe that there would have been in England in the following century the unity or the determination to undertake its destruction. The political history of Wales from 1066 onwards may be viewed in terms of an increasing subjection to the power of the crown of England, with the victory in 1282–3 as a natural and inevitable climax; on the other hand, it would be legitimate to stress the increasing ingenuity of the leading Welsh rulers, to emphasize the potential of the embryonic state created by them, and to consider its downfall, not as an inevitable happening, but as the result of an unexpected combination of factors.

Evidence of the way in which that potential was developed is scarce. There are references to the names of a number of Llywelyn's officials, the sons of Ednyfed Fychan among them. Few direct records of their activity have survived, but there is indirect evidence of the work of the financial, legal and military advisers of Llywelyn. It has already been noted that Llywelyn's financial obligations caused him to press heavily upon his subjects. Between 1267 and 1272, he paid the king of England sums amounting to £11,500, proof of the growth of a money economy in Wales and testimony of the effectiveness of the Principality's financial administration. In legal matters, the decline of the *galanas* (blood-fine) was further encouraged and use was made of some elements of English Law, such as the jury system. A direct relationship was developed between his subjects, as individuals, and the prince, and it was emphasized that he was the lord of all the land of his Principality. In military matters, the chain of castles defending the heartland of Gwynedd was strengthened and the system of provisioning them was perfected. A massive investment was made in cavalry horses, despite the galloping rise in their cost. The practice of granting land in exchange for military service was expanded; the land of Goronwy ap Heilyn, the most faithful of the servants of the house of Aberffraw, was held on military tenure.

A few dozen of the documents produced by Llywelyn's chancery have survived, mainly in the archives of the kingdom of England, the archdiocese of Canterbury and the Papacy, and they testify to the high standard of the work of his clerks. His correspondence with

Gregory X (1271–6) shows that the Pope had considerable sympathy for him, and in 1275 a message came from Rome insisting that a Welshman appearing before the court of the province of Canterbury should receive a hearing within the borders of Wales. Llywelyn's relations with the friars – the Franciscans and the Dominicans – were cordial. By his time, there were eight friaries in Wales. Cardiff had one of each; like Florence or Siena, the town was flanked by the Black and the Grey Friars. Equally acceptable to Llywelyn was the support of the Cistercians, whose abbots were eager to commend him to the Pope when conflict arose between the prince and Anian, bishop of St Asaph.

The conflict with Anian was an episode in the Church's struggle to win sovereignty over its own interests, and by 1274 its increasing bitterness had made the bishop a determined enemy of the prince. By then such enemies were numerous. Chief among them were the Marcher Lords whose lands Llywelyn had seized or threatened – the powerful barons, Clare, Bohun and Mortimer. Llywelyn's ambition received a severe check as a result of the 'second conquest of Glamorgan' – Gilbert de Clare's campaign to bring the lordships of northern Glamorgan under his complete control by abolishing any residue of Welsh rule there, an object which he had successfully accomplished by 1272. From 1272 onwards, Bohun and Mortimer redoubled their efforts to repossess the Marcher Lordships granted to Llywelyn under the Treaty of Montgomery. In 1274, there was a dramatic addition to the ranks of the prince's enemies when his brother, Dafydd, and his chief vassal, Gruffudd ap Gwenwynwyn, fled to England, leaving behind them evidence of a plot to kill him.

The enmity of Gruffudd was not surprising. In accordance with the tradition of his family, he was a reluctant vassal of the house of Aberffraw; he had spent the first twenty-five years of his life in England and he tried to escape from Llywelyn's clutches by seeking recognition as a Marcher Lord, a foretaste of the fate of Powys Wenwynwyn. Dafydd's conduct is more difficult to understand. He had deserted Llywelyn on a previous occasion, but in 1274 he, it must be presumed, was the heir to the Principality; of the other brothers, Owain was still a prisoner, and Rhodri had sold to Llywelyn in 1272 any claims that he might have had upon Gwynedd. After Dafydd's defection, and possibly as a reaction to it, a plan, perhaps originally aired in 1265, was resurrected – marriage between Llywelyn and

Elinor, a daughter of Simon de Montfort. Elinor's lineage was highly distinguished; among her uncles were a king of England, a king of France and a Holy Roman Emperor. Nevertheless, by 1275, when a proxy marriage took place, there was no political advantage to the union, for the opposition movement which her father had led was moribund. The king of England took the view that the marriage was a plot to rekindle dissension within his kingdom, and such a notion may also have been present in Llywelyn's mind. Elinor sailed from France to Wales in 1275, but the seizure of her ship led to her imprisonment at Windsor.

Elinor's incarceration was part of a deepening crisis in the relationship between Llywelyn and Edward I. Edward had inherited the crown of England in November 1272 on the death of his father, Henry III, but he did not set foot in his kingdom until August 1274, when he returned from the Crusade. By then, Llywelyn had a number of complaints against the administrators of the kingdom of England, among them their readiness to give refuge to his enemies, Dafydd and Gruffudd, and their unwillingness to uphold his treaty rights against the aggression of the Marcher Lords. They also had complaints against him, among them his reluctance to swear an oath of allegiance to the new king and to pay the remaining sums due under the Treaty of Montgomery. Llywelyn did not attend Edward's coronation in August 1274, and by April 1276 he had received five summonses to do homage to the king, all of which he had disregarded. He stressed that he was not refusing but rather postponing homage, because he feared for his safety at a court which harboured his enemies and imprisoned his wife, and because he was not being granted his rights under the Treaty of Montgomery. Yet, according to that treaty, those rights were dependent upon doing homage to the king of England. Although Llywelyn had legitimate complaints, he trod a dangerous path in refusing full recognition of the king's overlordship, and there has been much speculation about his reasons for treading it. In September 1275, Llywelyn explained his position in a letter to the Pope, who supported his protest against the incarceration of Elinor. In countering Llywelyn's arguments, Edward denied the validity of the Treaty of Montgomery, asserting that because of the Welsh custom of dividing land equally among all the sons Llywelyn's rights were no greater than those of his three brothers. Edward was encouraged in that view by his guest, Dafydd, who sought a share of Gwynedd, and it is difficult not to agree with John Speed that Dafydd was 'the chiefest firebrand in this fatall combustion'.

Between November 1276 and February 1277, Llywelyn wrote three letters to Edward expressing his readiness to discuss their differences and offering to accept the arbitration of the king of France. Edward was not prepared to entertain such a suggestion. In November 1276, Llywelyn was declared a rebel and free rein was given to English chauvinism, a phenomenon with which the Welsh would perforce become increasingly familiar. By November 1276, Edward had acquiesced in the Marcher Lords' seizure of the territories between Powys and Glamorgan which had been granted to Llywelyn by the Treaty of Montgomery, and the king was preparing to attack the prince with an army larger than any seen in Britain since 1066. That army marched through the south in the spring of 1277, and Rhys ap Maredudd of Dryslwyn hastened to make his peace with Edward. The rest of the Welsh rulers were not quite so Pétainistic (to quote Keith Williams-Jones's trenchant adjective), and after hesitating briefly Rhys Fychan, the ruler of northern Ceredigion, fled to Gwynedd. The lords of Powys Fadog submitted to the king, who burned their stronghold of Dinas Brân, a castle than which 'there was not a mightier in Wales nor a better in England'.

By August 1277, Edward's army of eight hundred knights and fifteen thousand foot soldiers (nine thousand of whom had been recruited in Wales) was in the heartland of Gwynedd. The army was provisioned from Chester and Dublin, and Edward showed that he understood the secret of Gwynedd's position as a natural fortress. His counsellors may well have read the works of Giraldus Cambrensis, for Edward's strategy followed Giraldus's advice in detail. Anglesey's grain harvest was seized by three hundred and sixty reapers and the campaign was continued into the winter months when Snowdonia, lacking pasture for herds and flocks, was unable to offer a refuge to the defenders of Gwynedd. It would appear that Edward originally intended utterly to destroy the Principality, but he probably came to the conclusion that the task would be excessively onerous. With no hope of victory, Llywelyn had little choice but to submit to the king, and the terms of the submission were agreed at Aberconwy on 9 November 1277. The Treaty of Aberconwy confined Llywelyn's authority to Gwynedd Uwch Conwy, although he was allowed to retain the title of prince of Wales and the homage of Rhys Fychan and four of the lords of Powys Fadog. Of the four *cantrefi* of the Perfeddwlad, the king took possession of Tegeingl and Rhos, and Dafydd received Rhufoniog and Dyffryn Clwyd, while Owain was granted lordship over Llŷn.

Despite the calamity of 1277, Llywelyn was not wholly bereft of power and dignity. There had been previous occasions when the authority of the rulers of Gwynedd had been confined to the lands west of the Conwy, and they had repeatedly shown their ability to use those lands as the springboard for the creation of a more extensive realm. If the house of Aberffraw had been able to continue to hold Gwynedd Uwch Conwy, a further opportunity to create such a realm could have arisen if the kingdom of England had again experienced dissension or feeble government. In the years immediately following the Treaty of Aberconwy, however, Edward's determined leadership precluded such a possibility. Northern Ceredigion was seized by the king, and on 1 August 1277 work began on a new castle at Aberystwyth. It was more ambitious in its design than anything previously seen in Wales, except at Caerffili, and was part of a chain of fortifications including the new castles of Flint, Rhuddlan and Builth. In 1279, Edward repossessed the lordships of Cardigan and Carmarthen which had been held by his brother Edmund since 1265. The county system which was already in place there was extended; a justice for south Wales was appointed in 1280 and the remaining Welsh lords of Deheubarth were enmeshed in a developing royal administration.

Thus, by 1280, Edward was firmly in control of his Welsh territories, which were far more extensive than those of any previous occupant of the throne of England. Llywelyn's behaviour towards the king was punctiliously correct; he made homage to Edward in December 1277; he married Elinor in the king's presence at Worcester Cathedral in October 1278; he promptly paid the sums due from him under the Treaty of Aberconwy and in his letters he fully acknowledged Edward's suzerainty. Yet there was no scarcity of issues which could cause conflict: the inhabitants of Tegeingl and Rhos were writhing under the oppressive rule of the king's officials; many of Llywelyn's ex-subjects were longing, as an inhabitant of Powys Fadog put it in 1278, to be restored to the 'unity of the prince'; in the lands of Dafydd, as well as in Deheubarth, the autonomy of the Welsh rulers was being undermined and English practices were being imposed, causing Dafydd in about 1280 to make a dignified defence of the traditions of his people. There were many problems relating to land, in particular those concerning Gwynedd's right to territories on the borders of Powys. Above all, there was the question of which Law should be used in deciding such cases, an issue which became so central that F. M. Powicke interpreted the relationship between Wales and England in the age of Llywelyn I and Llywelyn II in terms of 'The Conflict of Laws'.

Conway Davies argued that from 1277 onwards, Edward, by enlarging the districts administered under the English system and by insisting upon the use of the Law of England, was seeking to incite the Welsh to challenge him in order to give him an excuse to extirpate Welsh rule. To support his argument, Conway Davies referred to the obvious prejudice shown by the commission established in 1278 to investigate Welsh customs, to the unwillingness of the king to permit the use of the Law of Wales in the case relating to the ownership of the *cantref* of Arwystli, to the many afflictions which Llywelyn suffered at the hands of Bogo de Knoville, the justice of south Wales, to the legalistic stratagems employed by royal officials and to Edward's determination to strengthen his strategic position in Wales. Nevertheless, although historians agree that Edward was pedantic in his interpretation of his legal and constitutional rights, most of them are unwilling to accept that he deliberately plotted the destruction of Llywelyn and his Principality. Yet, his policies almost inevitably led to that outcome.

The war of 1282–3 had its origins, not in Llywelyn's Principality, but in those parts of north-east Wales administered by the crown. It began with an attack upon Hawarden Castle on Palm Sunday (21 March) 1282. The revolt, led by Dafydd, rapidly won widespread support; by 24 March it had spread to Ceredigion and by 26 March to Ystrad Tywi. Llywelyn was in a quandary for weeks, and it seems that he did not give the revolt his full support until late June. If his actions were to be consistent with his instincts and career, he would have hardly been able to avoid involvement, but the death of Elinor on the birth of their only child, Gwenllian, on 19 June 1282 was probably relevant to his state of mind when he finally made his decision.

Edward reacted to the revolt with the same strategy as he had employed in 1277. The insurgents had a considerable degree of success: they captured a number of castles -- Rhuthun, Aberystwyth and

Builth among them; the men of Gilbert de Clare, the leader of the
royal forces in the south, were defeated near Dinefwr on 16 June;
Welsh control of the uplands between the rivers Wye and Severn was
stubbornly defended; the king's hope of a rapid crossing of the Perfeddwlad was frustrated. Above all, on 6 November, when Luc de
Tany, seneschal of Gascony, sought during a time of truce to cross
the Menai Straits on a bridge of boats, his army was utterly
destroyed.

The truce was the result of an attempt by John Pecham, archbishop
of Canterbury, to mediate between Llywelyn and Edward, a plan
which had probably received the blessing of the Pope, for at Rome
there was considerable sympathy for the prince. Pecham spent three
days (3–6 November 1282) at Llywelyn's headquarters at Aber near
Bangor. His mission produced valuable evidence of the reaction of
Llywelyn and the members of his court to the grievous pressures
which were being brought to bear upon them. Indeed, the documents
which resulted from the mission are among 'the most sublime composi-
tions of the Welsh nation'. In answering Pecham's request for an
explanation of his attitude, Llywelyn declared that it was his wish that
the Welsh should be allowed to follow their customs and their Law as
did the other peoples who recognized the overlordship of the king.
Pecham suggested that Edward could be persuaded to grant Llywelyn
an income and an exalted position in England if the prince yielded his
territories to the crown. Llywelyn answered on 11 November stating
that the plan had astonished 'everyone who had heard of it, for its
purpose was to destroy and undermine my people and myself rather
than to offer me honour and safety'. About the same time, Pecham
received a letter from the leading men of Snowdonia in the name of
the *Walenses* (the Welsh), a letter which is a foretaste of the noble
declaration of the Scots at Arbroath almost half a century later. 'The
prince should not,' it stated, 'throw aside his inheritance and that of
his ancestors in Wales and accept land in England, a country with
whose language, way of life, laws and customs he is unfamiliar . . .
Let this be clearly understood: his council will not permit him to
yield . . . and even if the prince wishes to transfer [his people] into the
hands of the king, they will not do homage to any stranger as they
are wholly unacquainted with his language, his way of life and his
laws. If they were to accede, they may have to suffer imprisonment
and cruel treatment as have the inhabitants of other *cantrefi* . . . in

ways harsher than those of the Saracens.' Following the failure of his mission, Pecham gave expression to his innate English chauvinism: he execrated the Law of Wales as the work of the devil and urged conquest as the only method of delivering the Welsh from their sins, their sloth and their barbarity.

The victory of the Welsh on the Menai Straits was a severe blow to the king. As a result, he was obliged to increase his efforts to obtain money, men and resources for his war. The debts which Edward amassed as a result of his Welsh wars would have far-reaching implications. A large proportion of them arose from his need to pay his soldiers, for as the Welsh revolt was so protracted and so unexpected the old feudal host could not adequately meet the king's requirements – indeed, the war of 1282–3 is considered to be among the factors which caused its demise. Yet Edward had obligations to those of his vassals who had brought substantial forces to assist him, and by November 1282 he had rewarded the most prominent of them by creating Marcher Lordships for them in Powys Fadog and the Perfedd-wlad. He also had to put pressure upon the men of Gascony and the sheriffs of the counties of England. The sheriffs were informed on 24 November 1282 that the king believed 'it would be more fitting and suitable at this time to burden himself and the inhabitants of his kingdom with the cost of wholly overthrowing the malice of the Welsh rather than to face in the future, as in the present, the afflictions of the conflict which they have caused'.

When these words were written, Llywelyn had led a proportion of his army to the lordship of Builth – a region which had always been central to his strategy – with the intention of stiffening resistance there and possibly as the result of the deceitful suggestion of the sons of his cousin, Roger Mortimer, that that powerful family was prepared to assist him. There, on the bank of the river Irfon on 11 December 1282, he was killed by a Shropshire soldier who did not realize that he was in combat with the prince. When Llywelyn was recognized, his head was sent to London as proof of the king's success. The prince was under excommunication at the time of his death; the excommunication of Welsh insurgents was a long-standing habit of the archbishop of Canterbury. On the earnest entreaty of his cousin, Maud Giffard of Llandovery, and after assurances that he had asked for a priest in his dying moments, his trunk was buried in the holy ground of the abbey of Cwm-hir and the White Monks sang a mass for his soul.

In December 1282, the course of the Welsh revolt had still many months to run and it would not come to an end until Dafydd died in agony in Shrewsbury in October 1283, when the senior line of Aberffraw was utterly uprooted from Gwynedd. Other royal lines survived, in Powys Wenwynwyn in particular, but also in Glamorgan, Powys Fadog and Deheubarth. But the continuance of the revolt and the survival of some of the branches of the stock of Rhodri Mawr do not diminish the significance of 11 December 1282 in the history of Wales. Among his enemies and his supporters there was clear recognition of the meaning of the demise of Llywelyn. Edward was so anxious to inform the Pope that Wales no longer had a ruler worthy of papal patronage that his messenger hastened over the wintry Alps and reached Rome in five weeks, halving the usual duration of the journey. In Rome, the king's friends took the news to mean the eternal extirpation of the Welsh. To the author of *Brenhinedd y Saesson*, 1282 was the year when 'the whole of Wales was thrown to the ground', and to Gruffudd ab yr Ynad Coch the cosmos itself could not but be part of the torrent of grief for Llywelyn. Llywelyn, said Gruffudd, was *'Arglwydd neud maendo ymandaw – Cymry'* (the lord who was the keystone where the Welsh congregated). With his death, the keystone was destroyed and the Welsh polity which he and his ancestors had fostered was uprooted, a polity which, as yet, has had no successor. Henceforth, the fate of the Welsh in every part of their country would be to live under a political system in which they and their characteristics would have only a subordinate role, a fact which would be a central element in their experience until this very day and hour.

=====

CHAPTER FIVE

1282–1530: Rhuddlan, Sycharth and Penmynydd

In Wales, as in other parts of Europe, historians have been reluctant to come to grips with the Later Middle Ages. Admirable studies have been published on aspects of the period, but attempts to survey the experience of the Welsh people in its entirety during the years 1282 to 1530 have been rare. In his *Hanes Cymru* (1842), Carnhuanawc gave fifty pages (out of 748) to those years, and they received sixty-five pages (out of 495) from Jane Williams in her *History of Wales* (1869). Until very recently, the standard studies of the history of Wales were the works of J. E. Lloyd and David Williams; Lloyd's volumes come to an end in 1282 and Williams's book does not begin until 1485. The reluctance of the historians is not surprising. Although the manuscript sources for the period are more plentiful than those of previous centuries, most of them were fairly inaccessible until recently, and they are more difficult to interpret than the sources of subsequent centuries. Furthermore, with plague and depression and the mood of pessimism which came in their wake, the Later Middle Ages give the impression of being a period when society was at a low ebb, and there was a natural tendency to hasten past them to exciting themes such as the Renaissance, the Protestant Reformation, the 'new' monarchies and the expansion of Europe.

In Wales, the failure of the house of Aberffraw's great venture meant the end of the powerful theme which gives unity to previous centuries – the attempt to create a Welsh polity. For a quarter of a millennium after 1282, lack of unity was the essence of the Welsh experience. In some countries – England in particular – the totality of their history is greater than the totality of the histories of their regions, but in Wales it can appear that the reverse is true. This is a factor which weakened the appeal of the period for earlier generations of historians, scholars who considered that their chief task was to analyse the constitutional and administrative growth of sovereign states. Indeed, it was necessary to wait until other forms of history – social, economic, cultural and demographic – won acceptance before any period of the history of Wales after 1282 received the attention it deserved.

The lack of general studies of the Later Middle Ages can lead to the belief that it was a period of little significance in Wales – a tedious hiatus between the fall of Llywelyn and the coming of the Tudors. To take such a view would be a gross misconception, for during the years 1282 to 1485 there were developments which would be central to the experience of the Welsh people for many subsequent centuries. Despite numerous checks, the economy of Wales had stabilized by about 1450, and there would be very few changes in its main characteristics until the rural economy was overwhelmed by the growth of industry four hundred years later. By 1450, landholding systems associated with the *bonheddwyr* and the *taeogion* – the *gwely* and the *tir cyfrif* – were in the final stages of decay; they were replaced by the estates of the gentry, estates which would dominate Welsh society until very recently. Henceforth, as the poets no longer had princely patrons, they were adopted, as the famous comment in *Statud Gruffudd ap Cynan* put it, by the lesser nobility and, under their patronage, a body of literature was created which (according to Saunders Lewis) has no equal in Europe except in the works of Dante. The work of the poets proves that the Welsh did not lose their identity as a result of the Edwardian Conquest. When the princes enjoyed power, the allegiance of the Welsh was fractured, but the Conquest and the adversity which followed served to strengthen their self-awareness. That awareness was expressed in a series of anti-English revolts, but it was also expressed in delight in the achievements of those Welshmen who served the English crown and in pride in the Welsh connections of the king himself. This ambiguity in the attitude of the Welsh towards England, the complex interweaving of sympathy and antipathy which developed in the centuries after the Conquest, would be characteristic of many Welsh patriots to the present day.

After the death of Llywelyn, resistance was led by Dafydd, who also styled himself prince of Wales. Castell y Bere in Meirionnydd, whose defenders surrendered on 25 April 1283, was the last stronghold to withstand the forces of the English crown. Dafydd was captured on the slopes of Cadair Idris on 28 June and he suffered the appalling death of a traitor at Shrewsbury on 3 October. His two sons lived out their lives as prisoners in Bristol Castle and his daughter, Gwladus, was sent to the nunnery of Sixhills, Lincolnshire, where she died in 1336, a year before Llywelyn's daughter, Gwenllian, died in the neighbouring nunnery of Sempringham. Of the other brothers of Llywelyn, it would appear that Owain died childless before 1282, but Rhodri, who was a landowner in Tatsfield, Surrey, lived until 1315 without showing any desire to have a role in the life of Wales. His son, Thomas (1295–1363), had a greater interest in the land of his ancestors: the estate of Mechain came into his possession, he sought to claim Llŷn as the heir of his uncle, Owain, and he inspired his son, Owain Lawgoch, with an ambition to restore the honour of his family.

Thus, of the main line of Aberffraw, Rhodri's branch was the only one to survive the tribulations of 1282–3. The fate of the other Welsh families of royal descent was less dismal. Gruffudd ap Gwenwynwyn died in 1286, in his bed, and the status of his eldest son, Owain, was essentially that of a Marcher Lord. Owain rejoiced in that status, as the surname he adopted – de la Pole – suggests. After his death in 1311, his lordship passed in accordance with English custom to his son-in-law, John Charlton, much to the anger of his brother, Gruffudd, who would have inherited it if Welsh custom had been followed. Powys remained in the possession of the Charlton family until 1421, when it passed by marriage to John Grey, and it was still in the hands of the Grey family when the privileges of the Marcher Lords were abolished in 1536.

Powys Wenwynwyn was the only region of Wales to become part of the March through metamorphosis rather than through conquest. Gruffudd ap Gwenwynwyn's retention of his ancestral lands was his reward for deserting Llywelyn. Rhys ap Maredudd of Dryslwyn had been almost equally ambivalent towards the prince and he expected to be rewarded in the same way. In 1283, his landholdings were augmented so that they extended from the river Aeron to the river Tywi, but Rhys was disappointed by the king's decision to take into his own hands the old royal seat of Dinefwr and most of the other territories previously owned by those members of the house of Deheubarth who had remained loyal to Llywelyn. Edward's acquisitions were administered by the officials of the crown at Carmarthen and Cardigan and soon Rhys's commotes were also drawn into the web of royal authority. He rose in revolt in 1287 and, after the capture of his castles at Dryslwyn and Newcastle Emlyn, his lands were added to those directly administered by county officials. The revolt of 1287 did not attract much support; in view of the record of the lords of Dryslwyn, it is unlikely that Rhys appeared a credible national leader. A fugitive for four years, he was captured by men who had served Llywelyn and was put to death at York in 1292. Of the rest of the branches of the house of Deheubarth, Rhys Wyndod, lord of Dinefwr, and Rhys Fychan, lord of northern Ceredigion, were imprisoned, and Maelgwn, the son of Rhys Fychan, died in the revolt of 1294. Within a generation of the Conquest, it was only in southern Ceredigion that the house of Deheubarth survived in the male line. There, Llywelyn ab Owain, the representative of the senior branch of the descendants of Rhys ap Gruffudd, held parts of the commotes of Is Coed and Gwynionydd, and his grand-daughter would be Elen, the mother of Owain Glyn Dŵr.

Llywelyn ab Owain had the status of a Welsh baron. The same status was enjoyed by those of the line of Madog ap Maredudd who had succeeded in retaining possession of some of the land of their ancestors in Powys Fadog. They included the descendants of Owain Brogyntyn, Madog's youngest son; they were known for a quarter of a millennium as the barons of Edeirnion, and so conscious were they of their royal lineage that they rarely married outside their caste, although they were hardly more than minor squires. The lands of the descendants of Gruffudd Maelor I, Madog's eldest son, were more extensive: Gruffudd's great-great-grandson, Gruffudd ap Gruffudd, held an estate in Glyndyfyrdwy as well as half the commote of Cynllaith, and in 1328 he conveyed his lands to trustees in order that his son, Gruffudd Fychan II, the father of Owain Glyn Dŵr, should inherit them undivided.

Morgan Fychan, lord of Afan, was also a Welsh baron. A descendant of the last king of Glamorgan, he was the only Welsh lord in the kingdom of his ancestors to retain a degree of authority following the 'second conquest' of Glamorgan. Under his father and his grandfather, Afan had been a centre of Welsh resistance, and Morgan's younger son, Rhys, remembered with bitterness the expropriation of his forefathers. By 1300, however, Morgan's eldest son, Lleision, was known by the surname de Avene, a suggestion that there was very little difference between him and others of the vassals of the Clare family. When the last of Lleision's descendants in the male line died about 1350, Afan came under the direct rule of the lord of Glamorgan. Senghennydd, which had previously been held by Gruffudd ap Rhys, a descendant of Ifor Bach, had already been absorbed by the Clare family, but Gruffudd's son, Llywelyn Bren, would have enough influence in Glamorgan to lead a revolt there in 1316. The fate of Maredudd of Caerleon, the representative of the line of Caradog ap Gruffudd ap Rhydderch, was similar: his lands in Gwent and Gwynllŵg were seized by Gilbert de Clare in 1272, but the family continued to be highly regarded by the Welsh of the uplands and when they rose in revolt in 1294 they were led by Maredudd's son, Morgan.

The revolt of 1294 was a reaction to the post-Conquest settlement. Edward spent the greater part of 1283 and 1284 in Wales; a son was born to his wife, Elinor, at Caernarfon on 25 April 1284 – their eleventh child – and in midsummer 1284 the king celebrated his victory by holding an Arthurian Round Table at the old princely court in Nefyn, where the floor gave way under the weight of the festivities. The Conquest did not lead to the assimilation of the Welsh by the English. Although the whole of *Pura Wallia* was at Edward's disposal by the summer of 1283, it was not united with the kingdom of England and its inhabitants did not become subjects of the crown on the same terms as the inhabitants of England. Edward's hands were tied by the existence of the Marcher Lords, and he had neither the will nor the resources to abolish their privileges. Indeed, as has been seen, he created new Marcher Lordships: he gave Denbigh (the *cantrefi* of Rhos and Rhufoniog) to Henry de Lacy, earl of Lincoln, Rhuthun (the *cantref* of Dyffryn Clwyd) to Reginald de Grey, Bromfield and Yale (the commotes of Iâl and Maelor Gymraeg) to John de Warenne, earl of Surrey, and Chirk (parts of the commotes of Cynllaith, Mochnant and Nanheudwy) to Roger Mortimer, and thus a chain of lordships was created between England and the westerly conquests of the crown.

As the administrative structures of England were sufficiently mature to be exported, a colonial system was established in those parts of Llywelyn's Principality which were by 1284 in the hands of the king. In that year, they were provided, through the Statute of Rhuddlan, with a governmental framework. That document is sometimes referred to as the Statute of Wales, although it was only immediately relevant to Gwynedd Uwch Conwy and one commote to the east of the Conwy – that of Creuddyn, the district around Degannwy. The commotes were retained as the basic units of local government, and in Gwynedd Uwch Conwy and Creuddyn they were grouped to create three counties – Anglesey, Caernarfon and Meirionnydd. On 20 March 1284, sheriffs were appointed to administer them. Their chief duties were to collect the rents and taxes owed to the crown, to hold a county court once a month, to preside over a *magnus tournus* in each commote twice a year and to supervise the work of the commote officials. The sheriffs of the counties of England were directly responsible to the Exchequer at Westminster, but between that institution and the counties of Gwynedd another layer of officials was established consisting of a justice and a chamberlain and representing a colonial extension of the central power. There had been a justice for the counties of Carmarthen and Cardigan since 1280. As a result of the war of 1282–3 and of the revolt of 1287, the territories directly administered by him were considerably enlarged, but because the structure in the southern part of the Principality had developed in a piecemeal fashion it was never as systematic as that which was imposed upon the three northern counties. A justice was appointed for them in 1284, and the administration of the county of Flint (a combination of Tegeingl and Maelor Saesneg) became the responsibility of the justice of Chester.

Among the chief functions of the new administration was the introduction of English Criminal Law, and much of the Statute of Rhuddlan is a description of the means of doing so. The statute was one of a series of highly significant legal measures; the reign of Edward I was a period of much defining and reforming of the Common Law, which was becoming increasingly isolated as it followed a path different from that followed by the legal systems of others of the countries of Europe. Edward permitted the use of the Law of Wales in matters relating to land, but he was determined to prohibit its use in cases of murder, theft and arson. To older generations of historians, providing the Welsh with strong royal Law was Edward's greatest achievement. Their approval was based upon the mistaken notion that the Law of Wales was primitive and upon the assumption that strict order is society's greatest glory. The Law of the crown could be merciless and, as late as 1470, Dafydd ab Edmwnd –

whose friend Siôn Eos had been hanged for accidentally killing a man
– would be yearning for the benignity of the Law of Hywel. That
Law decayed rapidly in Gwynedd, where the hostility of the English
authorities towards it was at its most intense, but it remained for
centuries in at least partial use in the north-eastern March and in the
two counties of the south. Texts of the Law produced in Ceredigion
in about 1480 testify to the fact that some aspects of it were still
evolving, but by then it had long ceased to be a complete expression
of the legal genius of the Welsh. As the Law of Hywel became
increasingly moribund, an element which had been central to Welsh
identity was lost. In Scotland, the indigenous Law was (and is) the
corner-stone of the principle of the common citizenship of the entire
population. That principle did not develop in Wales. As a consequence, language came to be viewed as the touchstone of Welsh
nationality, although the Welsh word *iaith* had a meaning wider than
that of mere speech.

The spread of English Law, with its emphasis upon the relationship
between the transgressor – as an individual – and the state, helped to
undermine the importance of the bonds of kinship, a development
which was already afoot in Gwynedd in the age of Llywelyn II. The
process of undermining was also furthered by the growth of a money
economy, one of the most striking consequences of the Conquest and
another development which had its beginnings in the age of the
princes. The *bonheddwyr* (freemen) of most of the *gwelyau* (clan lands)
of Anglesey and Llŷn contributed to the maintenance of their lord in
money rather than in produce before 1282, but the practice had not
spread to the free population of the more mountainous regions nor to
the villein communities. In the generation after the Conquest, all the
inhabitants of the Welsh territories of the crown were obliged to pay
their taxes in cash, the sums being equivalent in value to the produce
which they had previously paid to Llywelyn. Although the evidence
is incomplete, it appears that the financial obligations of the *bonheddwyr*
of Gwynedd rose by about 75 per cent as a result of the Conquest.
The increase for the *taeogion* (villeins) was 600 per cent and more.
Their burden was particularly heavy: although they constituted only
a small minority of the population, they paid well over half the taxes
and each settlement was obliged to maintain its payments even if the
number of its inhabitants slumped. In material terms (apart from the
Welsh rulers themselves), it was the lower classes who suffered most

severely as a result of the Conquest and it was they also who suffered the greatest humiliation. As will be seen, elements among the *bonheddwyr* succeeded in profiting from the new order, but the social subjection of the classes beneath them was reinforced by their subjection as members of a defeated ethnic group.

The speed with which payments in produce and labour were abandoned caused great stress, and in 1315 and again in 1318 the inhabitants of the southern counties petitioned the king for a return to the old system. Nevertheless, the ability of officials to collect crown taxes suggests that the circulation of money expanded rapidly in Wales in the decades immediately following the Conquest. That expansion was aided by the economic growth characteristic of those decades, growth which was a continuation of developments seen in the age of Llywelyn II. The number of ships visiting the port of Llan-faes in Anglesey rose from thirty in 1280 to eighty in 1290; the wealth produced by the mines of Tegeingl and Snowdonia increased following Edward's recruitment of German miners; income from the fertile lands of the south-east rose in the wake of the expansion of commercial farming, and the profits of the wool trade grew as the export of fleeces yielded to the export of flannel. The Conquest cost the king huge sums: Edward spent £150,000 on the war of 1282–3 and almost £90,000 on his other campaigns in Wales, and although it would be perverse to claim that the Welsh benefited from the expenditure, it certainly promoted the circulation of money among them. That was further promoted by Edward's vast castle-building programme. During his reign, over £80,000 was spent on the royal castles of Wales, including nearly £20,000 on the four major castles – Rhuddlan, Aberystwyth, Flint and Builth – built following the war of 1277, and about £60,000 on the five major castles – Caernarfon, Conwy, Harlech, Cricieth and Beaumaris – built after the war of 1282–3 and the revolt of 1294.

In all, Edward's activities in Wales cost him about a third of a million pounds, more than ten times his regular annual income. In the later years of his life (he died in 1307) he was also spending heavily on wars in Scotland and Gascony, so it is hardly surprising that his debts loom large in the history of his reign. His main bankers were the Riccardi Company of Lucca in Tuscany, the most sophisticated financiers in Europe. Between 1276 and 1287 he borrowed £122,000 from them, specifically to finance his campaigns in Wales. Their business expanded substantially as a result of the Conquest, which therefore must be considered a factor in the growth of international capitalism. It may also be considered a factor in the growth of the power of the English parliament, for, as his need for money was growing so rapidly, Edward was obliged to acknowledge that his right to tax his subjects was to some extent dependent upon their consent. Furthermore, Edward's hopes of subjugating the Scots were vitiated by the debts he amassed because of his activities in Wales. The success of the Scots in withstanding the power of the king of England was an element of importance in the history of Wales, for it allowed Scotland to build up such reserves of strength as to preclude the possibility that the country would be completely assimilated to England, and thus it was ensured that Britain would never become a totally uniform centralized state.

The fact that much of the money spent on the Edwardian castles came from Lucca is characteristic of the far-flung connections of those splendid buildings. As A. J. Taylor's fascinating research has shown, the man mainly responsible for them was James of St George, an architect of genius from Savoy. He incorporated in them features from Palestine, Byzantium and Gascony as well as from his own homeland in the heart of the Alps. Of the Edwardian castles, Beaumaris is the most superb in plan, with its moat, its outer walls and its inner walls creating a perfect concentric pattern. But the most remarkable is Caernarfon. Caernarfon Castle, with its octagonal towers and its bands of light-coloured stone, cannot be other than a conscious imitation of the fortifications of Constantinople, the city which had been the capital of the Roman Empire for almost a millennium. St George probably knew of the legends which linked Caernarfon with Magnus Maximus and with Constantine, and in planning a headquarters for Edward he created on a strait at the western edge of Europe something of the splendour which had existed for centuries on a strait on its eastern edge. St George's intention was not to glorify Welsh traditions, but rather to symbolize the appositeness of the repossession of Caernarfon by an imperial power. The extinction of the autochthonous order was highlighted: at least four of the courts of the princes were destroyed and the monastery of Aberconwy, the spiritual heart of Gwynedd, was demolished; a new home was built for the monks at Maenan, twelve kilometres away, and Conway Castle was built above the original tomb of Llywelyn the Great. The site at Aberconwy was rapidly cleared; the work had started by March 1283 and the king attended the service of consecration at Maenan on Easter Sunday 1284.

The history of the building of the castles offers many similar examples of the scale of the resources available to Edward. There were 968 labourers at Rhuddlan in 1277 digging a canal to link the castle to the sea; by 1283 there was an army of three thousand men at work in Wales and they hailed from all parts of England — 150 excavators from Yorkshire, for example, and forty carpenters from Lincolnshire. In six months in 1295, a total of £6,736 was spent at Beaumaris; in 1296, despite Edward's desire to channel all his resources into his Scottish campaign, expenditure continued to be substantial there, St George arguing that the king's hold upon Wales could not be secure without the most elaborate fortifications, for 'Welshmen are Welshmen'. The castles can be considered to be shameful memorials to the subjugation of the Welsh — 'the magnificent badges of our subjection' as Thomas Pennant put it. Yet, when it is considered that the medieval military architect's science and art at the height of their development were necessary to ensure that subjection, the castles may be seen as a tribute to the tenacity of the resistance of the Welsh, as eloquent testimony to the immensity of the task of uprooting from Wales the rule of the Welsh.

Alongside each castle a town was established, as had been done two hundred years earlier at the time of the Norman invasions. About a dozen towns were created in Wales at the time of the Conquest, and the Marcher Lords, as well as the king, were eager to promote them. The rights of the burgesses were defined in the town's charter. The charters of the towns of Gwynedd were versions of the charter of Rhuddlan (1277), which in turn was based upon the charters of Hereford and Breteuil. Thus the burgesses of the second wave of town-building in Wales had broadly the same privileges as those of the first. They enjoyed a measure of self-government, legal and economic, which distanced them from the feudal world around them. As in the rest of Europe, it was intended that the boroughs should be the sole centres of trade; in Arfon, for example, the inhabitants could sell their goods only at Caernarfon, in the Saturday market there or in one of the town's five annual fairs. If they failed to develop a commercial function the boroughs had very little future, for the needs of the castle garrison were insufficient to ensure their prosperity. Within a generation of the Conquest, the major castles were manned by no more than a dozen soldiers and the smaller castles had ceased to be manned at all. As more towns had been established in Wales than the economy could sustain, the country would come to have a number of boroughs which were virtually defunct. The most prosperous boroughs were those established before 1150, a fact which may be overlooked if attention is concentrated upon the activities of Edward I. By 1300, the towns of the southern coast, from Chepstow to Haverfordwest, were sizeable and thriving; there were 421 burgages in Cardiff, 360 in Haverfordwest and 281 in Carmarthen, compared with only 70 at Caernarfon and 112 at Conwy. It was the ports which succeeded best, and from the scanty evidence it is possible to trace the growth of sea-borne trade between Cardiff and Bristol, Carmarthen and Bordeaux, Haverfordwest and Ireland.

Although they were not as substantial as the towns of the southern coast, the northern boroughs established by Edward I had a central role in the new order. They were not as new as is sometimes suggested: there had been a trading post at Caernarfon in the time of the princes, Dafydd had had a quasi-urban centre at Denbigh and the origins of Pwllheli and Nefyn were wholly Welsh. Pecham had recommended urban life as a way of civilizing the Welsh people, but in establishing towns Edward was not aiming to create a class of Welsh burgesses. There were elements of such a class – 43 per cent of the burgages of Aberystwyth were in Welsh hands in 1307 and 60 per cent of the burgesses of Rhuthun had Welsh names in 1346 – but in Gwynedd Uwch Conwy, the heart of Welsh resistance, the boroughs of Conwy, Caernarfon and Beaumaris were intended to be wholly alien colonies. The greater part of their inhabitants were English – from the border counties in the main – but they also included colonists from Ireland, Gascony and Savoy. Around the three towns, an area amounting in all to fifteen hundred hectares was cleared of its Welsh population in order to establish fields for the crops and livestock of the burgesses. The colonists were granted land rent-free for ten years and were given an assurance that if they came before the courts their trial would be in English before an English jury.

Attempts were also made to establish rural colonies, and in the Vale of Clwyd in particular a number of Welsh families were evicted to make room for newcomers, among them the cook of the earl of Lincoln, who was granted thirty-four hectares of land at Galltfaenan.

As in the Englishries created two hundred years earlier, the colonists were subject to courts, officials and taxation systems different from those of the native population. Nevertheless, the extent of the English influx should not be exaggerated; in the case of the rural population, they represented only one in five in north-east Gwent, one in ten in the eastern part of the lordship of Brecon and one in fifteen in Tegeingl.

The rural colonization which followed the wars of Edward I was less extensive than that of the Normans, and the incomers were more successfully assimilated than were those who had earlier colonized Pembroke and the Vale of Glamorgan. Many of the Edwardian rural settlers stayed only briefly – the earl of Lincoln's cook had abandoned Galltfaenan by 1290; this was also the case in the new boroughs, where no more than half the incomers proved to be permanent settlers. Nevertheless, they were numerous enough to be the object of the hatred of the Welsh, and the boroughs would be the primary target of any Welsh uprising. Caernarfon was burned during the rising of 1294, and as a result the anti-Welsh sentiments of the burgesses were intensified. They saw themselves as 'the king's friends' and as the chief guarantors of the permanence of the new order. For almost a quarter of a millennium, they gave expression to that mixture of arrogance and paranoia which is characteristic of privileged racial minorities.

The Edwardian colonization was less merciless as well as being less extensive than that of the Normans. When the Englishries of Pembroke and Glamorgan were created it is probable that no consideration was given to the dispossessed natives, but arrangements were made to relocate those made homeless in the wake of Edward's victory. The inhabitants of Llan-faes were moved to Newborough, those of Aberystwyth to Nantyrarian and those of Lleweni to Tre-prys, and although they received a poor bargain (Tre-prys is near the summit of Mynydd Hiraethog) the relocation did fulfil Edward's intention of compensating those who suffered as a result of his policies. He followed the same principle in his dealings with the Church. Much Church property was destroyed during the war of 1282–3, and by 1285 the king had paid almost £2,300 to indemnify a total of 107 churches and individuals, the compensation ranging from the £250 received by the bishop of Bangor to the 6s. 8d. received by the rector of Llanbeblig. The payments were made at the request of Archbishop

Pecham, who, although contemptuous of the Welsh as a people, was anxious to protect the interests of the Welsh Church and to foster the allegiance of the Welsh clergy to Canterbury. During 1284, Pecham made a thorough investigation of the religious institutions of Wales. He visited the four bishoprics and published a series of edicts for their reform; he insisted upon obedience to the latest decrees of the Church, rebuked clergy and monks for their low morals and lack of zeal, and condemned those who excited the people by glorifying the ancestry of the Welsh (the bards, no doubt).

In many respects, the Conquest did not prove prejudicial to the Welsh Church; indeed, the half century after 1282 is considered to be something of a golden age in its history. It was served by bishops of ability and energy, most of them Welshmen or men with Welsh connections. A body of Welsh religious literature was created, the continuation of a tradition of writing which had been established before the Conquest. The devotional prose and poetry in *The White Book of Rhydderch* and *The Book of the Anchorite* are proof that the Welsh language, like the other major literary languages of Europe, was becoming 'one of the dialects of the revelation of God'. At the same time, the work of consolidating the framework of the Church was continuing; it appears that it was the decades around 1300 which saw the completion of the division of Wales into parishes, and a number of notable religious buildings in the Decorated style were erected, the choir of St David's Cathedral among them. In the generation after 1282, there is hardly any evidence suggesting that Welsh clerics were critical of the system imposed upon their country, but implicit in the Conquest were factors which could cause bitterness among them. By the later years of the reign of Edward I, the Welsh Church in its entirety was under the control of the crown of England and it was tempting to exploit it in the interests of the English state. In 1294, it was taxed for the first time, and thereafter Welsh ecclesiastics would have to become accustomed to frequent and heavy impositions. More threatening was the tendency of the king to use the richer livings to reward his officials, almost all of whom were clerics. This practice increased rapidly under Edward's successors, partly in order to compete with Rome's claim that any living could be filled through Papal provision. The same practice was followed in England, but as the appointees in both countries were almost always Englishmen, state exploitation of livings had racial implications in Wales.

Edward's destruction of Llywelyn's Principality was not the only factor which gave the king full control over the Welsh Church. He also succeeded in greatly restricting the ability of the Marcher Lords to exploit the Church. Their ability to do so had deep roots. The lords of Glamorgan enjoyed at least as much influence over the diocese of Llandaf as had the house of Aberffraw over the diocese of Bangor, and in all the chief lordships the lord seized diocesan property when a bishopric was vacant. Llandaf lacked a bishop from 1287 to 1295; in accordance with custom, Gilbert de Clare, lord of Glamorgan, took most of the lands of the diocese into his own hands and intervened in the appointment of diocesan officials. Edward was not prepared to countenance his activities and after considerable controversy Clare acknowledged in 1295 that the authority of the lord of Glamorgan over the diocese of Llandaf would cease after his lifetime. The king was equally determined to resist the claims of other Marcher Lords and his resistance led to a victory which proved to be final.

The conflict over Church property was part of a wider campaign to curb the powers of the Marcher Lords. As a result of the Conquest, the lords had lost their *raison d'être*, for as inner Wales would henceforth be under the control of the English crown the need for a *cordon sanitaire* along the borders of Wales had vanished. At the same time, the destruction of the Principality strengthened the position of the Marcher Lords, for they were no longer threatened by the forces of the princes. Their power was also enhanced by their successful efforts to convert vague lordship over men into precise lordship over land, exactly as Llywelyn I and Llywelyn II had done in the Principality. That policy was at its most successful in the Clare lordships, where the lord's income rose from £850 in 1266 to £2,500 in 1317, but the results of the endeavours of Bohun, Fitzalan and Mortimer were almost as striking. The great men of the March were Edward's leading vassals – seven of his ten earls had territories there – and their pride and presumption were legendary. 'In the parts of the March where he now resided,' it was said of John Fitzalan, 'he was obliged to do nothing at the king's mandate and nothing would he do,' and in Glamorgan the king was greeted by Gilbert de Clare in 1284 as a fellow sovereign rather than as suzerain.

Edward was a masterful man. He insisted that his authority should be recognized in its fullness, and he had greater interests in Wales than had any of his predecessors among the kings of England. Yet, as he was pedantically legalistic, he lacked a pretext for abolishing the privileges of the Marcher Lords; furthermore, he did not have the resources which would have been needed if he were to crush the most powerful men of his kingdom. Nevertheless, he seized every opportunity to undermine the unique status of the Marcher Lords; against all precedents, he taxed them and undertook direct military recruitment within them; he restored Wigmore, which had been drawn into the March by the Mortimer family, to the administration of Shropshire, and he urged the inhabitants of Gower to demand a charter of rights from their lord. Above all, he sought to restrain the aggression of the Marcher Lords. In 1292, when a dispute between Bohun and Clare over the boundary separating Glamorgan from Brecon had developed into open warfare, he summoned both to appear before his council at Abergavenny; they were imprisoned and their lordships were distrained. Despite Edward's efforts, the Marcher Lords did not cease to engage in private warfare, and for generations to come the inhabitants of Wales would be burdened and the politics of the kingdom of England would be bedevilled by the conflicts which would arise among them.

The explosive nature of the March was consistent with its origins. From the beginning, the great men of *Marchia Wallie* had been lords of war above all else. That was equally true of the rulers of *Pura Wallia*; there, as Giraldus Cambrensis noted, the constant necessity to be ready to resist the invader had caused the Welsh to develop strong military traditions. After the Conquest, *Pura Wallia* had a reservoir of experienced warriors lacking an indigenous cause for which to fight, a reservoir ideal for a war-state such as the kingdom of England. Service in the king of England's armies, a tradition which already existed before the Conquest, expanded rapidly thereafter. In the century and a half after 1282, recruitment by the forces of the crown was as important to the Welsh as it would be to the Scottish Highlanders after 1745. In both cases, the central power could take advantage of the periods of idleness which are characteristic of quasi-pastoral societies. Soldiers (and horses) from Wales played a key role in the attempts of the kings of England to conquer Scotland and in their multifarious campaigns in mainland Europe. At Falkirk in 1298 – a battle which proved the superiority of the long bow, the speciality of the men of Glamorgan – 10,500 of Edward's 12,500 infantrymen came from Wales and a third of the horses had been bred in Powys. There were 5,000 Welshmen in Edward II's army at Bannockburn in 1314, and 6,200 served in the Scottish campaign of 1322. The distinctiveness of the customs and the clothing of the Welsh was the subject of comment in Flanders, where 5,300 of them served in Edward I's campaign of 1297. There were 4,000 Welsh soldiers in Gascony in 1326, and 5,000 at the battle of Crécy in 1346; at Crécy, they were dressed in green and white, perhaps the first national uniform in the history of European warfare. The few pence a day earned by the soldiers were important to the Welsh economy; the many wanderings of the Welsh recruits enriched the culture of Wales and their valour gave rise to new tales of heroism.

The Welsh were troublesome soldiers; they tended to get drunk and to pillage and vandalize, and as they were accustomed to the savagery of racial conflict they were reluctant to conform to the conventions of dynastic warfare; they killed their prisoners instead of offering them for ransom. They were prone to desert, and in August 1294 a large number of them refused to obey the order to embark for France. This was the spark which ignited the revolt of 1294, the most serious challenge to royal authority in Wales until the rising of Owain Glyn Dŵr. It was led by members of the old Welsh royal houses. The most prominent of the leaders – Madog ap Llywelyn, the son of the last of the lords of Meirionnydd and a descendant of Owain Gwynedd – assumed the title of prince of Wales. The Edwardian settlement had created much racial bitterness among the Welsh; a few months before the revolt began, Iorwerth ap Cynwrig of Llannerch near Denbigh prophesied that the English would soon hear 'such rumours that they will no longer wish to come to Wales'. The Welsh were also angered by the tax of 1292, which was heavier than that levied in England; it was intended to raise £10,000 and officials were in the process of collecting it when the rising began. By October 1284, the whole of Gwynedd except for a few castles was in the hands of the insurgents, and there was much unrest in the counties of Flint and Cardigan and in the lordships of Brecon and Glamorgan. Edward led an army of 35,000 men to subdue the Welsh. He was at Conwy by Christmas 1294 and the revolt came to an end when Madog ap Llywelyn was defeated at Maes Maidog in Caereinion on 5 March 1295. Five days later five hundred Welshmen were slaughtered in their sleep.

Despite the revolt, there is no lack of evidence of the readiness of elements within Welsh society to come to terms with the new order – indeed, to cooperate enthusiastically with it. Not everyone, even in Gwynedd, had warmly endorsed Llywelyn's policies. The descendants of Ednyfed Fychan, for example, were conspicuously absent from the ranks of the prince's supporters in 1282. In 1283, ten of the leading men of Gwynedd hastened to present Edward I with the chief treasure of the house of Aberffraw – a fragment of the true cross – and they and their kind were eager for patronage and office at the hand of their new master. In some of the Marcher Lordships – those of Bohun, Mortimer and Marshal in particular – there was already a tradition of serving the conquerors, and they saw merit in it, for as the men of the lord of Pembroke put it in 1244: 'In our part of Wales it is not easy to govern the Welsh except through one of their own race.' It was unusual, however, for a Welshman to be appointed to high office; in the century after the Conquest, no Welshman was appointed to the stewardship of the lordship of Ruthun nor to that of Bromfield and Yale, and such appointments were made only once in Glamorgan and in Denbigh and only twice in Brecon.

The situation was similar in the royal counties. After the revolt of 1294, it appears that an ordinance was published prohibiting the appointment of Welshmen to public positions and, although adherence to it was not absolute, very few Welshmen received anything beyond the most modest offices in the generation after the Conquest. The minor officers of the commotes were Welsh almost without exception, but the chief administrators were foreigners, often men who had had experience of government in others of the king's dominions, Gascony and the Channel Islands in particular. An occasional Welshman had slunk into the office of sheriff by 1308, much to the distress of the chamberlain of the north. He received a promise that Welshmen would not be appointed if there were Englishmen available and it appears that the promise was kept, for sixty-six of the eighty-four sheriffs appointed to the three northern and two southern counties between 1284 and 1348 bore English names. Nevertheless, Welsh names appear fairly frequently in lists of the middle-range officials; Ieuan ap Morgan, for example, was seneschal of Cardiganshire in 1305 and Adda ap Llywelyn was deputy steward of that county in 1347. Perhaps they felt that by accepting such offices they would be able to be of assistance to their fellow-Welshmen, for it was noted that Ieuan did not 'over-burden the Welshries'; however, to that lovable patriot, Carnhuanawc, the readiness of Welshmen to accept office only 'tended to consolidate alien authority over [Wales] and to ease the way towards its total subjugation'. Adda was dismissed because he was a Welshman, but it would appear that such dismissals occurred only during periods of severe tension.

Edward I and his successors sought to steer a middle course between the anti-Welsh fanaticism of the English colonists and the royal desire to employ anyone who could be of use to the crown. They were particularly anxious to reward those Welshmen who laboured to recruit soldiers for them – and such men had to be Welsh, for recruits were unwilling to serve under anyone except a Welshman, and a Welshman of distinguished lineage at that. Chief among the recruiters were the descendants of Ednyfed Fychan. Gruffudd Llwyd of Tregarnedd, Anglesey, the grandson of Ednyfed, was the leading recruiter of Welsh forces between 1279 and 1314, and Rhys ap Gruffudd of Llansadwrn, the son of Gruffudd's nephew, was diligent in the same activity from 1310 until 1341. These were the men who penetrated the centres of royal power in Wales as deputies of the leading officials, and they also amassed a number of more modest offices. They gathered around them men who were equally eager to benefit from the patronage of the king, and by 1300 it is possible to detect the existence of an embryonic Welsh official class.

The desire to create a focus of allegiance for this class was probably among Edward I's motives for granting the title of prince of Wales to his heir, Edward, in 1301. The prince, a youth of seventeen, was the son who had been born to the queen at Caernarfon in 1284; the legend that he was presented to the Welsh people as a baby was not recorded until 1584 and had his elder brother, Alphonso, survived his boyhood, he would probably have been the first English prince of Wales. The ceremony of 1301 was held at Lincoln, where Edward was invested with all the territories of the crown in Wales. He was also granted the allegiance of those barons holding lordships which had been in the possession of Llywelyn II, an indication that Edward's Principality was seen, not as a new creation, but rather as the re-establishment of the Principality created by Llywelyn in 1267. The income of the Principality – it was worth about £4,000 a year – was granted to the prince, who was also invested with the earldom of Chester and the dukedom of Aquitaine. His Principality was intended to provide him not only with an income but also with a sphere of activity, and until the long hiatus in the history of the title which began in 1509 it would not be an empty honour. The investiture of 1301 proves that Edward I was prepared to grant Wales some measure of distinctiveness, and this was done by grafting upon Llywelyn's dream an institution which was meaningful to those Welshmen who sought opportunities for themselves under the new order. Thus, the identity of Wales received expression, at least as a heraldic image, on the same grounds as Dauphiné, Asturias, the Lordship of the Isles and others of the peripheral regions of the kingdoms of Europe.

During his brief period as prince, Edward of Caernarfon won the affection of the Welsh. In 1305, for example, he examined with sympathy the petitions they had presented to him. In the Later Middle Ages, such petitions were numerous. They emanated from the community of the Welsh of the north and of the south, and sometimes from both together – *la communauté de Galeys*. The attitude of the Welsh towards Edward II was an important factor in his unhappy reign (1307–27). Those years were a period of almost continuous conflict between the king and his barons, almost all of whom had territories in the March. The victory of the Scots at Bannockburn (1314) was a severe blow to Edward's authority. Gilbert de Clare, lord of Glamorgan, the last of the male line of his family, was killed in the battle, a misfortune which cast a deep shadow over the March. Glamorgan passed into the hands of royal officials. Chief among them was Payne de Turberville of Coety, who had won the enmity of the Welsh by advocating their expulsion from his lordship. Ever since the coming of the Normans, there had been instability in northern Glamorgan, for the alien settlement in the Vale had sundered the linkages between upland and lowland. Matters worsened as a result of the poor harvests of the years 1314–18, the prelude to the severe distress which the Welsh, like the other peoples of Europe, would suffer in the following decades. In February 1316, Llywelyn Bren, the great-grandson of Ifor Bach, rose in revolt. Although the insurrection lasted for only a few weeks, it spread to nearly all the Welshries of Glamorgan. Llywelyn Bren was a man of culture; he owned a copy of the French poem *Roman de la Rose* and four Welsh books – unnamed alas – and he showed great dignity when surrendering to Bohun, lord of Brecon. Llywelyn was executed at Cardiff in 1317 and a fine of £2,330 was imposed upon the Welsh of Glamorgan.

It was Hugh Despenser, the brother-in-law of Gilbert de Clare and the new lord of Glamorgan, who insisted upon the execution of Llywelyn Bren. By 1318, Despenser was the leading supporter of the king's campaign against the Lords of the Ordinance, the reform party which was seeking to restrict the powers of the crown. With the king's support, Despenser created an extensive domain for himself in southern Wales; his activities sparked off a war in the March in 1320 and led to Despenser's exile in 1321.

While the inhabitants of the March were suffering from the ambition of Despenser, those of the Principality were burdened by the oppressive rule of Roger Mortimer of Chirk, justice at Caernarfon and Carmarthen for most of the period 1308–22. The Welsh set out their complaints against Mortimer in a series of petitions and in 1316, eight days after the beginning of the revolt of Llywelyn Bren, the petitions received the sympathetic consideration of Edward II. His desire to placate the Welsh was strengthened by the fear that the victory of Robert Bruce at Bannockburn would encourage the Welsh to defy the English crown. There was concern that Bruce, who had sent an army to Ireland in 1315 under the leadership of his brother Edward, would extend his activities to Wales. Edward Bruce, who was crowned king of Ireland in 1316, sought to establish a Celtic alliance against England. In that year, he wrote a letter to Gruffudd Llwyd which reflected something of the attitude of the author of *Armes Prydein*. There is at least a suggestion that Gruffudd responded positively to Edward Bruce's letter, although if he did so he was probably motivated by hatred of Mortimer rather than by hostility towards the king of England. Gruffudd was imprisoned from 1316 to 1318, and in 1322 he led an armed attack which was once considered to be a Welsh revolt. It is now believed that it was an important contribution to the success of the king in defeating the reform party, a party which included almost all the Marcher Lords. Following that success, the earl of Lancaster, lord of Denbigh and leader of the reform party, was executed, Roger Mortimer of Chirk and his nephew, Roger Mortimer of Wigmore, were imprisoned and the influence of the Despensers was restored. A parliament was held at York in 1322. It included forty-eight representatives from Wales, and its members endorsed an extreme interpretation of the authority of the crown.

From 1322 to 1326, power in the kingdom of England lay in the hands of Hugh Despenser and his father, another Hugh, and the reforms they undertook have earned the praise of historians. They were monstrously acquisitive, however; in Wales, Hugh the Younger linked lordship with lordship until his lands extended from Pembroke to Chepstow. In 1323, Roger Mortimer of Wigmore succeeded in escaping from prison; fleeing to France, he became the lover of Isabella, the wife of Edward II, who was in Paris on a mission for her husband. They were agreed upon their enmity towards the Despensers, and increasingly towards the king himself. They invaded England on 24 September 1326 and the king retreated before them to Wales. He was seized on 16 December, probably at Pen-rhys in the Rhondda. The two Despensers were executed, and in January 1327 the deposition of the king was announced in parliament, an assembly which included twenty-four members from Wales. Edward was imprisoned at Berkeley Castle on the banks of the Severn. Rhys ap Gruffudd failed in his attempt to free him and he was murdered at Berkeley in September 1327.

The king was buried at the monastery of St Peters, Gloucester, and his tomb became a place of pilgrimage for his supporters – the Welsh in particular. The first English prince of Wales's only mourners were the natives of the country of his birth, and the chronicler Walsingham noted 'the remarkable way in which he was revered by the Welsh'. As Edward's son, the new king, Edward III, was only fourteen years of age (he had not been granted the title of prince of Wales), the government was controlled from 1327 to 1330 by Roger Mortimer. Mortimer concentrated, as had Hugh Despenser, upon consolidating his power in Wales. He appointed himself justice of the Principality and made himself master of a chain of lordships extending from Denbigh to Pembroke. In 1328, he took the title of earl of March, thus recognizing that *Marchia Wallie* was the foundation of his power. His supremacy was brief. In 1330 he was hanged and his property was confiscated. His son Roger was not permitted to take possession of his ancestral lands until 1354, when the Mortimers once again became holders of more territories in Wales than any other of the Marcher Lords. Roger's son, Edmund, married Philippa, the heiress of Lionel, the second son of Edward III, a marriage from which the royal house of York was to descend. The Mortimers could, therefore, boast that they did not spring from kings; rather did kings spring from them.

With his extensive territories in the March and his offices in the Principality, Roger Mortimer's position in Wales was more powerful than that of any of the native Welsh princes. Edward, the Black Prince, the eldest son of Edward III, was invested with the Principality in 1343 and his councillors sought to re-create the supremacy once enjoyed by Roger Mortimer. In doing so, they followed the example of Llywelyn II by seeking to make the lords of Wales the prince of Wales's vassals. They insisted that the prince was the suzerain of the lords of Denbigh and of Bromfield and Yale, they interfered in the affairs of the lordship of Brecon, they attempted to make Gower dependent upon the princely administration at Carmarthen, they claimed that the prince had essentially royal powers over the Welsh bishoprics and they sought to make his council an effective instrument for the exploitation of the military and financial resources of Wales – particularly in order to promote Edward's campaigns in Aquitaine, his other Principality. Edward III was not prepared to allow his son to enjoy full regal rights over the whole of Wales, and in 1354 it was determined that the Marcher Lords owed allegiance directly to the crown. After the death of the Black Prince in 1376, his son, Richard of Bordeaux, was invested with the Principality; his powers were carefully defined and therefore the division between the March and the Principality was perpetuated, bringing to an end a development which could have given a measure of unity to the administration of Wales.

Edward's early years as prince coincided with another wave of unrest among the Welsh. The English were puzzled by the propensity of the Welsh to revolt – they must, it was argued, be 'light-headed' – but disaffection in Wales aroused deep fears among them. 'At one time,' wrote Edward II's biographer, 'the Welsh were noble and had sovereignty over the whole of England . . . and according to the sayings of the prophet Merlin they will one day repossess England. Thus the Welsh frequently revolt in the hope of fulfilling the prophecy; but as they know not the hour, they are often deceived and their labour is in vain.' These myths were sustained by the tradition of vaticinatory verse which had a new lease of life after the Conquest, the work of those poets and seers who had been condemned by Pecham in 1284 and who had been perceived as a threat by the advisers of Edward I in 1307.

The clergy and the monks were also concerned to sustain the identity of the Welsh, and the English authorities sought to uproot Cistercian communities with strong Welsh connections, a task made easier after the severance of the links with Cîteaux as a result of the Hundred Years' War with France. The composers of vaticinatory verse received the patronage of some of the members of the class of Welsh officials. As those officials were not full citizens of the state they served, they may on occasion have been ambiguous in their attitude towards it; there is at least a suggestion of such ambiguity in the career of Gruffudd Llwyd. At the same time, the pride of the English and their consciousness of their identity were strengthened by the long war with France which began in 1337; the English language came to be seen as the symbol of Englishness and Edward III addressed parliament in English in 1362, the first time since 1066 for a king of England to use the language in public.

The chauvinism of the English and the 'light-headedness' of the Welsh became apparent in the conflict which broke out in several parts of Wales in the 1340s. In 1344, the English of Rhuddlan, fearing the hostility of the local Welsh population, retreated to the safety of their borough, and Henry de Shaldeforde, one of the attorneys of the Black Prince, was murdered on St Valentine's Day 1345 as he was travelling to Caernarfon. The malcontents included men of substance, lay and ecclesiastical. Chief among them were Tudur and Hywel of Penmynydd, Anglesey; they were the sons of Goronwy ap Tudur, a cousin of Gruffudd Llwyd and the representative of the senior line of the stock of Ednyfed Fychan. The causes of the unrest were probably personal and social, but to the English burgesses in Wales it was proof of a Welsh plot to exterminate them and to undermine the authority of the English crown in Wales. 'If the Welsh have their way,' they declared, 'there will shortly be not a single Englishman alive in Wales.' 'The Welsh,' stated the burgesses of Denbigh, 'are now more prone than ever to rise against the king – the English of Denbigh dare not leave the town.' 'The Welsh are becoming arrogant and cruel and malicious towards the English,' stated the burgesses of Caernarfon, while those of Rhuddlan declared that if firm action were not taken 'the English will be exterminated from the land'. Evidence of the fate of the malcontents is not available, but their activities and the reaction to them are a foretaste of what was to happen on a much larger scale half a century later during the rising of Owain Glyn Dŵr.

Despite the vaticinatory verse and the racial bitterness, there is evidence of considerable stability and tranquillity in Wales in the age of Edward II and Edward III. The purpose in drawing attention to the stability and to the unrest is not to present two models of Wales, the one contradicting the other; rather it is to emphasize the complexities and ambiguities which confronted a people who, although aware of their defeat and ready to nurse their wrath, were conscious of the need to make the best of the world as it was. In reconciling the two attitudes, the myths undoubtedly had a role to play; they were a cry against the extinction of identity and against the tyranny of fact. This duality manifests itself particularly in the literature of the period; on the one hand there is the underground current of prophetic verse, and on the other the tradition of the 'recognized' poets which offers a very different portrayal of Welsh society.

In 1340, that tradition was on the threshold of the most glorious period in its history. In the generation immediately following the Conquest, the bardic order fell into decay, but in the succeeding generation 'the gentlemen who sprang from the blood of the princes took unto themselves the practitioners of the poetic arts', and under the patronage of *uchelwyr* (gentry) such as Gruffudd Llwyd Welsh literature was given a new lease of life. In about 1325 Einion Offeiriad wrote his *Grammar* as a guide for the poets, a work which was firmly rooted in the medieval tradition of rhetoric. At the same time Wales received new influences from France: it has already been noted that Llywelyn Bren had a copy of *Roman de la Rose*; in the towns, particularly in the south, the Welsh were in daily association with Francophones, and Welsh-speakers were so numerous in Bordeaux that the Pope was moved to question the city's archbishop in 1366 as to the ability of a candidate for the see of Bangor to preach in Welsh. These developments – together with his own innate genius – gave birth to the superb work of Dafydd ap Gwilym, although his 'passionate awareness of the validity of sensuous experience' would hardly have won the approval of that zealous cleric, Einion Offeiriad. Dafydd was in the flower of his manhood between 1340 and 1360, but his poems contain virtually no suggestion of racial tension or national bitterness. Born into the class of Welsh officials, he was the great-grandson of the castellan of Cardigan, the nephew of the castellan of Newcastle Emlyn and the son of a cousin of Gruffudd Llwyd. He wandered, as did all the poets, to every part of Wales, and on the banks of the Rheidol, the Usk, the Teifi and the Dee he sang the praises of nature, women and life.

Dafydd ap Gwilym embraced life in all its fullness, aware, as everyone was in the Middle Ages, that it is a brief and fragile thing – it is unlikely that he survived his forties. But he did not, as did mány of his contemporaries, dwell upon the horrors of death and the tortures of hell. He made no mention of the central happening of his age – the Black Death, the greatest tragedy to strike western Europe in historic times. The plague which caused it originated in the depths of Asia; it was sowing the seeds of mortality in the Crimea at the beginning of 1347 and in Sicily by the end of the year. It had reached Dorset by August 1348 and Carmarthen and Abergavenny by March 1349. There are two varieties of the plague – the pneumonic and the bubonic; the one is caught through breathing and the other through being bitten by the fleas of the black rat. Those struck by the plague suffered from fever and vomiting, and until the coming of modern medicine most of those affected died within a few days. Between 1347 and 1350, the Black Death killed about a third of the inhabitants of the Old World – twenty-five million people in Europe alone – and it struck again and again, especially in 1361 and 1369.

Evidence of the course of the plague in Wales is scarce. There is some suggestion that it was less severe in the upland regions; nevertheless, the poet Ieuan Gethin of northern Glamorgan noted that it had carried off all his sons. In 1349, officials were unable to collect more than a third of the rents of the lordship of Abergavenny. In Rhuthun, the only lordship whose court rolls have survived, courts in that year could be held only intermittently. In 1349–50, the plague probably killed about a quarter of the inhabitants of Wales. It is likely that the *taeogion* (villeins) suffered disproportionately, for they were less well nourished and were at their most numerous in the lowlands.

The tribulations of 1348–9 were the climax of decades of adversity. The economic decline so evident in the years after 1300 has been attributed to soil exhaustion, although the theory is not universally accepted. The growth in population characteristic of the High Middle Ages led, it has been alleged, to an expansion in the amount of land under the plough and to a decrease in stock-raising. As less manure was available, the fertility of the soil declined. If the theory is true, it would probably be relevant to such areas as Abergavenny and Rhuthun, but it would hardly explain the distress of the upland regions with their pastoral agriculture. In those regions, diseases among animals, which were particularly severe in 1315, 1348 and 1363, would have had more impact. Assuming that the Welsh

economy was in decline long before 1349, it is likely that the population of Wales was falling even before the coming of the plague. The
country may well have had at least three hundred thousand inhabitants
in 1300; it is doubtful whether it had as many as two hundred
thousand in 1400.

Similar or worse afflictions affected the rest of Europe, giving rise
to morbid obsessions and millenarian hopes. All over the continent,
the pattern of land tenure was disrupted, a matter of central importance
in a largely agricultural economy. It was especially central to the
Welsh, for tenure lay at the heart of the 'Conflict of Laws', one of the
basic themes of the history of medieval Wales. After the Conquest,
the Welsh had been allowed (or had been obliged) to continue to use
the Law of Wales in matters relating to land tenure. This was the case
in the March as well as in the Principality, for the Marcher Lords, like
the king, could exploit the Law of Hywel for their own ends. It
permitted them to claim a variety of payments: an *ebidew* on the death
of a tenant, an *amobr* on the marriage of a tenant's daughter, a mise
when the lord came into his inheritance, a share in the *galanas* (blood-
fine) and many a *cymhortha* (obligatory gift). Above all, they could
take advantage of the *gwely* (clan land) system; as that system did not
allow women to inherit land, the land of a man without male heirs
escheated to his lord. Escheat was central to the ability of the lord to
gain full possession of land over which he had previously enjoyed
only vague rights. Furthermore, the holder of *gwely* land could not
sell it, and anyone who was of the 'condition of a Welshman' could
not hold land in accordance with English tenure. In the conservative
communities of the south, these restrictions counted for little compared
with the security which came from adhering to native traditions, and
their inhabitants drew up several petitions in favour of the maintenance
of the Law of Hywel. In Gwynedd, however, where the privileges
which the Law of England bestowed upon the English burgesses were
a constant affront to the more ambitious of the Welsh, and where the
Law of Hywel had already been modified in the age of Llywelyn I
and Llywelyn II, there was the desire to abandon native law and
custom. This was the brunt of the petitions of the men of Gwynedd in
1305, 1315, 1321 and 1330. They were largely ignored and the Law of
Hywel was fossilized for the benefit of the English authorities; it is
fitting that the protests against that fossilization came from the men of
Gwynedd, the prime movers in the reform of the Law of Wales.

The Gwynedd petitions can be interpreted as pleas for release from the restrictions of the *gwely* system. *Cyfran*, the custom of dividing land equally among male heirs, was the essence of that system. In about 1600, John Wynn of Gwedir described *cyfran* as the 'curse of Wales' but, as he was the owner of a large estate which would not have come into existence had his ancestors not abandoned the custom, the only possible way of commenting upon his condemnation of *cyfran* is to quote the immortal words of Mandy Rice-Davies: 'He would, wouldn't he.' *Cyfran* could certainly lead to the creation of a host of scattered strips of land, too small to be economically viable. This happened in an extreme form in the case of Iorwerth ap Cadwgan, who flourished around 1220; so prolific were his progeny that by 1313 his land was shared among twenty-seven of his descendants. Nevertheless, no basic problem was solved by abandoning *cyfran* and adopting the English system of making the eldest son the sole heir. The consequence of the change would be to turn communities of fairly poor small landowners into communities with a few wealthy estate owners and a large landless proletariat. The majority of the members of the *gwelyau* could hardly have wished for that, and the petitions of the men of Gwynedd were probably inspired by the select few who yearned for opportunities to accumulate landed property. Even under the Law of Wales, they were not wholly bereft of such opportunities, and in the century after 1350 the *gwely* system collapsed under the pressure of native venturers and wealthy English burgesses and was replaced by consolidated farms and expanding landed estates.

The Black Death was among the most important factors contributing to the decline of the *gwely* system. In one respect, admittedly, the plague retarded that decline, for the high death rate among the members of the *gwelyau* lessened the need to divide the property of many a *priodor* (holder of clan lands). John Wynn was grateful for 'God's mercie and goodness' in killing so many of the relations of his forefathers. Nevertheless, escheats increased dramatically after 1349. Therefore, ample opportunities arose for energetic men to lease land free from the restrictions of the *gwely* system. Furthermore, the slump in the market and the labour shortages created by the high death rate among the *taeogion* (villeins) caused the Marcher Lords and the monastic houses to abandon the practice of direct farming of their demesne lands, a practice which was already in decline before 1349. The lands were offered on lease, providing golden opportunities for ambitious members of the class of *bonheddwyr*. By 1360, some of the *taeogdrefi* (villein townships) were virtually uninhabited. The shrinkage in the number of *taeogion* was not accompanied by a corresponding lightening of the burden of taxation; as the 'exaccions in those days [were] soe manyfould', as John Wynn put it, many of the *taeogion* fled to England, where they could command good wages for their services. The *taeogdrefi* represented another reservoir of land to exploit; in Eifionydd, where the nucleus of the estate which would later be held by the Barons Harlech was being formed, the ancestors of the Ormsby-Gores were busily turning the scattered strips of the villein holdings into consolidated farms.

It was rare for a family to be able to establish an estate solely through the profits of farming. Other sources of wealth were necessary. The availability of land was highly attractive to the merchants of the boroughs; by 1420, the Bolde family of Conwy had amassed 800 hectares in Arllechwedd, land which later became part of the Bulkeley family's estate in Caernarfonshire. The profits of office were also useful, as was booty from the campaigns in France. Yet the collapse of the *gwely* system should not be antedated. *Gwely* land was still common over much of Wales in 1400, although by then the factors which would overwhelm it by 1450 were clearly apparent.

The Welsh mortgage, or *tir prid*, was one of the most important of those factors. On average, a member of the *gwely* had three or four hectares of land; in addition, he had the use of the grazing land, woodland and waste land of his *gwely* and on the waste he could carve out new holdings for his sons. The stock of a typical *priodor* consisted of two oxen, three cows, six sheep, a pig and a few hens; his arable land produced wheat or oats, his garden yielded cabbage and leeks and he could supplement his family's diet with game. Like the vast majority of people throughout the ages until this century, he lived on the edge of penury; the death of the bread-winner, the costs of a funeral or a marriage, a poor harvest, destruction caused by war, diseases among stock or the burden of heavy taxes could all be disastrous to him. Although obligations of kinship were probably a safeguard against total destitution, it was tempting for a penurious *priodor* to seek to turn his land into money, and that was also a temptation for a man who owned a scattering of uneconomical strips. As the *priodor* could not sell his land, the Welsh mortgage was devised to enable him to use it to raise cash. Through *tir prid*, the *priodor* could mortgage his land, and after a mortgage had been renewed for sixteen years the land was considered to be in the absolute ownership of the mortgagee. The first record of *tir prid* dates from 1289, but it was rare before 1350; in the following century, its incidence increased rapidly and it has been claimed that it was the Welsh mortgage above all which caused the collapse of the *gwely* system.

Other factors were at work undermining the old order. Although the Black Death was a severe blow to the towns and to commercial and industrial ventures, Wales did not wholly lack such ventures. The Black Prince, as earl of Chester, received £5 a year from the lead mines of Tegeingl in the 1340s, and in the same region there were coalmines at Mostyn and iron works at Hope. The Clare family had collieries in Glamorgan and coal was also mined in the lordship of Pembroke. Despite the generally adverse conditions, there were occasional periods of prosperity, and the poverty of Wales has been exaggerated. In 1371, Richard Fitzalan, the most powerful of the lords of the northern March, had £1,900 in his coffers at Holt and Clun, and waggons full of treasure were conveyed to London from Roger Mortimer's lordships in 1387. A number of Welsh towns had a thriving commercial life which gave rise to wealthy burgher families; the Boldes of Conwy were not the only merchants to enter the land market, and in towns such as Caernarfon and Cardigan the ownership of burgages became concentrated in the hands of leading burgesses.

Some of the ports were particularly prosperous. In 1326, Carmarthen was recognized as a staple – a head port for export purposes, one of the fourteen in the territories of the king of England. In the 1350s, an average of 525 stones of fleeces was exported annually from the port, and in the 1390s the leading wool trader there was John Owen, who had a business worth £450 a year. Each year several ships entered the port of Carmarthen laden with the wines of Bordeaux. Doubtless some of the cargo reached the home of Llywelyn ap Gruffudd of Caeo, where sixteen tuns of wine a year were consumed in the 1390s; that represents fifty-five bottles of wine a day, Sundays included – it is hardly surprising that the poets praised the gentry.

Side by side with the growth of coastal trade, and of equal importance, was the spread of the fulling-mill, a development central to the expansion of the wool trade; indeed, it has been argued that the mills gave rise to an industrial revolution in the Later Middle Ages.

As in the later industrial revolution, the mills were dependent upon the power produced by rapidly flowing streams. Such streams were plentiful in the uplands, and 111 fulling-mills were established in Wales in the century after 1300. Initially, the main centre of the industry lay in the south-east, where the mills could rely upon the enterprise of the Bohun family – their flocks produced 18,500 fleeces in 1372 – and upon the thousands of sheep kept by monasteries such as Margam, Neath and Tintern. The fulling-mills spread to other parts of Wales, in particular to the north-east. A series of them came to be established on the river Ceiriog, and in 1380 there were thirty-six weavers in the lordship of Rhuthun. The prosperity of the woollen industry in places like the Ceiriog valley goes far to explain why the north-east was for centuries the most advanced part of Wales.

Nevertheless, in the half century after 1350, periods of prosperity were patchy and intermittent. With the plague striking again and again, and with constant pressure from the crown for resources to finance the war with France, that half century was bleak indeed. This is reflected in the Church, which experienced intellectual fatigue and economic depression. The tradition of writing religious literature declined, and with the last entry in *Brut y Tywysogyon* – that of 1332 – the monks ceased to be the chroniclers of the history of their people. The Papacy, which had been meaningful as a supranational power, became nothing more than another state, greedy for wealth and power. Its reputation suffered severely between 1379 and 1417, when there was one Pope in Rome and another at Avignon, both of them having partisans among the states of Europe. No new religious order arose to revitalize spiritual life and there was a dramatic fall in the number embracing monasticism. A document of about 1380 notes that the thirteen Cistercian monasteries of Wales had a total of only seventy-one monks. The friars – the members of the mendicant orders – were rather more lively. Yet their intellectual pre-eminence was fading and they were becoming subject to increasing criticism, as the bitter comments of Iolo Goch and the mocking poem of Dafydd ap Gwilym testify. Welsh literature was slipping out of the control of the Church; in Iolo Goch's remarkable poem to the labourer, the poor man of the soil is portrayed as the only true Christian, and it is suggested that the Day of Judgement will be the day when the lower orders will be avenged.

Such anti-clerical attitudes – and they were mild compared with those found elsewhere in Europe – gained sustenance from the attempts of ecclesiastics to safeguard their incomes in the face of depression. The monks became increasingly eager to lease their lands; they were thus abandoning any economic role that they might have had, and were therefore hastening the time when it would be doubted whether they had any role at all. They sought to restore their receipts by impropriating benefices in order to profit from parish tithes, an activity in which Margam was especially prominent. Many Welsh benefices were impropriated by monasteries in England and this caused considerable racial bitterness. The lower clergy were pushed into the ranks of the proletariat and some of them were prepared to countenance violent protest. The higher clergy sought to maintain their standard of living by holding more than one benefice, the resulting neglect of religious duties inciting further anti-clericalism.

Royal and princely policies deepened the crisis of the Welsh Church. The diocese of St David's, which had been substantially re-endowed by Edward I, was considered to be a worthy prize for one of the leading advisers of the crown, but the other three dioceses were pawns in contests between the Pope and the prince of Wales. Until about 1350, the Pope's appointments respected the sensibilities of the Welsh, in accordance with Gregory IX's ordinance of 1234, which laid down that the shepherd should be familiar with the language of his flock. This was not the case with the English authorities. Between 1347 and 1496, only two of the bishops of St David's had any connection with Wales. Most of the richer Welsh benefices came to be filled by Englishmen. An attempt was made to impose a non-Welsh bishop upon St Asaph in 1344 despite the stubborn resistance of the canons; the canons were supported by the Papacy, but after 1350 its enthusiasm for Welsh bishops waned. Thomas Ringstead was appointed bishop of Bangor by Innocent VI in 1357, Bangor's first non-Welsh bishop since Hervé; in his will, Ringstead left a hundred pounds to his successor on condition that he was not a Welshman. As a result of such appointments, the belief arose that able Welsh clerics could not expect promotion in their own country, and that the Welsh, as Hopcyn ap Thomas of Ynystawe put it, were 'suffering pain . . . and exile in their native land'.

Welshmen who had spent lengthy periods at the universities in the hope of climbing the ecclesiastical ladder were particularly conscious of the 'pain' and the 'exile'. The number of Welsh graduates increased rapidly after the Conquest. There is evidence of the presence of students from Wales at the universities of Paris, Lyon, Perugia, Bologna and Cambridge, but it was Oxford, where the registers record the attendance of 106 Welshmen between 1282 and 1400, which attracted the largest number. In that period, about one in forty of the students at Oxford was Welsh and the English students rioted against them in 1388 and 1389. Oxford was the cradle of Lollardy, a movement based upon the teachings of John Wycliffe (died 1384). Wycliffe challenged the Church's interpretation of the sacraments and the authority of the Pope, and the degree of support he received indicates the prevalence of anti-clerical and anti-papal sentiments. Two Welsh students at Oxford were excommunicated in 1386, but there is little direct evidence of Lollardy in Wales; attempts to show that some of the Welsh poets of the period were influenced by the movement are unconvincing, and there are no records of campaigns against the Lollards by the bishops of Wales, although as Welsh diocesan records have many gaps it cannot be stated as a fact that such campaigns did not occur. William Swinderby, a disciple of Wycliffe, sought to spread his ideas in the borderlands of Wales, retreating to the mountains in 1391. Swinderby's followers included the Welshman Gwallter Brut, who declared in 1391 that the Welsh had been chosen by God to overthrow the Pope, the Anti-Christ – an example of the millenarianism which was so marked a phenomenon in later medieval Wales.

Millenarianism, in a secular guise, drew sustenance from the career of Owain Lawgoch, the grandson of Rhodri, the brother of Llywelyn II. Owain was born in about 1330 on his father's estate at Tatsfield in Surrey, and in about 1350 he bound himself to serve the king of France. He constantly boasted that he was the true heir of Aberffraw – the French knew him as Yvain de Galles – and, as he was a talented soldier, he attracted other Welshmen to serve with him. Among the military leaders of France, Owain's reputation as a determined enemy of England was second only to that of du Guesclin, and so wide-ranging were his activities that he figures in the folk literature of France, Brittany, Switzerland, Lombardy and the Channel Islands. He won renown in Wales also; an unknown poet prophesied: '*Taleithiog frenin a ddaw,| A'i fonedd o Aberffraw*' (a territorial king will come, rooted in the stock of Aberffraw), and a native of Anglesey was condemned in 1370 for being in correspondence with him. In 1369,

Owain gathered a fleet at Harfleur to invade Wales, but his plans were frustrated by storms. The English authorities were seriously concerned and arrangements were made to fortify the castles. In 1372, Owain received 300,000 francs from the king of France to finance his campaign, and the prospects of a successful invasion of Wales rose following the destruction by the French of an English fleet near La Rochelle. Owain enjoyed considerable support in Paris, and there was probably a network of Welsh supporters preparing to welcome him to the land of his ancestors. But he sailed no further than Guernsey, perhaps because the readiness of the French to support him waned when they realized that their victory at La Rochelle offered them an excellent opportunity to drive the English out of large areas of Poitou and Gascony. In 1377, there were again fears among the English authorities that Owain would invade Wales, and it would appear that they plotted his assassination. The plot was carried out (by a Scot) in 1378, and Saint Léger on the banks of the Garonne (opposite Château Calon Segur – not a Welsh name, alas) became the burial place of the last of the male line of the house of Aberffraw.

Following the extinction of that line, the poets and the soothsayers sought another representative of the stock of Rhodri Mawr. There was a highly plausible candidate available in the person of Owain ap Gruffudd of Glyndyfrdwy and Sycharth, a man who combined the claims of Mathrafal and Dinefwr and who also had links with the house of Aberffraw. Owain Glyn Dŵr was born about 1354, and there were by the 1380s men in Wales who were grooming him for the role of the second Cadwaladr. *'Barwn, mi a wn dy ach'* (Baron, I know your lineage), sang Iolo Goch; Owain was *'yr edling o hen genhedlaeth'* (the atheling of an ancient lineage), and Gruffudd Llwyd (the poet, not the *condottiere*) composed a poem to him in about 1385 which explicitly linked him with the old prophecies. Furthermore, Owain, with an income of about £200 a year, was undoubtedly the wealthiest of the class of Welsh squires. Until his forties, his career, marked as it was by a readiness to cooperate with and to serve the English authorities, was typical of the careers of the members of that class. The Sycharth family lived under the shadow of the power of the Fitzalans, earls of Arundel; a document of 1370 notes a loan of £20 from Fitzalan to Owain's mother – *Elene, iadys le Femme Gruff. de Glendorde* – and it is likely that Owain had been sent to the earl's household as a youth. It was probably the influence of the Fitzalans which enabled him to spend some time at the Inns of Court and, when the English invaded Scotland in 1387, Owain was a member of Fitzalan's retinue.

By 1400, Owain Glyn Dŵr was a man with considerable experience of the ways of the world. Shakespeare provides a sympathetic portrayal of him as a man of breeding and education who was also in touch with mysterious powers. In about 1390 Iolo Goch composed his famous poem to Owain, and excavations at Sycharth have proved the accuracy of his description. The remains of the fishpond and the moat were discovered and the outlines of the 'fine wooden house on the top of the green hill' were traced. It was a building 13 metres by 5.5 and alongside it, in an outbuilding 3 metres by 3, the high level of phosphate in the soil suggests the existence of a urinal. It is difficult to get nearer than this to the poets and their patrons, for the phosphate provides evidence of the consequences of the much-praised hospitality of the lord of Sycharth.

The Glyn Dŵr rising began in September 1400. To some degree, it was a reaction to the events of the reign of Richard II. Richard, the son of the Black Prince, was ten years old when he inherited the throne of England on the death of Edward III in 1377. The next in succession to Richard was Roger Mortimer, earl of March, the grandson of Lionel, Edward III's second son. The most powerful man in the kingdom was Edward's third son, John of Gaunt, duke of Lancaster; he was the owner of vast estates, among them the lordships of Cydweli and Monmouth, while the lordship of Brecon was held by his son, Henry Bolingbroke, the husband of the co-heiress of the Bohun family. The early years of Richard's reign were a period of struggle between the barons for control of the young king, but in 1389 Richard seized the reins of government, and his leading vassals feared that he was intent upon creating an absolute monarchy. He won the support of the squires of Wales – men such as the sons of Tudur ap Goronwy of Anglesey; forces from Wales and from Cheshire wearing his badge, the white hart, were employed by Richard to browbeat the parliament of 1397.

In 1399, on the death of John of Gaunt, the king exiled Henry Bolingbroke and took possession of the property of the house of Lancaster, an act which triggered the crisis which terminated his reign. Bolingbroke landed on the coast of Yorkshire in July 1399 when Richard was campaigning in Ireland. Henry's intention was to claim his inheritance, but when he realized how fragile was the support for Richard he aimed for the throne. The king landed at Haverfordwest on 28 July 1399; after wandering disconsolately from castle to castle in Wales, he was seized by Bolingbroke's men on 19 August and was taken to Flint Castle. Dethroned in September, he was murdered at Pontefract Castle, probably in January 1400. Bolingbroke ascended the throne as Henry IV on 29 September 1399, and his son (later Henry V), who had been born at Monmouth in 1387, was invested with the Principality on 15 October 1399. To the gentry of Wales, with their strong dynastic traditions, the usurpation was a severe shock, and as in 1327 many of them felt that they no longer had an anchor in the kingdom of England.

Despite the impact of the usurpation, it would be superficial to view the Glyn Dŵr Rising as nothing more than turmoil caused by the removal of an English king. The half century after 1350 was marked by insurrections in many parts of Europe, and, although it would be unwise to seek a model which would include them all, the general crisis of the age had a bearing upon each one of them. To a great extent, the Glyn Dŵr rising was the protest of the poor. In 1401, the English parliament recorded that Welsh villeins working in England were returning home to take part in it, and it was accompanied by the extensive destruction which is considered to be a characteristic of peasant revolts. Its participants included *priodorion* distressed by the insecurity caused by the collapse of the *gwely* system, and lower clergy embittered by lack of opportunity and by the pretensions of their superiors. The millenarian tradition played a central role: it was widely believed that the world would come to an end in the year 1400; Glyn Dŵr referred to the ancient prophecies in 1401 when writing to the king of Scots, and he was encouraged by the comet which appeared in 1402; Gwallter Brut joined the insurgents; like Bruce at Bannockburn, the abbot of Llantarnam sought to inspire Glyn Dŵr's warriors with passages from the Book of the Maccabees, and the English parliament stressed the important part played in the rising by *divinations, messonges et excitations*.

But although many of the causes of the rising sprang from the depression and the tumult of the age, it would be perverse not to recognize that it was, above all, a national revolt. That was certainly the way it was interpreted by the House of Commons, and the anti-Welsh prejudice of the parliamentarians was fed by the xenophobia of the members from the English border counties. The first act of the insurrectionists was to proclaim Owain prince of Wales, proof that from the beginning their revolt was no mere local protest. In his letter to the king of Scots, Owain declared that he would deliver the Welsh 'from the oppression and captivity they had suffered since the time of Cadwaladr', and in 1401 he wrote to Henry Dunn of Cydweli stating that he had been appointed by God to release the Welsh from bondage to their English enemies. It was undoubtedly national motives which impelled the Welsh students at Oxford to abandon their studies in order to join him, and it was racial bitterness which caused the English boroughs to be the chief target of the insurgents. Owain attracted to his side the ablest Welshmen of the age, and the policies they prepared for him were distinctly national.

In addition to the mass support which Owain received from the *taeogion* (villeins) and the poorer *priodorion* and clergy, he also won the allegiance of most of the members of the lower ranks of the Welsh official class. The allegiance of the gentry was more divided. Much has been made of those Welsh squires – Dafydd Gam, for example, or Gwilym ap Gruffudd of Penrhyn – who either opposed him or who benefited from his eventual defeat, but the list of the leading Welshmen who supported him is impressive. It includes men who had served as sheriffs for the counties of Anglesey, Caernarfon, Cardigan, Carmarthen and Flint and, of the twelve Welshmen appointed to organize resistance to him in Flintshire, eleven went over to his side. The Cistercians, with their tradition of loyalty to Welsh rulers, provided Owain with some of his most prominent advisers, among them the abbots of Aberconwy, Strata Florida, Whitland and Llantarnam. Many of the friars (who had warm memories of Richard II) were eager partisans of Glyn Dŵr; they included John Sperhauke of Cardiff, who was executed for supporting Owain's claims. Sperhauke was undoubtedly of English extraction, as were other of Glyn Dŵr's followers – his wife's family, the Hanmers, among them – and the legislation of the English parliament proves that Englishmen who had married Welsh women were considered to be hardly more reliable than the Welsh themselves. Yet despite the degree to which the rising depended upon the allegiance of local leaders and upon the contribution of able clerics, it was above all the rising of Glyn Dŵr; he was its inspiration and its leader for almost half a generation, and there is no suggestion that his leadership was challenged. There can be no doubt that he had a magnetic personality, and there is every reason to endorse Trevelyan's comment that he was 'an attractive and unique figure in a period of debased and selfish politics'.

The origins of the rising lay in the north-eastern March, the region of those 'oppressive and fickle' magnates, the earls of Arundel. As Owain had been disappointed by the refusal of the new king to support him in his dispute with Reginald de Grey, lord of Rhuthun, he and his relations raised the banner of revolt at Glyndyfrdwy on 16 September 1400. In the following week, they attacked eight of the towns of the north-east and their example was followed in Anglesey by Owain's cousins, the sons of Tudur ap Goronwy. The first phase of the revolt was brief. Henry IV and his army were in Wales by October 1400 and although not one of the leading insurgents had been captured, large numbers of Welshmen came to make peace with the king. Henry of Monmouth, the youthful English prince of Wales, established his headquarters at Chester; the chief offices in the Principality were granted to Henry Percy (Hotspur), the son of the earl of Northumberland, and by the end of 1400 it appeared as if the trouble was over.

But although Owain, in the winter and spring of 1401, was a fugitive in the hills of central Wales, his rising had aroused deep feelings among the Welsh. The conflict was rekindled on Good Friday 1401 when Rhys and Gwilym ap Tudur ap Goronwy attacked Conwy Castle. In June, Owain defeated an English force at Hyddgen on the slopes of Pumlumon; as a result, the road to the south was open to him and during the summer of 1401 he was enthusiastically received by the inhabitants of the Tywi valley. The king made a second visit to Wales in October 1401; he was present at Llandovery when Llywelyn ap Gruffudd, the bibulous squire of Caeo, was executed, and he set up his headquarters at Strata Florida, much to the detriment of the monastic buildings. Nevertheless, he failed to check the progress of the rising. Owain was at Caernarfon early in November waving the dragon banner, the Britons' symbol of victory. He had not yet adopted the arms of the house of Gwynedd (*quarterly de Gu et Or en les quartiers leopards passans de contre coleur*, to quote the splendid language of the herald). This suggests that in 1401 his ideas were still rooted in the apocalyptic tradition of the legends of Nennius and Geoffrey of Monmouth, and that he had not adopted (as he was to do) the more pragmatic vision of Llywelyn I and Llywelyn II. This is confirmed by the letters, heavily influenced by mythical traditions, which he wrote in November 1401 to Robert III of Scotland and to leading figures among the Irish.

The year 1402 was a victorious one for Owain. In April he captured his chief enemy, Reginald de Grey, freeing him in November for a ransom of 10,000 marks (£6,666). In June, at the battle of Bryn-bras in Maelienydd, he captured Edmund, brother-in-law of Hotspur and brother of Richard II's heir, Roger Mortimer. Roger had died in 1398, and his son, also called Edmund, represented the true succession to the kingdom of England. Rumour had it that Richard II was still alive, and by November 1402 Edmund (the elder) had agreed to cooperate with Glyn Dŵr to restore Richard to the throne, or if he were dead to make Edmund (the younger) king of England. He also promised that he would ensure Glyn Dŵr's rights in Wales, and the agreement was sealed through marriage between Edmund and Catrin, Glyn Dŵr's daughter. Wales therefore became the centre of the hopes of the considerable number of Englishmen who were worried about the legitimacy of Henry IV's claim to the throne, a development helpful to the cause of insurgents. That cause was further advanced in August 1402 when Owain, on a march through Gwent and Glamorgan, received a warm welcome from the Welsh of the southeast. By then, the greater part of the countryside of Wales recognized his authority, although he had not yet gained possession of any of the chief castles. English campaigns against him were hindered by such appalling weather that the belief arose that even the elements were in alliance with him. In its frustration, the English parliament, in September 1402, passed the notorious Penal Laws which prohibited the rebellious Welsh from gathering together, gaining access to office, carrying arms and dwelling in fortified towns, and the same restrictions were placed upon Englishmen who married Welsh women.

The success Owain had enjoyed in 1402 continued into 1403 and 1404. Hotspur, stationed at Chester and increasingly antagonistic towards Henry IV, rose in rebellion in July 1403, thereby opening up the possibility of an alliance between the Welsh and the men of northern England. Hotspur's resistance lasted for less than a fortnight, for he was defeated and killed on 21 July 1403 at the battle of Shrewsbury before help from Wales and Northumberland could reach him. His failure did not lessen the momentum of the Welsh insurgents. Late in 1403 Owain, with the help of French sailors, led attacks upon

Caernarfon and Cydweli. In April 1404, the castles of Aberystwyth
and Harlech came into his possession and the region between the two
castles became a solid base for his authority. It was in that region – at
Machynlleth – that he held a parliament in 1404; according to tradition, it was there too that he was crowned prince of Wales in the
presence of envoys from France, Scotland and Castile.

In May 1404, *Owynus dei gratia princeps Wallie* (Owain, by the
grace of God, prince of Wales) sent a letter to Charles VI, king of
France, a document preserved in the French national archive. In the
letter, Glyn Dŵr referred to Owain Lawgoch's service to the French
crown; he requested arms and soldiers and authorized his two
representatives – his brother-in-law, John Hanmer, and his chancellor,
Gruffudd Young – to come to an agreement with the king of France.
Hanmer and Young were courteously received in Paris, and it appears
that the king – who was having one of his rare periods of sanity –
promised to help the Welsh insurgents. However, no material assistance was forthcoming until July 1405, when a fleet conveying 2,600
men sailed from Brest. In the meantime, Owain was busy consolidating his power and seeking new allies. He probably held court at
Aberystwyth Castle, where Gruffudd Young's chancery, the centre of
the administration of the Principality, was located. Young was a
highly experienced cleric who had once enjoyed the patronage of
Anne of Bohemia, Richard II's queen. He was the man mainly
responsible for attempting to make Owain's achievement the basis of
a Welsh lay and ecclesiastical polity and for persuading Owain to seek
inspiration from the policies of Llywelyn I and Llywelyn II rather
than from ancient Brythonic legend. By 1404, Young had attracted to
him men of similar experience, including John Trefor, the bishop of
St Asaph, and John Byford, the bishop of Bangor, both of whom
probably felt that by then Owain's success was beyond doubt. So
great was the prince's authority and so feeble was the reaction of
Henry IV that English officials, Marcher Lords and the inhabitants of
the border counties were making their own local agreements with the
new force that had arisen in Wales.

At the same time, Owain was seeking an alliance with the Percy
and Mortimer families, and there is evidence that a plan was drawn
up in Bangor in February 1405 to divide the territories of the kingdom
of England into three: Mortimer was to receive southern England,
and Percy, earl of Northumberland, central and northern England,

while Owain's share was to be Wales and five of the English border counties. The authenticity of the Tripartite Indenture has been questioned, partly because of the extensiveness of the territories claimed by Glyn Dŵr. Yet it is probably a genuine indication of the boldness of Owain's ambitions: he was a man of the borderland – Sycharth is only a kilometre from the present boundary with England – and there was a considerable Welsh population in many of the areas he is alleged to have claimed; furthermore, Owain was to be even more ambitious in laying down which of the English dioceses should be subject to a Welsh archbishop. Hopes of implementing the Tripartite Indenture were dashed by the foiling of the plan to smuggle Edmund Mortimer (the younger) into Wales, and by the failure in June 1405 of the rising of the earl of Northumberland. Percy fled to Scotland where there was considerable interest in Owain's cause. Young and Byford went on a mission to the Scottish court in 1405, but following the capture of the heir to the king of Scots by the English in 1406, hopes of assistance from Scotland evaporated. The Welsh rising lived on in the memory of the Scots; in 1442, a monk of Dunfermline wrote that the campaigns of the English 'against the Scots, the Welsh, the French and the Irish proved that they were the cruellest nation in the world'.

At the beginning of August 1405, French soldiers landed at Milford Haven. They marched towards England in the hope that the English followers of Richard II would rise against Henry IV. By the end of the month, they and the forces of Owain had reached Worcester, but as English support did not materialize they retreated to Wales, and in November 1405 the French soldiers embarked for France. By then, Owain's prospects were in decline. Henry IV's efforts had been ineffectual, but his son – the English prince of Wales – who had received full authority over the royal forces in Wales in 1405, was beginning to show signs of the military genius which would bring him fame at the battle of Agincourt. In the spring of 1405, the insurgents were defeated at Pwllmelyn near Usk, a battle in which John ap Hywel, the abbot of Llantarnam and the 'Savonarola of the Rising', was killed; by the beginning of 1406, the peripheral regions of Owain's Principality were slipping from his grasp.

Yet his position in central Wales remained secure, and given substantial help from France his prospects could still have been bright. It was probably in the hope of obtaining such help that he agreed in

1406 to Charles VI's request that the allegiance of the Welsh should be transferred from the Pope at Rome, recognized by England, to the Pope at Avignon, recognized by France and Scotland. There were dangers in the transfer, for it would cause the English authorities to view the insurgents as schismatics as well as rebels. There were also advantages, for the switch in allegiance would seal off the Welsh Church from exploitation by the English government and would create a barrier between England and Wales in ecclesiastical matters. Young probably considered that the transfer offered an opportunity of winning from Avignon concessions which would enable the Welsh Church, not only to be independent of England, but also to become an instrument at the service of a Welsh state. Young, no doubt, was the author of the letter to Benedict XIII, the Avignon Pope, written at Pennal near Machynlleth on 29 March 1406. The 'Pennal Policy' demanded that the Church of David, 'a Metropolitan Church since the time of St David, archbishop and confessor, should be restored to its original dignity'; it was to be granted authority over the other dioceses of Wales and over five in England, thus creating an archdiocese extending to Cornwall. Appointments to benefices in Wales were to be restricted to clerics who could 'speak our language'; the practice of 'the appropriation of churches in our Principality by monasteries and colleges in England' was to cease; two *studia generalia* (universities) were to be established in Wales; Henry 'of Lancaster' was to be excommunicated and the insurgents were to receive full remission for any sins they might commit in their struggle against him.

By 1406, the prospects of that struggle were increasingly bleak. It was acknowledged in Paris in October 1406 that no more assistance would be sent to Wales, and before the end of the year the inhabitants of Anglesey and of the southern coastlands had yielded to Henry IV. Nevertheless, the uprooting of Owain's power in the mountains and in central Wales was a difficult task. Aberystwyth Castle did not surrender to the king until September 1408, when Owain and his court moved to Harlech Castle. Harlech surrendered in 1409, when the prince's family was captured. Owain and his closest associates – Young, Trefor, Philip Hanmer and the sons of Tudur ap Goronwy – fled to the mountains and until about 1413 they were involved in sporadic attacks upon centres of English power. Thereafter, Young and Hanmer attempted to continue the struggle by other means.

They were seeking support in Paris in 1415, and it was almost certainly Young – Avignon's nominee for the archbishopric of St David's – who inspired the declaration at the Council of Konstanz (1414–18) that the Welsh were a *natio particularis*. He was appointed bishop of Ross in Scotland in 1418 and, like Augustine, he ended his life as bishop of Hippo, a diocese which had been *in partibus infidelium* for seven and a half centuries. After 1413, nothing is known of Owain Glyn Dŵr himself, although it is likely that he died in about September 1415, perhaps at Monnington in Herefordshire, the home of his daughter Alys Scudamore. Glyn Dŵr's death, like many aspects of his life, was mysterious; a manuscript copied about 1560 noted: 'many say that he died; the *brudwyr* [the prophetic poets] say that he did not.'

For a generation after 1415, the Welsh lived under the shadow of the failure of the Glyn Dŵr Revolt. There was nothing inevitable about that failure. Bruce succeeded under more difficult political circumstances (although easier geographical ones) in re-establishing the kingdom of Scotland; if the numerous enemies of Henry IV had been able to unite against him, doubtless the Welsh Principality would also have been re-established. Owain's abilities, the courage of his sons, the vision of his advisers and the loyalty of his people suggest that its prospects would have been promising. All the social discontents which had contributed to the rising were intensified by its failure. Even among the gentry who had supported Owain – perhaps among them in particular – there was a strong desire to forget him. They sacrificed their past to their future; for centuries to come, most of the members of the Welsh squirearchy would maintain that Glyn Dŵr was no more than a half-crazed rebel. Yet his memory was treasured by the less exalted classes, and at the end of the eighteenth century it was among them that Thomas Pennant collected the traditions which established Glyn Dŵr in his rightful position as the chief hero of the Welsh people.

The racial bitterness that had been fanned by the rising faded as the years passed. Nevertheless, for a century and more to come the burgesses of Gwynedd would give vent to their anti-Welsh sentiments, and an English poet wrote in 1436: 'Beware of Walys ... That it make not our childeis childe to wepe.' In 1431, 1433 and 1447, the English parliament insisted upon reaffirming the Penal Code and it was not removed from the statute book until 1624. The bitterness of the Welsh also found expression, and the Welsh literature of the century after 1415 is considered to be more nationalistic than that of any other period. This was not true of all the poets. The events through which he lived led Gruffudd Llwyd to conclude – as did Siôn Cent to an even greater degree – that the only reality is the grave and the life beyond the grave. Yet most of the dozen or so Welsh poets of distinction who rose in the generation after the rising gave expression to the grievances of their people. *'Gwae ni ein geni yn gaeth'* (Woe unto us, born into slavery), sang Guto'r Glyn, and Lewys Glyn Cothi longed for the day when no Englishman would hold office in Wales. *'Dwg Morgannwg a Gwynedd,/ Gwna'n un o Gonwy i Nedd'* (Bring Glamorgan and Gwynedd together,/ Make us one from Conwy to Nedd) appealed Guto'r Glyn to William Herbert (the grandson of Dafydd Gam), and in addressing Richard, William's brother, Ieuan Deulwyn declared: *'Chwi a ellwch â'ch allwydd/ Rhoi clo ar Sais rhag cael swydd'* (You can with your key lock the English out of office).

In accordance with the Penal Code, offices – at least the higher ones – were the monopoly of Englishmen. Following the rising, no Welshman would be a bishop in Wales until 1496 and none of the chief offices of the Principality would be held by a Welshman until 1461. Nevertheless, ambitious Englishmen were not anxious to live and work in Wales; what they wanted was the title and the income of office, and the duties of bishops, justices, sheriffs and others were undertaken by their deputies, men generally drawn from the ranks of the Welsh gentry. Shortly after its passage, Henry IV sought to lessen the severity of the Penal Code, for the Lancastrians like their predecessors were desirous of employing anyone who could be of use to them. Doubtless the king hoped that the code would gradually pass into disuse, but the government sometimes yielded to anti-Welsh pressure, as in 1433, when John Scudamore was dismissed from the office of deputy justice of the southern Principality because his wife was Welsh.

Ambitious Welshmen could escape from the restrictions inherent in their lineage by petitioning parliament to turn them into Englishmen. It would appear that the first such petition was that made in 1413 by Rhys ap Thomas, the sheriff of Carmarthenshire. His example was followed in subsequent decades by a handful of prominent Welshmen. One of them was Gruffudd Fychan of Penrhyn near Bangor. Following the failure of the rising, Gruffudd's father, Gwilym ap Gruffudd, succeeded in gaining possession of the greater part of the lands of his relations, the sons of Tudur ap Goronwy of Penmynydd, losses which caused the Penmynydd family to fade into obscurity. Gruffudd ap Nicolas, the founder of the gentry house of Dinefwr, followed the same course. It is difficult to fathom the complex emotions of such men as they pleaded publicly for permission to abandon the condition of being Welsh, while at the same time they were boasting of their distinguished Welsh lineage and were providing generous patronage for Welsh culture. This 'back-door' method of allowing a Welshman to rise in the world led to protests from the burgesses of Gwynedd. In about 1447, they declared that the granting of offices to Welshmen was likely to lead to 'the extinction of the population of the English districts of Wales, thus endangering the king and his kingdom'; as a result, the practice of turning Welshmen into Englishmen ceased for at least a decade.

Henry of Monmouth had hardly won full control of his Principality before he was elevated to the throne of England following the death of Henry IV in 1413. Henry V embodied the concept of the warrior king and he relaunched the war to assert the Plantagenet claim to the crown of France. For Henry, as for his predecessors, Wales was a useful source of soldiers; it was the only part of his kingdom where the inhabitants had had extensive experience of war over the previous generation. In the battle of Agincourt (1415) – the victory which gave Henry a degree of control over the kingdom of France – hundreds of Welshmen took part, some of them on the side of the French. The second phase of the Hundred Years' War, like the first, produced Welsh heroes; chief among them was Mathau Goch, a nephew of Glyn Dŵr's wife, who was immortalized by the words: *Morte Matthei Goghe/ Cambria clamitavit, Oghe*. Until the war came to an end in 1453 with a complete victory for France, it was central to the experience of the people of Wales: the gradual revival of the Welsh economy was hindered by the crown's constant demand for money to finance it; the violent attitudes encouraged by it undermined respect for law and order; the effectiveness of the government was weakened by the conflicts which arose from it; so various were the experiences of the Welsh who participated in it that Guto'r Glyn came to the conclusion that the role of the Welsh poet was hardly more than that of praising 'the periphery of the world'.

The conflicts arising from the war were exacerbated by the untimely death of Henry V in 1422. He left a young widow, Catherine (the daughter of Charles VI of France), and a one-year-old son. The early years of the reign of Henry VI were a period of struggle between his relations, and when he attained manhood it became apparent that the English throne had not been occupied by so incompetent a king since the reign of Aethelred the Unready. The problems of the government were aggravated by the ambitions of the aristocracy. The knight's fee – the core of the old feudalism – had long been in decay. In its place a different relationship arose between the lord and his followers, men who were often footloose veterans of the fighting in France. Henceforth, the great men of the kingdom raised private armies through indenture and rewarded their followers with wages.

Thus developed what has been called bastard feudalism, a system which allowed many an aristocrat to maintain forces of armed men who wore their lord's livery and who dwelt in the courts of his castle. This development was particularly evident in the March of Wales. Intermarriage among members of the English upper class had by 1450 concentrated the Marcher Lordships in the hands of a very few families. The duke of York – the nephew and the heir of Edmund Mortimer – held a broken chain of territories extending from Denbigh to Caerleon; with their 'capital' at Ludlow, the Yorkist lordships almost constituted an independent state. In addition to holding the Principality, Henry VI was lord of Monmouth and Cydweli as heir to the dukes of Lancaster, and of Brecon as heir to the Bohuns. The only other Marcher Lords of substance were Stafford, duke of Buckingham, at Newport, Mowbray, duke of Norfolk, at Chepstow and Gower, and the Neville family. the greediest and most prolific of the aristocratic families, who had obtained the lordships of Glamorgan and Abergavenny through marriage.

These families were newcomers to Wales. They did not have the same awareness as their predecessors of their position as barons of the March. Three quarters of the income of the Mortimers and two thirds of that of the Despensers had originated in Wales, but their territories in the March were peripheral to the interests of the aristocracy of the age of Henry VI. Those territories were useful as a source of soldiers, but they had decayed greatly as a source of income. By 1450, the Marcher Lords had long since abandoned the practice of directly farming their demesne lands, and rents had contracted severely as a result of the depression and the rising of Owain Glyn Dŵr. The Marcher Lords sought to maintain their income by imposing arbitrary fines and by increasing their receipts from courts of law, devices detrimental to order and good government. Nevertheless, the tendency to portray the March as a region of anarchy and as a haven for criminals has been carried to excess. For a century and more after the Conquest, courts were held there regularly, as the court rolls of Rhuthun amply demonstrate. The Law of the March was in no sense a charter for wrongdoers and was in fact becoming increasingly assimilated to the Law of England. Administration in the March was less disjunctive than is often assumed; although many of the individual lordships were small, a number of them were held by a single lord, and between one lord and another there were agreements and methods of arbitration – the Days of the March, for example – which served to limit tumult and crime.

The vilification of the Marcher Lordships as sanctuaries for criminals arose in part from the desire to praise the Tudor legislation which abolished the privileges of the lords, and in part from the undoubted decline in the administration of the lordships which occurred for long periods in the last century in which those privileges were in existence. The administrative decline resulted from an increasing unwillingness on the part of the Marcher Lords to fulfil their duties, and from lack of leadership from the government of Henry VI. One symptom of maladministration was the tendency of the lords to curtail or not to hold sittings of the Great Sessions of the lordship, imposing instead a fine upon the entire community. Bolingbroke at Brecon in 1373 seems to have been the first to 'redeem' the sessions, but by 1450 the practice had spread to most of the lordships. Thus the sessions of Chepstow were 'redeemed' in 1415, those of Newport in 1476 and those of Hay in 1518, examples of a tendency which brought short-term benefits to the lord and to his tenants: he received a substantial sum of money, and they were released from the tedium of attending the session. Nevertheless, the practice was certain to undermine respect for the law, and the gentry of Glamorgan declared that 'The redempcion of the sessions is . . . no admynistracion of justice at all.'

The quality of the administration of the Principality was also deteriorating. There too the receipts of the lord had fallen sharply; Edward, the son of Henry VI – who was invested with the Principality in 1457 – could expect less than a quarter of the £4,000 received by the Black Prince. The contraction of the villein class, the chief source of rents and taxes, was a heavy blow to the prince's income. By 1420, all the inhabitants of the *taeogdrefi* (villein townships) of eastern Caernarfonshire and southern Meirionnydd had fled from their homes, and attempts to force them 'to reinhabit their lands so that they should provide profit for the king' proved unsuccessful. The Principality was the responsibility of the central government, but the record of the Lancastrians was not distinguished. Henry IV's policies lacked the firmness, as well as the occasional generosity, which characterized those of Edward I. Henry V was rather more energetic, but matters worsened markedly following his death. In accordance with his will, the kingdom of England was placed under the care of his younger brother, Humphrey, duke of Gloucester. Humphrey had links with Wales, for the lordship of Pembroke had been granted to him in 1414, but according to Ralph Griffiths, the leading authority on the Lancastrians, he was hardly more than a tourist there. He became justice of the north in 1427 and of the south in 1440 and he showed an occasional interest in the Principality, mainly in order to nurture a party of supporters in Wales. But his leadership was weak. The practice of 'redeeming' sessions spread to the southern counties of the Principality; of the fifty-two sessions recorded in Carmarthenshire between 1422 and 1485, only ten ran their course. Henry VI attained his majority in 1437. He allowed the members of his court to use the offices of the Principality as rewards for their followers, high and low. Between 1437 and 1440, a third of them were granted for life to members of the king's household. It is hardly surprising that the inhabitants of the Principality complained in 1440 that the counties of Wales 'dayly habundeth and increseth in misgovernaunce'.

With the Marcher Lords and the central government abandoning their responsibilities, a power vacuum was created in Wales. It was filled by the Welsh gentry. During the reign of Henry VI, the foundations were laid of many of the landed estates which would be central to the history of Wales over the following five hundred years. It was recorded in 1883 that there were in Wales twenty estates exceeding eight thousand hectares (twenty thousand acres) in extent; fifteen of them were already in existence, at least in embryonic form, in 1450. Gruffudd ap Nicolas (*c.*1400–*c.*1456), a man who rose on the coat-tails of Duke Humphrey, was the most powerful of the Welsh gentry of his day. He was appointed sheriff of Carmarthenshire in 1436 and deputy justice of the south in 1437, and he was granted the supervision of the estates of the diocese of St David's in 1447. He ruled west Wales from his home at Carmarthen Castle, and so great was his authority that he was able to flout any commands he received from London. He used his influence to build an estate and his example was followed by his son and grandson. Among his contemporaries, there were men who were equally acquisitive – John ap Maredudd of Clenennau in Eifionydd, for example, and Hywel ap Ieuan Fychan of Mostyn, Flintshire, and Ieuan ap Llywelyn ap Morgan of Tredegar, Gwynllŵg. Some of the squires of Wales – families such as the Hanmers of Maelor and the Salusburys of the Vale of Clwyd – were English by origin, but the majority were men deeply rooted in the old lineages.

As a result of intermarriage over a number of generations, it is difficult to find much difference between gentry families of English origin and those of Welsh origin. Although the Penal Code was still on the statute book, the barrier between the Welsh and the English was being eroded, at least among the members of the upper layers of society. The squires of Wales were being fused into a single class, although it would appear that the anglicization of the Welsh was greater than the cymricization of the English.

Of all the estate builders, the most successful was William ap William of Gwent, the grandson of Dafydd Gam. His father, William ap Thomas, bought the Raglan estate in 1430 and amassed a number of offices in south-east Wales. The son built upon the achievements of the father and won a prominent position at court. In accordance with the increasingly common practice of the Welsh gentry, he adopted a fixed surname. William Herbert of Raglan was summoned to parliament as Baron Herbert in 1461, the first Welshman of full blood to join the ranks of the English titled aristocracy. A Marcher Lordship was created for him at Crickhowell in 1463 and another at Raglan in 1465 and he became the Yorkist earl of Pembroke in 1468, a title worthy of his income of £2,400 a year.

The career of a member of the lineage of *Ŵyrion Eden* (the descendants of Ednyfed Fychan) was even more remarkable. In about 1420, Owain ap Maredudd, the grandson of Tudur ap Goronwy of Penmynydd, and a nephew of Rhys and Gwilym, the cousins and allies of Owain Glyn Dŵr, went to London to seek his fortune.

There, in about 1431, he married Catherine, Henry V's widow; the marriage was secret, for even although it may not have been illegal it was certainly highly audacious. Like William Herbert, Owain adopted a surname. If he had taken his father's name, the throne of England would have been occupied for over a century by the Maredudd dynasty, but the name he chose was that of his grandfather, Tudur (Tudor); it was a prescient choice, for the name means territorial king. His sons, Edmund and Jasper, were Henry VI's half-brothers and were among the most enthusiastic supporters of the Lancastrian dynasty. In 1452, Edmund was made earl of Richmond and was married to Margaret Beaufort, the great-grand-daughter of John of Gaunt. He was given the task of re-establishing the power of the crown in west Wales and by 1456, shortly before his death at Carmarthen, he had succeeded in prising the castle there from the hands of Gruffudd ap Nicolas. His work was continued by his brother Jasper, the Lancastrian earl of Pembroke, and by 1460 Jasper had collected so many offices in the Principality and the March that he was, to all intents and purposes, the king's viceroy in Wales.

These were the men whom the poets delighted in praising. Robin Ddu of Anglesey hailed Edmund and Jasper as worthy descendants of Tudur ap Goronwy; Lewys Glyn Cothi described Gruffudd ap Nicolas as the 'Constantine of great Carmarthen', and Guto'r Glyn called upon God to protect William Herbert, 'the guardian of Gwent'. The volume of Welsh verse composed increased markedly in the decades after 1440. In about 1451, Gruffudd ap Nicolas held an eisteddfod at Carmarthen at which the chair was won by Dafydd ap Edmwnd, a relation of the Hanmers, and the Twenty-four Metres of Welsh prosody were agreed. The work of the team of researchers led by Dafydd Bowen has shown how dependent were the poets upon a network of patronage throughout Wales. Dafydd Nanmor's poem to Dafydd ap Thomas of Faenol in Cardiganshire is one of the most delightful acknowledgements of that dependence: '*Llety a gefais gerllaw teg afon/ Llawn o ddaioni a llawen ddynion*' (Lodging I have by a river clear/ Full of laughter and all good cheer). In a notable article, Saunders Lewis argued that Dafydd Nanmor and his fellows were expressing in their poetry a love for a stable, deep-rooted civilization. Lewis maintained that the poets were the leading upholders of the belief that a hierarchical social structure, 'the heritage and the tradition of an ancient aristocracy', was the necessary precondition of civilized life and that there were deep philosophical roots to their belief – although it could be argued that the poets praised hierarchical structures because it was only through the ability of the gentry to profit from the labours of other social classes that they were able to provide the luxuries craved by the poets.

The lay gentry were not the only patrons of the poets. Dafydd ap Thomas, so lavishly praised by Dafydd Nanmor, was an ecclesiastic. Rhys, the abbot of Strata Florida, was the first of the patrons of Guto'r Glyn, and Gutun Owain was much indebted to Sion ap Rhisiart, abbot of Valle Crucis. It is difficult to discover any significant difference between poems addressed to clerical patrons and those addressed to laymen. '[His] wines and viands made a heaven of earth,' sang Gutun Owain of Sion ap Rhisiart, and the tradition of praising the hospitality of the monasteries reached its climax with Tudur Aled licking his lips over the food and drink offered by Dafydd ab Owain, abbot of Strata Marcella.

Scholars have used the work of the poets to support the argument that the lives of the monks and clerics of the Later Middle Ages were essentially secular. As the monks – now much reduced in number – yielded control over their economic life to the squires, the inner life of the monasteries was opened to lay influence and the abbots themselves adopted an essentially squirearchical style of life. Monastic buildings were adapted so as to provide the abbot with a mansion, and the refectory, where austere meals had once been served, became a hall for feasts and revelry. Nevertheless, it has been claimed that the quality of monastic life in some at least of the forty-seven religious houses of Wales improved in the decades after 1440, allowing Welsh monasticism to enjoy something of a St Luke's summer before its end. As the scholarly activity of the monasteries was slight, probably their greatest contribution to culture was their patronage (or the patronage of a handful of them) of poetry, providing the poets with succour not only when they were in full vigour but also in their old age and debility.

The increase in poetic activity after about 1440 suggests that the Welsh economy was enjoying some degree of prosperity, for a society close to destitution is not one which can maintain the servants of the muse through the long years of their apprenticeship and provide them with lavish hospitality. There is evidence from other sources also that the black shadow of depression was lifting and that the population was once again increasing. Doubtless it would have increased sooner but for the devastation caused during the rising of Owain Glyn Dŵr by the one side and the other. That devastation was a severe blow to a number of towns and to extensive parts of the countryside, particularly in the north-east, where the lordship of Denbigh produced no income for years and where the fine mansion at Sycharth was completely destroyed. It had little impact upon towns such as Tenby, however, and prosperity had returned to Conwy by 1413 and to Beaumaris, Caernarfon and Carmarthen by 1420.

The following decades offer increasing evidence of the activities of the ports of Wales, and a pattern of trading developed which would be central to the Welsh economy for three hundred years and more – the importation of necessities and luxuries from mainland Europe, the conveyance of people and goods to Ireland, the activity of the fishing ports and, above all, the coastal trade between the Welsh ports themselves and between them and the ports of south-west and north-west England. Beaumaris imported goods ranging from iron to ginger, while the trade of Tenby included salt, figs and resin. A close association developed between Ireland and the ports of the south-west. Carmarthen held its own in the wine and wool trades, while the ports of the south-east were caught in the web of Bristol, a city of ten thousand and more inhabitants. The agricultural surplus of the southern coastal plain of Wales was sold there, at the Welsh Back near the quay. A wealthy class of Welsh merchants came into being at Bristol and the Welsh also migrated to London, establishing the basis of a community which would loom large in the history of Wales. There was a marked increase in the number of Welsh settling in the towns of the English border; they were heartily disliked in Chester, but there were large numbers of them at Hereford, Tewkesbury, Shrewsbury and Ludlow, while Oswestry, Guto'r Glyn's favourite town, was almost entirely Welsh. In Wales itself there was growing reconciliation between the natives and the burgesses of the walled towns. By 1450, it was only the inhabitants of Caernarfon, Conwy and Beaumaris who retained colonialist attitudes; most of the other towns were largely Welsh and even at Tenby men bearing Welsh names were appointed to borough offices.

There was a revival in the rural economy also. Indeed, it is argued that the period 1430 to 1480, as well as being a time of opportunity for the gentry, was something of a golden age for the lowest classes of society. As villeinage had largely collapsed and as the decline in the population had led to a degree of equilibrium between people and land, the labourer won a measure of bargaining power and it is believed that his position around 1480 was as good as if not better than it would be in any subsequent period before the twentieth century. Furthermore, as villeinage contracted in the manors of the southern lowlands – lands which had been seized from the native Welsh at the time of the Norman invasion – the Welsh of the hills infiltrated into them, beginning a process of recolonization of the plains which would last for centuries. The revival of the rural economy was aided by the development of the cattle trade. Welsh beef had been in demand since the Age of the Princes, but there is evidence that the trade was being organized on a more ambitious scale after about 1470, partly in order to supply the needs of the carnivores of London, a city of at least fifty thousand people. Droving came into existence; it was the most important channel for introducing money to the countryside, and would be central to the economic, social and cultural life of Wales until it was destroyed by the coming of the railways a little over a century ago. There was also growth in the wool trade. The industry, particularly in the north-east, suffered severely during the Glyn Dŵr Rising, but it revived thereafter and sixty-two new fulling-mills were built in Wales between 1400 and 1500. The border towns were the centres of the trade; Shrewsbury was its focal point and the town's Drapers' Company sought to dominate it completely.

The houses built in Wales in the decades around 1450 are further proof that some at least of the regions of Wales were enjoying increasing prosperity. Apart from the ruins of castles and the magnificent palace built by Bishop Gower at St David's, virtually the only evidence of the dwelling-places of the Welsh people before about 1450 consists of that which can be obtained through excavation, as at Sycharth. Castles continued to be built: William Herbert erected a splendid tower at Raglan and some of the older castles were adapted to make them more comfortable, a sign of the development among the aristocracy of notions of domesticity. There were castle elements in some of the mansions of the gentry – the 'tower houses' that were built around Pembroke, for example – but the majority of the buildings erected by the Welsh squires were uncastellated 'hall houses'. In Tretower in Ystrad Yw – the finest existing example of a home of a Welsh gentry family – the two traditions were combined; in about 1451, Roger Vaughan, a cousin of William Herbert, built in the valley of the Rhiangoll a fortified gatehouse and a range of luxurious buildings, including a mess for his indentured soldiers, Guto'r Glyn among them.

The homes of the yeomen – the substantial farmers – are more important as indications of increasing prosperity, and numbers of these have survived in the north-east and along the borders. In them use was made of the local oak, and in Powys in particular there developed the tradition of 'black and white' houses which is one of the glories of that region. Evidence of increasing prosperity may also be found in the tombs of the period, the work of talented schools of masons. Throughout the ages, a substantial portion of the surplus of the community has been spent on the burial places of its leaders, but after about 1450 there are signs of expenditure upon the commemoration of less distinguished members of society – the early growth (or the revival) of the notion that everyone has the right to be interred beneath masonry.

The Church shared in the economic revival. Although the ecclesiastical institutions of Wales, when considered in a wider European context, were not as impoverished as is sometimes believed, they were poor compared with similar institutions in England and they had suffered grievously during the Glyn Dŵr uprising. The combined income of the three least-endowed dioceses of Wales was less than that of the poorest English diocese, and the total wealth of the Welsh religious houses was not as large as that of the great monastery at Glastonbury. The Welsh Church continued to suffer from the practice of siphoning off its income for the benefit of institutions and individuals in England and, increasingly, for the benefit of the Welsh gentry. Nevertheless, it was not wholly bereft of resources to beautify its buildings and enrich its services. In the decades after 1450, many of the churches of Wales were rebuilt in the Perpendicular style, England's chief gift to architecture. Fine towers were erected in the villages of Gwent and Tegeingl, handsome town churches in Cardiff, Wrexham and Tenby and two-aisled churches in the parishes of the Vale of Clwyd. Masterpieces were created even in isolated places, as the splendid rood screens at Llananno (Maelienydd), Llanegryn (Meirionnydd) and Patrisio (Ystrad Yw) testify. Church walls were decorated with frescoes, the clergy wore rich vestments and the devout knelt before elaborate shrines. The richer churches vied with each other in collecting appendages to worship – crosses and candlesticks, bells and chalices, pyxes and paxes.

The climax of these developments came in the years after 1485, but they were all in train a generation and more before Henry Tudor ascended the throne of England. It is difficult to reconcile the evidence of an increasingly prosperous and cultured society with the portrayal of Wales in the decades before 1485 as a country racked to a unique degree by violence and lawlessness. That portrayal is a gross exaggeration; although the Welsh legal and administrative system had fundamental weaknesses, there is ample evidence that the country was hardly more riotous than some other territories of the king of England – Northumberland, for example, or Devon or East Anglia – and the notion that the coming of the Tudors brought immediate pacification is a myth. The entire kingdom was shaken by struggle between the houses of York and Lancaster which flared up intermittently in the generation after 1455, and by the local quarrels which erupted under the mantle of that struggle. Yet, although the 'Wars of the Roses' lasted for over thirty years, it has been estimated that the two factions were engaged in arms for a total of only thirteen weeks. The dislocation caused by the 'wars' should not therefore be exaggerated. They were a struggle between consanguineous aristocrats, and all efforts to endow them with a wider constitutional significance have failed. Between the battle of St Albans (1455) and the battle of Stoke (1487), the two factions were involved in about a dozen armed encounters. The most important of them were Wakefield, 1460 (where the duke of York was killed), Mortimer's Cross, 1461 (a victory which enabled his son to become King Edward IV), Banbury, 1469 (which led to the restoration of Henry VI), Barnet and Tewkesbury, 1471 (which ensured the restoration of Edward IV), and Bosworth, 1485 (where Edward IV's brother, Richard III, was killed and where Henry Tudor seized the crown).

These battles were of great interest to the Welsh. This is hardly surprising, for both factions depended heavily upon their territories in Wales for troops – the Lancastrians upon the Principality and Jasper Tudor's lordship of Pembroke, and the Yorkists upon the lordships of the earldom of March and upon Glamorgan, which was owned by their chief supporter, Richard Neville, earl of Warwick (the 'Kingmaker'). Mortimer's Cross was a battle between two Welsh armies; about a third of Henry Tudor's soldiers at Bosworth were Welsh, and so great were the losses among the Welsh at Banbury that Lewys Glyn Cothi considered the battle to be a national calamity. Carnhuanawc lamented that the Welsh had shed their blood in a contest for the crown of England rather than in efforts to ensure 'their innate rights as the inhabitants of Wales'. But to the poets, the contest was endowed with specific Welsh significance. They sang to the Yorkists and to the Lancastrians, seeking among the various leaders a man fitting in terms of ancestry and credible in terms of power to be the second Cadwaladr. In the 1450s, their favourite hero was Jasper Tudor of the stock of Ednyfed Fychan, and in Pembroke and Gwynedd in particular, allegiance to him survived the deposition of Henry VI. When the Yorkists seized the throne, the poets warmed to Edward IV, who through the Mortimers was a descendant of Llywelyn Fawr. It was said that Guto'r Glyn delighted in 'wearing the fine collar of the guard and the livery of King Edward'.

William Herbert, the chief upholder of the power of the Yorkists in Wales, was also hailed with enthusiasm. Herbert was executed following the battle of Banbury, and as his son was a nonentity the Yorkists of Wales lacked after 1469 a figure suitable to be the focus of allegiance. Henry VI and his heir, the prince of Wales, were murdered following the battle of Tewkesbury. The claims of the house of Lancaster then devolved upon Margaret, countess of Richmond, the mother of Henry Tudor. Henry, declared Edward IV, 'was the only imp now left of Henry VI's brood'. The hopes of the Lancastrians were centred upon Jasper, Henry's uncle. Jasper sailed with his nephew to France in 1471 in the hope of obtaining the assistance of his cousin, Louis XI. Their ship was blown on to the Breton coast, and for thirteen years Jasper and Henry were kept in semi-captivity by Francis, duke of Brittany.

As the kingdom of England had been won in 1461 by Edward IV, the heir of the earldom of March, the inheritance of the Mortimers became part of the estates of the crown, as had the lands of the dukes of Lancaster in 1399. In consequence, the king owned over half the lordships of the March. Furthermore, he held other Marcher lordships, for several members of the aristocracy were either under age or had been deprived of their lands through attainder. Thus the king had the opportunity to give a degree of cohesion to the administration of Wales. He responded by making the country the responsibility of

William Herbert, and in Charles Ross's biography of Edward IV fifteen lines are needed in order to list all the Welsh offices held by Herbert. Although somewhat insouciant, Edward IV was a more vigorous ruler than was his predecessor and it appears that Herbert, with the support of the central government, had a fair degree of success in making Wales answerable to his authority. The earl of Warwick's resentment of Herbert's unfettered power in Wales was one of the reasons why he abandoned Edward IV and initiated the campaign which led to the restoration of Henry VI in 1470–71. It was Warwick who insisted upon the execution of Herbert, an act which deprived Edward, following his restoration, of an adequate representative in Wales.

With the country leaderless, it became increasingly tumultuous. By 1472, the petitions of the inhabitants of the English border counties were bitter and fulminatory. The king sought to fill the vacuum by establishing a council for his son, Edward, who had been invested with the Principality shortly after his birth in 1471. In 1473, the council settled at Ludlow, the centre of the earldom of March, and in that year Edward held a meeting with the remaining Marcher Lords and reminded them of their duty to maintain order within their territories. The records of Edward's council have not survived, but it appears that it acted fairly efficiently. Its leading members were the queen's relations, scions of the Woodville family. They used their authority to undermine the influence of the Herberts in Wales and to create a party favourable to them in the March. The brothers Thomas and William Stanley, the former the justice of Chester and the latter the steward of the household of the prince of Wales, were prominent among the allies of the Woodvilles. Thomas, Baron Stanley, married Margaret, the mother of Henry Tudor; no doubt Edward IV hoped that the heiress of the Lancastrians would offer little threat if wedded to a man who had received extensive favours from the Yorkists.

Concern over the power possessed by Anthony Woodville, the queen's brother, in Wales was one of the factors which caused Richard, Edward IV's brother, to seize the crown from his nephew, Edward V. He did so in June 1483, eleven weeks after Edward V, a twelve-year-old boy, had inherited his father's kingdom. The usurpation split the house of York and raised the hopes of Henry Tudor. The council at Ludlow came to an end when the prince of Wales became king, and an attempt was made to fill the gap by granting the chief offices of Wales to the duke of Buckingham, lord of Brecon and heir to the rights of the youngest of the sons of Edward III. In September 1483, Buckingham rose in rebellion at Brecon, ostensibly in the name of Henry Tudor, although he probably considered that his own claim to the throne was sounder than Henry's. His rebellion aroused no enthusiasm in Wales and within a month he had been defeated and executed. With the execution of Buckingham, the administration of Wales lost all cohesion. In the north, the most powerful magnate was William Stanley, the owner of a chain of lordships, the rewards of a family which had played a double game throughout the dynastic troubles. In the south-west, the chief figure was Rhys ap Thomas, the grandson of Gruffudd ap Nicolas, a man who adhered instinctively to the Lancastrianism which had been responsible for the elevation of his family.

It was the administrative weaknesses of Wales which permitted Henry Tudor, with his army of about four thousand Frenchmen and Lancastrian exiles, to land without opposition at Dale on the Milford Haven and to march unhindered through west and mid-Wales in August 1485. Henry was not the first aspirant to the throne of England to land on the coast of Wales – the duke of York had done so in 1450 and in 1460 – and his attempt to land in Dorset in 1484 proved that Wales was not central to his plans. Apart from Pembroke, where there were fond memories of Jasper, Henry did not receive a particularly warm welcome. No one in Wales resisted him, but neither was there a rush to join his ranks; the days of his march through Wales (8–14 August 1485) were a vexatious period for him. He had corresponded with Rhys ap Thomas, and it appears that Henry had promised to entrust Rhys with the government of Wales. Nevertheless, Henry had reached the border before he was joined by Rhys and about a thousand men from Ystrad Tywi. The machinations of his mother, the wife of Baron Stanley, were central to Henry's success. Stanley had an army of five thousand soldiers, while his brother, William, had recruited about three thousand troops in Cheshire and north-east Wales. The forces of the Stanley brothers had been raised in the name of Richard III, but when Henry engaged in battle with Richard at Bosworth on 22 August 1485, Baron Stanley remained aloof and William Stanley fought against Richard. Thus did Henry Tudor win the victory which enabled him to assume the crown of England as Henry VII and to found the Tudor dynasty.

A hundred years and more after the battle of Bosworth, the spokes-men for the Welsh gentry – John Wynn and George Owen in particular – portrayed Henry's victory as the greatest blessing ever experienced by the Welsh people. That view was reiterated by historians, at least until this century, and the coming of the Tudor was seen as the climax, often as the conclusion, of the history of Wales – 'the long struggle over, the victory won' to quote Owen Rhoscomyl (1912). It is not difficult to understand the approval of the gentry. What they sought was the opportunity to build up their estates unhindered, to be free from the interference of English officials, to become the masters of local government in Wales and to be assured that the Penal Code was a dead letter. Some of these aspirations had been achieved under the Yorkists and, if that dynasty's history had been more fortunate, perhaps Wynn and Owen would have applauded 1461 rather than 1485. They were all achieved under the Tudors. When that dynasty came to an end in 1603, the Welsh gentry were firmly in place as the ruling class of Wales. Attributing their success to the fact that a dynasty of Welsh descent – of the same stock as themselves – had been on the throne of England for over a century was an intelligible and patriotic reaction. With a descendant of *Wyrion Eden* wearing the crown of England, it was possible to believe that the prophecies of the vaticinatory poets had been fulfilled; to Dafydd Llwyd of Mathafarn, the most enthusiastic composer of *canu brud*, Henry Tudor had won the battle lost by Cadwaladr.

It is unlikely that Henry Tudor interpreted his victory in such a way. It was not a matter of the Tudors identifying themselves with the Welsh but rather of the Welsh identifying themselves with the Tudors. Tudor enthusiasts among Welsh historians delighted in portraying Henry's court as a place where the Welsh were held in high honour. The portrayal had some substance, but there was little advantage for the king in vaunting his Welsh connections in London, where Cambrophilia was hardly rampant. By descent, Henry VII was a quarter Welsh, a quarter French and half English, and it was his English blood which gave him a claim to the throne of England. Indeed, recent research suggests that the Welsh connections of the king received almost as much attention at the court of Edward IV as they did in that of Henry VII. The Yorkist genealogies stressed that Edward was a descendant of *Gladus diw, filia Lewellin et heredis Brut*, and it has already been noted that David Powel considered Henry

VIII to be the successor of the Welsh princes through his mother, the daughter of Edward IV, rather than through his father, Henry Tudor. Edward, it was claimed, was the red dragon who had defeated the white dragon, Henry VI, in accordance with the prophecy of Nennius. Henry VII also used the dragon motif – it is particularly prominent in St George's Chapel, Windsor – but it was part of the heraldry of the house of Tudor rather than that of Wales. Edward IV, like Henry VII, had a son named Arthur but, as has been seen, Arthur had, since the age of Henry II, been a symbol not of Wales but of the English royal house.

In his Welsh policies, Henry VII did little more than build upon the work of the Yorkists. In 1489, when he was three years of age, Arthur, the king's heir, became prince of Wales. Within a year, his council was at work at Ludlow under the supervision of Jasper. Arthur died in 1502 and his brother Henry was invested with the Principality in 1504. The council was not abolished on the death of Arthur. It continued in existence as the Council of the King in the Dominion and Principality of Wales and the Marches, and a version of it would remain in existence until 1688, although there would be no prince of Wales during most of the period 1489–1688. Henry insisted, as had Edward IV, that the Marcher Lords should bind themselves through indenture to maintain order within their territories and it is known that Jasper, lord of Pembroke and Glamorgan, sealed such an indenture. Jasper, the architect of his nephew's success, obtained the chief offices in the Principality and the March, despite Henry's alleged promise to Rhys ap Thomas. Jasper died childless in 1495 and his lordships passed to the crown. In the same year, Henry, on somewhat flimsy grounds, grasped the opportunity to execute William Stanley as a traitor. His lordships also passed to the crown and Henry seized his wealth, valued at more than £25,000.

While Jasper lived, Rhys ap Thomas's rewards were small. In 1496, however, he was appointed justice of the southern principality, and he ruled his territories with considerable pomp from his luxurious castle at Caeriw. Rhys was the third Welshman (the two William Herberts were the first and second) to be appointed to a justiceship in Wales. By 1496, the flood-gates had opened and more and more public offices in Wales were held by Welshmen. Opportunities for Welshmen in England also multiplied. As has already been noted, Welshmen had pursued careers in England under the Yorkists, but the numbers doing so were increasing rapidly by 1500. In the Church also the richer livings were tending progressively to be held by members of Welsh gentry families, and at the same time Welsh laymen were tightening their hold over ecclesiastical estates. A few Welshmen were elevated to the bench of bishops, but most of the men appointed to the dioceses of Wales under the early Tudors were civil servants of English origin. In 1496, a Welshman was appointed to St David's for the first time since 1389; St Asaph had a Welsh bishop by 1500, but no such appointment was made in Bangor until 1542 or in Llandaf until 1566.

The fulfilment of the ambitions of the Welsh gentry indicates that the age of the Marcher Lords was coming to an end. When Henry VII died in 1509, the only powerful ones remaining were the duke of Buckingham at Brecon and Newport, Charles Somerset (the son-in-law of the second William Herbert) at Chepstow, Crickhowell, Raglan and Gower, and Edward Grey in part of Powys. With so much of the March in the hands of the king, the administration of the lordships increasingly resembled that of the Principality. The separate existence of the earldom of March came to an end in 1489 (that of the duchy of Lancaster still exists today) and thereafter it was administered under the king's great seal. This was a significant step towards uniting the March with the Principality, a process completed through the legislation of 1536.

Other elements of that legislation had been foreshadowed during the reign of Henry VII and earlier. According to John Wynn, Henry, during his march through Wales, had promised to deliver the Welsh from 'such miserable servitudes as they have piteously long stood in', and George Owen states that Henry VIII was charged by his father to have 'a special care' for the Welsh; the one story and the other may be doubted, for neither was recorded until after 1600. The substance of the 'servitude' may also be doubted. Between 1467 and 1485, only one Welshman bothered to obtain letters of denizenship, a suggestion that the Yorkists did not make use of the Penal Code. The most oppressed of the inhabitants of Wales were the members of what remained of the *taeog* (villein) class, a class which still existed in parts of the north. The *taeogion* of Ceri and Cedewain were emancipated by the duke of York in 1447, a precedent for the series of charters granted by Henry VII in 1505, twenty years after he had ascended the throne. A charter was granted to Bromfield and Yale in 1505, to

Denbigh and to Chirk in 1506, to the three northern counties of the Principality in 1507 and to Rhuthun in 1508. In addition to emancipating the *taeogion*, the charters declared that the Welsh had the right to be officials and burgesses, to hold land according to the Law of England and to be dealt with by the courts in the same way as the English. *Taeogdrefi* (villein townships) had survived only in the north, and to the *taeogion* inhabiting them Henry VII was literally the man who freed them from servitude. Henry did not grant the charters because of pressure from the *taeogion*. As the *taeog* communities were in an advanced state of decay, most of their land had passed into the possession of freemen, and the status of a freeman who held unfree land was ambiguous. In order to permit the gentry to pursue estate building unrestrained, a new theory of landholding was necessary and this was accomplished by abolishing unfree land and recognizing the right of Welshmen to practise primogeniture. Nor were Henry's charters granted in order to promote the interests of his kinsmen, the gentry of the north. The gentry paid heavily for the charters; the king received at least £5,000 for them, an important consideration for so prudential a ruler. There was a twist in the tail of the grants: as they were charters, not parliamentary statutes, and as the English of the boroughs protested bitterly against them, there were doubts about their legality and it appears that neither the *taeogion* nor the gentry could be certain of their validity.

Previous generations of historians considered that Henry VII transformed England into a 'new monarchy' and thus guided the kingdom into the modern age. It is now realized that too much has been made of this notion. In many ways, Henry did little more than revitalize governmental machinery, which had not changed in its essentials since the reign of Edward I. That machinery had been paralysed in the feeble hands of Henry VI, but the work of rendering it effectual was already in train under Edward IV. Thus, very little political or constitutional significance should be assigned to the year 1485; yet, because so many history courses start in that year, a mistaken notion of its significance has become deeply rooted in the consciousness of successive generations of pupils and students.

Henry VII's great achievements were to keep his throne and to bequeath a secure title to his son. Nevertheless, Henry VIII saw fit to sweep away potential claimants to the throne with a ferocity which makes Richard III appear tender-hearted. One of them was the duke of Buckingham. He was executed in 1521 and his lordships – Brecon and Newport – were added to the territories of the crown. After 1521 there were in Wales only two men of substantial power – Rhys ap Thomas and Charles Somerset (who was promoted to the earldom of Worcester in 1514). Rhys died in 1525; his estates were inherited by his grandson, Rhys ap Gruffudd, but most of his offices were granted to Walter Devereux, the steward of the household of the king's daughter, Mary. In 1529 a quarrel arose between Devereux's men and those of Rhys. Rhys was accused of plotting with the king of Scots to make himself ruler of Wales. Part of the evidence against him was that he had sought to stress his links with the ancient Welsh kings by adopting the name Fitzurien. He was executed in 1531 and much of his land passed to Walter Devereux, estates which were the basis of the authority of Devereux's descendants, the earls of Essex, in west Wales.

Rhys ap Gruffudd was executed in the last month of the first year of the 1530s, a decade that saw legislation which represented the culmination of developments which had been afoot in Wales for a quarter of a millennium, and which would provide a framework for the life of the Welsh people, in matters secular and religious, for the next quarter of a millennium.

===

CHAPTER SIX

1530–1770: Ludlow, Gwydir and Llangeitho

In the years between 1530 and 1770, the Welsh were a people sustained by an agrarian economy; this had been true of them before 1530, but in the decades after 1770 industrial communities, revolutionary in their implications, would arise among them. Between the 1530s and the 1770s, the Welsh were members of an episcopalian church which rejected the claims of Rome; this had not been true of them before 1530 and they would progressively abandon the episcopalian tradition in the generations after 1770. Wales was incorporated into England in 1536 and would remain in that condition after 1770. If any unity can be ascribed to the experience of the Welsh in the years between 1530 and 1770, it arises from the fact that they were in that period a rural people of 'Anglican' faith who were bereft of political structures specific to themselves.

Yet these statements need to be modified. Pre-industrial Wales was not wholly lacking in industry. By 1770, some areas – the Swansea region, for example, or parts of Flintshire – had a long-established industrial tradition. Even in regions which appeared to be exclusively agricultural, large numbers of people were partly dependent upon the contribution they made, in their homes, to the woollen industry, an industry organized upon large-scale capitalist lines. It is misleading to assert without qualification that Wales between 1534 and 1770 was an 'Anglican' or Protestant Episcopalian country. For generations after the break with Rome, many of the people of Wales – perhaps the majority – looked back upon the old order with nostalgia, and some of them laboured heroically to restore their country to the authority of Rome. Although the vast majority of the Welsh attended the parish church and although members of the Church of England contributed massively to the culture of Wales, it is difficult to determine when the nation in its entirety took that Church to its heart, assuming indeed that that ever happened at all. Puritanism was slow to strike roots in Wales and even in 1770 only a small proportion of the population supported the sects which had sprung from it. By then, however, it is possible to discern some of the factors which were to cause the majority of the devout to abandon the parish church and to choose the chapel as their spiritual home. Although Wales was incorporated into England in 1536, the country continued to have a degree of administrative distinctiveness, and its ruling class developed political loyalties which had Welsh characteristics. There was no doubt about the social and cultural distinctiveness of the Welsh. To their English neighbours, theirs seemed a strange – almost a closed – society. It has recently been argued that Wales is an 'internal colony'. This can hardly have been true of the country in its industrial heyday when its commercial links stretched across the globe, but it can be claimed with some conviction that this was precisely what it was in the years between 1530 and 1770.

Those years were the era of the gentry. Evidence about members of other classes is scarce, although new techniques and more detailed research are shedding increasing light upon their laborious lives; in consequence, the claim made by A. H. Dodd in 1951 that the history of Wales in the Tudor and Stuart periods is the history of the privileged few is now less tenable. Nevertheless, much more is known about the privileged few and their activities are of central importance, for they exercised power over the rest of the population and received the greater part of whatever surplus the economy produced. Society was organized so as to promote the interests of the gentry, and those interests were consolidated further by measures passed by parliament in the 1530s. In that decade, the link with Rome was broken and Wales was incorporated into England. The two events were interdependent. By breaking with Rome, Henry VIII was challenging the Roman Catholic states of Europe, and the Tudors had particular reason to be aware that the condition of Wales was such that its coasts were open to invasion. In abolishing the authority of the Pope in his territories, Henry VIII was declaring that his kingdom was a totally sovereign state. 'This realm of England is an empire,' states the Act of Appeals of 1533. Henry's policy in Wales and elsewhere was an expression of the same principle: by abolishing anomalies such as the privileges of the Marcher Lords, he was seeking to ensure the exercise of that sovereignty throughout his kingdom.

The intensification of the sovereignty of the crown was the essence of what Geoffrey Elton has described as the 'Tudor Revolution'. The revolution is associated in particular with Thomas Cromwell, the chief administrator of the kingdom between 1532 and 1540. Cromwell rose to prominence because of his readiness to fulfil the king's desire to divorce Catherine, his wife, in order to enable him to marry Anne Boleyn. It was only the Pope who could end a marriage and, as he was reluctant to do so, the anti-papal sentiments of the English ruling class were given free rein in the parliament called in 1529. As a consequence, a process was set in train which had a momentum of its own; by 1535 parliament, on the initiative of Cromwell and with the acquiescence of Henry VIII, had passed a series of statutes which totally abolished the authority of the Pope in the territories of the crown of England and which elevated the king to the status of the Supreme Head of the Church of England.

The Protestant Reformation had been under way since 1517, when Luther had nailed his theses to the door of the Schlosskirche in Wittenberg, but in breaking with Rome Henry was not intending to embrace the Protestant faith. His intention was to take unto himself the authority of the Pope and to transform the Church in England (and in Wales) into the Church of England. He sought a revolution in authority, not a revolution in religion. The Ten Articles of the Faith, promulgated in 1536, confirmed the central position of the mass and the Catholic dogma of salvation. Nevertheless, in denying the authority of the Pope, the keeper of the keys of heaven, much of that dogma was abandoned; this was a cause of great concern, for in a society in which everyone believed in the awesome reality of heaven and hell, nothing could be more important than salvation. Thus a vacuum was created which could only be filled by Luther's theory that salvation came through faith alone. As a result, some form of Protestantism was implicit in Henry VIII's attempt to establish a Pope-less papism.

As the Welsh had no representation in parliament, their ruling class had no opportunity to express its views on the parliamentary measures which terminated the link with Rome. It is unlikely that the legislation was welcome in a conservative country like Wales, where there was no tradition (as there was in England) of regarding the Pope as a focus of xenophobic feelings. There is at least a suggestion that it was his loyalty to the old order, together with his dislike of Anne Boleyn –

who married the king in 1533 – which was the true cause of the execution of Rhys ap Gruffudd in 1531. In 1534, Rowland Lee, the bishop of Lichfield, was appointed president of the Council of Wales and he initiated a reign of terror. His activity has been interpreted as an attempt to suppress the lawlessness which prevailed there, and doubtless that was what it was, in the main. At the same time, Lee's campaign served to remind the Welsh of the power of the kingdom to which they belonged and of the futility of any attempt to challenge it. If Lee had such intentions, they were achieved; the men of Yorkshire rose in revolt against the religious changes in 1536, and those changes were challenged in arms by the Cornish in 1549. The Welsh showed no inclination to tread the path of armed revolt against the policies of the Tudors although, as Christopher Hill has argued, that fact in itself is not proof of the absence in Wales of tension between the old and the new.

It is probable that awareness of the religious changes was not widespread until 1536. In that year, as a result of the attack upon monasticism, all but three of the twenty-seven monasteries of full status in Wales were dissolved. The impact of even that change was not felt everywhere. Indeed, it is possible that the population in its entirety was not conscious that the old order was under attack until the initiation of the campaign against pilgrimages in 1538, or perhaps not until 1549, when fundamental changes were imposed upon all parish churches. But in those districts where monasticism had been a dominant feature for time out of mind, the dissolution must have been a strange and dramatic experience for the neighbours of the monks. It happened rapidly: the agents of the crown visited Margam on 26 June 1536, and by 23 August the lead of the monastery roof had already been melted down. Apart from the castles, the monasteries were the most splendid of the buildings of medieval Wales; they were mercilessly vandalized at the time of the dissolution and subsequently – a cruel blow to the architectural heritage of the Welsh. That destruction was the greatest loss caused by the dissolution, for the spiritual, educational, cultural and philanthropic contribution of the monks had for generations been slight. No new monastery was established in Wales after 1250, and probably no new friary after 1300, and thus the country had no experience of the orders which remained faithful to asceticism. By 1536, the intellectual climate had, for a century and more, become increasingly hostile to the monastic ideal. At the time of the dissolution, the thirteen Cistercian monasteries of Wales had a total of only eighty-five monks, and the houses of the Benedictines, the Augustinians and the Friars were even emptier. The Cistercians included men of substance such as Leyshon Thomas, the abbot of Neath, a scholar and administrator of renown. But there is ample evidence from Wales, as there is from the rest of Christendom, of the inability of monks to be faithful to the exalted, almost unattainable, demands of their calling. There were highwaymen among the friends of the abbot of Valle Crucis, and one of the monks of Strata Florida was accused of coining counterfeit money in his cell; the abbess of Llanllŷr expressed a wish for an ape as a pet, and Richard, the son of Robert ap Rhys, Wolsey's agent in Wales, was a mere stripling when he was appointed abbot of Aberconwy.

The weaknesses of the religious houses had been known for generations. Yet they were dissolved, not because of their weaknesses but because of their wealth, although it was the general awareness of their inadequacies that enabled the king to seize that wealth with very little opposition. The property of the Church was recorded in the *Valor Ecclesiasticus*, a remarkable document compiled in a few months in 1535, its compilation testifying to the increasing efficiency of the administrative machine which Cromwell was developing for his royal master. Henry VIII's finances were rickety. He had long since exhausted the wealth bequeathed to him by his prudential father and therefore he coveted the property of the religious houses. He was in full possession of that property by 1540. The smaller monasteries were dissolved in 1536, the friaries in 1538 and the larger monasteries in 1539; had the king kept all their property in his own hands, it is estimated that his annual income would have doubled to about a quarter of a million pounds.

The Welsh religious houses played a minor part in this story. There were forty-seven of them, if various cells and hospices are included as well as the monasteries, the nunneries and the friaries. According to the *Valor*, their total income amounted to £3,178. It was very unevenly apportioned: the annual income of Tintern was £192 and that of Valle Crucis was £188, but the monks of Caldey received no more than £5 and the Benedictine cell at Cardigan was worth only £13. Most of the receipts of the religious houses came from their lands (their 'worldly' income), but some monasteries enjoyed substantial 'spiritual' income (the profits of the ecclesiastical livings they possessed). The Church owned perhaps as much as a quarter of the land of Wales; as ten of the country's abbots had incomes larger than that of the bishop of Bangor, it would be reasonable to assume that the holdings of the monastic wing of the Church were at least as large as those of the secular wing. The dissolution of the monasteries therefore involved a change in the ownership of hundreds of thousands of hectares of Welsh land. Yet as the monks had long since abandoned direct farming and had leased their lands to gentry families on long leases, the religious houses only had a tenuous hold upon their territorial inheritance. The leases were confirmed at the time of the dissolution, and the land of the monks rapidly slipped through the king's fingers into the absolute possession of the squires. Some landowners had to pay heavily for that possession; Rice Mansel gave £2,482, as much as twenty times the annual rent, for the lands of Margam, but the earl of Worcester obtained the lands of Tintern for next to nothing.

The dissolution did not lead to the creation of a new class of landowners, for it benefited almost exclusively those families who were already in the ascendant. It is sometimes suggested that the loyalty of the gentry to the religious changes of the Tudors was bought by permitting them to gain possession of the property of the religious houses. Admittedly, there were members of the gentry class – John Prys, for example, who bought Brecon Priory – who were eager reformers. Yet most of the squires of Wales were conservative in their religious beliefs, and some of the Welshmen who profited from the dissolution – men such as Edward Carne, who made his home in Ewenni Priory – would be prominent in Mary's attempt to re-establish Roman Catholicism. It was the gentry too who obtained the 'spiritual' property of the monasteries. As a result, a high proportion of the livings of Wales – the majority, indeed, in the dioceses of Llandaf and St David's – were owned by laymen from the dissolution until the disestablishment of the Welsh Church in 1920. In those appropriated parishes, the landowner received the greater part of the tithe and it was he who appointed the incumbent. From the beginning, therefore, Welsh 'Anglicanism' was seriously compromised.

The path followed by Cromwell and Henry VIII was a dangerous one. By 1534, there were signs that France and Spain were prepared to put aside the enmity which had existed between them in order to challenge heretics and schismatics. Chapuys, the ambassador of Charles

V, the Holy Roman Emperor, reported that some of the great men of England had promised their support if Charles invaded the kingdom, and the ambassador believed that such a campaign would win general backing in Wales. Chapuys's hopes were not fulfilled, for the rivalry between the Roman Catholic states proved stronger than their desire to defend the unity of Christendom. Nevertheless, Rowland Lee was alive to the possibility that Wales would be invaded and he was active in recruiting soldiers, defending the coasts and seeking resources to repair the royal castles, most of which had long been falling into ruin.

As there was no invasion, Lee was able to devote his energy – which was stupendous – to the suppression of the unruly elements of Wales. His policy amounted to little beyond the hanging of wrong-doers publicly and frequently. It was all to the good, he believed, if those hanged were of exalted status. The execution of a gentleman, he believed, did more good than 'dispatching a hundred petty wretches', and he boasted that he had executed 'four of the best blood in Shropshire'. The chronicler Elis Gruffydd stated that Lee had hung five thousand men in six years, an exaggeration no doubt, but such was the impression he made that his methods were cited as a cure for the rebelliousness of the Irish. It appears that his campaign was effec-tive: he claimed in 1538 that 'order and quiet such as is now in England' prevailed in even 'the wildest parts of Wales'.

His efforts were reinforced by measures relating to Wales passed by parliament in 1534. The legislation sought to ensure that juries would be less indulgent towards defendants and that the cattle trade would not be impeded by thievery; those who committed crimes in the Marches were to be brought before the courts of adjoining English counties; the practice of *cymhortha* (the imposition of obligatory gifts) – a significant source of income for the Marcher Lords – was forbid-den, and the Council of Wales was authorized to punish Marcher lordship officials guilty of dishonesty or oppression. By 1534, there was very little substance to the principle that the March was beyond the reach of royal power. Indeed, there were very few Marcher Lords left. A list of the lordships was drawn up in 1531 and, although it contains eighteen names, most of those listed owned little beyond a few manors. Almost all the old families, descendants of the original *conquistadores*, had disappeared. 'Where is Bohun? Where is Mowbray? Where is Mortimer? . . . Above all, where is Plantagenet?' asked Chief Justice Crewe. As members of the old aristocracy were scarce in

Wales, the country lacked men confident enough to challenge royal policies. That is another reason why the Welsh did not rise against the Tudors as did the inhabitants of others of the territories of the crown – northern England, for example, where members of old lineages had survived. The most prominent of the Lords of the March was the earl of Worcester; he, it has to be admitted, was a kind of Plantagenet, but he held his lordships because he had married a descendant of the Herberts, a family which had newly risen to the ranks of the great men of Wales. It was acknowledged in 1524 that Worcester possessed *juria regalia* (regalian rights) in the lordship of Gower, but such recognition was becoming increasingly meaningless as royal officials and the Court of Star Chamber were resolutely seeking to undermine the autonomy of the lordships.

Worcester was a venal and oppressive figure and it appears that complaints against the rapacity of his officials were among the factors which caused Cromwell to give serious consideration to the situation in Wales. Lee had no wish to go beyond a policy of bloody suppression, for he despised the Welsh; they were congenital thieves, he argued, and it would be futile to invest anyone among them with authority. Cromwell, however, was prepared to listen to other opinions. It is likely that he received different advice from such men as John Prys of Brecon – his relation by marriage – and Richard Herbert of Montgomery, the son of the Richard Herbert who Ieuan Deulwyn had hoped would rid Wales of English officials. Richard's great-grandson, Baron Herbert of Cherbury, mentions a petition begging the king to grant the Welsh the privileges enjoyed by the rest of his subjects.

A step in this direction was taken with the act of February 1536 which authorized the appointment of justices of the peace in the counties of the Principality, in the county of Flint and in Pembroke and Glamorgan – lordships which over the years had developed features which allowed them to be considered to be counties in some respects. For centuries, justices of the peace had been key figures in the local government of England, and the administration of the counties was to remain in their hands until the establishment of county councils in 1889. The act of February 1536 (the provisions of which were extended to the rest of Wales through statute 27 Henry VIII c. 26) was the central feature of Tudor policy in Wales, for it meant that the country's administration was to be entrusted to the Welsh gentry. When the antiquarian George Owen sought to encapsulate the activity of the Tudors in Wales, he stressed that it was they who granted the Welsh 'magistrates of their own nation'.

The act of February 1536 was followed a few weeks later by the statute already referred to: clause 26 of the legislation passed in the twenty-seventh year of the reign of Henry VIII. This is the famous Act of 'Union', although it was not known as such until 1901, when Owen M. Edwards made tentative use of the title. The title is misleading, for it suggests that the statute was of the same nature as the statutes which united Scotland with England in 1707 and Ireland with Britain in 1800. Those Acts of Union were pieces of legislation passed by the parliaments of both the countries concerned, parliaments which were, in theory at least, of equal authority. Deception and trickery were necessary in order to induce the members of the parliaments of Scotland and Ireland to acquiesce in their abolition, but at least there was acquiescence; the Welsh Act of 'Union' was passed solely by the parliament of England, a body lacking members from Wales. Furthermore, 27 Henry VIII c. 26 claimed that union between Wales and England already existed. The preamble states: 'Wales . . . is and ever hath bene incorporated, annexed, united and subiecte to and under the imperialle Crown of this Realme as a verrye membre . . . of the same.' The preambles to statutes were propaganda, particularly those written by Cromwell. But, according to Goronwy Edwards, the statement was correct in its essentials; Edwards argued that the Principality of Wales had been united with England in 1284 through the Statute of Rhuddlan and that the clauses in the statute of 1536 are declaratory clauses confirming union rather than mandatory clauses creating union. Furthermore, he argued that what was accomplished in 1536 was not union between Wales and England but union between the Principality and the March, for the administrative system established in Gwynedd in 1284 was extended to the new counties carved out of the March and it came to be considered that the Principality embraced Wales in its entirety.

The most prominent element in the act of 1536 is a list of the lordships which would make up the new counties. The counties of Pembroke and Glamorgan were created by attaching other districts to the old lordships. Most of the rest of the March was divided into five counties – Denbigh, Montgomery, Radnor, Brecon and Monmouth – but some of the more easterly lordships were added to the counties of Shropshire and Hereford. Thus was created the border between Wales and England, a border which has survived until today. It did not follow the old line of Offa's Dyke nor the eastern boundaries of the Welsh dioceses; it excluded districts such as Oswestry and Ewias, where the Welsh language would continue to be spoken for centuries, districts which it would not be wholly fanciful to consider as *Cambria irredenta*. Yet, as the purpose of the statute was to incorporate Wales into England, the location of the Welsh border was irrelevant to the purposes of its framers.

Central to the incorporation was the abolition of any legal distinctions between the Welsh and the English. This meant that the Penal Code would be abandoned (but not formally repealed) and that the Law of England would be the only law recognized by the courts of Wales. It has already been noted that the Penal Code had long fallen into virtual disuse and that the Law of Hywel was in terminal decline. Indeed, there was little that was revolutionary about the Act of 'Union'; in many ways it did no more than consolidate changes which had long since manifested themselves in Wales. Nevertheless, before 1536, the status of the Welsh in the kingdom of England had been anomalous. Some of them petitioned for letters of denizenship exactly as did immigrants from Flanders or Spain. The anomaly came to an end in 1536. Thereafter, in the eyes of the law, the Welsh were English. Yet it would be equally valid to argue – as there was no longer any advantage in boasting of the condition of being English – that henceforth everyone living in Wales was Welsh, a principle which would be built upon over succeeding generations.

In the wake of the incorporation, the Welsh received representation in the English parliament, a right not previously granted save in 1323 and 1329. In 1536, twenty-six members of parliament were granted to Wales, the number rising to twenty-seven in 1543. At the time, the English parliament had 349 members; if the estimate that Wales had about 278,000 inhabitants and that England had 3.75 million is correct, then the Welsh percentage of the population (6.9) was close to the Welsh percentage of the membership (7.2). Wales was not granted the exact English pattern of representation. That pattern was two members for each county and two members for each borough; the Welsh pattern was one apiece. As Wales had thirteen counties, this added up to precisely twenty-six members, but the arrangement was not as neat as that. No town in Meirionnydd was considered worthy

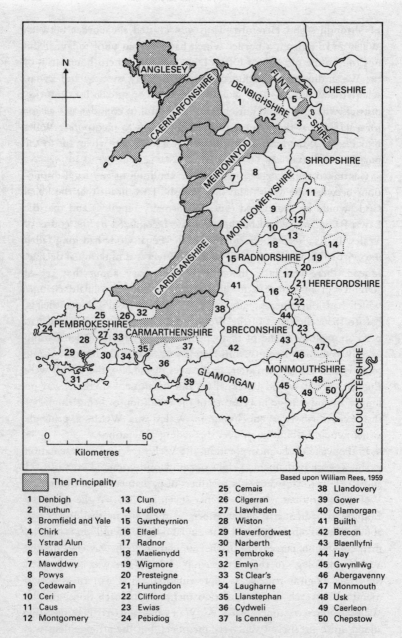

Based upon William Rees, 1959

The Principality

1 Denbigh	13 Clun	25 Cemais	38 Llandovery
2 Rhuthun	14 Ludlow	26 Cilgerran	39 Gower
3 Bromfield and Yale	15 Gwrtheyrnion	27 Llawhaden	40 Glamorgan
4 Chirk	16 Elfael	28 Wiston	41 Builth
5 Ystrad Alun	17 Radnor	29 Haverfordwest	42 Brecon
6 Hawarden	18 Maelienydd	30 Narberth	43 Blaenllyfni
7 Mawddwy	19 Wigmore	31 Pembroke	44 Hay
8 Powys	20 Presteigne	32 Emlyn	45 Gwynllŵg
9 Cedewain	21 Huntingdon	33 St Clear's	46 Abergavenny
10 Ceri	22 Clifford	34 Laugharne	47 Monmouth
11 Caus	23 Ewias	35 Llanstephan	48 Usk
12 Montgomery	24 Pebidiog	36 Cydweli	49 Caerleon
		37 Is Cennen	50 Chepstow

The Act of 'Union', 1536

of borough status; two members were granted to Monmouthshire, and in 1543 Haverfordwest was made a parliamentary borough. The Welsh members first attended parliament in 1542 (it appears that they were not summoned to the parliaments of 1536 and 1539), a crucial time in the history of that assembly. As Cromwell had used the statute as the chief weapon of the Tudor 'Revolution', the members of the House of Commons gained an awareness of self-importance that they had not previously possessed. They and their successors would be increasingly jealous of their privileges, thus ensuring that the parliament of England, unlike the parliaments of other European states, would not fade away as power was centralized in the hands of the sovereign.

There are about 7,500 words in the Act of 'Union'. Of these, 150 deal with the Welsh language, but that 2 per cent of the statute has been the subject of more discussion than the other 98 per cent. English was to be the only language of the courts of Wales, and those using the Welsh language were not to receive public office in the territories of the king. It is unlikely that the authorities were intent upon the demise of Welsh. As will be seen, the government would be prepared to promote the language in worship, showing more sympathy towards Welsh than it showed towards Irish in Ireland or French in Calais and much more than the government of Scotland showed towards the Gaelic of the Highlands. Cromwell's aim was uniform administration, an aim which any formal recognition of the Welsh language would have hindered. It was an aim which could be achieved without seeking the demise of the only medium of expression possessed by the vast majority of the people of Wales. Nevertheless, as Cromwell was intent upon placing the administration of Wales in the hands of the Welsh gentry, implicit in the Act of 'Union' was the necessity for the creation of a Welsh ruling class fluent in English.

In the High Middle Ages, the Welsh gentry had had little reason for learning English; the epithet *Sais* was given to a Welshman who knew the language, a suggestion that such knowledge was rare and viewed with contempt. As the *Francigenae* were anglicized, as English became the language of the courts of England, and as the pleasures of London began to appeal to the Welsh gentry, they undoubtedly felt the need to learn English. John Wynn of Gwydir states that his great-grandfather – presumably around 1470 – attended a school at Caernarfon for that purpose. Thus a proportion of the Welsh squires knew English before 1536. The proportion rose very rapidly thereafter, but two centuries and more would go by before English would wholly oust Welsh from the homes of the gentry. Yet that is what eventually happened, thus divorcing the Welsh ruling class from the language which had been its medium since the birth of the nation. The Act of 'Union' was not the only factor involved, but the language clause in the act is the clearest statement concerning the processes which were impoverishing the Welsh language and restricting its areas of use. The first part of the clause must have been impracticable. As the greater part of the population had no English, it would have been impossible to exclude Welsh from the courts and interpreters must have been used on a considerable scale. The monoglot Welsh cannot but have felt disadvantaged under such a system, and over the centuries awareness of the privileges enjoyed by English-speakers would give rise to attitudes to Welsh which would threaten the existence of the language.

There were obvious weaknesses in the act of 1536: its lists of Marcher Lordships were full of errors, some of its clauses were imprecise and the king was granted the power to revoke it. It appears that it was framed in haste and that the government was uncertain about the direction of its policy where Wales was concerned. The preamble stresses total incorporation, but the country was allowed a degree of administrative and legal distinctiveness wholly inconsistent with Cromwell's expressed intentions. He was executed in July 1540 and a document compiled a few months later suggests that the government was considering strengthening the distinctiveness of Wales, in particular with the aim of maintaining the Principality as the appanage of the heir to the throne. A second Act of 'Union' was passed in 1543. That corrected the weaknesses of the original act and added to the distinctiveness of Wales.

Those colonial extensions of the central power – the chanceries and exchequers established at Caernarfon and Carmarthen by Edward I – provided precedents for the legislators of 1536. Particular emphasis was placed upon the pattern in Gwynedd, for Caernarfon, with three counties answerable to it, became the model for the rest of the country. Pembrokeshire was added to the two counties which had been answerable to Carmarthen; a chancery and an exchequer were established at Denbigh to serve the three north-eastern counties, and Brecon became the centre for the counties of Radnor, Brecon and Glamorgan. The neatness of the four circuits of three counties seems to have appealed to the government, for in 1543 the circuits were used as the framework for a system of courts to serve twelve of the counties of Wales. The courts were the Great Sessions of Wales, which provided the Welsh with a cheap and efficient system of justice until their abolition in 1830. Monmouthshire was made directly answerable to the courts of Westminster, and as a result the notion arose that the county had been annexed by England. Monmouthshire was no less Welsh in language and sentiment than any of the other eastern counties and it would generally be treated as a part of Wales in the rare examples of specifically Welsh legislation passed between 1536 and 1830. With the abolition of the Great Sessions, almost all the differences which had existed between Wales and Monmouthshire came to an end; thereafter, it was increasingly assumed to be part of Wales, although the imprecision of its status did not disappear until 1974, when it was reborn as the county of Gwent.

The Great Sessions were not the only specifically Welsh institution referred to in the act of 1543. The act gave statutory recognition to the Council of Wales, a body which had hitherto been based solely upon the king's prerogative. The authority of the council extended over four of the counties of England as well as over the thirteen counties of Wales. It continued to sit at Ludlow, a town which developed some of the characteristics of a provincial capital. The existence of the Council of Wales, the Great Sessions and the three-county circuits, together with the unique features of Welsh parliamentary representation, prove that Wales was not totally absorbed into the English order of things as a result of the acts of 1536 and 1543. Furthermore, had the Tudors been more procreative, or had Henry VIII lived longer, the position of prince of Wales – with his Principality now extending over the whole of Wales – would also have served to stress the continuance of a degree of Welsh constitutional distinctiveness.

Nevertheless, the administrative and legal differences between England and Wales would henceforth be small in comparison with the similarities. To the spokesmen of Welsh public opinion, this was a cause of contentment, indeed of delight. For centuries, the 'Union' was considered to be an unmixed blessing to Wales and there can be no doubt that it was vastly favourable to the interests of the Welsh gentry. As justices of the peace, they dominated the local government of Wales; as members of parliament, profitable and entertaining doors were opened to them in London; as the statutes had outlawed *cyfran* and enthroned primogeniture, their efforts to build up their estates were facilitated; as the restrictions upon the Welsh as merchants and burgesses had been totally abolished, the possibilities of lucrative careers for the gentry in England as well as in Wales were greatly expanded. They rapidly seized their opportunities. In the Wales of the Tudors there was a marked widening of the gulf between the social classes; indeed, it has been claimed that the era saw a revolt by the rich against the poor. 'For nowe,' wrote George Owen, 'the poore tenante ys taught to singe unto his Lord a newe songe.' Until this century, the Act of 'Union' attracted nothing put praise. It is only over the last generation or two that it has been criticized, for its economic and social as well as for its cultural and national implications. The praise reached its peak with the comments of Edmund Burke in 1780: 'As from that moment, as by a charm, the tumults subsided . . . peace, order and civilization followed in the train of liberty.' It would, however, be equally apposite to quote another of Burke's speeches: 'When any community is subordinately connected with another, the great danger of the connection is the . . . self-complacency of the superior, which in all matters of controversy will probably decide in its own favour.'

When the act of 1543 was passed, the first Welsh heretic had newly been burned. He was Thomas Capper and his life was ended at Cardiff in 1542. By then, the monasteries and friaries and reliquaries had all been destroyed. Yet Henry VIII remained committed to Catholic orthodoxy concerning the mass, burning those who denied it, while executing those who denied his right to be Supreme Head of the Church. Luther's ideas were winning considerable support in the populous areas of England, but it appears that in Wales Capper was a lonely figure. Although anti-clericalism had been common among the Welsh for generations, criticism of clerics is not the same as a reasoned attack upon the creed they hold. The nurseries of the new ideas were the universities. Wales had no university, nor did the country have more than a few small groups of educated townsfolk, the backbone of the reformed religion. Parts of the Marches (where there was still, perhaps, some echo of the teaching of the Lollards), a few eastern towns such as Wrexham and Cardiff, and also south Pembrokeshire, a region where commerce and a knowledge of English were connecting links with the large ports of England – these were the only areas of Wales where Protestantism could be expected to strike roots. In the same way, there were only a few centres open to the impact of the efforts made, with knowledge and energy, to defend the tenets of Roman Catholicism. Although pilgrimages, respect for the rood and the cult of the Virgin were never more popular in Wales than they were on the eve of the Protestant Reformation and although the Welsh had a deep affection for sacred places such as Pen-rhys in the Rhondda and for images such as that at Llandderfel, their popular religion had little intellectual content. As there were among them only a few with the ability and motivation effectively to defend the old, and only a few eager to embrace the new, their general reaction to religious change was a sullen acceptance of the ordinances of the government.

But Wales was not wholly lacking in advocates of the old and of the new. The career of John Prys of Brecon proves that by about 1530 at least one Welshman had been attracted by the theory of justification by faith. Prys was responsible in 1546 for publishing the first book in the Welsh language. The invention of the printing press, the achievement of Gutenberg in Mainz in 1445, was one of the great turning-points of history. In its essence, the new device favoured widely spoken languages and it might reasonably have been expected that Welsh would not become a published language. The resources of its speakers were slight, hopes of an efficient system of distribution were slighter and the numbers literate in the language were small. Nevertheless, between 1546 and 1660, 108 books were published in Welsh, an infinitesimal number compared with the numbers published in English or French, but one which compares favourably with other languages which were not languages of state; in that period, only four books were published in Scottish Gaelic and only eleven in Irish.

Prys's book contained the Credo, the Lord's Prayer and the Ten Commandments. It was an attempt to introduce the scriptures to the people in their mother tongue. Rome frowned upon such attempts, for, as Pope Gregory VII had argued, the 'Scriptures . . . if available to everyone . . . will be misinterpreted by those of little learning . . . who will then be led to perdition.' Nevertheless, Church leaders, Pecham among them, had urged priests to 'explain to the people in ordinary language' the essentials of the Faith. To satisfy the needs of the priests, some of the key passages of the Bible were translated into

Welsh in the Later Middle Ages. There are twenty-two manuscripts of *Y Bibyl Ynghymraec*, a translation of a synopsis of the Bible. It is their existence, no doubt, which gave rise to the belief that the Bible had been translated into Welsh centuries before the Protestant reformers elevated the mother tongue to a central position in worship.

That principle came to prominence in 1549 with the publication of the first version of the English Prayer Book. Henry VIII had died in 1547 and the book was the work of the advisers of his son, Edward VI, a convinced Protestant. It led to a rebellion in Cornwall, where Cornish speakers considered the new service to be a piece of mummery. The English service must have been at least as strange to the Welsh, and this, no doubt, was the motive for the publication in 1551 of *Kynniver Llith a Ban*, a translation of the main texts of the Prayer Book. It was the work of William Salesbury, the most learned of the Welsh Protestants and a member of a gentry family of English origin. In the previous year, Salesbury had published *Ban wedi ei dynnu o Gyfraith Hywel Dda*, a volume seeking to prove that, under the Law of Hywel, clerics had been allowed to marry. That right was granted in 1549, a change which had far-reaching implications for the lives of the clergy – above all where their financial needs were concerned. Cohabiting clerics were a phenomenon throughout Latin Europe, and the sons or 'nephews' of priests were a constructive, if rather grasping, element. Canon lawyers thundered against the uxoriousness of clerics but they had very little success – particularly in Wales. To the ordinary priest, respectability for his wife and legitimacy for his children were above all the factors which made Protestantism acceptable to him. A far more Protestant version of the Prayer Book was authorized in 1553. It abandoned transubstantiation – the belief that the bread and wine turn into flesh and blood by means of the mass. In consequence, it can be claimed that it was in 1553 that Protestantism was established in the territories of the crown of England, for the distinction between the mass and the communion service is the essence of the distinction between Protestantism and Roman Catholicism.

Edward VI died in 1553. He was succeeded by his sister, Mary, who had inherited the unyielding Roman Catholicism of her grandparents, *los reyes católicos*. Because of her determination to re-establish the Roman Catholic religion, almost five hundred of her subjects fled to mainland Europe, where Protestantism, particularly in Switzerland, was developing a more radical form than that represented by Luther. There were about a dozen Welshmen among the exiles. The most prominent of them was Richard Davies, the son of the vicar of Gyffin near Conwy, who had embraced Protestantism while a student at Oxford. During her five-year reign, Mary burned about three hundred heretics. Most of them were from London and its surroundings, for it appears that it was only in the more central parts of the kingdom that Protestantism had won widespread support. Three were burned in Wales – White at Cardiff, Nichol at Haverfordwest and Ferrar, bishop of St David's, at Carmarthen. The majority of the Welsh people probably supported Mary's efforts. That, at least, is what is suggested by the work of the poets; to them, Protestantism was 'the English religion'. It was a Welshman, Edward Carne of Ewenni, whom Mary sent to Rome to offer the Pope the submission of her kingdom, and William Glyn, bishop of Bangor and brother of the founder of Friars School, was among the most zealous of her bishops. Carne and Glyn were inspired by the new energy flowing through their Church as the result of the campaign to reform it. They were sons of the Counter-Revolution, and had Mary lived longer they would probably have succeeded in making Wales a stronghold of renewed Roman Catholicism.

Mary died in 1558. She was succeeded by her half-sister, Elizabeth, the daughter of Anne Boleyn. With such ancestry, Elizabeth could not but be anti-papal, although it is doubtful whether she had any dogmatic religious convictions. All but one of Mary's bishops rejected her; the exception was Kitchin, bishop of Llandaf, and it was principally through him that the episcopate of the Church of England retained the apostolic succession, a matter of central importance to High Anglicans. Elizabeth's ideal was the restoration of the Pope-less Catholicism of her father, but she was obliged to cooperate with men of far more Protestant views, among them the returning exiles who were eager to purge the Church of everything which savoured of popery. Elizabeth compromised by re-establishing the essence of what had existed in 1553. The order of service of the Church of England was set out in the Prayer Book of 1559, the Church was defended in the *Apologia* of Bishop Jewel in 1562 and its doctrine was defined in the Thirty-Nine Articles of 1563. Elizabeth was so cautious with her religious changes and so clever in her dealings with Roman Catholic states that the Pope was not convinced until 1570 that she was an enemy of Rome. By then her Religious Settlement had begun to strike roots, as the noble English of the Prayer Book attracted the allegiance of congregations and as the majority of her subjects came to the conclusion that compromise was preferable to the religious wars which were tearing apart others of the states of Christendom.

Most of the people of Wales, clerical and lay, accepted the compromise. The notion that Protestantism was the 'English religion' faded, partly because of the dissemination of a myth concerning the origins of Welsh Christianity. According to the myth, the Celtic Church was a Protestant Church whose purity had been defiled by the Romish practices imposed upon it in the centuries following Augustine's arrival at Canterbury. Thus the Welsh were not being forced by England to embrace a new and dangerous heresy; rather were they returning to the faith of their forefathers, a faith which sprang directly from the era of the Apostles, for tradition maintained that it was Joseph of Arimathea who had converted the Britons to Christianity. This theory had an appeal in England too, for the reformers were concerned, not to create the new, but to re-create the old – the aim of all revolutionaries until very recently. The theory excited the imagination of Matthew Parker, archbishop of Canterbury from 1559 to 1575, who was eager to support attempts to stress the innately Welsh nature of the 'Anglicanism' of Wales.

The myth concerning the Protestantism of the Celtic Church was given prominence in *Epistol at y Cembru*, the introduction to the Welsh translation of the New Testament published in 1567. The *Epistol* was the work of Richard Davies, bishop of St David's from 1561 until his death in 1581. The translation was prepared in obedience to a parliamentary statute. In 1563, the bishops of Wales and Hereford were commanded to ensure that a Welsh version of the Bible and the Prayer Book would be available in every parish church in Wales by St David's Day, 1567. Thereafter, Welsh would be the language of the services in those parishes where the language was in general use. The statute was ironic, for it meant that parliament was authorizing the use of Welsh in spiritual matters barely a generation after declaring that it was to be banned in secular matters. In the situation that existed in the age of Elizabeth, however, the authorities considered religious uniformity to be more important than linguistic uniformity. The intention that the Welsh should learn English was not abandoned; the act of 1563 insisted that in the churches of Wales the English Bible should be available alongside the Welsh Bible in the hope that the

Welsh, in dealing with both languages together, would rapidly master English – the 'naturall mother tonge used within this Realme', as the act of 1536 described it.

The translation of the New Testament was put together at the bishop's palace at Abergwili, a place which in Richard Davies's day was one of the rare examples, before the establishment of the University of Wales, of a centre cherishing Welsh learning. Of the translation, 85 per cent was the work of William Salesbury, with Richard Davies and Thomas Huet contributing the rest. The translation was based upon the most correct texts of the Greek Testament as they were established by the tradition of biblical scholarship initiated by Erasmus in 1516. Salesbury held eccentric views concerning Welsh orthography; he ignored many of the mutations and over-emphasized the Latin elements in the language. The polished Cymricist, Morris Kyffin, declared that the ear of a true Welshman could not bear to listen to the work of Salesbury. But despite the weaknesses, the translation is masterly, and Welsh scholars have been prepared to defend Salesbury's achievement unto tears.

Perhaps the criticism of his work offended Salesbury, for it appears that he abandoned his original intention of preparing a translation of the Bible in its entirety. No such translation was available until 1588. In that year, through the efforts of William Morgan, the vicar of Llanrhaeadr-ym-Mochnant, Welsh joined the other mother tongues, thirteen in all, which were already the medium of a published Bible. The translation of the Old Testament was the work of Morgan, but with the New he did little more than 'cleanse', as he put it, the work of Salesbury and his colleagues of 'that incorrect method of writing which characterizes it throughout', rejecting (to quote Isaac Thomas) 'the archaic and the strange and the Latinized in favour of the contemporary, the familiar and the Cymric' – although some doubtless may regret that he swept away familiar words such as *cwny, can* and *ceser* used by the southerner, Thomas Huet, the translator of the Apocalypse.

William Morgan's Bible is a 'necessary, excellent, masterly, godly and learned' work, to quote Morris Kyffin. It appears that sufficient copies of it were published to answer the needs of all the parish churches of Wales – almost a thousand in all. Within a generation, Richard Parry, bishop of St Asaph, claimed that 'the majority of the Bibles in our churches have either been lost or have worn out', a consideration which led him in 1620 to publish a new edition. Parry's Bible is an adaptation of that of 1588, in which Morgan's work was corrected wherever it strayed from 'the strict purity of the literary language'. The adaptation was undertaken by John Davies of Mallwyd, Parry's brother-in-law and one of the most learned Welshmen of his day. The Bible of 1629 is the version of the scriptures in which generation after generation of the godly and literate among the Welsh were steeped. A large book, about twice the size of that of 1588, it was republished in a smaller form in 1630, and this 'Little Bible' was the first to reach the homes of the people. Between 1620 and 1800, 'Parry's Bible', or parts of it, was published twenty-eight times. Scores of further editions appeared between 1800 and 1900, thus ensuring that Welsh-speaking Wales would be awash with Bibles.

The Welsh Bible which resulted from the labours of Salesbury, Morgan, Davies and the others was as central to the experience of the Welsh as was Luther's Bible to that of the Germans or the Authorized Version to that of the English. Indeed, it could be argued that it was more central, for as German and English were languages of state they had secular means to maintain their unity, purity and dignity. This was not true of Welsh, a language which had for centuries been excluded from the courts of rulers, and which was increasingly excluded from the courts of law and the mansions of the gentry; the language was not fostered by school or college, and the bardic system which had cherished it since the birth of the nation was in decay. The language of the Bible was the language which had been nurtured by the bardic system, for Salesbury, Morgan and Davies had been immersed in the rich idiom of the poets of the 'Great Century' of Welsh literature. That richness was safeguarded – only just in time, probably – in the translation of the Bible. In about 1488, the abbot of Valle Crucis had appealed to Guto'r Glyn to 'give unto God part of the old understanding'. This was done, effulgently, a century later.

It is sometimes suggested that the Welsh Bible 'saved the language'. The claim has little substance in view of the fact that most of the non-state languages of Europe were fairly secure as spoken languages for centuries after 1588. What it did ensure was the continuance of the Welsh language as something more than a spoken language. As parsons throughout Wales were addressing their congregations, Sunday after Sunday, in the solemn rhythms of the Welsh of the Bible (and as importantly, if not more importantly, in the Welsh of the Prayer

Book), they familiarized the Welsh with an exalted image of their language. In imbuing their congregations with the language, they themselves became steeped in it, and thus there developed a tradition of 'literature-loving parsons' to which Welsh culture would be deeply indebted. Welsh was the only non-state language of Protestant Europe to become the medium of a published Bible within a century of the Reformation. This consideration is one of the most important keys to an understanding of the difference between the fate of Welsh and the fate of other non-state languages – Irish and Gaelic, in particular, the one lacking a Bible until 1690 and the other until 1801. Yet, it is not the only key, for some of those languages – Finnish, for example, which was Bible-less for generations after 1588 – is now sovereign in its territory in a way in which Welsh is not.

In translating the Bible, William Morgan was seeking to promote preaching in Welsh. Without the Bible in the mother tongue, he argued, the clergy lacked 'the words to explain in Welsh the sacred mysteries contained in the Holy Scriptures'. There had been very little tradition of preaching in Catholic Wales, for Catholicism stressed the Sacrament rather than the Word. There was a contrary emphasis in Protestantism, and the bishops of Elizabethan Wales lamented the scarcity of clergy fit to be licensed as preachers; there were only about twenty in the whole country in 1561. Those bishops were generally conscientious – and generally Welsh also. They succeeded in attracting some of the younger sons of gentry families into the ranks of the clergy, and the Anglican ministry also recruited graduates who had experienced the Protestant atmosphere of the universities of England. It was in those universities – Cambridge in particular – that the Puritan ethos crystallized. From about 1570, Puritanism was a serious challenge to the Elizabethan Religious Settlement. The Puritans were inspired by their vision of the early Church, particularly as that was interpreted by John Calvin, who had from 1536 until his death in 1564 conducted his theocratic experiment in Geneva. The followers of Calvin wished to transform the Church of England into a Presbyterian Church; they demanded a bishopless Church of intense moral consciousness; they embraced the theory of Election and sought to place laymen under the strict discipline of ministers of the Gospel – a system which John Knox partly succeeded in creating in Scotland. The Presbyterian Puritans were a continual affliction to Elizabeth, for they were numerous in parliament and influential among members of the court, the merchant class and the aristocracy. To the authorities, the Separatists were even more of a threat, for they denied the need for a 'Church of England', believing that the only true Church was the congregation of saints separated from the world.

In the England of Elizabeth, the influence of the Separatists was slight compared with that of the Presbyterians. In Wales, both were almost wholly absent. During the reign of Elizabeth, it would appear that the only Puritan to represent a Welsh constituency was Edward Downlee, the member for Carmarthen in the parliaments of 1584–5 and 1586–7. Although Downlee was the heir of the Dunn family of Cydweli, his home was in Buckinghamshire. The attacks of the Puritans reached their peak in the course of the parliamentary session of 1586–7. During that session, Downlee presented to parliament *The Aequity of an Humble Supplication*, a treatise which pleaded for preachers to expound the gospel to the Welsh. It was the work of John Penry, a native of Breconshire who had embraced Presbyterianism while a student in Cambridge. Penry composed two other treatises in 1588, both vicious in their condemnation of the Welsh clergy; the bishops of Wales, for example, were described as 'excrements of romish vomits'. Because of his links with the printing press which produced the Marprelate Tracts – witty and scathing attacks upon the weaknesses of the Church of England – Penry fled to Scotland in 1589. In 1592, he made his home in London, where he joined the Separatists. He, therefore, was the first Welsh Dissenter. In 1593, he was brought before the Court of High Commission, a body which had gained extensive authority on religious matters in the age of Elizabeth. He was sentenced to death by a verdict of doubtful legality and was hanged on 19 May 1593. Penry believed passionately that 'eternal damnation is the consequence of ignorance of God's saving mercy as it is expressed through Christ'. Side by side with his religious convictions, his Welsh patriotism was a secondary matter, although the *Aequity* and his comments on the eve of his execution show that he had a sincere concern for Wales. Penry was an impulsive and narrow-minded man, but there is dignity in his plea for the sovereignty of the individual conscience. Religious tolerance was implicit in that plea, but that virtue is absent in Penry's works. His ideas won no sympathy among his contemporaries in Wales, although the appearance of the *Aequity* in 1587 may have caused Whitgift, the archbishop of Canterbury, to be more positive in his support for the publication of William Morgan's Bible in the following year. Penry was ignored for centuries. He was elevated, just over a hundred years ago, to the position of Wales's leading martyr, a notable example of the ability of that age, like all ages, to discover and to produce the heroes it needs.

Penry's impulsiveness stemmed in part from the fear that Roman Catholicism would reassert itself in Wales if the people were not imbued with Protestant beliefs. It was not a baseless fear. The allegiance of most of the Welsh people to the Church of England was superficial, and it was reported in 1577 that some of the clergy of Wales were saying mass in secret and conducting baptisms and funerals according to the Catholic rite. The hearts of many of the gentry were with the Old Faith and members of some of the most distinguished lineages of Wales – Morgan, Herbert, Turberville and Salesbury among them -- were prepared to offer protection to the Catholic loyalists who dwelt on their estates. For centuries, the common people adhered to many of the elements of the Old Faith; they made the sign of the cross, they went on pilgrimage, they cherished holy wells, they celebrated patronal festivals and, although they attended services of the Church of England, it would appear that the parish church was less central to their lives than it had been for their ancestors.

Only about fifteen of the clergy of Wales were deprived of their livings because of their refusal to accept the Elizabethan Settlement. They included men of ability and energy such as Morys Clynnog, the prospective bishop of Bangor, Gruffydd Robert, the archdeacon of Anglesey, Morgan Phillips, the precentor of St David's, and Owen Lewis, a fellow of New College, Oxford. They fled to mainland Europe to plan the restoration of their country to Rome. Their ranks were strengthened in subsequent decades by men such as Hugh Owen of Llŷn, Rhosier Smith of St Asaph, Thomas Morgan of Monmouthshire and John Jones of Breconshire. The exiles had a number of options: they could seek to depose Elizabeth and replace her with a sovereign loyal to Rome; they could arrange for trained priests to infiltrate her kingdom; they could write and distribute Catholic literature. The Welsh were prominent in all these activities. From 1570, when Elizabeth was excommunicated by the Pope, until 1587, when her heiress, Mary Queen of Scots, was executed, there was a series of plots to place Mary on the throne of England. Thomas Morgan and Hugh Owen were prominent in most of them; it was

Morgan who arranged in 1586 for Mary to be introduced to Anthony Babington, the author of the plot which sealed her fate.

As the result of the threat to Elizabeth – which greatly intensified when Philip II of Spain claimed in 1587 that he had inherited Mary's rights (a claim which led to the Armada in 1588) – the government's attitude towards Roman Catholicism became increasingly severe. Serious efforts were made to prevent infiltration by Catholic priests. The chief centre for their training was Douai near Calais, where Morgan Phillips and Owen Lewis had assisted in 1568 in establishing a college to promote the restoration of England and Wales to the Church of Rome. By 1642, 119 prospective Welsh priests had been trained in mainland Europe, sixty-four of them at Douai. The rest attended various places, including Reims, Valladolid, Salamanca and Rome. The English College at Rome was established in 1578; its first head was Morys Clynnog, but he left the office after two years because of opposition from the English and the Jesuits. William Davies, the first Welsh priest to be executed under Elizabeth, had been trained at Reims; he was hanged for treason at Beaumaris in 1593. He had been preceded to the scaffold by Richard Gwyn, a schoolmaster from Llanidloes, who was executed at Wrexham in 1584.

In 1568, the year of the establishment of the college at Douai, a booklet of sixty-three pages was published in Rome. This was *Athrawaeth Gristnogawl* (Christian Doctrine), an exposition of the Catholic faith in the form of a catechism. It was the work of Morys Clynnog and contained an introduction by Gruffydd Robert, a canon of Milan and the confessor of Carlo Borromeo, the archbishop of Milan and the holiest of the leaders of the Counter-Reformation. In 1585, an essay on loving God – *Y Drych Gristianogawl* – appeared. According to tradition, it was printed in a cave near Llandudno; if so, *Y Drych* was the first book to be printed in Wales. These two volumes, together with three volumes of translations by Rhosier Smith, are the sum total of Counter-Reformation publications in Welsh. Although slight, they represent, according to Thomas Parry, 'a more substantial effort in some respects than that of the Protestants at home who had every advantage'.

There is no more romantic chapter in the history of Wales than the activities of the Catholic exiles, ranging as they did from Valladolid to Milan, from Rome to Douai. Yet those activities were almost a total failure. Despite every plot and deception, sacrifice and martyrdom, it was recorded in 1603 that there were only 808 people in Wales who shunned the services of the Church of England, compared with 212,450 who attended them. The figure probably understates the number of recusants; Glanmor Williams suggests that 3,500 would be more correct and he stresses that recusants were numerous in some districts, particularly in the dioceses of St Asaph and Llandaf. Nevertheless, they were a tiny minority. The coercive power of the state, which was a reality everywhere in Wales by the age of Elizabeth, was the factor chiefly responsible for the failure of the Counter-Reformation in Wales. This provides a striking contrast with Ireland, where the government was unable to prevent the campaign of the Catholic orders. In 1574, the unwillingness of the Welsh gentry to give sanctuary to Roman Catholic priests was a cause of distress to Robert Gwyn, a relation of Hugh Owen. The unwillingness intensified after 1586, following the execution of Thomas Salusbury, the heir to the Lleweni estate, for his part in the Babington Plot.

The work of the exiles was hindered by their internal divisions and by the *émigré* mentality which developed among them. The Roman authorities paid little attention to the Welsh campaign; of the Welsh priests trained in Douai and elsewhere, only about a quarter were sent back to their country, and the Papacy ignored Owen Lewis's earnest plea for resources to publish Welsh books. Furthermore, what the exiles were offering the Welsh was unfamiliar to them. The ethos of the Catholicism of the Counter-Reformation, with its emphasis upon priestly privilege and its respect for the fanaticism of the Jesuits (although not all Welsh *émigrés* warmed to that fanaticism), was very different from the old religion, leisurely and corrupt, for which the Welsh conservatives yearned. The way in which the old practices were attacked by the supporters of the Counter-Revolution is strangely similar to the strictures of the Protestant reformers. Indeed, it is striking how little difference there was between the two groups. Like Calvin and Loyola, they were brothers under the skin. Nevertheless, in the great struggle between Catholicism and Protestantism, each group considered itself to be right and the other to be wrong – and there cannot be a wider divide than that.

The similarity between the zealous Protestant and the zealous Catholic is at its most evident in the careers of William Salesbury and Gruffydd Robert. They shared the same cultural aspirations, for both

were heirs to the humanism of the Renaissance. Humanism developed
from about 1350 onwards in the prosperous, capitalist cities of Italy,
the result of a desire for a wider perspective on life than was offered
by the feudal system and the medieval Church. To the humanists, the
civilizations of Greece and Rome represented the pinnacle of man's
achievement; they delighted in the literature, philosophy and
architecture of the Old World; they sought manuscripts of the works
of classical authors; they acclaimed the polish of Latin writers such as
Cicero, nourishing the hope that their mother tongues could become
equally perfect in lineage, richness and purity. Alongside the respect
for literary learning was a curiosity about man and his world.
Although the scientific method of thinking had not yet been
established (the Renaissance was the golden age of alchemy and astrol-
ogy), the era saw significant advances in linguistics and history,
geography and mathematics, medicine and astronomy and, above all,
astounding success was achieved in portraying human beings in paint
and sculpture.

As languages could aspire to exalted virtues, so also could men, for
the humanists abandoned the pessimism concerning the achievements
of man which had characterized the Middle Ages. In 1514, Baldassare
Castiglione wrote a highly influential description of the ideal of a
gentleman: skilful in public affairs and in the amusements of life, but
also imbued with learning, wisdom and culture. In the urban economy
of Italy, literacy and education – previously the virtual monopoly of
clerics – were becoming essential for laymen. They were becoming
increasingly essential in other countries of Europe also as their
economies and administration evolved, and the combination of ideal
and necessity led to an explosion in educational provision.

The life of Wales was enriched, to some degree at least, by every
one of the elements of the Renaissance. The 'New Learning' did not
take root in England until about 1530, when it won the allegiance of
Welsh students such as John Prys and Edward Carne. William
Salesbury obtained his mastery of Greek at Oxford in the 1540s, a
period when Greek studies – a central feature of the Renaissance –
enjoyed high prestige in the universities. Gruffydd Robert favoured
the Latin authors and when he had passed three score years and ten he
published a Welsh translation of part of Cicero's dialogue, *De
Senectute*. The translation was appended to his *Gramadeg Cymraeg*
(Welsh Grammar), printed in parts in Milan between 1567 and about

1590. Gruffydd's work may be placed side by side with the grammars and dictionaries of William Salesbury, Siôn Dafydd Rhys, Thomas Wiliems and John Davies as proof of the Welsh humanists' intense interest in the Welsh language. They sought to portray its richness in idiom and proverb, and laboured so to adapt it as to make it a suitable medium through which to treat all aspects of culture.

The publications of the humanists contain prefaces which express concern that the circumstances of the age were hostile to the development of Welsh as a language of learning – indeed, were threatening its very existence. But equally often they express confidence in it, for its lineage and richness were proof that it was equal, as Gruffydd Robert put it, 'to the best of languages if it is set out in accordance with its own spirit and image'. It was cognate with Latin, if the stories of Geoffrey of Monmouth were to be believed. It had been the vehicle of bardic learning since the earliest ages, and the means of transmitting Christianity to the Britons in the time of the Apostles. It was therefore worthy to be included among the learned languages. 'Demand learning in your language,' urged Salesbury, and Siôn Dafydd Rhys longed to see a library of Welsh books containing every branch of knowledge.

Respect for the virtues of the Welsh language – virtues which had been sustained by the bardic tradition – was the basis of the aspirations and the achievements of the humanists. Yet they did not succeed in grafting the learning of the Renaissance upon that tradition. That was their ambition, as can be seen from the debate conducted from 1581 to 1587 between Edmwnd Prys, a graduate of Cambridge, and Wiliam Cynwal, a poet who was, through Gruffydd Hiraethog, an heir to the tradition of Tudur Aled and his fellows, the poets of the 'Great Century'. There were numerous similar debates in other parts of Europe where the New Learning came into conflict with the Old. Cynwal's responses are proof of the conservatism of the poets; he declared unequivocally that he would not yield an iota of the 'old understanding', for, in the making of a poet, nothing more was needed. In the century after the Act of 'Union', a far more abundant body of verse was composed in the strict metres than in the previous century. The authorities were concerned by the 'intollerable multitude [of] mynstrelles, Rithmers and Barthes' that wandered the country, and through the queen's commission an eisteddfod was held at Caerwys in 1567 in order to license the bards and to disown the less reputable elements. But despite such efforts, the work of the poets was declining in quality. They themselves were aware that their tradition was ebbing. '*Swydd y bardd sydd heb urddas*' (The office of poet lacks dignity) lamented Siôn Tudur in 1580. There was worse to come: in 1655 Edward Dafydd was to mourn: '*Nid yw'r byd hwn gyda'r beirdd*' (This world has abandoned the poets). They blamed the gentry for being reluctant to give them patronage, and that reluctance became increasingly apparent as the greater gentry became anglicized and the lesser gentry became impoverished through inflation and the pressure of their wealthier neighbours. There was also a change in taste: as the literary wealth of Europe came within the reach of the gentry through the printed book, the recitations of the poets became inadequate as entertainment; with the desire for family seclusion increasing – a development reflected in the architecture of the period – the 'hall culture', the mainstay of the poets since the time of Taliesin, was being abandoned; as other ways of expressing gentility became available – coats of arms, grandiose tombs, extravagant expenditure – there was a decline in the role of the poets as arbiters of social status. They believed that their muse was of divine origin and that the gentry were, as Simwnt Fychan put it, 'rejecting the Holy Spirit'. Yet Siôn Tudur and others recognized that the poets themselves, with their empty phrases and their fake genealogies, were bringing their art into disrepute, while their distrust of the values of the Renaissance and of the printed book were signs of the closed minds which would condemn their tradition to virtual oblivion.

Nevertheless, the extinction of the bardic order should not be antedated. For generations to come, there would be poets eager to praise the gentry: in 1691, Owen Gruffydd was generously rewarded for his elegy to Roger Mostyn, and the Nanneys of Nannau maintained a household bard until 1694. By then, however, the bardic schools had long become extinct and the tradition of the strict metres had greatly decayed. In consequence, the status of free verse was enhanced, thus demonstrating the remarkable tenacity of the Welsh literary tradition. Free verse had previously been too insignificant to preserve, but the skill of the composers of songs, carols and *cwndidau* (conduts or motets) of the Elizabethan age is proof that their craft had deep roots. That craft is seen at its best in the metrical psalms of Edmwnd Prys (printed with the Prayer Book in 1621), a foretaste of the wealth of hymns which would be among the glories of the literature of Wales.

The Welsh literary tradition did not succeed in coming to terms with the challenge of the Renaissance. It is doubtful, however, whether much evidence of the splendours of that tradition would have survived at all but for the example provided by the humanists who collected and copied the work of the writers of Antiquity. John Prys, the earliest Welsh humanist, was an avid collector of manuscripts, an activity which reached its peak with the career of Robert Vaughan (1592–1667), whose house at Hengwrt near Dolgellau contained *The Book of Taliesin*, *The Black Book of Carmarthen*, *The White Book of Rhydderch* and a host of other treasures. It was Vaughan also who provided a home for the vast collection of John Jones, Gellilyfdy (*c.* 1578–1658), the most industrious and skilful of the Welsh copyists. There were some who showed the manuscripts less respect: Protestant zealots destroyed a great deal of 'popish' material, and Siôn Dafydd Rhys grieved over the fate of manuscripts which 'passed into the hands of infants who tore them up . . . or of shop maids who packed vegetables in them, or of tailors who used them to make dummies'. Much ancient wealth was therefore lost, but all of it would have vanished but for the bibliomania of a few squires and the tireless labour of men such as John Jones, Gellilyfdy.

This antiquarian urge was not confined to language and literature. As the humanists sought to comprehend the world that had created the classical writings they treasured, they came to have an understanding of the flow of history. This development was encouraged by the awareness of time inculcated by the striking clocks which were increasingly within the hearing of urban populations. There arose a desire to do more than simply compile chronicles. The ability to assess and interpret sources was fostered. In Wales, the development of this instinct was hampered by the determination to defend the central myth of Welsh identity – the work of Geoffrey of Monmouth. Following the publication of *Anglica Historia*, the work of the Italian, Polydore Vergil, in 1534–5, it became fashionable to deny the truth of Geoffrey's work, much to the distress of patriotic Welshmen. From the time of John Prys until that of the Morrises of Anglesey two centuries later, a great deal of the energy of Welsh historians was expended upon answering mockers such as Vergil. As they were reacting to a threat from outside, their works were composed in Latin or in English; as a result, the tradition of writing the history of Wales in Welsh developed very slowly, if it developed at all. The most ambitious attempt to write the history of the nation was *Historie of Cambria* published in 1584, the work of David Powel of Ruabon. The basis of the book was Humphrey Lluyd's adaptation of *Brut y Tywysogyon*, although it also contained material collected by John Prys and Edward Stradling. A revision of it was published by William Wynne in 1697, a work republished in 1702, 1774, 1812 and 1832. This was to be the standard version in English of the early and medieval history of Wales until the publication of Jane Williams's *A History of Wales Derived from Authentic Sources* in 1869, or indeed until the appearance of J. E. Lloyd's splendid volumes in 1911. Through the work of Powel and Wynne, Geoffrey of Monmouth's stories remained part of Welsh consciousness long after scholarship had rejected them.

Local studies were not vitiated to the same extent by obsession with myth. The decades around 1600 were a golden age of local history. Historians were inspired by Camden's topographical masterpiece (*Britannia*, 1586), by the gentry's desire to learn about their origins and their locality, and by the county loyalty fostered by the increasing importance of that unit. Volumes were written on the history of the counties of Anglesey, Pembroke, Glamorgan and Meirionnydd, and in 1602 George Owen compiled his 'Description of Wales', an attempt to chronicle all the features of the country. George Owen's work on Pembrokeshire was the most mature product of this school of Welsh antiquarians; it testifies to the thoroughness of his research, to his analytical powers and to his intense affection for his native place. Owen also drew a map of Pembrokeshire which was published in the sixth edition of Camden's *Britannia*, the first book to contain individual maps of all the counties of Wales.

Delight in maps was one of the features of the Renaissance. There had been medieval maps in which Wales had been included, but they were crude at best. The first map which is specifically a map of Wales was that drawn by Humphrey Lhuyd and published in Antwerp in 1573 by Abraham Ortelius as an appendix to his atlas. It had its imperfections. The north, for example, was portrayed as being smaller than it is, and the south larger – very odd in view of the fact that it was the work of a native of Denbigh. Over the succeeding generations, far more accurate maps of Wales would be published, including a skilful one by Speed in 1611 and a splendid one by Blaeu in 1645, but Lhuyd's map retained its appeal, for it was reprinted almost fifty times between 1573 and 1741.

The popularity of the map resulted in part from the rediscovery of the cartographic tradition of the classical world and in part from the desire to chart the remarkable ocean voyages of the Europeans. The Welsh were involved in those voyages, and it would be agreeable to be able to believe in the story that it was Richard Amerik (ap Meurig) of Glamorgan, a Bristol merchant and one of the patrons of John Cabot's second voyage, who gave his name to America. Cabot's ambition was to discover the north-west passage to India and China. He was succeeded in the search by Robert Mansel of Margam and Thomas Button of St Lythan's, and the place-names Mansel Island and New Wales in Hudson's Bay commemorate their efforts. Robert Vaughan of Llangyndeyrn had rather more ambitious ideas about a new Wales, and between 1616 and 1632 he sought in vain to establish a Welsh colony in Newfoundland. The same period saw the creation of New England and Nova Scotia, and, had Vaughan succeeded, the three nations of Britain would have had colonies on the eastern seaboard of North America.

The north-west passage had already excited the imagination of one of the most remarkable figures of the Renaissance. He was John Dee, a London Welshman who claimed descent from Rhodri Mawr. In 1577, Dee claimed that King Arthur had won a vast empire in the north Atlantic, and that the voyages of Madog ab Owain Gwynedd (a story he borrowed from Humphrey Lhuyd) had confirmed the title of the Welsh to those territories. By the age of Elizabeth, he asserted, they were under the sovereignty of the queen as successor to the Welsh princes. It was Dee, it would appear, who coined the term British Empire – British in the sense of Brythonic. Gwyn A. Williams, in his uniquely provocative way, has argued that it is fitting that the term was coined by a Welshman. Inventing the British Empire would be a sufficient source of pride or shame, but this was only a minor part of Dee's activities. He was one of the magi, the seers of immeasurable knowledge and inexhaustible curiosity, the shapers of the chrysalis of that gadfly, the scientific mind. Dee published the work of Euclid and he prepared an edition of the mathematical studies of Robert Recorde of Tenby, the inventor of the equals sign ($=$), a work which had been published twenty-six times by 1662.

Dee's name is one which can be placed side by side with the great polymaths of the Italian Renaissance. Their genius found particularly fertile ground in architecture, painting and sculpture, fields in which the Welsh intellect did not flourish. The artistic vision of the Renaissance was slow to strike root in England also; the English tended to import their artists, and Inigo Jones was the first Englishman (all efforts to make a Welshman of him have failed) fully to understand the architectural principles developed in Italy. The earl of Pembroke formed a magnificent collection of the work of the great masters, but that was displayed in his London house and in his mansion at Wilton rather than in Wales. Some gentry houses contain portraits painted by Welsh artists in the decades after 1550, but the country was not visited by any of the great artists of mainland Europe. A few tombs were built – that to Richard and Magdalen Herbert in St Nicholas, Montgomery, for example – which prove that there was at least an echo in Wales of the glory which Michelangelo initiated in San Lorenzo, Florence. But most Renaissance sculpture in Wales is naïve in its appeal, as Bishop Rudd's delightful tomb at Llangathen demonstrates. Wales had very few men with the money and the taste to erect buildings reflecting the style of the Renaissance, although commercial links with Flanders inspired Plas Bachegraig in the Vale of Clwyd (1576) and Plas-mawr, Conwy (1576–95). Plas-mawr contains a great deal of skilful plasterwork, rich in device, and similar work may be found in the gallery of Powis Castle, which was built in about 1592. Hardly any churches were erected in Wales in the century after the Protestant Reformation and it is only an occasional private chapel, such as that at Gwydir, which carries a suggestion of the influence of Renaissance notions of ecclesiastical architecture. The Welsh economy was less able to offer patronage to artists and architects than it was to writers and publishers, and it is this, rather than theories about the inability of the 'Celts' to appreciate the visual arts, which explains the feeble contribution of the Welsh to the art of the Renaissance.

It was difficult to transplant to Wales other aspects of the Renaissance. The country's economy was very different from that of places such as Urbino, where Castiglione found his ideal of the cultured gentleman. Yet, as will be seen, the Welsh economy was becoming more complex and opportunities for education and openings leading to profitable careers were multiplying – at least for males belonging to the upper and middle levels of society. Thus Wales did not wholly lack men of the kind praised by Castiglione: Thomas Prys, for example (squire, soldier, pirate and poet), or Morris Kyffin (soldier, administrator, poet and translator), or William Midleton, who fought – as did Kyffin and Prys – in Elizabeth's campaigns in the Low Countries and who published a study of poetry and a collection of metrical psalms. There was also the Herbert family, the two brothers, the earls of Pembroke and Montgomery, Shakespeare's patrons, and their kinsman, William Herbert – scholar, planter in Ireland, the first Welshman known to have addressed the House of Commons, and a pioneer of education who in the 1590s sought to establish a college for the Welsh in the ruins of Tintern Abbey.

Herbert's hopes were not fulfilled, but some years earlier, in 1571, Jesus College, Oxford's first Protestant foundation, was established. Although it was not intended exclusively for the Welsh, it became increasingly to be considered the pinnacle of the academic ambition of the young men of Wales, particularly after it was re-endowed by Leoline Jenkins of Cowbridge in 1685. The universities of England became more important to the Welsh following the Protestant Reformation, partly because Welshmen (apart from the papist minority) were no longer acceptable in the universities of Catholic Europe. About twenty-five Welshmen were entering Oxford and Cambridge annually in the later decades of Elizabeth's reign. At both universities, the teaching of law was virtually a monopoly of the Welsh. They were also prominent in the Inns of Court: at least four Welshmen a year were joining Lincoln's Inn by the beginning of the reign of James I. With the rise in the commitment to formal education, the Welsh gentry became increasingly eager to send their sons to English public schools. Shrewsbury School, founded in 1552, was especially popular, but Welsh pupils were also to be found at Westminster, Eton, Winchester, Bedford and St Paul's. Schools for the less wealthy were established in the market towns of Wales – about eighteen in all by 1603. They were grammar schools – that is, centres to master the elements of Latin – and their equivalent could be found throughout those parts of Europe inspired by the principles of the Renaissance. English was tolerated in them but Welsh was not, for the language was irrelevant to their purpose – the fulfilment of the desire for gentility and a career.

The achievements of the Welsh humanists fell far short of their aspirations. The library for which Siôn Dafydd Rhys yearned did not materialize; only a tiny proportion of classical culture found expression in Welsh and the Old Learning failed to blossom under the influence of the New. The aristocratic literary culture of Wales was excluded from the grammar schools and from the 'Welsh' college at Oxford, just as the country's popular literary culture would be excluded from its county schools and university colleges four hundred years later. Men who epitomized the ideals of Castiglione were rare among the gentry of Wales, and there are small towns in Italy with more evidence of the architectural genius of the Renaissance than exists in the whole of Wales. Yet what was achieved was substantial. The greatest feat was ensuring that Welsh should be a language of religion, an achievement attributable as much to cultural pride as to religious zeal. The few books published proved that there was substance to the boasts of the humanists, and allowed Welsh to set out upon its halting journey as a published language. There were at least a few Welshmen whose careers show that the ideals nurtured in Florence and Urbino were not wholly irrelevant to Wales, and the range of activities of the Welsh was never wider that it was in the age of the Renaissance. In comparing the Welsh – a conservative people, bereft of control over their fate and lacking any centres of wealth – with others of the peripheral peoples of Europe, what is striking is not the inability of the Welsh humanists fully to realize their hopes, but rather the scale of their accomplishment and the fact that such people and such hopes existed at all.

All this suggests that the Welsh of the Tudor age had a dynamic spirit and an urge for modernization which differentiated them from some of the other peripheral peoples in Europe, their fellow Celts above all, perhaps. The difference may largely be attributed to political and economic factors. The lawlessness of pre-'Union' Wales has undoubtedly been exaggerated, but it is impossible to deny that the country experienced increasing stability as the system imposed by the acts of 1536 and 1543 struck roots. That stability helped to promote the economic growth which was a marked feature of the century following 1536, growth which consolidated developments which were already apparent in the Welsh economy.

Economic growth facilitated population growth. Although all statements relating to the population of Wales before the first census in 1801 are largely guesswork, it is likely that Wales had about 278,000 inhabitants in 1536. By then the population had been increasing slowly for some three generations. Growth accelerated in the following century, and by 1600 the country probably had as many inhabitants as it had had in 1300. By 1620, the population may have been as high as 400,000, although recent research favours a figure around 360,000. The growth was not a smooth upward curve: there was rapid advance in times of plenty but increases were scythed down with dreadful suddenness in times of dearth. Nor was it a uniform growth throughout the kingdom. In Britain as a whole, the greatest increase occurred in London; by 1600 the city was the largest in western Europe with a population of 200,000, about a hundred times more than that of Carmarthen, the largest town in Wales. Within Wales, it was the counties of the north-east which experienced the most rapid increase, a factor of importance when considering the central contribution made by that region to the Renaissance in Wales. The growth in the population of Denbighshire and Flintshire was in part the consequence of English immigration. Yet migration from Wales to England was certainly greater than that from England to Wales; indeed, Glanmor Williams asserts that historians have hardly begun to appreciate the extent and significance of the Welsh diaspora in Tudor and Stuart England.

As historical sources for the age of Elizabeth are far more plentiful than are those for previous ages, it is possible to provide a rather more detailed description of the main features of that age, features which would remain central to the life of Wales until the country was transformed by the rise of industry two hundred years later. Among the most important developments were the intensification of rural settlement and the increase in the demand for agricultural products – two of the keys to the rise in population. The Black Death had halted the attack upon waste land which had characterized the High Middle Ages, but, about two generations after that tragedy, assartment and enclosure recommenced. In 1537, Leland, the English antiquarian, was told that the inhabitants of Anglesey were building walls round their fields, and in 1578 Rhys Meurig recorded that the Vale of Glamorgan had, by his time, been wholly enclosed. The number of farms was increasing as landowners formed consolidated units from the scattered strips of the old *gwelyau* and from the open fields of the *taeogdrefi*, developments which led to extensive litigation. There were pressures to turn the *hafotai* (summer homes) of the uplands into independent farms and, in consequence, the practice of transhumance, which had been a central feature of the Welsh economy since time immemorial, went into decline. Despite enclosure and consolidation, grazings on the waste continued to be vital to farmers. The waste was coveted by greedy landowners and quarrels over common land were frequent – one of them exploded into a bloody riot at Denbigh in 1563. Extensive tracts of the country remained common land; a quarter of the surface area of Wales was still unenclosed as late as 1790. Nevertheless, in 1587, Churchyard, the English poet, praised the efforts of Welsh farmers as they ploughed land where sturdy oaks once stood, cleared the fields of stones and fertilized them with lime. In the richer lowlands, the new arable land was suitable for growing corn and in favourable times a surplus was produced which was exported to Bristol and to Ireland.

Yet, in the age of the Tudors as in every age, the profit from selling corn had little significance for the Welsh economy compared with the earnings from the raising of stock. Although mixed farming was the pattern throughout the country, most Welsh farmers grew wheat, barley and oats for domestic purposes only. Cattle and sheep were the basis of the economy and, because of the periods of leisure characteristic of pastoral farming, English visitors were prone to accuse Welsh farmers of laziness. The number of cattle in Wales was increasing. In 1571, Morus Wynn of Gwydir had 1,209 beasts at Dolwydd-elan, and the stock of John, his famous son, would be considerably greater. John Wynn acknowledged in 1613 that he would be short of ready money until the return of the drovers who had driven his cattle to the markets of England, and his kinsman, John Williams, archbishop of York, described the droves of cattle as 'the Spanish fleet of Wales, which brings hither the little gold and silver we have'. Some of the cattle were driven to Northampton, where their skins were used in the town's leather industry, but Smithfield in London was their most famous, if not perhaps their most important, destination. Even the honest drover (and the verses of Rhys Prichard, written about 1630, suggest that dishonesty was not unknown among them) could earn a hundred pounds a year, as much as fifteen times the earnings of a labourer. The drovers were the lubricant which oiled the Welsh economy, and in remote localities their visits had a significance beyond the merely economic. The black cattle of the uplands were raised as stores, but in the lowlands, the home of breeds such as the red cattle of Glamorgan, oxen were bred as draught animals. There, dairy produce was also important, and in 1620 £12,000 was received for the butter exported to Bristol from the Vale of Glamorgan.

Even in the hills, cattle were more important than sheep: in Merthyr Tydfil in 1535, the tithe on the former was twice that on the latter. But as a single sheep was less valuable than a single cow, there were probably more sheep than cattle in Tudor Wales; recent research suggests that a hill farmer had five sheep for every two cows. The price of wool trebled between 1500 and 1550 and the desire of landowners to take advantage of the rise caused great distress among the labourers of the lowlands. Most of the wool of Wales was woven into long rolls of cloth, the friezes and Welsh cottons mentioned so often in the documents of the period. The cloth was coarse and uneven, despite the efforts of parliament to lay down minimum standards. Nevertheless, it was in demand from Guinea to Archangel, from the Caribbean to Cadiz. The weavers were concentrated in mid- and north-east Wales, particularly after about 1560 when the industry in the south-west was struck by depression. Generally, the cloth was produced in the home; every member of the family played a part, and it was claimed in about 1610 that a hundred thousand people in Wales and the borders were dependent upon the industry. It is unlikely that it made the fortune of anyone in Wales. The profits were made in London and Shrewsbury; although parliament abolished the monopoly of the Shrewsbury Drapers' Company in 1624, it survived in its essentials because the weavers of Wales, lacking capital and isolated from each other, failed to create a system which would have given them control over the industry.

Compared with breeding cattle and making cloth, other activities were marginal in their contribution to the livelihood of the Welsh. They were not without importance, however. As the vast majority were dependent upon their immediate neighbourhood for their needs and their luxuries, a variety of crafts – those of the carpenter, smith, shoemaker, turner and tanner – provided a livelihood for between 5 and 10 per cent of the population. On the coasts, there were communities of fishermen. Some of them were quite populous: in 1550, the density of population in the commote of Cafflogion in Llŷn was among the highest in Wales. There were also developments in heavy industry, a notable feature of the reign of Elizabeth – so notable indeed as to cause J. U. Nef to argue that her reign experienced an industrial revolution as significant as the 'real' Industrial Revolution two hundred years later. The present tendency is to reject this notion, for the heavy industries represented growth in sectors which were not central to the economy. Nevertheless, they are highly interesting as indicators of the future. They were extractive industries producing raw materials – coal, iron, copper, lead – rather than finished goods, a foretaste of a situation which would exist on a far greater scale three hundred years later.

Small-scale digging of coal had taken place in Wales for centuries, and Leland noted in 1537 that coal was burned in the hearths of Carmarthen. Wood fires, however, were more popular; to Henry Sidney, president of the Council of Wales, coal was a 'noxious mineral' and it found favour only in the wake of the contraction of the woodlands. Its virtues were recognized by the makers of products such as bricks, soap and glass but, as Wales had few such industries, most of the coal produced was exported. Transport over land was slow and costly, causing collieries distant from the sea to have only very local markets. The main activity was therefore concentrated near the coast – in the district around Swansea, in south Pembrokeshire and in Flintshire. Efforts to break into the profitable London market failed; that continued to be the monopoly of the coalfield of Newcastle-upon-Tyne, but there was a demand for Welsh coal in Ireland, in south-west England and in France. The coal exports of Swansea Bay, the most important centre of the trade, rose from about five hundred tons in 1550 to over three thousand in 1607, a minute foreshadowing of the thirty-seven million tons which would be exported from the south Wales ports in 1913. Production was increased largely through multiplying the number of small levels and collieries, for the industry experienced very little technological advance.

It was otherwise with iron, an industry in which a new invention was of central importance. The first blast furnace in Britain was built in 1496 and a century later the island had about a hundred of them. The blast furnace allowed the process of smelting to continue without pause and high levels of heat could be produced by water-powered bellows. The centres of the industry were Sussex and Kent, but as the demand for iron increased – to make agricultural implements, tools for craftsmen and cannon for the navy – there were fears that the Weald Forest would be totally destroyed, so greedy were the furnaces for charcoal. Other regions having iron-ore, timber, limestone and streams were sought, and by 1600 a third of the blast furnaces of Britain lay outside south-east England. About a dozen were built in Wales, mainly in Monmouthshire, east Glamorgan and east Denbighshire.

They cost about two hundred pounds to build and many of them were short-lived. Most of the entrepreneurs were English – it was the 'Englishmen of the black iron' who were blamed by a Glamorgan poet for 'cutting the trees of Glyn Cynon' – but they also included the Mathew family of Radyr, the pioneers of the Pentyrch works, and Thomas Myddelton of Chirk, owner of the furnace at Pont-y-blew.

Owners of land also owned the coal and iron beneath their land, and they could profit from mineral exploitation either directly or through leases. The precious metals – gold and silver – belonged to the crown, as did the other metals used in coinage – copper and tin. Elizabeth was anxious to exploit the resources of her kingdom, partly in order to save on imports, and she drew upon the skills of the mineralogists of Germany, the home of metallurgical science, to achieve her aims. In 1568, the Mineral and Battery Company was established to produce brass, and the Company of Mines Royal to promote the copper industry. In 1566, the former built a works at Tintern to produce wire; by 1603 the Tintern works, with a labour force of six hundred, was by far the largest industrial enterprise in Wales; it was also to be the longest-lived, for a version of it survived until 1900. The works needed a supply of iron, which was provided by a number of furnaces established around Pontypool by Richard Hanbury, the ancestor of a family which would loom large in the industrial history of Wales. The first Welsh venture of the Company of Mines Royal was the works it established in Neath in 1584 to smelt copper ore from Cornwall. As the supply of ore was not reliable, the enterprise came to an end in about 1602, but the link with Cornwall was later to be a key factor in the industrial development of west Glamorgan. At the time, the lead mines of Cardiganshire were more significant. In 1617, Hugh Myddelton of Denbigh leased the works at Cwmsymlog at a rent of £400 a year, a very profitable bargain, for it was claimed that the annual return on the venture could be as much as £24,000. He sent three thousand ounces of silver to the Royal Mint in 1624, and Thomas Bushell, his successor as lessee, obtained a licence in 1637 to coin money at Aberystwyth Castle. There were also prosperous lead mines in the counties of Glamorgan, Montgomery and Flint, and John Wynn of Gwydir was tireless in his efforts to exploit the mineral resources of his estate.

The economic growth which occurred in Wales in the century

after the 'Union' did not lead to a higher standard of living for the population as a whole. The period saw a rate of inflation more dramatic than anything experienced until this century. After generations of comparative stability, there was between 1530 and 1640 a four-fold increase in the price of ordinary goods. The inflation in food prices was greater, for, despite the increase in agricultural production, it appears that it failed to match the increase in population. The rise in rents was greater still, particularly when the lessor, in granting a new lease, insisted upon commuting payments in produce into payments in money. Geraint H. Jenkins notes the example of a farm in Cardiganshire where the annual rent rose in 1621 from 11s. 8d. to £4, in addition to an entry fine of £30. The landowner and the substantial freeholder could benefit from inflation, but it is believed that the purchasing power of the labourer halved between the beginning and the end of the age of the Tudors. The gentry's lust for land had sound economic foundations. Land offered returns which were not only substantial but also more stable than those offered by other forms of investment, a factor of importance in considering the finance available for industrial development. It is claimed that in the period 1588–1630, in particular, there was a major redistribution of wealth at the expense of the wage-earner and the tenant and to the advantage of the gentry; it is hardly surprising that the gentry were so lyrical in their praise of the regime which made this possible.

There were many possibilities open to a man intent upon rising in the world: he could marry an heiress; he could amass money through office, royal favour, commercial venture, distinction in law, or – as a smuggler or a pirate – through bold lawlessness; he could break the spirit of a less wealthy opponent through merciless litigation; he could usurp the property of the Church and the crown; he could grab the land of the lowly through naked bullying. All these methods were employed in Wales. They were effective, as the rise in the income of the most successful squires testifies. Although the Welsh gentry were poorer as a class than their fellows in England, at least a dozen of the landowners of Wales enjoyed an annual income of a thousand pounds or more by the accession of James I, and their increasing wealth was reflected in the houses they built and the luxuries they enjoyed.

The richest of the squires – the Bulkeleys of Beaumaris, for example, or the Wynns of Gwydir or the Perrots of Pembrokeshire – were almost equal in their economic circumstances to some of the aristocratic families. But in a society which placed such emphasis on degree and honour, a particular distinction belonged to those men (about fifty throughout the kingdom under Elizabeth, twice that number under her successor) who had a title and a seat in the House of Lords. Four aristocratic families had interests in Wales during the reign of Elizabeth: Robert Dudley, earl of Leicester, who was granted the lordship of Denbigh in 1563; the Devereux family, earls of Essex, who had extensive interests in the south-west; the Somerset family, earls of Worcester, the owners of most of the manors of Monmouthshire and Gower; and the Herbert family, earls of Pembroke, the chief landowners in Glamorgan. Leicester and Essex were luminaries of Elizabeth's court, where Worcester and Pembroke were also influential. There was a wide gulf between Henry Herbert, the second earl of Pembroke (of the Tudor creation), with his receipts of £5,000 a year, and men such as the squire of Clenennau whose income was less than a tithe of that of the earl. Yet, compared with the members of the social groups beneath them, they belonged essentially to the same class. As receivers of rents, they seized much of the economic surplus, and as members of the one or the other of the Houses of Parliament, and as state and county officials, they had an assured role in the system of government.

The members of the landed class sought to emphasize their dignity by stressing their gentility. Nevertheless, the majority of the Welsh belonged to the degree of gentleman, and families who did not rise to the rank of squire would remember for generations to come that their lineage was as honourable as that of more fortunate families. However, lineage unsupported by adequate wealth was increasingly considered insufficient to maintain the status of a gentleman; in England, the genealogical pride of a poor Welsh *uchelwr* (gentleman) was an object of derision. In the age of Elizabeth and for centuries to come there would be a craving to define gentility. Although lineage remained a factor of importance (which explains the faking of genealogies for those who had abruptly risen from obscurity), there was an increasing tendency to include within the rank of gentleman only those who could maintain themselves without soiling their hands. They, with their families, constituted 5 per cent of the population at most. In addition to the landed gentry, the rank of gentleman also included the members of the higher reaches of the legal, ecclesiastical and military professions, along with the wealthier merchants. To a large extent, they also sprang from landed families; the younger sons of the landed gentry were numerous, for the squires were philoprogenitive. The more successful sought to found a new line of squires, as did the judge David Williams at Gwernyfed, Breconshire, and the merchant Richard Clough at Plas Clough, Denbighshire.

Yet the advancement of a son of a substantial farmer was not wholly exceptional; it would be wrong therefore to underestimate the social mobility of pre-industrial communities. The substantial farmers were usually freeholders, although there were among them tenants who leased their farms on favourable terms. These were members of the yeomen class, men who could afford a degree of comfort, as can be seen from the eight-room house built by Richard Love, who farmed fifty hectares of land at Penmark, Glamorgan. They, along with the craftsmen, were in many ways the backbone of Welsh society, and religious, cultural and educational movements were highly indebted to them. In about 1570, Glamorgan had perhaps a thousand yeomen, and they with their families constituted about 10 per cent of the population.

The landed class, the professional class, the merchants, the more substantial craftsmen and the yeomen accounted for about 20 per cent of the population. That percentage had a standard of life which varied from prudential sufficiency to luxurious abundance. The 80 per cent below them were less fortunate, particularly in famine years such as 1585–7, 1593–7 and 1620–23. As vast numbers of the less fortunate suffered from malnutrition at some period of their lives, they were shorter and less physically developed than were their more prosperous fellows, a fact which further convinced the upper classes of their innate superiority. At least half the population belonged to the class of husbandmen – the lesser farmers and smallholders. There could be wide differences of wealth within that class; in Glamorgan, a smallholder could leave property worth £70, but in view of the fact that the holdings of the majority rarely exceeded ten hectares (less on good land) and that the land produced hardly a quarter of what it would today, most of them must have lived on the edge of destitution.

The boundary between the smallholder and the labourer was imprecise. Many labourers had a holding of a hectare or two, although their main support came from their wages of about sixpence a day. Their earnings were controlled by the Statute of Labourers of 1563, an act based upon the assumption that those without property are fundamentally unfree and which sought to ensure a reservoir of cheap labour for landowners and industrialists. Their homes were temporary hovels of a single room without windows or chimney – 'dung heaps shaped into cottages' to quote William Richards, the author of the satirical volume, *Wallography*. As the work available failed to match the increase in population, many labourers were only intermittently employed. In their wretchedness, some of them were prepared to break the law, and two men were hanged in Cardiff in 1596 for stealing ten loaves of bread. As unemployment and underemployment were rife, it is impossible to distinguish clearly between the labourers and the poor. Many of the poor – the old, the sick, and the mentally and physically disabled – were unemployable, but the able bodied among them were numerous. Emphasis was placed upon the distinction between the 'impotent poor' and the 'sturdy beggars'. While the former were considered a legitimate charge upon society, official attitudes towards the latter hardened as their numbers increased and as the belief that idleness was sin became more widespread. They were whipped and branded, and some of them became forced labour for the mines. Others were press-ganged into the army: 6,611 Welshmen were recruited to fight in Ireland between 1594 and 1602. In 1601, an act was passed which was to be the basis for the treatment of the poor for a quarter of a millennium and more. It authorized each parish to raise rates to maintain the poor, to apprentice orphan children and to punish 'sturdy beggars'.

Many of the poor believed that they could better themselves by migrating to the towns. In consequence, the growth of an urban proletariat was a cause of concern to members of corporations, as the protest of the borough of Swansea in 1603 testifies. It is unlikely that the circumstances of the migrants improved by moving to the towns. There, they were more at the mercy of the market economy than they were in the countryside, and because of the restrictions of the craftsmen's guilds there was little work available to the unskilled. Yet the gulf between town and country should not be exaggerated. Townspeople, with their herds on the corporation fields and their cows and pigs in back-street byres and sties, were half country people, and the town's main role was to provide a focus for the agricultural economy which surrounded it. The market and the fair were central to its prosperity as, increasingly, were permanent shops; the number of such shops in Pwllheli, for example, rose from one to five between 1580 and 1600. During the reign of Elizabeth, a hierarchy of towns became established in Wales and it lasted until it was overwhelmed by the rise of industry. Harold Carter has shown that the towns with the fullest functions were the four centres of the Great Sessions – Caernarfon, Denbigh, Brecon and Carmarthen – the capitals, so to speak, of the four corners of Wales. In about 1560, around two thousand people dwelt in Carmarthen ('the chiefe citie of the country' according to Camden), and rather less in Brecon, while Caernarfon and Denbigh each had about a thousand inhabitants. Swansea, Tenby, Pembroke and Monmouth also probably had about a thousand inhabitants apiece, and there were perhaps slightly more in Wrexham, Abergavenny, Haverfordwest, Cydweli and Cardiff (the handsomest town in Wales, according to George Owen). None of the other towns of Wales had more than a few hundred inhabitants. Although the country had fifty-four centres which claimed some civic features, most of them were little more than villages. According to Leland, many of the towns of Wales in the 1530s were 'wonderfully decayed', but at that time the most viable towns were on the eve of a century of considerable growth. Growth depended upon an overflow from the countryside. There, on the whole, the inhabitants were Welsh and thus the Welsh character of the towns of Wales was strengthened. The English element was almost wholly overwhelmed in the towns of the old *Pura Wallia*, and to a large extent that also happened in many of the towns of the old March. The towns of south Pembrokeshire remained English, but by 1600 Swansea and Cardiff were bilingual communities. Abergavenny came to be considered so Welsh that standard English was unlikely to be mastered there, and in 1698 only 10 per cent of the population of Brecon bore English surnames.

Towns depended upon an overflow from the countryside because the urban environment of Wales, like that of every country until very recently, did not permit a natural increase in population. With their piles of filth and their impure water, and with their inhabitants packed together, the towns were nurseries of pestilence and a threat, above all, to the survival of infants. But although the countryside produced a population surplus when harvests were good, conditions there were not much better. Virtually everyone, for much of the time, was in some degree of pain, and it would appear that there were more diseases in the Tudor era than there had been previously. It is believed that the sweating sickness, which killed five hundred people in Oswestry in 1559, was brought to Wales by the army of Henry Tudor, and it is possible that syphilis was a gift from America. Typhus and smallpox attacks were increasing and the population of Presteigne was devastated by the old enemy, the plague, in 1593.

All classes of society faced disease and sickness; ill-health was probably the cause of the choler which was so much a part of the personalities of men such as John Perrot and John Wynn. But it was the members of the lower classes – who were often deficient in vitamins A, C and D – who suffered most. Among them, there was deep faith in herbal remedies and magic potions, for they could not afford the services of a doctor. Indeed, only a small proportion of the population was within reach of such services. In 1620, the family at Lleweni had to send to Chester for a doctor, although as medical methods were so crude the scarcity of doctors was probably advantageous to the sick. Everyone believed that they were at the mercy of mysterious powers. Those powers could be placated by spells and magic, or aggravated by associating with the devil, as witches were believed to do. The fate of the condemned witch, the ferocity of many of the amusements of the age, the barbarity of the frequent executions (about two thousand a year in the kingdom as a whole) and the pleasure people obtained from watching savagery prove that there was very little sensitivity towards suffering – something to be expected, perhaps, in a society where pain and cruel afflictions were part of the common experience.

With so many dying in their infancy or in the flower of their youth, consciousness of the fragility of life was omnipresent. As people were so vulnerable in the face of disease and so defenceless in the face of tribulations such as fire, floods and crop failures, it is hardly surprising that the teaching of the age stressed the burdens of life and urged everyone to submit to their fate. This was the message of many of the sermons of the period. The clergyman in his pulpit was virtually the only means of educating the people and of making them answerable to social discipline – the aim of the Puritans as well as of the government. It was only from the clergy that the common people would regularly hear (in theory at least) a point of view based upon experiences beyond the boundaries of the parish, for pre-industrial Wales was not one integrated society but rather a network of small local communities. This could nurture deep local loyalties – as can be seen from the propensity of successful men to endow charities in their places of birth – but it could also give rise to suspicion of the inhabitants of neighbouring parishes and hatred towards more distant strangers. The strongly local nature of society was intensified by the appalling condition of the roads. Entire districts could be isolated for long periods, as was south Caernarfonshire in the 1630s after the bridge over the river Dwyfach had been destroyed in a storm. Travel was slow and expensive; the journey from west Wales to London took up to ten days. As a result, apart from men such as drovers, it was only the wealthy or the exceptionally poor who had the money or the time to wander from their homes.

It is likely therefore that most people lived and died in their native parish, although if the evidence were fuller – if parish registers, for example, had survived on a larger scale – this statement would perhaps have to be modified. The government feared mobility, for it sought stable communities characterized by conservatism or inertia. The desire to promote social stability, particularly by emphasizing the authority of heads of households, was central to the values of the age. That authority was strengthened by the fact that children, in pre-industrial societies, constituted a far higher proportion of the population than they do in modern western societies. It was not only the children (and the wife) of the head of the household who were answerable to his worldly and spiritual discipline; the unmarried among his servants and employees were also subject to his authority. It was believed that the only fully responsible people were married males – a drover did not receive a licence unless he were married. The vast majority got married; although the economic status of a man declined when he had a wife, his social status rose.

In the age of Elizabeth and for centuries to come, marriage was the only path to any kind of social recognition for women, the queen herself being the only exception to the rule. There were occasional Welsh women of outstanding character; Catherine of Berain, a kinswoman of the queen, was the most prominent of them, but she is remembered largely because of her numerous marriages. Of the 3,223 individuals listed in the *Dictionary of Welsh Biography*, only fifty-eight (1.8 per cent) are women, which suggests that Welsh historiography conspires to ignore over half the population. The making of amends for this male prejudice is only just beginning, but the research already undertaken indicates that the history of women in Wales, as in the rest of the world, is a story of deprivation. Under the Law of England – the only law in force in Wales after 1536 – the wife yielded to her husband all control over her property, but she received in return a more exalted status than that of her unmarried compeers. From the time of her marriage, the wife was the mistress of her home, for, unlike the traditional societies of the east with their extended families, societies in Europe were based upon the nuclear family. In theory, this meant that a man did not marry until he could afford to maintain a family, but as up to half the wives gave birth within less than nine months of the wedding it would appear that the time of marriage was not always determined by prudence.

Such marriages reduced the number of illegitimate children. About 10 per cent of births took place out of wedlock; this, at least, is what is suggested by the evidence that has survived for the parish of Ceri in Montgomeryshire in the 1630s. The courts had a great interest in such matters, for sex outside marriage was an illicit act; between 1633 and 1637, 31 per cent of the punishments meted out by the Council of Wales related to sexual offences. They were considered to be as subversive as violence and riot, offences which accounted for 37 per cent of the punishments of the council. The records of the council relating to the 1630s prove that violence remained a feature of Welsh life a century after the 'Union'. That century was an unruly one in Wales. In the 1540s, hardly a week passed in Caernarfonshire without a bloody assault, a riotous assembly or a violent quarrel, and the Red Bandits of Mawddwy ambushed and killed Lewis Owen, the sheriff of Meirionnydd, in 1555. A generation later, the gentry were still maintaining bands of followers which aroused such fear among jurors that members of the landed class were rarely successfully prosecuted. A quarrel between members of the squirearchy, with their numerous retinues, could rapidly become a bloody affray, and during Elizabeth's reign no county in Wales was free from such violence. There were conflicts at sea also and landowners such as John Perrot were eager to profit from the piracy which was rife along the coasts of Pembrokeshire.

The aristocracy continued to expect their tenants to follow them on military service; in the year of the Armada, the earl of Pembroke was able to offer the queen an army of eight hundred men. Following the death of the earl of Leicester in 1588, Pembroke was the most powerful of the great men of Wales; he was president of the Council of Wales from 1586 until his death in 1601 and he could depend upon support from other branches of his multifarious family. In the counties of Glamorgan, Monmouth and Montgomery, factions arose which were hostile to the Herberts; in about 1588, Richard Herbert's skull was split in Llanerfyl churchyard, and in a series of brawls in Cardiff in 1597 two men were killed and a woman's nose was split so that it 'did hang downe over her lipps'. In the 1590s, the power of Pembroke was challenged by the earl of Essex; through royal favour and through the efforts of his right-hand man, Gelli Meurig, Essex built up a position of authority for himself over much of Wales. His Welsh followers and allies were drawn into his thirteen-hour rebellion in London on 8 February 1601; the rebellion led to the execution of Essex and Meurig and caused much alarm along the borders.

Essex's rebellion was an echo of a dying world – the world of bastard feudalism. Although violence was common in Elizabethan Wales, the problem was coming increasingly under control. Penry Williams has claimed that by 1601 almost all cases of open violence were coming before the courts, and Glanmor Williams has argued that the greatest achievement of the Tudors in Wales was to induce the people to accept the rule of law. The achievement sprang from the readiness of the Welsh ruling class to be an integral part of the kingdom and from the increasing efficiency of the machinery of government.

The central element of that machinery was the Privy Council, the almost daily meeting of the queen and her advisers. The Privy Council sent its orders and directives to the Council of Wales at Ludlow. The Council of Wales was primarily a court of law; its task was to fill the gaps in the system of Common Law and to enforce a wider authority than that of the justices of the peace and the judges of assize. The council represented a remarkable experiment in regional government. It administered the law cheaply and rapidly; it dealt with up to twenty cases a day and George Owen stated that the 'oppressed poor' flocked to it. It was at its most effective during the presidency of Henry Sidney (1560–86). In the 1590s, with the earl of Pembroke at the helm, it was accused of various misdemeanours and many Welsh cases were taken before the Court of Star Chamber in London. The four English border counties provided most of the judges and about half the cases tried at Ludlow, but the council's authority over those counties was greatly resented. That authority was relaxed in 1606 but it was restored by royal command in 1609. The activity of the council reached its peak between 1610 and 1620, when 1,200 cases came before it annually.

The president of the Council of Wales was also lord lieutenant of the Welsh counties and was therefore responsible for ensuring that the counties contributed to the armed forces. This was a matter of central importance, for during most of Elizabeth's reign her kingdom was in dire danger. The president also recommended to the Lord Chancellor the names of men suitable to be appointed as sheriffs and justices of the peace. The sheriff was the executive officer of the Quarter Sessions, the three-monthly assembly of the magistrates. Almost all felonies could come before the sessions, but the more serious tended to be sent to higher courts, leaving the magistrates to deal only with minor transgressions. As the legal duties of the Quarter Sessions declined their administrative duties increased, for almost all the statutes passed by the parliaments of the Tudors and the early Stuarts added to the work of the magistrates. The act of 1536 provided for eight magistrates in each county; this proved insufficient and by the reign of James I most of the Welsh counties had at least twenty apiece. Without exception, they were chosen from the ranks of the gentry. In Glamorgan, a county which had thirty-three magistrates by 1642, the heads of the twenty most prominent families could be confident of a seat on the bench. As it was the gentry who administered the law, they were conditioned to accept that they were answerable to it and thus their violent instincts were progressively curbed. Nevertheless, as their activities were only intermittently supervised, the magistrates could use their position to exploit less privileged classes; they were reluctant to insist upon obedience to measures not to their taste, and their power as a class was strengthened by their monopoly of the bench.

The county commission of peace was not operative everywhere. Some towns – Haverfordwest, Carmarthen, Cardiff and Beaumaris, for example – had their own Quarter Sessions, and all incorporated towns boasted of some degree of autonomy. They were governed by a hierarchy of officials – the mayor, the alderman and the bailiffs – who were generally elected annually by the burgesses. Only a small minority of the townsfolk were burgesses; it is estimated that in Swansea in 1600 the dignity belonged to about 8 per cent of the population. In theory, borough charters gave extensive rights to the corporations, but in practice town governments were increasingly falling into the hands of powerful landowners. The earl of Worcester was the final authority at Swansea, and the earl of Pembroke at Cardiff, while the corporation of Beaumaris was wholly dependent upon the Bulkeley family.

By gaining influence over the corporations, landowners could be confident that their nominees would be elected to represent the boroughs, for in the Welsh borough constituencies (there were thirteen of them) the burgesses alone had the vote. In some prosperous boroughs – Haverfordwest, for example – a prominent burgess was sometimes elected, but that was unusual. The vast majority of borough representatives were members or clients of gentry families, and the earl of Leicester was enraged when the burgesses of Denbigh challenged him in 1572. A member of parliament enjoyed a higher status and received greater expenses by representing a county rather than a borough constituency. In the county seats of Wales (there were fourteen of them), the voters were freeholders owning land with an annual value exceeding forty shillings, a class for whom the gentry were the natural leaders and representatives. During the reigns of Elizabeth and James I, the status of the House of Commons grew rapidly and as a result the competition for seats became increasingly keen. Representatives were chosen by agreement rather than by vote: in Wales, no more than a dozen elections are known to have been decided by balloting during the reign of Elizabeth.

It appears that Welsh MPs were rather taciturn in the first decades of Welsh representation in parliament, but from about 1570 onwards a number of them won prominence at Westminster. Between 1571 and 1603, thirty Welsh representatives had experience of the committee work of the House of Commons, and in James I's first parliament (1604–11) four out of five of them contributed to the business of the House. They concentrated upon local matters, and A. H. Dodd has analysed their increasing skill in defending the interests of Wales. Men like John Perrot were also prepared to air their views on the great issues of state, and by attending parliament the Welsh gentry were progressively drawn into the political and social life of London, a development which promoted their absorption into the English ruling class. As they sought membership of the House of Commons mainly in order to enhance the prestige of their families in their own localities, few Welsh MPs were intent upon a political career. William Cecil,

Elizabeth's chief adviser, took pride in his partially Welsh descent, and it was probably he who ensured that the queen's government was not inconsiderate towards Wales. (It may be doubted whether Elizabeth I had more interest in the cradle of her line at Penmynydd than Elizabeth II has in the cradle of hers at Saxe-Coburg.) The most successful Welsh politician of the period was John Herbert, the member for Glamorgan. He served as Second Secretary of State between 1600 and 1610 and was prominent in the unsuccessful attempt to unite the parliaments of England and Scotland in the wake of the union of the two crowns in 1603. In that year, the kingdom of Great Britain came into existence, an event of importance in the history of the Welsh. Unlike the Bretons, who were incorporated into the state and the nation of the French, the Welsh henceforth could feel that they were partners in a state which represented the union of three nations. It was difficult for them to consider themselves to be both Welsh and English, but to be Welsh and British was acceptable, particularly in view of the central role of the concept of Britain in the Welsh national myth. It is hardly surprising therefore that it was a Welshman – William Maurice, the member of parliament for Caernarfonshire – who most vocally advocated that James I should adopt the title of king or emperor of Great Britain.

James, the great-great-grandson of Henry VII, inherited the allegiance the Welsh had shown to the Tudors. He was eager to praise his Welsh subjects for their obedience and loyalty, loyalty which was strengthened when his son, Henry, became prince of Wales in 1610. Apart from the stubborn hispanophile Hugh Owen – one of those involved in the Gunpowder Plot (1605) – even the Welsh Catholics were loyal to James, while the Puritans hoped (in vain) that a man nurtured in the Presbyterian environment of Scotland would be sympathetic to their views. Puritanism struck a few roots in Wales during his reign, particularly in towns such as Cardiff, Swansea, Wrexham and Haverfordwest. It was promoted by wealthy London merchants. They endowed lecturers to preach the gospel; they bought the advowson of parishes in order to further the careers of Puritan clergy; they established schools and paid for the publication of Bibles and devotional books. In creating Puritans, they were concerned not only to save souls but also to disseminate London values throughout the kingdom. Early Puritanism was a tendency rather than a movement, and some of its elements – moral seriousness for example –

were adopted by men wholly loyal to the Established Church. Lewis Bayly, the author of the Puritans' favourite book, *The Practice of Piety*, was presented to the see of Bangor, and the book was translated into Welsh by the royalist conservative Rolant Fychan of Caer-gai. Rhys Prichard of Llandovery was an ardent Churchman and chancellor of the diocese of St David's, but the severe morality of the Puritans finds expression in his rhymes. Nevertheless, the more zealous Puritans sought reform in Church and State, and they were increasingly critical of the government of James I, particularly of its reluctance to persecute Catholics and its readiness to warm to Spain, Protestantism's arch enemy. These were issues raised in the eloquent speeches of James Perrot, MP for Haverfordwest, in the parliaments of 1614 and 1621.

James I died in 1625. After his experiences with the parliaments of 1625, 1626 and 1628–9, his son and successor, Charles I, decided to rule without parliament. There was little protest from Wales against the 'personal' government of the king. The Welsh gentry found most aspects of it to their taste; as the coasts of Wales were open to invasion from Spain or Ireland, they approved of the king's efforts to strengthen the navy, and between 1634 and 1638 the Welsh counties were among the readiest to pay Ship Money; as their society was largely rural and conservative, they sympathized with the paternalistic nature of royal government; as they were zealous members of the Church of England, they warmed to the attempts of William Laud, archbishop of Canterbury (and former bishop of St David's), to emphasize the hierarchical character of the Church and to elevate the dignity of its services. Yet, by the end of the 1630s, with the burden of Ship Money increasing, the Scots mobilizing against Charles's policies, the king's supporters (it was believed) recruiting Catholic soldiers in Ireland, and Catholic aristocrats such as the earl of Worcester and the heir of Baron Powys rumoured to be raising a Welsh papist army to greet them, even the Welsh gentry were becoming perturbed.

The threat from Scotland obliged the king to summon parliament. The Short Parliament lasted only from March to May 1640, but the Long Parliament was to continue in some form from November 1640 until March 1660. Between 1640 and 1642, parliament passed a series of statutes which destroyed the royal bureaucracy – the most significant happening, according to Christopher Hill, in the entire history of Britain. The old paternalism was dismantled and monopolies were forbidden, allowing the unfettered private enterprise which would enable Britain to be the pioneer of the Industrial Revolution. The government was obliged to withdraw from many spheres of activity which had previously been considered to be part of its responsibility. The Court of High Commission – Laud's weapon to ensure religious uniformity – was abolished and the Presbyterian majority in the House of Commons sought to get rid of the bishops and the Book of Common Prayer. The religious upheavals which followed gave the sectarians an opportunity boldly to challenge the clergy. By then, there were congregations of Separatists in two of the Welsh dioceses: a group of 'Baptists' at Olchon in the see of St David's on the borders of Herefordshire, and a group of 'Independents' at Llanfaches near Chepstow in the see of Llandaf.

During the first months of the Long Parliament, only one Welsh member – Herbert Price, the MP for Brecon – wholly supported the king. The rest were suspicious of him, and there was vocal criticism particularly from John Vaughan (Cardigan boroughs), Thomas Myddelton (Denbighshire) and John Bodvel (Anglesey). They were infuriated by the Irish revolt of October 1641 and feared that an Irish army would land on the coast of Wales. The notion that the Welsh were uncritical loyalists is therefore mistaken. Nevertheless, by the summer of 1642, as the Parliamentary leaders were attacking the Church Establishment and the king's right to his prerogative, there was a decline in the reforming zeal of the Welsh members – Vaughan and Bodvel among them. When Charles raised his standard in Nottingham in August 1642, only five of them – two from Pembrokeshire, two from Denbighshire and one from Glamorgan – still adhered to the Parliamentary cause.

It is not difficult to find reasons for the reluctance of the bulk of the Welsh ruling class to defy the king in arms. It is true that recent research has modified the interpretation of the Civil War as a struggle between the south and east of the kingdom, the ports and the large towns on the one hand, and the north, the west and the remoter pastoral regions on the other. It is now realized that local and personal considerations were central in determining the attitude of families and localities towards the struggle and that isolated districts could produce ardent Parliamentarians. But it cannot be denied that it was the regions which in economic, social and religious terms were the most progressive that provided the greater part of the support for the Parliamentarian cause and that outside south-eastern England such regions were few. In Wales, there were probably no more than two: south Pembrokeshire (where trade links with Bristol together with the influence of the earl of Essex, the leader of the Parliamentary army, encouraged attitudes sympathetic to the Parliamentary cause), and the Wrexham area, where there was a handful of Puritans of remarkable zeal. Wrexham was the locality of Thomas Myddelton, a man who had extensive interests in the city of London and who shared in the frustrations aroused in the merchant class by the policies of the crown. In the rest of the country, the natural conservatism of an agrarian society was strengthened by specifically Welsh factors. In the century since the 'Union' the Welsh gentry had profited from royal government; they had learned to respect the law and were appalled by the prospect of the troubles which might ensue if the existing order were overturned. They cherished the Church, believing in its Brythonic origins, regarding it – as they regarded the monarchy, with its descent from Brutus – as a corner-stone of their identity.

But reluctance to fight against the king did not imply an enthusiasm to fight for him. In Wales, more than in any other part of the kingdom, there were many who were genuine in their indifference and sincere in their neutrality. The majority of the ordinary people were probably unaware of the issues at stake, for nothing was published in the only language they understood by either one side or the other. The leaders of both armies tended to be contemptuous of the Welsh, and the poet, Huw Morys, grieved to see them become 'constant sacrifices to the sword'. They were mistaken for the despised Irish by the Parliamentary forces, while they also suffered at the hands of the Irish forces of the crown. Although the Welsh gentry sympathized with the values represented by the king, few of them were prepared to sacrifice their all for his sake. Most of them were primarily concerned to hold on to their estates, and according to John Vaughan the best way of doing so was 'to keep out of trouble'. Despite the royalism of Henry Vaughan – the first English poet of distinction to live all his life in Wales – his attitude towards the struggle is considered to have been one of 'epicurean unconcern'. Some of the most zealous supporters of the crown were disillusioned by Charles's policy and leadership. In 1643, John Williams, archbishop of York, laboured to defend Conwy, his native town, against the

Parliamentary forces; by 1646, however, he was prepared to cooperate with the Parliamentarians in its capture. In 1645, the squires of Glamorgan, wearying of the struggle, established a Peace Army to save their county from being a battleground, and some of them were so disgruntled that they considered delivering the king to his enemies in order to bring the fighting to an end.

Yet, although the unconcern and the neutrality were real enough, the support Charles received from Wales was central to his ability to resist the Parliamentary forces for four years and more. His first action, after challenging his opponents at Nottingham, was to march to Shrewsbury to meet the forces conscripted on his behalf in Wales. The description of Wales as 'the nursery of the king's infantry' was therefore not wholly without foundation. It is possible that Charles would not have challenged his opponents at all had he not been sure that the wealth of the Somerset family would be at his disposal; it was asserted that the earl of Worcester spent three quarters of a million pounds on the royal cause, and it was to the earl's home at Raglan that Charles retreated following his defeat at Naseby in June 1645 – the first crowned head to visit Wales for nearly a quarter of a millennium.

The history of the campaigns of the Parliamentarians and the Royalists in Wales between 1642 and 1646 is complex and fragmentary; indeed it borders upon the incomprehensible when divorced from the pattern of fighting over the kingdom as a whole. After their crucial success in preventing the king from seizing London in October 1642, one of the aims of the leaders of the Parliamentary forces was to isolate Wales in order to prevent Charles from recruiting soldiers there, and to break the link between Ireland and the royal headquarters at Oxford. Control over the route from Pembroke through south Wales and on to Bristol and Oxford was therefore important to the strategy of the war. It changed hands several times between 1643 and 1645; by the winter of 1643, as a result of the efforts of Richard Vaughan of Golden Grove (the earl of Carbery), only Pembroke remained outside the control of the Royalists; the situation changed during the spring of 1644 when the Parliamentarians, under the leadership of Rowland Laugharne and with the support of the navy, captured all centres of importance in south Wales. From the summer of 1644 to the spring of 1645, Royalist control was reimposed by Charles Gerard, an able and ruthless soldier; Laugharne had some success against the Royalists in April 1645, but Gerard was again the master by early summer; by August, when Gerard was serving in England, Laugharne, with some assistance from disillusioned Royalists, had succeeded in recapturing almost the whole of south Wales; he was challenged by the Royalists during the winter of 1645–6, but following the fall of Raglan Castle in August 1646 all the counties of the south yielded to the Parliamentary forces.

In the context of the connection with Ireland, the northern coastal counties were equally important. In October 1643, the Parliamentarian Thomas Myddelton sought to capture the main centres, but he was prevented by an army from Ireland. During the summer of 1644, Myddelton undertook a new campaign and defeated the Royalist forces near Montgomery on 14 October. Thereafter, although the Royalists fought stubbornly, the war in the north became a series of sieges. The First Civil War came to an end when Harlech Castle yielded to the Parliamentary forces in March 1647.

Peace was short-lived. The victory of the Parliamentarians brought a host of problems in its train. They were obliged to raise heavy taxes, and their relations with the army which had won them their victory were ambiguous. The moderate element among the victors wished to restrict the power of the king and to presbyterianize the Church; the more radical elements wished to overthrow the monarchy, encourage the sects and 'turn the world upside down'. Late in 1647, Charles seized the opportunity to ally with the Scots and the Presbyterians, and in 1648 there was a strong reaction in his favour. The spark which led to the Second Civil War was ignited in Pembrokeshire. There, the death of the earl of Essex in 1647 had weakened the personal ties which had bound the inhabitants to the Parliamentary cause. In April 1648, John Poyer, the castellan of Pembroke, declared in favour of the king. He was followed by Rice Powell, the castellan of Tenby; they marched to Cardiff, where they were joined by Rowland Laugharne. There were also uprisings in Kent and Essex and unrest in the navy, while John Owen of Clenennau and others challenged the authority of the Parliamentarians in north Wales. By May 1648, Laugharne had an army of eight thousand men, but it was defeated at the battle of St Fagans on 8 May. Cromwell, the most vigorous of the leaders of the Parliamentary army, swept through the south, and fighting ceased there following the capture of Pembroke Castle on 11 July 1648. The hopes of the northern insurgents were dashed when the Scots were defeated at the battle of Preston in August 1648, and their resistance ended after fighting in Anglesey in the autumn.

To Cromwell and his followers, Charles's readiness to re-ignite the flames of war was proof that he was unreliable and responsible for shedding innocent blood. He had, they asserted, caused many to sin against the light. In December 1648, parliament was purged of those not wholly hostile to the king, Thomas Myddelton among them. Charles was executed at Whitehall on 30 January 1649. His death warrant bears fifty-nine names, including two 'regicides' representing Welsh constituencies: John Jones, the member for Meirionnydd since 1647, and Thomas Wogan, the member for Cardigan boroughs since 1646.

Twenty-six days before the execution of the king, the Commonwealth was established, and a version of it was to last until the elevation of Charles I's son to the throne in May 1660. The Welsh reacted sullenly to the new order. To the leaders of the Commonwealth, Wales was one of the 'dark corners of the land', for its resistance to the Parliamentary cause proved that it was bereft of the saving light. That which had been won by the sword could be preserved by the Word. In 1650, parliament passed the Act for the Better Promotion of the Gospel in Wales, a measure which authorized, as R. Tudor Jones put it, 'the unexpected experiment of granting Wales religious home rule'. Implicit in the act was the desire to strengthen the ties which bound Wales to the values and the morals of London, and Christopher Hill has argued that it was the evangelical campaign of the Commonwealth which above all hastened in Wales the demise of the old order and its values.

Even before 1650, the success of the Parliamentary cause had permitted the dissenting sects to gain support among the Welsh. The Parliamentarians offered succour to Puritan refugees – the congregation at Llanfaches among them – and they were eager to remove unworthy clerics and to replace them with godly ministers. In 1646, some of the wealth of the Church was set aside to pay the wages of six itinerary preachers in Wales. The most experienced of them was Walter Cradoc, one of the leaders at Llanfaches and a former curate at Cardiff; so great was his fame that for generations to come Welsh Puritans would be known as Cradocians. He was assisted by his disciples, Morgan Llwyd and Vavasor Powell, and Cradoc claimed that their campaign caused the gospel to spread over the mountains like 'fire in the thatch'. Cradoc and his fellows were 'Independents', but in 1649 John Miles established a congregation of Baptists at Ilston in Gower, the earliest Baptist church within the borders of Wales.

The act of 1650 was intended to facilitate these developments. It transferred the income of the Church to two committees of commissioners. In the following three years, the commissioners dismissed 278 clerics whom they considered to be unworthy; they employed some scores of itinerant preachers and established a school in every urban centre of importance in Wales. The act ceased to be operative in 1653, but part of the work continued under the supervision of the Commission for the Approbation of Public Preachers, established in 1654. The evangelizing campaign had exhausted itself by 1658, and there was substance to accusations from Royalists that it had served mainly to promote the ambitions of the greedy and the notions of the addle-pated. Despite the weaknesses and the brevity of the campaign, Puritanism was to be heavily indebted to it, and Cromwell claimed that God had planted in Wales 'a seed ... hardly to be paralleled since the primitive times'. It was the Independents who benefited most, but Baptist congregations also multiplied and the Presbyterians won a foothold in Flintshire. Growth was not free from controversy. There were disputes over Calvinism and over forms of church government, and the Baptists split into two groups of communicants – strict and free. The more fervent proselytizers – particularly Vavasor Powell, the 'archbishop of the new saints' – were embittered when Cromwell made himself Lord Protector in 1654, an elevation which to Powell and his supporters was injurious to the millenarian potentialities of the Puritan revolution.

The sects already in existence proved unable to contain all the spiritual excitement of the age, in particular the yearning for a deeper and more intense devotion. It was this yearning which inspired Morgan Llwyd, the author of *Llyfr y Tri Aderyn* (The Book of the Three Birds, 1653), one of the greatest Welsh prose classics and the most mature and complex fruit of the Puritan muse. Llwyd believed that 'an inner burning light may show the way', a belief held by George Fox, the founder of the Society of Friends (the Quakers). Fox undertook a missionary tour in Wales in 1657 and his message was enthusiastically received by some of the inhabitants of mid-Wales and south Pembrokeshire. As they spurned the sacraments, had no formal ministry and adopted unique social habits, the Quakers suffered the hostility of even their fellow Puritans, and when the hour of persecution came they would bear the brunt.

The army was the basis of the authority of the Commonwealth. Its leaders shrank from an appeal to the 'people', for the Commonwealth's primary object was to ensure that the political revolution would not become too much of a social revolution. Every effort to embody that authority in permanent constitutional structures failed. As the bulk of the members of the ruling class were Royalists, it was difficult to find suitable men to serve on the County Committees, the basis of Commonwealth local administration. As a result, men of lowly origins were recruited, and in 1646 the gentry of Glamorgan claimed that the country was in the hands of men of inferior birth. To the squires and the poets, the most distressing consequence of the Parliamentary victory was the overthrow of the 'natural' hierarchy in Church and State, and it was reported in 1652 that 'the gentry and the people of substance in Wales were sad and downhearted'.

Nevertheless, the 'people of substance' survived the experience of the Civil War and the Interregnum remarkably well. A few powerful Roundheads seized the opportunity to build up estates. The most prominent of them was Philip Jones of Llangyfelach, who by 1658 had created a substantial estate at Fonmon in the Vale of Glamorgan, but there were others equally greedy, if not so successful. The efforts of Jones and his fellows were promoted by the market in land which resulted from the confiscation of Church possessions and from the fines imposed upon refractory Royalists. The victors were not, however, excessively revengeful towards the vanquished; the glory of the house of Raglan was temporarily dimmed and a number of squires were obliged to sell some of their land, but hardly any of the major estates of Wales came to an end as a result of the events of 1642–60. Indeed, members of the old Welsh ruling class proved remarkably eager to cooperate with the new system. Perhaps that should not be a matter for surprise; contemporaries were not to know that the Commonwealth would not last; in war and in its foreign and commercial policies it was highly successful. Furthermore, those who have had power instinctively align themselves with those who possess power. By the 1650s, members of staunchly Royalist families such as the Salesburys of Rhug and the Vaughans of Caer-gai were serving on the County Committees and the heir of the house of Raglan was accepting honours from Cromwell. The role of the gentry was limited between 1655 and 1657; those were the years of the experiment in military government when Wales was under the authority of Lieutenant-General Berry. Cromwell died in September 1658 and his son, Richard, resigned in May 1659. The gentry were elated. Philip Jones, the mainstay of Cromwellianism in Wales, was fiercely attacked, and some of the leading figures of the north-east plotted to restore the monarchy. Charles I's son was proclaimed king by Thomas Myddelton at Wrexham in August 1659. The action was untimely, but Myddelton was able to repeat it ten months later when General Monck ensured the restoration of the Stuart dynasty.

Surviving evidence suggests that the accession of Charles II was enthusiastically welcomed by most of the inhabitants of Wales. That evidence comes from the conservative elements of society – the gentry and the poets, the natural upholders of monarchy. Yet it probably also reflects the feelings of the bulk of the ordinary people of Wales, for few among them had warmed to the message of the Puritans or to the ideas of the political radicals. In welcoming the Restoration, the Welsh gentry presumably hoped that the government of Charles II would be essentially the same as that which had existed when his father was at the height of his authority. Outwardly, that appeared to be so. The king and the court, the Church and the bishops, the aristocracy and the House of Lords were all restored. But the legislation of the Long Parliament was not abrogated and it was impossible to disregard the experience of the Civil War and the Interregnum. Henceforth, the king would be able to rule only with the consent of the classes represented in the House of Commons, and he would be bereft of the prerogative courts which had allowed his predecessors to circumvent Common Law. The machinery which had enabled Charles I to oversee local government, to superintend the economic activities of his subjects and to insist that they conformed to the State Church had been swept away. As monopolies could no longer be granted, the king could not restrict private enterprise. The abolition of feudal tenures meant that there was no limitation upon the ability of landowners to deal with their estates as they pleased. Despite the arrogant confidence of the supporters of Crown and Church in 1660, they were advocates of institutions whose power was ebbing.

Those who benefited most from the outcome of the struggles of the years 1640 to 1660 were the greater landowners and the leading figures in the City of London. The century after 1660 was a golden age for the members of the landed class. They were virtually free from royal control and were not seriously threatened by social upheaval; for several generations, no other class would be able to compete with them in wealth, power and status. In the years following the Restoration, almost every substantial landed family adopted the practice of granting its landed property to trustees. This system of strict settlement ensured that, generation after generation, the head of the family would inherit the estate in its entirety and that his relations would receive maintenance from it. The income and wealth of the leading families grew rapidly. They were the main beneficiaries of the attempts made following the Restoration to compensate Royalists who had suffered during and after the Civil War. They had the resources to buy the best legal advice and to invest in the most efficient administrative procedures. They were also the best placed to take advantage of the advances in farming, advances which were, it has been claimed, initiating a revolution in agriculture. The larger estates grew as their owners obtained possession of the property of lesser gentry burdened by debt and as they bought out the survivors of the yeoman class. The greater landlords took advantage of the inability of copyholders to obtain firm titles to their land, and they were avid appropriators of common and crown lands.

The most favoured instrument in adding land to land was marriage. In the decades around 1700, a demographic crisis hit landowning families; many of them produced only one child, and that a daughter. Such an heiress was extremely attractive; frequently she married the heir of another estate and thus the lands of two families were united. In Wales, the most remarkable example of this phenomenon was the Williams Wynn family of Wynnstay, Denbighshire; through a series of marriages, the Wynns succeeded in uniting seven estates, bringing together holdings which would, by the second half of the nineteenth century, extend over 60,000 hectares. As the circle of acquaintances of the Welsh squires widened, and as they became wealthy enough for their estates to be coveted by men from the eastern side of Offa's Dyke, the marriage of an heiress frequently resulted in an English family obtaining possession of a Welsh estate. The marriage of Mary Wynn in 1679, for example, gave the Gwydir estate to the Bertie family. This was a highly significant factor in the anglicization of the ruling class of Wales.

As the result of the uniting of estates and of the decline of the smaller squires, many gentry mansions became undistinguished farmhouses. In the age of the Tudors, those mansions had produced members of parliament, but in the age of the later Stuarts the parliamentary representation of Wales came to be dominated by a tight caste of about two dozen families, a pattern which would continue until it was overwhelmed just over a century ago by new economic, social and intellectual forces. Between 1660 and 1714, there were sixteen general elections; in Denbighshire, fifteen of them were won by members of the Myddelton family of Chirk, and similar feats were accomplished by the Bulkeleys in Anglesey, by the Vaughans of Llwydiarth in Montgomeryshire and by Vaughans of the stock of Golden Grove in Carmarthenshire. In other counties – Cardigan, Pembroke and Monmouth among them – the representation of the county and the boroughs was shared among two or three of the leading families, while in Glamorgan there were battles between the aristocrats and the squires of the county. The struggle for a seat very rarely led to an electoral contest. In the twenty-seven constituencies of Wales, the sixteen general elections of the period 1660–1714 yielded a total of 432 election returns. Of these, only about forty were decided through the casting of votes. The rest were settled through private deals between landowners, thus avoiding the enormous cost of an electoral contest.

Almost all the Welsh members of parliament in the later Stuart age were natives of Wales, but their tendency to act as a Welsh block was in decline. This had been a feature of the history of the first hundred years of the parliamentary representation of Wales, but it did not survive the rise of party politics. The ministers of the crown sought to build a party loyal to the court, a group which around 1679 became known as the Tories. By then about two thirds of the Welsh members had Tory sympathies, from conviction in most cases, although bribery was also a factor. Those who had doubts about the policies of the ministers of the crown adhered to the Country party, which came to be known as the Whig party. The most eloquent of the Welsh Whigs was John Vaughan, the member for Cardiganshire, a man who had already made a name for himself in the Long Parliament, and the ablest of the Welsh lawyers who were so prominent in public life in the period 1660–88.

The party divisions crystallized during the Exclusion Crisis (1679–

81), the unsuccessful attempt of the Whigs to exclude Charles II's brother, James, duke of York, from the succession on the ground that he was a Roman Catholic. The papist bugbear of which the crisis was an expression would be a central feature in the politics of Britain for generations. With Louis XIV of France driving the Protestants out of his kingdom and with the Inquisition in the ascendant in Spain, it was not a groundless prejudice. It was fostered in Wales by publications such as *Y Ffydd Ddi-ffuant* (The Sincere Faith) by Charles Edwards (1667, 1671 and 1677) and, on a more popular level, the almanacs of Thomas Jones, which were published annually from 1680 onwards. The Roman Catholics of England and Wales were subject to at least fourteen penal laws, but it was believed that they were numerous and powerful, and the influence of Catholic aristocrats such as the earl of Powis and members of the Somerset family of Raglan was much feared. In fact, the Catholics were a tiny minority; according to a religious census conducted by the archbishop of Canterbury in 1676, they did not amount to more than 1 per cent of the population of Wales. The chief stronghold of Catholicism in southern Britain was Monmouthshire, the result of generations of succouring by the Raglan family. There, on the border with Herefordshire, the college of Cwm was founded in 1622 as a centre for the Jesuits, the order most deeply detested by Protestants. On the eve of the Exclusion Crisis, anti-papal hysteria was promoted throughout the kingdom; Cwm was ransacked and four of its priests were executed. Laymen were also persecuted, and between the Papist Plot of 1678–9 and the Irish immigration of the nineteenth century, the Old Faith in Wales would languish almost unto extinction.

Parliament was more given to persecution than was the king. Indeed, Charles II was a crypto-Catholic and was received into the Roman Church on his death-bed. In 1672, he sought to use his prerogative to relieve the burdens of Catholics. In order to win support for his efforts, he offered the same concessions to Protestant Nonconformists. Protestant Nonconformity had come into existence as a result of the desire of Royalist Anglicans to drive their Puritan enemies out of their Church. In 1660 and 1661, ninety-three Welsh clerics were deprived of their livings. In 1662, the same fate was experienced by twenty-five clergymen who refused to use the Book of Common Prayer in accordance with the Act of Uniformity passed in that year. In a series of measures known as the Clarendon Code, restrictions were placed upon the career and residence rights of the ousted clerics and upon the size of their congregations, and those who refused to take communion in the Church of England were deprived of any role in public life. But henceforth the refusal to take communion was not in itself an illegal act, for the ideal of including the entire population within the State Church had been abandoned. Implicit in that abandonment was the recognition of the existence of Nonconformity, although those who embraced it would not enjoy the full rights of citizenship for over two hundred years.

Their rights were very few in the years 1660 to 1688. Although it was only the Quakers who were subjected to a ferocious campaign aimed at eliminating them, persecution varying from arbitrary insult to periods of imprisonment was suffered by those who belonged to the Presbyterian, Baptist and Independent traditions. (And it is to traditions rather than to formal denominations that they belonged.) The campaign against the Quakers was successful. By 1700, most of the Friends of central Wales had joined the 'Holy Experiment' in Pennsylvania. They flourished there, although William Penn, the author of the experiment, did not adhere to his promise that they should be granted a distinct and separate Welsh colony. Other groups of Nonconformists also set sail for America, among them the Baptists of Ilston, who settled as a body in Swanzey, Massachusetts. But apart from the Quakers, no section of Welsh Nonconformity was terminally weakened through migration. In the face of persecution, the worldly and the ambitious returned to the Anglican fold. As a result, Nonconformity in Wales came to depend upon the middle ranks of society – the craftsmen and the yeomen. As they, in the main, had little knowledge of English, Nonconformity in most parts of Wales became thoroughly Welsh in language. Some of the faint-hearted also returned to the Established Church, and the conviction of the faithful remnant was strengthened by the adversity they suffered. It was a small remnant. The archbishop of Canterbury's religious census of 1676 suggests that no more than one in twenty of the population of Wales attended Nonconformist services in that year.

Although they were few, these were the people who laid the foundations of Welsh Nonconformist culture, a culture which would play a central role in the history of Wales in subsequent generations. As with the early Puritans, the sermon was the chief feature of worship among the Nonconformists. As preachers were scarce, the value of the printed word was stressed as an appendage to the pulpit. In 1674, a trust to evangelize among the Welsh was founded by Thomas Gouge, a London clergyman ejected from his living in 1662. The intention of Gouge and his London patrons was to give the children of Wales a knowledge of the English language so as to enable them to read English devotional books. Between 1674 and the death of Gouge in 1681, about three thousand pupils attended the schools of the Welsh Trust. To Stephen Hughes, the leader of the Independents of Carmarthenshire, it was repugnant that the Welsh should have to master English before their souls could be saved. 'It would be good,' he wrote, 'if everyone in Wales understood English. But, Oh Lord, how will that be possible if thou dost not commit wonders.' It appears that Hughes persuaded Gouge to devote some of the money of the Trust to the publication of religious texts in Welsh, and thus a crucial stimulus was given to the Welsh press. Between 1546 and 1670, about 116 Welsh books were published, less than one a year on average; 139 were published between 1670 and 1700, an average of over four a year. Among Hughes's publications was a Welsh version of *Pilgrim's Progress* (*Taith y Pererin*, 1688), one of the numerous translations from English produced by Hughes and his associates. He was also responsible for publishing the verses of Vicar Prichard, *Canwyll y Cymru* (The Welshman's Candle, 1681), and for the printing of eight thousand Bibles in 1678 and a further ten thousand in 1690.

Gouge and Hughes were Nonconformists, but Nonconformists were not the only promoters of education and publishing. Despite the persecuting zeal of some of the bishops, there were in the late Stuart period examples of cooperation between Churchmen and Nonconformists, especially as the political threat of Puritanism disappeared and fears of the political threat of Catholicism intensified. The Welsh Trust received the support of prominent Anglicans, some who were of a Puritan mentality (for not all clergy of that mentality were ejected from the Church in 1662) and others who were increasingly impatient of minor sectarian differences. Their views owed much to the Cambridge neo-Platonists, men who believed that Christianity was a rational religion and that its fundamental simplicity had been obscured by rigid abstractions. With their emphasis upon rationalism, the Platonists promoted a doctrine that could be theologically fairly contentless. This was the Latitudinarianism which was so characteristic of the leaders of the Church of England in the following generations.

Their ideas were given intellectual substance by the work of the philosopher John Locke. Locke was inspired by the scientists of his day – Newton, in particular – and so great was their achievement that the reign of Charles II is considered to be a key period in the rise of the scientific mind.

The attitudes and the circumstances of life of the Welsh of the twentieth century were to be determined to a high degree by the intellectual revolution initiated by men such as Newton and Locke. At the time, however, that revolution had little impact upon the lives of the ordinary people of Wales. Nevertheless, the scepticism promoted by the new ideas was among factors which undermined the notion of the divine right of kings and which brought to an end the persecution of Nonconformists. These were two of the chief consequences of the 'Glorious Revolution' of 1688, the revolution which swept James II from his throne. Throughout his three-year reign, James sought to improve the condition of his fellow Roman Catholics. Through his clumsy efforts, he alienated many members of the aristocracy and the episcopate, men who had previously been the natural upholders of his dynasty. In this maelstrom, Welshmen were prominent on the one side and the other. James's opponents included William Lloyd, bishop of St Asaph, the most eloquent of the seven bishops prosecuted for challenging the king's Declaration of Indulgence to Catholics. The bishops were declared not guilty on 30 June 1688, partly because of the arguments of one of the judges, John Powell of Llanwrda. On the same day, Arthur Herbert, one of the Herberts of Montgomeryshire, set sail for the Netherlands to plead for the intervention of William of Orange, James's son-in-law and nephew, and the most prominent of the Protestant rulers of Europe. On the other hand, James's advisers included his Lord Chancellor, George Jeffreys of Acton near Wrexham, and his Solicitor General, William Williams, the ancestor of the house of Wynnstay, and the Speaker of the sole parliament he convened was John Trevor of Bryncunallt near Chirk. Furthermore, the son born to the queen on 10 June 1688 was entrusted to the care of Elizabeth Herbert who, as the wife of the marquess of Powis and the daughter of the earl of Worcester, was related to the most powerful of the Catholic landowners of Wales.

It was the birth of the prince of Wales – an occasion for celebration among some of the inhabitants of Wales – which sparked off the crisis which terminated the reign of James II. James had two daughters – Mary, the wife of William of Orange, and Anne, both of whom were Protestants. Having a son whom he was determined to raise as a Catholic meant that James's Catholicizing policies were likely to survive him; the birth of the prince of Wales also threatened William's hopes of seeing his wife inherit the British throne.

A rumour was therefore started to the effect that the baby was not the queen's child. William landed on the coast of Devon on 5 November 1688, an auspicious date for a Protestant; James fled to France on 23 December and William III and Mary II were accepted as joint sovereigns on 13 February 1689. The architects of the 'Revolution' were the Whigs. The clergy of Wales were natural Tories; nevertheless, so great was their fear of Roman Catholicism that less than two dozen of them joined the Non-Jurors, the body established by those who refused to swear an oath of allegiance to William and Mary – the Puritans of the Right, to quote Thomas Richards. The most dedicated Tory among the landowners of Wales, Henry, earl of Worcester (who had become a Protestant and had been elevated to the dukedom of Beaufort in 1682), had promised to raise an army of ten thousand men in Wales to fight for James but, in the face of the king's readiness to abandon his kingdom Beaufort's efforts proved feeble. As president of the Council of Wales, he had aided James in his attempts to interfere with constituencies in order to bring the electoral process under central control, attempts which had angered both Whigs and Tories. Above all, the gentry of Wales were disturbed in 1688 – as they had been in 1642 – by a rumour that the king was seeking the assistance of a Catholic army from Ireland. Any surviving allegiance to James was undermined when he landed in Ireland in 1689 in order to use the one island as the base for an attack on the other. He was defeated by William III at the battle of the Boyne on 1 July 1690. That victory opened a sorrowful chapter in the history of the Irish, but to the Welsh it provided an assurance that their coasts would no longer be vulnerable; in consequence, they were enthusiastic supporters of William III's Irish policy.

Welsh approval of William manifested itself in the oath of allegiance sworn to him in 1696 by the greater part of the prominent men of his kingdom, the result of a proposal by Rowland Gwynne of Llanelwedd. Yet as the royal succession had been broken by the 'Revolution', it would henceforth be impossible to consider kingship as sacred and inviolable. It had been proved that the government could exist independently of the sovereign and that the king was no more than one of the servants of the state. Although he still retained substantial prerogatives, parliament had proved that it could make and unmake a sovereign. Implicit in the 'Revolution' was the erosion of the power of the king and the growth of the power of the landed oligarchy which dominated parliament. In 1694, the Triennial Act laid down that there should be a parliamentary election every three years at least; in the wake of the growing importance of the sittings at Westminster, London's appeal for members of the Welsh ruling class was vastly strengthened. The attraction of Ludlow, 'the lost capital', had long vanished. When the council at Ludlow was abolished in July 1689, there was very little protest in Wales. Instead, the Welsh gentry embraced London with its half a million inhabitants, among them Welshmen who would play a central role in the history of their country.

The growth of London was greatly promoted by the development of the 'City', which by 1700 was the pivot of world capitalism. The reign of William III saw the establishment of the Bank of England, the Stock Exchange and Lloyd's Insurance, institutions central to the Commercial Revolution, the necessary precursor to the Industrial Revolution. The ethos of the age was more and more favourable to business interests. Following the union of the English and Scottish parliaments in 1707, Britain was the largest state lacking any internal restrictions on trade, and the work of Gregory King in 1696 showed that the non-agricultural aspects of its economy were more important and more varied than they were in any other of the states of Europe. Those aspects were fostered by the long war with France (1689–97; 1702–13), and, as a result of the treaty which brought the conflict to an end, Britain won extensive commercial advantages. At the time, Wales was on the periphery of these developments, but so dynamic were the capitalist forces they nurtured that the Welsh would progressively become enmeshed in them.

Economic considerations were among the factors which ensured a measure of tolerance for Nonconformists. Toleration had proved profitable in the Netherlands, and the persecuting policies of Louis XIV were a severe blow to the prosperity of France. It has already been noted that the increasing scepticism of the age promoted toleration. An additional complication was the situation in Scotland, where the government was obliged in 1689 to recognize Presbyterianism as the official religion; it would therefore be perverse to continue to persecute the Presbyterians of England and Wales. Furthermore, the Nonconformists had firmly rejected James's policies, despite his readiness to include them in the Declaration of Indulgence which he had proclaimed for his fellow-Catholics. The Whigs (and the moderate Tories) were prepared to reward the Nonconformists. The reward was the Act of Toleration of May 1689 which permitted Trinitarian Protestant ministers to conduct services without hindrance provided they swore the relevant oaths and registered their places of worship. It was a niggardly concession; the Corporation Act (1661) and the Test Act (1673), which restricted public office to Anglican communicants, were not repealed; the obligation upon all – whether or not they attended the parish church – to pay rates and tithes to maintain the buildings and the clergy of the Church of England remained; university degrees continued to be granted only to those who subscribed to the Articles of Faith of the Established Church; the Church kept a firm hold upon the endowments of the grammar schools and upon a host of philanthropic institutions. Of the status and power enjoyed by Anglicanism as the State Church, not a jot was yielded, thus ensuring that Nonconformists would be conscious that their status was that of second-class citizens.

Despite the inadequacies of the Toleration Act of 1689, its passage meant that Nonconformists, who had previously been persecuted by the courts, could henceforth look to the courts to defend them. Immediate steps were taken to profit from the measure. The chief need of the Nonconformists was suitable buildings in which to worship – hitherto, they had had to be content with services in private houses, in barns or in the open air. Cefnarthen, near Llandovery, which was built in about 1692, was probably the earliest of the chapels of the Independents, and it is believed that Llanwenarth, near Abergavenny, which had been completed by 1695, was the earliest of the chapels of the Baptists. They were the first fruits of a building campaign which would be one of the most remarkable episodes in the history of Wales. By 1715, there were about seventy Nonconformist chapels in Wales. Nonconformity was strongest in Carmarthenshire, Glamorgan and Monmouthshire, counties which had about thirteen chapels apiece; there were only eight chapels in the counties of the north-east and only two in the whole of Gwynedd. A single church could serve an extensive district – Cilgwyn Church, for example, served the needs of the Independents over a wide area of Cardiganshire – and decades would pass before a daughter of the mother church attained the status of a separate congregation.

The Independents and the Baptists stressed the sovereignty of the individual congregation. (The Presbyterians had a centralized form of government, but they had very little support in Wales; the present Presbyterian Church of Wales has no links with the old Presbyterianism.) The congregational emphasis, however, did not prevent the Nonconformists of Wales from associating with movements having a wider influence. They needed support, for despite the Toleration Act of 1689 they were still vulnerable. They could feel fairly secure during the reign of William III, but his successor, Anne (1702–14), had no sympathy for them. The enthusiastic welcome received in 1710 by the high Tory, Henry Sacheverell, on the borders of Wales indicates that the people of the chapel were a target for the hostility of the rural gentry and the urban mob. The Toleration Act found no favour among diehard Tories; their success in 1711 in outlawing occasional conformity (a back-door method of allowing Nonconformists to hold public office) and their enthusiasm for the Schism Bill (which would have banned Nonconformist academies) were expressions of their opposition to the principle of toleration. The vengefulness of the Tories was restrained by the Whigs of the House of Lords, and the alliance between the Nonconformists and the Whig party (and its successor, the Liberal party) was to become a central feature of Welsh politics; as late as 1910, a Welsh chapel-goer could declare: 'If a Nonconformist can be a Tory, then I have not understood my Bible.' Welsh Nonconformity was also heavily indebted to the wealthy English Nonconformists. The financial assistance of the Boards of the Presbyterians and the Congregationalists came from London, as did the legal assistance of the Protestant Dissenting Deputies.

As they were aware of their English origins and were grateful for the patronage of their English co-religionists, the Nonconformists of Wales did not embrace any specifically Welsh aspirations; the Baptists did not feel the need for a distinctly Welsh organization until 1866 nor the Independents until 1871. Although Nonconformity contributed greatly to what came to be considered characteristic of Wales, that contribution was not concerned with furthering the claims of Wales as a nation. The links with London were at their most obvious in the attempts to train ministers. The Nonconformist academies sprang from the readiness of learned ministers to welcome students to their homes. The famous academy at Brynllywarch near Llangynwyd was the home of Samuel Jones (1628–97), but the need for a more permanent and endowed system soon became apparent. Assistance from London was forthcoming for the academies of the Baptists, the Independents and the Presbyterians; indeed, the most famous of the academies, the 'beloved learned nest' at Carmarthen, was indebted in turn to the Independents and the Presbyterians.

The educational standards of the academies were high; they often surpassed those of Oxford and Cambridge. Respect for education and literacy was central to the values of the Nonconformists. Their services were primarily training schools and the tone of their sermons was philosophical rather than evangelical. When persecution declined, the millenarian tradition ebbed away. The grandsons of the revolutionary Puritans were men of formal correctness. They spent much of their energy on theological debate – on the nature of the person of Christ, the doctrine of the atonement, the sacrament of baptism and the forms of ecclesiastical government. As a result, the members of the varying dissenting traditions, who had drawn together during the era of persecution, came to make much of the differences between them. These scholastic discussions were not always characterized by brotherly love, and the hymn-writer William Williams remembered with abhorrence the bitter debate which split Cefnarthen, the Independent chapel attended by his family. Despite the intellectual energy of the Nonconformists, there was very little increase in their ranks in the fifty years following the passage of the Toleration Act. Indeed, it has been claimed that the numbers attending Nonconformist places of worship in England declined by 40 per cent between 1700 and 1740, partly because wealthy dissenting families tended to return to the Established Church. Such families were less numerous in Wales (although they were not wholly absent), but it appears that the proportion of the Welsh population adhering to Nonconformity in 1715 was the same as it had been in 1676.

With Nonconformity weak and Roman Catholicism almost expiring, nine out of ten of those of the Welsh who attended a place of worship frequented the parish church. The Methodists created a portrait of the Established Church as it was before their revival which stressed its corruption and neglectfulness. It is now realized that their portrayal was partial and unfair, and that much of the harvest reaped by the Methodists had been sown by others. In the age of the later Stuarts (1660–1714), the Church had conscientious bishops – many of them Welsh – and its members, high and low, held it in great esteem. 'To God be thanks,' wrote Edward Samuel, rector of Llangar, in 1715, 'for the light of the Gospel now shines more brightly in Wales than in almost any other country . . . More useful, godly books have been printed . . . and there are better preachers . . . amongst us than there have been for a thousand years and more.' The Church certainly had its weaknesses. As has been seen, the landowners had, at the time of the dissolution of the monasteries, obtained possession of a large number of livings; where that had happened, the tithes – as much as £500 a year in some parishes – were paid to the landlord, who was not obliged to pay more than £6 or £10 a year to the curate who ministered to the flock. It was therefore natural for a curate to undertake duty in a number of parishes, rushing from church to church on Sundays to reel off the liturgy. When describing the state of the diocese of St David's in 1721, Erasmus Saunders noted the long hours which congregations spent in their half-ruined churches waiting the coming of the clergyman. These weaknesses were at their worst in the southern dioceses, where lay patronage was more common than it was in the sees of Bangor and St Asaph; in 1708, half the livings of St David's were worth less than £30 a year and a quarter were worth less than £10.

Not all lay patrons were heedless of their responsibilities, and religion in Wales was much indebted to the patronage of devout laymen. The most prominent of them was Sir John Philipps of Picton Castle near Haverfordwest (1662–1737), the wealthiest of the landowners of Pembrokeshire. The Society for the Propagation of Christian Knowledge (the SPCK) was founded in 1699 and Sir John was one of its earliest members. Although most of the society's supporters were Tory High Churchmen, they had something of the zeal of the old Puritans. Their activities savoured strongly of social control – many of the publications of the SPCK promised rewards, on earth and in heaven, for those of the poor who followed the path of meekness and obedience. Nevertheless, it would be perverse to impugn the sincerity which motived the philanthropy of men such as Sir John Philipps.

The SPCK was chiefly concerned with establishing and maintaining charity schools. Between 1700 and 1740, it established ninety-six schools in Wales, almost half of them in Pembrokeshire and Carmarthenshire, the region most amenable to the influence of Sir John. By his time, parents able to afford to educate their children sent them to the private schools which were increasingly available, and literacy was becoming fairly widespread among families enjoying a modicum of prosperity. It was with those beneath them that the SPCK was concerned. In the areas of its greatest exertions, the society had a considerable impact, for those areas were to be the centre of the religious and educational developments of the following generation. In most of Wales, however, the SPCK only touched the edges of the need for education. Its efforts were hindered by the inability of many children to attend school because their parents needed their services as beggars and farm labourers, and by the presumption that English should be the language of the schools. Yet, although the SPCK did not advocate education in Welsh, the use of the language was condoned in many areas, particularly in the north. Education through the medium of Welsh was practical because there was already a considerable tradition of publishing religious works in the language. (This was in marked contrast with the situation in Scotland, where the society was for years wholly hostile to Gaelic.) The SPCK made an honourable contribution to that tradition, for it was largely responsible for the 'useful and godly books' praised by Edward Samuel in 1715. Between 1700 and 1730, an average of fourteen Welsh books a year was published, a considerable advance upon the four a year published in the previous thirty years. Many of the books were translations of rather uninspired devotional works, but they included Ellis Wynne's *Gweledigaetheu y Bardd Cwsc* (The Vision of the Sleeping Bard, 1703). Wynne was a cleric and a minor landowner, and his work is proof that there were still gentry, at least in Meirionnydd, who had a superb command of the Welsh language. *Y Bardd Cwsc* is a satirical portrait of the ills of the age, and a classic of Welsh High Anglicanism; to Ellis Wynne, the Established Church was the only vehicle of salvation and Queen Anne was the most beloved of heroines.

Wynne's respect for the queen was not without foundation, for she cherished the lesser clergy and appointed godly bishops who supported the work of the SPCK. This was not true of the bishops appointed by her successor; in 1720 Bishop Bisse of St David's condemned all attempts to publish Welsh religious works. It was the coming of the Hanoverian dynasty which caused the change in the disposition of the bishops. At least a dozen people had a better claim to the British throne than had George, the elector of Hanover, but as they were all Roman Catholics it was he who assumed the crown on the death of Anne in 1714. Hereditary royal succession had been infringed in 1689 but it was assailed in a far more fundamental way in 1714. In the more conservative parts of the kingdom – Wales among them – this caused much anguish, and decades would pass before Welsh land-owners and clerics abandoned their loyalty to the house of Stuart. Therefore, Hanoverian governments needed bishops who would restrain the Jacobite zeal of the clergy. They found them among the Latitudinarian divines, men who believed that Christianity was a matter of good conduct and who condemned all forms of religious enthusiasm. They began their episcopal careers in the poorer dioceses and were promoted in accordance with their readiness to support the government in the House of Lords. As Welsh bishops were not lavishly rewarded (incomes varied from £500 in Llandaf to £1,400 in St Asaph), an apprentice bishop tended to be sent to Wales. If he showed himself to be useful, he would be translated to a richer diocese (Durham was worth £6,000), and it was claimed that the bishop of Llandaf was immortal, for no one ever died in the office. The time the bishop could devote to his flock was limited by the demands of the House of Lords and some bishops never visited their dioceses at all.

The Hanoverian bishops were gracious and learned men, and their Latitudinarianism was more commendable than the intolerance of some of their predecessors. Yet, because the Welsh religious tradition in later generations came to glorify zeal above all other attributes, they have been vilified more, perhaps, than any other group in the history of Wales. Their greatest disfavour to the Welsh Church was undoubtedly to associate it with anglicization. The Church of England had made a distinguished contribution to the life of Wales, but under the Hanoverians its higher ranks became totally English. All the bishops were Englishmen – scions as often as not of aristocratic families who had rediscovered that the Church could be exploited. They cherished the culture of London, a culture increasingly cosmopolitan in nature and unprepared to tolerate 'regional' peculiarities. As most of the lower clergy were Welsh speakers, inadequately educated and rustic in manner, they were considered not to be gentlemen; in consequence, Welsh clergy rarely advanced beyond the most modest offices, a cause of great bitterness among Welsh intellectuals.

To the Hanoverian government, the attachment of the Welsh landowners to the house of Stuart was far more threatening than the Jacobitism of the lesser clergy. As has been noted, the landowners were largely Tory; in the general election of 1713, only four of the twenty-seven constituencies of Wales were won by Whigs. During the reign of Charles II, the Whigs had been the Country party – the Opposition – but their victory in 1688 caused them to become the natural party of government. After 1688, Tories only occasionally became ministers of the crown. This did not happen, even occasionally, in the generation after 1714. Although most Tories were prepared to acquiesce in George I's elevation to the throne, decades would pass before the accusation that they lacked loyalty to the new dynasty would be dispelled. Following the Jacobite Rising of 1715, the Whigs seized the opportunity to dismiss many Tory magistrates. In Wales, it was difficult to do so, for there were few to take their place. The leading Welsh Whig families included the Mansels of Margam in Glamorgan, the Owens of Orielton in Pembrokeshire, the Vaughans of Trawsgoed in Cardiganshire, the Wynns of Glynllifon in Caernarfonshire and the Myddeltons of Chirk in Denbighshire, but they were cast into the shade by the Tory legions led by the duke of Beaufort, the earl of Powis, the Wynns of Wynnstay and the Philippses of Picton Castle. As late as 1743, the advisers of the Young Pretender (Bonnie Prince Charlie, the grandson of James II) believed that the whole of Wales was controlled by men such as Beaufort and Wynn, and the presumption that their support would be forthcoming played an important part in Charles's plans during the Jacobite Rising of 1745. The Welsh Jacobites, however, showed no inclination to join him, one of the considerations which caused him to venture no further south than Derby.

It is easy to make too much of the Jacobitism of Wales, with its secret messages, its fanciful societies and its sentimental toasts. It probably would not have received so much attention had the great men of the kingdom been divided by more substantial ideological differences. After the failure of the rising of 1745, and particularly after the accession in 1760 of George III, the first Hanoverian to 'glory in the

name of Briton', that division faded away and the labels Whig and
Tory lost all significance. Politics in the eighteenth century was a
matter of family faction rather than party ideology. Parliamentary
elections were not contests over policy but trials of strength between
leading families and their followers. In seeking entry to the House of
Commons, the Welsh squire was mainly concerned to enhance the
status of his family in county society and to influence the dispensation
of government patronage in his locality. Nevertheless, Welsh MPs
were not unmindful of the activities of parliament; they tended to
believe that government is essentially corrupt and oppressive and that
every man of substance should keep it under a hawk-like scrutiny. At
the same time, they recognized that the crown was obliged to maintain
some form of government, a consideration which – aided by considerable corruption – gave Walpole's Whig administration (1715–41) the
reluctant support of the majority of the representatives of Wales.

Some Welsh members of parliament loathed Walpole. Sir Watkin
Williams Wynn was the most prominent of them. In 1716, Sir Watkin
succeeded in capturing the Denbighshire constituency from the control
of the Myddelton family, and when he was challenged in 1741 he
spent £20,000 on preventing the county from reverting to its former
allegiance. A great deal of electoral expenditure went on 'wet canvassing' and parliamentary contests were scenes of wild drunkenness. Sir
Watkin and his fellow landowners could create voters by granting life
leases to their tenants – for voting purposes, a life tenant was
considered to be a freeholder. As the number of enfranchised tenants
increased, the number of genuine freeholders decreased, allowing the
leading landowners to consolidate their hold over county representation. Tenants voting in defiance of the wishes of their landlord were
liable to be evicted, but such evictions were rare, for the estate was a
natural unit and obedience to landlords was instinctive in tenants. It
was possible to create borough voters also. As landowners dominated
the corporations, they could control entry into the burgess-ship, an
honour which carried with it the right to vote in parliamentary
elections. Most of the borough constituencies of Wales included
several boroughs and the patrons of each could compete in creating
voters. This happened in 1769, when the squire of Gogerddan created
a thousand burgesses in Aberystwyth and Cardigan, and the squire of
Peterwell (Sir Herbert Lloyd of infamous memory) retaliated by
creating twelve hundred at Lampeter. Nevertheless, such struggles

were rare. As during the years 1660–1740, so also in the century after 1714, the vast majority of the Welsh members of parliament were elected unopposed, proof of the basic unity of the ruling class to which the landlords of Wales belonged and of their desire to avoid huge disbursements of money.

They, or at least the richest of them, had been wholly assimilated into the ruling class of England by the mid eighteenth century. As has already been noted, a number of prominent Welsh families had become extinct in the male line early in that century. This tendency was to continue. Although it was masked to some extent by the readiness of some new lineages to adopt the surnames of the old, unfamiliar names proliferated: Stuart in place of Herbert at Cardiff Castle, Campbell in place of Vaughan at Golden Grove, Stanley in place of Owen at Penrhos. Nevertheless, with very few exceptions (the Smith family, granted the Faenol estate by William III, being the most prominent), the newcomers were not alien landlords imposed upon the Welsh. (In Ireland, alien landowners were imposed; this was a vital factor in determining that the 'Land Question' in Ireland was very different from that in Wales.) It was their few drops of Welsh blood which entitled them to their estates in Wales and they could be quite well disposed towards Welsh activities; they took pride in regiments such as the Royal Welch Fusiliers (founded in 1689) and were prepared on occasion to subscribe to a Welsh book or to support a cultural venture. But they expended only a minute part of their time and their resources on such matters, and by the middle of the eighteenth century there were no organic links between the leading men of Wales and the literary culture of the country.

But literature is not the sum total of culture. Between 1720 and 1750, the landscape of Wales was enhanced by mansions such as Leeswood, Nanteos and Wynnstay, gracious buildings in the Palladian tradition. The country was also endowed with something of the baroque tradition, particularly through the splendid ironwork of the Davies family, and there were suggestions too of the rococo style, as in the library at Fonmon. Members of the wealthier gentry families undertook the Grand Tour; three of the Mansels of Margan did so between 1715 and 1740 at a cost of over £2,000 a head. In consequence, they developed a taste for French furniture and Italian pictures, and by 1750 Louis Quinze cabinets and Renaissance paintings might be seen in some of the mansions of Wales. Parks were created around the mansions: the enchanting glades of Dinefwr were laid out by 'Capability' Brown in 1775. New species of trees were planted and distinguished gardeners arose among the Welsh squires; the most distinguished of them was Thomas Hanmer of Flintshire, one of Europe's most renowned tulipomaniacs. London periodicals such as the *Spectator* and the *Gentleman's Magazine* were eagerly read; the most recent novels were bought and gossip from London was avidly discussed. Not all landowners, of course, could afford – or wished for – such things, and there were many among them who had no interests beyond their dogs, their horses and their liquor. But they also were under pressure to be 'polite', part of the social discipline which was to transform the nature of the Welsh squirearchy by the end of the eighteenth century.

The same processes were at work among other classes of society. The view that the schools of the Commonwealth hastened the extinction of the old world in Wales has already been noted. Native traditions were further undermined by the activities of both Churchmen and Nonconformists, and the work of Ellis Wynne shows that even a conservative such as he lacked sympathy with the older culture. Of the 406 Welsh books published between 1700 and 1730, only a handful had any bearing upon Welshness as such; most of the publications, with their pietistic seriousness, were fundamentally inimical to the high Welsh culture of the past. The bardic schools were in advanced decay and the native musical tradition was being abandoned; parents no longer gave their children Welsh names, many old customs were reviled as meaningless and scholars were contemptuous of the story of Brutus, the central myth of Welsh identity. In 1686, William Richards prophesied the imminent death of the Welsh language ('Englished out of Wales', as he put it), and there would be many in the succeeding generation who would agree with him. Thomas Jones, the compiler of almanacs, went so far as to express the fear that the Welsh as a people would be expunged from history. To the commentators of the period – and subsequently – the anglicization of the gentry was the root cause of the erosion of Welsh identity, but that class was perhaps the scapegoat for a more fundamental debility.

Out of enfeeblement came renewal, not through the restoration of the old but rather through adapting it and through creating new traditions. It is increasingly recognized that the national cultures of countries such as England and France are conscious creations rather than the fruit of organic development. So was it also in Wales, and the *Cyffroawd Cymreigyddawl* (The Welsh Excitation) was imbued with a self-conscious seriousness. This can be seen in one of the most influential books of eighteenth-century Wales. The aim of Theophilus Evans, the curate of Llangamarch, Breconshire, in writing *Drych y Prif Oesoedd* (The Mirror of Past Ages, 1716, 1740) was to reinforce the pride of the Welsh by portraying their history as a glorious epic. In the book he sought to 'give an account of the experience of the Welsh . . . from the time when the Language was first mixed in the Tower of Babel'. He asserted that the Welsh were descendants of Gomer, the grandson of Noah – a notion he borrowed from that strange Breton scholar, Abbé Pezron. The Gomer myth and the belief that Welsh was among the very oldest of languages was to help to sustain Welsh consciousness until this century. *Drych y Prif Oesoedd* drew renewed attention to the story of the mission of Joseph of Arimathea and emphasized the central role of Brutus in the history of the Britons – an eighteenth-century Welsh patriot could not abandon Geoffrey of Monmouth. In 1723, Welsh mythology received a further dimension through the publication of the work of Henry Rowlands, *Mona Antiqua Restaurata*. This was the book which launched the druidic fad, a fad which, through the genius of Iolo Morganwg, would do much to muddy the stream of Welsh historiography.

The obsession of the Welsh with myth was strange, particularly in view of the fact that scientific study of their history and language had already been undertaken when *Drych y Prif Oesoedd* was published. Edward Lhuyd (1660–1709) was the first Welshman to train himself in the experimental ideas of the new science and the first to place Welsh studies on a firm foundation. He visited all the countries where Celtic languages were spoken and analysed the linguistic links between them; he offered considered theories concerning the monuments of his country and through a vast correspondence collected an abundance of material relating to the customs and traditions of the Welsh. In addition, he was an expert geologist and botanist and won recognition as the 'finest naturalist now in Europe'. He was unable to complete his work (he died in his forty-ninth year) and only a tiny proportion of his writings was published. As Wales lacked institutions capable of developing and disseminating his ideas, the Welsh were for generations to view their past through the romantic eyes of Theophilus Evans rather than through the scholarly eyes of Lhuyd.

Nevertheless, some of the seed sown by Lhuyd bore fruit. His disciple, Moses Williams, was the pioneer of Welsh bibliographical studies, and William Wootton, another disciple, was the first to publish the Laws of Hywel Dda. The ideals of Lhuyd also influenced the Morrises of Anglesey. The correspondence between the three brothers, Lewis, Richard and William Morris, and their friends is proof of the breadth of their interests and of their longing to convince the anglicized Welsh, as Lewis put it, 'of something of which they have never heard – that there was formerly scholarship and knowledge in Wales'. To this end, Lewis in 1735 published *Tlysau yr hen Oesoedd* (The Treasures of the Ancient Ages), the first attempt to establish a Welsh periodical.

The Morrises saw the need for an institution on the lines of the Royal Society to promote the interests of Wales. Although some Welsh towns – Carmarthen, in particular – were becoming cultural centres of importance, London was the only possible location for such an institution. It is difficult to estimate the size of the Welsh community in London, but there were certainly more Welsh people living there than in any of the towns of Wales. Almost all Welsh families of substance visited the city and it also attracted a host of seasonal workers from Wales. The Society of Ancient Britons was established in 1715 with the intention of proving that some, at least, of the London Welsh were loyal to the Hanoverian dynasty, but its activities were limited. The Honourable Society of Cymmrodorion, established in 1751, was far more ambitious. Its founder was Richard Morris, a clerk in the Admiralty, and so great was his contribution that the Cymmrodorion (of the first creation) faded away after his death in 1779. The society was stamped with the image of Richard's brother, Lewis, the deputy-steward of crown lands in Cardiganshire, and he sought to guide it from his home at Pen-bryn near Aberystwyth. As with other societies of the eighteenth century (a century which saw the rapid growth of freemasonry), the members of the Cymmrodorion indulged in elaborate ceremony, rituals which the London Welsh enjoyed re-performing in 1951. The Morrises were reluctant to recruit those of lowly status: they sought members among the leading landowners of Wales, men who were – with a few exceptions such as William Vaughan of Corsygedol, the society's president – ignorant of the Welsh language. According to the 'Ordinances of the Cymmrodorion', its members vowed to defend the purity of the Welsh language, to stimulate interest in the history and literature of Wales and to promote economic and scientific ventures beneficial to Wales.

The work of the society was vitiated by its snobbish and anglicizing tendencies, and its achievements were small compared with its ambitions. But the contribution of the Cymmrodorion to the Welsh 'Renaissance' of the eighteenth century should not be totally dismissed. It inspired attempts to publish the early literature of Wales, including that magnificent publication, *Some Specimens of the Poetry of the Antient Welsh Bards* (1764), the result of the tireless research of Ieuan Brydydd Hir (Evan Evans) into the wealth of manuscript material. Like Edward Lhuyd, the Morrises were eager to enlighten English intellectuals. They sought enlightenment, in part because the songs of Ossian (the forgeries of the Scots poet James Macpherson) published in 1763 had aroused widespread interest in Celtic literature. The members of the Cymmrodorion gave assistance to that awkward genius, Goronwy Owen of Anglesey, the man who gave renewed prestige to the strict metres and who inspired the poets to seek to compose a Welsh epic – an aspiration which was to absorb their energies for a century and more. By the time of Goronwy Owen, the succession of the poets writing in the classical tradition had been broken; he learnt his craft from books rather than from living exponents of the art. The most important of those books was that of Sion Rhydderch (1728), the first of a series of studies and dictionaries (the best of which came from Glamorgan, much to the astonishment of the Morrises) which would provide a lexical quarry for the poets and a key to an understanding of the early poetry.

It was the high literary tradition of Wales which excited the interest of the Morrises. Although there were still some country poets, Lewis Morris believed that they did no more than delight in beer, buffoonery and foul language (though he himself was not unacquainted with such things). Nevertheless, the Welsh 'Renaissance' had truly popular aspects. The prominence which Thomas Jones gave to poetry in his almanacs – reading material which reached the homes of the most lowly of the literate – shows that interest in the poetic tradition was not confined to intellectuals. 'The people,' wrote R. T. Jenkins, 'insisted upon some sort of literature,' and there were those eager to satisfy them by composing ballads, interludes, halsings, lays, carols and hymns. The meetings of the poets were advertised in the almanacs.

The almanac *eisteddfodau* – often drunken and bootless occasions – preceded the more formal *eisteddfodau* held after 1789, the beginnings of an expression of popular culture unsurpassed anywhere in Europe. At the beginning of the eighteenth century, popular literature was an oral tradition, but it was increasingly overtaken by the printed word. The first publication of the press founded by Isaac Carter at Atpar near Newcastle Emlyn in 1717 (the earliest permanent printing press on Welsh soil) was a ballad in praise of tobacco, a foretaste of the abundance of ephemera which was to flood from the presses of Wales in subsequent generations.

These developments suggest that literacy in the Welsh language was spreading rapidly by the middle decades of the eighteenth century. That was the period of the great campaign of Griffith Jones of Llanddowror to endow his compatriots, as quickly as possible, with the ability to read their mother tongue. Griffith Jones (1683–1771) was a farmer's son from the Teifi valley, one of the most cultivated districts of Wales. In his youth, he had a religious experience so intense that he was overwhelmed with the desire to save souls. His career was strongly influenced by Sir John Philipps; in 1708, Jones began to keep a school under the auspices of the SPCK, he became a correspondent of the society in 1713, Sir John presented him to the living of Llanddowror in 1716 and he married the baronet's sister in 1720. The support of the squire of Picton Castle was of crucial importance to Griffith Jones; a Hanoverian bishop would have been unlikely to present him to a valuable rectory, and the patronage of Sir John saved him from the anger of the ecclesiastical authorities when his fellow-clerics complained of his custom of visiting their parishes and arousing the emotions of large congregations.

Although highly talented as a preacher, Griffith Jones considered that sermons in themselves did not suffice, and that there was a need to ensure that the mass of the population had a firm grasp of the Christian religion through indoctrinating them with the catechism and through enabling them to read the Bible. In about 1734, when he was over fifty and in poor health, Jones devised a scheme for establishing temporary schools which would concentrate entirely upon teaching children and adults to read their mother tongue. Every feature of the plan for circulating schools had been at least suggested before. Griffith Jones had little originality; what he did have was the energy and single-mindedness to fulfil his aspirations. He received the enthusiastic support of Bridget Bevan of the Vaughan family, squires of Derllys near Carmarthen. Her links with wealthy patrons in London and Bath were an important element in his success, for England was the source of most of the money which went to pay the meagre wages of the teachers and to buy reading materials for the pupils. Griffith Jones sent an annual report, *Welch Piety*, to his patrons; in it he appealed for funds, noted the progress of the campaign and sought to allay any doubts concerning his efforts. One of the chief doubts arose from his emphasis upon the Welsh language, for, outside anglicized areas such as south Pembrokeshire, the circulating schools were conducted in Welsh. The argument he presented to his English patrons was the practical necessity for teaching through the mother tongue, although Griffith Jones certainly had a warm affection for the Welsh language. He also emphasized that the language was a barrier which prevented the Welsh from adopting dangerous ideas and loose morals, for to him as to almost all Welsh patriots, at least until the late eighteenth century, the Welsh language was a weapon of reaction.

Welch Piety provided details year by year of the number of pupils attending the circulating schools. They can be interpreted to imply that over two hundred thousand people, almost half the population of Wales, had attended them by 1771, the year of Griffith Jones's death. The work continued under Bridget Bevan until her death in 1779. The circulating schools were at their most numerous in the three south-western counties, where there were districts in which schools were held and held again over a quarter of a century and more. But apart from Flintshire, where there was virtually no campaign, numerous classes were held in all the counties of Wales and they were warmly praised by northerners such as William Morris of Holyhead and Robert Jones of Rhos-lan. The circulating schools offered a very limited education and the reading materials used in them were heavily pietistic. Griffith Jones stressed that he did not wish the pupils to have ideas above their station. 'The purpose of this spiritual charity,' he wrote, 'is not to make gentlemen, but Christians and heirs to eternal life.' His efforts led to a fundamental transformation of the life of Wales. By the second half of the eighteenth century, Wales was one of the few countries with a literate majority. Griffith Jones's schools aroused interest outside Wales, and do so still; Catherine, empress of Russia, commissioned a report on them in 1764 and they were suggested as a model by UNESCO in 1955.

As has been seen, the Welsh press benefited from widening literacy, and the notion that Wales had a *gwerin diwylliedig* (cultured peasantry) won currency. The success of the circulating schools widened the gap between the experience of the Welsh language and that of other languages not officially recognized, especially between Welsh and the other Celtic languages. Sober and well-regulated behaviour came in the wake of literacy, and Griffith Jones delighted in the ability of his pupils to improve the conduct of their parents. Furthermore, as the Welsh became increasingly literate, they were prepared for the immense social changes which they were soon to encounter, thus ensuring that their experience of industrialization, although traumatic, would not be as traumatic as that of peoples who had not received such preparation.

The history of Griffith Jones and his schools intertwined with that of the Methodist Revival. The region where the schools were most numerous was the cradle of the revival and Griffith Jones was a friend and spiritual father to its leaders, although their impulsiveness – they were a generation younger than he was – caused him grave concern. Like him, they were loyal members of the Established Church. Daniel Rowland was a clergyman and Howel Harris applied for Anglican holy orders, as did William Williams after he had abandoned the Nonconformity of his family. Traditionally, the beginning of the revival is dated to Whit Sunday 1735, when Howel Harris experienced religious conversion at Talgarth, Breconshire. He began to evangelize among the inhabitants of the enchanting villages around Llangors Lake, and in 1737 he met Daniel Rowland, who was similarly occupied in the Aeron valley. By then revivals were afoot in England, Scotland, Germany and North America, for Methodism was part of a religious awakening which was experienced throughout the Protestant world. There were close links between the Welsh revivalists and the leaders of English Methodism – George Whitefield and John Wesley – although it would be mistaken to believe (as some historians have done) that the initial stimulus for the Welsh revival came from England.

The message of the revivalists was terrifyingly simple: eternal torment in hell would be the fate of those who did not have a personal awareness of Christ's suffering and sacrifice. This message, together with descriptions of the torments of the damned, was the theme of Daniel Rowland's eloquent sermons, particularly in his earlier years, and Howel Harris's voluminous diaries show that the Judgement was the central subject of his orations. William William's interests were more complex and manifold. In his abundant writings (he published over ninety books and pamphlets), there are discussions of almost every aspect of life, along with hymns which are incomparable expressions of the Christian view of the sacrifice of the Saviour and the love of God. But if knowledge of the seed sown by the revivalists is extensive, historians' knowledge of the soil in which it was sown is inadequate, as are the attempts to explain why the seed germinated and blossomed. Indeed, as the Methodist Revival has been given such a prominent place in the historiography of Wales, there may be a tendency to overstress and antedate the blossoming. In 1750, after fifteen years of strenuous evangelization, probably no more than eight thousand people in Wales had embraced Methodism. It did not become a popular movement, especially in the north, until the last decade of the eighteenth century, and the forces released by the revival were not to be central to the experience of the devout among the Welsh until the following century.

Nevertheless, it is clear that the fervour of the revivalists did find a response: Howel Harris attracted large congregations and thousands came to Llangeitho to hear Daniel Rowland. The forces of social control which were impressing the need for religion upon the mass of the population were growing in strength, and the excitement of a Methodist meeting was more appealing than the formality of the parish church or the aridity of the Nonconformists. The revivalists, with their challenging exhilaration, were talented artists; their meetings were theatre, as their opponents recognized by seeking to compete with them by commissioning an anti-Methodist *anterliwt* (interlude). The appeal of the flesh was not absent either. Howel Harris was a man of strong passions and his relationship with Madam Griffith of Cefnamwlch caused the movement much concern; the jubilant singing of hymns with their occasional erotic images was a sensuous experience, and the leaping characteristic of the more exultant of the saved was even more sensuous. As a high proportion of those following the revivalists were unmarried young people, there arose insinuations which would reach the pages of the Blue Books a century later. The Methodists were deeply pained by such accusations, for they sought above all to inculcate seriousness. 'I had a temptation to laugh last night,' wrote Harris in his diary. (He resisted it, of course.) He and his fellows despised the old customs of the Welsh – their merriment, their tippling and their neglect of the Lord's Day – and the revivalists have frequently been blamed for annihilating the traditional culture of Wales.

Yet, as has been seen, the old world was in retreat before the coming of the revival, and Methodism may have filled a vacuum in Welsh life which already existed. The emphasis upon seriousness was increasingly acceptable, for the Welsh economy was becoming more complex and opportunities for the industrious and the prudent were multiplying. With the growth of education, lay people sought a greater role than they were allowed in the parish church, an ambition which Methodism, with its network of counsellors, was well placed to fulfil. Above all, the revival led to the development of cohesive societies with clearly defined rules, a fundamental consideration in a world where the old bonds were slackening.

The core of Methodist organization was the *seiat*, an institution created by Howel Harris 'to keep the believer from back-sliding'. The *seiat* was the 'soul's clinic', in which the faith was strengthened and declared under the leadership of a counsellor. By 1750, there were 428 *seiadau* in Wales, over half of them in the counties of Carmarthen, Brecon and Glamorgan. In 1742, they became part of an integrated system with superintendents and monthly and quarterly meetings, for the Welsh Methodists, almost without being aware of it, adopted an essentially Presbyterian form of government. The initial arrangements were made in 1742 at Dugoedydd, a farmhouse in the upper Tywi valley, and they were completed the following year at Watford near Caerffili. Whitefield was present at Watford. Welsh Methodists looked upon him as the leader of their movement, and they took his part in the theological debate which arose between him and John Wesley. Whitefield believed that only a portion of mankind had been elected by God, whereas Wesley, although he accepted justification by faith, rejected the complementary doctrine of predestination. As the Welsh movement was Calvinist in doctrine, Wesley did not seek to foster in Wales followers who accepted his Arminian beliefs, although he visited the country on almost fifty occasions. Had this division not arisen, Welsh Methodism would have probably been absorbed by the English and centralist Wesleyan movement. It was its Calvinism (and its language – Wesley became restless on hearing Welsh) which gave the Methodism of Wales its separate identity. But it is easy to exaggerate the Calvinism of the revival; it was later generations which elevated it into an overweening doctrine. The revivalists embraced the moderate Calvinism embodied in the Thirty-Nine Articles of the Church of England, and it could be argued that the act of evangelization – of giving everyone knowledge of salvation – indicates an attitude far removed from the strictest forms of Calvinism.

As they were Calvinist, the Welsh Methodists were closer to the Nonconformists than were their English counterparts. Dissenting ministers such as Edmund Jones of Pontypool and Philip Pugh of Llwynpiod warmly welcomed the revival. Indeed, the movement first rooted itself in those regions in which Nonconformity already had a following. In its early years, it could almost be claimed that Methodism was an interdenominational movement, with Anglicans, Independents and Baptists following the 'Methodist way'. But the aim of the revivalists was specifically the renewal of the Established Church and in 1743 the members of the *seiadau* were instructed to take communion in the parish church. As the Nonconformists had been offended by Howel Harris's arrogance and as they feared that he was seeking to entice their members back to the Established Church, their enthusiasm for the revival waned. They were also suspicious of some of the beliefs of the Methodists and they disagreed with the Methodist emphasis upon centralized organization; in addition, as the Nonconformists belonged to an austere tradition, they disapproved of the emotionalism kindled by the revivalists. But although the Methodists distanced themselves from the Nonconformists, Nonconformity adopted some of the features of the 'Methodist way' – the emphasis upon inner experience, for example, and the eloquent sermon and also the use of hymns. (The first collection of the hymns of Dafydd Jones of Caeo was published in 1753, a notable date in the history of worship among the Independents.) As a result, the nature of Nonconformity changed; by the end of the eighteenth century, its churches had a strong popular appeal and there was to be a great increase in their membership in the following generation.

In distancing themselves from the Nonconformists, the revivalists were partly motivated by their desire to allay the suspicions of the authorities. In the same way, they resisted any tendency to turn Methodism into a denomination; when the society at Groes-wen near Caerffili, the first of the *seiadau* to build a meeting-house, sought permission to ordain its counsellors, it met with a curt refusal. The revivalists hoped that when Frederick, George II's heir, inherited his father's throne, Whitefield would become a bishop. Frederick, like the Methodists, had aligned himself with the Tories, and it was believed that the influence of the countess of Huntingdon, the patron of the Methodists, over the Tory leaders would ensure Whitefield's promotion. He would then be able to ordain Harris and others of the lay preachers. This hope perished when Frederick died in 1751, but the Methodists persisted in maintaining that they were not Nonconformists, although they were thereby depriving themselves of the protection of the Toleration Act. They needed protection, for in many districts, especially in the north, there was savage antagonism towards them among the gentry and the common people. William Seward died following an attack at Hay in 1742; Howel Harris was almost killed by a mob at Bala, and Peter Williams was imprisoned in the Wynnstay kennels by Sir Watkin Williams Wynn.

The position of the Nonconformists was more secure than that of the Methodists; their leaders had the dignity of ministers with the right to administer the sacraments to their flocks. These were considerations which caused the *seiat* at Groes-wen to become an Independent congregation in 1745, an example followed by a number of other *seiadau* in the 1750s. The ambiguity of their situation was not the only motive for the change, for the 1750s were years of crisis in the history of Methodism. The crisis was caused by Harris, a man whose temperament was not dissimilar to that of Mao Tse-tung. He was much indebted to the Moravians, the Pietists from Germany; they belonged to a German tradition which had already influenced Welsh religious life, as the activities of Morgan Llwyd, Sir John Philipps and Griffith Jones testify. Through his links with the Moravians, Harris developed an obsession with the wounds of Christ and he embraced Patripassionism, the belief that God the Father had died on the cross. In 1750, Harris was disowned by the Methodists, and over the following twenty years he expended most of his enormous energy on establishing a 'Holy Family' at Trefeca, one of the strangest chapters in the history of Wales. During the 'schism', Daniel Rowland continued to consolidate the Methodism of the western counties, but many of the *seiadau* in the eastern counties – Harris's sphere of activity – went into decline or joined the Nonconformists.

Thus Methodism, which had originated in 'outer' Wales, came to be strongest in 'inner' Wales, a development greatly assisted by the vigorous campaign in the late eighteenth century to evangelize the north. The stimulus for that campaign was the 'second revival' at Llangeitho, the result, according to Robert Jones of Rhos-lan, of the publication of William Williams's volume of hymns, *Caniadau y Rhai sydd ar y Môr o Wydr* (The Songs of Those Who Are on the Sea of Glass). In the wake of the new revival, Harris rejoined his old companions, and he died in 1773 at peace with everyone.

Many attempts have been made to assess the impact of the Methodist Revival upon Wales. They are almost all commendatory, for they are largely the work of those who cherish the chapel culture which developed from the revival. Indeed, Welshness was so redefined as to raise doubts that those who did not cherish that culture could be considered heirs to the true traditions of Wales. This was a highly ironic development, for in the eighteenth century the defenders of those traditions saw Methodism as a threat. Lewis Morris believed that the culture of Wales faced extinction if the people continued to 'get drunk on religion'; Theophilus Evans claimed that the revivalists were destroying the true heir of the Church of the Britons; William Jones, the antiquarian from Llangadfan, thought the Methodists were turning Wales into a dreary and morose country. To a large extent, these were the voices of reaction, but men of progressive views were even more critical. 'Zeal,' wrote the philosopher David Hume, 'is responsible for the most cruel divisions of Society.' 'Methodism,' claimed Richard Greaves in 1773, 'has reintroduced the powers of darkness in an age of enlightenment'; indeed, it is possible to consider Methodism as a reaction to the 'Age of Reason', as an attempt to postpone the realization of the potential of the human race. The distinguished historian Edward Thompson has argued that the chief significance of the Methodist Revival was that it induced the mass of the population to accept the discipline of the industrial system, and Élie Halévy asserted that Britain did not experience revolution, as did France, because Methodism had taught the people to bow to their fate. The historian Lecky believed that there had never been religious terrorism as appalling as Methodism, and it is possible to appreciate his argument when considering the eagerness of the Methodistical Independent, John Thomas of Rhaeadr, to provoke children to weep 'as if the Day of Judgement had dawned'.

Yet although the negative aspects of Methodism must be acknowledged, they do not represent the entire truth. In criticizing the excessive seriousness of the movement, it is possible to romanticize the merriment of the pre-Methodist society of Wales; crudeness was the hallmark of that society, and beneath its merriment lay widespread deprivation, savage customs and brutal behaviour. Although the Methodists 'wasted much of their intellect . . . on Calvinistic Scholasticism,' as R. T. Jenkins put it, minds were sharpened and articulate men and women were nurtured by such activities. Despite the fact that Methodism helped to sustain the reactionary forces of society for generations, the intellectual tradition it fostered was eventually to become a weapon against such forces. Although Methodists were conditioned to bow to their fate, they were also animated to accept their fate with dignity and pride.

When Howel Harris died in 1773, the heroic era of Welsh Methodism had come to an end. The ambiguities of its position, however, continued and there would be many vicissitudes before those ambiguities were resolved by the leaders of the following generation. During that generation, there was a dramatic increase in the numbers of Methodists, an expansion which occurred in a very different world from that which had seen the beginnings of the revival. The growth and increasing complexity of the Welsh economy has already been noted, and by 1773 Wales was on the threshold of changes which would revolutionize the life of its people. It has been assumed that those changes were entirely English in origin and that they were imposed upon a country wholly unprepared for them. By now – although historians have an incomplete understanding of Welsh society in the generation or two before 1770 – that society is not believed to be as passively old-fashioned as was once thought. English influences were of central importance, of course. In 1530, England was one of the smaller kingdoms of Europe; by 1770, it was the most progressive of states and much of the world had felt the impact of its power. London, with a population of three quarters of a million, was the largest city in Europe, and resources were drawn from every corner of the kingdom to supply the needs of the 'great wen'. In consequence, England's economy was more integrated than that of its neighbours, and even the remotest areas of Wales knew something of its power and appeal. England was the centre of the Atlantic capitalist economy, the economy which sustained the prosperity of Bristol and Liverpool. The coast of south Wales was drawn into the web of Bristol and that of the north into the web of Liverpool, and thus the extremities of Anglesey and Pembrokeshire were linked with the most progressive developments of the age.

Although the links with England were central to the experiences which were to transform Wales after 1770, changes within Wales itself had long been preparing the country for that transformation. An attempt was made above (pp. 259–75) to portray the nature of Welsh society in the age of Elizabeth and the early Stuarts. The main features of that society – the dependence upon agriculture, the emphasis upon hierarchy, the fragility of human existence, the intense localism – were still the main features of Welsh society in the mid eighteenth century. Nevertheless, it is possible to give too static a portrait of the experience of the Welsh in the pre-industrial era. Change did occur. The population increased: it is estimated that Wales had 500,000 inhabitants in 1770 compared with perhaps 360,000 in 1620. This is a field where more research is urgently needed, and until it is undertaken any comments can be no more than tentative. It would appear that the growth in population had slowed down by about 1620; indeed, it is possible that the population of Wales declined somewhat as a result of the dislocation which came in the wake of the Civil War and the distress caused by the worsening climate of the years 1645–1710. There were some later checks. Although the plague ceased to be a threat (the townsfolk of Haverfordwest in 1652 were the last of the inhabitants of Wales to suffer from it), and although attempts were made to control smallpox through inoculation with cowpox, the attacks of lethal diseases could still be ferocious. Crises of subsistence – occasions when death would strike the weaker and more marginal members of society because of inadequate food supplies – could still be oppressive. There was a severe crisis in 1699–1700, when the death rate was three times its normal level. By then, however, such crises were rare in the more developed parts of the kingdom, although they could still be lethal in remote areas such as the mountainous parishes of Montgomeryshire. But they were on the decline there also; the crisis of 1699–1700 was perhaps the last occasion on which the inhabitants of Welsh communities were felled by local dearth. With the retreat of crises of subsistence, the population of Wales was on the threshold of sustained growth and, as will be seen, a complexity of factors would lead that population into the Modern Demographic Cycle, one of the central happenings in the history of Wales.

Although agriculture continued to be the basis of the economy, there were significant developments in other sectors. The industries established during the reign of Elizabeth did not experience unbroken growth, but they partook of a new liveliness in the first half of the eighteenth century. Their growth was encouraged by statutes of 1693 which ended the monopolies of the Elizabethan age and which confirmed that landlords owned the minerals beneath their estates. There was wild speculation in the lead and silver mines of Cardiganshire and Flintshire, greatly to the advantage of Humphrey Mackworth (one of the founders of the SPCK) and much to the distress of Lewis Morris. Mackworth was also responsible for the re-establishment of the copper industry at Neath. Neath was rapidly overtaken by Swansea, which in 1727 became the home of Robert Morris, the father of the creator of Morriston; by 1750, the Swansea district was producing half the copper needs of Britain. The growth of the copper industry led to the manufacture of vessels decorated with Japanese lacquer, the innovation of the Allgood family of Pontypool and one of the most curious of the products of industrial Wales.

Pontypool was the chief centre of the Welsh iron industry, but in the period 1700–1770 ironworks were established which were to loom large in the history of Wales, among them Bersham near Wrexham and Dowlais and Cyfarthfa near Merthyr Tydfil. The iron was smelted with charcoal and therefore the expansion of the industry was not associated as yet with the mining of coal. However, the demand for coal increased in the wake of the general industrial growth. The levels driven into the hills of northern Glamorgan and Monmouthshire multiplied, as did pits around Swansea, which continued to be the main centre of the industry. Swansea's coal exports rose rapidly, largely because of demand from Ireland, a market which was also responsible for stimulating the development of the Flintshire coalfield.

Yet, although the exploitation of mineral resources was increasing, and although there were in Wales districts inhabited by families who could look back upon several generations of industrial experience, the heavy industries continued to be marginal to the Welsh economy. In 1770, the experience of the great majority of the Welsh still lay in agriculture and in the activities dependent upon it. Those activities were expanding rapidly in the first half of the eighteenth century. Indeed, it is increasingly recognized that the phenomenon known as the Industrial Revolution was to a great extent the fruit of developments in the agricultural sector. Droving was as central as ever, and as towns expanded the demand for Welsh cattle expanded also. Thirty thousand cattle were driven across Herefordshire annually, and a partnership of Llŷn drovers was reputed to have a yearly turnover of £16,000. Through the activities of such men, the rural population became progressively used to handling money, an essential preparation for the capitalist world into which they were being drawn. The woollen industry was equally central. By 1770, the grasp of the Shrewsbury Drapers was slackening; in the 1770s, the port of Barmouth exported woollen products worth £50,000 a year to all corners of the earth. Although the organization of the industry was fairly primitive, it gave a large number of Welsh people experience of sub-industrial employment (proto-industrialization, to use a term which is rapidly winning acceptance), a factor of importance in considering their ability to adapt themselves to a more intense experience of industrialization.

There were developments in the primary processes of agriculture also. To the majority of the farmers of Wales in 1770, and for generations to come, the practice of agriculture was a hereditary custom rather than a rational science; yet there were progressive Welshmen who were eager to disseminate the ideas of the pioneers. Thomas Jones included useful hints in his almanacs; Henry Rowlands, the Anglesey antiquarian, published his *Idea Agriculturae* in 1704, and in 1717 Moses Williams urged landlords to introduce to Wales the 'Cultivation and the Husbandry of the English'. Some of them did so: by 1770, there were farmers, particularly in the border counties, who rotated their crops; fields planted with turnips and potatoes multiplied and there was a great increase in the use of lime with kilns being built by creeks and harbours. These improvements were fostered through the establishment of county agricultural societies, with Breconshire (1755) in the vanguard. At the same time, land available for agriculture expanded as forests contracted, because of the demands of the navy and the furnaces' greed for charcoal, and as the commons were enclosed. Enclosure was seen as the key to improvement. 'Inclose, inclose, ye swains! . . . in fields/ Promiscuous held, all culture languishes,' wrote John Dyer, the poet from Aberglasni, in 1757. As manorial villages were rare in Wales, only a few places such as Gower and the Vale of Clwyd had open fields on good land – the object of most enclosures in England. It was the moors and mountain pastures which were enclosed in Wales, through surreptitious encroachment or by local agreement. In 1733, however, enclosure began to be carried out through act of parliament, a foretaste of an activity which would be at its height at the end of the eighteenth century.

These developments must have resulted in an increase in agricultural production. Although there are few reliable statistics, it is reasonable to assume that the gap between what was produced by farmers and what was kept by them for their own use was widening. Without that widening gap, the expansion in the urban population, a marked feature of the history of Wales in the generation after 1770, would not have been possible. The growth had begun before 1770. Wrexham, with about three thousand five hundred inhabitants, was the largest town in Wales in 1700, but Carmarthen had re-established its lead by 1770, when there were at least four thousand people living in the town. By then, about 15 per cent of the Welsh were town-dwellers; they were a small minority, but forces would stem from them which would in the long run transform the rural areas around them. Carmarthen and Brecon, with their theatres, their 'season' for the gentry and their dignified Georgian houses, were considered to be towns of distinction. Richard Steele, the editor of the *Spectator*, settled in Carmarthen in 1724; 'Beau' Nash (1674–1762) was educated there, and the great actress Sarah Siddons (1755–1831) was born in Brecon. Towns fostered the growth of the middle class, a class whose prosperity was to be one of the leading themes in the history of Wales in the century after 1770. There was a rapid rise in the status of professional men – lawyers, doctors, ships' captains, surveyors, government officials – men such as the Morrises of Anglesey and their associates. *Embourgeoisement* was contagious. It affected the gentry, and Philip Jenkins has shown that landowners, at least in Glamorgan, were almost as capitalistic in their attitude by 1770 as were the businessmen of the City of London. The growth of such attitudes saddened Ellis Wynne; he complained in 1704 of the merchants, speculators, usurers and profiteers who were undermining the world he loved. They were to be even more influential two generations later. By 1770, Wales was on the verge of being wholly ensnared by them, for its fate was to become a part – a central part, indeed – of a capitalistic system whose tentacles would reach to all corners of the earth.

=====

CHAPTER SEVEN

1770–1850: Holywell, Dowlais and Llanover

Wales had about 500,000 inhabitants in 1770; it had 1,163,000 in 1851. The population doubled in about two generations, an increase which previously had needed twelve generations to accomplish. In 1770, most of the people of Wales were directly dependent upon the soil for their livelihood; by 1851, the proportion had fallen to a third. A nation can hardly experience a greater change than that the cultivation of the soil, the occupation of the vast majority since the invention of agriculture in the Neolithic Age, should become the experience of a minority. Politics in 1770 was the business of a narrow class of squires and hardly a voice had been raised in favour of the right of the mass of the people to be consulted about the way in which they were governed; by 1850, interest in politics was increasing phenomenally and demands for a way of giving expression to the 'voice of the people' were yearly becoming more vocal. In 1770, it took days to travel to London from the extremities of Pembrokeshire or the further reaches of Anglesey, journeys which could be accomplished in a matter of hours by the 1850s. In 1770, there were no Welsh-language periodicals and the *Cyffroawd Cymreigyddawl* was merely beginning; by 1850, dozens of Welsh periodicals had appeared and the language had become the medium of a wealth of cultural activities. In 1770, there were only a few districts in Wales in which the majority of worshippers had abandoned the parish church; by 1851, Anglicans were a minority almost everywhere and eight out of ten of the Welsh who attended religious services were opting for the Nonconformist chapel. 'I never heard,' wrote a commentator in 1770, 'of any one travelling in Wales for pleasure.' In the following decades, visitors came in great numbers; Wales was 'discovered', and by 1850 many parts of the country were increasingly reliant upon tourism.

There were other spheres also in which transformation occurred in the period 1770–1850. All periods, of course, are 'periods of change', but it is difficult to avoid the conclusion that the changes which the people of Wales underwent between 1770 and 1850 were of a fundamental nature. It seemed as if the nation was changing gear and, although the Welsh were to have even more eventful experiences, particularly in the twentieth century, they can be considered to be consequential upon the changes initiated in the period 1770–1850. As those were so far-reaching, it is not easy to appreciate that they happened within the lifespan of a single individual – that of Gwallter Mechain (Walter Davies, 1761–1849), for example, or Robert Owen (1771–1858) or Robert ap Gwilym Ddu (Robert Williams, 1766–1850).

The various spheres of change were interrelated, although it would be difficult to discover a primary cause which would account for them all. Priority must, however, be given to factors relating to the population, for to a large extent the nature of any community is determined by its demographic features. Knowledge of the population of Wales before the compilation of the first census in 1801 is very incomplete, for little work has as yet been done on the extensive but flawed evidence available in sources such as the parish registers. Following the publication of the authoritative study by Wrigley and Schofield (1981), much is known of the demographic history of England in the eighteenth century and, although the authors stress that they are exclusively concerned with England, some of their conclusions may be considered relevant to Wales.

The population of a country increases because the number of its immigrants exceeds the number of its emigrants, or because of natural growth – that is, there are more births than deaths. Wales received immigrants: in 1851, the country had almost 140,000 inhabitants who had been born outside its borders. But between 1770 and 1850 there was a rapid growth in Welsh communities in England and considerable Welsh migration to America, the emigration more than compensating for the immigration. Thus the population of Wales must have increased because of natural growth; that is caused by a rise in the birth rate or a decline in the death rate or a combination of both. It was once believed that the decline in the death rate was the most important factor, a decline which was attributed to advances in medicine. The present tendency is to doubt whether medical advances were, at least until 1850, as important as they were once supposed to be. The emphasis is rather upon an increase in fertility, the result of a rise in the marriage rate and a lowering of the age of marriage. Wrigley and Schofield maintain that in England the ratio between births and deaths rose from 1.1 to 1 at the beginning of the eighteenth century to 1.6 to 1 at its end. In consequence, population growth in England accelerated from 0.1 per cent a year in the early decades of the century to 1.0 per cent in the later decades.

The pattern in Wales was probably broadly similar, although it would appear that the increase there in the second half of the eighteenth century was not as rapid as it was in England. This is what is suggested by the tables prepared by John Rickman, the organizer of the census of 1801, although he recognized that his material was very incomplete. In the first half of the nineteenth century, however, the two countries had a similar rate of growth: between 1801 and 1851, the increase was 98 per cent in Wales and 94 per cent in England. It is probable therefore that the reasons considered to be responsible for the rise in fertility in England are also relevant to Wales. Chief among them was the confidence of young couples that there would be a livelihood for them if they married and had a family. The factors underlying that confidence are the primary key to the growth in the population. It could stem from the knowledge that adequate sustenance would be available from a hectare or two of potatoes, or from a holding carved from the common land; marriage was also fostered by bidding (the *neithior* – payments by neighbours in order to enable a young couple to 'begin life'), and by the assumption that poor relief would ensure that a family would not starve. The economy was quickening almost everywhere in the late eighteenth century. The increase in employment which ensued probably encouraged couples to marry earlier than they would have done in more unfavourable economic circumstances, and to believe (mistakenly, no doubt) that having a numerous progeny was economically advantageous.

The quickening in the economy is the phenomenon known as the Industrial Revolution and there have been efforts to associate the growth in the population of Britain with the fact that the island was the cradle of that revolution. The association is dubious. The population upsurge was an international phenomenon; if the population of Wales more than doubled between 1770 and 1851, there was an even higher rate of growth in Ireland, Quebec and Finland, none of which experienced an Industrial Revolution during that period. In Wales,

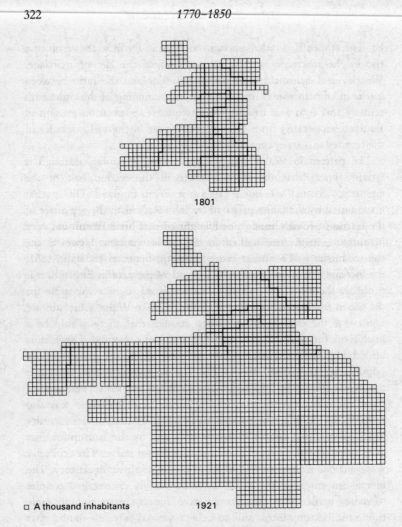

1801

□ A thousand inhabitants   1921

The population of Wales, 1801 and 1921

there was a dramatic increase in the number living in entirely rural parishes: in Nancwnlle on the slopes of Mynydd Bach in Cardiganshire, for example, the population increased by 74 per cent between 1801 and 1851. It would therefore be misleading to assert that the Demographic Revolution occurred as a result of the Industrial Revolution (or *vice versa*), but it would also be unwise to deny that there were linkages between the one and the other. After all, the districts which experienced the greatest demographic upsurge were those which were rapidly industrialized. If there was a growth of 74 per cent in Nancwnlle between 1801 and 1851, there was a growth of 1,795 per cent in the parish of Bedwellte, Monmouthshire, during that period.

But if the pattern and the causes of population growth have not been wholly elucidated, the consequences are vividly clear. The growth was the source of the multitudes who were drawn to the furnaces, the collieries and the quarries of industrial Wales, the footloose surplus from rural Wales who colonized their own country. Population growth made possible the rise of mass communities in Wales, a central development in the country's social, political and cultural history. The Welsh were fairly fortunate in the balance they experienced between numbers and sustenance (remarkably so, in comparison with the Irish), but there were regions of Wales where the upsurge in population exceeded the increase in resources; that was the key to the deprivation and unrest in many rural districts in periods such as the 1790s and the 1840s. So great was the growth in population that emigration seemed to many to be the only salvation, and substantial Welsh communities came into being on the banks of the Mersey, the Thames, the Hudson, the Ohio, the Salt Lake and the Chubut.

Nevertheless, migration from their country was not as central to the experience of the Welsh as it was to that of others of the nations of Europe, largely because industrial Wales could offer a livelihood to much of the rural surplus. It was the Industrial Revolution, therefore, which insured that population growth did not lead to tragedy in Wales as it did in Ireland. There was a fashion a generation or more ago of avoiding the term Industrial Revolution, for it gave excessive prominence, it was claimed, to the economic changes of the late eighteenth century – changes which were the consequence of centuries of development, with their climax decades in the future. The revolution is, however, back in favour, for it is recognized that those changes, in their essence and in their significance for future generations, deserve such prominence. It is futile, it is argued, to seek to determine when the revolution reached its climax, for its most prominent feature is its ability to generate accelerating change.

Traditionally, the cotton industry (the source of half Britain's exports in 1820) has been considered the pivot of the Industrial Revolution. It was the first to centralize its activities in factories (a nail in the coffin of the age-old tradition that the home was the place of production), and it gave rise to the vast proletariat which stirred the emotions of Engels in 1844. A few cotton-mills were established in Wales, and the prosperity of Lancashire, the headquarters of the industry, had a profound effect upon the history of Wales. But it was not through producing consumer goods such as cotton, but through producing capital goods – metals and fuel – that the chief industrial areas of Wales developed. Although the factory system which sprang from the consumer-goods industries is central to the concept of the Industrial Revolution, it could be argued that the development of a new source of energy is of even greater importance. That development sprang from the capital-goods industries, the speciality of Wales. Before the eighteenth century, the only sources of energy were the strength of men and beasts and the power of wind and water, and none of these was tireless or wholly reliable. Following the invention of the steam-engine (Newcomen, 1712; Watt, 1765), production was revolutionized and the new power could be harnessed to produce cheap and rapid transport. Wales had a leading role in these developments: the ironworks of Wales were among the first to adopt the steam-engine; the first experiments with locomotion were made in Wales and many of the world's locomotives were to travel along rails of Welsh manufacture; above all, Wales contributed wholly disproportionately and on a world scale to the supply of fuel for steam power and transport.

The full implications of the invention of steam power and its offspring, the locomotive, did not become apparent until the middle and later years of the nineteenth century. One of the chief implications was the tendency to concentrate production in or near coalfields. The pattern was very different in the early years of the Industrial Revolution. Then there was a degree of industrial liveliness in almost all parts of the kingdom; indeed, A. H. Dodd argued that it was by no means obvious in 1800 where 'the centre of gravity of Britain would ultimately lie'. It has already been noted that by 1770 Wales had many of the prerequisites for industrial growth. Nevertheless, it must be acknowledged that England provided the stimulus which transformed the Welsh economy, although that fact should not be considered (as sometimes it is) as proof that industry is something alien, incompatible with the character of the Welsh. After all, as the English were the pioneers of the industrial system, industrialization throughout the world represents an overspill from their activities.

The north-east, with its close association with Merseyside, received the greatest variety of industries. Lancashire interests built a cotton-mill at Holywell in 1777 and at Mold in 1792. A pottery was established at Buckley in 1757 and by 1780 there were fourteen potteries in the district, a development which gave rise to one of the most interesting communities in Wales. Vitriol was produced at Holywell and a variety of salts at Saltney, manufactures which depended upon the metal industries of Flintshire. Holywell was the chief centre of metal-working; in 1774, Dr Johnson counted nineteen different works within two miles of St Winifred's Well. The Holywell Level was considered to be the richest lead-mine in the kingdom, and five thousand tons of lead were exported from the ports of the Dee estuary in the 1770s. Mines were opened from Prestatyn to Llanarmon and smelters were built to process zinc and silver, the by-products of the lead industry. Lead ore from Cardiganshire, Ireland and Scotland was transported to the smelting works of Holywell, Bagillt and Whitford, for Flintshire was one of the few regions containing coal as well as ore. As a result of the demands of the metal-works and the needs of the Buckley potteries, the coalminers of Flintshire were freed from their dependence upon the markets of Chester and Dublin, and they enjoyed considerable prosperity in the last decades of the eighteenth century.

The metal-works were also responsible for encouraging the growth of the coal industry around Wrexham, a district which had not profited greatly from the coastal trade. Charles Lloyd (of the stock of Lloyds of Dolobran, the family which gave its name to Lloyds Bank) was smelting iron with coke at Bersham from about 1721 onwards. He was among the first to follow the example of Abraham Darby of Coalbrookdale, Shropshire, who had discovered that centrally important process in 1709, a process which freed the iron industry from the limitations imposed by the charcoal supply. John Wilkinson gained possession of the Bersham works in 1761; he began to sink pits from Ruabon to Chirk and his example was followed by other ironmasters settling in Denbighshire. By 1780, Bersham was one of Europe's leading ironworks. Wilkinson produced almost all the cylinders used in Watt's steam-engines, and the armies of several countries depended upon the cannon he developed. The progressiveness of the north-east may be seen in the fact that it was the first region of Wales to tackle the appalling condition of its roads. Five turnpike companies had been established there by 1760, and they built roads linking the main centres of the region with Shrewsbury and Chester and thus with the English road network.

Lead was not the only ore transported from districts lacking coal to the smelting-works of Flintshire. In about 1750, a copper-works was established at Holywell which benefited greatly from the demand for copper from the army and the navy. The copper industry, like the iron industry, prospered in the wake of war. Initially, the ore came from England, but in 1768 the rich veins of Mynydd Parys near Amlwch were discovered, opening a remarkable chapter in the industrial history of Wales. Mynydd Parys flourished so mightily that by 1801 there were in Wales only five parishes which exceeded Amlwch in population. Control of the copper-mines came into the hands of Thomas Williams, a solicitor from Llanidan. His career is clear proof that the Welsh did not lack entrepreneurial skills, for there is nothing comparable in the history of any industry with the dominance which Thomas Williams won over the copper industry from 1780 until his death in 1802. Forty ships continually transported ore from Amlwch to the copper and brass works established by Williams at Holywell. He also built smelting-works in Swansea and in Lancashire, part of an empire which controlled half the world's copper production. In the late eighteenth century, the copper industry was Britain's leading metal industry. In 1788, it was estimated that its output was worth twice as much as that of the cast-iron industry. North-west Wales was combed for veins equal in richness to those of Mynydd Parys, and prosperous mines were opened at Drws-y-coed, Llanberis, Cwm Glaslyn and the Great Orme.

Thus it was the copper industry which gave the inhabitants of Gwynedd their first experience of large-scale industry. Slate quarrying, the industry which would come to dominate the economy of that region, was far less important in the late eighteenth century; in the 1780s, when the earl of Uxbridge received £2,000 a year in royalties from the ore extracted from his land, Richard Pennant received only £80 a year for the slate quarried on his Penrhyn estate. But the 1780s were a crucial decade in the history of the slate industry also. Richard Pennant was a capitalist to the tips of his fingers, and he could draw on the wealth amassed by his family through their Jamaican slave plantations. He consolidated his hold over the scattered quarries of his estate and his example was followed by the owners of the Faenol and Glynllifon estates, for the slate industry of Caernarfonshire was developed by local landowners rather than by incoming capitalists. By 1790, Pennant had built a road to link his quarries with the coast. There, near Bangor, he established Port Penrhyn, the first port created specifically to serve the slate industry.

The growth of small ports such as Port Penrhyn was a central factor in the increasing vitality of the Welsh economy. In 1737, Lewis Morris drew a detailed chart of the coast from Pembroke to Anglesey and he foresaw a prosperous future for the coastal trade. As Aled Eames has shown, there was a highly developed maritime culture in Gwynedd by the later decades of the eighteenth century. About 360 ships a year sailed from its ports, some of them to destinations in North America and the Caribbean. After centuries of being largely dependent upon trade overland with England, the Welsh economy was profiting increasingly from maritime trade with the rest of the world; the western sea-routes were rediscovered, routes which had been so important to Wales over many millennia.

Something of the same tendency may be seen in the woollen trade. Instead of being transported to England, flannel and other woollen goods were exported from the ports of Wales, largely to America. There they were used to clothe soldiers and slaves – one of the numerous examples, as Gwyn A. Williams has emphasized, of the imperial context of the development of the Welsh economy. The thread, the webs, the flannel and the stockings were produced in the home, for before 1800 the factory system had been adopted hardly anywhere in Wales. Woollen production expanded dramatically in the last decades of the eighteenth century. The annual value of the stocking sales at Bala rose from £10,000 to £18,000, and the yearly profit on the Montgomeryshire flannel sales exceeded £40,000.

In the eighteenth century, the counties of the south-west did not experience growth comparable with that of the north. Wool was produced there, but the prosperity of the Teifi valley woollen-mills belonged to the future. Some of the small ports of the region were lively enough and the town of Milford was established in 1790 to serve the whaling industry, but the coastal trade of the south-west received no stimulus comparable with that which the north received through the copper and woollen trades. There was not the same necessity rapidly to reach the southern counties of Ireland as there was to reach Dublin (the second city of the Empire), and thus there was a turnpike road and a daily coach to Holyhead long before the ports of Pembrokeshire had such facilities. Lead was mined in Cardiganshire; although the county had rich veins, the mines were remote and as there was no coal at hand little of the ore was smelted there. The south-west had a scattering of ironworks, but they did not develop into a large-scale industry because the anthracite coal of Carmarthenshire and Pembrokeshire was unsuitable for smelting. Slate-working in the Preseli Mountains had a long tradition, but the amount of rock suitable for quarrying was small compared with the vast reserves of Snowdonia. Thus, despite the religious and educational progressiveness of south-west Wales in the eighteenth century, its economic development was slow compared with the rest of Wales. For centuries, the material culture of the region was far poorer than that of the north and the south-east, as Peter Smith's admirable study of the houses of the Welsh countryside amply demonstrates.

The variety in the pattern of development in different regions is part of the appeal of the history of the industrialization of Wales. While the south-west lagged behind, Flintshire – where there was already a long industrial tradition – experienced rapid growth. In Anglesey, a county which had previously been almost wholly rural, development was so rapid that it would be perverse not to use the word revolutionary to describe it. In the south-east, there was a similar diversity – rapid growth on old foundations in places such as Swansea, Neath and Pontypool, and revolutionary changes in places such as Merthyr Tydfil, Ebbw Vale and Blaenafon, districts which had previously been almost wholly uninhabited. In 1801, Swansea, with over ten thousand inhabitants (if all the areas now constituting the city are included), was the most populous place in Wales. Some of Swansea's inhabitants lived in the old town, which was a holiday resort and a centre of fashion, but the majority lived around the copper-works of the lower Tawe valley. At the end of the eighteenth century, the Swansea region was Britain's chief copper-producing area, and the smelters and colliers of the district were heirs to an industrial tradition extending over at least two hundred years.

On the other hand, Merthyr Tydfil, the home of 7,700 people in

1801, wholly lacked an ancient industrial tradition. The narrow strip from Hirwaun to Blaenafon – with Merthyr at its centre – was the cradle of the industrial community of the south Wales coalfield. That strip is therefore the starting-point of the central happening in the modern history of Wales. Its significance was hardly obvious in 1801. At that time, about 10,000 people lived in an industrial belt, twenty-nine kilometres long, between Hirwaun and Blaenafon, less than half the number dwelling in the twenty-nine kilometre industrial belt between Holywell and Wrexham. Despite the industrial expansion of northern Monmouthshire, Monmouth, with a population of 3,345, was the largest urban centre in the county in 1801. If there were 7,700 people in Merthyr, there were almost 5,000 in Amlwch. Yet, part of the function of the historian is to identify the winners, and it was undoubtedly Merthyr that won. Amlwch experienced an industrial revolution which failed. The revolution which was afoot in Merthyr in 1801 succeeded, and the majority of the people of Wales were sucked into the pattern of life which was pioneered there.

It is fitting therefore to examine the beginnings of Merthyr's industrialization in some detail. To industrialists, the appeal of the region was the fact that iron ore, coal, timber, limestone and water power were all available in convenient proximity. 'The whole district,' enthused a commentator, 'seems to have been intended to be one great ironwork' – and he had no doubt that Providence had ordained the universal deluge specifically to create such convenience. The realization of the wealth of the region's resources coincided with an upsurge in the demand for iron. As Britain in the eighteenth century was at war as often as not, armaments were in great demand. At the same time, as more efficient means of production led to a fall in the price of iron, the metal became more widely used; agriculturalists bought more iron implements and householders more iron utensils, and ways were found of using the metal in construction. Few of the implements and utensils were made in Wales, for the country specialized in producing iron, not in producing things made of iron. Welsh production was characterized by its bulk rather than its refinement, for the metallurgical crafts which were so important to the prosperity of places like Sheffield and Birmingham struck few roots in Wales. Production was assisted by stirring or puddling the molten iron, the discovery of Henry Cort in 1784. By puddling, it was possible to make fifteen tons of iron bars in twelve hours rather than one ton as before, and so rapidly was the invention adopted by the ironmasters of Merthyr that it became known as the 'Welsh method'.

The Merthyr ironmasters were enterprising men. Their ventures were assisted by the leases granted to them by local landlords; they were ridiculously cheap, for no one in the mid eighteenth century realized that a major industry would develop in so isolated a place. In 1748, Viscount Windsor (who had inherited the Welsh estates of the earls of Pembroke) granted a ninety-nine-year lease of the minerals of the common of the lordship of Senghennydd Uwch Caeach to a group of industrialists at a rent of £26 a year. In 1760, the enterprise, which was located on the Dowlais brook near Merthyr, came under the direction of John Guest, a native of Shropshire, and by the end of the century it was producing over five thousand tons of iron a year. In 1765, Anthony Bacon, an ironmaster from Cumberland, received terms almost as favourable from the landlords of Cyfarthfa, establishing an ironworks there which came into the possession of Richard Crawshay (1739–1810) of Yorkshire in 1794. Cyfarthfa was so successful that Crawshay on his death was one of Britain's first millionaires. In addition to Dowlais and Cyfarthfa, the ironworks of the parish of Merthyr Tydfil included Plymouth (1763) and Penydarren (1784), while further west works were established at Hirwaun (1780) and at Aber-nant (1801). To the east of Merthyr, a chain of ironworks was built in the upper reaches of the narrow valleys of Monmouthshire, among them Rhymney, Sirhowy, Tredegar, Ebbw Vale, Nant-y-glo and Blaenafon.

The ironworks of northern Glamorgan and Monmouthshire were large-scale enterprises from the beginning. In Lancashire, a local man of little capital or experience could establish a small textile factory and build it up into a major concern. That was not an option in the south Wales coalfield. There, because of the scale of the unit of production, outside capital was essential. If the original investment succeeded, the profit of the business was sufficient to fund expansion, for the take-off (to use W. W. Rostov's term) to self-sufficient growth could be very rapid. By 1798, £100,000 had been invested at Cyfarthfa, and a decade or so later there were around Merthyr at least a dozen enterprises in which similar amounts had been invested – a concentration of capital in heavy investment without parallel anywhere in the world. Large-scale expenditure on transport was also necessary, for the winding paths linking the iron districts with the ports of Cardiff and Newport were wholly inadequate to the needs of the industry. In the mid-1760s, Anthony Bacon's iron bars were carried to the coast on pack horses; he built a road from Merthyr to Cardiff in 1767, but the cost of transporting such heavy goods on carts was burdensome. The situation was transformed by the building of canals, the great enterprise of the 1790s. By 1800, Swansea, Neath, Cardiff and Newport had all been linked to the uplands of the coalfield by water transport at a total cost of over £400,000.

The cost of the canals was inflated by the geographical nature of the coalfield – by the need, for example, to build fifty-two locks between Merthyr and Cardiff. The south Wales coalfield is the only mountainous coalfield in Britain, a fact which was to be central to the experience of the communities of northern Glamorgan and Monmouthshire. The uplands have an unfavourable climate – Hirwaun has an annual rainfall of 200 centimetres – and the shape of the new settlements was determined by the contours of the valleys and the moors. The iron districts had no urban traditions. Although a mass society developed there, it happened in a frontier world, a world lacking the graces of civic life. The people who created the communities which grew up under the shadow of the ironworks brought with them the traditions and the values of the countryside from whence they came. At first, the area was populated through short-distance migration – the parishes of the mountains of Breconshire were the earliest to record a decline in their population – but with the growth of the 'works' people were attracted to them from more distant parts of Wales, and from other countries also.

In the wake of increasing urbanization, there was a fall in the proportion of the people of Wales working on the land. It has already been noted that it had decreased to a third by 1851, but it is difficult to be precise about the situation before the mid nineteenth century because of the shortcomings of the early censuses. If the population of a country increases and if the percentage abandoning agriculture rises, it is necessary either to improve agricultural productivity or to import food from elsewhere – otherwise tragedy ensues. By the end of the nineteenth century, Britain was heavily dependent upon food imports, but up to the middle of the century 90 per cent of the food consumed was produced within the country itself. British agriculturalists supplied the needs of seven million people in 1750 and of eighteen million in 1850. The achievement was not great enough to satisfy the demand, for there is considerable evidence (although the issue is contentious) of a decline in the standard of nourishment of the bulk of the population between 1770 and 1850. Yet it was an achievement, the achievement known as the Agricultural Revolution, the essential precursor and sustainer of the Industrial Revolution.

It is easier to chronicle the latter than the former. The rise of great industrial enterprises is amply documented, but it is difficult to generalize about the history of a host of farms. There were at least fifty thousand agricultural units in Wales in 1770, but very few farmers kept a record of their activities. Yet, although the farm was the unit of production, the estate was the unit of ownership, and estate records are a voluminous source. Traditionally, landlords had not interfered to any great extent with the farming practices of their tenants. They usually let their land at a fixed rent on leases of ninety-nine years or three lives. The urge for improvement which characterized the last decades of the eighteenth century and the huge inflation which accompanied the wars with France (1793–1802, 1803–15) caused landlords to be eager to influence the activities of their tenants and to raise rents. Both ambitions could be fulfilled by letting their land by the year rather than renewing long leases. Almost all the tenants of the progressive Faenol estate held their land on annual lease by 1800, although more conservative and inattentive landowners were slower to adopt the new practice.

With a stronger hold upon his estate, the conscientious landowner could reorganize his holdings to make them more productive and could coerce or cajole his tenants into adopting more efficient agricultural methods. 'Every field will be kept to the Culture I shall dictate,' declared the enthusiastic improver, Philip Yorke (1743–1804), the owner of the Erddig estate. The chief aim of the improvers was to make more effective use of arable land through ensuring that it was not necessary to keep part of it fallow. The key to that was the rotation of crops. Many Welsh landowners became enthusiastic rotationists but, as the growing of crops was not central to the agriculture of Wales, the practice was relevant only in a few parts of the country – the Vale of Clwyd, for example, and the Vale of Glamorgan. Yet, as the profit from corn-growing soared during the war (the price of wheat rose from 6s. a bushel in 1794 to 18s. in 1800), arable land in Wales was greatly expanded. The emphasis of Welsh agriculture, however, was upon raising stock; the growth of crop rotation was therefore less central to its advance than were the efforts to improve the standard of farm animals and to produce food (turnips, in particular) to sustain them over the winter. Edward Corbett of Ynysymaengwyn near Tywyn was a tireless breeder – he could demand three times the usual price for his cattle – and the *Acreage Returns* of 1801 show that there was a considerable increase in the amount of land devoted to turnips, particularly in the border counties.

Publicity was given to the new methods through the agricultural societies. There was one in every Welsh county by 1817; they rewarded industrious farmers, held shows, distributed seeds and drew attention to new machinery. Agricultural improvements received extensive coverage in the periodicals established in the early nineteenth century; between 1808 and 1814, a quarter of the space of the *North Wales Gazette* was devoted to them. A few booklets on the subject were published in Welsh, including a translation of the advice offered to his tenants by Thomas Johnes of Hafod. Johnes (1748–1816) was the most tireless of the improvers; he covered the bare slopes of the upper Ystwyth valley with trees, he printed the reports of the Husbandry Society on his private press, he experimented with breeds and crops and he considered planting a colony of hardy Swiss mountain folk on the heights of Pumlumon. The exertions of Johnes and his fellow-improvers are impressive, and official reports and accounts of travellers suggest that by the beginning of the nineteenth century they were yielding results. Yet, what was achieved should not be exaggerated. In the 1790s, food supplies were frequently cruelly inadequate, as the corn riots of the decade testify. In the remoter regions of Wales, farmers had hardly been touched by the commercial forces which were transforming agriculture in the lowlands of England. Even in more favourable districts, most farmers were innately conservative and lacking in capital, and thus they were unable – or unwilling – to abandon the practices of their forefathers.

Johnes and his fellow-landowners could spend freely on their estates and on their own comfort, for their income was increasing rapidly. As they were receiving inflated prices for their produce, the farmers' standard of living rose, and the pianos they bought for their daughters and the education they sought for their sons were objects of mockery. They were, however, obliged to yield a large proportion of their surplus to their landlords. Where the old leases expired, the increase in the rent could be dramatic – from £8 to £40 at the farm of Blaengwrelych near Rhigos, for example. The rentals of the Trawsgoed and Nanteos estates in Cardiganshire trebled between 1790 and 1815, and the receipts of most of the landlords of Wales probably doubled at least during those years. Squires who had known austerity became accustomed to living lavishly, and they were to be reluctant to forgo their inflated incomes when circumstances changed after the war ended. Wales became adorned with sober late-Georgian mansions – and with handsome rectories too, for the Church also profited from inflation. The richer estate owners developed a craving for land, avidly buying the property of debt-ridden squires and yeomen. Between 1790 and 1815, there was an increase of 25 per cent in the size of the Cardiff Castle estate, a property which had come into the possession of the Bute family, heir to the Pembrokes and the Windsors, in 1766. The concentration of land in the hands of the few, a development which had been afoot in Wales since the Later Middle Ages, was coming to its climax. Nineteenth-century Wales was a country of great estates, and the implications of that fact would be one of the chief themes of its history during that century.

Enclosure of common lands also led to the expansion of estates. The transformation of the landscape into fields had been proceeding in Wales since the Neolithic Age and three quarters of the country had been enclosed by 1770. The process accelerated vastly during the war. Between 1793 and 1818, parliament passed almost a hundred acts authorizing the enclosure of eighty thousand hectares of the land of Wales. Some commons became fertile land – the enclosure and drainage of the sea marshes of Saltney, Malltraeth and Traeth Mawr, for example, were certainly a benefit to agriculture. The benefits accruing from the enclosure of moorlands are more doubtful. The most ambitious of the enclosure acts – that relating to Fforest Fawr, fifteen thousand hectares in southern Breconshire – was an abject failure. Yet, the main aim of the promoters of enclosure was not the improvement of agriculture but rather the intensification of landlord rights. Among the members of the ruling class, a deep prejudice had developed against anything which savoured of public or communal possession, and they could use their control of parliament to abolish such possession. As a result of enclosure, land over which the leading landowners had previously enjoyed only limited rights came into their absolute possession. As the enclosures were carried out by the agents of the great estates, and as small landowners lacked the legal resources to insist upon their share, the greater part of the old commons passed into the hands of the leading landowners. The Glynnes of Hawarden (ancestors of the Gladstones) obtained four hundred hectares of Saltney Marsh and the marquess of Bute seized three quarters of the Heath at Cardiff, while vast sheep walks were added to estates such as Golden Grove, Trawsgoed and Faenol.

There were bitter protests against enclosure, particularly from the squatters who had built *tai unnos* (shacks erected in a single night) on the common. As they had no legal title to their land, the fate of many squatters was to be cleared away, and there is a distressing description of the way this was done at the Heath in 1799. The most favourable outcome they could hope for was to be allowed to pay rent for the holding their labour had created, while being deprived of the various resources they had previously obtained from the common – fodder for their animals, timber and stone for their dwellings and peat and wood for their hearths. A commentator in Caernarfonshire lamented in 1806 that it was impossible to carry out improvements without harming individuals, but his was a lonely voice. The enclosures were part of a wider process – that of elevating the rich and of pushing the poor to the margins of the society, all in the name of progress.

For the people who had been pushed aside by progress, emigration offered hope of deliverance. It has already been noted that Merthyr proved attractive to the inhabitants of the moorlands of Breconshire, but people faced with destitution were prepared to go further afield. There was a numerous Welsh community in Liverpool by 1815, and the appeal of London increased, not only for seasonal workers such as *merched y gerddi* (the garden women), but also for more permanent settlers.

America, once the refuge for persecuted Puritans, became a favoured haven for the deprived. The voyage could be made for two pounds, and a dozen people from Llanbrynmair – a village famous in the annals of migration – crossed the Atlantic in 1795. They were welcomed and assisted in the New World, for the Cambro-Americans, descendants for the most part of the Puritan exiles of the previous century, were an influential community. Their contribution to the universities of their country was considerable; they played a significant part in the development of the key state of Pennsylvania and it was claimed that a third of the signatories of the Declaration of

Independence were of Welsh descent. They had retained a loyalty to the culture of their ancestors; the publication of Welsh books began in Philadelphia in 1721 and a St David's Society was established in the city in 1729. To the Nonconformists of Wales, the New Wales across the Atlantic offered a prospect of paradise and it was suggested that the Independents of the north should migrate, in their entirety, to Ohio. Although the hope of a better life in material terms was the main motive of the emigrants, there were millenarian aspects to the propaganda urging them to make the crossing. It was claimed that the Welsh community in America had been founded in about 1170 by Madog, son of Owain Gwynedd. In the late eighteenth century, there were increasing rumours that a tribe of Welsh-speaking Indians, the Madogwys, dwelt in the heart of the continent. John Williams, a Presbyterian minister, published an account of the Madog story in 1791, and the book inspired the strange journey of John Evans of Waunfawr, the first man to map the course of the Missouri river. In the 1790s, the Madog fever, along with the distress of the period, was responsible for a rapid growth in the number of Welsh migrants to America, people intent upon fulfilling their aspirations, material and spiritual, in the new republic of the United States.

It was the struggle which led to the establishment of the new republic that aroused for the first time in Wales a popular interest in political issues. During parliamentary elections, people of all classes displayed great enthusiasm, but elections were hardly concerned with fundamental principles. The interludes of Twm o'r Nant contained social criticism, and wars and troubles were the subjects of many ballads, but before the 1780s there was virtually no tradition of discussing politics in the Welsh language. The beginnings of such a tradition may be traced to the American War of Independence (1775–83), when a few ballads were composed which deplored the struggle between 'brothers' and when a Welsh translation of a pamphlet explaining the causes of the war was published. It was believed that Britain's failure to retain its colonies was proof of basic weaknesses in the system of government. Economic Reform – the abolition of sinecures in order to limit the ability of the government to buy the votes of members of parliament – was the remedy according to some, Thomas Pennant of Plas Downing, Flintshire, among them. Political Reform – increasing the number of voters in order to limit the government's influence over parliamentary elections – was the remedy according to others. Parliamentary Reform was strongly supported by some of the Welsh Whigs; a group in Flintshire presented a petition on the matter in 1782 and attempts were made, particularly in the north-east, to familiarize the population in general with the issue.

The ideas of the reformers were given philosophical justification (more radical than most of the Whigs would have wished for) by Richard Price, a native of Llangeinor, Glamorgan, a cousin of the maid of Cefnydfa and the most original thinker ever born in Wales. In his volume *Observations on the Nature of Civil Liberty* (1776), Price argued that parliamentarians are the trustees of the people, a theory further developed by David Williams of Waenwaelod near Caerffili in his volume *Letters on Political Liberty* (1782). By the middle of the nineteenth century, the ideas of these men were to be the commonplaces of Welsh political discourse, but in their day they found support only among small groups of progressives.

The most prominent of the radical intellectuals were those Nonconformists who had abandoned Calvinism. Almost all the Presbyterians had done so – both Price and Williams were Presbyterian ministers in England. In addition, a number of the Independent congregations of Wales rejected Calvinism, largely because of the influence of ministers educated in the liberal atmosphere of Carmarthen Academy, the *alma mater* of David Williams. John Jenkins, a former Carmarthen student, established Llwydrhydowen Chapel near Llandysul in 1733. The congregation adopted the doctrine of Arminius, the Dutch divine who taught that Christ had died for all and that into His work of salvation God weaves man's response and his freedom. By 1770, there were half a dozen Arminian congregations in the Teifi valley and another in Cefncoedycymer near Merthyr Tydfil. The Calvinists considered the growth of Arminianism to be a dire threat to Christian orthodoxy. They were right to do so, for Arminianism rapidly developed into Arianism (the belief that the Son is not of the same substance as the Father) and then into Socinianism or Unitarianism (the belief that Christ was no more than a man and that human reason is the key to salvation). Thus there were two distinct streams in the religious history of eighteenth-century Wales. While the majority were attracted to revivalist zeal (zeal which represented a reaction against the Age of Reason), a small minority sought to modify religious doctrines in the light of reason. And in the long term, the few who rejected traditional dogma were to be at least as influential as those who adhered to it.

Almost all those who reacted positively to the French Revolution came from the ranks of those influenced by Arminianism or Arianism. Chief among them was Richard Price. 'Tremble, all ye oppressors of the world . . . you can not now keep the world in darkness' were the closing words of his sermon welcoming the revolution. The sermon provoked Edmund Burke to write his *Reflections on the Revolution in France* (1790), a classic statement of conservative values. Burke was answered in turn by a number of radicals, among them Tom Paine, the author of another classic, *The Rights of Man* (1791, 1792). When Price died in 1791, he was officially mourned in Paris, and the following year David Williams was honoured with French citizenship. Williams's theology as well as his politics appealed to the revolutionaries. He had rejected all forms of Christianity, embracing Deism and establishing a chapel where the cult of reason and nature was celebrated. Something of his doctrine may be discerned in the ideas of Iolo Morganwg (Edward Williams, 1747–1826), for the 'religion' which Iolo invented for the *Gorsedd* of the Bards was a curious mixture of his own antiquarian obsessions and Williams's 'theophilanthropia'.

Iolo was closely associated with the Gwyneddigion, a society of Welsh patriots founded in London in 1770 with a livelier and more populist membership than the Cymmrodorion. To the Gwyneddigion, the French Revolution was an inspiration. 'The purpose of the Society is Freedom in Church and State,' declared its president, Owain Myfyr, and 'Liberty' was the subject of the chief prize in the eisteddfod organized by the Gwyneddigion at St Asaph in 1790. The anthem of the society was a liberty hymn (to Madog), the work of Jac Glan-y-gors (John Jones), a man who sought through his volumes, *Seren Tan Gwmmwl* (Star under a Cloud, 1795) and *Toriad y Dydd* (The Break of Day, 1797) to acquaint the Welsh with the ideas of Tom Paine. Another of the members of the Gwyneddigion was Thomas Roberts of Llwyn'rhudol near Pwllheli, the author of *Cwyn yn erbyn Gorthrymder* (A Complaint against Oppression, 1798), an attack upon tithes and the Church Establishment and a plea for the recognition of the Welsh language in the administration of justice. Members of the society supported the efforts of Morgan John Rhys of Llanbradach, Glamorgan, to publish a Welsh periodical. Five issues of his *Cylch-*

grawn Cynmraeg (Welsh Magazine, 1793–4) appeared, and their contents are proof of his zeal for education, freedom of conscience, social reform and the Welsh language. Morgan John Rhys was a strange and complex man. He was a Baptist minister, but he published the work of the atheist Volney; he interpreted the French Revolution as a reaction against popery and in 1791 he went to Paris to distribute Bibles. He hoped that the profits from his periodical would finance a mission to the Madogwys, and in 1794 he emigrated to America, where in 1796 he founded the town of Beula, Pennsylvania, as a centre for a Welsh colony.

Morgan John Rhys's successor in the attempt to establish a Welsh periodical press was the Unitarian and enthusiastic reformer Tomos Glyn Cothi (Thomas Evans), the editor of *Y Drysorfa Cymysgedig* (The Mixed Treasury, three issues, 1795). He was succeeded by David Davies, Holywell, the editor of *Y Geirgrawn* (The Magazine; nine issues, February to October 1796), a boldly radical journal which published a Welsh translation of the *Marseillaise*. *Y Geirgrawn* was suppressed by the state and the authorities also prosecuted Tomos Glyn Cothi, for the radicals were considered to be highly dangerous. Although they were a tiny minority, ideas such as theirs had been responsible for the overthrow of the *ancien régime* in France. The authorities feared that the mass of the population – who were close to starvation in such desperate years as 1795–6 and 1800–1801, and who were suffering the scourge of the press-gang – would come to embrace revolutionary doctrines. As Britain, from 1793 onwards, was at war with the home of the revolution, the government could interpret any political radicalism as proof of sympathy with the enemy. The result was reactionary repression; all hope of constitutional reform vanished; Habeas Corpus – the act which insisted that every prisoner must appear before a court of law – was suspended; statutes were passed to outlaw political meetings, to confirm the Treason Acts and to strengthen anti-trade-union legislation. A number of the Nonconformists of Pembrokeshire were prosecuted following the French landing at Fishguard (February 1797); five workers from Swansea were imprisoned in 1806 for plotting to raise wages and there were large numbers of court cases arising from riots over food and land.

By 1800, the hopes and the vitality of the Welsh radicals had been almost totally extinguished. The iron fist of the state was not the only factor involved. The Reign of Terror in France (1793–4) and the

Fishguard invasion helped to cool the ardour of the radicals; by the beginning of the nineteenth century, Iolo Morganwg was prepared to laud the Glamorgan Volunteers and Jac Glan-y-gors was singing the praises of Nelson.

When reaction was at its height, any anomalous or dissident group was open to attack. Attempts were made to vilify the Methodists by suggesting that their *seiadau* were nurseries of sedition. According to the *Gentleman's Magazine*, their meetings were 'instruments of Jacobinism', an accusation which Thomas Charles sought to refute in his pamphlet *The Welsh Methodists Vindicated* (1802). The accusation was ludicrous. To the Methodists, with their belief in the innate corruption of man and the eternal damnation he faced but for the sovereign grace of God, the principles of the revolution – the talk of progress and the rights of man – were trumpery vapourings. According to Thomas Jones of Denbigh, the author of *Gair yn ei Amser* (A Word in Time, 1798), the revolution was the result of sin. 'Whosoever attacks authority,' he wrote, 'opposes the ordinances of God.' More than ten thousand copies of his pamphlet were distributed, and it probably reached more homes than the entire publications of the radicals. The dissemination of this passive doctrine was as important as the persecution of the state in limiting the impact of the French Revolution, in stifling the vision of the Gwyneddigion and their associates of a Welsh nation being reborn in freedom.

The vilification of the Methodists could become persecution. In the 1790s, the press-gang singled out their counsellors; their congregations were fined and the militia menaced their services. As recognized denominations, the Baptists and Independents were safeguarded by the Toleration Act of 1689, but the Methodists, who were merely a faction within the Church of England, had no such protection. They reacted by registering their meeting-houses in accordance with the act of 1689 and were thus well on the way to becoming a separate denomination. Their meeting-houses proliferated: over a hundred and fifty were built between 1790 and 1810.

The appeal of Methodism was strengthened by the growth of Sunday schools, which by 1810 were part of the activity of almost all Methodist congregations. The Sunday schools (which were attended by adults as well as children) were particularly associated with Thomas Charles, the chief leader of Welsh Methodism in the late eighteenth and the early nineteenth centuries. Charles had been brought up near

Llanddowror but, after he had settled at Bala in 1783, that town became the centre of the movement, testimony of Methodism's increasingly northern orientation. The Sunday schools were intended to fill the vacuum left by the demise of the schools of Griffith Jones and Madam Bevan. As with the circulating schools, the emphasis of the Sunday schools was upon reading the Bible. To assist such reading, Charles published his *Geiriadur Ysgrythyrawl* (Biblical Dictionary, 1805–11) and his *Hyfforddwr* (Manual, 1807), thus continuing the tradition of biblical scholarship among the Methodists initiated by Peter Williams's annotated Bible of 1770 – a work which led to the excommunication of Williams for heresy in 1791. The chief requirement of the Sunday schools was cheap Bibles. In his efforts to supply them, Charles was probably inspired by Mari Jones's willingness in 1800 to walk the forty kilometres from Llanfihangel-y-Pennant to Bala to buy a Bible. Two years later, while in London, he planted the seed which developed into the British and Foreign Bible Society, a body which by now has published the entire Bible in 283 languages, including its first venture – the publication of twenty thousand Welsh Bibles. Thomas Charles also persuaded the Methodists to accept the principle that elders should be elected by the local congregation rather than be appointed by the Association, an important step towards the Presbyterianism which was to be characteristic of the Calvinistic Methodism of Wales.

The developments of the period 1790–1810 only served to deepen the anomalous position of Methodism. It had begun as a tendency but had, to all intents and purposes, become a church. Yet it was a church which lacked the authority to offer the sacraments to its members. By 1800, there were only about a dozen clerics of the Established Church – Thomas Charles of Bala and David Jones of Llan-gan, Glamorgan, foremost among them – who were wholly acceptable to the Methodists, and the number of clergymen prepared to welcome a Methodist to the communion table was decreasing year by year. 'I have never read in any ecclesiastical history,' wrote Michael Roberts of Pwllheli, 'of any Church similar to ours.' Thomas Charles had no desire to break away from the Established Church. 'We agree entirely,' he declared in 1801, 'with the Principled Articles of Faith of the Church of England ... Our intention is not to create a schism, a sect or a party, no in the name of God.' There is nothing in the Welsh language comparable with the earnestness of the discussion of the following decade – the discussion which led, in 1811, to the establishment of the Calvinistic Methodist denomination. The Moravians had ordained ministers in Britain since 1753, the Wesleyans began administering the Lord's Supper in their services in 1795, and Calvinistic Methodist counsellors were highly envious of the status of the reverend pastors of the Nonconformists. David Jones of Llan-gan died in 1810 and in that year Thomas Jones, a layman, administered the sacraments of baptism and communion in Capel Mawr, Denbigh. Thomas Charles was forced to accept that separation from the Established Church was unavoidable; he ordained nine men to the ministry in the Bala Association in June 1811, and a further thirteen at the Llandeilo Association in August of the same year.

Although they were not to make use of the word for decades, the Calvinistic Methodists from 1811 onwards were Nonconformists. That fact fundamentally changed the denominational balance in Wales, for it meant that the vast majority of the devout among the Welsh were associated with denominations other than the Established Church. In joining the ranks of the Nonconformists, the Methodists were strengthening those ranks not only in numbers but also in organization, for, unlike the denominations which had sprung from old Dissent, the Methodists were subject to central leadership and discipline. The time would come when the Connexion's centralized machinery would be at the service of the leaders of Welsh radicalism, a development which would transform the politics of many of the constituencies of Wales. The first leaders of the new denomination, however, had no sympathy for radicalism. They were concerned above all with doctrinal orthodoxy and Calvinist scholasticism, and their yearning for authoritative unity may be seen in their desire to define the credo of the denomination. For Thomas Jones of Denbigh, the Connexion's most learned theologian, the Church of England's Articles of Faith sufficed. After his death in 1820, it was considered necessary, as Owen Thomas put it, 'to have a more detailed and definitive Statement of the Connexion's vision of the specific truths of the Gospel'. In 1823, the Confession of Faith of the Calvinistic Methodists was drawn up in 'a spacious and fitting upper room' in Great Dark Gate Street in Aberystwyth. In accordance with the views of John Elias of Anglesey, 'the idol of the Associations', the document bound the Connexion to High Calvinist doctrines, much to the discomfiture of more liberal Methodists in later generations.

Owen Thomas suggested that the leaning to High Calvinism could partly be explained by the fact that 'the coming of the Wesleyans to Wales caused some to be driven to extremes on the opposing side'. The Wesleyans were Arminians, but of an unusual kind, for they had no sympathy for theological liberalism such as that which sprang from the Carmarthen Academy. It has been noted already that Wesley had not sought converts among the Welsh. Yet his frequent visits to Wales had not been without effect and by 1770 there were about half a dozen Wesleyan societies in the anglicized parts of the country. Attempts were made to convey the message in Welsh, and in 1800 Edward Jones of Bathafarn (a farm in the Vale of Clwyd and a name of resonance among Welsh Wesleyans) founded a Wesleyan society at Rhuthun. In the same year, on the recommendation of Thomas Coke, a native of Brecon and a leading figure among the Wesleyans, the conference of the denomination founded a mission to the Welsh. The mission had rapid success and by 1810 it was supervising more than a hundred congregations. The Wesleyan Conference was a highly centralized organization – a 'systematic denial of local autonomy', to quote Élie Halévy. It could launch a mission, but it could also emasculate a mission. That is what happened. After the death of Coke in 1814, the mission's resources were curtailed, its abler preachers were moved to England and Welsh chapels were linked to English circuits. Wesleyanism did not fade away in Wales. It would have numerous adherents, particularly in the southern coastal towns, in the lead-mining districts of Cardiganshire and in parts of the north-east, but its remarkable advance in the period from 1800 to 1814 was not sustained.

To those concerned with the traditional culture of Wales, this Methodist advance, whether Calvinist or Wesleyan, was highly unwelcome. The Methodists were barred from participating in the worldly activity of the Welsh societies, and on becoming a focus for Methodism Bala ceased to be a centre of *eisteddfodau*. 'The north, by now,' wrote Iolo Morganwg in 1799, 'is as Methodistical as the south, and the south as Methodistical as hell.' Yet, as they sought their converts among monoglot Welsh-speakers, the Methodists were obliged to promote the Welsh language as a medium of evangelical zeal. They used the language in a less self-conscious way than did the scholars and the patriots, and, if the culture they created was narrow and pietistic, its medium was Welsh and its productions were prolific.

The contribution made by the radicals to the growth of the Welsh press has already been noted. This was a field in which the Methodists were also active, with *Y Drysorfa Ysbrydol* (The Spiritual Treasury, six issues, 1799–1801) and *Yr Eurgrawn Wesleyaidd* (The Wesleyan Magazine, 1809–1983), the longest-lived of all Welsh periodicals. Neither did the Methodists wholly lack interest in the older culture: Thomas Jones had a sound command of the strict metres, Thomas Charles's *Geiriadur* contains considerable material on Welsh traditions and many cultural works found a market through the Sunday school network.

Yet the contribution of the Methodists was marginal to the scholarly, literary and antiquarian activities of the period 1770–1815, activities which would become the basis of some of the most characteristic manifestations of the culture of mid- and late-nineteenth-century Wales. The Gwyneddigion were the fulcrum of this enthusiasm for Welsh culture. The disciples of Edward Lhuyd and the Morris circle had aspired to prove the richness of Welsh tradition by publishing the contents of the ancient manuscripts. Owain Myfyr, the president of the Gwyneddigion, shared that aspiration. As he was a wealthy businessman, he had the means to fulfil it. The work of Dafydd ap Gwilym was published in 1789 and that of Llywarch Hen in 1792, and *The Myvyrian Archaiology*, three substantial volumes of early Welsh literature named after the publication's patron, appeared between 1801 and 1807. Although these works had their weaknesses, they provided the main foundation for nineteenth-century Welsh literary scholarship.

The weaknesses were largely the result of the inventiveness of Iolo Morganwg; the volume of the works of Dafydd ap Gwilym contained a number of *cywyddau* (poems consisting of rhyming couplets in strict metre) composed by Iolo, and there are a host of his forgeries in the *Archaiology*. Iolo was not content merely to study the culture of the past; he felt impelled to add to it, and the scholarship of the day lacked the skills to distinguish between the fake and the genuine. Other eighteenth-century writers – in England, Scotland, Bohemia and Finland – allowed their enthusiasm for the past to run riot, but there can hardly ever have been so tireless a forger as Iolo. Only a small proportion of his work appeared in the volumes financed by Owain Myfyr. When Iolo died in 1826, his cottage at Flemingston in the Vale of Glamorgan was found to be crammed to the ceiling with manuscripts, material which has been a quarry and a perplexity to Welsh scholars ever since. His exertions were inspired by his love of his county, by his ardent desire to prove that the contempt of the Morrises and their fellow-northerners towards the Welsh culture of Glamorgan was wholly unwarranted. By the late eighteenth century, northern Glamorgan was one of the few places in Wales where the bards still followed their craft, a fact inflated by Iolo into a splendid extravaganza. He asserted that the traditions of the Welsh were older than those of any other country in Europe. The guardians of those traditions were the druids, an order that had died out everywhere except in Glamorgan. Even there, only two men knew the secrets of the druids of the Isle of Britain, and Iolo himself was one of them. He persuaded the Gwyneddigion to embrace his theories; they were published as part of the work of Llywarch Hen in 1792, the year in which Iolo organized his gorsedd (assembly of bards) on Primrose Hill in London. Many *gorseddau* were subsequently held and in 1819 at Carmarthen Iolo succeeded in linking the gorsedd with the eisteddfod, a linkage which has lasted until today, although it has gone through some stormy episodes.

The meeting of 1819 was an attempt to root the eisteddfod in the south. A number of gatherings of poets and musicians had been held in the eighteenth century, mainly in the north-east, where the tradition of the *eisteddfodau* of Caerwys was held in high regard. They were fairly chaotic occasions, and in 1789 members of the Gwyneddigion were invited by Thomas Jones of Clocaenog near Rhuthun to provide them with patronage and leadership. Owain Myfyr readily agreed, not only in order to promote music and literature but also in order to have a platform for political radicalism. From 1789 onwards, a series of Gwyneddigion *eisteddfodau* was held in the towns of the north-east, and in them were developed the features characteristic of the festivals of the nineteenth century.

The poets of the *eisteddfodau* did not produce a distinguished body of verse. There is little merit in the works of Gwallter Mechain and Dafydd Ddu, and the thirteen thousand lines which Dafydd Ionawr wrote on the Trinity are hardly inspiring. Nevertheless, the poets adhered, as Thomas Parry put it, 'with secure instinct and judgement to Welsh tradition in language and metre'. In the following generation, that virtue would be lost, largely because of the dissemination of mistaken notions concerning the Welsh language. While Iolo

Morganwg, one of the editors of *The Myvyrian Archaiology*, sowed confusion about the history and literature of Wales, his fellow-editor, William Owen Pughe, sowed confusion about its language. Pughe considered that the function of the grammarian was to describe a language, not as it is, but as it ought to be. He believed that Welsh was closely related to the original language of mankind, a language which could be reconstructed through an analysis of Welsh. He developed these notions in his *Geiriadur* (Dictionary, 1793–1803), his *Gramadeg* (Grammar, 1803) and his *Cadoedigaet yr Iait Cybraeg* (The Conservation of the Welsh Language, 1808). His publications offered a reformed orthography, a revised grammar and a vast quarry of neologisms – there are a hundred thousand words in Pughe's dictionary. Many of the weaknesses of the Welsh literature of the following decades – the faulty syntax, for example, and the empty ostentation – may be attributed to the influence of Pughe, influence which lasted until the advent of more securely based scholarship at the end of the nineteenth century.

Yet, although Pughe had his weaknesses (including his infatuation for that strange prophetess, Joanna Southcott), it is impossible not to admire his industry. He was responsible for the *Cambrian Register* (1795–6), among the first of a series of English periodicals dealing with Wales, and *The Cambrian Biography* (1803), the first Welsh biographical dictionary. Such publications are proof of an increasing demand for material on the history of Wales. William Wynne's *History of Wales* was republished in 1774 and 1812 and David Powel's *Historie of Cambria* in 1811, and six editions of William Warrington's *History of Wales* appeared between 1786 and 1823. The Elizabethan tradition of studying the history of the Welsh counties was revived. Between 1775 and 1818, substantial volumes were written on the history of the counties of Anglesey, Caernarfon, Meirionnydd, Monmouth, Brecon, Cardigan and Radnor. *History of the County of Brecknock* (1805–9), the work of Theophilus Jones, the grandson of Theophilus Evans, is the most detailed and learned of them. A tradition of writing parish histories was also initiated with the volume of Edmund Jones, the zealous Independent of Pontypool, *Historical Account of the Parish of Aberystruth* (1779), and that of Thomas Pennant, *The History of the Parishes of Whiteford and Holywell* (1796).

Thomas Pennant was the most learned of the Welsh antiquarians of his age, but it is as a naturalist that he won international fame. (It was through his friendship with Joseph Banks, the chief scientist on James Cook's second voyage (1768–71), that the east coast of Australia came to be known as New South Wales.) His *Tours in Wales* (1778, 1781) are an informal portrayal rather than an organized historical discussion, but they contain a great deal of valuable material, including a spirited defence of Owain Glyn Dŵr. Pennant's *Tours* were a central factor in the growth among the English of the notion that the Welsh were intellectually interesting. The notion had been abroad in England since about 1750, as may be seen from Thomas Gray's poem 'The Bard' (1757), a version of the myth that Edward I had slaughtered the bards of Wales. (The myth was borrowed by Arány as the theme of one of the most famous poems in Magyar, thus causing Hungary to be one of the few countries where the inhabitants have an inkling of the Welsh and their history.) Interest in Wales was promoted by the Celtomania which followed the publication of the poems of Ossian in 1763, by improvements in the roads which facilitated the journeys of travellers and by the spread of aesthetic theories associated with the Romantic movement.

In the early eighteenth century, a wild landscape was something to avoid. Wales was considered 'the fag-end of creation, the very rubbish of Noah's flood' and sensitive travellers drew down the blinds of their coach lest they should be pained by the barbarity of mountain scenery. There was a transformation in sensibility in the second half of the century, and philosophers, artists and men of letters came to glorify the wild, the sublime and the picturesque. They praised Wales, for the country was rich in cliffs, waterfalls and ruins. Although the country could conveniently be reached from London, its attractions had an appealingly foreign context and, following the completion of the turnpike roads and the development of a network of hotels, they could be appreciated in some degree of comfort. Between 1770 and 1815, eighty books describing tours in Wales were published. Much of their contents consist of Rousseauesque rhapsodies, but when they contain more substantial material it can be very valuable. The tourists included some of the chief figures of English literature, including Wordsworth, Coleridge, Shelley, Southey, Scott, Peacock, Landor and De Quincey.

The writers were following in the footsteps of the painters. The French artists Claude Lorrain (1600–1682) and Nicolas Poussin (1613–75) had promoted the notion of the ideal landscape with mountain,

lake and ruin in splendid asymmetry. Among the most famous of
their followers was Richard Wilson (1713–82) who succeeded through
his paintings in creating a powerful image of Wales. Wilson's disciples
included Thomas Jones of Pencerrig, Radnorshire (1743–1803), and
there were other Welsh painters of talent including Moses Griffith,
who illustrated the works of Thomas Pennant, Penri Williams, who
received the patronage of the Crawshays of Cyfarthfa, and Hugh
Hughes, the portrayer of the emerging Nonconformist middle class.
While great painters such as Wilson (and Turner, who visited Wales
almost annually in the 1790s) were creating their masterpieces, hosts
of topographical artists were seeking to record the Welsh landscape.
Copper engravings of their work were published – the three volumes
of the brothers Buck (1740–42), for example, and the volume *Twelve
Views in Aquatinta* (1775), the work of Paul Sandby, the pioneer of
the aquatint. Copper was displaced by steel around 1820, a development which led to a vast increase in the sale of engravings. One of the
earliest collections of steel engravings was the volume of Finden and
Batty, *Welsh Scenery* (1823), and in the following decades thousands
of prints of Welsh scenes were produced, a large number of them
based on the drawings of the prolific artist Henry Gastineau. In
addition, there were growing efforts to map Wales, with the polished
work of cartographers such as Kitchin, Cary, Greenwood and
Teesdale. The Ordnance Survey was founded in 1791 and the
triangular system, the basis of accurate mapping, had been completed
by 1852. Between 1805 and 1875, inch-to-a-mile maps were published
of every part of Wales. This was the first phase of the Ordnance
Survey maps, by far the best record of the Welsh landscape.

Interest in Wales among Englishmen in the late eighteenth and the
early nineteenth centuries was partly the result of the fact that the war
with France impeded travel to more distant places. That interest
waned after 1815, when mainland Europe was again open to travellers
from England. The year 1815 was a turning-point in other spheres
also. Between 1815 and 1816 the collapse in the market for war
material caused the price of iron bars to fall from £12 to £8 a ton.
'The day peace was signed,' wrote Robert Owen, 'we lost our best
customer.' The boom in the prices of agricultural produce came to an
end, and tenants were burdened with the inflated rents imposed upon
them during the war. As conservatism had defeated the forces of

revolution, reaction was in the ascendant. The earl of Liverpool was for fifteen years the head of a Tory administration (1812–27); all discussion of reform, constitutional and social, was suppressed and the authorities reacted harshly to the frequent protests of the frustrated and the deprived. The south Wales coalfield was among the most discontented areas of the kingdom. There were troubles in Tredegar in 1816 and they quickly spread to the rest of the iron-producing districts. As the only police were unpaid constables, the suppression of rioting was a matter for the army and the militia, and the inhabitants of many coalfield communities became accustomed to periods of military occupation. Most of the rioters were probably reacting instinctively, but from 1816 onwards there are suggestions of more organized protests. This was particularly true of the 'black domain' of the Monmouthshire coalfield, an area often considered to be an eastern adjunct of Merthyr, although its history has features which cause Merthyr's experience to seem fortunate.

Monmouthshire was the home of the Scotch Cattle, a group of men who sought to use terror and vandalism in order to create working-class unity. The Scotch Cattle were a reaction to the unrestricted power of the employers and to the uncertainty of employment in the coalfield. The ironmasters were not merely employers; frequently they were the owners of their employees' homes and through the truck system many workers were obliged to buy their goods in company shops; the masters sat on the magistrates' bench and they dominated the parish meeting, the only form of local government in the coalfield communities. They believed that they had absolute power over the ventures created through their capital and enterprise; employees who appeared intractable were liable to be dismissed and, as the majority of the workers in the coalfield were at best only semi-skilled, the over-populated countryside offered an inexhaustible supply of people to replace them. The masters sought a disciplined workforce and there were those among them who believed that this could be achieved only by making hostages of their employees, particularly by ensuring that they were constantly in debt.

The autocracy of the owners was part of a pattern of deprivation. It has already been noted that the lives of the inhabitants of the industrial districts were affected by the mountainous environment and the unfavourable climate. They were also threatened by the lethal dangers of the furnaces and the collieries, the appalling scarcity of

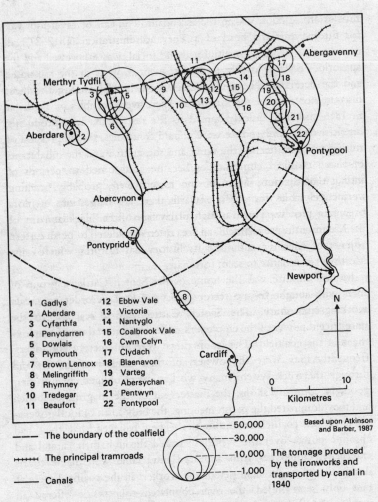

1 Gadlys
2 Aberdare
3 Cyfarthfa
4 Penydarren
5 Dowlais
6 Plymouth
7 Brown Lennox
8 Melingriffith
9 Rhymney
10 Tredegar
11 Beaufort

12 Ebbw Vale
13 Victoria
14 Nantyglo
15 Coalbrook Vale
16 Cwm Celyn
17 Clydach
18 Blaenavon
19 Varteg
20 Abersychan
21 Pentwyn
22 Pontypool

Based upon Atkinson
and Barber, 1987

- - - - The boundary of the coalfield
++++++ The principal tramroads
——— Canals

—— 50,000
—— 30,000
—— 10,000
—— 1,000

The tonnage produced
by the ironworks and
transported by canal in
1840

The iron industry in the south Wales coalfield

services such as sewage disposal and a supply of pure water, the
horrifying infant mortality rate and the frequent attacks of a variety
of diseases. It may therefore appear surprising that migrants flooded
into the coalfield. But flood they did. Of all the counties of the
kingdom, Monmouthshire experienced the most rapid rise in population in the first half of the nineteenth century, and Glamorgan was

third on the list. At least 27,000 people lived in Merthyr by 1831 and the increase in the numbers of inhabitants in parishes such as Aberystruth, Bedwellte and Trefethin (Pontypool) was even more dramatic. The high level of natural population growth – a consistent feature in areas of heavy industry – was partly responsible for the increase, but much of it can be ascribed to migration. Not all the migrants intended to settle: many of the smallholders of Cardiganshire came to the 'works' for the winter, returning to their homes for the harvest, and it is estimated that 10,000 people circulated through Merthyr annually. The most numerous element among the migrants were males in their teens and twenties; there were 1,255 males for every 1,000 females in Aberystruth in 1831. As young men were such a high proportion of the population, and as they often had nowhere but the tavern in which to spend their leisure hours, it is hardly surprising that the communities of the coalfield were inflammable. This was undoubtedly part of their appeal.

Despite the arrogance of the owners, the perils of the work-place and the filthiness of the environment, the coalfield was an exciting place. Although Merthyr was described by a Meirionnydd preacher as 'a kind of Samaria – the place to throw one's rubbish', rural young men were attracted by the experience of living in a crowded, cheerful and Welsh-speaking society. Despite the inadequacies of the houses, they were better than the primitive cottages of the countryside and they were warm, for coal was cheap in the coalfield. There was pride there too – pride in understanding the ways of the furnace and the vagaries of the seam. Above all, it was a place where a livelihood could be obtained. Despite the instability of employment in the iron industry – the frequent dismissals, the sudden reductions in wages, the periods of short-term working – the ordinary worker in Dowlais earned at least three times as much as the shilling a day received by a farm servant. In Merthyr, even a labourer owned a watch.

The increase in the population of the coalfield proves that the depression which hit the iron industry in 1815 was short-lived. Although its social consequences were severe and although the price of iron remained low for decades after 1815, more and more furnaces were built and their efficiency was improved by the adoption of the hot blast and by the spread of the use of the steam-engine. The output of the south Wales ironworks rose from about 100,000 tons in 1815 to

277,000 in 1830. New markets were discovered. Iron was used increasingly in building: the chains of the Menai Bridge (1819–26) were manufactured at Penydarren, and those of Brighton Pier at Pontypridd. Thousands of kilometres of tram-rails were laid down. The trains between Stockton and Darlington – the world's first public railway (1825) – travelled on rails produced at Ebbw Vale, and by the 1840s there would be an almost inexhaustible demand for the rails produced by the ironworks of Wales. Foreign markets were developed. In 1827, almost thirty thousand tons of iron were exported from Cardiff, mainly to the Netherlands, Turkey, Portugal and Italy. The Cardiff trade represented about half the iron exports of Britain and the south Wales coalfield was recognized as the chief centre of the industry. In discussing the future of the Bute ironworks in the Rhymni valley in 1824, the surveyor David Stewart expressed the hope that they would become 'the first works in Wales and consequently in the world'.

With the growth of the iron industry, the output of coal increased, for 4.5 tons of coal were needed to produce a ton of iron. By the 1820s, enough was raised to supply the needs of the iron industry and to permit a rapid growth in the coal trade, largely because richer and deeper seams were worked as a result of the development of the steam-engine and the adoption of the Davy lamp. In the late eighteenth century the coal of the upper reaches of the coalfield had only a very local market. 'We have no coal exported from this port,' stated the customs officer at Cardiff in 1782, 'nor ever shall, as it would be too expensive to bring it down here from the internal part of the country.' The situation was transformed by the building of the canals, a development which benefited Newport in particular. No tolls were levied on Newport's coal trade and in 1830 the port exported over 450,000 tons, more than four times the exports of Cardiff. But significant developments were afoot in the areas served by Cardiff also, with the activities of Coffin in the lower Rhondda, of Powell in the Taff valley and of Brocket near Llantrisant, and the abolition of all coal tolls in 1831 led to a marked increase in the coal trade of Cardiff.

With the growth of Newport, Swansea lost its position as the chief coal port of Wales. Its trade did not decline, however, largely because of the link between west Glamorgan and Cornwall. After the exhaustion of the Amlwch mines, Cornwall was the source of almost all the ore smelted in the copper-works of the Swansea region, and coal was cheaply conveyed on the boats which returned to ports such as Penzance and St Ives. By 1820, the area between Aberafan and Llanelli – with Swansea at its centre – produced 90 per cent of Britain's copper and a large proportion of its zinc, lead and silver. The area was the world's chief centre for the production of non-ferrous metals and 'the Welsh method' of smelting ore was considered 'one of the finest examples of the metallurgist's art'. The copper industry was less labour-intensive than the iron industry and thus the growth in population in west Glamorgan was slower than it was in Merthyr. The copper-works were especially filthy: tens of thousands of tons of sulphuric acid were released annually in the Tawe valley, grossly injuring the health of the inhabitants and the fertility of the soil. The area between Llanelli and Aberafan was also the centre of the tinplate industry – the process of coating thin sheets of iron with tin. Here again the link with Cornwall was central, for Cornish mines were the chief source of tin ore. There was a considerable demand for tinplate to make a variety of kitchen utensils, and – as the song suggests – Llanelli was especially associated with the craft of making saucepans. In 1825, tinplate was used for the first time to can food, a development which was to lead to a large-scale trade, especially with the United States.

While the south Wales coalfield was experiencing increasing prosperity, several of the industries of mid and north Wales were falling into decay. The richest seams of Mynydd Parys had been exhausted even before the death of Thomas Williams in 1802. Distress befell the people of Amlwch. There was bitter rioting there in 1817, and by 1831 the parish had only a handful of miners. Some of the small mines of Snowdonia – Drws-y-coed in particular – remained fairly prosperous until the second half of the century, but they also would eventually be abandoned. As there was no longer much copper ore within convenient reach of Holywell, the copper industry of Flintshire came to an end; there are no references to any smelting works in the county after 1842. The lead industry was weakened by wild speculation and by competition from foreign ores. British lead exports halved between 1820 and 1830, although the mines, especially those of Cardiganshire and Montgomeryshire, experienced occasional revivals. The iron industry of the north also declined. Litigation among the descendants of John Wilkinson had led to the closure of the famous

Bersham works by 1826. Attempts were made to reopen the works at Brymbo, but their proprietor fled to Paris as a bankrupt in 1829. Other works in the area had periods of prosperity, but they were all in difficulties by 1830. Between 1830 and 1850, there was a 150 per cent increase in the amount of iron produced in the south Wales coalfield, but in the north the industry stagnated. The prospects of the coal industry of Denbighshire and Flintshire were more promising. The two counties had three thousand colliers between them in 1831. Following the abolition of the tolls on the coal trade in that year the industry experienced substantial growth, although nothing comparable with the dramatic developments in the south.

The prospects of the Welsh woollen industry also seemed promising – at first glance at least. The industry was located in areas where water-power could be harnessed and between 1800 and 1830 many spinning and weaving factories were established, particularly in the Severn valley, an area which was linked with the canal system of the kingdom in 1821. The population of the towns of the valley tripled between 1801 and 1831, and by 1831 Welshpool, Newtown and Llanidloes were essentially industrial towns. Yet they were minute compared with Bradford and Leeds; the capital of the owners of their factories was insufficient and every financial crisis was followed by a crop of failures; when the woollen industry in Yorkshire adopted steam power, the industrialists of the Severn valley soon came to feel the disadvantage of being a considerable distance from a coalfield. Although the Welsh woollen industry appeared to be prosperous enough in the early 1830s, its future was highly uncertain.

By the second quarter of the nineteenth century, only one of the industries of the north had substantial prospects. That was the slate industry. By the first decade of the nineteenth century, Richard Pennant's enterprise was bearing fruit. When he died in 1808, his quarries in the parish of Llandygái were yielding £7,000 a year. Assheton Smith sought to emulate him at Llanberis and the industry was becoming sufficiently prosperous to attract capital from outside Gwynedd, particularly to Ffestiniog, the only quarrying area where capital from England was central to its development. The coming of peace in 1815 was beneficial to the industry, for there was a need to make good the lack of investment in building during the war. Its growth was hindered by over-speculation and by uncertainty concerning the ownership of many a cliff and rock, but despite a slump between 1828 and 1830 the

Welsh slate industry had firm foundations. In contrast with the other industries of the north, the quarries of Gwynedd had no competitors of significance. Transport problems were solved by building tramways to link the quarries with the sea and by establishing ports; in 1821, Porthmadog was created specifically to serve the slate industry. The demand for the products of the quarries increased because of the meteoric growth of towns – in northern England in particular – and the abolition of the toll on slates in 1831. The prosperity of the industry was reflected in the expansion of the quarrying communities: there was an increase of 61 per cent in the population of the parish of Llanddeiniolen between 1831 and 1841, a decade when the rate of population growth in Caernarfonshire (21 per cent) was twice that of any of the other counties of the north.

Yet despite the significance of the rise of industrial communities, agriculture continued to be the mainstay of the majority of the people of Wales, at least until 1830. There were eighty-eight hundreds in Wales; in 1811 more than half of the inhabitants of seventy-nine of them depended directly on the soil for their livelihood. For decades to come, the population of the countryside would continue to increase and in those areas where small-scale industry and crafts were in decline, reliance upon agriculture was intensifying. With the coming of peace, the position of agriculturalists worsened. The price of corn was halved despite the efforts of parliament to keep it high by means of the Corn Laws. Many upland farms abandoned corn growing and even in favourable areas such as the Vale of Glamorgan arable farmers were severely hit. There was also a marked fall in the price of meat and dairy produce, and, following the severe weather of the years 1816–18, many farmers were obliged to sell their stock on highly unfavourable terms. While most landowners were prepared to grant rent abatements during difficult times, they were reluctant to allow permanent reductions. As the countryside was over-populated, there was no lack of applicants for farms even at inflated rents, and as most landowners had committed themselves to heavy expenditure during the prosperous war years they were unable to accept a substantial fall in their income. In consequence, almost every estate recorded a massive increase in arrears in the years immediately following the war. Arrears rose again in 1826, when ready money was in short supply because of the banking crisis of 1825–6. In the course of that crisis, many of the banks that had been established in the market towns of Wales from

1790 onwards failed. They included all the banks of Pembrokeshire, along with romantically named institutions such as the Bank of the Black Sheep. A large number of prudent farmers lost all their savings, a severe, perhaps even a lethal, blow to what remained of the old class of small freeholders.

The circumstances of the age were even more merciless to the labourers (about a hundred thousand of them, two on average to each farmer), with their low wages and with underemployment rampant among them. According to Dewi Wyn of Eifion in 1819, the labourer 'shared the needs of one between nine', and J. R. Jones of Ramoth wrote of 'that hard and restrictive time . . . when . . . almost everyone was under his full burden'. The distress in the countryside was expressed in riots – at Carmarthen in 1818, at Aber-miwl in 1819, at Maenclochog in 1820, on Mynydd Bach in Cardiganshire from 1820 to 1827 ('the war of the Little Englishman'), at Dryslwyn in 1826 and at Llanwnda in 1827. Conscientious landowners believed that the answer lay in reorganizing farms in order to create units large enough to offer a tenant an adequate living. This policy further reduced the number of holdings available for letting, and some landlords were prepared to assist their more impoverished tenants to emigrate to America, a practice which savoured of the clearances which the lairds of the Scottish Highlands were so eager to promote. The distress of the inhabitants of Penllyn is vividly described in the autobiography of Ap Vychan, and the poverty of the people around Llangwm (Denbighshire) is portrayed in Hugh Evans's remarkable book, *Cwm Eithin* (The Gorse Glen), but it would appear that deprivation was at its worst in the three counties of the south-west, where the condition of the inhabitants was frequently compared with that of the Irish.

The impoverished were protected from starvation by the Poor Law. For a century and more after its passage, the act of 1601 was a dead letter in most of Wales. In the first half of the eighteenth century, Wrexham was the only parish in the diocese of St Asaph which regularly levied a poor rate. In the second half of the century, under the pressure of population growth, Wrexham's example was followed by most parishes, thus causing a marked increase in the expenditure upon poor relief. The total poor rate collected in England and Wales in 1785 amounted to two million pounds; it was over seven million in 1819. (The severe inflation of the period should be borne in mind.) In 1819, £40,000 was spent in Denbighshire and a similar sum in Montgomeryshire, which, although considerably less populous, was burdened by frequent depressions in the woollen industry. Originally, the Poor Law was an expedient reserved for times of crisis, but by 1819 it had become a regular feature of society. Assistance was not restricted to the old and the infirm. No district of Wales adopted the Spleenhamland system, the system whereby labourers' wages were regularly supplemented from the rates; nevertheless, there is evidence that Welsh parishes made payments to large families even if the head of the household was employed. In some areas, attempts were made to solve the problem of unemployment by building workhouses. There was one within the walls of Caernarfon Castle in the 1790s, but such schemes were rarely successful.

Landlords were prepared to assist the poor; in the 1820s, the marquess of Bute spent 8 per cent of the income of the Cardiff Castle estate on philanthropic activities. Doubtless such expenditure was inspired by charitable motives; openhandedness was, however, an essential attribute for a landlord intent upon winning elections, and he was also anxious to ensure that his supporters remained on the list of voters – those who received parish relief were deprived of the vote. To the grossly deprived, begging was an option and Ap Vychan records that his father sent him to Cardiganshire, of all places, to beg. The more prudent elements sought security through the Friendly Societies. There were over thirty such societies in Merthyr in 1830, but they were also established in rural areas – in Llansilin, for example, and in Llanymynech and in Ysbyty Ifan.

With the cost of poor relief rising so rapidly, the parish authorities were under increasing pressure to be niggardly in responding to the claims of the needy and to remind them that it was a disgrace to be 'on the parish'. Families with possessions of any value were denied relief, and Ap Vychan remembered with horror his bedridden father being deprived of his mattress by the overseer of Llanuwchllyn. The responsibility of the parish was limited to those who had dwelt within its boundaries for a year or more. Those who had not were obliged to return to their birthplace, and in 1829 J. H. Moddridge, a conscientious Monmouthshire magistrate, complained that the task of sending them home was absorbing almost all his energies. The kingdom was well able to afford its seven million pound annual expenditure on the poor. At the time, however, it seemed an unsupportable burden, and there were eloquent demands for a reduction in taxation. In the wake of fears that a social explosion was imminent, the question of the 'condition of the people' attracted the attention of many in public life.

It was a question which received extensive consideration in the press, a medium which expanded rapidly in the early decades of the nineteenth century. *The Cambrian*, Wales's first weekly newspaper and the voice of the Whiggery of the businessmen of Swansea, was founded in 1804; it was followed by *The North Wales Chronicle* (1807) and *The Carmarthen Journal* (1810), weeklies more inclined to Toryism. The first Welsh language weekly, *Seren Gomer*, was established in 1814 by Joseph Harris (Gomer), a Baptist minister at Swansea. Apart from *Yr Eurgrawn Wesleyaidd*, all previous efforts to establish a Welsh periodical had failed, and the *Seren Gomer* also perished within a year. In the early nineteenth century, the launching of a periodical was a considerable venture; its publishers were burdened by a duty of fourpence per issue and by taxes on paper and advertisements; all periodicals faced the hostility of the authorities and their distribution was hampered by the high cost of postage. The launching of a Welsh periodical was even more of a venture, for its potential readers belonged to the poorer classes of society and it could not – as could a paper like *The Cambrian* – depend upon extensive advertising. It is hardly surprising, therefore, that so many Welsh periodicals failed; indeed it could be considered a matter of some astonishment that the Welsh periodical press became established at all. But it did. *Seren Gomer* was revived as a fortnightly in 1818 (a monthly from 1820) and, before the end of the 1820s, *Y Gwyleidydd*, *Y Dysgedydd*, *Lleuad yr Oes*, *Goleuad Cymru*, *Y Drysorfa* and *Yr Efengylydd* had also appeared. The greater part of these periodicals consisted of theological and literary articles, but they also discussed the issues of the day and it was through them that the Welsh people received their political education.

In the publications of the Nonconformists, the cause most frequently ventilated was the need to redress the grievances of chapel-goers – tithe, church rate, the obligation to marry in the parish church, and the varied privileges of the State Church. These were issues which concerned the middle-class Nonconformists of the great towns of England. Under their leadership, with the Unitarians in the vanguard, the Test and Corporation Acts – the acts which confined public office to members of the Established Church – were repealed in 1828. In itself, this victory had little significance, for little use had been made of the acts for generations; yet the repeal was a foretaste of more ferocious battles in the future, when the relationship between religion and the state would become the central issue of Welsh politics.

Following legislation enhancing the status of Protestant Nonconformists, it was difficult to deny the claims of Catholic Nonconformists. The struggle which came to its climax in 1829 with the Catholic Emancipation Act was far more bitter. In the 1820s, Roman Catholicism hardly existed in Wales: in 1829, the country had no more than five centres where mass was regularly celebrated. But so strong was the anti-papal tradition that the *Carmarthen Journal* asserted that for every Welshman supporting emancipation there were two hundred who opposed it. The leaders of Nonconformity were forced to choose between their sectarian prejudices and their political beliefs. Although they hated papism as a religion, the logic of their liberalism forced some of them – including the editors of *Y Dysgedydd* and *Seren Gomer* – to support the rights of Roman Catholics. It was argued that 'all legislative interference on religious matters is unreasonable, unjust . . . and an attack upon the entire community'. Such comments were not only made by the Old Dissenters, for the above words are part of a statement by the members of Jewin Calvinistic Methodist Chapel in London. The members of Jewin were reprimanded by the leaders of Welsh Calvinistic Methodism for their forthright declaration, but the fact that it was made is proof that by the late 1820s not all Methodists agreed with the reactionary attitudes of the leaders of their denomination.

It was John Elias who insisted upon reprimanding the progressive members of Jewin Chapel. Following the death of Thomas Jones in 1820, Elias became the leader of Welsh Methodism and despite (or perhaps because of) the narrowness of his vision he presided over a rapid expansion in the history of his denomination. Indeed, the first half of the nineteenth century was a period of remarkable growth for all the Nonconformist denominations of Wales. By 1851 there were 2,813 chapels in the country, the result of a building programme which is among the most striking happenings in Welsh history. Between 1801 and 1851, it is estimated that a chapel was completed in Wales every eight days. The growth of Nonconformity was promoted by a number of factors. The first half of the nineteenth century was the golden age of the itinerant preachers, with stars such as the Methodist, John Elias (1774–1841), the Baptist, Christmas Evans

(1766–1836) and the Independent, William Williams (Williams o'r Wern; 1781–1840). Preaching tours were in great vogue and as Elias and his like were effective communicators they attracted thousands of listeners. In the parish of Llanynghenedl (Anglesey), the vicar reported in 1814 that 'nine out of ten follow the itinerant preachers without caring to what sect they belong'. The enthusiasm was fed by recurrent revivals; some of them were local in their influence, but others, such as those of 1806, 1809, 1819, 1825, 1839 and 1849, aroused passions over a wide area.

The growth of Nonconformity in the industrial areas was particularly striking. There, the rigid organization of the Established Church, with its parish churches frequently situated far from the new communities, proved unable to meet the needs of those who flooded to work in the furnaces, the collieries and the quarries. The vacuum was filled by the chapels, the creation of the people themselves. The appeal of the chapels was strengthened by their atmosphere of equality, their emotional services, their emphasis upon self-culture and the opportunity they provided for laymen to play a prominent role. To many an intelligent member of the working class, Nonconformity was a private, controllable world – in stark contrast with the public world, where no clear role was available to him. These factors were also at work in England; by the mid nineteenth century, that country had many districts, especially in the industrial areas of the north, which teemed with chapels. Nevertheless, the appeal of Nonconformity was weaker in England than it was in Wales. In 1851, 52 per cent of the seats available in places of worship in England were those of the Established Church; in Wales the proportion was 32 per cent. The Welshness of Nonconformity was the chief cause of the difference. The Church of England had made an honourable contribution to Welsh culture, but by the early nineteenth century the upper ranks of the Anglican ministry in Wales had for generations been totally anglicized. Although there were a number of Welsh enthusiasts among the clergy, many parsons considered that their primary duty was to be chaplain to the local landowning families, families which had long been wholly English in speech. In the chapel, there were at least three Welsh services on Sunday and through the chapel the monoglot Welsh could participate in a host of other activities held in the only language they understood.

The growth of Nonconformity was not without its troubles. There were lengthy debates concerning Calvinism, some of them very bitter. Ieuan Gwynedd (1820–52) shuddered on remembering quarrels such as that between Michael Jones, the Independent minister at Llanuwch-llyn, and the 'Old People', advocates of a strict interpretation of the exclusiveness of redemption. 'They shrink the souls of men,' he declared, 'so that they cannot tolerate anything, nor feel anything, except their own shibboleths.' The autocracy of John Elias caused distress to such men as John Jones (1796–1857) and Lewis Edwards (1809–87), the leaders of the younger generation of Methodists. A host of talentless preachers sought to imitate the eloquence of the stars of the pulpit. Their antics were made the subject of satire by David Owen (Brutus) and caused distress to Lewis Edwards, who was troubled by the 'great folly of nurturing an ignorant ministry'. Despite the increase in the support for Nonconformity, only a minority of those attending the chapels were full members. Many of the 'hearers' slipped from the narrow path and there were frequent complaints that religion was in decline. Nevertheless, in the first half of the nineteenth century the range of the activities of Welsh Nonconformists was astonishing, as they 'crystallized the revival', to quote R. Tudur Jones. Campaigns were conducted to evangelize the 'black districts' of Wales, in particular the large towns and the anglicized rural areas, and missions were organized to Tahiti, Madagascar, Brittany and Assam.

Challenged by the growth of Nonconformity, the members of the Established Church were obliged to consider the implications of their inability to retain the allegiance of the bulk of the population. This was a matter of great concern, particularly to the Anglican evangelicals, a powerful group within the Church in the early decades of the nineteenth century. It was thought that the influence of the Establishment could be restored through creating a network of schools in which the children of the poor would be trained in the principles of the State Church. That was the purpose of the National Society, established in 1811. The British authorities – unlike those in France, Austria and Prussia – did not believe that the provision of education was part of the responsibility of the state. Thus the National Society and the British and Foreign Society (established in 1814 to promote non-sectarian education) were obliged to depend upon voluntary contributions. By using the monitor system, few teachers were needed, and it was estimated that a child could be educated for a year at a cost of five shillings. The National Society benefited from the diocesan system and from the readiness of landowners to endow Anglican education, advantages not available to the British Society. In consequence, by 1833, when the government first made financial contributions to schools, there were almost a hundred and fifty National schools in Wales compared with only about fifteen British schools. This was a serious imbalance in a country which was becoming increasingly Nonconformist and was to be the cause of widespread discontent in later years.

The Established Church also succeeded in establishing in Wales a centre for the training of clergy. Before the opening of St David's College, Lampeter, in 1827, the grammar schools – some of which were of a high standard – were virtually the only places of education available for the training of prospective Welsh clerics, for few of them could afford to go to Oxford or Cambridge. The college at Lampeter was intended to serve the diocese of St David's, which included over half the surface area of Wales, and in its early years it was in many ways a curious institution. Nevertheless, the college was the harbinger of the revival of the Anglican Church in Wales. Its founder was Thomas Burgess, bishop of St David's from 1803 to 1825, the first Welsh bishop for generations to devote himself to his duties. In the 1820s, the Anglicans came to realize the extent of the challenge represented by the condition of their Church in the diocese of Llandaf. There, the cathedral was in ruins, the bishop was homeless and Nonconformists in the industrial areas were ten times more numerous than were the adherents of the Church. Yet, as the ecclesiastical structure was still essentially medieval, it was impossible to solve such problems until the administration of the Church was reformed, and that did not occur until the 1830s.

Burgess was a believer in the distinguished and Protestant origins of the Welsh Church and was enthusiastically in favour of clergy who could preach in Welsh, in particular in order to counteract the tendency of the monoglot Welsh, in their desire to attend services in their mother tongue, to become chapel-goers. He was equally enthusiastically in favour of giving church patronage to Welsh cultural activities. It was his suggestion which led in 1818 to the creation of the Cambrian Societies, the bodies responsible for organizing the provincial *eisteddfodau*. The scheme was put together at the Bishop's Palace in Abergwili, an echo in some ways of the age of Richard Davies. By the first decade of the nineteenth century, the *eisteddfodau* of the Gwyneddigion had come to an end and, when the festivals were revived in 1819, the leadership came, not from political radicals, but from *'yr hen bersoniaid llengar'* (the old literature-loving parsons), to quote R. T. Jenkins's evocative phrase. A score and more of the clergy were active in Welsh literary and antiquarian studies in the 1820s and 1830s, a period when such matters had little appeal for Nonconformist ministers. Unlike the ministers, the parsons had generally received a classical education and they had the learning and the leisure to study and write. They were aware of the appeal of the romanticism which was responsible for inspiring cultural nationalism throughout western and central Europe. The border counties were the main centre of the activities of the 'literature loving persons'. Until his death in 1829, John Jenkins, who lived in the vicarage of Ceri in Montgomeryshire, provided the meeting-place of the promoters of the Welsh awakening, and in the two subsequent decades Abergavenny, the centre of the 'excitation in Gwent', was to play a key role. Those areas where native traditions were under threat were the first in which efforts to safeguard them were made, a phenomenon seen in other parts of Europe. It was accepted that leadership should be in the hands of the London Welsh, and to that end the Society of Cymmrodorion was revived in 1820.

Linked with this upsurge in Welsh activities was the attempt to win over the landed gentry. It was partly successful – the squire of Wynnstay, the owner of the largest estate in Wales, was the president of the revived Cymmrodorion. But the price paid for the patronage of the anglicized gentry was the acceptance of English as the medium of the provincial *eisteddfodau*, and also of music, largely of English if not of Italian origin, as the principal form of activity. Perhaps the chief contribution of the eisteddfod movement was that it led to the establishment of a large number of local *eisteddfodau*, a central development in the cultural life of nineteenth-century Wales. The literature produced by the provincial *eisteddfodau* was mediocre, although there are some fine passages in *Dinystr Jerusalem* (1824), the work of Eben Fardd, one of the few Methodists involved with the eisteddfod. Indeed, the greatest glories of Welsh literature in the early nineteenth century are to be found in the works of those who were not straining consciously to make a contribution to the literary tradition. The work of the hymn writers was especially distinguished, with Ann Griffiths shining forth in a talented company. There were also substantial contributions by prose writers, in particular Robert Jones of Rhos-lan, the historian of the Methodist Revival.

While institutions were created to give expression to the cultural identity of Wales, the country was deprived of the only legal and administrative institutions which were uniquely Welsh. In 1830, after being in existence for almost three hundred years, the Great Sessions and the chanceries of Wales were abolished, thus causing Wales to be wholly absorbed into England in legal and administrative matters. The Great Sessions had for centuries been the butt of the mockery of Welsh satirists and the object of the jealousy of the upholders of the chief courts in London. Yet they had their defenders, in particular the Tory members of parliament from west Wales. Their main argument was the cost and inconvenience which the Welsh would suffer as a result of abolition, although John Jones, the member for Carmarthen, praised the Great Sessions because they were a specifically Welsh institution. To men like the earl of Cawdor, this was precisely the argument against them, and he expressed the hope that Lyndhurst, the Lord Chancellor, would be recognized as the 'greatest benefactor in Welsh history' as he 'completed the work began by Henry VIII by abolishing all differences and truly uniting the inhabitants of England and Wales'.

The abolition of the Great Sessions was almost the last action of the duke of Wellington's government before it fell amidst bitter recriminations in November 1830. The political crisis was intensified by the severe depression of the winter of 1830, a period of widespread protest by farm workers, the labourers of the Vale of Glamorgan among them. There were also protests by industrial workers, including marches in the wool towns of Montgomeryshire and demonstrations by the colliers of the north-east. There, in Bagillt, Flintshire, a branch of the Friendly Associated Coal Miners Union was founded in November 1830, the first evidence of formal trade-unionism in Wales. The reaction of middle-class leaders to the problems of the age was to demand the reform of parliament. The issue had been raised in the 1790s, but a succession of reactionary governments had caused it to be deleted from the political agenda. Wellington's successor, the Whig, Earl Grey, had no choice but to introduce a Reform Bill. With the masses fervently in favour of the bill, and with the Tories fervently against it, the years 1830–32 were a period of political excitement without parallel since the Civil War.

The Welsh electoral system was not as full of abuses as was that of England. In England, some constituencies were virtually uninhabited while large towns such as Birmingham and Manchester had no representation at all. Although the representation of Wales was firmly under the influence of the landowners, there was hardly a constituency which was totally subservient to a single family, the situation in many English boroughs. Yet the Welsh system of representation had little to commend it. With twenty-seven members compared with forty-four from Cornwall, Wales's voice at Westminster was weak. Radnorshire had 25,000 inhabitants and Glamorgan 127,000, but the two counties had the same representation. The populous town of Merthyr was outside the system of contributory boroughs, although that system included a number of small villages. In the boroughs, the franchise was determined by a complexity of rules and the number of voters could vary from half a dozen to many hundreds. The vote was restricted to one in eight, at most, of adult males. The opportunity to vote did not often occur; there were no contests in any of the seats of Wales in the general election of 1830 and when voting did occur it was done publicly under the scrutiny of the agents of landed estates. During a contest 'most men have to drink beer enough to make them mad' to quote *Seren Gomer*, the supporters of William Paxton swallowed 200,000 pints of beer and 11,068 bottles of liquor during the electoral campaign in Carmarthenshire in 1802, and in Pembrokeshire in 1831 one candidate spent £15,000 in the taverns of Haverfordwest alone.

Jac Glan-y-gors and others had drawn attention to the abuses of the system thirty years previously, and this was done again, rather less boldly, by the Welsh periodicals of the 1820s. In 1831, reform meetings were held throughout Wales, with the industrialists – who resented the power of the landowners – being particularly vocal. The notion arose that the reform of parliament would lead to a new world and there was a ferocious reaction when Grey's bill was defeated in April 1831. A riot occurred at Carmarthen, a town with a long history of electoral violence, and the reform agitation played a significant part in the great upheaval which shook Merthyr in June 1831.

When the Reform Bill became law in June 1832, the Welsh celebrated with bands marching and church bells pealing. The act gave Wales five additional members: the representation of the counties of Glamorgan, Carmarthen and Denbigh was raised from one to two, a borough seat was created for Merthyr and the boroughs of Glamorgan were split into two, with one seat centred on Cardiff and the other on Swansea. The borough franchise was reformed by granting the vote to men who held real estate worth at least £10 a year. In the counties the rights of the forty-shilling freeholders were confirmed, but the vote was also granted to tenants who paid an annual rent of £50 or more. Although the working class had campaigned vigorously in favour of the Reform Bill, hardly any members of that class obtained the vote as a result of it; indeed, in some boroughs the new franchise was less 'democratic' than the old. After 1832, about one adult male in five had the vote, but as the £50 tenant was wholly under the thumb of his landlord and as the secret ballot was not granted, the ability of the landowners to control the parliamentary representation of Wales was hardly impaired. The squire of Nanteos was elected to represent Cardiganshire in 1816 and he was succeeded by the squire of Trawsgoed in 1852, one of the many examples which prove that the old representative pattern did not end in 1832. The situation was similar in the boroughs, apart from Swansea and Merthyr where industrialists were successful. Yet the 'industrial feudalism' which ensured the success of J. J. Guest at Merthyr was in many respects similar to the system which allowed the squire of Nanteos to maintain his hold upon Cardiganshire.

The fact that there was a seat available to J. J. Guest can be attributed to insurrection, for the government had originally rejected demands to give Merthyr its own member. The Merthyr Rising in 1831 (and it was a rising rather than a riot) was the most ferocious and bloody event in the history of industrial Britain. Since its beginning as an industrial community, Merthyr had been a stronghold of radicalism, with the Unitarians in the lead. In the spring of 1831, when the inhabitants were already excited by the reform agitation, they were angered by the decision of William Crawshay, owner of the Cyfarthfa Ironworks, to lower the wages of his employees. Huge crowds gathered and strong feelings were expressed, especially concerning the Court of Requests, the institution which dealt with small debts. The court-house was destroyed on 1 June; by the following day, the town was in the hands of the crowd and the magistrates were under siege in the Castle Hotel. There, J. Bruce Pryce, Merthyr's stipendiary magistrate, wrote a dramatic letter to the marquess of Bute, the lord lieutenant of Glamorgan, declaring that 'we need every soldier we can get hold of'. Eighty men of the Argyll and Sutherland Highlanders reached Merthyr on 3 June and they were faced by a crowd of perhaps ten thousand. In a confrontation outside the Castle Hotel, about twenty members of the crowd were shot dead. By 1831, at least eighty thousand people lived within fifteen miles of Merthyr. Their feelings were inflamed by the slaughter. Yeomanry sent from Swansea were disarmed and the red flag was raised – probably the first time for that to happen in Britain. More soldiers were sent to Merthyr and after a number of fierce struggles the town was again in the possession of the forces of the state by 8 June.

In the court cases which followed the rising, two men were condemned to death. The sentence on Lewis Lewis (Lewsyn yr Heliwr) was commuted to exile for life, although he seems to have been the most prominent of the leaders of the crowd. Richard Lewis (Dic Penderyn) was found guilty of wounding a Scottish soldier and was hanged in Cardiff Gaol on 31 July 1831. The inhabitants of Merthyr were convinced that he was innocent; indeed, years later, another man confessed to the crime for which Dic was executed. Over eleven thousand people petitioned against the sentence and J. Tregelles Price, the Neath ironmaster and Quaker, visited Viscount Melbourne, the Home Secretary, to plead for Dic's life. '*O Arglwydd, dyma gamwedd*' (Oh Lord, this is an injustice) were Dic's last words, and a vast crowd accompanied his body from Cardiff to the churchyard at Aberafan, his place of birth. Because his execution was believed to have been unjust, Dic was seen as Wales's first working-class martyr. He had no more of a role in the rising than had thousands of others. As Gwyn A. Williams argued, he was not the face above the crowd but a face in the crowd, a face which the Welsh worker could perceive as his own.

The rising was not the only tribulation suffered by the people of Merthyr in 1831. During the summer of that year, the example set by Flintshire was followed and branches of the miners' union were established in Merthyr and its surroundings. The rising was an instinctive reaction; joining a union was a considered reaction. Gwyn A. Williams suggests that the step from the instinctive to the considered was proof that the primitive era in the history of the working class of the south Wales coalfield had come to an end. To the authorities and the employers, unionism was more dangerous than insurrection. In condemning the union, they received the support of Nonconformist leaders who were appalled by the secret oaths sworn by unionists. In May, most of the ironmasters insisted that their workers should choose between the union and employment. At least four thousand unionists were dismissed, and the employers – in defiance of the law – ensured that poor relief should not be available to them. With soldiers harrying the people and with hunger oppressing the families of those dismissed, the union had ceased to exist by November 1831. Similar steps were taken by employers in the north Wales coalfield, where there was considerable unrest during the winter of 1830–31. There also the mining districts experienced military occupation, and unionism had been stamped out in Denbighshire and Flintshire by the end of 1831.

As the attempts to create an effective unionism had failed, violence seemed to be an option once more. The years 1832–4 saw the peak of the activity of the Scotch Cattle, with the most ferocious campaigns occurring in the Monmouthshire valleys. The property of employers was destroyed, mass meetings were held on the mountains to discuss wages and conditions of employment, and those workers who ignored the decisions made in them were threatened. The protesters were particularly incensed by the continuance of the custom of paying workers in tokens which could be exchanged in company shops, a practice specifically outlawed by the Anti-Truck Act of 1831. In 1834, one of the protesters, Edward Morgan, was hanged in Monmouth Gaol, the climax of the successful campaign by the authorities to suppress the Scotch Cattle.

In the same year, Robert Owen sought to establish a single movement for the working class through his Grand National Consolidated Trades Union. Owen was a native of Newtown, although he lived there only for the first ten years and the last year of his long life (1771–1858). Through his prolific writings, he brought a more specifically socialist emphasis into the thinking of the British working class. It was not sufficient to demand fairness for the workers within the system as it stood; as it was the workers who created the wealth of the country, the system was fundamentally wrong. Owen's ideas were promoted by the bilingual monthly *Y Gweithiwr/The Worker*, Wales's first working-class periodical, but as Owen had highly unorthodox religious views he was opposed by the devout of all denominations. Owenite unionism was shallow in its foundations and rickety in its structure. The exiling of the Tolpuddle Martyrs (April 1834) was a death blow to it, and decades would go by before unionism again became a dynamic force in Wales.

Yet social unrest did not fade away and the years 1834–45 were among the most troubled in the history of Wales. One of the reasons for the unrest was working-class reaction to the act passed in 1834 to reform the Poor Law. Concern over increasing expenditure on poor relief has already been noted, expenditure which by the 1830s represented a quarter of the costs incurred by the British state. Had it produced social stability it would have been considered a price worth paying, but following the rural unrest of 1829–30 it was argued that poor relief encouraged rather than averted instability. The Poor Law Amendment Act of 1834 laid down that no one was to receive relief at home. The indigent would have to move to the workhouse before receiving assistance, and it was intended that conditions of life there should be worse than anything experienced by even the poorest-paid worker in the outside world. As the authors of the act had accepted Malthus's ideas concerning the dangers of population growth, married couples were not allowed to cohabit in the workhouse and, as it was believed that females would be more chaste if the burden of maintaining a bastard child fell upon the mother alone, the insistence that fathers should contribute to the maintenance of an illegitimate child was largely abandoned. Parishes were grouped into unions – Wales had forty-eight of them – and each union was obliged to build a workhouse. The unions were administered by boards consisting of justices of the peace and elected members, and the boards were answerable to the Poor Law Commissioners at their headquarters at Somerset House in London. The architect of the act was Edwin Chadwick, a disciple of Jeremy Bentham, and it reflected the faith in efficient centralization which was one of the hallmarks of Utilitarianism.

The new system had its virtues – there was, for example, a marked improvement in the medical care received by the poor – but it was almost universally loathed. The gentry considered it to be an attack upon local autonomy, and magistrates were annoyed at having to share their power with elected members. As residents were not permitted to leave the workhouse, they could not attend Nonconformist services, a fact condemned by Nonconformist leaders. To the humane, it appeared appalling that families should be separated and that the poor should be treated as if they were criminals – indeed, in Carmarthen better food was served in the prison than in the

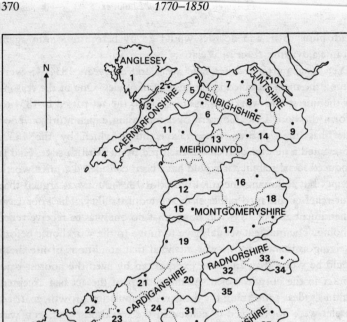

——— The boundaries of registration counties
··········· The boundaries of registration districts and Poor Law Unions
•   Workhouse built by 1871

1	Anglesey	13	Bala	25	Haverfordwest	37	Hay
2	Bangor	14	Corwen	26	Narberth	38	Crickhowell
3	Caernarfon	15	Machynlleth	27	Pembroke	39	Swansea
4	Pwllheli	16	Llanfyllin	28	Carmarthen	40	Neath
5	Conwy	17	Newtown	29	Llandeilo	41	Merthyr Tydfil
6	Llanrwst	18	Montgomery	30	Llanelli	42	Bridgend
7	St Asaph	19	Aberystwyth	31	Llandovery	43	Cardiff
8	Rhuthun	20	Tregaron	32	Rhayader	44	Abergavenny
9	Wrexham	21	Aberaeron	33	Knighton	45	Monmouth
10	Holywell	22	Cardigan	34	Presteigne	46	Pontypool
11	Ffestiniog	23	Newcastle Emlyn	35	Builth	47	Newport
12	Dolgellau	24	Lampeter	36	Brecon	48	Chepstow

Poor Law Unions, registration counties and registration districts

workhouse. The decline in the level of poor rate which occurred immediately after the passage of the act was welcomed, but ratepayers were angered when it increased again because of the cost of building workhouses and paying union officials. For the poor themselves, the workhouse was a nightmare, and it was claimed in Carmarthenshire in 1843 that people preferred to die rather than to enter it. The Welsh authorities were slow and reluctant in implementing the act; many unions continued to provide relief in the home, and at Merthyr the guardians delayed building a workhouse until 1853. An Assistant Poor Law Commissioner was attacked by a crowd in Llanfair Caereinion in 1837; the militia had to be called to defend Carmarthen workhouse in 1838, and an attempt was made to burn down the workhouse at Narberth in 1839.

The Poor Law Amendment Act was one of a number of reform measures passed in the 1830s. As parliament had been reformed in 1832, it was difficult to deny the need to reform the borough corporations. Commissioners were appointed to investigate them in 1832; although their report was prejudiced, they recorded a mass of examples of corruption, of interference by powerful landowners and of the subjection of the interests of boroughs to party purposes. The report of the commission provided evidence relating to fifty-six places in Wales which enjoyed some degree of borough status. The Municipal Corporations Act of 1835 recognized only twenty of them. The twenty were to have councils elected by all adult male ratepayers, and the councils were given wide powers to provide public services. But they were not obliged to provide them, for almost all legislation relating to local government was permissive rather than mandatory. Most of the Welsh boroughs recognized in 1835 proved dilatory. The situation was worse in boroughs not recognized, some of which – Llanelli, for example, with six thousand inhabitants – were places of considerable size. Furthermore, there were many urban centres which the commissioners did not consider at all. Wrexham succeeded in gaining borough status in 1857, but Merthyr did not do so until 1905. Despite the act of 1835, most of the heavily populated areas of Wales would have to depend, at least until the last years of the nineteenth century, upon a hotchpotch of boards and committees. That would also be the fate of the counties, units bereft of any representative element until 1889. It is hardly surprising that words such as 'rudimentary', 'chaotic' and 'corrupt' were those most frequently

used by commentators on nineteenth-century British local government.

   In view of the reforming zeal of the 1830s, the Church of England
could not avoid coming under scrutiny. The ecclesiastical establishment was the favourite target of the radicals, while among the Whigs
and even some of the Tories it was accepted that the arguments in
favour of its reorganization were unanswerable. The task was begun
in 1833, when the number of Irish dioceses was halved. The Ecclesiastical Commission was founded in 1836, and it was given extensive
powers to administer the finances of the Church and to reform its
organization. Among the recommendations of the Commission were
the union of the sees of Bangor and St Asaph, and of those of Llandaf
and Bristol, plans abandoned following a vigorous campaign by Welsh
Anglicans. Between 1834 and 1840, a series of bills was passed to
reform the Church: the ability of clerics to hold numerous livings was
curbed; tithe was to be paid not in produce but in money; the state
was given the authority to register births, marriages and deaths; the
duty of the Church to hold services in the Welsh language was
reasserted; efforts were made to equalize the salaries of clerics; money
was set aside to establish new parishes. These measures proved the
necessary precondition for a remarkable revival in the history of the
Church – in Wales perhaps more than anywhere.

   Nevertheless, it was a distressful experience for Churchmen to
realize how helpless the Church was when faced by a state determined
to reform it and to redistribute its property. That experience gave rise
to the Oxford Movement, a sincere attempt to consider where lay the
source of authority within the Church of England. The leading
theologian J. H. Newman could not tolerate the notion that the source
was parliament, an assembly that was no longer necessarily Anglican.
Newman and his associates insisted that the authority of the Church
derived from the fact that its bishops were in the apostolic succession,
an argument they emphasized in a series of tracts published between
1833 and 1841. To zealous Protestants, this was a notion which
savoured of popery. The fears of the opponents of the Oxford Movement were intensified as the followers of Newman – Isaac Williams
of Llangorwen near Aberystwyth among them – adopted elaborate
ceremonies and polished ritual. Fear became terror in 1845 when
Newman was received into the Roman Catholic Church. In the
following decades, some of the most prominent of the clerics of

Wales would belong to the 'high' wing of the Church. Through their efforts, the ancient heritage of the Welsh Church came to be increasingly appreciated and the beauty of holiness was offered to some of the most deprived communities in Wales.

Yet, in the Wales of the mid nineteenth century, the ideas of the Oxford Movement could not but add to denominational bitterness. The Calvinistic Methodists felt little antagonism towards an Anglicanism which was Protestant, but their anger was aroused by an Anglicanism which emphasized its Catholicism – one of the chief reasons why the Connexion was prepared to warm to the Old Dissenters. The Dissenters were increasingly eager to challenge the privileges of the Church of England. In 1833, the Protestant Dissenting Deputies declared that the Church Establishment was unjust and unscriptural, and they collected a petition bearing 343,000 names. The Nonconformists won a victory in 1836 when marriages were permitted in chapels, but the Tithe Act of that year was a blow to them. As a result of the act, maps were compiled which are a splendid source of information on the ownership and use of land, but more relevant at the time was the fact that the change in the method of collecting the tithe added to the burdens of farmers.

The increasing confidence of the Nonconformists may be seen at its clearest in their resistance to the Church Rate, the rate levied upon parishioners in order to maintain the building and the ceremonies of the parish church. That resistance had particular significance, for it represented the beginnings of the radical Nonconformist protest which was to be so central a feature of the politics of late-nineteenth-century Wales; indeed, it is in the context of the protest against the rate that the word 'radical' was first used in Welsh. Most of the grievances of the Nonconformists could be alleviated only through legislation, but it was the parishioners who determined the rate and thus it was the perfect target for a local campaign. Merthyr levied no rate after 1836, an example followed by a large number of the parishes of Wales in the following years, much to the detriment of many old buildings and to the distress of churchwardens. Churchwardens could be Nonconformists, as was David Jones of Llan-non, Carmarthenshire, who died as the result of troubles relating to the rate.

The Nonconformists' resistance to the Church Rate suggests that they were increasingly prepared to assume leadership. The same readiness may be found in the history of the Temperance Movement, a movement which struck deep roots in Wales in the 1830s. Old rural Wales had been a country in which lord and peasant tippled with enthusiasm. The gentry sobered somewhat in the early nineteenth century, but it was quite otherwise among those who flooded into the industrial districts, where almost every feature of life served to intensify the innate beer-loving character of the Welsh. Following the Beer Act of 1830, there was a huge increase in the number of drinking places; in Blackwood in 1842 there was one for every five inhabitants, and the Dowlais Ironworks was surrounded by two hundred taverns. Over-indulgence was a cause of concern to many: to the employer, for it undermined his efforts to create a disciplined workforce; to working-class wives who were jealous of the public house, 'the masculine republic', and who were bitter when the household's meagre resources were spent on drink; to the more serious of the working class, who were saddened by the sodden state of their fellow-workers; to the respectable of every rank, who were disgusted by public drunkenness. There was therefore an eager welcome for the temperance societies, organizations first established in the United States in the 1820s. The first such society among the Welsh was that set up in 1831 by Welsh migrants to Manchester, but by 1835 there were twenty-five societies within the borders of Wales itself.

The emphasis of the earliest societies was upon moderation, and the members of the Ebbw Vale Temperance Society were allowed to drink two pints of beer a day. But soon the virtues of total abstinence were advocated and the first teetotal society in Wales was founded in Llanfechell (Anglesey) in 1835. With its emphasis upon the nurturing of moral and self-reliant individuals, temperance was remarkably well-suited to form part of the ethos of nineteenth-century Nonconformity. It was the ministers who led the societies and the methods of religious revivalism were used to spread the message. A temperance sub-culture of considerable energy emerged, with periodicals, meetings, songs, orders, ceremonies, hotels and pledges, and by 1850 teetotalism had been absorbed into the moralistic system of Nonconformity. The original intention of the temperance advocates was to create a sober society through example and persuasion, but by the middle of the century the demand arose for legislation to restrict or prohibit the liquor trade. Thus the temperance movement was transformed from a moral crusade into a political campaign and became another element in the legislative programme of the Nonconformists.

The temperance societies can be interpreted as part of the urge for self-improvement which played such a significant part in the history of the nineteenth-century working class. The leaders of working-class movements argued that it was the failings of the poor which allowed the rich to retain authority and that the workers needed to prove themselves worthy of the power they sought. This belief was central to the ideas of the Chartist Movement, the main channel for the unrest which swept through the industrial communities of Britain between 1836 and 1842. It crystallized around the six-point charter compiled by the London Workingmen's Association in 1838, a manifesto for transforming Britain into a democracy (for men at least). The movement, however, had wider implications. The Chartists were motivated in part by the anger felt by members of the working class when they realized that they had gained nothing from the Reform Act of 1832. Furthermore, the supporters of the movement were embittered by the effects of a severe depression, the iniquities of the new Poor Law and the frustration which sprang from their inability to create a viable trade-union movement. Above all, they wished to give shape and meaning to their increasing consciousness of their existence as a class.

Of the violent outbreaks associated with Chartism, the most serious occurred in Wales; they reflected not only the unique nature of the experience of Welsh industrial communities but also – as Ivor Wilks has argued – the essential Welshness of those communities. The strongholds of Chartism in Wales were the south Wales coalfield, the town of Carmarthen and the wool towns of Montgomeryshire. The most prominent Chartist in Carmarthen was the solicitor Hugh Williams, a brother-in-law of the radical politician Richard Cobden and a friend of Henry Hetherington, one of the compilers of the Charter and a disciple of Robert Owen. Hetherington's friends also included Thomas Powell and Charles Jones, the leaders of Montgomeryshire Chartism. In Llanelli, the Charter was warmly welcomed by David Rees, the editor of *Y Diwygiwr* (The Reformer, established in 1835), a periodical which was among the most powerful agents in creating a radical public opinion in Wales. The leading Chartists in Glamorgan were the Unitarian, Morgan Williams of Merthyr, and that astounding phenomenon, Dr William Price of Llantrisant. The chief figure in Monmouthshire was John Frost, a man who had proved his radicalism in struggles concerning the corporation of Newport. The

Chartists of the coalfield attended mass meetings where they were excited by the oratory of Henry Vincent, editor of the *Western Vindicator*, a paper published at Bristol which included articles in Welsh.

Most of the Chartists sought to achieve their aims through 'moral suasion' – by spreading propaganda, organizing petitions and arranging demonstrations. At the General Assembly of the movement, held in London from February to May 1839, the Welsh Chartists were represented by Williams, Jones and Frost, and a petition was presented in parliament in July bearing 1,280,000 names. Nevertheless, many of the speeches and publications of the Chartists, with their powerful imagery, seemed to the authorities to be appeals to violence. There was extensive correspondence between the magistrates and the Home Office; spies were employed, soldiers were sent to the most disturbed districts and talk arose of arming middle-class vigilantes. There was substance to the fears of the authorities, for not all Chartists adhered to 'moral suasion'. The advocates of physical force held that there would be no advance without armed protest. Such ideas had a particular appeal in the coalfield, with its tradition of violence and insurrection, and some of its inhabitants began to collect arms and to make pikes. Vincent was struck by the defensible nature of the south Wales coalfield; Wales, he declared, would make 'an admirable republic'. In London, there was much concern over the militant spirit of the inhabitants of the coalfield. 'Nowhere throughout the Empire,' stated the *Courier* in 1839, 'is there a population more discontented than they.' 'The south Wales coalfield,' said Melbourne (a man who had good cause to remember the Merthyr Rising), 'is the most terrifying part of the kingdom.'

Nevertheless, the first violence linked with Chartism occurred not in the south but in the upper Severn valley – although it is likely that the root cause of the unrest among the inhabitants of Montgomeryshire was hatred of the workhouse rather than a concern to advance democracy. Three London policemen were sent to Llanidloes on 20 April 1839 at the request of the local magistrates. On the following day, they were attacked in the Trewythen Hotel. The men they had arrested were released, the hotel was ransacked and a week went by before the magistrates dared to interfere, a week during which Llanidloes was controlled by local Chartists. The crisis that was coming to a head in the south was far more serious. The Chartists of the coalfield were angered by the imprisonment of Henry Vincent in May 1839, and in Monmouthshire in particular the initiative was increasingly passing to the supporters of 'physical force'. Frost sought to reason with them, but by October 1839 it seems that he also had come to the conclusion that armed protest was inevitable.

There is considerable doubt about the purpose of the attack on Newport by five thousand of the men of the coalfield on 4 November 1839. Was it a procession intended to display the power of the Chartists, as David Williams claimed, or was its purpose to launch an insurrection which would overthrow the government, as Ivor Wilks and David Jones maintain? Part of the uncertainty stems from the failure of those in authority fully to grasp what was happening in the coalfield; they knew little of the interior life of the industrial communities, partly because to a large extent those communities conducted their affairs through the medium of the Welsh language. If the document written by one of the most colourful of the Chartists, Zephaniah Williams of Nant-y-glo, is to be believed (and Wilks argues that it should be) the Chartists intended to capture the towns around the coalfield and to defend the boundary represented by the Wye and the Severn Sea. Thus south-east Wales (the 'Silurian Republic', as Harri Webb described it) would become a working-class fortress and the centre for revolutionary activity which would sweep through the kingdom. If this were the intention, it was a total failure. No support came from the Chartists of England and Scotland; there was no attack on any town apart from Newport and that attack was bungled. A group of soldiers was stationed at the Westgate Hotel; the hotel was stormed and in the struggle there and elsewhere in Newport at least twenty Chartists were killed. In the court cases that followed, eight were condemned to death as traitors. The sentences of five of them were commuted to imprisonment, and the three others (Frost, Zephaniah Williams and William Jones, the leader of the Chartists of Pontypool) were exiled to Van Diemen's Land.

The fiasco in Newport was a severe blow to Chartism. It gave the supporters of the status quo an opportunity to lambast all forms of radicalism; the first Chartist, argued Evan Jenkins, the Dowlais clergyman, was the devil, because he sought equality with God; similar notions were expressed by the Calvinistic Methodists, who were gratified that no members of their denomination were among the ranks of the Chartists. The rising caused distress to the leaders of Old Dissent;

a number of them, including David Rees of Llanelli, hastened to condemn all tendencies to violence and to associate themselves with more respectable, middle-class protest movements, in particular the Anti-Corn Law League. Yet the Newport Rising did not lead to the extinction of Welsh Chartism. In 1842, Morgan Williams of Merthyr became one of the five directors of the National Association of the Charter, and he attempted to spread Chartist ideas through his periodicals, *The Advocate and Merthyr Free Press* (1840) and *Utgorn Cymru* (1840–42). As late as the 1850s, meetings would be held in the name of the movement, and the petitions of 1842 and 1848 bore more Welsh names than had the petition of 1839. In 1850, the remnants of the movement were captured by men of specifically socialist views; they sought to create a working-class political party, and a thin connecting thread may be traced between their activities and the successful attempt to create such a party at the end of the nineteenth century.

While the industrial areas of the south-east were being agitated by Chartism, the agricultural areas of the south-west were being disturbed by the protests known as the Rebecca Riots. The tollgate at Efail-wen near St Clears was destroyed on 13 May 1839, and it was again attacked in June and in July. Then there was a pause until October 1842. The rioters – who wore women's clothes – were known as Rebecca and her daughters, probably a reference to Genesis 24, 60, a verse which claims that the seed of Rebecca shall inherit the gates of those that hate her. Although the tollgates were the chief targets of the rioters, it would be wrong to assume that hatred of the gates was the main cause of their protests. The tollgates were convenient objects of attack, but the will to attack and destroy sprang from a deep-rooted sense of deprivation.

The rural society of south-west Wales in the first half of the nineteenth century was a society in crisis. Demographic factors were at the root of the crisis. Between 1801 and 1841, many of the rural parishes in the counties of Carmarthen, Cardigan and Pembroke experienced population increases as high as 50 per cent, increases which were more rapid than those experienced by similar communities in other parts of Wales. In accordance with Malthus's prediction, the standard of living declined as numbers exceeded resources, particularly among those living on former common land, where farming was, at best, only marginally profitable. The most deprived inhabitants of the countryside were the labourers. Nevertheless, it was the small farmers who felt most strongly the threat to their standard of living. It was they who paid the tolls to the turnpike companies when transporting their produce to market or when carting lime from the kilns; it was they who paid rent, rates and tithe, three of the burdens about which Rebecca was especially vocal; it was they, also, it may be assumed, who were most perturbed by the possibility that they might end their days in the workhouse – the object of the most daring of Rebecca's attacks. Although many labourers participated in the Rebecca Riots, the riots primarily reflected the interests and the fears of the small farmers. The distress of the small farmers was intensified by the weaknesses of the legal system – the negligence of the magistrates, for example, and the high fees of the courts – and by the arrogance of the landed class, which by the 1840s was divided from its tenantry by religion as well as by language.

Although the Rebecca Riots were not simply a protest against the obligation of road users to pay tolls, hatred of the tollgates was the spark which ignited the protest. The appalling condition of Welsh roads has already been noted. In Britain, unlike France, the building of a network of roads was not considered to be the responsibility of the government, and therefore British roads developed piecemeal in response to local demand and initiative. There were occasional exceptions. The link with Ireland was the most important of these; the government spent heavily on it, and in consequence the journey from London to Holyhead took twenty-seven hours in 1836 compared with forty-eight hours in 1784. The rest of the highways of Wales came under the control of turnpike companies. As has been seen, the first Welsh company was founded in Flintshire in 1753; between 1753 and 1839, parliament authorized over two hundred schemes to improve the roads of Wales, the work to be financed by levying tolls. Road improvement was central to the changes experienced by Welsh society between 1770 and 1850, but it was not trouble-free. The efforts of many of the trusts were feeble and a number of them were crippled by corruption or inefficiency. The burdens of the trustees could be lightened by leasing out the tollgates, and by the 1830s many of the gates of south Wales had come to be controlled by the entrepreneur Thomas Bullin. His toll-collectors were rigorous and there were numerous complaints against them. When using the roads of a single company, only one payment had to be made but, where there were several companies, a journey could be expensive. There were eleven companies in Carmarthenshire, five of which had tollgates around the county town.

It is sometimes claimed that the Rebecca Riots were a rural version of Chartism. There is some substance to the claim. Bitterness caused by the Poor Law Amendment Act was a significant element in both. The Carmarthen workhouse was destroyed on 19 June 1843, and Rebecca's activities attracted the attention of the editor of *The Times*, a newspaper eager to gather evidence detrimental to the act. It sent the talented journalist T. C. Foster to west Wales. Foster spent six months among the rioters; he won their confidence and his reports provide a valuable analysis of their motives. As in the coalfield, so also in the countryside, communal pressures promoted protest, and Rebecca's daughters, like the Chartists, could draw upon a long tradition of violence. It is believed that several of Rebecca's statements were written by the Chartist Hugh Williams, and the violence in the west, like that in Monmouthshire, caused perplexity among radicals who, while eager to condemn oppression, were appalled by the implications of disorder and lawlessness. Yet, as R. T. Jenkins argued, 'Chartism was a truly political movement, inspired by a theory; Chartism was a plan; Beca was a commotion.' The authorities believed that the riots also were the result of a plan, and the identity of Rebecca was the subject of much speculation. The name of Hugh Williams was suggested, and there were occasions when there was a specific leader – Thomas Rees (Twm Carnabwth) in Efail-wen in 1839, for example, and Michael Bowen in Carmarthen in 1843. But it is unlikely that the riots had one leader and organizer. They spread as the success of protesters in one district inspired others to imitate them in another district. As the distinguished historian George Rudé argued, the Rebecca Riots were a remarkable example of the crowd acting upon its own initiative. 'Beca is the country,' wrote *Seren Gomer* . . . 'it was Beca who obtained the Charter from King John, who severed the head of Charles I and who won the Independence of America; Beca executed Louis XVI, Beca won the Reform Bill.'

In its first phases, the rioting, which restarted in October 1842, was confined to the district between Narberth and St Clears. It spread to the Teifi valley during the spring of 1843 and to the industrial areas around Llanelli in the summer. By then Rebecca's activities were not restricted to tollgates; among the objects of her attacks were monoglot

English stewards, tithe receivers, builders of weirs, encroachers on the commons, greedy landowners and tenants who leased more than one farm. Rebecca also punished sexual offenders, and many private wrongs were avenged under the cover of the riots. By the end of the summer of 1843, protest was becoming anarchy as more turbulent elements were attracted to the ranks of the rioters. The keeper of the tollgate at Hendy near Pontarddulais was killed in September 1843, the only murder that can indisputably be laid at Rebecca's door.

The able soldier Colonel Love was sent to west Wales in July 1843 and by the autumn he had 1,800 soldiers under his command. Catching wrongdoers as elusive as Rebecca's daughters was a difficult task, but gradually the forces of the crown won the upper hand. Three of the rioters were exiled to Van Diemen's Land in October 1843, a punishment which was also meted out to those two ruffians Dai'r Cantwr and Shoni Sgubor Fawr in December. The enthusiasm of the farmers waned as their labourers caught the fever of protest; in the wake of demands for higher wages and the burning of an occasional rick, they increasingly supported efforts to bring the lawlessness to an end. The three counties of the south-west had been pacified by the end of October 1843; there were some later troubles in Glamorgan and in mid-Wales, and the last attacks associated with Rebecca were probably those on tollgates in the Builth area in September 1844.

The Conservative government of Sir Robert Peel reacted rapidly and constructively to the Rebecca Riots. In October 1843, a commission to inquire into their causes was established under the leadership of Thomas Frankland Lewis of Harpton Court, Radnorshire, the first chairman of the Poor Law Commission. The causes were ventilated in a series of mass meetings held throughout the west during 1843, as rioting yielded to more legal protest. The report of the commission, published in March 1844, led to an act which received royal assent in August. The act provided for the establishment of a Roads Board in each of the counties of south Wales (except Monmouthshire), boards which were to take over the management of the turnpike roads. Experienced surveyors were appointed to advise the boards, and in consequence the roads of the south by the 1850s were of a higher standard than those of most other parts of the kingdom. Reminiscing about the riots in 1852, Frankland Lewis declared that they were a 'creditable portion of Welsh history'. The people were oppressed by the turnpike companies and 'they saw that their only remedy was to take the law into their own hands'. 'The Rebecca Riots,' said Frankland Lewis, 'were organized with much skill . . . and, the instant that [their] purpose seemed likely to be attained, they came to an end.'

Rioting by Rebecca and the Chartists proved how unsatisfactory it was to rely upon unpaid constables to keep the peace. The Metropolitan Police had been founded by Peel's act of 1829, and a number of London policemen were sent to Wales during periods of commotion; there were at least seventy-seven in west Wales in 1843. The Municipal Corporations Act of 1835 obliged boroughs to establish police forces financed by the rates; of the twenty Welsh corporations recognized by the act, a half had regular forces by 1839. In that year, with unrest at its height, the magistrates were given the authority to establish county police forces, although the legislation was permissive rather than mandatory. To many in Britain, a paid police force savoured of the authoritarian states of mainland Europe, and a more powerful argument against them was their cost. The measure was rapidly adopted by Glamorgan on the earnest entreaty of its lord lieutenant, the marquess of Bute. Glamorgan's example was followed, although rather reluctantly, by the counties of Carmarthen, Denbigh, Montgomery and Cardigan, but the rest of the counties of Wales did not have police forces until the act of 1856 obliged magistrates to establish them. There were strange and amusing episodes in the early history of the police forces. Nevertheless, they made an important contribution to social stability; the second half of the nineteenth century was a far less riotous period than the first, a fact which can be attributed, in part at least, to the establishment of the county police forces.

Yet there were more fundamental causes for the comparative equipoise of the decades after 1850. The census of 1851 showed that the increase in the population of agricultural parishes – the chief cause of the troubles of the countryside – had come to an end, and that the number of the inhabitants of many rural areas was in decline. The decline can mainly be ascribed to the increasing ability of the industrial areas to offer a livelihood to the rural surplus. Part of that surplus moved out of Wales altogether; there was no slackening in the appeal of the United States and there was substantial migration to England. It was recorded in 1851 that over 48,000 people born in Wales lived in Cheshire and Lancashire, and that there were almost 18,000 in London. Nevertheless, it was possible to retain in Wales a large proportion of those who migrated from the rural areas, largely because the south Wales coalfield was able to attract and maintain them. There was an increase of 117,000 in the population of Wales in the decade 1841–51, 80 per cent of it occurring in the industrial districts between Llanelli and Pontypool.

The 1840s was a key period in the history of the coalfield, with the coming of docks and railways and the beginnings of the trade in steam coal. Wales was transformed by the railways. The creation of the country's railway network belongs to the second half of the nineteenth century, particularly to the period 1850–70, but the coalfield had felt the impact of the invention of locomotion decades earlier. The ironmasters were eager to profit from the demand for rails. They had an extensive market within Britain; almost every railway company in England bought rails from companies such as Dowlais, Cyfarthfa and Ebbw Vale. The foreign market was almost limitless; from the early 1830s onwards, Cyfarthfa had a lively trade with the United States, and by 1850 Crawshay had invested a quarter of a million pounds in American railways. Rails of Welsh manufacture were laid between Warsaw and Vienna in 1837. In the 1840s, there was extensive business with Russia and it was probably on a rail bearing the letters GL (Guest Lewis, the trade mark of Dowlais) that poor Anna Karenina met her end. The rail trade was a vast stimulus to the iron industry of the south: its production rose from 277,000 tons in 1830 to 706,000 in 1847, a year in which J. J. Guest made a profit of £172,746. At that time, he was the owner of the world's largest iron company; indeed, it is likely that he had more people working for him than had any other employer on the face of the earth.

Although the iron industry expanded greatly as a result of the growth of the railways, it was dethroned from its pre-eminent position in the Welsh industrial economy as a result of their coming. The railway from Llanelli to Pontarddulais, which was opened in 1839, was the first to be built in Wales. It was an important venture, but it was cast into the shade by the Taff Vale Railway which linked Merthyr with Cardiff in 1841. Branches of the TVR were built – up the Cynon valley in 1846 and up the Rhondda valley in 1854 – and by the 1870s the company was paying higher dividends than any other railway company in Britain. A barge made the voyage by canal from Merthyr to Cardiff six times a month, carrying a cargo of twenty-four tons of coal each time; after 1841, the entire month's load could be conveyed in little more than an hour. With such a revolution in transport, the coal trade could develop rapidly, independently of the iron trade. In 1840 the south Wales coalfield produced about 4.5 million tons of coal; half of it was consumed by the iron furnaces and over a million tons by the other industries and the domestic consumers of the region. The remaining 1.5 million tons were exported, but only 5 per cent of the exports were sales to foreign countries. In 1854 8.8 million tons were produced; exports amounted to 2.6 million tons, 31 per cent of which represented sales to foreign countries. The most rapid growth in production occurred in the areas served by the Taff Vale Railway. The total tonnage mined in the parish of Aberdare rose from 177,000 in 1844 to 477,000 in 1850. The steam coal of the Cynon valley was of a high standard, and the demand for coal to feed steam-engines – a demand which increasingly came from every corner of the world – caused coal to replace iron as the chief industry of Wales.

The growth of the coal trade was much assisted by the initiative of the marquess of Bute. He spent £350,000 on the dock opened at Cardiff in 1839 – one of the most remarkable ventures ever to be financed by one man. With its position at the mouth of the river which drained the richest part of the coalfield, with a dock superior to that of its rivals, and with a patron – the marquess of Bute – who was determined to ensure for the town every advantage which could result from the power he enjoyed as the greatest of the landowners of the coalfield, the prospects for Cardiff were bright. In 1801, Cardiff was twenty-fifth in size among the towns of Wales; in 1851, it was exceeded in size only by Merthyr, Swansea and Newport and it was to overtake them also by 1881.

With the economy of the industrial areas of Wales being strengthened by developments in transport, those areas could accept an increasing number of immigrants. Indeed, David Williams argued that the Rebecca Riots would not have happened had the railways come to Wales a decade earlier. Rural Wales was not the only source of migrants. The industrial areas of Llanelli and the Tawe valley were wholly Welsh, and few people from outside Wales had reached the Cynon valley before the middle of the nineteenth century, but further east the non-Welsh element increased progressively. It was estimated in the 1840s that the proportion of the inhabitants of English origin was 12 per cent in Merthyr, 38 per cent in Blaenafon and 44 per cent in Trefethin (Pontypool). The census of 1851 noted that 115,000 of the inhabitants of Wales, representing almost 10 per cent of the population, had been born in England. The country attracted migrants from Ireland also, at times of scarcity such as 1817 and 1822, and above all during the famine years of 1846–9; there were in Wales in 1851 20,000 people who had been born in Ireland. As they were in dire straits, they were prepared to work for wages lower than that which the Welsh considered to be a bare livelihood. Consequently, there were bitter protests against them – in the Rhymni valley in 1825, in Swansea in 1828 and on many other occasions in subsequent decades. The Irish were forced to live in insalubrious areas – the slums of Cae-draw and Ynys-gau in Merthyr, for example, or the filthy closes that peppered the back streets of Cardiff. Thus the belief arose that uncleanliness and unruliness were an intrinsic part of their character. Most of the Irish of Wales came from south-western Ireland, a region which was almost wholly Catholic, and thus the hostility between Orange and Green which was such a burden to cities such as Glasgow and Liverpool was not imported into Merthyr or Cardiff. But as the Welsh had a long anti-Catholic tradition, the Irish among them had to suffer indignities far greater than those suffered by the Nonconformists at the hands of the Anglicans. Strong feelings were aroused by the spread of Catholic churches; twenty-one of them were recorded in Wales in 1851. Their priests were subjected to considerable harassment and in Merthyr mass was celebrated in a loft above a slaughter-house.

The influx from Ireland declined later in the nineteenth century, but that from England increased. As a result, it has been argued that the industrial development of Wales was detrimental to the Welsh language – an issue which will need to be examined later. The history of the language in the nineteenth century is not known in detail, for the first census to record the number of its speakers is that of 1891. The claim that two thirds of the inhabitants of Wales spoke Welsh in the 1840s is, however, probably correct. Although many English people migrated to the eastern industrial districts, those districts also attracted many Welsh-speakers and were the scene of a vigorous Welsh-language culture in the early and mid nineteenth century. David Williams claimed that half the inhabitants of Newport had a knowledge of Welsh in the 1830s and it would seem that that was also true of Cardiff. There were lively Welsh communities in industrial

Monmouthshire, as the exciting research of Sian Rhiannon has shown. Dynolwyr Nantyglo (The Humanists of Nant-y-glo), a body which gave expression to a radical and practical Welsh nationalism, was established in 1831. Saron Chapel, Tredegar, had as its pastor a succession of prominent Welshmen, among them Hugh Jones (Cromwell o Went) and Evan Jones (Ieuan Gwynedd), while John Davies (Brychan) was tireless in furthering the Welsh-language culture of the district. Merthyr had a particularly vigorous Welsh cultural life, organized by its *Cymreigyddion*, its *Cymmrodorion*, its *Gomeriaid* and its *Brythoniaid*. It was one of the chief centres of publishing in Welsh, as Aberdare was to be somewhat later. It was in Merthyr that the foundations of the Welsh tradition of choral singing were laid, largely through the work of John Thomas (Ieuan Ddu), the man who introduced Handel's *Messiah* to the Welsh. Lady Charlotte Guest, the wife of the owner of the Dowlais works, was attracted by the Welshness of Merthyr, and between 1838 and 1845 she published her English translation of the *Mabinogi*. In the mid nineteenth century, the most learned literary figure in Merthyr – and, indeed, in Wales – was Thomas Stephens, a chemist in the town. He was the author of *The Literature of the Kymry* (1849), a critical survey of Welsh literature in the period 1100–1350 which is still valuable today.

The activities of the industrial districts were linked with the tradition of the 'literature-loving parsons' through the labours of Thomas Price (Carnhuanawc), a clergyman who served in parishes around Crickhowell, Breconshire, from 1813 until his death in 1848. He was one of the great Welshmen of the nineteenth century. Throughout Europe, in the first half of the century, energetic and gifted men – clerics as often as not – were concerned to give dignity to the culture of deprived ethnic groups or nations. In Wales, Carnhuanawc is the most striking example of this phenomenon. He was inspired by ideals similar to those of the German philosopher Herder (1744–1803), who held that every ethnic culture is uniquely valuable and that it is the common people who are the true guardians of those cultures. Carnhuanawc constantly expressed his admiration for the 'ordinary people who embrace the language and the literature of the nation'; he thundered against non-Welsh-speaking clergy; he sought to establish Welsh-medium schools; he established the Welsh Minstrelsy Society to train harpists, and the Welsh Manuscripts Society, which sought to publish the wealth of manuscript material, found in him a dedicated supporter. In the nineteenth century, many patriots were eager to create links with nations of similar lineage, thus giving rise to Pan-Slavism, Pan-Latinism and Pan-Teutonism; Carnhuanawc was among the first of the Pan-Celts and he played a key role in the Bible Society's efforts to publish a Breton translation of the scriptures.

His greatest achievement was his *Hanes Cymru* (History of Wales), which appeared in fourteen parts between 1836 and 1842, a substantial work illuminated by his warm and enlightened patriotism. As a historian, he was anxious 'not to assert anything except upon authority', but bearing in mind that the revolution which would transform historiography was already afoot in Germany, his treatment of sources was frequently uncritical. Carnhuanawc was mainly responsible for the success of the *eisteddfodau* of the Abergavenny Cymmrodorion. They were held annually from 1834 to 1853 and were the connecting link between the regional *eisteddfodau* of the 1820s and the first National Eisteddfod. Through Carnhuanawc, the *eisteddfodau* received the patronage of Lady Llanover, one of the numerous contributions of that wealthy and patriotic woman. Despite the mockery of her fellow-gentry, she sought to make Llanover Court the focus of Welsh culture; it became the repository of the manuscripts of Iolo Morganwg and it was there that the image of what came to be regarded as the traditional Welsh costume was created. Lady Llanover was also anxious to collect the folk songs of Wales and it was at her instigation that Maria Jane Williams of Aberpergwn published her valuable collection of songs in 1844.

Gentry and clerics such as Lady Llanover and Carnhuanawc were not numerous. To many commentators, the curse of Wales was its distinctiveness – the fact that it was not English, linguistically and otherwise. That distinctiveness, it was argued, lay at the root of the Welsh readiness to riot, a readiness much exhibited in the years between 1839 and 1844. The Welsh language was the quintessence of the distinctiveness. Insurrection could be expected in Wales, claimed the *Morning Chronicle* in 1839, because there was a linguistic division between the upper and the lower classes. It was the existence of the Welsh language, argued the Rebecca Commission in 1844, that hindered the Law and the Established Church from civilizing the Welsh. The attacks upon the language were interwoven with the racism which was rampant in nineteenth-century Europe. The undisciplined Irish proved that the Celts were shaped from materials inferior to those which formed the Teutons, and Carnhuanawc was obliged in 1829 to refute the argument that mankind in its entirety did not derive from the same origins. There were Welshmen who had succeeded in rising above their fellows, and that was attributed to their desire and ability to integrate with the English. Thus the wildness of the Welsh could be tamed by steeping them in an English education. It was a task that would cost less than the suppression of insurrection and riot; as H. L. Bellairs, author of the report on the condition of the south Wales coalfield, put it: 'A band of efficient schoolmasters is kept up at a much less expense than a body of police or soldiery.'

As has already been emphasized, compared with others of the states of Europe, educational provision was startlingly inadequate in Britain – or, to be more exact, in England and Wales, for the situation in Scotland was different and better. It was a strange paradox that the dominant state in economic terms offered its citizens virtually no education. A network of schools had been established in the Austrian Empire in 1774, almost a century before such a network was created in Britain. It is difficult to overestimate the consequences of this educational backwardness. Efforts to overcome it were to be one of the major themes in the history of Wales in the second half of the nineteenth century. The lack of an adequate system of education was at the root of many of the features of Welsh life during that century – the inability of members of the working class to enter the professions (apart from the Christian ministry), for example, or the uncritical nature of Welsh scholarship, or the tardy development of positive ideas concerning the value of Welshness.

In the last resort, Britain's primitiveness in the field of education, as in other fields, sprang from the success of the enemies of the crown in dismantling royal paternalism on the eve of the Civil War. Thus the growth of *étatisme*, a central feature in the development of other European states, was stifled. Furthermore, every attempt to create an educational system was wrecked by denominational bitterness. The Established Church wanted education to be under its control. This was also what most politicians would have preferred, but they were unable to ignore those who were members of other Churches. Thus, when the government in 1833 began to contribute towards the cost of erecting schools, it opted to share its money between the National Society and the British Society. The supporters of the State Church rapidly seized the opportunity: between 1833 and 1847, 231 National schools were added to the 146 which already existed in Wales. In 1843, Robert Peel's Conservative government introduced a bill to establish schools for the children of the poor, and provision was made to ensure that there would be an Anglican majority on the boards supervising them. The reaction of Nonconformists, both Protestant and Catholic, was fierce, and two million people signed the petition protesting against the measure. The government yielded and a generation was to pass before a complete network of elementary schools was established.

The challenge represented by the bill of 1843 and by the achievements of the National Society caused Nonconformists to interest themselves in elementary education. For many who belonged to the old dissenting tradition, state interference in education was a dangerous concept; state-supported schools, argued Ieuan Gwynedd, represented oppression of the grossest kind. For him and those who thought like him, education was an aspect of religion and they were convinced that it would be impossible to create a state educational system which did not favour Anglicanism. The task of organizing and financing day schools should be left to the denominations; in 1845, a campaign to implement the voluntary principle was launched in the regions where Old Dissent was well represented, but because of lack of funds it was abandoned in the 1850s.

The reaction was different in the west and north, the stronghold of Calvinistic Methodism, a denomination which did not have an instinctive antipathy towards the patronage of the state. There, the initiative of Hugh Owen, a Methodist from Anglesey and an official with the Poor Law Commission in London, was warmly welcomed. In 1843, he published his *Llythyr i'r Cymry* (Letter to the Welsh) which explained how to establish British schools and obtain government grants. He was stating what had been common knowledge for years and the enthusiastic reaction to his letter can only be understood by presupposing the extreme isolationism of Welsh Methodist culture. There were only twenty-eight British schools in Wales in 1843; a further seventy-nine were established by 1847, almost all of them in the west and north, where John Phillips, a native of Pontrhydfendigaid, was from 1843 until 1863 the British Society's indefatigable representative. Because of the readiness of the Methodists to accept state patronage, it was in the districts where they were strongest that the chief institutions born of the educational upsurge of the mid nineteenth century – the Normal College at Bangor and the University College at Aberystwyth – came to be located; they were sparsely populated agricultural districts, and therefore the most important fruits of that upsurge were situated in places remote from the populous communities of Wales.

The interest in education turned to white-hot excitement following the publication of the infamous report of 1847. The proposal which led to the establishment of the commission responsible for the report was put forward by William Williams, the MP for Coventry and one of the most radical of the members of the House of Commons. He was a native of Llanpumsaint, Carmarthenshire, and a successful businessman in London. On 10 March 1846, he urged the government to inquire into the state of education in Wales, and in particular to examine the means available for members of the working classes to obtain a knowledge of English. The commission was set up by the distinguished civil servant James Kay-Shuttleworth, the first secretary of the Education Committee of the Privy Council. The three commissioners had completed their report of 1,252 pages by April 1847. Most of it consists of a conscientious description of the schools offering education to the working-class children of Wales. The commissioners acknowledged that the only schools available in all parts of Wales were Sunday schools; in the counties of Glamorgan, Carmarthen and Pembroke – the region which was the responsibility of the commissioner, R. W. Lingen – thirty thousand children attended day schools, while eighty thousand attended Sunday schools. The limitations of the education provided by the Sunday schools were emphasized, but it was noted that the schools enabled the young (and others) to be literate in Welsh and trained them to use the language to discuss abstract ideas.

The report offers ample evidence that the facilities for elementary education were abysmally inadequate. Although Wales had a number of schools of high quality, particularly those maintained by the National Society and the British Society, the condition of the buildings of many private schools was appalling and the education they offered was paltry in the extreme. In the 1840s, hardly more than half the bridegrooms of Wales could sign their names, and there were virtually no facilities enabling the children of the poor to rise above their circumstances. The situation in some of the regions of England was similar or worse. In East Anglia, for example, less than half the bridegrooms could sign their names, but the weaknesses of education in Wales were intensified by the custom of teaching monoglot Welsh children through the medium of English, a language in which the teachers were often only partially fluent. (In England also, few of the children of the poor had a grasp of standard English, but their vernacular was not fundamentally different from the language in which they were taught.) Because of the ignorance and the prejudice of the three young commissioners, the report of 1847 exaggerated the weaknesses of education in Wales. Although they were able and energetic men, Wales was wholly alien to them and they had no experience of teaching working-class children. As they asked complicated questions and depended upon inadequate translation, they misinterpreted the answers of the children they questioned. Furthermore, they were prone to accept uncritically the comments of those clergymen who had been embittered by the successes of Nonconformity, comments which gave the impression that the Welsh were uniquely lax in their sexual habits. Less than ten of the pages of the report discuss this issue but it was those pages which gave London journals the opportunity to vilify the Welsh and which aroused the anger of Welsh patriots. Some clergymen went further, insinuating that the immorality of the Welsh was a by-product of their allegiance to the chapel.

As the mythological tradition was still part of the heritage of the Welsh, the report of 1847 came to be known as *Brad y Llyfrau Gleision* (The Treachery of the Blue Books). The epithet was an echo of the Treachery of the Long Knives – the plot which had furthered the interests of the English in the age of Vortigern. The treachery consisted of the readiness of Welsh clergymen to slander their compatriots. In consequence, the clerics of the Established Church began to be considered as internal enemies, an unjust notion in view of the clerical contribution to Welsh culture. Furthermore, staunch Anglicans were prominent in the efforts to refute the report, as the trenchant comments of J. H. Cotton (the dean of Bangor), the warm-hearted arguments of Jane Williams (a disciple of Carnhuanawc) and the weighty tome of Thomas Phillips (the mayor of Newport in 1839) testify. Yet, in the atmosphere that existed in mid-nineteenth-century Wales, the report could not but inflame sectarian passions. In the Nonconformist reaction to it – the eloquent speeches of Henry Richard, the heart-felt essays of Ieuan Gwynedd, the satirical drama of R. J. Derfel and the incisive articles of Lewis Edwards – it is possible to discern the seed of the notion that the chapel people were the only true Welsh and that Welshness was synonymous with Nonconformity.

Despite the ferocity of the reaction to the report, the activities of the leaders of Welsh Nonconformity in the following decades may be considered as evidence that they agreed with its conclusions. Those years saw the climax of campaigns against wantonness, drunkenness and lawlessness, efforts which fully conformed to the moral atmosphere of the Victorian age. Although such campaigns could lead to hypocrisy and insincerity, they enjoyed considerable success; in the second half of the nineteenth century, there was substance to the boast that the Welsh were at least as respectable as other nations. Yet national leaders intent above all upon proving the respectability of their nation are unlikely to be audacious. The faint-heartedness of national movements in Wales in the second half of the nineteenth century may to a great extent be attributed to aspirations for a virtuous nation – the fruit of the reaction to the 1847 report. This faint-heartedness was at its most obvious in the history of the Welsh language. The panacea offered to Wales by the commissioners was schooling through the medium of English. This is precisely what the leaders of the Welsh laboured to establish. Hostility towards English was widespread among the ordinary people of Wales, for they considered, as Ieuan Gwynedd Jones put it, that 'the Welsh language was a precious and singular possession of the masses of workers at a time when the inhuman, dehumanizing and brutalizing forces of industrialism were alienating them from nature and from society.'

The perception of the emerging Welsh Nonconformist leaders was different. To them, the key battle was that in favour of the rights of the Welsh as Nonconformists. It was a battle in which there would be allies and sympathy in England; neither would be available in a battle for the rights of the Welsh as a nation, and therefore that battle was not fought. This is perhaps the chief significance of the 'Treachery of the Blue Books' – that it proved the hypersensitivity of the leaders of Welsh to the criticism of the English. Those leaders sought to promote a national revival but it failed to win full credibility, not because it was too Welsh, but because it was not Welsh enough.

The report of 1847 was a particularly painful experience for the Calvinistic Methodists. As they had been anxious not to annoy the Church Establishment, it was especially galling to read insinuations that institutions specifically theirs – the meetings of the *seiat* (fellowship) and the *pwnc* (Bible study class) – were nurseries of licentiousness. The 'Treachery' was one of the main reasons for the increasing readiness of the Methodists to cooperate with their fellow Nonconformists. After the death of John Elias in 1841, his successors as leaders of the denomination were anxious to give it a new image. The influential quarterly *Y Traethodydd* (The Essayist) was founded in 1845, with Thomas Gee of Denbigh as publisher and Lewis Edwards of Bala as editor. In the spring issue of 1848, Edwards concluded his comments on the 1847 report by expressing his hope that 'principled Nonconformists would be elected to Parliament by every county and every borough in Wales'. It was the existence of the Established Church, he argued, which allowed a state commission to slander Nonconformists. 'The great issue of this age,' wrote Edwards, 'is the union between Church and State,' a remarkably bold statement for a Methodist to make in view of the fact that the Association had unanimously decided in 1834 that the Connexion should have no involvement with those who sought a 'divorce between Church and State'.

By 1848 there was a society specifically working for that divorce. The Anti-State-Church Association was founded in 1844; it was renamed the Liberation Society (the Society for Liberating the Church from the State) in 1853. Most of those attending the inaugural meeting hailed from the English Midlands, but they also included representatives from Wales. A London Welshman, J. Carvell Williams, was appointed secretary of the society, and under his leadership cells were established in Wales. Their members were mainly adherents of the old dissenting tradition from the industrial districts, but the society was increasingly to win support in rural areas and among the Methodists. The Liberation Society was the most important means whereby staunch Nonconformists became political activists, a central fact in the political history of Wales in the second half of the nineteenth century.

The debate in favour of and against the Church Establishment dealt with fundamental issues, for it concerned two different views of the nature of the state. Was the state an institution hallowed by tradition and sanctified by religion, or was it merely a useful structure which deserved only minimal powers? In the mid nineteenth century, aspects of this question lay at the root of almost every debate on public issues. The most influential of the economists, disciples of Adam Smith, asserted that the state had no role in matters relating to commerce and industry; if economic laws were allowed to operate unrestricted, the 'invisible hand' would ensure that the self-centred interests of businessmen would produce general prosperity. This was the classical theory of capitalism, a theory which in the nineteenth century gave rise to incomparable economic growth and to appalling social injustice – in Wales as much as anywhere.

It was faith in the 'invisible hand' which inspired the campaign in favour of Free Trade which came to its climax in 1846, when Peel repealed the Corn Laws. The Irish famine was the immediate cause of the repeal, which was passed despite the opposition of the majority of Peel's fellow Conservatives, but it was the Anti-Corn-Law League which had created a public climate hostile to protection. The leaders of Welsh Nonconformity were vocal in their support of the league and from it they learnt useful lessons about how to put pressure upon the government. To the Nonconformists, Free Trade was a religious and moral issue, for they considered that interference with trade was a challenge to the intentions of God. The league was a notable example of middle-class activism. Cheap food was useful to the employer, for it meant that he was under less pressure to raise the wages of his employees. Furthermore, the campaign against the Corn Laws was a useful weapon in attacking the power of the landowners, a class which had benefited from the inflated rents caused by the high price of corn. Little corn was grown in Wales, and the league succeeded in persuading the Welsh farmers that Free Trade was in their interests, a factor which further alienated tenants from their landlords. If Free Trade were to be achieved, it would have to be defended; in the second half of the nineteenth century and subsequently, this was the *raison d'être* of the Liberal party – the alliance of Whigs, Radicals and Peelites – for hostility to protection was almost the only principle which united those disparate factions.

Free Trade was an aspect of *laissez-faire*. In the mid nineteenth century *laissez-faire* found advocates in Wales who were prepared to defend the ideology in its entirety. The most vocal and consistent of them was S.R. (Samuel Roberts of Llanbrynmair). S.R. attacked everything that could be considered inimical to a free society – slavery, war, landlordism, monopolies, tolls, hierarchy in state and church; he believed passionately in progress, embracing every improvement from the railways to the penny post; he denounced anything savouring of collectivism – trade unions, state support for education, paternalistic legislation. Above all, he sought to nurture upright and independent individuals; this is what caused him to oppose the secret ballot, which he saw as a device for the cowardly. Yet *laissez-faire* was an ideology impossible to achieve in its entirety. Implicit in the circumstances of the age, if not in its philosophy, was the need for legislation to modify the more pernicious consequences of unrestrained capitalism. Anthony Ashley Cooper, the Tory earl of Shaftesbury, was mainly responsible for the act of 1833 which ended some of the worst excesses of the factory system. As the statute dealt mainly with the textile industry it had little relevance for Wales, although the supervisory system it established was to be a significant precedent when legislation came to be applied to the heavy industries which dominated the Welsh economy.

In 1840, on Cooper's initiative, a commission was appointed to examine those industries, and the commission's report on Children's Employment (Mines) was published in 1842. It revealed that boys as young as four years old worked in the pits, and that the employment of boys was more common in the south Wales coalfield than in any other of the coalfields of the kingdom. Girls were also employed, especially in Pembrokeshire and in the collieries of the Monmouthshire iron companies, but outside Pembrokeshire it was unusual for women to work underground. No one was surprised to learn that the children of the poor worked – that was part of an age-old pattern – and the commissioners found little evidence to suggest that the young colliers were ill-treated. Yet the report, with its startling drawings, had an immediate impact.

Before the end of 1842, parliament had prohibited females of all ages from working underground, a prohibition which also extended to boys under the age of ten (thirteen until the amendment of the House of Lords). A decade went by before the law was fully obeyed, despite the efforts of Seymour Tremenheere, the conscientious inspector. It caused grave problems for families with numerous daughters, for as a consequence of it the Welsh industrial economy ceased to offer much employment to females, a fact which lay at the root of some of the most distinctive features of coalfield society. It was one thing to legislate to protect the interests of women and children, beings who were not considered to be fully responsible; it was quite another to legislate to protect the interests of adult males. But that could not be avoided either. Many tender consciences were distressed by the appalling death toll in the coal industry; in the 1840s, up to two hundred colliers a year were killed in the pits of south Wales alone. In 1850, an act was passed which was the first of a series of safety measures and the basis of a system which was eventually to recognize the principle of compensation.

The principle of *laissez-faire* was further eroded by the necessity to address the problems of the populous districts. As Young and Handcock put it, 'economic individualism in the hour of its victory over the Corn Laws, found itself challenged by a sanitary doctrine that involved innumerable interferences with private property'. Conditions of life in the towns were probably not dirtier than they were in the countryside, but the effects of filth are more dire when people are crowded together. The situation was greatly exacerbated by the rapid urbanization of the first half of the nineteenth century, and at the same time the material available to measure and analyse it multiplied: with the Registration Act of 1837, the state began to collect statistics on the death rate, and the Poor Law Commission gathered much information on the links between poverty and ill-health.

In 1842, Edwin Chadwick, the secretary of the Commission and one of the most determined and influential figures of the nineteenth century, prepared a report on the condition of the health of the people. It showed that typhus, typhoid, dysentery and tuberculosis were rife in the populous districts; although scientists could not yet show exactly how filth caused sickness, Chadwick could prove that disease was more widespread among the disadvantaged masses squeezed together in insanitary parts of towns and cities. He demanded legislation which would empower the central government to insist that local authorities should provide pure water, clean the streets and build sewers. To Chadwick's many enemies, his plans savoured too much of the dictatorial system which it was considered he had already created through the Poor Law Commission. Nevertheless, the government was forced into action by the most dramatic of nineteenth-century diseases – cholera, with its 'fearfully sudden destructions'. Cholera was first recorded in Britain in 1832, when it killed 160 in Merthyr and 152 in Swansea. The epidemic of 1848–9, when 1,682 died in Merthyr alone, was much more serious. The striken communities reacted by praying, and ministers spoke of the debt of religion to 'this terrible preacher'. Parliament reacted by passing the Public Health

Act of 1848, the starting-point of a revolution in sanitary matters. It was a feeble measure compared with what Chadwick had sought. A local Board of Health would be established if an effective petition were organized; the board had the power to appoint a public health officer and to wrestle with the various problems arising from filth. By 1856, twenty-five places in Wales had boards of health, and the local arguments in favour and against the petition represented a significant political awakening. Before a board was established, a report on the sanitary condition of the district was prepared; such reports – the two compiled by T. W. Rammell on Merthyr and Cardiff, for example – contain some of the most unsavoury material ever to appear within the covers of an official publication.

The act of 1848, together with the legislation on safety and employment, prove that the unrestrained era of industrial capitalism in Wales was coming to an end. Indeed, the middle of the nineteenth century can in many ways be considered a turning-point. With the growth of the coal trade, a new age was dawning in the south Wales coalfield, and with the decline in the rural population the countryside was entering into a different phase. The edge of social protest was blunted by both these developments, and the second half of the nineteenth century would experience nothing comparable with the series of insurrections which had been such a feature of the first. With the widening of opportunities to give legal expression to political aspirations, the struggle to win constitutional power was to absorb the energies of an increasing number of the people of Wales. With more and more industrialists able to compete in terms of wealth with the landed gentry, the simplicity which had previously characterized the class structure of Wales came to an end. These developments sprang from the revolutionary changes set in train at the end of the eighteenth century. The first chapter in those changes may be considered to have come to a close by 1850.

CHAPTER EIGHT

1850–1914: The Rhondda, Aberystwyth and Bethesda

In 1851, Wales had 1,163,139 inhabitants; it had 2,523,500 in 1914, an increase of 117 per cent in sixty-three years. By the middle of the nineteenth century, the majority of the people of Wales no longer earned their living through agriculture, although it was still the most important single industry. In 1851, 35 per cent of the male labour force were employed in agriculture and 10 per cent in the coal industry, the second biggest source of employment. In 1914 the positions had been reversed, with almost 35 per cent employed in the collieries and 10 per cent on the land. In 1850, south Wales exported overseas a total of 450,000 tons of coal; in 1913, the figure was 36,832,000 tons and by that time economic development fuelled by an energy source of Welsh origin had been experienced by much of the world. In 1850, only one adult male in five in Wales had the right to vote; by 1914, it was a right enjoyed by the majority of Welshmen and the extension of the franchise had led to a fundamental change in the nature of Welsh parliamentary representation. In 1850, almost all the constituencies of Wales were represented by members of the landowning class; they also dominated local government and their estates were continuing to increase in size. In 1914, hardly more than three of the thirty-four Welsh members of parliament were of gentry stock; only a handful of landlords sat on local councils and the estates were in the process of breaking up. With the striking exception of the Calvinistic Methodist denomination, there were virtually no specifically Welsh organizations in 1850, and few people would have defended the notion that Wales was an entity comparable with England, Ireland or Scotland. By 1914, Wales had a national university, library and museum; in a number of sports – rugby, in particular – it had a national team; there was some degree of administrative devolution and a tentative tradition of specifically Welsh legislation had been established. Although it was still considered that the United Kingdom represented the union of three kingdoms, it was increasingly acknowledged that it contained four nations.

In 1850, two out of three of the inhabitants of Wales spoke Welsh – a total of about 750,000 people – and most of them had no knowledge of any other language. By 1914, there were almost a million Welsh speakers; yet they represented only two fifths of the population, and four out of five of them had some command of English. In 1850, the Nonconformists of Wales were well acquainted with contemptuous treatment and the privileges of the members of the Established Church were a constant affront to them. By 1914, most of those privileges had been abolished and a measure to disestablish the Church in Wales was on the statute book. In 1850, able and energetic members of the working class had little opportunity to rise above their circumstances. In 1914, mainly as a result of increased educational provision, they were entering the professions, and the beginnings of the social mobility which was to be so characteristic of the twentieth century could be seen. To the vast majority in 1850, the world was full of omens and enchantment and of the supernatural acts of God and the devil, and many magical rites had functional significance. By 1914, the agents of modernity – education, mobility, machines, policemen, science – were rapidly leading to the 'disenchantment of the world' as mysticism yielded to rationalism.

Industrialization and urbanization, and the new mentality which developed in their wake, were the root causes of this transformation. This can be seen particularly in the demographic history of the period. Population distribution in Wales was fundamentally changed by the growth of the south Wales coalfield. In 1851, broadly speaking, a third of the population lived in the counties of Glamorgan and Monmouth, a third in the rest of the southern counties and a third in the six counties of the north. By 1914 the proportion living in Glamorgan and Monmouth had doubled and the proportion living in the two other regions had halved (see the diagram on p. 322). On the eve of the First World War, 1,100,000 people lived in the south Wales coalfield and 600,000 in the towns bordering the Severn Sea; the remaining 800,000 lived in essentially rural surroundings, although there were 60,000 in the quarrying areas of the north-west, 100,000 in the coalfield of the north-east and 50,000 in the seaside towns which stretched from Llanfairfechan to Prestatyn.

There was an increase in population in all parts of Wales between 1770 and 1850, a period when the number of people living in the five counties of mid-Wales rose by 70 per cent. The pattern was very different between 1850 and 1914, when there was in those counties a decline of 10 per cent and when many rural parishes experienced a population decrease of 40 per cent or more. Brinley Thomas calculates that 388,000 people migrated from the rural areas of Wales to other parts of the United Kingdom between 1851 and 1911, a period when 320,000 moved into the south Wales coalfield. As the experiences of rural and industrial Wales were so fundamentally different, the demographic characteristics of the one area were, by the end of the nineteenth century, diametrically opposed to those of the other, a consideration of the utmost importance in analysing the structure of Welsh society (see the diagram on p. 401).

In the 1850s, the parish of Aberdare, where the population increased from 14,999 in 1851 to 32,299 in 1861, was the most dynamic place in Wales. Those involved in coal production were astounded by the quality of the coal from the four-foot seam at Aberdare, and as early as 1851 the Admiralty's experts had acknowledged that it was the ideal fuel for the British Navy. The long-established coalfield of Newcastle-on-Tyne reacted with hostility to the Admiralty's findings. After a long dispute, the Admiralty made a firm decision in favour of Welsh steam coal, and such was the reputation of the British Navy in the nineteenth century that its seal of approval opened up world-wide markets for the produce of Welsh pits. Until the 1870s, the Cynon valley was chiefly responsible for satisfying the increasing demand for steam coal. There, in the mid nineteenth century, businesses were established which would loom large in the history of Wales. They included the collieries of Samuel Thomas (the father of D. A. Thomas, Viscount Rhondda) and the companies of David Davis and Sons and of Nixon's Navigation. Above all, there were the pits of Thomas Powell, the foundation of the empire later known as Powell Duffryn, which was acknowledged in the twentieth century to be the largest coal company in Europe.

Aberdare's supremacy was short-lived. In the 1870s, the Cynon valley yielded its primacy to the Rhondda. Although Walter Coffin had been mining bituminous coal in the lower Rhondda valley since 1807, the upper reaches of the valley were described as late as 1847 as a pastoral paradise. In 1851, fewer than a thousand people lived in the

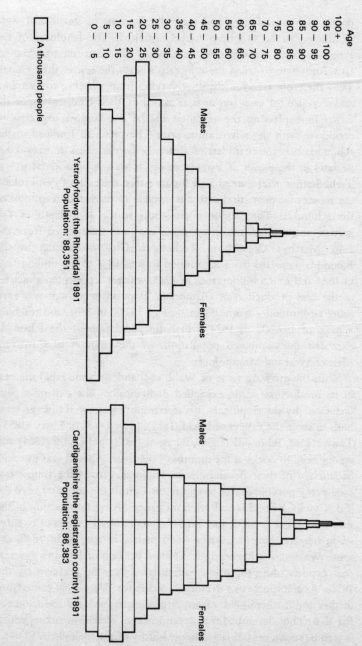

Age

| 100 + |
| 95 — 100 |
| 90 — 95 |
| 85 — 90 |
| 80 — 85 |
| 75 — 80 |
| 70 — 75 |
| 65 — 70 |
| 60 — 65 |
| 55 — 60 |
| 50 — 55 |
| 45 — 50 |
| 40 — 45 |
| 35 — 40 |
| 30 — 35 |
| 25 — 30 |
| 20 — 25 |
| 15 — 20 |
| 10 — 15 |
| 5 — 10 |
| 0 — 5 |

☐ A thousand people

Males

Ystradyfodwg (the Rhondda) 1891
Population: 88,351

Females

Males

Cardiganshire (the registration county) 1891
Population: 86,383

Females

The contrast between demographic profiles in industrial and rural Wales in the late nineteenth century

parish of Ystradyfodwg and the valley's seams of steam coal were considered to be too deep to be exploited. The landlords of the Rhondda were eager to prove otherwise, since according to English Law landowners owned the minerals beneath the soil of their estates. They therefore received royalties varying from sixpence to a shilling and sixpence for each ton of coal mined on their land, an important factor in explaining the readiness of the old landowning class to cooperate with the new industrialists. The principal landlord in the Rhondda was the marquess of Bute, the owner of more than 3,000 hectares in the parish of Ystradyfodwg. It was he who initiated – at Treherbert, a place named after his ancestors, the earls of Pembroke – the business of proving that it was possible to reach the steam coal of the Rhondda. The four-foot seam was struck at a depth of 115 metres, and in 1855 the first load of coal was transported from the Bute Merthyr Colliery in Treherbert. Coal production in the Rhondda increased from 2.1 million tons in 1874 to 5.5 million tons in 1884 and to 9.5 million tons in 1913, when it represented a quarter of the coal production of Glamorgan. Population growth was even more astonishing – from 951 in 1851 to 55,000 in 1881, and reaching a peak of 167,000 in 1924, when the population of the Rhondda exceeded the combined populations of the counties of Cardigan, Meirionnydd and Montgomery.

With the growing fame of Welsh coal and with the rapid increase in its production, trade expanded dramatically. The expansion was facilitated by developments in the transport system. Railways were built to serve the valleys of Nedd (1851), Llwyd (1854), Ebwy (1855), Tawe (1856), Rhondda (1856), Rhymni (1858) and Llyfni (1861) and were linked to docks at the mouths of the rivers. Cardiff was the chief beneficiary of these developments. The managers of the Bute estate used every possible device to ensure for Cardiff the entire trade of the Taf, Cynon, Rhondda and Rhymni valleys. After the opening of the East Bute Dock in 1859, the Cardiff docks covered an area of twenty-seven hectares and had quays 4,650 metres in length. In 1840, the south Wales coalfield contributed only 4 per cent of Britain's overseas coal exports; the proportion had risen to over 30 per cent by the 1870s. As transport costs decreased, orders for Welsh coal came from further and further afield – from Argentina, from India and from the Far East. Thus developed that dependence on overseas markets which was to be such a central factor in the history of the coalfield.

The new coal-producing communities differed in many ways from the old centres of the iron industry. In Merthyr, at least, the valley was sufficiently wide to accommodate a town; this was not the case in the Rhondda nor in many of the valleys of Monmouthshire and mid Glamorgan. There, chains of villages developed with virtually no sign of an urban centre and with no street more than a few steps away from the open mountain. As most of the houses in places like the Rhondda were built after the outcry over public health, and as building was increasingly controlled by local by-laws, the houses were better designed and more convenient than were the cottages of the iron districts. By the 1870s, the terraced house which was to be so characteristic of the coalfield had developed, providing a dwelling which compared favourably with working-class housing in others of the industrial areas of Britain. Because the steam coal companies were, initially at least, much smaller units than the leviathans of the iron industry, the collieries were not overshadowed by mansions such as Dowlais House and Cyfarthfa Castle. Yet, although the majority of the coal-owners were local men who often worshipped in the same chapel as their employees, it seems that they had a less paternal attitude towards the communities which developed around their pits than had the more enlightened of the ironmasters.

Higher wages were paid for mining coal for sale than for mining coal for use in the furnaces. As a result, workers from the iron districts were attracted to the new coal-mining villages. The population of Merthyr decreased by 6 per cent between 1871 and 1881. Welsh workers were also attracted to new centres of iron production outside Wales, for industrialists in England and overseas were eager to take advantage of their skills. The readiness of workers from the iron districts of Wales to migrate indicates that employment in those areas was in decline. By 1860, only 25 per cent of the pig iron produced in Britain came from south Wales, compared with 40 per cent in 1830. The technology of the industry developed rapidly and only a few of the ironmasters could afford to invest in the new techniques. In 1856, Henry Bessemer proved that steel, a much more versatile metal than cast iron, could be produced quickly and efficiently, but it was very expensive to adapt the old works to the new processes. This had been done at Dowlais by 1866 and during the next twenty years Dowlais's example was followed by five of the other ironworks of the uplands of Glamorgan and Monmouthshire. The rest – about a dozen in all – were closed, and as early as 1860 the editor of the *Merthyr Telegraph* was of the opinion that the town's prosperity was declining. The Bessemer process needed iron ore free of phosphorus. The local ore was unsuitable and in 1872 Dowlais, in cooperation with the German firm of Krupp, established a company to import ore from Bilbao, a venture which gave rise to a close relationship between Wales and the Basque Country.

As Merthyr and its surrounding area were no longer self-sufficient in the materials necessary for iron production, the location of the industry in the upland regions of Glamorgan and Monmouthshire could be considered a liability rather than an asset. As a harbinger of the future, it is significant that in 1868 C. W. Siemens chose to locate his pioneering company, Landore Steel, at Glandŵr near Swansea. At Glandŵr, steel was produced by means of the Siemens open-hearth process; it was expensive, but the steel produced was of a high standard. Siemens steel proved to be ideal for the manufacture of tinplate, a fact which strengthened Swansea's position as the centre of the tinplate industry. Swansea also kept its place as Britain's chief centre of copper production. In 1860, fifteen of the eighteen copper works in the United Kingdom were in Wales. More than half of these were situated in the lower Tawe valley, where there were constant protests over the filth they produced. As in the case of the iron industry, there was an increasing dependence on imported ore, from Chile, Cuba and Australia, although a few Welsh mines – at Llanfachreth, for example, and at Trawsfynydd – continued to be worked until the end of the century. The Swansea area was also the main centre for the smelting of zinc, a metal which became important in the building industry after the discovery of galvanization in 1837. The zinc industry of Swansea flourished at the expense of that of Flintshire, as did the lead industry of Llanelli, a port which in the 1860s dealt with more than half the lead imported into Britain. In that decade the greater part of the lead mined in Wales was also transported to Llanelli. Lead-mining reached its peak in 1862 when Wales produced 27,800 tons of ore. According to the census of 1861, six thousand people were employed in the lead-mines, more than half of them in the mountainous districts around Pumlumon. Mining declined rapidly after 1870, but speculators remained perpetually optimistic: considerable investments were made in railways to serve the mines – lines to

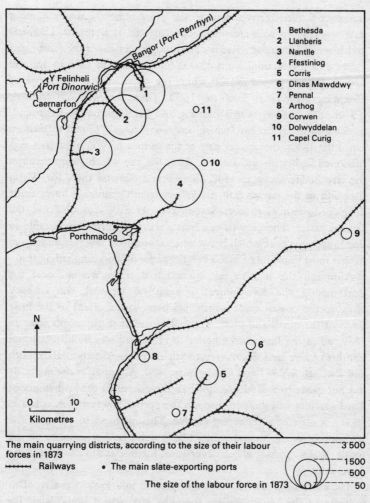

1 Bethesda
2 Llanberis
3 Nantlle
4 Ffestiniog
5 Corris
6 Dinas Mawddwy
7 Pennal
8 Arthog
9 Corwen
10 Dolwyddelan
11 Capel Curig

The main quarrying districts, according to the size of their labour forces in 1873

┼┼┼┼ Railways   • The main slate-exporting ports

The size of the labour force in 1873

3 500
1 500
500
50

The slate quarries of north Wales

Dalar Goch and Minera in 1855, to Van in 1871, to Esgair-hir in 1883 and to Devil's Bridge in 1902.

The quarry-owners of Gwynedd made similar investments. Between 1840 and 1869, ten railways were built to serve the quarrying districts; one of them was the Ffestiniog line, the first narrow-gauge railway in the world to use locomotion. The improvement in transport facilities proved fatal to the more remote quarries, causing slate-working to be increasingly concentrated at Bethesda, Llanberis and Blaenau Ffestiniog. Blaenau Ffestiniog experienced the most rapid increase in production, from 45,000 tons of slate in 1851 to 150,000 tons in 1881, a period during which the population of the parish of Ffestiniog grew from 3,460 to 11,274. There the rock was worked, not in open quarries as in Dinorwig and Penrhyn, but underground, in the enormous caverns which are today such a tourist attraction. Until the 1840s, the greater part of the output of Welsh quarries was marketed in Britain and Ireland. After the fire which swept through the city of Hamburg in 1842, there was a demand there for Welsh slate and in the second half of the nineteenth century a lively trade developed with Germany, Scandinavia, France, Australia and the United States. The growth in exports was particularly favourable to Porthmadog, a port which between 1860 and 1890 saw the golden age of that most beautiful of man's creations, the ocean-going sailing ship.

Although the increase in international trade was a boost for Porthmadog, the development of a railway network was a heavy blow to the coastal trade which had been so important to the little ports of the north and west. The railway reached the north coast in 1849, when the line from Chester to Holyhead was built; it reached Pembrokeshire in 1856, Aberystwyth in 1864, Aberdyfi, Barmouth and Pwllheli in 1867 and Cardigan in 1880. Although maritime trade did not come to a sudden end – half the output of the lead-mines of Cardiganshire was shipped through the port of Aberystwyth as late as 1900 – it suffered accelerating decline. The inheritors of the maritime tradition of the north and west set their sights on Liverpool or on the south Wales ports, where several of them established flourishing companies.

The coming of the railways also proved injurious to the woollen industry of the Severn valley, the chief industry of mid-Wales. By 1850, production was concentrated in the towns of Llanidloes and Newtown at the expense of the smaller enterprises of the countryside. Between 1850 and 1870, there was heavy expenditure on factory buildings and steam-driven machinery in an attempt to compete with the modern woollen mills of Rochdale and Bradford. The attempt was made too late and much of the investment was unwise. It was hoped that the railway, which reached the woollen towns between 1861 and 1863, would enable the goods to win new markets. Instead it had the opposite effect, facilitating a deluge of mass-produced products from the factories of northern England into mid-Wales. The direction of the railway was unfortunate, for, as J. Geraint Jenkins has argued, if the line had led south instead of east, the industry of the Severn valley might well have been saved by the demand for flannel which existed in the south Wales coalfield – a demand which the woollen mills of the Teifi valley were to exploit extensively in the last decades of the century.

A new industry came into existence in Wales as a result of the creation of the railway network. That was the tourist industry. The custom of taking annual holidays developed in the wake of the Industrial Revolution, and even before the coming of the railways some of the seaside towns of Wales – Aberystwyth, Swansea and Tenby, in particular – were eager to attract visitors. Horse-drawn conveyances, however, were insignificant carriers compared with the train. This fact was quickly grasped by Baron Mostyn, the owner of the Gloddaith estate in the old commote of Creuddyn. In 1849, the year in which a railway was built across the commote, he began to plan a holiday resort on his land between the Great and the Little Orme. This was the beginning of the town of Llandudno, which by 1856 had accommodation for eight thousand visitors. Colwyn Bay, the result of developments initiated by the owners of the Pwllcrochan estate, had similar origins, but the development of Rhyl, a town which attracted a less middle-class type of tourist than its two neighbours, was more haphazard. The entrepreneur Thomas Savin had such faith in the flood of visitors which the railway would bring to Aberystwyth that he offered packages which included the journey and accommodation in his hotel on the town's promenade – a vast edifice designed by the architect J. P. Seddon. The Cambrian railway reached Aberystwyth in 1864 and a branch line to Pwllheli was built in 1867, thus accelerating the development of Aberdyfi, Barmouth and Cricieth as holiday resorts. Tenby was connected to the network in 1866 with similar results, and the building of railways in the Vale of Glamorgan permitted convenient trips from the coalfield to the resorts of the Severn Sea. In 1864 the railway reached Llandrindod; the town's springs had been famous since at least 1750, but the fact that they could now be reached by train gave a decided boost to Llandrindod's prosperity. Snowdonia had been encircled by railways by 1880. A strong tradition of mountain-walking already existed, and

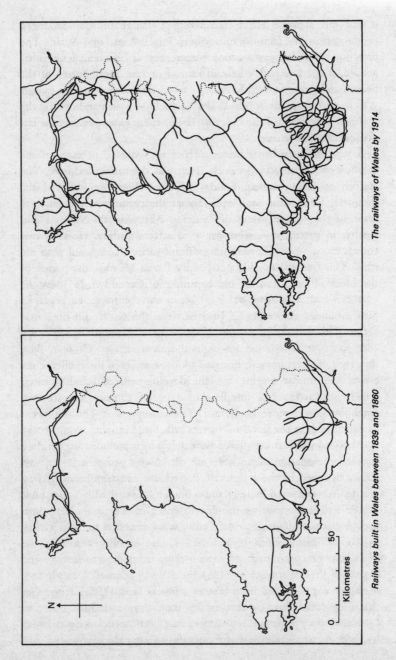

The railways of Wales by 1914

Railways built in Wales between 1839 and 1860

0   50

Kilometres

N

it was noted in 1831 that hardly anywhere was so public as the slopes of Snowdon in midsummer. It was the coming of the railway, however, which opened up Snowdonia to climbers and which made it one of the chief nurseries of the art of mountaineering. Although tourism first came to Wales in the wake of tastes and interests which became fashionable in the period 1775–1800, it was the railways, in the period 1850–75, which gave rise to tourism as an industry – an industry which by now employs more people than the iron and coal industries put together.

It is difficult to discover any aspect of the life of Wales which was not transformed by locomotion. Between 1840 and 1870, 2,300 kilometres of railway were built in the country, an investment, if the cost per kilometre is taken as averaging £10,000, of twenty million pounds in less than a generation. It was the achievement of private capital. Although parliamentary authorization was necessary before railways could be built, the government did not invest a penny in them. Furthermore, unlike the governments of most of the countries of Europe, the government in Britain took no part in planning the railway network; parliament merely responded to schemes put forward by those intent upon making money. Since no one thought of creating an overall plan which would give unity to Wales, railway development there was a matter of connecting different regions of the country with populous areas of England. 'From the national point of view,' wrote the editor of *The Welsh Outlook* in 1920, 'our railway system is the worst in the world.'

Many commentators assumed that the railways would destroy the distinctiveness of Wales – indeed, that was what some of them hoped. A woman in a petticoat and gown trying to restrain the new monster was a favourite subject with cartoonists. Most of the people of Wales, however, eagerly embraced the train; it is difficult now to imagine the thrill of travelling for the first time at a speed of sixty kilometres an hour. Men of progressive ideas such as Thomas Gee and Samuel Roberts doted on the 'steam stallion', and a body of what Tecwyn Lloyd calls 'locomotivistic literature' was composed in praise of it. Although English was the official language of the railways, their coming was a central factor in the cultural history of Wales in the second half of the nineteenth century; the growing popularity of the National Eisteddfod, the vastly increased distribution of books and magazines and the elevation of many ministers to the status of national heroes can all be attributed to the development of the railway network. Above all, national consciousness became more intense as the railways undermined the age-old isolation of the communities of Wales.

The coming of the railways was also central to the agricultural history of Wales. A pattern of trade which had developed over at least half a millennium vanished in their wake. By 1870, the custom of driving cattle along the drovers' roads had come to an end, and the ancient fairs were losing ground as marts were established near railway stations. The railway built between Newport and Haverfordwest (1850–54) was well adapted for the conveyance of produce from the agrarian south-west to the industrial south-east, and therefore the agricultural surplus of south Wales ceased to be exported to Bristol. It cost 17d. a kilometre to carry a ton of butter by cart from the Tywi valley to Merthyr; the equivalent cost by rail was 1·9d. For farmers whose land was near a railway station, the price of lime fell to a quarter of what it had been and they could also make use of other fertilizers such as guano and later, basic slag. With more assured markets for meat and dairy produce, the acreage devoted to corn declined. As a result, the demand for farm-workers fell and their numbers contracted from 73,300 in 1851 to 44,900 in 1871. The railways were mainly responsible for the comparative prosperity of the countryside during 1850–75, a prosperity which was reflected in chapel and church building and in the ability of landowners to rebuild or extend their houses. The more conscientious landlords were prepared to invest heavily in the new prosperity of agriculture, the earl of Powis spending almost a quarter of his rents on improvements between 1859 and 1879. New farmhouses and outbuildings were built on an extensive scale – by Cawdor in Carmarthenshire, for example, and by Talbot in Glamorgan and Grosvenor in Flintshire. W. G. Hoskins claimed that England experienced 'a great rebuilding' between 1575 and 1625; it would appear that it was in the period 1850–75 that such an experience came to the Welsh countryside.

Although the landowners – or some of them at least – made valiant attempts to raise the standard of agriculture in the years 1850–75, that period saw increasingly bitter criticism of landlordism in Wales. In the third quarter of the nineteenth century, the spread of the railways and the penetration of the countryside by capitalist values resulted in a rural awakening throughout Europe. The liberal ideology which had developed in the towns was the basis of the awakening, an ideology fundamentally destructive of the values of traditional rural societies. Samuel Roberts (S.R.) published his *Ffarmwr Careful, Cilhaul Uchaf* in 1850 and his *Diosg Farm* in 1854, pamphlets which mark the beginning of the Welsh attack upon landlordism. The burdens of farmers were also discussed in *Y Cronicl*, the journal founded by S.R. in 1843, and in *Yr Amserau*, the newspaper established by Gwilym Hiraethog in the same year. *Yr Amserau* was merged with Thomas Gee's paper, *Baner Cymru*, in 1859, and thereafter *Baner ac Amserau Cymru* (*Y Faner*) would be the principal scourge of the landlords of Wales.

S.R. declared that landlordism 'soiled, and burdened, and slandered, and humiliated, and degraded, and trampled underfoot the most diligent and hardworking farmers that our old valleys have ever seen'. Consequently, he saw no salvation but through emigration. 'Your hands,' he wrote, 'can earn four times as much on the plains of Ohio and Mississippi as they earn in the valleys of the Dyfi and the Severn.' There were many who were eager to listen to the urgings of S.R. and others. Although the statistics present considerable difficulties, it seems likely that between 1850 and 1870 at least sixty thousand people emigrated from Wales to the United States. To S.R., the main appeal of America was the opportunity to own land. Welsh emigrants were drawn to already existing Welsh rural communities such as Cambria in Pennsylvania, Gallia in Ohio and Oneida in the state of New York, but Welsh migrants also established new farming communities, especially in Wisconsin, where the state's constitution was translated into Welsh for their benefit. The majority of the Welsh, however, settled in towns and areas of heavy industry. Indeed, by the middle of the last century, an increasing number of Welsh emigrants came from non-rural backgrounds. Aberdare was the home of *Y Gwladgarwr* (1858–82), the most pro-American of the periodicals of Wales, and it published a host of letters praising America and urging more people to cross the Atlantic.

As industrialization in the United States proceeded apace, experienced workers were in great demand in places like the ironworks of Pittsburgh and the coalmines of Scranton and Wilkes Barre. Thousands of Welsh people from the industrial areas were

ready to answer the call, especially in view of the declining prosperity
of the Welsh ironworks, and it has been argued that emigration to
America was one of the factors which weakened the Welsh language
in industrial Monmouthshire. The United States was not the only
country to covet the skills of Welsh workers. In 1869, John Hughes
left Merthyr for the Ukraine, where he established the industrial
centre of Yuzovka (Hughesofca), the home of about a hundred Welsh
workers and their families by 1875. (The name was changed to Stalino
in 1924; it later became Donetsk and may yet again become
Yuzovka.)

One of the most unusual migrations from Wales to the United
States had its origins in the industrial areas – in Merthyr in particular.
It resulted from the missionary activities of the Mormon, Daniel Jones
of Abergele. Jones emigrated to America in 1840 and in 1843 he
became a member of the Church of Latter Day Saints. He returned to
Wales in 1845 and, from his headquarters in Merthyr, he gained at least
five thousand converts to his faith. The religious census of 1851
records twenty-eight congregations of Mormons in Wales; the Saints'
periodical, *Utgorn Seion*, was published from 1849 to 1855 and Welsh
hymns were composed in honour of that extraordinary man, Joseph
Smith, the founder of Mormonism. In 1848, 249 Welsh Mormons
emigrated to Salt Lake City in Utah, and the famous Tabernacle
choir had its origins among them. Other groups followed, and
Mormonism in Wales declined in consequence. It was estimated in
1949 that there were twenty-five thousand Mormons of Welsh descent
in America and, since the Saints re-baptize their ancestors, Utah contains
an excellent collection of genealogical material relating to Wales.

The Welsh Mormons were the first non-English-speaking migrants
to settle in Utah. As the mother tongue of most of them was not
English, the experience of the Welsh in America was closer to that of
emigrants from central and eastern Europe than to that of emigrants
from England and Scotland. They felt little allegiance to the state
from which they came and were more ready than almost any other
group of emigrants to seek United States citizenship. It was their
language, particularly their desire for religious services in that
language, which made them eager to establish Welsh communities.
By 1872, there were 384 Welsh-language chapels in the United States
and some two dozen Welsh periodicals had seen the light of day.
Many of the emigrants sought to create a microcosm of Wales. It was

the inability to ensure the continuance of such microcosms that aroused interest in the notion of systematizing the direction of emigration in order to establish Welsh communities which would survive from generation to generation. Michael D. Jones, the minister of a Welsh church in Cincinnati from 1848 to 1850, was an ardent advocate of the notion. 'If we gather together,' he declared in 1849, 'we shall be much more content than we are now in our scattered condition, and we shall have a better ministry and our nation will be saved from extinction.' This was the motivation for S.R.'s clumsy and unsuccessful attempt between 1856 and 1867 to create a Welsh colony in Brynffynnon, Tennessee, and Michael D. Jones had plans for colonies in Wisconsin, Oregon, Vancouver and even in Palestine.

As North America was developing so rapidly, the notion arose that the uninhabited areas of South America would be more likely to provide a permanent home for the Welsh, a notion which fired the imagination of Thomas Benbow Phillips of Tregaron. In 1852, he established a settlement for about a hundred Welsh people, mainly from northern Monmouthshire, in the state of Rio Grande do Sul in Brazil. In 1856, the Welsh of the United States began to consider the merits of Patagonia, a region which was considered to be fertile and thinly populated and only nominally answerable to the government in Buenos Aires. In 1858, Michael D. Jones returned to America to discuss the idea of establishing a Welsh colony in Patagonia, presupposing that the colonists would be found among the Welsh of the United States. By 1860, the scheme had attracted support from some of the Liverpool Welsh, particularly Hugh Hughes (Cadfan Gwynedd) and Lewis Jones. In 1863 Lewis Jones and Love Jones-Parry, the owner of the Madrun estate in Llŷn, visited Argentina. In Buenos Aires, Guillermo Rawson, the Minister of the Interior, offered them a tract of land and promised that *Y Wladfa Gymreig* (The Welsh Colony) would be recognized as one of the states of Argentina when its population reached twenty thousand. This promise was not ratified by the Congress of Argentina because of fears that the British would use the presence of the Welsh as an excuse to seize Patagonia, as they had seized the Malvinas (the Falkland Islands) in 1833.

On 28 May 1865, 163 Welsh people sailed from Liverpool on the ship *Mimosa*, and on 28 July they landed at a place they were later to call Porth Madrun (Puerto Madryn), sixty kilometres north of the valley of the Camwy (Chubut). Most of the emigrants were drawn from the southern coalfield and from Welsh communities in English cities, and, although about half the adults had rural origins, only two had experience of farming. The Camwy valley was not, as R. Bryn Williams put it, *'tir addewid y taer weddiau'* (the fervently prayed-for promised land), for the notion of its innate fertility was completely misleading. The pioneers suffered great privation, and despite grants from the Argentinian government and help from the British Navy only ninety emigrants were left in the valley by 1867. Their efforts were heroic. They mastered the art of irrigating the wilderness, they began to produce a surplus of wheat, they developed a friendly relationship with the native inhabitants – the Tehuelche – and in 1866 they founded under the shadow of the Andes the settlement of Cwm Hyfryd, an offshoot of the original *Wladfa*. Some of the Welsh settlers in Brazil moved to the Camwy valley in 1868, and in 1875–6 about five hundred people from Wales and a few dozen of the Welsh of the United States emigrated to *Y Wladfa*. There was another wave of emigration between 1884 and 1886, and yet another at the beginning of the twentieth century; it is estimated that by 1914, when the migrations came to an end, about three thousand Welsh people had settled in Patagonia.

In the history of southern South America, *Y Wladfa* is of considerable importance. Its existence enabled Argentina to withstand Chile's claims to large tracts of Patagonia, and the activities of the Welsh, particularly the achievements of Ec. Em. Ec. (Cwmni Masnachol Camwy – the Chubut Commercial Company), were central to the economic development of the lower reaches of the continent. Nevertheless, R. Bryn Williams considered *Y Wladfa* to be 'one of the Welsh nation's most magnificent failures'. The intention of the pioneers was to create a society where there would be 'chapel, school and parliament, with the old language the medium of worship, trade, education and government', where 'a strong nation' would develop 'in a Welsh home'. This intention was realized in the years between 1865 and 1875. Every man and woman over the age of eighteen had the vote, and they elected the council of *Y Wladfa* in accordance with the state constitution. The courts of law were organized under the Law for Administering Justice, which was ratified by the council in 1873 and proclaimed by its president. Welsh was the language of these institutions; Welsh was also the language of the Irrigation Company, the Commercial Company, the schools, the chapels (about a dozen in all) and the newspapers. (Publication of the first of these began in 1868; layers of memory and myth lay beneath its title – *Y Brut*.) The government of Argentina was not prepared to allow this state of affairs to continue. Officials were sent to *Y Wladfa* from Buenos Aires in 1880; a bitter dispute arose over military conscription, particularly over the obligation to attend training sessions on Sundays. In 1896, it was enacted that Spanish should be the only medium of instruction in schools, and at the same time immigrants flooded into the Camwy valley from Spain, Chile and Italy. Thereafter, the population of Welsh descent became a declining minority, and in the early 1980s it was noted that 'a conversation in Welsh gets more difficult every day' in Esquel, the chief centre of Cwm Hyfryd.

As far as the history of Wales is concerned, the main significance of the establishment of *Y Wladfa* is the evidence it affords of the existence, in the middle decades of the nineteenth century, of aspirations to Welshness. 'Up to the present time,' declared Saunders Lewis in 1962, 'our lack of national awareness, our deficiency of national pride, prevents us comprehending the significance and heroism of the Patagonia venture.' That venture provides evidence of a desire to create political institutions which would protect and foster Welshness – evidence, in fact, of the existence of Welsh nationalism. This was a new phenomenon. Although consciousness of Welsh nationality was deeply rooted, the notion that there should be political structures which would give expression to that consciousness was not put forward until the second half of the nineteenth century. Similar aspirations emerged among other nationalities in Europe whose languages and cultures were not recognized by the states of which they formed a part – the non-historic nations, to use Friedrich Engels's term. The same pattern of development can be seen in each one of them – from a scholarly interest in the nation's traditions, to cultural rebirth among the populace at large and then on to mass nationalism. These developments should be considered an essential part of the process of modernization. In nineteenth-century Europe, the nationalism of non-historic nations was a progressive force; it challenged the old dynastic and feudal ideologies; it aimed at creating, in the most remote peoples, a consciousness of their cultural identity, and implicit in it was the ethos of democracy.

If the position of ethnic groups like the Slovaks or the Slovenes is compared with that of the Welsh, it will be seen that the nationhood of the Welsh in the mid nineteenth century had firmer foundations than had most of the non-historic nations of Europe. In any consideration of the first step towards nationalism – scholarly activity – the superiority of Wales is obvious. It was further strengthened by the periodical *Archaeologia Cambrensis* (first published in 1846), by the Cambrian Archaeological Association (established in 1847) and by the Honourable Society of Cymmrodorion (re-established in 1873). As far as the second step – the cultural reawakening of the general populace – is concerned, Wales was once more in the forefront. This can be seen from the popularity of the Welsh-language press. In the 1850s, books of poetry in Slovene were unlikely to sell more than a few dozen copies, and there were only three hundred subscribers to the leading literary magazine of the Croats, and this at a time when the readership of Welsh-language periodicals numbered tens of thousands. In 1866, Henry Richard claimed that five quarterlies, twenty-five monthlies and eight weeklies were published in Welsh, and that their circulation totalled 120,000. Welsh-language publishing was so profitable that Scottish companies such as Blackie and Mackenzie considered it to their advantage to enter the field. The most ambitious Welsh-language publishing venture of the century was *Y Gwyddoniadur Cymreig*, a ten-volume encyclopedia, the fruit of the labours of two hundred authors, published between 1854 and 1879 by Thomas Gee. (There was a second edition in 1889–96.) Gee spent £20,000 on the publication and its popularity allowed him at least to cover his costs. Apart from the Bible, the best-selling Welsh-language publication of the 1860s was *Oriau'r Hwyr*, a collection of the poems of Ceiriog; 30,000 copies were sold between 1860 and 1872. Following close on the heels of *Oriau'r Hwyr* were five other volumes of poetry published by Ceiriog in the same decade, incontrovertible evidence of his ability 'to please an audience that was as wide as the nation'.

The success of *eisteddfodau*, large and small, offers further proof of the mass appeal of Welsh-language culture. The first National Eisteddfod was held in Aberdare in 1861, and the following decade saw the shaping of an institution which was to become a central element in the lives of devotees of the Welsh language. Although some of the leaders and sponsors of the eisteddfod were ambiguous in their attitude to the language, and although the work of some prize-winning poets reached what Thomas Parry described as 'the nadir of sterility', the thousands who flocked to *Gwyl Gwalia* (the Festival of Wales) are proof that there was in Wales a hunger and thirst for Welshness. 'When I see,' said Matthew Arnold, who visited the National Eisteddfod at Chester in 1866, 'the enthusiasm which these Eisteddfodds [*sic*] awaken in your whole people . . . I am filled with admiration.' At the Chester Eisteddfod, *Hen Wlad fy Nhadau* (Land of my Fathers – composed in 1856 by Evan and James James of Pontypridd) was sung with such passion that it was adopted forthwith as the national anthem.

By the 1860s, there are indications that some at least among the Welsh saw political implications in their cultural allegiance. This was most obvious among those who had experience outside Wales, in particular in the United States and on Merseyside, the places in which the Patagonia venture had originated. In the nineteenth century, the most nationalistic sentiments published in Welsh were those to be found in Cambro-American periodicals such as *Y Drych*. Gwilym Hiraethog, the editor of *Yr Amserau*, who ministered to a Welsh congregation in Liverpool from 1843 to 1875, was eager to make the Welsh aware of what was happening among Hungarian and Italian nationalists. Although it was the anti-papal aspect of their activities which principally interested him, both Mazzini and the followers of Kossuth expressed their appreciation of his efforts. Manchester was the home of R. J. Derfel (1824–1905), who advocated in 1864 a university for Wales, a Welsh-language daily paper and a national museum and library.

It was no doubt his experience in the United States that made a nationalist of Michael Daniel Jones (1822–98). He insisted that there were economic and political dimensions to Welsh nationality, for he opposed the *laissez-faire* doctrine supported by most of his fellow-radicals. 'There is no consistency,' he said, 'in advocating personal liberty, and in opposing liberty for nations.' He believed that the subjection of the Welsh as a nation was interwoven with their subjection as peasants or industrial workers, and that salvation would not come unless they challenged the power structures which enslaved them. His arguments were nourished by the battle which he fought between 1862 and 1889 against attempts to presbyterianize the Independents. 'There is an obvious connection,' he wrote, 'between our conception of ecclesiastical organization and our political credo.' Hierarchy was anathema to him, and in the same way that he emphasized the value of a community of equal congregations so also did he campaign for a community of equal nations. In his opinion, the chief weakness of the Welsh was their servility – the result of English control of their land, their industries and their commerce, and the dominance of the English language over their courts and schools. He called for Welsh-medium educational establishments – his own college at Bala was the only one which gave the language a place of honour; he condemned the way in which those of the Welsh who achieved worldly success became alienated from their roots; he sought to promote an independent political party for Wales; he was a vehement supporter of trade-unionism and of plans for the nationalization of land, and he lamented that the same concern was not shown for the bodies of the Welsh people as was shown for their souls.

Compeers of Michael D. Jones, men who sought to create a progressive ideology for their people, may be found in others of the non-historic nations, particularly those of central Europe. There, their activities gave birth to mass nationalist movements, and as a result the nationality of peoples such as the Czechs and the Slovenes was placed upon firm foundations. This did not happen in Wales. It is difficult to explain why the Welsh did not tread a path more similar to that of other non-historic nations. Some Welsh historians hold that there is nothing to explain, for they take it for granted that the natural and inevitable fate of the Welsh, as their economy became more complex and their society more modern, was to be increasingly integrated into the state of which they were a part. Yet, as Robin Okey argues, 'set against the wider European background, this generalization does not hold water'. 'Industrialization and the emancipation of suppressed ethnic groups,' claims Okey, 'are the twin shaping themes of modern European history and far from being antagonistic they have proved largely complementary.' This was to some extent the Welsh experience, for, as Brinley Thomas emphasized, it was the ability of industrial Wales to offer a livelihood to a substantial population which provided the basis for a mass culture to flourish in the Welsh language. Nevertheless, the conditions which would have assured the continuance of that culture were not created; above all, the Welsh language did not win sovereignty in its own territory.

This failure is often explained by reference to the large numbers of English people who settled in Wales in the wake of industrial development and the growth of the railways. However, migration to Wales did not become a flood until the beginning of the twentieth century; in the mid nineteenth century, English speakers were hardly a higher percentage of the population of Wales than were German speakers of the population of Bohemia. The vital period was that between 1850 and 1880, a time which saw, from Slovenia to Finland, determined campaigns to secure education in the mother tongue and to win public status for languages which had hitherto enjoyed no official recognition.

There was no corresponding activity in Wales. It must be admitted that, in terms of geography, politics and economics, the circumstances of the Welsh were very different from those of other ethnic groups whose nationhood was more successful than that of the Welsh in wrestling with the challenge of modernization. Perhaps the greatest difference lies in the field of ideology. The universities were the nurseries of the nationalism of the non-historic nations. The ablest and richest of the Anglicans of Wales were educated at Oxford and Cambridge, lacklustre establishments compared with the universities of central Europe, which were benefiting from the intellectual excitement of the German-speaking world. By the second half of the nineteenth century, Anglicans were becoming alienated from Welsh culture as Welshness fell increasingly into the hands of the Nonconformists. The older English universities were not wholly opened to Nonconformists until 1871, and the educational background of the leaders of Welsh-language society was meagre compared with that of their fellows in central Europe. As a result, they borrowed their intellectual values from the middle-class Nonconformists of the large towns of England, people who laid great stress on the rights of individuals, but who had scant regard for the natural rights of communities.

Middle-class English Nonconformists were steeped in Utilitarianism, a creed which deplored everything which might hinder progress. Among such hindrances was the Welsh language. Leaders of the Welsh language community could not pour scorn on the language as did *The Times* or *The London Review*, but the convictions of most of them precluded them from having faith in its future. As a result, from the midst of the vitality of Welsh-language activity in the period 1850–80 came a deluge of statements voicing the conviction – occasionally, indeed, the hope – that the lifespan of the Welsh language was swiftly drawing to a close. As the leading figures of Nonconformity had an unshakeable belief in competition (ordained by heaven, according to John Roberts, S.R.'s brother), to resist the effects of competition, whether between men or between languages, was to flout one of the ordinances of Creation. Although Darwin's theory of evolution (1859) caused much distress to the orthodox, Darwinianism was rapidly adapted to the world of the social sciences. Consequently, it was claimed that the changes which would render inevitable the decease of the Welsh language could be proved scientifically, and that they were independent of the will of man.

Welsh patriots could console themselves with the theory that the demise of the language would not lead to the disappearance of those values which were implicit in Welshness. They had been assured by Matthew Arnold in 1867 that the genius of the Celts lay in their imagination and in their awareness of enchantment and magic, and that Celtic spirituality was an essential element in the 'eclectic imperial graces' (to quote Tecwyn Lloyd) which were at the root of Britain's greatness. Side by side with the honourable contribution which the Welsh could make to the British empire, the Welsh language could be considered an irrelevance – indeed, an impediment. During the following decades, Arnold's ideas were elaborated to such an extent that almost every English virtue was attributed to Celticism and Welshness, and thus was created a body of writing which ranks among the most pathetically comic in the history of the Empire.

As Hywel Teifi Edwards has demonstrated with a host of splendid quotations, it was the National Eisteddfod above all which provided a platform for the Utilitarian, Darwinian and Arnoldian notions of the leaders of the Welsh-speaking community. Their intention was to show that Welsh cultural activities did not constitute a threat of any kind to the unity and tranquillity of the kingdom, and that such activities merited the patronage of the wealthy and the aristocratic. At the same time Hugh Owen endeavoured, through the activities of the Social Science Section of the National Eisteddfod, to prove that Wales was capable of catching up with the rest of Britain.

Owen and his fellows were voicing the standpoint of the Welsh Nonconformist elite. Between 1780 and 1850 – the period when it attracted mass support – Nonconformity was the religion of the common people. But in the wake of the social and economic developments of the latter half of the nineteenth century, the chapels nurtured a leadership which was increasingly middle-class. As Merfyn Jones has written, Welshness was redefined by the members of the Nonconformist elite, and they were skilful in excluding their enemies – and some of their supporters. To quote again – this time from the work of Ieuan Gwynedd Jones – Welshness allied with the chapels on the chapels' terms. As a result, in striking contrast with the first half of the nineteenth century, almost nothing was published in Welsh in the second half which was not acceptable to the denominations, a development which opened the way for English to be the medium for expressing what could not be expressed in Welsh. There is a mass of evidence to prove that the common people of Wales had a lively awareness of their nationality. Welsh was marginal to the lives of the elite; English was their working language, to judge from their diaries and their correspondence. Welsh was the only language of the mass of the people. As Ieuan Gwynedd Jones observes, it permeated their institutions; in it was embodied their vision of their heroic past, for, as Glasynys in Meirionnydd and Morien in Pontypridd bear witness, they still cherished the national myths. 'The function of the giants of Nonconformity,' argues Robin Okey, 'was to abate the nationalist preconceptions of the common people.' It was a task they performed with zeal.

The complexities of the interweaving of Welshness and religion are apparent in the campaign to make the chapels acceptable to non-Welsh speakers. The Wesleyans had had English circuits in Wales since the eighteenth century; the Baptists established the 'English Assembly of Monmouthshire' in 1857; and the Established Church endeavoured, with more success than is generally allowed, to preserve a balance between the two languages. In the latter half of the nineteenth century, the Calvinistic Methodists and the Independents responded to the challenge of English immigration by establishing English-medium chapels. An 'English causes' campaign was launched by the Independents in 1853 and the Methodists followed their example in 1869. Both denominations were motivated partly by the desire to win adherents among wealthy incomers – Welsh congregations had enormous debts and their pastors were often inadequately paid. There were, however, authentic religious reasons for the campaign. Since most Nonconformist leaders in Wales had no faith in the future of Welsh, they were eager to ensure that their own particular spiritual witness should not die out with the language. In the opinion of Lewis Edwards, the desire to extend the blessings of

Calvinistic Methodism to those who spoke no Welsh was similar in essence to the Apostle Paul's desire to take the gospel to the Gentiles. The Independents' campaign proceeded without much controversy, but the efforts of the Methodists attracted the wrath of Robert Ambrose Jones (Emrys ap Iwan); through his attacks upon English causes, he gave expression to a passionate advocacy of the value of the Welsh language.

The campaign to establish English-medium chapels was the result of the belief of the leaders of Welsh Nonconformity that they could assimilate the incoming English religiously if not linguistically. Nonconformity was at its height in the middle of the nineteenth century, and its leaders felt justified in claiming that 'The Nonconformists of Wales are the people of Wales.' The evidence does not entirely support the claim. Religious statistics are a complex matter, and a contentious issue also in view of the bitterness of mid-nineteenth-century denominational rivalries. As the denominations had different criteria for assessing their supporters, it would be unwise to depend on the figures they published. The only fairly reliable source is the religious census of 1851. This gives details of the places of worship and the seating accommodation provided by each denomination and records the number of worshippers attending the services held on Sunday, 30 March 1851. The information is available on the basis of registration districts – forty-eight in all in Wales; they cut across county boundaries, a source of irritation to anyone studying the censuses of the period 1841–1911.

Horace Mann, the organizer of the census, considered that accommodation should be provided in places of worship for 58 per cent of the population; as there was provision for only 51 per cent of the population of England, that country needed seating for a further million worshippers. The situation in Wales was very different; there, 76 per cent of the population could be accommodated in places of worship; indeed, in the districts of Machynlleth, Dolgellau, Pwllheli and Conwy the accommodation was greater than the population. As Mann put it, the Welsh were 'basking in an excess of spiritual privilege'. The excess was the result of the building campaign of the Nonconformists. The chapels of Wales could seat 50 per cent of the country's inhabitants; the equivalent figure in England was 23 per cent. The provision of the Established Church, however, was by no means as inadequate as its enemies sometimes claimed. Of the

898,442 sittings recorded by the census, the percentages of the denominations were as follows: Anglicans, 32; Calvinistic Methodists, 21; Independents, 20; Baptists, 13; various Wesleyans (a denomination much given to schism), 12; others (Catholics, Unitarians, Mormons, Quakers and a few esoteric sects), 2. From the point of view of the provision of sittings, the Established Church was the strongest single denomination in twenty-five of the forty-eight registration districts; indeed, in five of the border districts its seating capacity exceeded that of all the other denominations put together. In the remaining areas, the Methodists were in the lead in thirteen, the Independents in six and the Baptists in four; in one district (Tregaron), a single Nonconformist denomination (the Calvinistic Methodists) had an absolute majority of the sittings.

The rural, Welsh-speaking areas were the strongholds of Methodism, while the strength of the Independents and the Baptists lay in the industrial districts, especially in those where the Welsh language was widely spoken. This suggests a connection between the Welsh language and Nonconformity, and points to a tendency for the industrialized Welsh to favour a congregational system of ecclesiastical government, and for the rural Welsh to favour a more presbyterian system. As the different traditions of Nonconformity appealed to different areas of Wales, none of the denominations apart from the Established Church had a complete network of places of worship in every part of the country. As A. G. Edwards, the first archbishop of Wales, put it: 'The Church is everywhere; Nonconformity only somewhere.' Because of this, and also because of the doctrine that the people of the chapel were a society which had withdrawn from the world, it was difficult for any Nonconformist denomination to think in terms of the well-being of the nation as a whole. The Independents and the Baptists had great influence in the south Wales coalfield, but there was almost no discussion of the problems of industrial Wales in their meetings. As E. T. Davies observes, although Nonconformity 'largely succeeded in dominating [Welsh] industrial society, [it] never became responsible for that society as a whole.'

If the evidence regarding the provision of places of worship is complex, that relating to the use made of the provision is even more abstruse. On 30 March 1851, there was a total of 976,490 attendances in the places of worship of Wales. As the population of the country amounted to 1,163,139, it would not be unreasonable to assume that

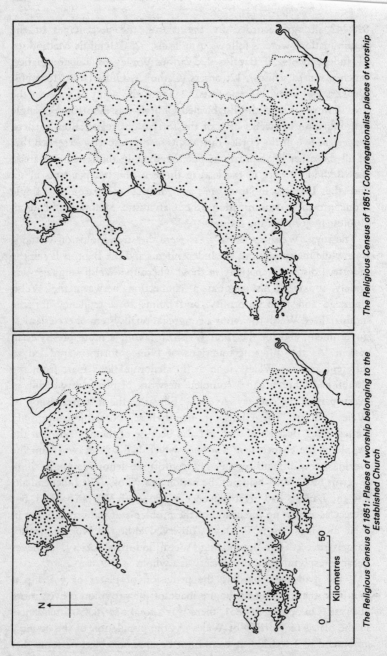

The Religious Census of 1851: Congregationalist places of worship

The Religious Census of 1851: Places of worship belonging to the Established Church

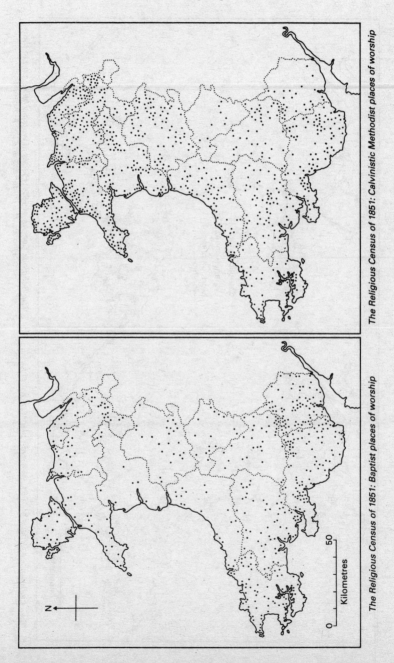

The Religious Census of 1851: Calvinistic Methodist places of worship

The Religious Census of 1851: Baptist places of worship

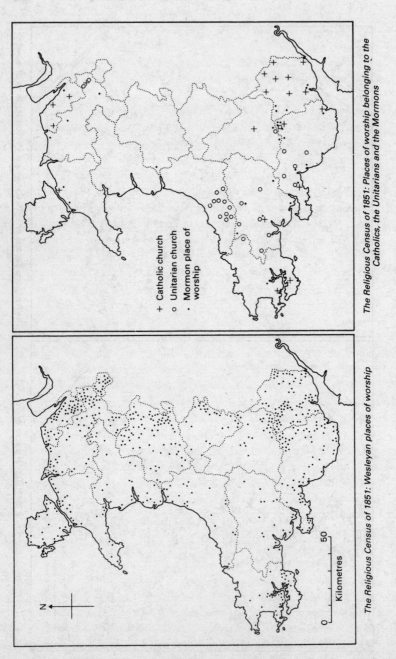

The Religious Census of 1851: Places of worship belonging to the Catholics, the Unitarians and the Mormons

+ Catholic church
o Unitarian church
• Mormon place of worship

The Religious Census of 1851: Wesleyan places of worship

N

Kilometres
0   50

everyone capable of attending a place of worship had done so. This accords with the traditional conception of Wales in the reign of Victoria – that the entire population was involved with organized religion. Of the attendances, 80 per cent were recorded in chapels and 20 per cent in parish churches, providing a basis for the oft-made claim that in the mid nineteenth century four Welsh people out of every five were Nonconformists. But the situation was not quite as simple as that. There were places of worship which returned highly optimistic estimates, and it must be borne in mind that the attendance figures were a record not of individuals but of attendances. As most places of worship offered two services on a Sunday and many offered three or more, and as the devout delighted in attending as many services as possible, large numbers of people must have been counted twice if not thrice; indeed, in the Aberystwyth district, the most religious in Wales, the attendance figures accounted for 121 per cent of the population. If only the attendances at the service which attracted the largest congregation are counted, then the total present in the places of worship of the five main denominations amounts to 480,000 people, or 40 per cent of the population. The percentage for each denomination was as follows: Calvinistic Methodists, 25; Independents, 23; Anglicans, 21; Baptists, 18; Wesleyans, 13. The Anglicans were the strongest denomination in the registration counties of Montgomery, Radnor, Pembroke and Flint, the Independents in Brecon, Glamorgan and Carmarthen, the Baptists in Monmouth and the Calvinistic Methodists in the rest. If it is accepted that about 40 per cent of the Welsh people attended a place of worship on 30 March 1851 (a day when there was pressure on adherents to make sure that they were counted), then large numbers of the inhabitants of Wales in the mid nineteenth century must have lacked any formal link with a place of worship; indeed, those of no religion when added to the Anglicans account for more than half the population; thus the Nonconformists were a minority in Wales.

The irreligious are a lost element in Welsh historiography; as they have left virtually no written record, the historians of the twentieth century have tended to ignore them. The religious leaders of the nineteenth century were well aware of their existence. They tried by means of missions, revivals and a flurry of temperance activity to entice them to places of worship or, if that failed, to legislate them into respectability. However, although the existence of an irreligious element must be acknowledged, it was much smaller in Wales than it was in England, a fact proudly proclaimed in countless speeches. Too much can no doubt be made of the difference between the two countries, for England had a greater variety of communities than did Wales. Wales, for example, had none of the enormous conurbations which were already, in 1851, a source of despair to the devotees of organized religion. Nevertheless, the contrast is striking, and Scott Latourette, a leading historian of Christianity, claimed that religion had been more successful in retaining the allegiance of the mass of the population in Wales than in any other country in Europe.

The religious census of 1851 underlined a fact of which the Nonconformists of Wales were already aware – that their adherents, when taken together, were far more numerous than those of the Anglican Church. In the second half of the nineteenth century, that awareness caused them to be increasingly ready to challenge the privileges of the Established Church. Those privileges were especially offensive to members of the chapel-going middle class, a class which was increasingly prosperous and which coveted social recognition and political power commensurate with its commercial and professional status. Its members could win full citizenship only through legislation, and accordingly a new conception developed of the kind of man suitable to represent a Welsh constituency. In the general election of 1852, the Cardiff constituency was won by the Unitarian Walter Coffin, Wales's first Nonconformist member of parliament, a victory which ended the Bute family's control of the seat. In the same election, the wealthy Methodist Richard Davies, a shipowner from Menai Bridge, stood as candidate in Caernarfon Boroughs. Although he was unsuccessful, his candidature had considerable significance, for it demonstrated that the Methodists were increasingly ready to be included, side by side with the denominations which had sprung from the old dissenting tradition, in a united Nonconformist political front.

In the general elections which followed – those of 1857, 1859 and 1865 – more candidates of the same type as Richard Davies entered the field. Yet, the rise of politicized Nonconformity should not be antedated. In those three elections, there were ninety-six returns for the thirty-two constituencies of Wales; of the returns, eighty-one were uncontested. In 1865, eighteen Liberals and fourteen Conservatives were elected, the first occasion for Wales to have a Liberal majority. This should not be attributed to a Nonconformist upsurge. Indeed, when seeking to analyse the growth of Liberalism in Wales, it is tempting to overstress the denominational factor. The influence of Whig landowners – families like the Stanleys, the Talbots, the Hanmers and the Lewises – was still considerable, and the Free Trade policy of the Liberal party was a key factor in determining the allegiance of the new industrialists. Free Trade meant cheap food, a matter of vital concern to the urban working class, while the Liberal emphasis on the individual, and on the ability of all citizens to improve their lot through industriousness and prudence, was an ideology exactly suited to the rising Welsh middle class. There is a tendency to depict Liberalism in nineteenth-century Wales as a moral crusade; it would be equally correct to look upon it as a convenient instrument for promoting the interests of various groups and classes within Welsh society.

Nevertheless, Nonconformity could be the central issue in an electoral battle. That was the case in 1859 in Meirionnydd, the most remote of all the Welsh constituencies. Meirionnydd had been represented time out of mind by a succession of Tory squires, and for a century and a half every member but one had been returned unopposed. In 1859, W. W. E. Wynne, the owner of the Peniarth estate, was the candidate for the third time, and his supporters assumed that in accordance with age-old tradition his path to parliament would be unimpeded. Wynne was a distinguished Welsh bibliophile; he was the owner of many of the most important Welsh manuscripts, and he himself had made intelligent use of them, as can be seen from his articles in *Archaeologia Cambrensis*. He was also a zealous supporter of the Oxford Movement; under his patronage, elaborate services were held in Llanegryn church in accordance with the tenets of High Anglicanism. It was Wynne's religious convictions and the threat to Protestantism that was implicit in them, rather than his Toryism or his membership of the landed class, that disturbed the leaders of Nonconformity in Meirionnydd, particularly the influential group of intellectuals centred upon the town of Bala. They provided the backing for the candidature of David Williams, a Liberal solicitor from Penrhyndeudraeth, and their efforts were bolstered by the religious revival which swept through Wales in 1859. Williams was beaten by 389 votes to 351, but the Meirionnydd squires were flabbergasted by their tenants' willingness to challenge them. On the whole, the squires were genial and generous men, but they did not understand the new forces – urban in origin – which were undermining their role as the natural leaders of rural society. Their reaction was bitter: twelve tenants were evicted – five on the Rhiwlas estate and seven on the Wynnstay estate – while various penalties were imposed upon the tenants of other estates. The evictions caused consternation among the inhabitants of Meirionnydd, proof that they were wholly exceptional acts on the part of the landowners. They cast a heavy shadow over the society and the politics of the county; by trying to safeguard the old estate bonds, the squires had ensured that they would speedily be loosened. They ensured also that Meirionnydd, formerly the most conservative of the Welsh constituencies, would henceforth be among the most progressive.

The following decade, from 1859 to 1868, was a period of considerable significance in the political history of Wales. Although, at first glance, the decade seemed comparatively placid, it was a period of rapid growth in the political consciousness of the Welsh. The press, in particular, flourished. 'Taxes on Knowledge' were abolished in 1855 and the duty on paper came to an end in 1861, bringing prosperity to a host of periodicals, many of which were far more political than those of preceding decades. The most famous was Thomas Gee's *Baner*, published in Denbigh, although papers published in the south, such as *Seren Cymru*, *Y Gwron* and *Y Gwladgarwr*, probably had a greater influence in the more populous areas of Wales. In addition, there was a reading public for working-class papers from England such as *The Beehive* and *The National Reformer*, while some of the English-language weeklies published in Wales were quite radical – *The Star of Gwent*, for example, and *The Cardiff Chronicle*. These papers gave coverage to the activities of the Liberation Society, a movement which, following its successful conference in Swansea in 1862, sought to establish cells in every part of Wales. The society was chiefly responsible for the fact that the politicization of the Welsh took place in a socio-denominational context. That context was analysed in Henry Richard's *Letters on the Social and Political Condition of Wales* (1866), a volume which proved influential in Wales and in England.

The Welsh radical press also gave publicity to the attempts to revive the issue of Parliamentary Reform. As has been seen, the Reform Act of 1832 had had only a minimal impact upon the size of the electorate; indeed, its scope was so narrow that the percentage of the population having the right to vote was tending to decline. Of the 1.3 million inhabitants of Wales in 1866, only 62,000 were entitled to vote. The National Reform Union was established in 1864 and the Reform League in 1866; branches of both bodies were formed in Wales although they were only intermittently active. The Liberal government's Reform Bill of 1866 was a failure, largely because of the opposition of elements on the right wing of the Liberal party. There were Welsh MPs among them, men who preferred, according to Henry Richard, to 'sacrifice their professed principles rather than see the representation of the kingdom slip from the grasp of their class'. It was the Tories under Disraeli who brought the matter to a successful conclusion. The Parliamentary Reform Act of 1867 gave the vote to every male householder in the borough constituencies and to every male householder occupying premises rated at £12 or more in the county constituencies. Increased representation was given to large towns, but voting continued to be a public act. The measure created 59,000 new electors in Wales, the vast majority of them in the boroughs. The Merthyr Tydfil constituency, which was given an additional member, experienced the greatest increase. There, the number of voters rose from 1,387 to 14,577; henceforward, Merthyr would be the most 'democratic' constituency in the kingdom.

Fifteen months after the Reform Bill became law, its provisions were put to the test in the general election of November 1868. That election was to have a central place in Welsh Liberal mythology. Forty years later, Lloyd George claimed that it had 'awakened the spirit of the mountains ... The political power of the landlords in Wales was shattered as completely as the power of the Druids.' Lloyd George was guilty of some exaggeration. Most of the twenty-three Liberals elected were Whigs of the landed class, and every one of the ten Conservatives came from the ranks of the landowners. Nevertheless, the results from about a quarter of the Welsh constituencies showed the way in which the wind was blowing. In Merthyr Tydfil, where it had been assumed that local industrialists would be returned for the two seats, there was a dramatic intervention by Henry Richard. His eloquent speeches in support of the rights of Nonconformists, and the sympathy which he showed for the economic problems of the working class, enabled him to poll 11,683 votes and to push H. A. Bruce, the trustee of the Dowlais works (later to be elevated to the Lords as Baron Aberdare), into third place. Richard Davies was elected unopposed in Anglesey, as was David Williams in Meirionnydd. Although Sir Watkin Williams Wynn kept his seat, his fellow member for Denbighshire – the Whig, Robert Myddelton Biddulph of Chirk Castle – was defeated by a barrister, George Osborne Morgan. Another barrister, Watkin Williams, who like Morgan was an Anglican who sympathized with the Liberation Society, won Denbigh Boroughs. In Cardiff, the Bute estate's costly attempt to regain the seat was unavailing; the failure was attributed to the lack of a local Conservative paper, and as a result the *Western Mail* was launched on 1 May 1869. In Cardiganshire, one of the Vaughans of Trawsgoed was beaten by E. M. Richards, a Baptist shipbuilder from Swansea, while there was a fierce battle in Carmarthenshire, where the Nonconformists were urged to plump for the radical landowner, E. J. Sartoris of Llangennech. In Caernarfonshire, George Douglas-Pennant, Baron Penrhyn's son, lost his seat to Love Jones-Parry of Madrun, one of the sponsors of the Patagonia venture.

Much of this Liberal upsurge may be attributed to the influence of Whig landowners. The backing of the squire of Gogerddan was a central factor in the success of Richards in Cardiganshire, and Davies would not have had a free run in Anglesey but for the Liberal leanings of most of the county's landowners. The squire of Cefnamwlch was praised by *Y Faner* for ensuring that his tenants 'formed a neat and organized procession' to vote for Jones-Parry. While the tenants of estates owned by Whigs were willing to obey their landlords, Tory landlords were dismayed by the disobedience of some of their tenants. The election of 1868, like that of 1859 in Meirionnydd, was followed by vengeance. It was claimed that eighty workers at the Penrhyn Quarry lost their jobs following Douglas-Pennant's defeat and that hundreds of tenants in the counties of Cardigan and Carmarthen were served with notice to quit; it is accepted that this was the fate of forty-three in the former county and of twenty-six in the latter. A fund for the relief of homeless tenants raised £20,000, and the subject was brought before the House of Commons by Henry Richard and others. The experience of the 'Martyrs of '68' was a potent symbol in the political awakening which was afoot in Wales. The secret ballot was achieved in 1872 partly because of the experiences of Welsh tenants. The power of the landlords did not disappear altogether with the advent of the ballot. The long-standing belief that the landlord was the natural leader of society did not vanish immediately. In addition, although voting, by the time of the general election of 1874, was a secret act, going to the poll was not. Being a political activist was even more of a public act, and an awareness of the power of landed Conservatives prevented many radicals from campaigning. Four years after the Ballot Act, Gwilym Marles and his Unitarian congregation were deprived of their chapel by a vengeful landlord.

The future of the Established Church in Ireland was the main issue of the general election of 1868. It could claim the allegiance of only 12 per cent of the people of Ireland, and Gladstone, the Prime Minister, succeeded in disestablishing and disendowing it in 1869. As has been noted, there was little brotherly love between the Welsh and the Irish, and many Welsh Protestants feared that with the ending of the Establishment the Catholic Church would consolidate its hold over Ireland. Nevertheless, the Welsh could not but discern a parallel between the position of the Established Church in Ireland and in Wales. Indeed, from 1868 until the First World War, the example of Ireland was to be important to Wales. In Ireland, disestablishment was followed by legislation on land tenure, education, temperance and home rule, and on each occasion the cry arose that Wales had the right to the same treatment as was accorded to the Irish.

The parallel can be taken too far, for there were quite as many contrasts as there were similarities between the experiences of the two nations. This was especially true in the matter of the Church Establishment. The 'Anglican' Church of Ireland was a distinct body with its own archbishops; the greater part of the Irish people had never been members of it and its contribution to native Irish culture had been meagre. The Anglican Church in Wales was part of the archdiocese of Canterbury; it had been the spiritual home of the majority of the Welsh for at least eight generations and its members had made an enormous contribution to the culture of Wales. There was in Wales no movement similar to the National Association which campaigned for the disestablishment of the Church of Ireland. Although the Liberation Society deployed a considerable amount of its resources in Wales, its aim was the disestablishment of the Church of England in its entirety.

From the standpoint of the Liberation Society, Watkin Williams's statement, within a month of the Irish disestablishment measure becoming law, that he intended to introduce a bill to disestablish the Church of England in Wales, was a rash act. The attempt was a failure – only seven of the MPs of Wales supported it – but it could be claimed that it was Williams's initiative which placed Welsh disestablishment on the political agenda. It was to remain there until 1920, when a disestablished province of the Anglican Communion was created in Wales. Although it would be mistaken to believe that the issue was central to Welsh politics throughout that period, it left its mark upon more than one aspect of the life of the nation.

By the 1880s, the Liberals of Wales had accepted that there was little hope of disestablishing the Church of England in its entirety. They therefore concentrated their efforts on disestablishment for Wales alone; at the same time, the Conservatives aroused themselves to defend the Establishment. By seeking disestablishment for Wales alone, the Liberals were obliged to prove that Wales was an entity which could reasonably demand separate legislation on such a delicate issue; that is, it became necessary for them to insist that the Welsh were a nation, and that that fact had political and legal implications. On the other hand, the defenders of the Establishment were obliged to deny such a premise; consequently, the Conservatives, who were not in origin more un-Welsh than the Liberals, were manoeuvred into a position in which they could be portrayed as an anti-Welsh party, a development which would cast a long shadow over the politics of Wales. As the Nonconformists won more and more concessions, the substance of their grievance against the Establishment was eroded. In 1912, a book entitled *Nonconformist Disabilities* was published; only thirteen of its 147 pages dealt with 'Disabilities still unredressed'. By that time, it was not repression but rather the memory of repression which fuelled the desire to bring the matter to a successful conclusion – 'a splendid example,' as W. J. Gruffydd put it, 'of the time-lag in history'. 'There was something distasteful to me,' Gruffydd declared in 1926, 'in the movement which eventually succeeded in disestablishing the Church.' He was dismayed by the energy expended and the denominational bitterness fostered in order to win what was portrayed as a national victory, energy which could have been better directed to activity based upon a shared consciousness of the national heritage.

Gruffydd considered that the Welsh character of the Church was more secure under a system in which the bishops were appointed by the government. By the last decades of the nineteenth century, there was substance to his argument, for from 1870, when Joshua Hughes was appointed bishop of St Asaph by Gladstone, until 1920, when the Church gained the right to elect its bishops, no non-Welsh-speaking cleric was elevated to a see in Wales. By 1870, the Anglican revival was at its height. Between 1851 and 1910, 347 new churches were built in Wales, a number of them admirable examples of the Neo-Gothic style; in addition, almost all the old churches – nearly a thousand of them – were renovated or rebuilt. Efforts were particularly striking in the diocese of Llandaf, where 170 churches were built during the episcopate of Alfred Ollivant (1849–82). By the end of the century, old failings such as plurality and non-residence had disappeared and the fifteen hundred Anglican clerics who laboured in the Welsh vineyard were industrious and well conducted. The fruits of the revival were to be seen in the numbers of communicants. They doubled between 1851 and 1910, a more substantial increase than was experienced by the Nonconformists in that period.

There was one field in which the Anglicans were exceptionally active. That was elementary education. By 1870, as a result of the campaign begun by Hugh Owen in 1843, the British Society had approximately three hundred schools in Wales; the National Society, however, had more than a thousand. The influence wielded by Anglican schoolmasters was a source of anxiety to Nonconformists, and Thomas Rees, in his influential book *A History of Protestant Nonconformity in Wales* (1861), expressed his fear that the schoolmasters might accomplish what centuries of persecution had failed to do. Despite the efforts of the two societies, a comprehensive network of elementary schools had not been established in Wales – or in England either. For decades, there had been calls for the state to create such a network, but every attempt had come to grief because of the unwillingness of the Anglicans and the Nonconformists to compromise over the kind of religious education that should be offered in state schools.

The Liberal government elected in 1868 sought to solve this thorny problem through the Education Act of 1870, an attempt to create a system of educational provision comparable with that of countries such as Prussia. The act was essentially a piece of class legislation. The intention was to ensure that there would be a complete network of elementary schools which would give basic skills to the children of the lower classes; the provision was to be complete in itself and would come to an end when the child reached the age of thirteen. It was not primary education, for there was no intention that the child should go on to intermediate and higher education – that was the privilege of middle- and upper-class children. The Education Act recognized the existence of the schools of the National Society and the British Society and government grants to them were continued. In places where educational provision was insufficient, the act authorized the setting-up of a School Board with the power to build schools which would be funded by local rates. The board was to determine whether or not there should be religious education in its schools, but such education, if given, was not to be denominational; however, under Clause 25 of the act, the boards were empowered to pay the fees of poor children attending denominational schools.

This was probably the best compromise attainable at the time, but it pleased nobody. The British schools were incorporated into the School Board system, but the National and Roman Catholic schools insisted on remaining apart. As they received no help from the rates, their resources could not compete with those of the Board schools, a cause of bitterness to members of the Church of England. The Nonconformists were bitter in their turn because Board schools were not set up in those localities where there were sufficient places in the schools of the National Society, even if the majority of the children of the locality came from Nonconformist families. It was claimed that Wales had three hundred such localities, and in them young chapel-goers were drilled in the catechism of the Church of England – a splendid way in which to rear a rebel, as Lloyd George's career bears witness. Nonconformists such as Henry Richard argued in favour of schools which would not offer any religious teaching at all, an argument which was accepted in its essentials by about half the 320 School Boards established in Wales. The Nonconformists were also angered by Clause 25, for it meant that the rates could be used to subsidize denominational education. As a result, School Board elections were ferocious sectarian battles. Nevertheless, the boards achieved considerable success. Their schools, often distinctive buildings with their high windows and their bell-towers, came to be familiar features in all parts of Wales. By 1880, when education became compulsory, provision was fairly adequate for the majority of children, although there were many overcrowded schools in the highly procreative society of the coalfield.

It has frequently been claimed that the 1870 act was mainly

responsible for the decline in the proportion of the population of Wales able to speak Welsh. Yet the tradition of teaching through the medium of English had taken a firm hold in Wales before 1870. It was strengthened by the system of allocating money to the schools on the basis of each child's performance in an annual test. The principle of 'payment by results' was adopted in 1861 and, as the tests were restricted to knowledge of arithmetic and the ability to read and write English, Welsh was driven out of the schools. There was little protest at the time. Some candidates for seats on the School Boards raised the issue – Jonathan Morgan in Swansea, for instance – but their weak voices were drowned by denominational dissension. The attitude of most of the public figures of Wales towards the Welsh language was ambiguous, and among working-class parents awareness of the usefulness of English was increasing; after all, literacy in Welsh could be attained in Sunday school. By 1891, when questions concerning linguistic ability were first included in the census, 54 per cent of the inhabitants of Wales could speak Welsh and 69 per cent could speak English. It seems not unreasonable to assume that it was in the decade 1870–80 that the ability to speak English (even if that ability was often elementary) became more common in Wales than the ability to speak Welsh. To a certain extent, the change can be attributed to the spread of the elementary schools; the completion of a network of English-medium schools was a heavy blow to Welsh, especially in those areas where the language was already in retreat. Yet a variety of other factors – demographic, social, economic and attitudinal – were also at work, and it is probable that in this century supporters of the Welsh language have subjected the act of 1870 to excessive condemnation.

The elementary schools were only one aspect of the surge of educational activity which swept through Wales in the second half of the nineteenth century. In many ways, this activity was the most significant development of the period. Between 1859 and 1914, education was by far the most frequently discussed topic in the leading articles of *Y Faner*. Because of the growth in the number of schools, it was necessary to provide training for teachers. Here again the Anglicans were in the lead: they established Trinity College, Carmarthen, in 1848, and a college (later St Mary's College, Bangor) in Caernarfon in 1856. The Nonconformists were satisfied for years with the training provided by the British Society in its college in

Borough Road in London, and it is known that 166 Welshmen attended the college between 1844 and 1856. To satisfy the increased demand, the Normal College, Bangor, was established in 1858, in the centre of the region which had been stirred by Hugh Owen's letter of 1843. Hugh Owen himself was chiefly responsible for the Normal College and it rapidly developed into a college for Nonconformists from all parts of Wales.

In 1858, Hugh Owen's contribution to education in Wales was merely beginning. He wanted to create a middle class for Nonconformist Wales – a well-conducted, ambitious and enlightened class. His efforts reached their apogee in his unwearying campaign to create a university for Wales. The idea had been ventilated in the 1840s by exiled Welsh clergymen in Yorkshire, and a committee to promote the idea was established in 1854. The scheme was modelled on the system in Ireland, where a government grant of £100,000 to build three non-denominational colleges had been provided in 1845. But the Welsh did not have the same power as the Irish to wring concessions from the government and they therefore had to rely upon voluntary contributions. The committee dithered for years and the response to its appeal for money was disappointing. In 1867, £10,000 was paid for the huge hotel built in Aberystwyth by the bankrupt entrepreneur Thomas Savin, a purchase which opened one of the most remarkable chapters in the history of education in Wales. Aberystwyth College was opened on 16 October 1872, with twenty-six students, a principal (T. C. Edwards, the talented son of Lewis Edwards), two professors and a registrar. Since the main aim of Hugh Owen and his associates was to provide young men (women were not accepted until 1884) with an education which would fit them to be successful applicants for posts throughout Britain and the Empire, Welsh had no place in the original curriculum. The college had to wait until 1885 before it received any state help and until then it was in continual difficulty. It was saved by the leadership of Edwards, the dedication of Owen, occasional substantial contributions from the industrialist David Davies and, above all, by the generosity of a host of ordinary Welsh people – seventy thousand people contributed to the costs of the college in 1875 alone. As will be seen, intermediate education in Wales was hugely inadequate and until the 1890s Aberystwyth was obliged to give many of its students an intermediate rather than a higher education. Among those students were some of the ablest Welshmen of their age and to a great extent the college was the cradle of the cultural and national revival of late-nineteenth-century Wales.

Although the title University College of Wales was conferred upon Aberystwyth, the time would come when the populous communities of the industrial south would expect a college of their own. Those communities were growing quickly in confidence and self-awareness. During the 1870s – a key period in their history – the population of Glamorgan increased by 113,574, while the population of almost all the rural counties of Wales declined. At the beginning of the decade, there was a huge boom in the market for coal; between 1869 and 1873, its price rose from 8s. 6d. to 23s. 3d. a ton and a dozen new pits were opened in the Rhondda valley alone. The decade saw a rapid increase in steam-ships, a development of which the Cory Brothers of Cardiff, with their eighty coaling stations located at key points along the world's sea-routes, took full advantage. By 1880, 32 per cent of the coal exported from Britain came from Wales, and Cardiff was acknowledged to be the most important coal port in the world. Between 1871 and 1881, exports from Cardiff increased by 120 per cent and its population rose by 44 per cent; the town, as Gwyn A. Williams put it, was transformed 'from a counting-house into a community'. In the process, Cardiff discovered that it had a Welsh dimension. Although the language of the town was increasingly English, its inhabitants realized that there was more dignity in being the principal town of Wales than in being merely one of a host of provincial English towns. In 1873, it was referred to for the first time as the metropolis of Wales, and Neil Evans maintains that it was from Cardiff that the first declaration of an Anglo-Welsh identity was heard.

The same tendency is to be observed in the movement which succeeded in 1881 in creating the Welsh Rugby Union. Although St David's College, Lampeter, was the cradle of the game in Wales, it spread quickly in industrial Wales in the 1870s. The union's principal founder, Richard Mullock of Newport, wanted a national rather than a provincial team, and as a result rugby was grafted on to Welshness and became a powerful symbol of the nation's identity. Rugby's popularity can probably be attributed to the particular nature of the industrialization in Wales. As Gareth Williams and Dai Smith argue, the more energetic the physical labour in which a workforce is

involved, the more strenuous the physical relief it craves. Rugby was
one of a series of games which developed in Britain in the third
quarter of the nineteenth century – the concept of leisure was twin to
the concept of work which had developed in the wake of the Industrial
Revolution. Organized games with their numerous rules fitted in
with the employers' desire to create a disciplined workforce, and the
sponsorship of industrialists was a central factor in the spread of
rugby.

The rugby clubs could draw upon the strong tradition of communal
activity which had taken root in the industrial districts of Wales. The
chapels were the most obvious products of this tradition, but it had its
secular aspects also. A network of friendly societies developed in the
coalfield, an attempt by the working class to create organizations
which would preserve them from the clutches of the Poor Law and
which brought colour and ceremony into lives which could otherwise
be drab. In 1864, five thousand of the inhabitants of Dowlais were
members of friendly societies; one of the most popular was the True
Ivorites, a movement thoroughly Welsh in language and culture. The
first cooperative shop in Wales was opened in Cwm-bach, Aberdare,
in 1860, and in the 1860s Mechanics' Institutes were established in
most of the towns of the coalfield. Their founders were men of
prudence and circumspection, for in the second half of the nineteenth
century there was a reaction against the violent protests and the
idealistic hopes which had been characteristic of the preceding
generation.

The members of the working class were taught by that astonishingly
influential volume, Samuel Smiles's *Self Help* (1859; Welsh translation,
Tonypandy, 1898), and by a host of other publications in both Welsh
and English that the existing order of things was in essence acceptable;
by working hard and living frugally, they could hope to rise in the
world. This was a philosophy which appealed strongly to the skilled
working class – the 'aristocracy of labour'. It was reflected in the craft
unions which were established by mechanics, carpenters and others,
the most successful union activity of the 1850s and 1860s. With their
suspicion of strikes and their emphasis on prolonged apprenticeship,
these unions, like the Trades Councils created by them, upheld all the
assumptions of Victorian Liberalism, and in Cardiff, Swansea and
other Welsh towns they played a central role in ensuring the success
of that Liberalism.

Viable unionism was slower to take root among the most numerous workforce of industrial Wales – the miners of the south Wales coalfield. This did not mean that there was no unrest among them. As the price of coal was so unstable and as wages were so high a proportion of production costs, hardly a year went by in the 1850s and 1860s without the employers reducing wages and the employees striking in protest. There is evidence of the existence of some local lodges and, on occasion, of more widespread organization. As a rule, however, protest was spontaneous, especially the bitter resistance to the remnants of the truck system and to the employers' use of strike-breakers.

Although G. T. Clark, the manager of Dowlais, claimed in 1867 that the Welsh had an innate talent for communal action, the development of unionism was hindered by a number of factors. One of these was the division between the collieries serving the iron industry and those producing coal for sale, a division which also prevented the employers from presenting a united front. It was the attempt by the owners of the steam-coal pits to reduce wages in order to bridge the division between them and the ironmasters which sparked off the 1871 strike in the Cynon and Rhondda valleys, an important milestone in the history of unionism. The Amalgamated Association of Mineworkers (the AAM) had been established in Lancashire in 1869, but initially it received only a lukewarm welcome from the workers of the south Wales coalfield. Following the AAM's support of the strike of 1871, they flocked to join it and by 1873 the association had 45,000 Welsh members. Its support also proved valuable during the strike of 1873 by the miners employed by the iron companies. With the help of the AAM, the miners succeeded in profiting from the boom of 1869 and 1873, but their success proved short-lived. The Monmouthshire and South Wales Coalowners Association was established in 1873, an alliance of eighty-five companies owning 222 pits between them. The boom came to an end in 1874 and reductions in wages were insisted upon. In the battle which followed between the employers and the AAM, the employers were able to use their new unity to lock out the entire workforce; it was not therefore possible to sustain the strikers through the assistance of men who remained at work. By the summer of 1875 the miners had been beaten and the union was bankrupt; it was dissolved before the end of the year.

This chapter in the history of miners' unionism came to an end with the system which was adopted in December 1875. From 1875 until 1903, pay in the coal industry was determined according to a Sliding Scale, which meant that wages rose and fell in accordance with the price of coal. The Sliding Scale had its virtues; it also had its weaknesses, for henceforth employers and employees shared in the risks of capital; furthermore, the system encouraged the employers to undersell and over-produce. After the adoption of the Sliding Scale, unionism had little part to play, for there could be virtually no collective bargaining over wages. Nevertheless, an attempt was made to build some kind of organization upon the remnants of the AAM, and by 1880 there were a number of small district unions in the coalfield.

The Cambrian Miners' Association established in the Rhondda was the strongest of these, and it was this body which appointed William Abraham (Mabon) as full-time organizer in 1877. For the rest of the century, Mabon was to be the most prominent of the miners' leaders of the south Wales coalfield. During that period, he, more than anyone else, symbolized the values of Welsh industrial society. A zealous Methodist and an enthusiastic *eisteddfodwr*, he embraced the Liberal consensus, believing that the interests of labour and capital were essentially the same. He had been deeply moved by the distress caused by the strike of 1875 and he welcomed the Sliding Scale as a means of avoiding conflict; this it did, for there were no great disturbances in the coalfield between 1875 and 1893. 'Half a loaf is better than no loaf at all' was Mabon's favourite saying, and he devoted himself to winning piecemeal concessions. He succeeded on more than one occasion in modifying the terms of the Sliding Scale in favour of the workers; he was prominent in pressing for legislation on safety and conditions of work; he laboured to obtain support for the Miners' Permanent Provident Society; in 1888, he won his most famous victory, a holiday for the miners on the first Monday of each month – Mabon's Day. Mabonism was acceptable as long as there was no divergence between the price of coal and the price of commodities in general. A time would come when there would be such a divergence and when faith in Mabon's interpretation of the relationship between capital and labour would be undermined. Until the beginning of the 1890s, however, his leadership received general support; in 1891, the wages of the miners of the south Wales coalfield were 50 per cent higher, in real terms, than they had been in 1869.

With the rise in the miners' standard of living, the coal valleys were able to attract increasing numbers of immigrants. Almost 130,000 people moved to them between 1881 and 1901. In the same period, more than 160,000 people left the rural areas of Wales. A substantial proportion of the migrants went to south-east Wales, but large numbers moved to England, a country which had 265,000 Welsh-born inhabitants in the year 1901. London accounted for 35,000 of them, and the London-Welsh community included 4,000 natives of Cardiganshire who were prominent in the dairying business. There were 60,000 in the midlands of England, but it was the north-west of England which was the favourite destination of Welsh emigrants. In 1901, Lancashire and Cheshire had 87,000 inhabitants who had been born in Wales, 70 per cent of them natives of the six northern counties. Between 1851 and 1911, Liverpool attracted at least 20,000 Welsh people in every decade. They were destined to be assimilated into the society around them, but, because of the constancy of the influx, Welsh culture flourished in the city for sixty years and more. *Yr Amserau*, the first real newspaper in the Welsh language, was founded in Liverpool, and from 1906 to 1939 the city was the home of the influential paper *Y Brython*. There were fifty Welsh chapels in the city, among them Princes Road, the 'cathedral' of Calvinistic Methodism. The Welsh were prominent in the business circles of Liverpool, in the building industry in particular; they tended to employ (and to exploit) their fellow-countrymen, thus making the chapels a labour exchange as well as a source of friendship, culture and discipline. A wealthy Welsh middle class arose in the city, and the 'swish of satin' in Princes Road came as a shock to many of the rural immigrants from Wales. Gareth Miles claims that Liverpool produced the only well-established bourgeoisie that the Welsh nation has ever possessed. Mervyn Jones has argued that if this group of urban, prosperous and confident Welsh people had come into existence within the borders of Wales, the history of the nation would have been very different. Some of the leading figures in the history of twentieth-century Wales – David Lloyd George and Saunders Lewis among them – were born in north-western England, and the Welsh of that region, through their frequent visits to the places from which they had sprung, were an important medium whereby urban values were introduced to the rural communities of the north.

Migration from rural Wales to Merseyside and to the south Wales coalfield reached its climax in the 1880s. That was a decade of great hardship in the countryside as depression struck agriculture. There were a number of poor harvests in the 1870s, and the harvest of 1879 was disastrous. In the past, such circumstances had led to rises in the prices of agricultural produce, but in 1879 a slump in prices began which did not ease until the first decade of the twentieth century. Imports – from North America and Australasia in the main – made possible by cheap transport were at the root of this phenomenon. It gave rise to a crisis throughout rural Europe, particularly in those areas where there had been heavy investment in arable agriculture. Between 1879 and 1895, the price of corn fell by half, a harsh experience for the landlords and the farmers of eastern England. The prices of meat, butter and cheese, the mainstays of Welsh agriculture, did not fall as sharply, but, as many Welsh farms were only marginally profitable, any decrease was a severe blow. Yet, as the countryside had not been fully penetrated by commercial values, there was no decline in the hunger for land. Therefore, despite the fall in prices, there was, it was claimed, no corresponding fall in rent. The number employed in agriculture – the primary rural population – shrank from 169,000 in 1851 to 114,000 in 1921 but the number of farmers remained fairly constant at around 35,000. The decrease took place among their relations and their labourers, as the farmers reduced the number of their employees and as the more deprived rural dwellers escaped from the poverty and the underemployment of the countryside. There was also a substantial reduction in the secondary rural population – those who supplied the needs of the primary population – as the inhabitants of the countryside came to depend increasingly upon products of urban provenance.

Landlords as well as tenants suffered as the agricultural depression deepened. Apart from those who had holdings in the towns or the industrial districts, every estate owner experienced a decrease in income in the last decades of the century, an important factor in any consideration of the erosion of the political power of the landed class. Information on landholding in Britain is increasingly available from the 1870s onwards. It proves that land in Wales had become concentrated in the hands of the few to a greater degree than elsewhere in the kingdom. In 1887, only 10.2 per cent of land in Wales was owned by the person who farmed it, compared with 14.0 per cent in Scotland and 16.1 per cent in England. There were in Wales almost four hundred estates exceeding a thousand hectares in size, and of these twenty were over eight thousand hectares. The concentration was at its most intense in Gwynedd and Glamorgan, although the largest estate in Wales was in the north-east, where the lands of Watkin Williams Wynn extended over sixty thousand hectares.

As has been seen, Samuel Roberts had claimed in 1850 that landlordism was at the root of the problems of rural Wales. Supporters of this opinion were winning growing support in the 1880s when there were also numerous attacks upon urban and industrial landlords – on the enormous income which the marquess of Bute, for example, received from ground rents and royalties on coal. The criticism was not altogether fair. There were other factors – problems of marketing, together with lack of enterprise, the scarcity of capital, and the conservatism of farmers – which hindered the development of agriculture. Many landlords gave rent rebates in difficult years; they invested extensively in improvements, and the eviction of a tenant was an exceptional action. The historian David Howell argues that much of the vilification of the landlords arose from the prejudices of sour radicals and bitter Nonconformists, and from the incorrect assumption that the 'Land Question' in Wales was of the same nature as the 'Land Question' in Ireland. This was precisely the opinion of those who defended the landed class in the late nineteenth century – men such as J. E. Vincent, the chancellor of the diocese of Bangor and the solicitor of the North Wales Property Defence Association. The argument has some substance. Nevertheless, it is unlikely that the criticism of landlordism would have won credibility if its main themes had not struck a chord in the minds of those who read them – and they, for the most part, were tenants with personal experience of landlords and their stewards. The 'Land Question' in Wales cannot be explained solely on the basis of a study of estate records and government reports. As W. J. Gruffydd put it: 'The unrest which led to the Land Question was not, at root, an economic or a political movement, but a social and national one, the traditions of an old culture which had been preserved among the *gwerin* [common people], breaking its bonds and claiming back its own kingdom.'

Criticism of landlordism was an important factor in the Liberal victory in the general election of 1880. Candidates drawn from landed families – Douglas-Pennant, Philipps, Morgan, Kenyon and Meyrick – were rejected; in Montgomeryshire, a constituency which had been

solidly under the control of the Wynnstay family since 1740, Charles
Williams Wynn was beaten by the wealthy industrialist Stuart Rendel.
Of the thirty-three Welsh members of parliament, twenty-nine were
Liberals, eight of whom were Nonconformists. In the kingdom as a
whole the Liberals, under Gladstone's leadership, won a majority of
137 over the Conservatives, and it was widely believed that a new
dawn was about to break. In addition, more than five dozen Irish
Nationalists were elected, and they constituted a disciplined army
under the leadership of Parnell. As a result of their activities, and of
the unrest organized in Ireland by Michael Davitt and the Land
League, an act was passed in 1881 which gave security of tenure and
arbitration on rents to tenants in Ireland, a victory which led Welsh
radicals to call for similar legislation for the tenants of Wales.

On the issue of land, therefore, as on the issue of disestablishment,
the Irish example was a key factor in the demand for specific legislation
for Wales. Although there were few examples of such legislation, an
act passed in 1881 came to be regarded as a significant precedent. That
was the Welsh Sunday Closing Act. For the supporters of total
abstinence – an increasingly vocal pressure group since the founding
of the United Kingdom Alliance in 1853 – the act was a step towards
total prohibition. The enemies of the public houses had already, in
1872, persuaded a Liberal government to restrict the licensed trade. As
a result, the public houses became recruiting centres for the Conservative party – a development central to the ability of that party to
survive in a world which was moving towards democracy. Although
going to the pub was the favourite form of relaxation among
working-class men, there was substantial backing among them for the
closure of public houses on Sundays: a public opinion poll held by the
promoters of temperance recorded that 90 per cent of the electors of
Mountain Ash favoured such a measure. Nevertheless, the act of 1881
was largely negative in its results. Evidence concerning its effect on
Sabbath drunkenness was ambiguous, for following its passage a host
of unregulated clubs came into existence. It was legislation aimed at
the working class, for most of the middle class imbibed at home. The
measure fostered hypocritical behaviour – the Welsh Pharisaism which
the *Western Mail* took such delight in unmasking. Above all, it connected Welshness with negativity. In the twentieth century, when the
appeal of teetotalism and Sabbatarianism had declined, this symbol of
specifically Welsh legislation came to be unacceptable to the majority

of the people of Wales, and some of the consequences of this were to be seen in the Referendum of 1979.

If it were possible to legislate specifically for Wales on the matter of public houses, it would also be possible to do so on other matters, the Church Establishment among them – a consideration which caused Anglican temperance advocates to take a lukewarm attitude towards the 1881 act. The Anglicans of Wales had reason to be concerned. Nine of the Welsh MPs elected in 1880 were subscribers to the Liberation Society and about ten others sympathized with its aims. The society's organization in Wales was restructured in 1883 and its leaders began to think seriously of specifically Welsh legislation on the matter of disestablishment. One of the most prominent members of Gladstone's cabinet was Joseph Chamberlain, a Unitarian from Birmingham and an uncompromising enemy of the Establishment. On a visit to Wales in 1884, he announced that he was in favour of the disestablishment of the Church of England in Wales. Gladstone was less enthusiastic. A fervent High Anglican, he deeply deplored attacks upon the Church. They were even more distasteful to the Whig aristocracy, a group which still had great influence over the policies of the Liberal party.

By 1880, therefore, the Church Establishment, together with temperance and land tenure, had become a specifically Welsh issue. There was a similar development in the field of education. One of the new government's first acts was to set up a committee under the chairmanship of Baron Aberdare to examine intermediate and higher education in Wales. The establishment of the committee was an acknowledgement that there was substance to the complaint that Wales was uniquely ill provided for in these fields. In Scotland, the ratio of university students to the population was 1:840; in Ireland it was 1:3,121. The corresponding figure in Wales was 1:8,200. The provision for intermediate education in Wales was even more inadequate. The number of boys attending grammar schools in Wales was 1,540, and a further 2,287 were educated in a variety of private schools. (There was even less opportunity for girls.) In order to make provision on the scale recommended for England by the Taunton Commission in 1869, it would be necessary to create in Wales over twenty thousand places for boys in intermediate education. In 1881, the Aberdare Committee published its report, together with the evidence it had collected – 1,008 pages in all. In marked contrast with the report of

1847, that of 1881 contains references sympathetic to the attributes of the Welsh. Nevertheless, the majority of the witnesses had a negative attitude towards the Welsh language, and the commissioners took it for granted that English would be the only medium of intermediate and higher education in Wales. It was also accepted that such education was intended mainly for the middle class; as that class was smaller in Wales than it was in England, it was considered that Wales would not need provision on the same scale as England.

Although the members of the Aberdare Committee, to quote J. R. Webster, 'saw Welsh educational problems through fundamentally English eyes', the effect of their report was far-reaching. It recommended that the government should pay an annual grant of £4,000 each to two university colleges, one in the north and one in the south. In 1883, Cardiff and Bangor were chosen as the sites of the two colleges. Aberystwyth was refused a grant and its prospects were therefore bleak. However, in 1885, because of the admiration engendered by the college's pioneering heroism and the loyalty and distinction of many of its former students, a grant was secured for Aberystwyth also. There was immediate action on the matter of the two colleges, but the government was more dilatory in putting into effect the recommendations of the Aberdare Committee in relation to intermediate education. In Britain, it was not considered that the government had a responsibility to provide financial assistance to schools beyond the elementary level. This was precisely what the Aberdare Committee had recommended, but there was no action on the matter until 1889, when one of the most influential pieces of legislation in the history of Wales was passed.

Despite some successes, Gladstone's government of 1880–85 proved disappointing to the radical elements within the Liberal party. During the general election campaign of 1885, Chamberlain published his 'Unauthorized Programme', an exciting manifesto which had a strong appeal in Wales. By 1885, the electoral pattern had been transformed by the Parliamentary Reform Act of 1884. The act gave the vote to all male householders and to a proportion of male lodgers in the county constituencies, a franchise system similar to that which had existed in the borough constituencies since 1867. As a result, the number of county voters in Wales rose from 74,936 to 200,373; henceforth, approximately 60 per cent of male adults were on the electoral register, although there were striking variations in the percentages from constituency to constituency. It is often claimed that the act of 1884 gave birth to democracy in Wales and in Britain. As not a single woman was enfranchised and as significant groups of men (sons who lived with their parents, for example, or those in receipt of poor relief) were not granted the vote, it is a misleading claim. Indeed, if it is accepted that one adult, one vote, is the minimal definition of democracy, there would not be a democratic general election in Britain until 1950. Nevertheless, the Reform Act of 1884 was a significant step along the path to democracy. Together with the Corrupt Practices Act of 1883 (a measure which severely restricted campaign expenditure) and the Redistribution Act of 1885, the act of 1884 opened the way to fundamental changes in Welsh parliamentary representation. As a result of the Redistribution Act, five thinly populated borough seats were abolished. In the more populous counties, constituencies were reorganized in order to create one extra seat for Caernarfonshire, one for Monmouthshire and four for Glamorgan.

The general election of 1885 was fought under this new system. Of the thirty-four Welsh MPs elected, thirty were Liberals. The owner of Wynnstay was beaten in East Denbighshire, and the heir of Golden Grove in West Carmarthenshire – the owner and the future owner of the largest and the second largest of the estates of Wales. Some scions of old Whig families held their ground, but most of the Liberals elected were lawyers and businessmen. This Liberal advance is often portrayed as a victory for Welsh national feeling. Yet the prominence of English businessmen among the MPs elected for the constituencies of Wales suggests that the country's parliamentary representatives in 1885 were less Welsh than it had been a generation earlier. When turning their backs upon their traditional leaders, the middle class of Wales had neither the confidence nor the resources to take the reins into their own hands. Although they were to do so increasingly in later years, Welsh Liberalism in the 1880s was highly dependent upon wealthy Englishmen.

The Liberal upsurge is also frequently portrayed as a victory for the 'common people'. Nevertheless, the essence of the change which occurred in the parliamentary representation of Wales between 1865 and 1885 was that wealthy members of the landed class yielded their place to wealthy industrialists and professional men – that is, one elite was replacing another. As a result of the 1884 Parliamentary Reform Act, a majority of the electors of Wales belonged to the working class, but decades were to go by before the implications of this fact became fully apparent. As no salary was paid to members of parliament and as openhandedness was considered to be one of the chief attributes of an MP, it was impossible to select a candidate who had no means at his disposal. As the electoral organization of the Liberal party was firmly in the control of the middle class, selection committees found it difficult to appreciate the appeal of a working-class candidate. In 1885, the caucus candidate was challenged in only one constituency – the new constituency of the Rhondda. There, the caucus selected Lewis Davis, a Rhondda Fach coal-owner, but he was beaten by Mabon, the miners' choice, by 3,859 votes to 2,992. Mabon was the first 'Labour' MP to represent a Welsh constituency, and his victory is an indication of the potentialities of the act of 1884. Nevertheless, as he was an upholder of the Lib–Lab tradition, Mabon took his place without difficulty within the progressive wing of the Liberal party.

The general election of 1885 gave the Liberals a majority of eighty-six, a figure exactly equalled by the number of Irish Nationalists elected to parliament. Gladstone, embarking on his third premiership, had therefore no choice but to give serious consideration to the demand of Parnell and his party for self-government. He introduced an Irish Home Rule Bill in parliament in April 1886. He was opposed by strong factions within his own party – specifically the Whigs, led by the marquess of Hartington, and the radicals, led by Joseph Chamberlain. The bill was defeated by 343 votes to 313, and those who voted against it included ninety-three Liberals. As Gladstone had lost the confidence of the House, he appealed to the electors. They proved even more hostile to his plans. In the general election of 1886, 315 Conservatives, 191 Gladstonian Liberals, and seventy-eight Liberal Unionists were elected.

The results were very different in Wales. The Welsh response to the troubles of 1886 shows to what extent Welsh politics had developed a distinctive character of its own. After the general election of 1886, Wales sent to Westminster twenty-seven Gladstonian Liberals, six Conservatives and one Liberal Unionist. (He was William Cornwallis-West, who was returned unopposed in West Denbighshire, and he lost his seat in the following election.) Thus, only a minority of Welsh Protestants supported the resistance of the Irish Protestants to self-government for Ireland; indeed, it was claimed that the Welsh were more determinedly in favour of 'Justice for Ireland' than were the Irish themselves. It must be admitted, however, that elements among the Welsh Liberals were drawn to the arguments of the Liberal Unionists, particularly those which stirred up the ancient anti-Catholic prejudice of the Welsh. Thomas Gee saw substance to Chamberlain's claim that Gladstone's obsession with Ireland would postpone consideration of the problems of Wales, and the young solicitor from Llanystumdwy, David Lloyd George, only just missed attending the inaugural meeting of the Liberal Unionists. At least half a dozen Welsh Liberal MPs had deep misgivings about Gladstone's policy. It was only after strong pressure from their constituency parties that Vivian (Swansea District) and Talbot (Mid Glamorgan) declared their support for Irish Home Rule. The Liberal Unionist, David Davies of Llandinam, failed by only nine votes to hold Cardiganshire, a result which caused him to distance himself from the college at Aberystwyth, an institution of which he had previously been the principal patron. In Meirionnydd, Robertson, one of the Liberals who had voted against Gladstone's bill, retired, thus opening the way for the candidature of Thomas Edward Ellis, a farmer's son from Penllyn, who brought a new and exciting emphasis to Welsh Liberalism.

Although it has to be acknowledged that Welsh support for the Unionists was stronger than the results of the general election of 1886 suggest, the fact remains that more of the Welsh were in favour of Home Rule for Ireland than were opposed to it. It was a fact which caused surprise both at the time and subsequently, for it would not have been unreasonable to suppose that the Welsh would have warmed to the Nonconformist radical, Chamberlain, rather than to the High Churchman, Gladstone. However, this supposition takes no account of the exceptional allegiance which Gladstone had won among the people of Wales. He lived in Flintshire, in the home of his wife, the heiress of the Glynnes of Hawarden; the firm morality which characterized his rhetoric and his statesmanship appealed strongly to the Welsh; he attended *eisteddfodau* at which he referred with sympathy to the attributes of the Welsh; time and again in parliament he expressed his readiness to give consideration to Welsh public opinion. Accustomed as they were to being ignored, such recognition was greatly appreciated by the Welsh, and the admiration of many of them for the 'grand old man' approached idolatry.

Although a sincere High Churchman, Gladstone was the only British politician who had disestablished a Church (Ireland, 1869). He gave the impression that he had an open mind on the subject of the disestablishment of the Church in Wales – he abstained from voting on the bill brought forward in March 1886 by Lewis Llewelyn Dillwyn (the member for Swansea), a bill defeated by only twelve votes.

Chamberlain claimed that disestablishment would be won by voting for the Liberal Unionists, but as he joined forces, first with the Whigs, then with the Tories, the number of those persuaded by him shrank rapidly. His followers stood in eight constituencies in Wales in 1892, but none of them came within reach of victory. After that, apart from an unexpected victory in Carmarthen Boroughs in 1895, Liberal Unionism in Wales languished to extinction. With Gladstone's party strong in Wales and weak in England, it was open to pressure from its Welsh members. Gladstone fully understood the situation, and his references to Wales became ever more flattering, as in the meeting in Swansea in June 1887 when he basked in the admiration of a crowd of some sixty thousand. (As Emrys ap Iwan commented: 'We would prefer to be without bread, Mr Gladstone, than without soap.') Gladstone realized that he could no longer resist the supporters of disestablishment and in October 1887 the disestablishment of the Church in Wales became part of the policy of the Liberal party.

The campaign against the Church Establishment was intensified by the 'Tithe War', a disturbance which was at its height during the summer of 1887. There had for generations been opposition to the Church's right to a tenth of the produce of the land. The resentment was aggravated by the agricultural depression, for outgoings on tithe had not fallen in line with the fall in prices – a particularly heavy blow to the arable farmers of eastern England. However, it was not the Anglicans of Norfolk but the Nonconformists of Wales who refused to pay tithes, a fact which suggests that sectarian and political issues were at least as important as economic grievances. Unrest arising from tithes occurred in the Tywi valley and in the counties of Pembroke and Cardigan, but the most violent protests were those in the area around Denbigh. Denbigh was the home of Thomas Gee and the headquarters of the Welsh National Land League which he had established in imitation of the Irish Land League. The violence oc-curred when the property of those who had refused to pay tithes was distrained and sold. Following troubles in Llangwm in May 1887, thirty-one men from the parish were summoned to court. A month later, during the skirmishes in Mochdre, eighty-four people – thirty-five policemen among them – were injured.

Y Faner made much of the 'Tithe Martyrs', and Thomas Edward Ellis used the 'War' to air the problems of rural Wales in parliament. According to the secretary of the south Caernarfonshire branch of the Anti-Tithe League, David Lloyd George, the 'tithe business [is] an excellent lever wherewith to raise the spirit of the people'. The Tory press published poignant descriptions of the plight of 'the distressed clergy of Wales' and to the Conservative government of the marquess of Salisbury their tribulations were proof that the unrest prevalent in the Irish countryside was spreading to Wales. In 1891, the responsibility for the payment of tithe was transferred from the tenant to the landlord and, as a result, the storm died down. While the Tithe Bill was making its way through parliament, Welsh MPs seized every opportunity to harass the government. For three weeks, the time of the House was almost entirely taken up by a Welsh issue – 'a glorious struggle for Wales' in the opinion of Lloyd George, who in April 1890 had been elected member of parliament for Caernarfon Boroughs.

Their ability to engross the attention of the House of Commons indicates that by 1890 the Welsh MPs had a degree of cohesion. Despite his epithet, the 'Member for Wales', Henry Richard had little sympathy for specifically Welsh legislation. He died in 1888 and his role as leader of the Welsh MPs passed to Stuart Rendel, a man who succeeded, through his close friendship with Gladstone, in deepening the old man's comprehension of the needs of Wales. Rendel organized a Welsh Parliamentary Party with a chairman, two whips, and distinctive policies – a development which gave rise to the fear, or the hope, that the Welsh were treading the same path as the Irish. The Parliamentary Party was strengthened by the victors of the seven by-elections held in Wales between the general elections of 1886 and 1892. Among them were D. A. Thomas, an independently minded industrialist (Merthyr, 1888), David Randall, a solicitor highly respected by the trade unions (Gower, 1888), S. T. Evans, another solicitor and a hot-headed radical (Mid Glamorgan, 1890) and, of course, Lloyd George. Stuart Rendel, an English Churchman who had made his fortune in the arms trade, seemed an unlikely leader for the Welsh. His parliamentary career is proof of the degree to which liberally minded Englishmen warmed to the aspirations of small nations in the last decades of the nineteenth century. Rendel considered that the Liberal party's commitment to self-government for Ireland was of fundamental importance for Wales. 'The Irish Question,' he said in 1886, '. . . is helping Wales by helping to made a Welsh Question.' There was talk of a coalition of radical Celts to resist the Toryism of England, and Michael Davitt, the leader of the Irish Land League, received a warm welcome in such places as Blaenau Ffestiniog and Tonypandy. As the arguments for self-government for Ireland were being constantly rehearsed, it is hardly surprising that there was a desire to apply them to Wales. That was done in particular by those devoted nationalists, Michael D. Jones and Emrys ap Iwan, both of whom expressed their admiration for the 'splendid example of the Irish'.

These two prophets were marginal to formal politics, but from 1886 there was a Welsh member of parliament who considered himself to be a disciple of Michael D. Jones. He was Thomas Edward Ellis. Ellis, in 1886, was the first to include self-government for Wales in an election manifesto. After taking his seat, he became one of a 'small company' in London who dreamt 'many dreams about Wales'. This was the group which adopted the name Cymru Fydd (The Wales To Be), a name apparently suggested by Ellis. Within a short time, some half dozen branches had been founded in London – the Caradog branch in Hampstead, for example, and the Hiraethog branch in Finsbury. Cymru Fydd adopted a programme which included a legislative assembly for Wales; it planned to campaign among Welsh voters in English constituencies which suggests that Cymru Fydd was originally conceived as a movement aimed at exiles. Indeed, no branch was established in Wales until 1891, when one was founded in Barry. In its early years, Cymru Fydd, with its vague policies and the idealistic rhetoric of its leaders, was an amorphous body. Was it a campaign to unite the Welsh, or a society to promote the political aims of Liberals and Nonconformists? Was it an organization fighting for self-government, or a movement aimed at fostering Welshness? T. E. Ellis sought to encompass all the implications of Cymru Fydd by developing a concept of nationality which connected history, literature, art, social values and political institutions in a single organic whole. He gave expression to his vision in a striking speech at Bala in 1890, when he called for a 'Legislative Assembly ... which would be a symbol ... of our national unity ... a means of achieving our social ideals and our cultural interests ... an embodiment and a fulfilment of our aspirations as a people'.

The Welsh were not inspired by his words. This was not surprising in view of the fact that they had little confidence in their Welshness. Some of the supporters of Cymru Fydd considered that their main priority should be to seek to strengthen that confidence. This was the aim of the talented young men at Oxford who established Cymdeithas Dafydd ap Gwilym (the Dafydd ap Gwilym Society) in 1886. The honorary president of the Dafydd was John Rhys, the first to occupy the Chair of Celtic established at Oxford in 1877. Under his leadership, the members of the society sought to comprehend the true characteristics of the Welsh language, a task to which John Morris-Jones, one of the founders of the Dafydd, consecrated his life. The society stimulated Owen M. Edwards's love for Wales, a love which inspired his untiring efforts to give his compatriots an understanding of their history and their cultural heritage.

In the 1880s, Welshmen at Oxford were not the only ones involved in opening up new vistas in Welsh-language culture. For the first time, novels of a high standard were written in the language; between 1879 and 1894, Daniel Owen's four novels were published – works which, as Thomas Parry put it, 'stand like a great mountain upon a wide plain'. In the same period, Emrys ap Iwan wrote more than fifty substantial articles which gave expression to his belief in the dignity of the Welsh language and which became a manifesto for the nationalists of the succeeding generation. The 1880s also saw the publication of the early poems of Elfed and John Morris-Jones, the first fruits of a renaissance which would transform the Welsh muse.

Above all, it was in the 1880s that the Welsh language gained a foothold in the education system. In 1890, the Education Committee of the Privy Council agreed to pay specified sums to those schools which successfully taught Welsh grammar and the history and geography of Wales and which followed a programme of translation from Welsh into English. To a certain extent, Welsh had been employed in the elementary schools before 1889; it is unlikely that the use of the 'Welsh Note' was as widespread as the mythology of the twentieth century maintains. Nevertheless, in most of the schools of Welsh-speaking Wales there were pupils whose main experience of education was a mechanical drilling in a language which they did not understand; as late as 1960, it was possible to meet old people who remembered nothing of their schooldays except the learning by rote of a book known to them as 'Redimarisi' (*Reading Made Easy*).

The starting-point of the campaign to win formal recognition for the Welsh language was the argument that it should be used to assist in giving the pupils a knowledge of English. The Society for the Utilisation of the Welsh Language was established at the National *Eisteddfod* at Aberdare in 1885, and the words 'for the better teaching of English' were often added to its title. It is likely that the emphasis on English arose partly from the desire to put forward an argument which would be acceptable to the authorities. The society's Welsh-language propaganda was more favourable to the language, and its Welsh title – Cymdeithas yr Iaith Gymraeg (the Welsh Language Society – of the first creation) – was less tentative. Its principal founder, Dan Isaac Davies, a deputy inspector of schools in the Merthyr district, was inspired by his confidence in the future of Welsh, by his fervent belief in the value of bilingualism and by his feeling that it was invidious to raise a generation of people who were illiterate in their mother tongue – a conviction which came to him on listening to an address by the marquess of Bute at the Cardiff National Eisteddfod in 1883. In 1885, he published a collection of his articles, *Tair Miliwn o Gymry Dwy-Ieithawg ymhen Can Mlynedd* (Three Million Bilingual Welsh People in a Hundred Years). In April 1887, a month before his untimely death, he presented the evidence of Cymdeithas yr Iaith Gymraeg to the Royal Commission which had been set up to inquire into elementary education (the Cross Commission). It was the recommendations of that commission which led to the decision of the Education Committee of the Privy Council in 1890. It was a grudging concession. No school was required to use Welsh; where it was used, it was merely grafted upon an entirely English curriculum, and decades were to go by before there was any movement from lessons on the mother tongue to lessons in the mother tongue. Nevertheless, the campaign of Dan Isaac Davies and his colleagues led to developments which were crucial to the Welsh language; it is only necessary to compare the fate of Welsh in the twentieth century with that of Breton – a language which did not succeed in winning a foothold in the educational system – to appreciate the scale of their achievement.

Thus, although the founding of Cymru Fydd and the ventilation of the issue of self-government indicate that the 1880s saw an upsurge in Welsh political nationalism, the cultural nationalism which manifested itself in that decade was probably of greater significance. Indeed, it can be argued that some of the aspirations of the advocates of self-government had been satisfied before Cymru Fydd had properly established itself, for what those advocates desired above all were reforms which would give the electors of Wales control over local matters. To some extent, that came about through the County Councils Act of 1888, one of the principal measures of the Conservative government of 1886–92. Following the first county council elections in 1889, the justices of the peace – almost all of whom were members of the landowning class – were relieved of their administrative duties and those duties were transferred to the new councils. In extensive areas of rural England, it was the justices who were elected as councillors and thus the 1888 act did not give rise to any fundamental change. An occasional landowner was elected in Wales – the earl of Lisburne, Viscount Emlyn and Baron Tredegar, for example – but others were defeated. In south Cardiganshire, four of the six squires who stood were rejected. Tenants and small businessmen made up half the members of Cardiganshire County Council; it also contained four Nonconformist ministers, the redoubtable Thomas Levi of Aberystwyth among them.

With the exception of the anglicized border districts, the pattern was the same in the rest of Wales. In the industrial areas (apart from some unexpected results, such as the success of four Tories in the Merthyr area), almost all the seats went to Nonconformist middle-class radicals. Party conflict was so intense that only 3 per cent of the candidates stood as Independents. Two Liberals were elected for every one Conservative, and the Liberals had a majority in every county in Wales except Breconshire. A large proportion of the men elected were elders and deacons; after generations of being content with the private world of Nonconformity, the doors of public life were opened to the occupants of the 'Big Seat'. They seized the opportunity, and as they immersed themselves in the work of the council chamber they were obliged to curtail their contribution to their denomination, a factor of importance in tracing the decline in the role of organized religion in the life of Wales.

It had taken decades for the squirearchy's control over the parliamentary representation of Wales to be undermined. Its control over county government was terminated much more abruptly, and the representative character of local government was further strengthened in 1894, when district and parish councils were established. Although the replacement of the aristocratic by the democratic principle was of great significance, the range of activity open to the councils elected in 1889 was limited. They soon received additional duties. That happened as a result of the Welsh Intermediate Education Act of 1889, an act which established county joint education committees, the majority of whose members were to be councillors. It was a private measure, introduced by Stuart Rendel. He was responsible for steering it through the House of Commons, although the support of members of the Conservative government was essential to his success. The joint committees were authorized to draw up plans for county schools which were to be financed from the rates, a treasury grant, the fees of pupils and by the reorganization of old endowments.

To spend public money on schools other than at the elementary level was a new departure, but to authorize such expenditure in Wales and in Wales alone was almost revolutionary. The programme was set in hand at once and by 1896 all the county schemes had received approval. Seventeen of the old endowed schools – Friars, Bangor, and Queen Elizabeth, Carmarthen, for example – chose to be included in the new system, but others insisted on remaining outside it, Brecon and Rhuthun among them. By 1902, Wales had ninety-five intermediate schools attended by over ten thousand pupils, an achievement which was the source of great pride. Most of the pupils came from the lower-middle and working classes; 80 per cent of them had received their early education in state elementary schools, a striking contrast with England, where the grammar schools depended heavily on the output of 'prep' schools.

Despite the pride taken in the county schools and despite the fact that they were answerable in matters relating to examinations and inspections to a Welsh body (the Central Welsh Board, established in 1896), there was little that was specifically Welsh about the education they provided. They slavishly imitated the ethos and the curriculum of the English grammar schools and, contrary to the intentions of the 1889 act, they neglected subjects which were relevant to the local economy and community. Many of the early headteachers came from England and the atmosphere of the schools was completely English; in

1907, only forty-seven of the county schools offered Welsh lessons, and nobody suggested that the language should be used as a medium of instruction. The act was particularly beneficial to the rural areas: the population of the area served by the school at Tregaron was 7,500; the corresponding figure for Porth, Rhondda, was 88,000, and the difference became greater as the population of the one area fell and that of the other rose. In the industrial areas, the gaps in the provision were made good by municipal schools, private academies, and the evening classes which were such an essential part of the culture of the coalfield.

Yet, while admitting that the intermediate schools had their weaknesses, their importance cannot be denied. They contributed to social mobility, to the erosion of class barriers, and to the advancement of the sons and daughters of families in poor circumstances. What would have been the fate of W. J. Gruffydd, wondered David Williams, 'had not the efforts of the Victorian reformers borne good fruit in the Education Act of 1889?' Furthermore, as there were more opportunities of receiving an academic education in Wales than in England, Wales came to produce a surplus of people with scholastic qualifications and too few with technical and commercial qualifications. As a result, the Welsh came to play a part in Britain not unlike that played by the Bengalis in India. Wherever a county school was built, a group of teachers came into existence. In many a market town and coal-mining valley, the teachers were the only significant group of educated people and the cultural life of the neighbourhood would be greatly indebted to them – particularly as ministers declined in number and prestige. Indeed, the coming of the teachers hastened that decline, for the secular education they provided was one of the heaviest blows suffered by Welsh Nonconformity. The county schools had an impact upon their pupils at the exact time when their minds were most open and sensitive to cultural influences; English was the medium of that impact, and Glyn Jones has argued that it was the Education Act of 1889 which gave rise to the Anglo-Welsh literature of the twentieth century.

The 1889 act whetted the appetite for more specifically Welsh legislation. By the general election of 1892, Welsh Liberal candidates had a ready-made programme. In their election manifestos, every one of them gave priority to disestablishment, but there was also a demand for legislation for Wales on matters such as land tenure, education, self-government and the liquor trade. Eleven of the candidates campaigned solely on Welsh issues, but the other twenty-three varied in their readiness to give precedence to Wales, an important consideration when measuring the extent to which the Liberal party had by 1892 been permeated by a commitment to Wales. Following the general election of 1892, the House of Commons consisted of 315 Conservatives and Liberal Unionists, 273 Gladstonian Liberals and eighty-one Irish Nationalists. With Irish backing, Gladstone became Prime Minister for the fourth time; he formed his cabinet in the house of Stuart Rendel who warned him that, if his ministry were to survive, it was important that it should fulfil the aspirations of the thirty-one Welsh Liberals.

The Liberal government of 1892–5 was the subject of lively debate both at the time and subsequently. Those years represented the climax of nationalism as a formative element within Welsh Liberalism. Because of the powerful leverage possessed by the Welsh MPs, important advances were won for Wales, but the momentum was not maintained and by the beginning of the twentieth century the vigour and confidence of Welsh political nationalism had evaporated. The attempt to create a viable Welsh political movement failed; as a result, the belief arose that Wales had somehow failed to take advantage of that upsurge of nationalism which gave to others of the non-historic nations of Europe control over their destiny. That belief was fed by the theory that the hopes of the 1890s had been wrecked on the rocks of a divided allegiance – that the desire to serve Wales had been distorted by the wish to remain faithful to the Liberal party. T. E. Ellis pondered this issue in 1892 after he had been invited to join the government. He came to the conclusion that he could best serve Wales, not through leading a movement which kept the Liberal party at arm's length, but through being at the power centre of that party. He accepted the office of Deputy Chief Whip, a key post in view of the variety of the factions supporting Gladstone. (He became Chief Whip in 1894 and retained that office until his death at the age of forty in 1899.) In Wales, his appointment was generally received with satisfaction, although that interesting man, Arthur Price – a High Church nationalist – spoke scathingly of the harm done to Welsh nationalism 'when Ellis grasped the Saxon gold'. If the Welsh Parliamentary Party had been similar to the Irish Parliamentary Party, it would of course have been highly inconsistent for its most prominent member to become responsible for the discipline of a British party. That, however, was not the situation, for the Welsh Parliamentary Party was, administratively and financially, an integral part of the Liberal party, and Ellis was strongly attracted by the intellectual and patrician atmosphere of the governing circles of Liberalism. Nevertheless, Ellis's dilemma in 1892 afforded a foretaste of the perplexity which was to confront many twentieth-century patriots – whether the interests of Wales could best be promoted inside or outside the power structures of Britain.

A consideration of the 'Land Question' in Wales was high on Ellis's list of priorities. His position of authority within the Liberal party enabled him to persuade Gladstone to set up a royal commission on the subject. Gladstone, like others of the older generation of Liberals – men who had close ties with the remnants of the Whigs – had hoped that Wales would be content with a select committee, a much less authoritative and dignified body than a royal commission. In Ellis's opinion, that would have been an insult to Wales, particularly as the problems of tenure in both Ireland and Scotland had been studied by royal commissions. The nine members of the commission were appointed in May 1893 and the last of its seven thick volumes was published in August 1896. Chiefly because of the untiring labour of Lleufer Thomas, the secretary of the commission and one of the great benefactors of the Welsh nation, those volumes are an inexhaustible source of information on the history of Wales. The commissioners sat in fifty-nine centres throughout Wales, including villages such as Reynoldston, Letterston and Hanmer; they examined 1,086 witnesses, 372 of them through an interpreter. As the commission had been specifically charged to study questions of tenure, two thirds of the witnesses were owners, stewards and tenants of the landed estates. One in every thirty of the farmers of Wales was examined, but little attention was given to the farm labourers, the most numerous and the most deprived of the inhabitants of rural Wales.

The evidence collected by the commission provided an ambiguous verdict on the validity of the accusations levied against the landowning class. As tenants rarely kept detailed records, their complaints were often vague; the response of the landlords was highly effective, largely because of the tireless work of J. E. Vincent, the solicitor of the North Wales Property Defence Association. *Y Faner* believed that the 'evidence proves to the hilt all that we have been saying over the years', while H. M. Vaughan, a squire from the Teifi valley, considered that the landlords had come through their ordeal unscathed. In their recommendations, six of the commissioners called for a land court which would arbitrate on matters of rent, compensation and tenure; a bill to establish a land court for Wales was brought before parliament in 1897, but by then, with the Conservatives in power, it received little attention.

Although the Land Commission did not result in any legislation, the opportunity to air the problems of rural Wales was beneficial. By the beginning of the twentieth century, those problems had lost something of their urgency. Between 1900 and 1913, prices of agricultural produce rose by 18 per cent, and in consequence there was a degree of prosperity in the countryside. Later generations were to have an appealing image of Welsh rural society at the turn of the century. As portrayed in the works of D. J. Williams and others, that society was cheerful, prudent, godly and Welsh-speaking. As David Jenkins has shown in his brilliant study, its communities were held together by a complex pattern of obligations. Indeed, a great deal of the Welsh literature of the twentieth century is an elegy for that golden age. There is, however, another side to the picture – the frequent deaths from consumption, the pitiful wages of farm servants, and the failings which are chronicled (hyperbolically, no doubt) in the stories of Caradoc Evans.

Another factor which contributed to the decline of rural unrest was the growth of freehold tenure. As landlords were dissatisfied with the income they received from land and were aware that the ownership of an estate was no longer the key to political power, they began to put their estates on the market. In 1902, the duke of Beaufort put his Monmouthshire lands – a total of seven thousand hectares – up for auction and by the First World War Welsh landowners such as Baron Harlech, Baron Glanusk and the earl of Powis had sold at least a part of their estates. The majority of the farms were bought by their tenants: of the fifty-four farms sold by the earl of Powis in 1911, fifty were bought by their occupiers. Landed estates, which had been a central feature in the history of Wales for half a millennium, were beginning to break up, and by the middle of the twentieth century the majority of the farmers of Wales would be freeholders. Nevertheless, at the end of the nineteenth century, the landowners still enjoyed considerable power, as a host of incidents recorded by the Land Commission bears witness.

Three months after the appointment of the members of the Land Commission, the charter of the University of Wales was laid before parliament. The promoters of higher education in Wales had aimed from the beginning at creating a national university, but there was some disagreement over the nature of the proposed institution. As the students of the colleges at Aberystwyth, Cardiff and Bangor sat examinations for the external degree of the University of London, the first necessity was the establishment of a Welsh body empowered to confer its own degrees. Some advocated a scheme whereby the degrees would be available, not only to the students of the three colleges, but also to those studying in a variety of other institutions or no institution at all – a truly radical plan which would have allowed people throughout the length and breadth of Wales to consider themselves students of the national university. However, the plan adopted was that of Viriamu Jones, the brilliant principal of the University College of Cardiff; it involved establishing a federation of the three colleges, with degrees restricted to those who had pursued courses in them. St David's College, Lampeter, was not included and as a result there was opposition in parliament to the charter, particularly from the bishops. Despite this, the charter received the Royal Assent on 20 November 1893. Baron Aberdare was elected chancellor, a fitting recognition of his contribution to higher education in Wales; Aberdare died in February 1895 and, since Gladstone refused the office, the University had to content itself with the prince of Wales as Aberdare's successor.

With the 'Land Question' under investigation and the University's charter confirmed, the Welsh Liberals could concentrate their attention upon the Church Establishment. In the programme of priorities adopted by the Liberal Party in Newcastle in 1891 (the Newcastle Programme), Home Rule for Ireland was placed at the top of the list, but it was immediately followed by Disestablishment for Wales. A bill preparing the ground for disestablishment was introduced in February 1893, a step which aroused the wrath of Churchmen. Their leader in Wales was A. G. Edwards, who had been bishop of St Asaph since 1886. Edwards could rely upon strong support in England, where it was feared that disestablishment in Wales would provide the basis for an attack on the Church Establishment in its entirety. The Anglicans were angered not so much by disestablishment itself as by a consideration which was implicit in it – that it would be inconsistent for the

Church, after disestablishment, to continue in possession of the endowments which it had held by virtue of its status as the Established Church. Thus, in the wake of disestablishment, the Church was to be deprived of a substantial portion of its property. From 1893 onwards, the issue of the State Church came to revolve around disendowment rather than disestablishment; the nature of the debate changed, and not for the better, as it moved from considerations of principle to considerations of property and income. To some men of vision – T. E. Ellis in particular – the Church endowments represented wealth which could transform the cultural life of Wales; to many vengeful Nonconformists, disendowment represented the fatal blow to the old enemy; to Anglicans, clerical and lay, it was desecration.

By the summer of 1893, it was obvious that disestablishment would not be won in that year, chiefly because the attempt to give Home Rule to Ireland was monopolizing the attention of parliament. In September, half the Welsh Liberal MPs voted in favour of forming an independent party if disestablishment were not given priority during the parliamentary session of 1894. A 'Welsh Revolt' had been threatened for some time, but when the threat was carried out in April 1894 (five weeks after the earl of Rosebery had succeeded Gladstone as Prime Minister) it did not pose a major threat. Only four Welsh MPs – Lloyd George, D. A. Thomas, Frank Edwards (Radnorshire) and Herbert Lewis (Flint Boroughs) – refused the Liberal Whip; although their action received widespread support, they were back within the fold by the end of May. Asquith, the Home Secretary, brought a disestablishment bill before parliament in 1894 and again in 1895; the bill of 1895 passed its second reading, but it was abandoned in June of that year when the government fell. The Conservative party did well in Wales in the general election of 1895. Partly because of vigorous campaigning by the supporters of the Church, the party's candidates won nine seats, a figure not bettered until 1979. They and their allies had a majority of 152 in the new parliament, and in the ten years of Tory rule which followed there was no likelihood of any advance on the issue of disestablishment.

At the time, it was claimed that the fall of the Liberal government had been brought about by Lloyd George and his associates, whose amendments to the disestablishment bill had created widespread confusion. Their intention was to graft on to the bill a national Welsh institution which would administer Church endowments. In the later years of the nineteenth century, there were several attempts to create some kind of Welsh national institution – in 1888, during the passage of the County Councils Bill, in 1889 as a part of the Intermediate Education Bill, and particularly in 1892 with the National Institutions (Wales) Bill which sought to establish an elected council and a Secretary of State for Wales. Rosebery claimed in 1895 that he was in favour of Home Rule for all the nations of the United Kingdom (Home Rule All Round). In the same year Lloyd George, assisted by Scottish home rulers, won a House of Commons vote approving of that principle. The policy of Home Rule All Round had been aired by Chamberlain in 1886; his motive, like that of Rosebery, was to remove Home Rule for Ireland from its place at the top of the political agenda. Irish nationalism contained a strongly republican element which thought in terms of total independence. There was no similar element in Wales. The most that was hoped for was the establishment of an elected body, securely under the sovereignty of the 'Imperial Parliament' at Westminster, which would deal with specifically Welsh matters. Such an aspiration was wholly in accord with the ideas of the champions of the British Empire, both Conservative and Liberal, who were at the height of their influence at the end of the nineteenth century. The modest ambitions of the Welsh home rulers go far to explain a fact which was to perplex subsequent generations – that a man such as T. E. Ellis could embrace both Welsh nationalism and British imperialism.

As the time seemed favourable to the cause of Home Rule for Wales, a movement which would campaign on the issue was deemed to be necessary. Such a movement was created between 1894 and 1896 when branches of Cymru Fydd were established throughout the length and breadth of Wales. A central structure for the movement was set up in 1894, and in 1895 Beriah Gwynfe Evans, the former secretary of the Welsh Language Society, was appointed full-time organizer. Cymru Fydd reached its apogee during the winter of 1895–6. It was widely expected that the first aim of the movement – the uniting of the Welsh organization of the Liberal party with that of Cymru Fydd in a national league – would speedily be achieved. That aim was supported by most of the leaders of Welsh-speaking Wales, from the venerable Thomas Gee to young intellectuals such as John Morris-Jones, J. E. Lloyd and Llewelyn Williams. About half the Welsh MPs, with Lloyd George at their head, joined the ranks of

Cymru Fydd. In the months following the fall of the Liberal government, Lloyd George travelled untiringly, winning the support of
audiences from Aberdare to Amlwch, from Llanelli to Rhosllannerchrugog. Before Lloyd George took over its leadership, Cymru
Fydd had been a vague, romantic movement, but the response to his
speeches suggests that there was in Wales the potential for a mass
nationalist movement. There were negative aspects to Lloyd George's
dynamism. The Welsh MPs were a particularly quarrelsome group
and they were very unwilling to see the youngest among them
establishing a power base for himself. Bryn Roberts, the member for
South Caernarfonshire, believed that Lloyd George's activities were a
threat to the unity of British Liberalism. D. A. Thomas, who, although
treasurer of Cymru Fydd, had no intuitive sympathy for Welsh
nationalism, considered that Lloyd George was wholly concerned
with his own advancement.

The North Wales Liberal Federation amalgamated with Cymru
Fydd in April 1895, and the South Wales Liberal Federation, which
had been more eager to act independently of the Liberal party, was
expected to follow suit. But that did not happen. The matter was
debated at Newport on 16 January 1896, in a meeting packed with
the enemies of Lloyd George. His speech was howled down by the
audience and Robert Bird, a native of Bristol, a fervent Wesleyan and
the chairman of the Cardiff Liberal Association, was particularly
hostile. 'There are,' Bird told the supporters of Cymru Fydd '. . .
from Swansea to Newport, thousands upon thousands of Englishmen,
as true Liberals as yourselves . . . who will never submit to the domination of Welsh ideas.' The *Western Mail* was full of glee, reporting the
meeting under the headline: 'A Radical Bear-garden; Outbreak of
Anti-Welsh Feeling in Newport'. Lloyd George was deeply angered.
'Is the mass of the Welsh nation,' he asked in *Y Faner*, 'willing to be
dominated by a coalition of English capitalists who have come to
Wales, not to benefit the people, but to make their fortune?' The
answer to his rhetorical question was 'Yes', for although capitalism
was to come under attack in Wales it would not be challenged in the
name of the nation. The meeting in Newport was a fatal blow to
Cymru Fydd. Further meetings were held in 1897 and 1898 but they
lacked conviction; by the end of the century the movement had
become moribund.

But the ideals of Cymru Fydd did not disappear. There were

stalwart efforts to realize its cultural aspirations, and hopes of realizing its political aims were not extinguished. Between 1910 and 1914, there were further efforts to raise the issue of Home Rule for Wales, particularly on the part of E. T. John, a native of Pontypridd who had made his fortune in the steel industry in Middlesbrough. John followed the strategy of Cymru Fydd, seeking to win the support of the institutions of Welsh Liberalism, an ambition aided by his election as Liberal MP for East Denbighshire in 1910. He brought new elements into the Home Rule debate. He was eager to cooperate with the Scots (who were much more relevant allies for the Welsh than were the Irish), and he laboured tirelessly to demonstrate that Wales had economic and social problems which would not be solved without a Welsh parliament. He was the first to pay detailed attention to the nature and powers of such a body, and in March 1914 he introduced a Welsh Home Rule Bill in the House of Commons. It received little attention and his efforts were soon drowned in the deluge of the First World War.

E. T. John's was a one-man campaign. After the demise of Cymru Fydd, a quarter of a century was to pass before another attempt would be made to establish a national political movement in Wales. This was Plaid Genedlaethol Cymru (the National Party of Wales); its founders were intent upon creating an entirely independent party, for they believed that Cymru Fydd had failed because of its dependence upon British Liberalism. That belief had considerable substance. The energies of Cymru Fydd had been dissipated by the struggle to capture the power structures of the Liberal party. The effort was fruitless; the wealthy Welsh upper middle class – the mainstay of official Liberalism – saw no advantage to themselves in the victory of Welsh political nationalism. The capitalist class of Wales, unlike that of Catalonia or Bohemia, had no need of an autonomous political system to further its material interests. The strain of social radicalism that had been present in Welsh nationalism from the beginning – the tradition of Michael D. Jones and R. J. Derfel, a tradition whose heirs Lloyd George and T. E. Ellis considered themselves to be – was unacceptable to the capitalist class. Yet, although that radicalism was sufficiently strong to estrange the capitalist class, it was not given enough prominence to make the nationalist movement attractive to the working class.

In the last decades of the nineteenth century, a desire arose –

chiefly, but not solely, in the quarrying districts – to combine labour
and national aspirations in a united Welsh political movement. The
desire was not realized, mainly because it involved challenging the
Liberal party, a step which the nationalists were not prepared to take.
In the mid-1890s, there were signs that Lloyd George was prepared to
take up the challenge, and it is interesting to speculate on what would
have happened if he, with his brilliant talents, had devoted himself to
the creation of an effective national movement. After the débâcle at
Newport, however, he decided to serve 'the juggernaut of my ambition' by advancing within the Liberal party. He continued to advocate
Home Rule All Round, and in 1898 he was prominent in the successful attempt to create a Welsh National Liberal Council. Nevertheless,
such activities were increasingly of marginal importance to him, and
by 1901 he was considered to be a 'below the gangway English
radical – nothing more'.

Although it may be acknowledged that the fundamental weakness
of Cymru Fydd was the desire of its leaders to cling to the Liberal
party, there were other factors at the root of the movement's failure.
Tension between the Welsh-speaking and the non-Welsh-speaking
Welsh was one of them, although it should be remembered that Bryn
Roberts, the representative of the most thoroughly Welsh-speaking
of all the constituencies of Wales, was among the strongest opponents
of Lloyd George's plans. It is sometimes claimed that Cymru Fydd
was destroyed by a split between the north and the south. This is a
misleading contention; there were many ardent Welsh patriots in the
south Wales coalfield, and such patriotism was as feeble in Rhyl and
Wrexham as it was in Newport. However, D. A. Thomas and his like
had reason to suspect that a movement which was led by a man from
the depths of Gwynedd would not give adequate attention to the
interests of the populous south-east. To Thomas, it was perverse that
the most dynamic areas of Wales should accept the leadership of the
least dynamic.

In the last decades of the twentieth century, with the industrial
areas of the south-east having suffered such calamitous blows, it is
difficult to appreciate how confident and full of energy they were in
the last decades of the nineteenth century. By 1895, two out of every
three of the Welsh people lived in them; the coal valleys and the
coastal ports embodied reality for the majority of the inhabitants of
Wales, but this situation had come into being so rapidly that the

image of Wales did not correspond with the substance of Wales. As Dai Smith has argued, within one generation a disparity arose between the experience of the majority of the Welsh and the image of Welshness, a disparity which has continued to trouble the life of Wales until the present day.

The upholders of Welsh rural values tended to be patronizing towards the communities which had developed in the south-east. Nevertheless, as agriculture was hit by depression, rural Wales came to depend increasingly heavily upon industrial Wales. For generations, a substantial proportion of the rural surplus had been saved from destitution by the work available in the coalfield; the severity of the agricultural depression was mitigated by the huge market for food which existed in Monmouthshire and Glamorgan; the woollen mills of the Teifi valley prospered as a result of the coalfield's needs; the hotels of the spa towns of mid-Wales and the seaside resorts of the west were filled by miners on holiday. As Gwyn A. Williams has argued, by the end of the nineteenth century the whole of Wales was responding to the rhythms of the industrial economy, and he notes that the rate of marriage, even in rural Wales, fluctuated in accordance with the price of coal.

The impact of the coalfield was not only felt in Wales. From their very beginnings as a nation, the Welsh had looked enviously towards the plains to the east, with their fertile soil and their prosperous communities. By the end of the nineteenth century, the situation had been reversed. In his youth in Herefordshire, the author B. L. Coombes had looked enviously towards the west, where the sky was lit up by the furnaces of Dowlais, sixty kilometres away. There had been a time when the people of Glamorgan had depended for their news on the *Hereford Journal*, which had been founded in 1713; in the late nineteenth century, the radicals of Hereford bought the *South Wales Daily News*, the Cardiff Liberal paper. For centuries, southern Wales had lived in the shadow of Bristol, the 'emporium of the west', but by the end of the nineteenth century the harbour at Bristol was a mere creek compared with the docks at Cardiff. In terms of tonnage exported, Cardiff in 1890 was the largest port in the world and the centre of a commercial empire which stretched to the farthest reaches of the globe. The industries and the railways of western France and northern Spain, of Italy and Egypt, of Brazil and Argentina, depended on Wales for their fuel, and the oceans were traversed by ships powered by Welsh coal. In 1890, those countries which produced a surplus of coal – about a dozen in all – exported a total of sixty-one million tons. Of that total, 62 per cent came from Britain; Welsh exports represented 40 per cent of the exports of Britain and 25 per cent of the total world exports. (Because of the nature of the statistics, these figures probably underestimate Wales's role.) As at least a quarter of the international trade in the sources of heat and energy originated in south Wales, the Severn Sea in the 1880s occupied a position in the world economy comparable with that of the Persian Gulf in the 1980s. The rest of the coalfields of Britain produced coal primarily for home consumption, but more than half of the coal mined in Wales was exported. As the south Wales coalfield was dependent upon international markets rather than upon the internal demands of the British economy, the pattern of its development differed from that of the coalfields of England and Scotland, a fact which, as Brinley Thomas has demonstrated, was of fundamental importance in its history.

Although the coalfield was served by a chain of ports stretching from Newport to Saundersfoot, Cardiff was handling 72 per cent of Wales's coal exports by 1880. Because of congestion there, the coal-owners succeeded in 1884 in obtaining an act of parliament which empowered them to build docks at Barry. The act became law after one of the most lengthy battles in the history of parliament, for the Bute estate and the Taff Vale Railway Company – both of whose interests were concentrated at Cardiff – opposed it fiercely. By 1901, Barry, which had previously been almost uninhabited, was a town of 27,000 people, while Cardiff had a population of 128,000, almost seven times as many as had lived there half a century earlier. Although the development of Barry was a blow to the Bute Docks, the position of Cardiff as the headquarters of the coal industry and as the pinnacle of the urban hierarchy of south Wales was wholly secure. In 1883, that remarkable building, the Coal Exchange, was opened in Butetown; in 1897, buildings worthy of the Welsh metropolis were begun in Cathays Park, and in 1905 Cardiff was elevated to the status of a city. The confidence of the wealthy among the citizens of the new city was boundless; with their huge banquets, their luxurious mansions and their appetite for honours, they were a notable part of the British capitalist class, which was then at the height of its power and wealth.

This prosperity was narrowly based. Coal exports accounted for 95 per cent of the business of Barry Docks, and Cardiff's dependence on coal was also overwhelming despite the efforts of the managers of the Bute estate to attract imports to their docks. In the coalfield, dependence upon coal was even more intense: in the Rhondda in 1901, 70 per cent of the male workforce were miners. On the northern rim of the coalfield – the cradle of the Industrial Revolution in Wales – the iron industry was languishing. Dowlais was still in high repute, and at the Blaenavon works the cousins Gilchrist and Thomas invented in 1877 a method of ridding molten iron of phosphorus, a discovery which was of revolutionary significance to the iron and steel industry. But most of the rest of the ironworks of northern Glamorgan and Monmouthshire were in terminal decline. By 1900, only 10 per cent of the iron of Britain was produced in south Wales; of the companies which had adopted the Bessemer system of making steel, Rhymney closed in 1891, Tredegar in 1900 and Cyfarthfa in 1910. On the eve of the First World War, the only works remaining in the old iron-producing area were Blaenavon, Ebbw Vale and Dowlais. Since 1891, the Dowlais Company had produced a proportion of its steel at East Moors, Cardiff, an acknowledgement that henceforth the advantage lay with works sited near ports.

The decline in the international demand for rails, the speciality of the Welsh ironworks, was a severe blow to the iron companies. As the industries of the coalfield were so dependent upon exports, they were seriously weakened by any contraction in overseas markets. This was clearly demonstrated in the history of the tinplate industry. The United States had taken three quarters of Welsh tinplate exports. Because the American government was anxious to boost home industries, it imposed a tariff (the McKinley Tariff) on tinplate imports in 1891. The annual value of tinplate exports from Britain declined from £7.2 million in 1891 to £2.7 million in 1898, and during the same period the industry's workforce decreased from 25,000 to 16,000. There was much suffering in the valleys of the Llwchwr, Tawe, Nedd and Afan and many of the tinplate workers emigrated to the new centres of the industry in Pennsylvania. In the first decade of the twentieth century, new markets were found, but the McKinley episode was a foretaste of what would happen in more important sectors of the Welsh economy as a result of changes in the conditions governing international trade.

At the end of the nineteenth century, hardly anyone believed that contraction could strike the most important sector of the Welsh economy. Indeed, faith in the boundless potential of the coal industry was chiefly responsible for the one-sided nature of that economy – what was the point in investing in something else when the profits from coal were so great? In the last decades of the nineteenth century, the output of the pits of the south Wales coalfield was increasing at a rate of a million tons a year. In 1900, sales of Welsh coal represented over 5 per cent of the export receipts of the United Kingdom. Nevertheless, fundamental problems lay beneath the surface. Indeed, the causes of the tragedy which was to overwhelm the south Wales coalfield can, with hindsight, be discerned in the 1890s. D. A. Thomas tried to establish a body which would regulate production and prices – an OPEC of the coal industry, as it were – but most of the coal-owners favoured untrammelled competition, particularly that master-ful man, W. T. Lewis, the agent of the marquess of Bute and the chairman of the Sliding Scale Committee.

Because of the geological formation of the south Wales coalfield, its pits were more dangerous than those of the other coalfields of Britain. Between 1880 and 1900, 2,328 British miners were killed in major disasters – that is, tragedies in which more than twenty-five lives were lost. Although the miners of south Wales constituted only 18 per cent of the miners of Britain, 48 per cent of the 2,328 deaths occurred there. Yet major disasters were responsible for only a small proportion of the total deaths: 80 per cent of fatal colliery accidents were the result of individual incidents – what John Benson has called 'the steady drip-drip of death'. For every fatal accident, there were a hundred which were not fatal, and dust-related diseases were at their worst in Wales as the hideous statistics for pneumoconiosis demonstrate. Geological factors were also the main cause of the high price of Welsh coal, a disadvantage which could be borne when the market was buoyant, but which would cause concern if the demand were to contract. Above all, the industry's rate of productivity was falling: the workforce mined 309 tons a head in 1883; the figure was 266 in 1900. As a result of this, and of the rapid increase in the amount of coal produced – from twenty-one million tons in 1880 to thirty-nine million in 1900 – there was an enormous rise in the size of the workforce: from 69,000 men in 1880 to 148,000 in 1900.

By 1880, and for half a century after that, between a quarter and a third of the male labour force of Wales worked in the coal industry. If the numbers engaged in providing services for the miners and those employed by the railways and docks which transported coal are added, there was a period when almost half the people of Wales were dependent on a single industry, a situation unusual if not unique in the history of industrial Europe. As they were such a significant element in the population of Wales, the nature of Welsh society was determined to a considerable extent by the circumstances of the miners and their families. Those circumstances were less lamentable than they had been in the early phase of industrialization. By the late nineteenth century, the industrial valleys had weather-proof houses, clean water, efficient sewerage and paved and lighted streets; indeed, to visitors from the countryside, they offered a cornucopia of marvels. A reformed structure of local government existed and there had been important developments in the fields of education and health. The mortality rate among infants continued to be distressingly high – as much as 135 per 1,000 as late as 1911 – but it did not compare with the appalling levels of the first half of the nineteenth century. As the pits offered virtually no employment to women, there was a lack of balance in the ratio between the sexes: in 1891 the Rhondda had 1,314 men for every 1,000 women (the ratio in Cardiganshire was 776:1,000). There was a young and prolific population in the coalfield, a complete contrast with the situation in the countryside. (See the diagram on p. 401.) The oppressive truck system had long disappeared and goods from all over the world could be bought in the shops and markets. The industrial districts had developed a lively and appealing culture – from the various chapel activities to the boxing booths, from the theatres to conversations in public houses and Italian cafés, from Carnegie libraries to greyhound and pigeon races.

Apart from a very small petit bourgeois class, the communities of the coal valleys were one-class (not classless, as some people assert) communities. Those who had won wealth through the coal industry lived outside the coal valleys, in rural mansions or in Cardiff and the other coastal towns. The principal significance of the coalfield in the history of Wales is that its growth gave birth to a mass working class, and one of the central themes of the recent history of Wales is the attempt of this class to assert its identity. After the bloody battles of the first half of the nineteenth century, the second half saw the emergence of a generation of working-class leaders who were willing to accept the direction of the middle class. They delighted in chapel values, they considered the Liberal party to be the natural guardian of their interests and they were eager to cooperate with the capitalist system. By the last decade of the nineteenth century, however, there were signs that this Liberal, Nonconformist consensus was becoming increasingly fragile. Yet its break-up should not be antedated, for the consensus still existed as late as 1914. But come to an end it did, under the pressures of militant unionism, a new interpretation of labour politics, and a decline in the importance of the Christian faith.

The years 1889–91 saw a significant growth in unionism, particularly in the coastal towns. It was stimulated by the 'New Unionism' which had developed in the large towns of England, a phenomenon which reached its peak during the London dock strike of 1889. A sudden increase in union activity took place among railway-men, dockers, sailors, clerks, and gas and shop workers – most of whom had not been eligible to join the craft unions which had existed since the 1850s. The railway companies were challenged in 1890 and the dock-owners in 1891, and workers in Cardiff, Newport and Swansea were stirred by the most eloquent labour leaders in the kingdom. The new unions belonged to a general British pattern of organization; they had no interest in specifically Welsh topics and, as L. J. Williams has argued, they were a powerful factor in the process of anglicizing the working class of Wales. The loyalties of the workers in the coalfield were more Welsh and local; subjects such as disestablishment and Home Rule for Wales were discussed in the union meetings of the miners and tinplate workers. Unrest was on the increase among them too. In 1893, the hauliers went on strike, the first important confrontation since 1875; there was bitter fighting in the Rhondda and in northern Monmouthshire, and a thousand soldiers were sent to the coal-mining valleys. The hauliers were expressing their hostility to the Sliding Scale. In their opinion, it impoverished the miners and prevented them from uniting with workers in the other coalfields of Britain to fight for a fair wage.

By 1893, there was a focal point for those miners who opposed the Sliding Scale. That was the Miners' Federation of Great Britain, founded at Newport in 1889. The policies of the Federation included willingness to use the strike weapon to further its main aims – legislation to restrict the hours of work to eight hours a day, and the creation of a Board of Arbitration to replace the Sliding Scale. The

miners of north Wales became part of the British Federation in 1893,
but the majority of the miners' organizations in the south were unable
to do so because they followed Mabon in supporting the Sliding
Scale. In some areas – particularly in Monmouthshire – Mabonism
was challenged, and William Brace of Risca became prominent as the
chief supporter of the Federation. In 1893, of the 118,000 men who
worked in the collieries of the south Wales coalfield, 6,000 belonged
to the Federation and 40,000 to unions which supported Mabon's
position; the rest belonged to no union at all, which suggests that the
part played by unionism in the life of the coal communities can be
exaggerated. Despite the support for Mabonism, a number of factors
were favouring the growth of the Federation. Between 1890 and
1896, the price of large coal on the dock in Cardiff declined from 13s.
to 9s. 2d. a ton. It was argued that the existence of the Sliding Scale
encouraged the owners to sell their coal cheaply, for by doing so they
could keep wages low. At the same time, the size of the coal companies
was growing rapidly and giants like Powell Duffryn were coming to
own pits in a number of valleys. As the employers became organized
in increasingly large units, there was added substance to the Federation's argument that a slack network of local unions was an insufficient
defence of the interests of the miners. The Mabonite unions reflected
the community values of Welsh industrial society, values which came
under increasing attack as immigrants who did not share them poured
into the industrial south-east. Between 1891 and 1901, 52,000 people
were attracted to Glamorgan, less than half of them natives of Wales.
Although the coastal towns were the favourite destination of English
incomers, they were sufficiently numerous in the coalfield by the end
of the century to weaken allegiance to Mabon, a man who depended
heavily upon his ability to charm Welsh and Welsh-speaking audiences. Above all, Mabonism was challenged by the growing support
for socialist ideas. As a result, the younger generation of miners'
leaders were increasingly hostile to Mabon's faith in the partnership
between labour and capital.

These developments reached their peak during the strike of 1898.
In September 1897, with a degree of prosperity returning to the coal
industry, the miners voted in favour of reforming the Sliding Scale so
as to include within it the principle of a minimum wage. The employers refused, offering instead minor adjustments to the scale together
with the abolition of Mabon's Day. As a settlement had not been

reached when the existing agreement ran out at the end of March 1898, the employers terminated their contracts with the workers; thus, the 1898 dispute was a lock-out rather than a strike. The pits were idle until September. The lock-out caused widespread suffering; the strikers were denied assistance from the Poor Law and the resources of the Mabonite unions were quickly exhausted; the Miners' Federation of Great Britain contributed £10,000, a pitifully inadequate sum to maintain a hundred thousand miners and their families. Mabon was under a cloud at the beginning of the strike, but as it dragged on the miners turned to him to seek a settlement. The employers, led by W. T. Lewis, aware that the workers were close to collapse, insisted upon total victory – although Lewis, after experiencing the troubles of 1898, decided that it would be pleasanter to live at Hean Castle, near Tenby, rather than at Aberdare.

To the miners' leaders, the chief lesson of the strike was the need for a more centralized organization. On 11 October 1898, the South Wales Miners' Federation (the 'Fed') was established, with Mabon as its president. At the beginning of the strike, the majority of the miners had wanted a revised Sliding Scale; by its end, they – Mabon among them – were firmly in favour of its total abolition. Thus, there was nothing to prevent the 'Fed' from becoming part of the Miners' Federation of Great Britain; the one federation was affiliated to the other in January 1899. The 'Fed' won immediate acceptance; 104,000 miners had joined it by the end of 1899, and it gained a notable victory in 1903, when the Sliding Scale was abolished. A time would come when it would have over a quarter of a million members; no secular body in the history of the Welsh people has ever had more members than the 'Fed', and for a generation and more after 1898 its activities were to be a central element in the life of that people.

The year 1898 was a turning-point in political terms also. Keir Hardie, the chairman of the Independent Labour Party (the ILP), made several visits to Wales during the strike. He contributed a number of sensitive articles describing the suffering of the miners to *The Labour Leader*, the socialist weekly he published. The ILP held a recruiting campaign in Wales, and by the end of 1898 some two dozen branches had been established in the south Wales coalfield. Before 1898, there had been little support for socialism in Wales. Thomas Halliday, the president of the Amalgamated Association of Mineworkers, had received 4,192 votes at Merthyr in the general election of 1874, but his efforts had not been followed up. There were socialist elements in the radicalism of Michael D. Jones and Dr Pan Jones, but their political views were primarily concerned with the countryside. Between 1892 and 1903, R. J. Derfel wrote a series of powerful articles on socialism for Welsh periodicals, but as he lived in Manchester he had little effect on Welsh public opinion.

Mabon's success in the Rhondda in 1885 proved that there was in Wales an awareness of the need for working-class political representation. That feeling increased in the decade which followed and in areas such as Merthyr, Cardiff and Swansea the Trades Councils succeeded in getting some of their candidates elected to School Boards and Boards of Guardians. This activity took place within the Lib–Lab tradition, a tradition which considered the labour cause to be one among a number of interests which could be accommodated under the umbrella of Liberalism. By the last decade of the century, however, there were those, particularly in the north of England, who were arguing that a party for the working class should be established. As the majority of the population belonged to that class, the labour cause was not one interest among many; it was the most important interest, and a realignment which would reflect the fact was an urgent political necessity.

No representative from Wales was present at the meeting in Bradford in 1893 which led to the establishment of the ILP, and until 1898 the party had only two or three weak branches in Wales. Most of the branches set up in 1898 proved to be short-lived, much to the disappointment of that lively journal *Llais Llafur* (The Voice of Labour), which was founded in Ystalyfera in that year. At the end of the century, there was a wide variety of views on methods of promoting the interests of the working class and there were deep divisions between the different factions. The Marxists of the Social Democratic Federation regarded the members of the ILP as weak-minded moderates; the intellectuals of the Fabian Society considered them to be naïve idealists; to most of the upholders of traditional politics, they were dangerous revolutionaries. The ILP functioned as a propaganda society rather than as a political party; it was therefore felt that a more widely based movement to promote working-class parliamentary representation was necessary. Such a movement was created in London in February 1900, when the Labour Representation Committee came into existence. It was established by the representatives of half a million trade-unionists, together with the leaders of the ILP and other socialist groups. This was the organization which from 1906 onwards was to be known as the Labour Party. Its chief aim was to promote the interests of trade unions; it was financed by a political levy on the unions and it did not at first adopt any specific ideology.

It was the Labour Representation Committee which sponsored the candidature of Keir Hardie in Merthyr in the general election of 1900. The election had been called early by the Conservative government in the hope that the party would profit from the jingoistic spirit which had resulted from the South African War (1899–1902). The war split the Liberal party, with the earl of Rosebery and his like fervently supporting it and younger progressives such as Lloyd George vehemently opposing it. As Kenneth O. Morgan has argued, there were those in Wales who enthusiastically supported the British forces, for the belief that the country was free of imperialist fever is a myth. Nevertheless, except for Ireland (where a battalion was raised to fight for the Boers), readiness to sympathize with the Boers was stronger in Wales than it was in any other part of the kingdom. In Merthyr, where pride in the pacific tradition of Henry Richard was still an important factor, a split arose between the two Liberal candidates, with D. A. Thomas criticizing the war and Pritchard Morgan ardently in its favour. Thomas, who detested Morgan, was ready to take the Labour anti-imperialist under his wing. As Merthyr was a two-seat constituency, the electors had two votes each, and 77 per cent of Hardie's votes were ones which he received jointly with Thomas. Thomas was supported by 8,598 of the electors, Hardie by 5,745 and Morgan by 4,004; thus it was under the aegis of the arch-capitalist, D. A. Thomas, that Wales's first socialist MP was elected. It was the exceptional circumstances at Merthyr which secured Hardie's return. Nevertheless, a Labour candidate could poll a high vote in a straight fight against a Liberal; John Hodge, the secretary of the British Steel Smelters Association, received 45 per cent of the vote in Gower, the only Welsh constituency, apart from Merthyr, where there was a contest between a Labour and a Liberal candidate in the general election of 1900.

In 1900, Merthyr was the sole constituency in the United Kingdom to return a convinced socialist. Despite the uniqueness of Hardie's position, a number of factors were working in his favour. He proved able to strike a note which appealed to Welsh voters. A Scot, he praised the attributes of the Celts, adopting as his slogan 'The Red Dragon and the Red Flag'. He gave the impression that he was in favour of Home Rule for Wales, claiming that the members of the ILP were the only true nationalists, for they alone wished the Welsh people to own the land and the resources of their country. Hardie was, above all, a Christian and his ideas appealed particularly to those who were attracted by the Social Gospel and the 'New Theology' of R. J. Campbell. It was Campbell and Hardie together, wrote James Griffiths, who had made him a socialist. Hardie's vision influenced those who were distressed by the glaring contrast between wealth and poverty. In the early twentieth century, there were many who abandoned the prudential respectability which had characterized the age of Victoria, and there was an eagerness among the wealthy to flaunt their wealth. At the same time, the studies of Rowntree, Booth and others proved that a third of the population were lacking in basic necessities. *Can a Man be a Christian on a Pound a Week?* was one of Hardie's most effective publications, although one wag maintained that a man could not be anything but a Christian on so pitiful an income.

While the moral reasons for drawing closer to socialism were being rehearsed, there arose a practical reason for seeking to make parliament more responsive to the concerns of trade-unionism. That reason was the judgement given in the case of the Taff Vale Railway Company (the TVR). In 1900, some of the employees of the company went on strike without the support of their union, the Amalgamated Society of Railway Servants (the ASRS). As the dispute dragged on, the union gave a degree of assistance to the strikers, thereby attracting the hostility of Amon Beasley, the manager of the TVR. He prosecuted the ASRS from court to court and in 1901 the House of Lords gave judgement in his favour. The union was ordered to pay £23,000 to the company for losses incurred during the strike and in addition it was burdened with legal costs amounting to £25,000. 'The TVR case,' asserted G. D. H. Cole, 'created the Labour party.' The judgement meant that the strike was powerless as a weapon and that the employers could use the law to destroy trade-unionism. As a result, union leaders considered that it was essential to obtain legislation which would safeguard trade-union rights; an increase in the number of working-class MPs came therefore to be seen as a matter of crucial importance. That goal could be achieved either through the Labour

Representation Committee or through the efforts of individual unions.

The Miners' Federation of Great Britain chose the second alternative. In 1901 the Federation established a political fund. The miners soon came to consider that they had a right to at least ten of the constituencies of south Wales, and their ambition was facilitated by the desire of the Liberal party, centrally if not locally, to avoid contests between Liberal and Labour candidates. Following the general election in 1906, Hardie was once more Wales's only independent Labour MP. But, in addition, four candidates sponsored by the miners were successful – Mabon in the Rhondda, John Williams in Gower, William Brace in South Glamorgan and Tom Richards in West Monmouthshire. The four had a close relationship with the Liberal party, but when the Miners' Federation of Great Britain became affiliated to the Labour party in 1909 they became – rather reluctantly, in some cases – members of the Labour party. In the general election of 1906, twenty-nine of the Labour Representation Committee's candidates won seats; in addition, twenty-five Lib–Labs were elected, thirteen of them members of the Miners' Federation of Great Britain. Labour had become a considerable force in the political life of Britain, and the progress it had made since 1900 was a matter of astonishment.

Yet, although Labour's success has to be acknowledged, the general election of 1906 was primarily a triumph for the Liberal party. In the new parliament there were 377 Liberals (including the Lib–Labs), 157 Conservatives and their allies, eighty-three Irish Nationalists and twenty-nine independent Labour members. Wales was represented by thirty-three Liberals (again including the Lib–Labs) and one Labour member. All the Conservative candidates were defeated, although the party had received the support of 33.8 per cent of the electors of Wales – a higher percentage than they were to win in 1987; in 1906, the Liberals were silent on the matter of proportional representation. The striking success of the Liberal party was chiefly the result of the Conservative party's advocacy of tariffs on foreign goods, a campaign mainly associated with Joseph Chamberlain. Hatred of protectionism had been one of the articles of faith of Welsh Liberalism ever since the time of Samuel Roberts of Llanbrynmair. Although farmers and tinplate workers were suffering from foreign competition, the prodigious success of the coal trade was proof of the Welsh economy's dependence upon Free Trade. Furthermore, the Liberals could make much of the threat to the standard of living of the working class if duties were levied on food imports.

The battle between the parties was given a sharper edge by the revival of sectarian bitterness. That was the result of the passage of the Education Act of 1902, an attempt by the Conservative government to reform the system of school administration. The School Boards were abolished and the Education Committees of the county councils were made responsible for elementary schools. Part of the purpose of the act was to safeguard the future of the Church schools. They were in difficulties, for in accordance with the Education Act of 1870 they, unlike the Board schools, did not receive assistance from the rates. The 1902 act had its merits; it was, however, bitterly opposed by the Nonconformists because it ensured that henceforth denominational education would be provided at the cost of the ratepayers. In many parts of Wales, Church schools were the only schools available, even in areas where the majority of the pupils attending them were the children of chapel-goers. Nonconformist leaders had hoped that this injustice would be brought to an end as the Church schools disappeared under the weight of their financial difficulties, but this hope was extinguished by the Education Act of 1902. There was an angry reaction from the Nonconformists of England, but the fiercest response came from Wales, where Lloyd George led a national revolt. The 1902 act was the main point at issue in the local elections of 1904, elections which gave a substantial majority to the opponents of the act on every one of the county councils of Wales. They refused to implement it, and the government replied with the Education (Local Authority Default) Act – the 'Coercion of Wales Act', as it came to be known. Some of the Welsh authorities were declared to have failed in their duties; they were deprived of grants, and plans were put in hand to teach the children of Nonconformists in chapels and vestries. In December 1905, when the uproar was at its height, deliverance came. The Conservative government fell, and its successor, the Liberal government of Campbell-Bannerman, announced that it would not implement the 'Coercion Act'. The emotion generated by the Welsh revolt was still operative at the time of the general election (10 January–7 February 1906). That emotion helped the Liberals of Wales to win an unequalled victory, and it strengthened their determination to do away with the Church Establishment.

As the Liberal government of 1906 had an absolute majority of 108 seats, the Welsh MPs did not wield the same influence as they had done in 1892–5. Rather than introduce a disestablishment bill, the government set up a royal commission to inquire into religious provision in Wales – a decision which was seen as an attempt to postpone legislation on the matter. The tortuous meanderings of the commission became a matter of ridicule, and it did not produce a report until 1910. The House of Lords rejected all attempts to solve the problems resulting from the 1902 Education Act, but the difficulties became less pressing as the number of council schools increased and the number of voluntary schools decreased. To Lloyd George, a leading figure in the new Liberal government, disestablishment and sectarian education were no longer issues of vital concern. He was appointed President of the Board of Trade in 1905 and Chancellor of the Exchequer in 1908. He was the first Welshman since Cornewall Lewis in 1855 to be a member of the Cabinet, and the first Welshman (and one of the first Britons) to reach such a position from the ranks of the common people. The Welsh people were enthralled by the exploits of the 'son of the cottage', and his success came to be regarded as synonymous with the elevation of the nation.

Lloyd George was the apostle of the 'New Liberalism', a body of broadly pragmatic ideas, but with a leaning to collectivism – a striking contrast with the old Liberal ideology. As President of the Board of Trade, he acknowledged the role of trade unions in collective bargaining; as Chancellor, he introduced Old Age Pensions in 1908, an act which almost deified him among the needy aged. To pay for his schemes, he introduced in 1909 his 'People's Budget' which included new taxes on the wealthy, particularly landowners – an echo of the hatred of landlordism which was so characteristic of Welsh radicalism. The House of Lords rejected the Budget, an act of folly which enabled Lloyd George to lead a campaign of demagogic invective against the aristocracy (dukes in particular – there were no Liberal dukes). After a constitutional crisis and two general elections (January and December 1910), the power of the House of Lords was drastically reduced. Then, in 1911, in the teeth of bitter opposition, Lloyd George established National Insurance against unemployment and sickness. In the same year he masterminded the investiture of the prince of Wales at Caernarfon, in the heart of his constituency; the willingness of the royal family to take part in so unwonted a ceremony was proof of Lloyd George's political importance. From then until the First World

War, he was busy with plans concerning land, health, housing, roads and income tax, while he also involved himself increasingly in international affairs. To the wealthy and the reactionary, he was the curse from Wales; because of him, the entire nation was vilified in many English circles, as the welcome given to volumes such as *Perfidious Welshman* (1910) and the readiness of some members of the aristocracy and their hangers-on to hiss at a band playing 'Men of Harlech' bear witness.

Most of the supporters of the Labour party were strongly in favour of the achievements of the Liberal government of 1906–10. In addition to the legislation associated with Lloyd George, that government also secured legislation to counteract the effects of the Taff Vale Judgement (the Trades Disputes Act, 1906), to restrict the miners' hours of work to eight hours a day (1908), to establish labour exchanges (1909) and to safeguard the interests of exploited workers (the 'Sweated Trades' Act, 1909). Indeed, between 1906 and 1914 the Labour party was not an independent party but rather a part of a progressive alliance. Labour enthusiasts found it difficult to counteract the argument that it was better to support a progressive and experienced Liberal party than to seek sterile independence. The growth of the Labour party was hindered by the Osborne Case of 1909, which adjudged that the unions' political levy was unlawful – a judgement which deprived the party of the greater part of its income. As MPs were not paid a salary until 1911, a political career was an impossibility for a working-class man bereft of union support. In the two elections of 1910 – contests which were fought almost entirely on the Liberals' plans to curb the power of the House of Lords – support for the Labour party remained stationary.

In Wales, Keir Hardie and the four miners' members were re-elected, but the rest of the handful of Labour candidates were defeated, Vernon Hartshorn, one of the leading figures in the South Wales Miners' Federation, among them. The Labour party had greater success in local elections, and their ability to win seats on county and district councils gave a huge boost to their credibility in the local community. The elevation of an occasional Labour supporter to the magistrates' bench also contributed to the growth of that credibility; in 1914, almost half the members of the executive committee of the South Wales Miners' Federation were justices of the peace. Nevertheless, in the years immediately before the First World War, the Labour party's record in parliamentary by-elections was dismal; in the contest in East Carmarthenshire in 1912, only 10 per cent of those voting supported the Labour candidate.

In 1914, therefore, over half the seats in the coalfield and almost all those in the rest of Wales were firmly in the grasp of the Liberal party. The party was still credible as the vehicle for the aspirations of Welsh electors, particularly those of the older generation. (It must be remembered that a substantial proportion of the younger men – the group for whom the appeal of the Labour party was strongest – had no vote.) As Liberalism, Nonconformity and Welshness were so closely intertwined, it was possible for Liberal enthusiasts to claim that those who embraced socialism were denying their religion and their nation. This was the theme of the Methodist minister W. F. Phillips in his book *Y Ddraig Goch ynte'r Faner Goch?* (The Red Dragon or the Red Flag?, 1913). The argument had some substance. For socialists with Marxist inclinations, religion was the weapon of the capitalist class. In his autobiography, *From the Valley I Came*, W. J. Edwards of Aberdare noted that after the death of his mother he removed the Bible and *Taith y Pererin* (Pilgrim's Progress) from their place of honour in the parlour and put the Communist Manifesto and *Das Kapital* in their place; he was acknowledging that one religion was supplanting another. Lack of patience with the Welsh language and with Welsh attributes was characteristic of many of the early Welsh socialists. They embraced what Robin Okey calls 'naïve cosmopolitanism', a feature of socialism in England, as it was in every dominant nation. As John Davies of *Llais Llafur* put it in 1911: 'There are too many people in the movement ... who are inclined to take no account of national feeling. They have learned to mumble something they do not understand about internationalism, and they neglect their own country – like the Imperialist, their eyes are fixed upon the furthest corners of the earth, and they ignore the existence of their next door neighbour.' Nevertheless, as the Liberals insinuated that they were the guardians of religion and Welshness, many socialists became increasingly doubtful of both. Feeling that they were required to choose between 'Socialism and Christ' or 'Socialism and Wales', they chose socialism and turned their backs on the chapel and the Welsh language, a turn of events which left a long shadow over the history of Wales.

This was not the experience of all those attracted to socialism. The patriotic Welsh element was numerous in the ILP, and there were many members who considered that Christianity was the foundation upon which their political beliefs were based. They included John Davies, the son of a miner killed in the Maerdy explosion of 1885, an enthusiastic socialist and a faithful Calvinistic Methodist. In the north-west, where between 1908 and 1914 active branches of the ILP had been established and where the poet–preacher Silyn Roberts was the chief inspiration of the movement, it was strongly felt that the adoption of a new political creed should not entail the rejection of the old values. Welsh was the language of socialism in Gwynedd, as the substantial volumes of David Thomas and the socialist paper *Y Dinesydd Cymreig* (The Welsh Citizen) bear witness. The membership of the ILP in the south-east was also more favourably disposed to the Welsh language than is often supposed. 'Literature in Welsh, that is our great need here,' wrote the secretary of the Bedlinog branch in 1911. Following correspondence between John Davies and David Thomas, discussions were held during the Carmarthen National Eisteddfod of 1911 on the need to set up a Welsh Labour party. A Welsh section of the ILP was created in 1912, an example which the Labour party was not willing to follow when its organization was restructured in 1918.

As has been seen, the Labour movement continued to be marginal to formal Welsh politics in the years immediately preceding the First World War. But if the movement was marginal electorally, it was becoming increasingly militant industrially. In the twenty years before the First World War, it is possible to trace wave after wave of working-class discontent, discontent which reached a peak in the period 1912–13. This was the 'Great Unrest'; it was an international phenomenon, and historians have been much exercised in seeking to account for it in its various aspects.

In Wales, the beginning of the twentieth century saw the longest-lasting dispute in the industrial history of Britain – the 'Great Strike' at the Penrhyn quarry, a struggle which began in November 1900 and did not come to an end until November 1903. The dispute arose from the special nature of the quarryman's craft, from the particular ethos of the quarrying communities and from the way in which the second Baron Penrhyn (1836–1907) interpreted his rights as an employer. A chasm yawned between the quarrymen in their drab villages and Penrhyn in his castle. They were almost monolingually

Welsh, regular chapel-goers and increasingly radical; he was arrogantly English, ardently Anglican and unyieldingly Tory. The
Penrhyn family, with its schools and its hospital. were paternalistic
employers, but in return they expected obedience and submissiveness.
The quarrymen had had their union since 1874; it was a moderate
body – their main leader, W. J. Parry, was a northern version of
Mabon – and it was only occasionally that it succeeded in attracting
to its ranks more than a third of the labour force.

With the quality of the rock so variable, the traditional way of
working was through the 'bargain' – an agreement between a group
of workers and the management. This system allowed the quarrymen
to regard themselves as contractors rather than employees. In each of
the main quarries, the management sought to undermine the
autonomy which the workers enjoyed through the 'bargain' system.
This was what motivated the lock-outs at Dinorwig in 1885–6 and at
Llechwedd in 1893; the chief ambition of E. A. Young, the accountant
from London who was appointed manager of the Penrhyn quarry in
1885, was the abolition of the 'bargain'. In order to defend the 'bargain'
and to obtain a pay rise (5s. a day was aimed at), it was necessary to
strengthen unionism among the quarrymen. Young and Penrhyn
responded in September 1896 by dismissing all the members of the
quarrymen's committee, and as a result the Penrhyn quarry was idle
until August 1897. Another dispute over the 'bargain' arose in 1900,
and then, on 22 November, the 'Great Strike' began. As it proceeded,
it became obvious that the bone of contention was the workers' right
to an effective union. Baron Penrhyn was praised by opponents of
unionism – the supporters of 'Free Labour' – from every corner of
the kingdom, while trade-unionists throughout Britain collected
thousands of pounds to assist the strikers. Union support encouraged
the quarrymen to think of themselves as members of the British
working class; the Liberals of Wales were reluctant to embrace their
cause, although Baron Penrhyn was the embodiment of everything
that was most hateful to the Welsh Liberal tradition.

The labour force at the Penrhyn quarry numbered about 2,800; by
the spring of 1902, 700 of them had returned to work and 1,300 had
left the area, mainly for the south Wales coalfield. The community
was angered by the strike-breakers, and soldiers had to be brought in
to protect them, particularly on those occasions when the men who
had left for the south returned home. The *cynffonwyr* (blacklegs) were

thrown out of the community in Bethesda; they gathered in pitiful bands in the upland villages and the ill-feeling between their families and the families of the strikers was to cause bitterness in the area for generations. The atmosphere in Bethesda in the last months of the strike was frenzied. As the hope of defeating Penrhyn vanished, the suffering of the strikers became a justification in itself. Steeped as they were in the rhetoric of Calvinism, they saw themselves as the Chosen Few, purified by their tribulations. The strike was a terrible blow to the slate industry. There were only 1,800 working at Penrhyn by 1907, and the labour force decreased in the other quarries also in the wake of the depression in the building industry. In 1898, 18,801 men had been employed in the slate quarries and mines of Gwynedd; the figure was 11,658 in 1914.

As a result of the contraction in the number of quarrymen, the coalminers were by the early twentieth century the most numerous non-agricultural workforce in north Wales. The number of miners in the counties of Denbigh and Flint increased from 10,176 in 1881 to 13,377 in 1901 and to 16,257 in 1914. In 1914, they produced about 3.3 million tons of coal; almost all of it was sold locally, particularly to the iron and steel industry, which was re-established in the north-east in the last decades of the nineteenth century. A modern steelworks was built at Brymbo in 1885, and the John Summers Company began to make steel in Shotton in 1896; by 1911, there were 3,384 metal-workers in the counties of Denbigh and Flint. There was a close connection between the industrial communities of the north-east and the bustling activity of Lancashire; nevertheless, as the miners of colliery villages such as Rhosllannerchrugog and Ffynnongroyw were thoroughly Welsh-speaking, they gave an enthusiastic welcome to visitors from the south, Mabon above all.

Although the distress experienced by the people of Bethesda and the marked growth of the industrial districts of the north-east were significant happenings in Welsh industrial history, both communities were marginal to the main course of working-class history in Wales. There were twenty times as many miners in south-east Wales in 1914 as there were quarrymen in the north-west, and fifteen times as many as there were miners in the north-east. The years immediately preceding the First World War were a stirring period in the history of the south Wales coalfield. Of all the industrial districts of Britain, south-east Wales offers the fullest testimony of the anguish of the 'Great Unrest'.

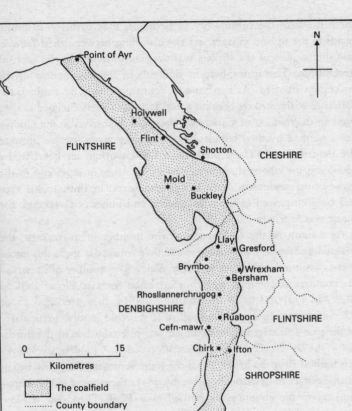

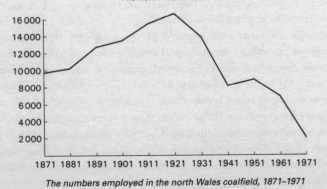

The north Wales coalfield

The numbers employed in the north Wales coalfield, 1871–1971

The unrest was largely the result of the astonishingly rapid growth of the coal-mining communities. Between 1901 and 1914, the population of the counties of Glamorgan and Monmouth rose from 1,158,007 to 1,821,310, and in some areas – Mynyddislwyn, for example, and Bedwellte – there was an increase of 100 per cent and more. Between 1901 and 1911, the coalfield gained 129,000 people through immigration; more people moved into Wales than moved out, thus causing the country to be unique among the nations of Europe. In that decade, only the United States excelled Wales in the ability to attract immigrants. With such a flood of incomers, some districts became grossly overcrowded; in 1911, there were nine thousand people to the square kilometre in Tonypandy in the Rhondda. It is significant that the districts which grew most rapidly were the ones which experienced the greatest unrest.

In the discussion of the growth of the coalfield in the period 1880–1900 (pp. 468–80), consideration was given to those factors which aroused confidence, created tension and promoted social and political change. These factors were greatly intensified by the developments of 1900–1914. The prosperity of the coalfield reached its peak in 1913, when over forty-six million tons of coal were produced and thirty-seven million were exported. H. S. Jevons, the author of *The British Coal Trade* (1915), was confident that production would rise to a hundred million tons by 1940; by then, Jevons believed, there would be half a million additional inhabitants in the south Wales coalfield. The tragic aspect of the coal industry reached its climax in 1913 with the explosion in Senghennydd which killed 439 men. The trend towards capital amalgamation intensified; by 1913, the Powell Duffryn Company was employing 13,600 men, while D. A. Thomas, the creator of the Cambrian Combine, was presiding over an industrial empire with a value of over two million pounds. The coal companies were generous to their shareholders: in 1911, the Ocean (the company owned by David Davies of Llandinam) granted a bonus of 50 per cent, and between 1910 and 1914 Powell Duffryn paid an annual dividend of 20 per cent.

At the same time, the income of the working class was being eroded as inflation struck the economy; the real value of miners' wages declined by 25 per cent between 1901 and 1912. The employers were slow to invest in mechanization; in 1913, 98.8 per cent of the coal produced in south Wales was cut by hand. Productivity continued to decline, particularly after the eight-hour day was introduced in 1908; by 1912 annual production per head had fallen to 222 tons. Between 1900 and 1914, there was a growth of 37 per cent in the total tonnage produced, but to achieve that growth the labour force had to be increased by 58 per cent (from 148,000 to 234,000). Most of the extra labour came from outside Wales. Of the immigrants to Glamorgan between 1901 and 1911, 63 per cent came from England, and the percentage was even higher in Monmouthshire. It is likely, therefore, that there was an ethnic dimension to the miners' readiness to embrace a more militant standpoint. More important, however, was the ideological generation gap. Members of the younger generation of Welsh miners – many of whom had lost touch with their rural origins – were becoming instinctively hostile to capitalism. Indeed, it was a Welshman with deep roots in the society of the coalfield, W. J. Edwards of Aberdare, who provided the liveliest picture of the ideological change experienced by the miners of south Wales.

By the first decade of the twentieth century, the ILP, with its moral appeal and its biblical rhetoric, seemed inadequate to the more radical elements in the coalfield. They were not satisfied with the South Wales Miners' Federation either, unless it were prepared to adopt a role beyond that of defending its members within the existing order of things. To Noah Ablett, the passionate socialist from Porth, the first step was to imbue the working class with an understanding of the nature of the forces which were oppressing them. He did not consider that this was the kind of education provided by Ruskin, the Labour college in Oxford where the 'Fed' sent some of its most promising young men – Ablett among them. In 1909, Ablett was in the forefront of the strike at Ruskin, a dispute which led to the establishment of the Central Labour College in London under the patronage of the South Wales Miners' Federation and the National Union of Railwaymen. The Central Labour College was to have extensive influence in the coalfield. Some of the principal miners' leaders – men such as Aneurin Bevan, James Griffiths and Ness Edwards – attended it; the college was also the centre of a network of classes in which large numbers of miners were steeped in Marxist theory. The classes were run by the Plebs League, a body which came, from 1910 onwards, under the influence of the syndicalist ideas which had already taken root in France and the United States. The syndicalists argued that the working class could win power through industrial action. Production was the basis of the capitalist system; with effective unionism, the workers could gain control of the system of production and become the co-owners of the industries in which they worked. The parliamentary path was a snare and a delusion. 'Why,' asked Noah Ablett, 'cross the river to fill the pail?' The priorities, therefore, were to reorganize the 'Fed' and to activate the ordinary workers. This was the aim of the various 'rank-and-file' movements, and also of the Unofficial Reform Committee which came into prominence in Tonypandy in 1911. In the following year, again in Tonypandy, the syndicalists' manifesto, *The Miners' Next Step*, was published, an explosive work by Ablett and his colleagues which describes the steps which had to be taken in order to ensure the downfall of the coal-owners.

The leading coal-owner in the Tonypandy area was D. A. Thomas, the owner of the Cambrian Combine and the employer of twelve thousand miners. It was a dispute between Thomas and the miners which led to the strike of 1910–11, a conflict which proved that the coalfield had become the most turbulent industrial battlefield in Britain. The trouble began with a disagreement over the pay for working in 'abnormal places' – a constant problem in the south Wales coalfield, with its disturbed seams, and one which had been complicated by the Eight Hour Act of 1908. When seventy miners refused the wage offered to them for working the Bute seam in the Ely pit at Pen-y-graig, the management responded at the beginning of September 1910 by locking out the 950 men who worked in the pit. By November 1910, the entire labour force of the Cambrian Combine was on strike and there were similar protests in other areas of the coalfield, particularly in the Cynon valley. The strike lasted until October 1911, when the strikers were forced by stark necessity to return to work.

Although they failed to achieve their ends, they succeeded in elevating their demands to the top of the agenda of coal politics in Britain. Legislation to ensure a minimum wage was seen as the answer to the problem of the 'abnormal places'. The Rhondda miners made up a third of the membership of the South Wales Miners' Federation, and the 'Fed' was the largest section within the Miners' Federation of Great Britain. Under pressure from the miners of the Rhondda, the British Federation held a strike in all the coalfields of Britain in 1912, the first time for the miners of the kingdom jointly to withhold their labour. The response was immediate and the Minimum Wage Bill became law in March 1912. The dispute of 1910–12 had far-reaching consequences. It strengthened those who favoured the reorganization of the 'Fed' and it was a deathblow to the influence of Mabon. He resigned the presidency of the 'Fed' in 1912, acknowledging that his policy of conciliation had been completely rejected. The miners of the south Wales coalfield – those of the Rhondda, in particular – came to realize how great was their influence, and henceforth they were to be in the forefront of every campaign involving the miners of Britain.

At the time, it was the violence which occurred in the wake of the strike which left the deepest impression. There was an inflammatory atmosphere in Tonypandy in November 1910. The pits were guarded by hundreds of policemen under the leadership of Colonel Lindsay, the chief constable of Glamorgan. There was a riot on 8 November 1910; more than sixty shops were attacked and one miner (Samuel Rays) was killed following clashes with the police. The Tonypandy riot was portrayed as an orgy of violence and destruction carried out by the hooligans of the Rhondda but, as Dai Smith has demonstrated, there was a pattern and a meaning to the protest. Before the riot, Lindsay had appealed to the Home Secretary, Winston Churchill, for soldiers. Churchill hesitated, sending in the first place hundreds of London policemen, mounted officers among them. After the riot, soldiers were sent to the coalfield, and the Rhondda and some of the neighbouring valleys were under a degree of military occupation for months. The soldiers were prudently deployed, but there were occasions when they were in confrontation with protesters and their presence was held to have deprived the miners of victory. Thus it is not a myth (as some insist) that Churchill used soldiers against strikers. The amity between the army officers and the owners of the pits was noted, and it was therefore difficult to deny the claims of men such as Ablett that the army, the owners and the Liberal government were leagued together in a conspiracy against the working class. According to the *Times* correspondent, there was in the Rhondda 'the same oppressive atmosphere that one experienced in the streets of Odessa and Sebastopol during the unrest in Russia in the winter of 1904. It is extraordinary to find it here in the British Isles.'

Tonypandy was not the only Welsh community to experience rioting at the time of the 'Great Unrest'. There was extensive trouble in the Cynon valley, where the miners were roused by the rhetoric of

C. B. Stanton, the most extreme – at the time – of the leaders of the South Wales Miners' Federation. The excitement reached its peak during the exceptionally hot summer of 1911. A temperature of 124° was recorded in Cardiff; during the seamen's strike at Cardiff Docks in July, ships were ransacked and the city's Chinese community attacked. In August the seamen's strike was followed by a strike of railway workers. It was in this context that the Llanelli riot, the most violent episode in this series of conflicts, occurred. The railwaymen and their supporters proved that they could prevent the trains from running, and six hundred soldiers were sent to Llanelli. On 19 August 1911, while a crowd was harassing the soldiers, two young men were shot dead. In the ensuing uproar, ninety-six trucks were destroyed, shops and stores were damaged and four people were killed in an explosion. On the same day, at the other end of the coalfield, Jewish shops were attacked at Tredegar; in the days that followed, the attacks spread from Bargoed in the west to Brynmawr in the east. Jews formed a mere 1 per cent of the population of Tredegar, and it is unlikely that there were more than four thousand of them in the whole of Wales. As the Jews in Russia were at that time suffering from the persecution inspired by Stolypin, this manifestation of Welsh anti-Semitism had terrifying connotations. The word 'pogrom' was used to describe the Tredegar attacks, and the young scholar Lewis Namier was sent to investigate them. There was an occasional undertone of anti-Semitism in socialist propaganda, and Welsh Nonconformity was not free of prejudice against Jews. The Jewish population in the towns of the coalfield declined after the attacks, and within a generation it was only at Cardiff that there was a substantial community of Welsh Jews.

Wales was not unique in experiencing riot and upheaval in the years immediately before the First World War; there were bloody confrontations in Liverpool and Hull; Glasgow and east London seethed with discontent, and the protests of the suffragettes caused a great deal of commotion. In Ireland, Nationalists and Unionists were arming themselves, and in Britain the Unionists' detestation of Irish Home Rule was so intense that they gave the impression that they were prepared to sanction rebellion against the government. According to the historian George Dangerfield, these occurrences were proof that the British state was verging upon being ungovernable; but for the First World War, Britain would have experienced revolutionary conflict. However, although the range and intensity of the unrest is striking, it is easy to exaggerate its significance. The union leaders who embraced a revolutionary standpoint were a small minority, and the resources of the state were almost limitless. Even in Wales, the stronghold of syndicalism, those who accepted the teaching of Ablett and his like were not numerous, consisting as they did of small groups, mainly in the Rhondda and Cynon valleys. The majority of the miners followed the leadership of men such as Hartshorn, Brace and James Winstone, and there was an ideological chasm between them and the syndicalists. Indeed, in considering the day-to-day life of the communities of industrial Wales, too much attention can be given to riot, to ideology and even to unionism. There were more people present in a boxing match in Tonypandy on 8 November 1910 than took part in the riot there that night. Despite the prominence given to clashes on the streets, clashes in boxing booths or on playing fields were more characteristic of the coalfield. The period 1900–1914 was the golden age of Welsh boxing, with champions like 'Freddie Welsh', Jim Driscoll and Jimmy Wilde. It was also the golden age of Welsh rugby, with Wales winning the Triple Crown six times in twelve years and defeating New Zealand in an unforgettable match in 1905.

Successes in sport were only one aspect of the vitality of Welsh life in the period 1900–1914. During those years there was a marked growth in the social conscience and a number of humanitarian bodies were founded to challenge the evils of the age. The appalling standard of housing in rural Wales and the drab townscape of industrial Wales were among the most obvious of those evils. The Welsh Housing Association was founded in 1908 with H. S. Jevons and E. L. Chappell as its tireless propagandists. The local authorities were urged to build council houses, and attempts were made through the garden village movement to prove that the masses could be housed in a pleasant environment. The cooperative societies sought to alleviate poverty among farmers, branches of the Workers' Educational Association were established and the Welsh School of Social Service was founded under the leadership of the energetic minister Gwilym Davies.

The periodical *The Welsh Outlook*, launched in January 1914, declared itself to be 'a monthly journal of social progress', and its chief purpose was to give publicity to these activities. It was founded by that remarkable man, Thomas Jones of Rhymni, and was financed by David Davies, the grandson of the industrial pioneer from

Llandinam. Cooperation between Thomas Jones and David Davies also ensured the success of the most ambitious venture of those years – the campaign against tuberculosis. In large areas of Wales, tuberculosis was responsible for 10 per cent of deaths. Young people in their prime were the principal sufferers, and the white plague killed slowly. It was a common experience for a family to have a son or daughter lying ill for years – a significant factor, argues Tecwyn Lloyd, when considering the morbidity of much nineteenth-century Welsh literature. The strongholds of tuberculosis were the regions where nourishment was inadequate, the houses dark and damp and the health services rudimentary. The disease was rampant in the western counties, proof of the deprivation among the rural Welsh. Fatalism was also rampant among them, and this added greatly to the problems of those battling against the disease. David Davies was the most prominent among them. In 1910 he used the desire to create a memorial to Edward VII as an opportunity to establish an anti-tuberculosis movement in Wales; he donated £125,000 to the Memorial Association and secured the services of Thomas Jones as its secretary. By 1914 the association had ten hospitals and its 'missionary caravans' were a familiar sight throughout Wales.

While the humanitarians were becoming increasingly active, there was growing vitality in the cultural scene. In the arts, Welsh horizons were expanding. Although cantatas and oratorios and other varieties of choral singing were never more popular than they were at the beginning of the twentieth century, the taste for symphonic music was growing, especially in the bigger towns. There was also a growth of interest in the fine arts, a development which Owen M. Edwards was particularly anxious to promote. Wales was producing professional painters such as Augustus and Gwen John and J. D. Innes, and in 1908 the Davies sisters began their superb collection of the work of the French Impressionists. In the field of architecture, there were splendid advances in Wales, including the powerful, uncluttered buildings of University College, Bangor (1905–11), and the Neo-Baroque magnificence of the City Hall, Cardiff, the most outstanding example of that style in Britain. The Welsh-speaking Nonconformists were prepared to venture away from the simple classical façade when planning their chapels (that strange hybrid, Capel Heol y Crwys, Cardiff, was built in 1899), while the English-speaking Nonconformists adopted Anglican styles, as the Neo-Gothic places of worship built by them bear witness. The art form which experienced the most remark-able flowering was probably drama. Between 1900 and 1914, hundreds of drama companies were founded in Wales and there was talk of the theatremania of the Welsh. John Williams of Brynsiencyn, one of the giants of Calvinistic Methodism, was seen attending a theatre in 1914, thus demonstrating that 'mummery' was acceptable even to the most conservative of the denominations. Historical pageants, most of them serving up dubious history, were very popular, but there were also thought-provoking plays on contemporary themes, especially those of J. O. Francis and D. T. Davies.

In the years 1900 to 1914, the achievements of Welsh scholarship were particularly remarkable. The National Museum and the National Library, institutions which came into being chiefly as the result of the efforts of Herbert Lewis, received their charters in 1907. There were important developments in the field of Welsh history: *The Welsh People*, by John Rhys and Brynmor Jones, was published in 1900 and it was followed in 1901 by *Wales*, by Owen Edwards. Then, in 1911, J. E. Lloyd's two volumes, *A History of Wales from the Earliest Times to the Edwardian Conquest*, appeared, a work which is an inspiration to all who are involved with Welsh history. As R. T. Jenkins put it: 'There are only two kinds of Welsh historian on the period prior to 1282. These are the two: (a) everyone *before* Lloyd: (b) Lloyd.' The work of John Morris-Jones on the Welsh language was equally important. His *A Welsh Grammar, Historical and Comparative* was published in 1913, sweeping away a host of mistaken ideas about the language. There were even more exciting developments in the field of poetry. The work of John Morris-Jones, T. Gwynn Jones, Silyn Roberts, W. J. Gruffydd, R. Williams Parry and T. H. Parry-Williams appeared between 1900 and 1914, providing evidence that a new age had dawned in the history of Welsh literature. The new 'school' was inclined to romanticism, a fashion which came late to Wales, as Alun Llywelyn-Williams has explained. The poets leaned heavily on the work of the historians, finding their inspiration in the legends and early history of the nation.

Yet, at precisely the moment when it was confirmed – or, rather, reconfirmed – that the Welsh language was capable of being the medium of exalted literature, it was revealed that that literature was beyond the reach of half the inhabitants of Wales. According to the census of 1901, 50 per cent of the population could speak Welsh and

85 per cent could speak English; by 1911, the one percentage had fallen to 43 and the other had risen to 92. There were still districts into which English had not penetrated: as late as 1921, 56 per cent of the population of the industrial parish of Llanddeiniolen had no knowledge of English and there was one parish in Llŷn (Bodferin) where everyone was monoglot Welsh. But by 1911 84 per cent of the Welsh-speaking Welsh aged between fifteen and sixty-five were bilingual, a development of great significance in the history of the language. Henceforth, over extensive areas of Welsh-speaking Wales, those with no knowledge of Welsh were more numerous than those with no knowledge of English, a justification for giving priority to English in local activities. Formerly, when the greater part of the population could be reached only through Welsh, there was a need for material in Welsh on every subject. Henceforth, it would be possible to draw upon the inexhaustible riches of the material published in English for information on every subject except those that were specifically Welsh; in consequence, there was a contraction in the number of subjects dealt with in Welsh, as can be seen from the list of the publications of the Gee Company of Denbigh.

With the growth of bilingualism, English came to influence the language spoken by Welsh-speakers, many of whom adopted a vernacular which denied the true characteristics of Welsh. There were striking developments in the English popular press in the first decade of the twentieth century, and Wales was flooded with a mass of shallow, lively publications with which the Welsh press could not compete. At the same time, many young Welsh people were enchanted by the splendours of English literature, a central experience for the Welsh-language poets of the early twentieth century. Bilingualism advanced most rapidly in the southern coastal counties and in the north-east. In 1911, 36 per cent of the population of Gwynedd were monoglot Welsh speakers, and in Gwynedd purity of speech was maintained, as O. H. Fynes-Clinton's pioneering study, *The Welsh Vocabulary of the Bangor District* (1913), demonstrates. Although only 20 per cent of the Welsh-speaking Welsh lived in Gwynedd, 80 per cent of Welsh-language periodicals were published there. Gwynedd was also the cradle of the Welsh literary revival; of the writers of the early decades of the twentieth century who receive special mention in *Llyfryddiaeth Llenyddiaeth Gymraeg* (The Bibliography of Welsh Literature) over three quarters were natives of Gwynedd.

Despite the rapid decline in the percentage of monoglot Welsh speakers and the more gradual decline in the percentage of those able to speak the language, the actual number of Welsh speakers continued to increase. There were 930,000 of them in 1901 and more than a million in 1911; if the Cambrophones living outside Wales are taken into account, it is likely that as many as 1,100,000 people spoke Welsh in 1911 – the language's highest point, so far, in terms of numbers. The linguistic fortunes of Wales between 1801 and 1911 can be broadly described as follows: there was a four-fold increase in the population of Wales, a two-fold increase in the number of Welsh speakers and a twelve-fold increase in the number of monoglot English speakers. Despite the disparity between the growth of the one language and the other, the flourishing state of Welsh-language culture in the nineteenth century was much indebted to the fact that the number speaking the language was increasing decade by decade. As Brinley Thomas argues, this increase is chiefly attributable to the ability of the industrial areas to retain in Wales people who would otherwise have been forced to emigrate. The situation was very different in Ireland, where the population haemorrhage caused grave damage to the Irish language. According to Brinley Thomas, 'the Welsh patriot should sing the praises of industrial development', for 'the Welsh language was saved by the redistribution of a growing population brought about by industrialism'.

There has recently been criticism of Brinley Thomas's theory. It has been claimed that it is misleading to portray the pattern of Welsh migration as if it had little connection with the English pattern; the theory is said to underestimate the number of Welsh people who migrated overseas; attention is drawn to the fact that, for migrants from rural Wales, England was at least as important a destination as was the south Wales coalfield. Furthermore, talk of 'saving' is very misleading. Demography was not the only factor involved, and the industrialization of the coalfield did not merely redistribute the Welsh. Until the last decade of the nineteenth century, many coal valleys succeeded in assimilating the non-Welsh-speaking elements. Dan Isaac Davies cited a pit in Treherbert where 353 Welsh miners taught their 120 English-speaking co-workers to speak the Welsh language. Nevertheless, as the schools and public and commercial life were firmly on the side of English, it is unlikely that the miners of Treherbert would have succeeded had the language ratio been more favourable to the English element.

In the following two decades, the ratio would become more favourable to English as a result of an enormous influx into the coalfield from England. 'Until some fifteen or twenty years ago,' noted a report in 1917, 'the native inhabitants had in many respects a marked capacity for stamping their own impress on all newcomers ... [but] of more recent years the process of assimilation has been unable to keep pace with the continuing influx of immigrants.' The comment of Gwyn Thomas, the Rhondda writer, was more blunt. Describing the various peoples who settled in the valley, he declared: 'The Welsh language stood in the way of our fuller union and we made ruthless haste to destroy it. We nearly did.' Thus, while acknowledging that Brinley Thomas has rendered a great service by rectifying the anti-industrial prejudice which is implicit in the work of some Welsh historians, his theory cannot be accepted in its entirety. The development of the coalfield was beneficial to the Welsh language, but the frenzied growth of the period 1890–1914 was harmful to it. It is significant that the quarrying districts, with their short-distance migration, have made a totally disproportionate contribution to Welsh-language culture.

As the Welsh-speaking Welsh, by 1911, were a minority in Wales, a problem of definition arose which was to cause increasing anguish over the succeeding generations. There was hardly a legal or a constitutional dimension to the condition of being Welsh. Scots can define themselves as persons subject to the Law of Scotland who dwell within the historic boundaries of the kingdom of Scotland; a Welsh version of such an argument has little credibility. In the nineteenth century, there were social, religious and communal dimensions to Welshness, but the linguistic dimension was central. To most Welsh speakers, the meaning of the word *Cymro* (Welshman) is Cambrophone, and the meaning of the word *Sais* (Englishman) is Anglophone. Nevertheless, the majority of the non-Welsh speakers of Wales consider themselves Welsh, and they have reacted angrily to insinuations that they are not a part of the nation. Over the years, attempts have been made to create a definition of Welsh nationality which would be relevant to the majority of the population; naturally, it has been based on the characteristics of Wales's most populous region – the south Wales coalfield. Emphasis is placed upon the political radicalism of the Welsh, their communal solidarity, their love of singing, their enthusiasm for rugby, their voluble and welcoming temperament and their lack of obsession with class divisions. Thus, two models of Welshness have emerged, and neither is particularly relevant to large areas of Wales, especially the rural border areas and the northern seaside towns. Consequently, it has been claimed that, in the twentieth century, there is no such thing as a common Welsh experience and that attempts to write the recent history of Wales are no more than exercises in metaphysics. Yet, to this day, a consciousness of Welshness, whether it is given expression through the Welsh language or the English, is a living reality to a host of people throughout Wales. During the twentieth century, national characteristics have found expression through an increasing variety of movements and institutions, and the concept of the territorial integrity of Wales is stronger today than it has ever been before. The writing of the history of any country is to some extent a metaphysical act, but the fact that there exists the will to undertake the task indicates that it is a substantive act also.

It was not only the Welsh language which reached its peak in terms of numbers in the early years of the twentieth century. That was also the case with church membership. In 1907, the churches of Wales had 750,000 communicants – the highest number ever – and they could also claim thousands of occasional 'hearers'. After the first decade of the twentieth century, the numbers regularly frequenting places of worship and the numbers of Welsh speakers were to contract continually, suggesting a marked congruence between the fate of the language and the fate of religion. This congruence nurtured the notion that the crisis of faith was synonymous with the crisis of the nation, the theme of R. Tudur Jones's admirable study, *Fydd ac Argyfwng Cenedl* (Faith and the Crisis of a Nation, 1981, 1982). He points out that at the beginning of the twentieth century the 'life of the churches' was 'a huge continent of Welshness', and that places of worship benefited from 'close marriage between Christianity and Welsh culture'. At least two thirds of the Welsh-speaking Welsh were church members; the equivalent figure among the English-speaking Welsh was a third at most. Gwenallt in his poetry gave eloquent expression to the image of Wales as a nation Christian from its beginnings, and there are today advocates of the view that a religious revival is a necessary precondition of a Welsh national revival.

The matter can, however, be viewed in a different light. In the second half of the nineteenth century, Nonconformity succeeded in 'highjacking' Welshness and a secular Welsh-language culture did not therefore emerge. As a result, the interconnection between chapel-going and Welshness was confirmed, for those who did not sympathize with the values of Nonconformity could turn their backs upon both. The English world was open to them; they could embrace the opportunity to 'escape into the universal' – to quote Sartre's comment on the reaction of the Jews in not totally dissimilar circumstances. Furthermore, it is an exaggeration to claim that the history of the Welsh people is uniquely Christian. The ancestors of the Welsh had a rich civilization, non-Christian and pre-Christian. Throughout western and central Europe, the origin of nations as literate societies is dated to the coming of Christianity among them. Although the majority of the 'heroes of the nation throughout the centuries are Christian heroes too', it must be remembered that it was the very people who sought that conjunction who selected the heroes of the Welsh people. In the twentieth century, secularization was to be part of the experience of all the countries which had formerly been part of Christendom, but there is hardly a general presumption that the decline of religion puts an end to all hope of a national future.

In the late twentieth century, with that decline apparent in every neighbourhood in Wales, it is difficult to realize how central religion was to vast numbers of the Welsh people at the beginning of the century. At that time, the extent of the activities of Welsh places of worship was amazing. They were served by 4,000 ministers and priests; they could draw upon the assistance of 25,000 deacons, elders and wardens; 11,000 sermons were preached in them every Sunday; their Sunday schools were attended by almost half the population; at least two million meetings were held annually in their vestries and halls; their members bought countless commentaries, hymn books and religious periodicals. The decline in this activity, together with the decay of belief in the Faith which was its foundation, is one of the most important changes in twentieth-century Wales. The activities took place within a denominational framework; there was much sectarian pride, the source of a great deal of bickering. Nevertheless, as commitment to Calvinism was on the wane, the differences between the denominations were slight. In their credo and in the values they upheld, almost all the Nonconformists could be considered to be part of an 'Evangelical Concord'. This also included most of the members of the Established Church, for despite the disestablishment dispute there were few theological differences between Low Churchmen and Nonconformists.

The High Churchmen were outside the 'Concord'. They had made substantial progress since the early days of the Oxford Movement. Their doctrinal ideas and the dignity of their worship had profoundly affected Anglicanism, although at the beginning of the twentieth century only about two hundred of the fifteen hundred Anglican churches of Wales were obviously ritualistic. The diocese of Llandaf was the stronghold of ritualism in Wales; there, particularly in Cardiff, incense and Eucharistic vestments were much prized, and there were young priests who were willing 'to become martyrs for their beliefs at any time'. The Roman Catholics were also outside the 'Concord'. In 1907, 65,000 Roman Catholic worshippers were recorded in Wales, ten times as many as in 1851. They were concentrated in the main towns – Cardiff, Swansea, Newport, Merthyr and Wrexham – and the overwhelming majority of them were the descendants of immigrants from Ireland. The Catholic Church, however, was eager to attract the native Welsh back to the Old Faith; in 1889, the Society of Saint Teilo was founded and a translation of the Prayer Book was published; a mission from Brittany was launched in 1900 and *Cennad Catholig Cymru* (the Welsh Catholic Messenger) was published from 1900 to 1914. In 1895, the Pope recognized the unity of Wales by creating the diocese of Menevia (that is, St David's) side by side with the diocese of Newport. The diocesan structure was reorganized in 1916 when Cardiff became an archbishopric, four years before the Anglicans consecrated an archbishop in Wales.

Despite the vitality of the Catholic wing of Welsh Christianity, it was the 'Evangelical Concord' which gave religion in Wales its special characteristics. As has been seen, the success of the denominations of Wales in retaining the loyalty of the mass of the people was one of the most prominent of those characteristics. Nevertheless, there was growing evidence that sizeable sections of the working class were outside the grasp of organized religion. The founders of the Calvinistic Methodist Forward Movement (1891) and the Home Missions of the Independents and the Baptists (1895) were motivated by an awareness of the need to reach the irreligious. The same motive gave rise to efforts of the Church Army, the activities of many Catholic orders and the campaigns of the Salvation Army.

Despite strenuous missionary activity, the anxieties of the devout were multiplying. Above all, they were distressed by the realization that the Faith itself was under attack. Between 1850 and 1914, almost every scholarly development appeared to be a challenge to orthodoxy, and the poems of Arnold, Tennyson and others illustrate the perplexity which tormented English intellectuals. The chronology of the growth of doubt in Wales was different, partly because the Welsh language, as Thomas Lewis of Bala-Bangor College noted in 1891, was a 'solid barrier to keep back the flood'. Nevertheless, as Harri Williams has demonstrated, the theories of the scholars received considerable attention in Welsh periodicals, particularly in *Y Traethodydd*. It was not the scientists but rather the historians and the textual critics who created the greatest perplexity. As the literal truth of the Bible was an article of faith to the members of the 'Evangelical Concord', they reacted angrily, initially at least, to Higher Criticism – research which emanated mainly from Germany. Higher Criticism was an attempt to use the same critical methods in analysing the Bible as were used for analysing any other body of literature; the practitioners of Higher Criticism came to the conclusion that there are mythological elements in the scriptures and that the authors of the books of the Bible, like any other authors, were capable of error. To Owen Thomas in 1849, this was 'German Atheism', a conspiracy to 'strip the gospels of their historical truth, to destroy the foundations of our faith and to rob us of our hope of everlasting life'. By the beginning of the twentieth century, however, Higher Criticism had become acceptable in educated circles in Wales. It was emphasized that it was the Word rather than the words which was divinely inspired, and it was claimed that Christians could, through their own experience, bear witness to the infallibility of the Bible in those matters which the scriptures were intended to reveal. It was a standpoint which acknowledged that the objective authority of the Bible was waning.

Parallel with the researches of the biblical critics were the discoveries of the geologists, which proved that the earth was vastly more ancient than the Old Testament suggests. Geology was successfully reconciled with Genesis by means of the hypothesis that the six days of Creation implied six long periods, but the evidence of the rocks was a further blow to the belief in the divine inspiration of the Bible. Darwin's theory was a much more grievous blow. This involved one of the corner-stones of the Faith – Adam's fall – and it strengthened the argument of those who denied that there was 'any purpose to the whole prodigious and glorious machine of Creation'. Yet, half a century after the publication of *On the Origin of Species* in 1859, many Welsh religious leaders had come to accept the essentials of Darwinism, and skilful attempts had been made by theologians to reconcile it with the biblical doctrine of God the Creator. Believers were also worried by the growth of relativism – a doctrine which led to a lack of faith in the abiding validity of any creed, and to reluctance to believe in the existence of absolute values. This intellectual turmoil gave birth to Modernism, or Liberal Theology, a body of ideas held by most of the religious leaders of Wales in the generation following the First World War. To some Christians today it was a mangy compromise, and it is claimed that it was the willingness of the devout to dilute the Faith that was principally responsible for the decline of religion. Yet, if the churches had refused to yield one jot of their beliefs, it is probable that they would have lost their congregations more quickly and more completely. It was Modernism, wrote R. T. Jenkins, that persuaded him to 'give a welcome to religion'.

The challenges to orthodoxy which resulted from the work of the historians, the scientists and the philosophers were not the only anxiety confronting the devout. Many problems were concealed behind the apparent success of the churches. Some of them sprang from that very success. In most Welsh communities, it was considered that everyone was a Christian; if that were so, did any particular virtue attach to the condition of being a Christian? Over much of Wales, the churches had succeeded in bringing almost all communal activities under the umbrella of religion. Consequently, many chapel-goers considered that the Faith was, as R. Tudur Jones put it, 'an aspect of Welsh cultural recreation'. Recreations which existed independently of organized religion were viewed with suspicion; this was one of the reasons why many ministers were so ready to condemn football, hiking and cycling, an attitude which led young people to regard the occupants of the pulpit as sour killjoys. While succeeding in putting disestablishment on the political agenda, the Nonconformists had learned that denominational size was an important factor; as the Royal Commission of 1906–10 demonstrated, sectarian arithmetic was an essential weapon in the battle against the Established Church. The idea that the people of the chapel were a society set apart from the world faded away; the rules for the acceptance and expulsion of communicants were relaxed, and full membership of a denomination became one of the unavoidable experiences of adolescence. Ministers who could entertain their congregations were highly praised, and sermons which dwelt on damnation became increasingly rare. (This was a development of great significance; once hell is abandoned, most people are unlikely to interest themselves in religion.) Nonconformist success on the matter of religious education in schools was a dubious victory. To Ieuan Gwynedd and his like, education had value only when it was grounded in religion, but their successors among the Welsh radicals were eager to promote a system which made secular education central and religious education marginal.

Thus, despite the range of Nonconformist activity in Wales in the early twentieth century, there was much uncertainty about the depth of the religious conviction of those involved in that activity. The uncertainty fanned the desire for a revival. There had been several local revivals in Wales in the last decades of the nineteenth century, but the whole country had not been stirred by a revival since 1859. It was stirred again by the revival of 1904–5, one of the most extraordinary happenings in twentieth-century Wales. It began in February 1904 in southern Cardiganshire; the 'foster father' of the revival, according to R. Tudur Jones, was the South Cardigan Calvinistic Methodist Monthly Meeting. By November 1904, it had spread to Treorci, Aberdare, Llangefni and Rhosllannerchrugog, and before the end of the winter there were congregations throughout Welsh-speaking Wales (and some in English-speaking Wales) which had experienced joy and anguish. No former religious ferment in Wales had been chronicled in detail by daily newspapers, and the attention the revival received from Cardiff journalists was a major factor in its spread. 'Blessed be the *Western Mail*,' wrote the editor of *Y Goleuad* in November 1904. Partly as a result of the reports in the *Western Mail* and the *South Wales Daily News*, with their emphasis upon the exciting and abnormal, the leadership of the revival fell increasingly into the hands of Evan Roberts, a twenty-six-year-old ex-collier from Loughor. His meetings were wholly extraordinary occasions: there were frequent references to 'the dam breaking', and there are descriptions of members of congregations in transports of anguish.

As a result of the revival, there was a decline in the popularity of *eisteddfodau* and theatre companies, and a number of rugby clubs were disbanded – Ynys-y-bwl, Ammanford and Creunant among them. In many a quarry, tinplate works and colliery the working day began with prayer, and over much of Wales children arranged their own religious meetings. Observers were drawn to Wales from England, France, America and Germany. As R. Tudur Jones has shown, the revival was the starting-point of a powerful reawakening which affected the Protestant churches of five continents. From it sprang the Apostolic Church, with its headquarters at Pen-y-groes near Llanelli, and also the Elim Movement – the Four Square Gospellers.

Many attempts have been made to account for the revival. To some extent, it was a movement of young lay persons of both sexes, and it was condemned by educated ministers like Peter Price of Dowlais. It can be seen as a revolt against theocracy, as an attempt to recapture the spirit of the popular, uneducated, unclerical enthusiasm which had formerly been characteristic of religion in Wales. It contained an undisciplined element which can be seen at the same time in other aspects of Welsh life – in the labour movement in particular. At the beginning of the twentieth century, the Welsh were experiencing prodigiously rapid social change. 'Revivalism,' says Dai Smith, 'is a frontier sport.' He claims that the mining valleys, with their vast numbers of immigrants, were frontier lands and that many of their inhabitants felt guilty because they had turned their backs upon the values they had inherited through their rural origins. Yet this interpretation is insufficient, especially when it is borne in mind that the revival affected people whose experience differed greatly from that of the Welsh. In any discussion of the causes of the revival, it is probably appropriate to repeat the words of the Frenchman de Fursac: *'Je suis très embarrassé pour y répondre.'*

Estimating the effects of the revival is an equally complex task. In 1904–5, the main denominations gained about eighty thousand new members, but three quarters of them had fallen away by 1912. Church membership was decreasing rapidly in the years immediately before the First World War, a fact which led to a great deal of cynicism about the value of the revival. Many chapels proved unable to handle the flood of converts, some of whom were eager to find other fields in which they could give expression to their new-found moral and spiritual earnestness. Indeed, it is sometimes claimed that the ILP and the socialist movement were the main beneficiaries of the revival. Nevertheless, the experiences of 1904–5 were a source of joy to those who remained faithful to religion. For fifty years and more, there would be throughout Wales congregations indebted to men and women who believed that the Holy Spirit had touched them at the time of the revival.

The spiritual excitement of 1904–5 had secular implications also. Revivalist passion was a factor in the struggle against the Education Act of 1902 and in the Liberal victory of 1906. It gave a significant boost to the Temperance Movement, as the campaign of 1908 to close three quarters of the public houses of Wales testifies. The Licensing Bill was thrown out by the House of Lords in 1908, but between 1908 and 1914 thousands of public houses closed under the weight of higher taxes on the licensed trade. The revival also envigorated the disestablishment campaign. As a result of the upsurge of 1904–5, chapel membership was at its height at precisely the time when the royal commission was collecting statistics on denominational membership. In spite of the progress made by the Anglicans since 1851, the commission recorded that there were in Wales three Nonconformists for every member of the Established Church. By 1911, because of the success of the attack on the House of Lords, disestablishment was politically feasible. In April 1912, a bill was introduced in parliament which would deprive the Anglican Church in Wales of its status as the State Church and take from it two thirds of its endowments. The bill passed the House of Commons in February 1913. As it was rejected by the House of Lords, it could not become law until the House of Commons had passed it again in two different sessions. This took place in July 1913 and in May 1914, and the Disestablishment Bill received the Royal Assent on 18 September 1914. As the war was by then forty-five days old, the implementation of the act was postponed and it did not come into force until 1 April 1920.

By 1920, Wales was a very different place. The confidence of the Nonconformists – the basis of the disestablishment campaign – had been undermined, and the Liberal consensus which had brought the campaign to a victorious conclusion had been shattered. The young were eager to challenge the achievements and the beliefs of their fathers, and the optimism concerning the national future of Wales was ebbing rapidly. Above all, the industrial economy of Wales was tottering and within a few years it was to collapse. In the 1920s, these changes were attributed in their entirety to the First World War. Yet some of the factors which caused them are to be found before 1914. As has been seen, the anxieties of the devout had been increasing for decades, and threats to the alliance between the working class and the middle class – the corner-stone of the Liberal consensus – were already apparent. There were many, before 1914, who lacked sympathy for Victorian values, and there was an awareness that the ability of the Welsh language to be the medium of a mass culture was on the wane. The problems of the coal industry – particularly low productivity and bitterness between employers and employed – had become manifest before the war, and the McKinley episode was a foretaste of the adversity which would hit the Welsh industrial economy as a result of over-specialization and over-dependence on overseas markets. Thus it could be claimed that the First World War merely hastened changes which were already afoot. Nevertheless, other, quite basic, changes occurred as the result of the war. After the war, everyone believed that the experiences of 1914–18 had been unique in their anguish and in their significance. They were correct in their belief.

CHAPTER NINE

1914–39: The Somme, Brynmawr and Penyberth

Franz Ferdinand, the nephew of the emperor of Austria–Hungary, was assassinated at Sarajevo on 28 June 1914. Three weeks later, Lloyd George declared himself confident that common sense and good will would solve the problems which faced Europe. That did not happen. By 3 August 1914 Germany and Austria–Hungary were at war with France and Russia. Britain joined in on the side of France on 4 August. When the fighting came to an end on 11 November 1918, more than ten million men had been killed, forty thousand Welshmen among them. Such was the horror of the war that T. Gwynn Jones longed for hell, since 'every devil was away from home'. The war, said Winston Churchill, had effaced 'the old landmarks and frontiers of our civilization'; the international economic system was undermined, and for many the barbarity of the war extinguished belief in the innate goodness of God and man.

The British government believed that the Royal Navy would be its greatest contribution to victory. Jellicoe, the admiral of the Grand Fleet, was said to be the only man who could lose the war in an afternoon, and it was emphasized that Welsh coal, the main fuel of the fleet, was among the most important of Britain's resources. However, the rapid successes of the Germans proved the need for a large army to resist the might of Germany's war machine. There was no military conscription in Britain, as there was in most of the other states of Europe. In order to encourage volunteers, it was necessary to foster the belief that a man's supreme duty and virtue was to kill Germans and to die for the Empire. This was a credo alien to the beliefs which the majority of the Welsh people claimed to profess. Among Nonconformists, military life was held in deep distrust. The officers of regiments such as the Royal Welch Fusiliers were drawn from the Welsh landowning class, but nine of every ten of the ordinary soldiers came from England. The Nonconformists were proud of the peace-loving tradition of Henry Richard; in 1913 the Union of Welsh Independents declared that 'every war is contrary to the spirit of Christ'. The labour movement considered that the stock-piling of armaments was a corrupt plot to benefit profiteers. The unions and the Labour party were bound by the resolution passed in 1907 by the International Socialist Conference. The resolution declared that it was the duty of the members of the working class to prevent the outbreak of war; if they failed, they should make every effort to transform a war between states into a war between classes. There were many in Wales who held Germany in high regard. Labour supporters admired the German socialist party – the largest in the world; the country was extolled as the birthplace of the Protestant Reformation; its theologians and its linguistic scholars were deeply respected; Heine and other German romantic poets were greatly esteemed; every choir in Wales knew of the works of Handel, Bach and Mendelssohn. There was little enthusiasm for France, the home of immorality and irreligion, or for Russia, the home of oppression and superstition.

It would therefore have been reasonable to assume that many in Wales would oppose the war. As will be seen, there was opposition on religious and on socialist grounds. However, only a small minority clung to their professed beliefs, a fact which throws doubt on the depth of those beliefs. Although the South Wales Miners' Federation adopted a challenging attitude on 1 August 1914, a week later its executive committee agreed to comply with the Admiralty's demand for an extra hour's work from those miners who supplied coal to the navy. Although the Labour party condemned the diplomatic system which had led to war, it announced on 29 August its willingness to take part in the recruitment campaign. A socialist firebrand could rapidly become a jingoistic warmonger, as can be seen from the career of C. B. Stanton, the most eloquent speaker on recruitment platforms in the coalfield. Stanton and others like him were highly successful; by the end of 1914, forty thousand of the miners of the south Wales coalfield had joined the armed forces. Keir Hardie was mocked because he clung to the international socialism of the I L P. In the by-election of November 1915 which followed Hardie's death in September, Stanton, standing as an Independent Labour candidate, polled 10,286 votes, while James Winstone, the Labour party candidate and the president of the South Wales Miners' Federation, polled

6,080. Winstone succeeded in keeping most of the support which had formerly been Hardie's, for Hardie had never been top of the poll in the two-seat constituency of Merthyr. Nevertheless, Stanton's victory received widespread attention; right-wing journalists claimed that it proved that the working class was casting off the pacific and revolutionary ideas of the ILP.

In order to induce young men to join the armed forces, it was necessary to portray the Germans as the destroyers of civilization. In the First World War (unlike the Second) their behaviour was hardly worse than that of their enemies, but such was the success of the British propaganda machine that they came to be regarded as a uniquely barbaric nation. This condemnation of Germany could give rise to the persecution of individual Germans, as can be seen from the sad fate of Hermann Ethé, the most learned of the professors of the University College of Wales. In October 1914, when he was returning to the college, he was tormented by a crowd of two thousand of the inhabitants of Aberystwyth, with the town's most respectable elements in the lead. Ethé was forced to resign his chair and he died, dejected and embittered, in 1917. It is some satisfaction to be able to record that the college has, by now, put up a memorial to him.

Although *The Welsh Outlook*, with its illustrations of Bach, Beethoven, Kant and Goethe, reminded its readers that love of war was not the only German tradition, the majority of Welsh intellectuals were eager to emphasize the evil elements in German culture. Academics like John Morris-Jones and ministers like Miall Edwards argued that the war was the inevitable result of the craving for power which had been fostered by nineteenth-century German philosophers. In their desire to dominate, the Germans had betrayed every principle. Thus, to oppose them was a moral and religious duty. As Eifion Wyn put it: '*Gwell rhyfel nag i elyn/ Herio deddf a sathru dyn*' (Better war than that an enemy/ Should defy law and trample upon mankind). If the tyrannical spirit of Germany were conquered, the world would be secure; as H. G. Wells declared in August 1914, this was the war to end war. As a result, a number of ministers of the gospel were prepared to bless British forces; some – John Williams of Brynsiencyn, the leading Calvinistic Methodist preacher, the most prominent among them – went so far as to conduct services dressed in military uniform.

The moral–religious argument was linked with an appeal to the patriotism of the Welsh. As the independence of Serbia and Belgium had been crushed by Germany and Austria–Hungary, it was possible to portray the war as a crusade in support of small nations – and it was implicitly suggested that Wales was one of them. This was the theme of a speech by Lloyd George to the London Welsh on 19 September 1914. His support for the war was a central factor in the history of Wales and of Britain. He had vacillated during the fateful days at the beginning of August 1914. There was a section of the cabinet which expected him, as the most prominent of the radical Liberals, to take a firm stand in favour of keeping Britain out of the war. He knew that if he were to do so he would harm his own career and threaten the unity of the Liberal party; indeed, it is likely that the German attack on Belgium was a relief to him, for it enabled him to cast aside his doubts. Once he had convinced himself that it was necessary for Britain to take part in the war, Lloyd George saw no other choice than to fling himself into the struggle with unflinching determination. Much to the benefit of his career, he became the chief symbol of Britain's commitment to the struggle. He became Minister of Munitions in May 1915, Minister of War in July 1916 and Prime Minister in December 1916. In the wake of his success, a number of his compatriots received advancement, and by 1917 Joneses, Davieses and Evanses were much in evidence in the corridors of power.

Among the Welsh, particularly the country dwellers, Lloyd George's enthusiasm for the war was one of the most important factors in inducing them to join the army. In 1914, there was widespread apathy among the rural Welsh. Robert Graves noted that only two of the inhabitants of Harlech had hurried to enlist – Graves himself and a caddie who was in trouble for stealing golf clubs. 'The chapels,' wrote Graves, 'held soldiering to be sinful, and in Merioneth, the chapels had the last word . . . However, Lloyd George became Minister of Munitions in 1915, and persuaded the chapels that the war was a Crusade, and we had a sudden tremendous influx of Welshmen.' Recruitment was encouraged by attempts to give recognition to the place of the Welsh within the British army. Lord Kitchener, Lloyd George's predecessor as Minister of War, had intended to scatter the Welsh among the various regiments of the army, and efforts were made to forbid them to speak Welsh on parade and in their billets. Lloyd George, who had promised publicly that a Welsh Division would be established, was infuriated. Following a row in the cabinet, the 38th (Welsh) Division was created; Nonconformist chaplains were appointed and the task of recruiting in north Wales was entrusted to Brigadier Owen Thomas, a Welsh-speaker and a zealous Congregationalist from Anglesey. Propaganda emphasizing the military prowess of the Welsh was produced, and it was suggested that the volunteers were following in the tradition of Llywelyn and Glyn Dŵr. Despite these efforts, most Welsh recruits found themselves in English regiments, and large numbers of them experienced the insults and the contempt of English officers. 'To fight for the freedom of the Belgian,' *The Welsh Outlook* claimed in 1917, 'it is not absolutely necessary to oppress and bully the Welshman.' Silyn Roberts wrote in 1919 of the 'scandalous indignities' resulting from the 'caddish and cowardly' attitude of English officers towards Welsh soldiers. 'The bitterness born of such unfortunate bungling', he wrote, 'will scarcely die with the present generation.'

Despite the bungling, the recruiters could be proud of their success. It was noted in 1919 that 13.82 per cent of the population of Wales had joined the armed forces compared with 13.3 per cent of the population of England. These statistics have little meaning, for in the early decades of the twentieth century there was a proportionately higher number of young men in Wales than in England. The oft-repeated claim that the Welsh were readier than the English to go to war is therefore based on very flimsy grounds. However, it can hardly be claimed that they were less ready either. Welsh soldiers fought on every one of the battlefields in which British forces were engaged. There was a substantial number of them in Salonica, and they were well represented in Allenby's army in Palestine, as the Welsh *englynion* on graves in the Negev bear witness. Others – W. J. Gruffydd, for example – served in the navy and many a Welshman went to '*Barlyrau'r perl, erwau'r pysg*' (the parlours of pearls, the fish's pastures), a thousand black seamen from Cardiff's Butetown among them. But it was in the trenches of France and Belgium that the vast majority of the Welsh experienced warfare. Their torment reached its height at the battle of the Somme, a deadly struggle in which the Welsh Division played a prominent part. In four months (July to November 1916), 420,000 British soldiers were killed, 19,000 of them on the first day. 'Hell! Hell! Hell!' wrote Lewis Valentine in August 1917, when the third battle of Ypres was at its height. 'Torn flesh, shattered bones. Halt, O God, the mad fever, halt the spitting of the demented dogs!'

But perhaps the degree to which the war was loathed by those who participated in it is sometimes exaggerated. '*Gwybu fy nghalon hiraeth dir*' (My heart knows a sincere longing) sang Cynan as he remembered the 'great adventure' of the Salonica campaign, and for half a century after 1918 there were in every community in Wales men who remembered the war as their only exciting experience. It is possible also to over-emphasize the anti-English feeling aroused by the arrogance of English officers. By suffering alongside Geordies and Brummies. Cockneys and Scousers, Micks, Jocks and Aussies, the Taffs became part of a new brotherhood; to become a soldier was to assume a new nationality. Robert Graves records that he considered that all those who had experienced the trenches (including the Germans) were comrades, and that the strangers were those who had not shared that experience, relations and friends at home among them.

In the early years of the war, it was difficult to resist the war fever. Nevertheless, there was among the Welsh intellectuals a handful who were distressed by the general eagerness to embrace the slaughter. T. Gwynn Jones walked out of Capel Tabernacl, Aberystwyth, in September 1914 when the minister made a 'barbarous appeal to the God of the tribe' by praying for a British victory. The war was a source of anguish to T. H. Parry-Williams, a colleague of T. Gwynn Jones in the Department of Welsh at Aberystwyth. Both of them contributed articles to *Y Wawr*, a student magazine which was closed down by the college authorities in 1917 because of its criticism of the war. Thomas Rees, the principal of Bala-Bangor Theological College, insisted on remaining loyal to the standpoint that 'every war is contrary to the spirit of Christ'. In September 1914, he wrote a letter to *Y Tyst* to express his 'shame that the Christianity of Europe had not been a sufficient buttress against the tempest of destruction'; the fighting would not put an end to war, he argued, but would instead sow the seeds of more terrible wars in the future. The Fellowship of Reconciliation was established in December 1914 and immediately gained members in Wales; chief among them was George M. Ll. Davies, the most intense and unyielding of the Welsh pacifists.

While Rees, Davies and others were trying to raise the banner of Christian pacificism, attempts were being made to keep alive the flame of international socialism. In September 1914, a powerful article by W. F. Hay, one of the authors of *The Miners' Next Step*, was published in *The Welsh Outlook*. In it Hay stressed that Welsh coal was an essential element in Britain's ability to wage war, and he expressed the hope that 'the Welsh [colliers] . . . and the colliers of Europe may presently learn to down tools and arms for the cause of human fellowship'. Arthur Horner, the Merthyr socialist, claimed that he had no intention of fighting against the Germans, for he had discovered 'in the mine-owners, and in the government which supports them, an enemy far closer to home than the Kaiser'. Fenner Brockway, the editor of *The Labour Leader*, established the No Conscription Fellowship to campaign against any attempt to introduce military conscription. The Fellowship had considerable support in the coalfield, especially in areas like Merthyr and Briton Ferry, where there were strong ILP branches. Religious and political considerations frequently overlapped: in Briton Ferry, for example, most of the members of the Baptist Chapel belonged to the ILP, and *vice versa*. The No Conscription Fellowship cooperated closely with the Quakers and the Fellowship of Reconciliation, and when military conscription was introduced in January 1916 it was opposed by a united front of Christians and socialists – although it must be acknowledged that there was only a small handful of the one and the other.

Military conscription was a shattering blow to Liberal values. The Prime Minister, Asquith, sought for as long as possible to cling to the principle of voluntarism, but he was forced to yield, chiefly because of pressure from Lloyd George and his Tory allies. Lloyd George's eagerness to abandon the principle of voluntarism shows that he had little loyalty to liberal ideology. Indeed, he associated increasingly with such Tories as Viscount Milner, a man who believed in an authoritarian state. Only three Welsh Liberals voted against the Conscription Bill. One, Llewelyn Williams, member for Carmarthen Boroughs, considered Lloyd George's support for conscription as proof that he was sunk in iniquity; from 1916 until his death in 1922, Williams was to be an implacable enemy of Lloyd George.

The Conscription Act laid down that all those who had a conscientious objection to war had the right to state their case before a tribunal; tribunals could force conscientious objectors to serve, grant them conditional exemption or exempt them unconditionally. The majority of the members of the tribunals were highly jingoistic, and a socialist speech could send them into paroxysms of anger. There is reason to believe that conscientious objectors were proportionately more numerous in Wales than in the kingdom as a whole. Of the 16,500 registered throughout Britain, at least a thousand were Welsh.

Nevertheless, in order to put the matter in perspective, it must be remembered that 280,000 Welshmen served in the armed forces between 1914 and 1918. Most of the conscientious objectors agreed to undertake non-combative war work, but 1,500 of them – the absolutists – refused to have any involvement with the war. Lloyd George promised that they would have a 'very hard path', a declaration which further undermined his credibility as a radical. In his autobiography, Ithel Davies described the harsh methods which were used to break the spirit of the absolutists; forty of them came close to being shot for disobedience, and nine died as a result of the treatment they received. George M. Ll. Davies's fate was to be sent from prison to prison, although the colonel who sentenced him acknowledged that he was passing judgement on a better man than himself. The experience of the conscientious objectors was recorded in *Y Deyrnas*, the monthly magazine of the Welsh pacifists, published from October 1916 to November 1919. It was edited by Thomas Rees, and he wrote at least a third of every issue. *Y Deyrnas*, wrote W. J. Gruffydd, was 'one of the strongest reasons why Wales did not completely lose its soul at the time of the great madness'.

As the war dragged on, the point of view of *Y Deyrnas* became increasingly acceptable in radical and Nonconformist circles in Wales. At the same time, unrest was increasing among the miners of the south Wales coalfield. This sprang not so much from criticism of the war itself as from the belief that the miners' willingness to respond positively to the demands of the government was being exploited by the coal-owners. That belief led to a strike in the south Wales coalfield in July 1915. As the price of coal had risen 50 per cent since the beginning of the war, companies like Powell Duffryn were paying startlingly high dividends. The wage agreement signed in 1910 came to an end in 1915. With the cost of living – particularly the price of food – rising rapidly, the miners were determined to obtain a new wage structure, one which would include a substantial rise and which would remain in force after the war ended. The employers rejected their claim and, when strike action was threatened, the mining valleys were placarded with a royal proclamation; this declared that the coalfield was henceforth subject to the provisions of the Munitions of War Act which made striking a criminal offence. The proclamation was a serious mistake; it infuriated the miners and it was completely unenforceable, for it was impossible to punish a workforce of over two hundred thousand.

The pits were idle from 15 to 21 July. There was a savage reaction from the press. It was claimed that the strike had been encouraged by German secret agents and that £60,000 in gold sovereigns had been used to bribe the miners. There was a suggestion (from the *Manchester Guardian*) that the coalfield should be blockaded so that the men would be forced back to work by lack of food. Bonar Law, the leader of the Conservative party and a member of Asquith's coalition government, considered that 'it would be better to shoot 100 men in suppressing a strike than to lose thousands in the field as a consequence of it'. James Winstone, the president of the South Wales Miners' Federation, urged a conference of the 'Fed' to send a deputation to London for further discussions. 'No,' said one of the delegates, 'you have gone to London, that city of the Philistines, too often . . . if the government wants discussion, let them come to us, here in south Wales.' That is what happened. On 19 July 1915, Lloyd George and two of his fellow-ministers travelled to Cardiff by a special train. There, the substance of the miners' demands was granted, and assurance was given that the coal-owners would be compelled to honour the agreement made between the government and the 'Fed'.

Of all the miners of Britain, it was only the men of south Wales who came into direct conflict with the government in 1915, proof of their militancy and of the unique importance of Welsh coal. The same defiant spirit became apparent in January 1916 when two thirds of the delegates of the 'Fed' voted in favour of a strike if the Conscription Bill became law – a policy which was rejected by the Miners' Federation of Great Britain. There was further unrest in the months which followed over the issue of the 'closed shop'; this was secured, at least until the end of the war, in April 1916, a victory which led to a rapid growth in the membership and the resources of the 'Fed'. The huge profits of the mining companies remained a source of bitterness, particularly in view of the employers' resistance to demands for wage increases. The 'Fed' demanded the right to inspect company accounts, and when that was refused unrest spread through the coalfield. The government responded in November 1916 by taking control of the coal industry of south Wales, a policy which was extended to the rest of the coalfields of Britain in February 1917. This partial nationalization of the pits encouraged renewed discussion of the role of private capital in the industry. The Marxist movement, which had been under a cloud since the beginning of the war, became active again.

During the winter of 1916–17, the Central Labour College held 120 classes in the south Wales coalfield; in those classes, wrote *The Welsh Outlook*, 'at least two thousand young miners will during the next year . . . be made relentless foes of Capitalism'. Ablett became increasingly vocal; so also did his pupils, especially A. J. Cook of Trehafod – 'by far the most dangerous . . . of the advanced syndicalists', according to Lindsay, the chief constable of Glamorgan – and Arthur Horner, the 'incorrigible rebel' from Merthyr and the only Welshman to join James Connolly's Citizen Army.

The unrest in the coalfield was encouraged by the revolution in Russia. The tsar abdicated in March 1917 and a government was formed under the socialist, Kerensky, in May. In Petrograd and other Russian cities, the Bolsheviks established councils of workers and soldiers (the soviets) which called for an immediate end to the war. 'There was no place outside of Russia where the Revolution has caused greater joy than . . . in Merthyr Tydfil,' proclaimed *The Merthyr Pioneer*, and the miners of Ammanford sang: 'Workers of the Vale of Amman/ Echo Russia's mighty thrust.' On 20 July 1917, the South Wales Miners' Federation agreed to contact the labour movement in Germany in order to create a united, working-class peace policy. Plans for establishing councils on the pattern of the soviets were discussed; in furtherance of this, two hundred representatives from the coalfield met in Swansea on 29 July, but their conference was broken up by soldiers and armament workers.

The Russian example, together with the rise in the price of living and the widespread war weariness, was among the factors which led to a series of strikes in May 1917. Lloyd George reacted by establishing a commission to inquire into industrial unrest. The report on Wales, by far the fullest of the commissioners' reports, is a very valuable document. It was largely the work of E. L. Chappell and Lleufer Thomas, and it stressed that the quality of life in industrial Wales was unsatisfactory and that the coalfield economy had given rise to tensions of an explosive nature. It noted that the entire trade-union movement was being rapidly penetrated by 'the propaganda of a small but earnest group of men', and that 'hostility to Capitalism has now become part of the political creed of the majority' of the miners. The commissioners did not consider that 'any serious disturbance would occur during the period of the War' but they took a 'grave view as to the situation that is likely to develop immediately after'.

Their anxiety was not groundless, for 1919 ushered in a period of industrial unrest unparalleled in the history of Wales and of Britain. The principal cause of the unrest was the determination of the working class to defend and consolidate the improvements which they had won during the war. Those were substantial. Although the cost of essential goods rose by 75 per cent between 1914 and 1920, the rise in the wages of industrial workers was, on average, 100 per cent. In addition, the war led to a vast expansion in work opportunities for women. For the first time, they were to be seen selling tickets on buses, driving vans and serving in paramilitary units. Secretarial posts – formerly almost monopolized by men – were increasingly held by women, and women were also employed by the hundreds of thousands in munitions factories. Where both husband and wife were working, the family income in 1918 could be worth double what it had been in 1914. The ability of women to earn a wage, and the new freedom which they won as a result, were the most significant social developments to stem from the war, for from them sprang the sexual revolution of the twentieth century. There was a rapid decline in the number employed in domestic service – traditionally by far the commonest form of female employment – and women were unwilling to return to such work when peace deprived them of better-paid and less confining jobs.

Among the male labour force, farm-workers probably made the greatest advances during the war. Their earnings rose 200 per cent between 1914 and 1920, partly as a result of the insistence of the government-established County Agricultural Committees that they should receive adequate earnings. The farmers complained bitterly, but they could afford to pay better wages, for the prices of agricultural produce rose by 300 per cent between 1914 and 1920. In the other main sectors of the Welsh economy, there was a substantial increase in employment in the steel industry, while W. J. Edwards claimed that the miners had never enjoyed prosperity comparable with that of the period 1914 to 1918. Indeed, probably the only group of Welsh workers to suffer during the war were the quarrymen. Little building took place while the fighting continued, and it was announced in 1917 that quarrying was a 'non-essential occupation'. There was high unemployment in the quarrying towns and the quarrymen had little choice but to join the army; as a result, Gwynedd had more reason than the rest of Wales '*i ddwys goffáu/Y rhwyg o golli'r hogiau*' (To remember with passion the wrench of losing the boys).

With wages and prices rising rapidly and with unemployment (except among quarrymen) low, the war provided ideal conditions for the growth of trade-unionism. The growth was assisted by the policies of the government. As the armed forces were taking skilled men from industry, less skilled men (and women) had to be employed in their place. This 'dilution' needed union consent, a fact appreciated by Lloyd George in particular. It was he who, in March 1915, ensured that most union leaders agreed to dilution, an agreement which elevated trade-unionism from being a movement existing on sufferance to being an indispensable part of the British organizational structure. Union membership in Britain rose from 4 million in 1914 to 6.5 million in 1918. As has been noted, all the employees of the south Wales coal companies were members of a union by 1916; there was also a marked expansion in unionism among engineers, railwaymen, dockers and farm-workers. This increase continued until 1920 when there were 8.25 million trade-unionists in Britain. The opportunity was taken to form large and powerful unions such as the Amalgamated Engineering Union, the Municipal and General Workers' Union and the Transport and General Workers' Union; the North Wales Quarrymen's Union was incorporated into the latter in 1922.

The war also favoured the growth of the Labour party. In 1914, there was a possibility that the party would split between the majority who supported the war and the minority who opposed it. The party's leader, Ramsay MacDonald, was one of the minority, although his remarks were frequently ambiguous. He resigned from the leadership in August 1914 and was succeeded by Arthur Henderson, under whose prudent leadership party unity was preserved. In 1915 three Labour MPs joined the government; they included Henderson and the South Glamorgan representative, William Brace. When Lloyd George formed his war cabinet in 1916, Henderson was one of the five members, a striking elevation in view of the fact that only one in fifteen of the members of the House of Commons belonged to the Labour party. While they were winning credibility for their party through serving in the government, Henderson and his colleagues could at the same time stress that Labour had no responsibility for the pre-war diplomacy which had led to the war. The leaders of the Labour party were prominent among the founders of the Union of Democratic Control, a body which condemned secret diplomacy and doubted the validity of the theory that Germany was solely responsible for the war. The members of the UDC put forward a highly influential interpretation of the causes of the war, one which appealed particularly to those Liberals who were appalled by the slaughter at the front.

The war was a disaster for the Liberal party. It deprived the party of an opportunity to solve its problems, in particular the tension between *laissez-faire* and the interventionist ideas of the social reformers. Some of the basic principles of Liberalism had to be abandoned, Free Trade and Voluntaryism among them. At the same time, the party's image was eroded by the split between the followers of Lloyd George and the followers of Asquith which had resulted from Lloyd George's elevation to the premiership. For many Liberals, therefore, the Labour party was highly attractive as the only party wholly untainted by association with pre-war governments. Labour's ability to win support received a boost from the new constitution which the party adopted in February 1918. For the first time, individuals were allowed to join it, and structures were created which enabled it to become an effective electoral machine. Clause 4 of the constitution committed the party to public ownership of 'the means of production, distribution and exchange', an avowal that the Labour party was a socialist party.

The collectivist system adopted in Britain during the war also served to promote the credibility of the Labour party. The fact that the power of the state was being used to defeat an external enemy lent force to Labour's contention that the same power could be used to abolish poverty and social injustice. Before 1914, the government hardly impinged upon the lives of the greater part of the population; according to orthodox opinion, the idea that good could come of governmental interference in the economy was a fantasy. During the war, merchant shipping, the railways and the collieries came under state control; prices and rents were controlled, exports were restricted and farmers were told which crops to plant; food was rationed, the opening hours of public houses were severely curtailed, and in 1916 – when clocks were put forward an hour during the summer – even time became a matter for legislation. This was 'War Socialism' – and it worked. Lloyd George was the key figure in this process of strengthening the sinews of government. The Munitions of War Act gave him, as Minister of Munitions, unfettered authority over the workers in the munitions factories; at the same time, he established welfare services for them, an initiative which led to a lasting improvement in the conditions of work in factories. As Prime Minister, Lloyd George created five new ministries, and it was he who appointed D. A. Thomas (Viscount Rhondda), his old enemy from the days of Cymru Fydd, as Food Controller, a post in which Thomas was a brilliant success.

'War Socialism' was not intended to outlast the war; indeed, some of its principal elements were dismantled soon after the Armistice. Nevertheless, the war greatly stimulated the growth of the welfare state. The Ministry of Pensions was established in 1916, mainly to assist the wounded and the widowed; schemes were developed to safeguard the interests of wives and children and to increase the number covered by National Insurance. In the field of education, H. A. L. Fisher's act of 1918 raised the school leaving age to fourteen. As the war dragged on, it was necessary to emphasize the hope that a more secure and just world would be created when the fighting should come to an end. This hope was the motive for the founding in 1915 of the League of Nations Society, a movement which was to achieve great prominence in Wales. Lloyd George realized how strong was the desire to believe that blessings would come out of suffering. In 1917 he appointed Christopher Addison as Minister of Reconstruction with the task of preparing plans which would make Britain a country worthy of its heroes. Addison gave special attention to health and housing; a promise was obtained that a Ministry of Health would be established after the war and consideration was given to methods of using public funds for decent housing. Faith in reconstruction was important to British morale in the last years of the war, and there were many who looked forward eagerly to the period when Lloyd George would be free to devote his energy and talents to the task of transforming the living conditions of the inhabitants of Britain.

There were constitutional aspects to reconstruction, for there was a widespread feeling that the British constitutional system would be inadequate to deal with the problems which would arise after the war. It was believed that those problems would be so complex and so numerous that the 'Imperial Parliament' would be overwhelmed by them. Thus the need to establish regional parliaments was widely canvassed, on the left and on the right. 'We have a vision of better things after the war,' declared Thomas Richards, the secretary of the South Wales Miners' Federation, in July 1918, and he claimed that that vision could not be realized without establishing a federal system in Britain. 'We are deeply impressed by the need for a far-reaching system of Federal Devolution for the United Kingdom,' declared a group of Conservatives in April 1918. 'We cannot see how otherwise ... we can escape from the most dangerous congestion.' By 1918, it was widely believed that Home Rule All Round was an essential part of the new order which would be created after the war. Woodrow Wilson, the president of the United States, emphasized in his 'Fourteen Points' (January 1917) that one of the conditions of peace was full autonomy for the peoples of eastern Europe. Therefore, self-government for small nations would necessarily be one of the main themes of any peace conference. Home Rule for Ireland had been on the statute book since September 1914, but the obstinacy of the Ulster Unionists and the new situation created by the Easter Rising of 1916 meant that the constitutional future of Ireland was still a very intractable problem. Indeed, the readiness of the Tories to consider Home Rule for Wales and Scotland sprang partly from their desire to avoid making a special case of Ireland. In May 1918, a conference was held in Llandrindod to discuss Home Rule for Wales; most of those present were Liberals, but a month later Home Rule All Round was included in the Labour party manifesto. A unanimous vote in favour of a federal system in Britain was passed by the South Wales Labour Federation, and Arthur Henderson expressed the belief that a self-governing Wales could be a 'modern utopia'. By the summer of 1918, it appeared that everyone in Wales (apart from the spokesmen of the Licensed Victuallers Association) was a Home Ruler. With the premiership held by Lloyd George, formerly the most zealous of the leaders of Cymru Fydd, it was not surprising that in 1918 *The Welsh Outlook* contained headlines such as 'The Imminence of Welsh Home Rule'.

Fundamental to the interest in federalism was the desire for a more effective system of representation. That desire was also the motive for the Representation of the People Act, which became law in June 1918. It was considered fitting that all who had served in the armed services should be included on the electoral roll; at the same time, it was difficult to refuse the franchise to women, especially as they had made such a sterling contribution to the war effort. In 1918, therefore, the vote was given to every man over twenty-one, except for conscientious objectors (they were disfranchised for five years); it was also given to women over the age of thirty. (Women in their twenties – the so-called flappers – were considered too immature to be full citizens.) As a result, the number of electors in Wales rose from 430,000 to 1,172,000, a much more dramatic increase than those of 1832, 1867 and 1884.

An attempt was also made to create roughly equal electoral districts, each with about 70,000 inhabitants. (Before 1918, the member for Cardiff represented 185,000 people and the member for Montgomery Boroughs 16,000.) This aim was not fully realized: the population in the new Welsh constituencies varied from 100,000 in Flintshire to 44,000 in Meirionnydd. Nevertheless, the redistribution was sufficiently thorough to ensure that the pattern of representation in Wales would henceforth reflect the fact that the majority of the Welsh lived in the industrial south-east. Of the thirty-four parliamentary seats in Wales before 1918, fourteen were in Glamorgan and Monmouthshire, eight in the other southern counties and twelve in the north. Of the thirty-six seats in Wales after 1918, twenty-two were in Glamorgan and Monmouthshire, five in the other southern counties and eight in the north. In addition, a seat was given to the University of Wales; its electors were the registered graduates of the University – 1,066 of them in 1918. From the earliest days of the parliamentary representation of Wales, a number of Welsh constituencies had consisted of groups of boroughs; in 1918 these were all abolished apart from Caernarfon Boroughs, the Prime Minister's constituency. The 1918 legislation also laid down that every constituency should poll on the same day and that every candidate should pay a deposit of £150.

A general election was held under the new legislation on 14 December 1918, thirty-four days after the Armistice. With the time so short, little attempt was made to obtain the votes of the soldiers at the front; only 57 per cent of the electorate voted, the lowest percentage this century. The campaign was dominated by the euphoria of victory and by the desire for revenge. Party divisions were blurred. The coalition headed by Lloyd George contained the Liberals who had supported him against Asquith in 1916 together with almost all the Conservatives; it also included the National Democratic party, which was composed of former members of the Labour party. The Conservatives were by far the strongest element in the coalition, and Lloyd George had to struggle to ensure the election of as many as possible of his Liberal supporters. He did so by ensuring that he and the Tory leader, Bonar Law, jointly endorsed coalition candidates, the endorsement disdainfully labelled 'the coupon' by the Opposition. Of the candidates who received the 'coupon', 339 Conservatives and 136 Liberals were elected; in addition, about sixty other supporters of the coalition were successful. Of the Liberals faithful to Asquith, only twenty-nine were returned. In Ireland seventy-three members of Sinn Féin were elected, but they refused to take their seats in the House of Commons. As a result, the Labour party, with fifty-nine members, was the largest of the opposition parties. As eight out of every ten MPs were supporters of Lloyd George, the results of the general election of 1918 appeared to be a paean of praise for the 'man who had won the war'.

In Wales too, the achievement of the Prime Minister, 'the greatest Welshman ever', was the main theme of the election. Of the Welsh seats, twenty-five were won by followers of Lloyd George (twenty Liberals, four Conservatives and one member of the National Democratic party); only one of Asquith's supporters – Haydn Jones in Meirionnydd – was elected. Every method was used to keep out the Prime Minister's critics – men such as Llewelyn Williams and E. T. John. As a result, many of the Welsh Liberals elected in 1918 were uninspiring yes-men. The Representation of the People Act had doubled the number of constituencies in the coalfield and had enfranchised a host of voters likely to be sympathetic to socialism, providing the Labour party with an unprecedented opportunity. Yet, because of the nature of the campaign, the party was unable fully to take advantage of the opportunity, and seats like Merthyr, Pontypridd and Llanelli were won by Liberals. Nevertheless, the Labour party, with ten seats in Wales and a third of the Welsh vote, had far more favourable prospects than it had had before the war.

The euphoria which characterized the last weeks of 1918 soon ebbed away. Not everyone had been euphoric, even on Armistice Day. On 11 November 1918, Robert Graves walked across Morfa Rhuddlan (the Flodden of Wales, as he called it), 'cursing and sobbing and thinking of the dead'. His mind, like that of a host of his contemporaries, had been 'seared by the experience of the trenches'. A reaction rapidly developed against the orthodox view of the war. The arguments put forward by members of the Union of Democratic Control won increasing support, and it quickly came to be considered that the Peace Treaty of 1919 contained clauses which were too vindictive. The Caerffili by-election of 1921 was won by Morgan Jones, the first conscientious objector to sit in the House of Commons; two years later, George M. Ll. Davies was elected as a Christian Pacifist to represent the University of Wales. A gulf opened as the younger generation reflected upon the willingness of the old to sacrifice the young, the theme of a powerful poem by W. J. Gruffydd. *The Welsh Outlook* asserted in 1920 that a revolution was under way. 'There are thousands of young men and women in Wales today,' it stated, 'who will attend the feast of the slaying of their political fathers with very little regret.'

The most prominent of the 'political fathers' was Lloyd George. It is often claimed that his attitude and that of his government between 1918 and 1922 were at the root of the disillusionment that was so obvious a feature of life in Wales and in Britain in the 1920s. The claim is not entirely fair. Sincere attempts were made to carry out the promises of reconstruction. A Ministry of Health was established in 1919, a development which led to major improvements in public health in the ensuing years. Addison, the Minister of Health, obtained legislation which allowed him to give generous subsidies to local authorities for the building of houses. Addison's act was the real beginning of council housing; he was responsible, therefore, for a revolution in the housing of the working class. Some of the urban authorities of Wales took eager advantage of the measure and 15,000 Welsh families were rehoused as a result of it. The Unemployment Insurance Act of 1920 was equally revolutionary. Through the Insurance Act of 1911, Lloyd George had provided unemployment insurance for some categories of workers, and there were piecemeal extensions during and immediately after the war. The 1920 Act created a far more comprehensive system by insuring almost the entire working-class labour force. Within a few years of 1920, the industrial south-east was to suffer horrific levels of unemployment; thus, by the late 1920s, the standard of living of a large number of the people of Wales would be determined by the act.

In 1920, when the economy had not yet been hit by depression, the extent to which the government was incurring new obligations was not fully realized. Before 1920, the unemployed were largely dependent for their maintenance upon the charity of the Poor Law; after 1920, most of them had a statutory right to maintenance, a change of far-reaching significance. In the field of education, the Fisher Act became the basis for new developments; in 1921, teachers' salaries were standardized through the Burnham Scale, an important change in view of the fact that teachers in Cardiganshire, before 1921, had to be content with salary scales 20 per cent lower than those of colleagues in Glamorgan. In agriculture, the state continued until 1921 to guarantee the prices of farm produce and to insist that farm labourers received a minimum wage. The Forestry Commission, a body which would be responsible for the transformation of many of the mountainous areas of Wales, was established in 1919. Efforts were made to find work for former soldiers, old-age pensions were doubled and the Whitley Councils were created to arbitrate between the employed and the employer. Thus, there was substance to the reforming efforts of the coalition government; indeed, Kenneth O. Morgan claims that its achievements were greater than those of the pre-war Liberal government. In foreign policy, the record of Lloyd George's government was not as bad as is often supposed. Without his common sense and mental flexibility, the peace treaties would undoubtedly have been more vindictive.

Nevertheless, there was disillusionment. By 1921, the right-wing newspapers and the leaders of the business world were vigorously campaigning against the alleged wastefulness of the government. As Lloyd George was totally dependent upon the votes of Conservative MPs, he had little choice but to yield. Addison and his housing crusade were sacrificed and at the beginning of 1922 the 'Geddes Axe' fell, entailing severe cutbacks in public expenditure on education, housing and health. At the same time, many of Lloyd George's supporters were dismayed by events in Ireland. Although he succeeded in 1921 in getting parliament to accept the Irish Free State – a remarkable achievement in view of the failure of giants like Gladstone – the use of the Black and Tans perturbed many liberal consciences and aroused protests from the labour movement. There was growing criticism of the coalition's foreign policy, with the left angered by the intervention of British forces in the Russian Civil War and the right apprehensive about the consequences of Lloyd George's enthusiastic support for Greek claims to large parts of Anatolia. The Conservative leaders remained loyal to the Prime Minister, but rank-and-file Tories were increasingly uneasy, particularly as Lloyd George was airing the notion of a new centre party under his leadership. There was much anxiety that the 'Welsh wizard' would split the Conservative party as he had already split the Liberals.

The government's credibility was seriously weakened by the suggestion that it was corrupt. This stemmed chiefly from its willingness to sell honours – a barony for £50,000, for example, and a baronetcy for £15,000 – with much of the money going to Lloyd George's personal political fund. The system led to the elevation of Welshmen such as Baron Glanely, and Cardiff came to be known as 'the city of the dreadful knights'. Commenting on the readiness of Welsh MPs to accept honours, Llewelyn Williams declared: 'You get into the House to get on; you stay in to get honours; you get out to get honest.' This nonchalant attitude to the decencies of political behaviour was characteristic of Lloyd George; combined with the slippery cleverness of his many manoeuvres, it was responsible for the belief that he was not trustworthy, a notion which would plague him for the rest of his life. The activities of the man from Llanystumdwy perplexed the prudent upholders of the political traditions of Wales. 'It is no advantage to Wales to have Lloyd George as Prime Minister,' wrote the editor of *The Welsh Outlook* in 1920. 'Indeed, it is a danger. It is a danger to our spiritual independence.'

The results of the by-elections held between 1919 and 1922 are proof of the growth of disillusionment with Lloyd George among the voters of Wales. In Welsh mythology, the most famous of the by-elections was that held in Cardiganshire in February 1921. Ernest Evans, one of Lloyd George's secretaries, stood as the coalition candidate, but the chosen candidate of the Cardiganshire Liberal Association was the Prime Minister's implacable enemy, Llewelyn Williams. This battle between two Liberals was a heavy blow to the Liberal party's credibility. The personality and policies of Lloyd George were the principal themes of the election campaign. Evans obtained the backing of the Conservatives of the constituency; as a result, he won by a majority of 3,590. However, as his opponent polled 10,511 votes, it could be claimed that more than half the Liberals of Cardiganshire had endorsed Williams's severe criticism of the Prime Minister. The by-election in Newport in October 1922 had a more dramatic result. There, only a quarter of the voters supported the Liberal candidate, and the seat was won by the anti-coalition Conservative, Reginald Clarry. The result was announced on 19 October, a few hours before the famous meeting of Conservative MPs at the Carlton Club. The news from Newport encouraged those who sought the demise of the coalition, and at the Carlton Club it was agreed by 187 votes to eighty-seven to put an end to it. Lloyd George resigned at once; he was fifty-nine years old and he would never be in government again. (He was never lucky in his dealings with Newport.)

As far as the long-term trends in Welsh politics are concerned, however, the results of by-elections in the coalfield were far more significant than those of Cardiganshire and Newport. Between 1920 and 1922 there were six by-elections in Welsh mining constituencies and all of them were won by the Labour party. The Liberals did not bother to put up a candidate in Ebbw Vale in 1920, and in Pontypridd in 1922 a Liberal majority of 3,175 was turned into a Labour majority of 4,080. The implications of the Representation of the People Act were now clear, and it was obvious that at the next general election the Labour party would overtake the Liberal party as the leading party in Wales.

This upsurge in support for the Labour party in the immediate post-war years went hand in hand with a rising working-class militancy. That militancy was an international phenomenon. 'All Europe,' declared Lloyd George in March 1919, 'is filled with the spirit of revolution.' While the Bolsheviks were consolidating their power in Russia, soviets of soldiers and workers were established all over the continent, and there were Communist revolutions in Hungary and Bavaria. Tension was further increased during the winter of 1918–19 by the ravages of the influenza epidemic which killed twenty-seven million people, including about ten thousand of the inhabitants of Wales. The millions of men under arms were increasingly dissatisfied, for demobilization proved to be a complex process; there were fifty mutinies in the British army in 1919. One of the gravest took place at Kinmel Park, near Abergele, where five Canadian soldiers were killed. Problems arising from the war were at the root of the widespread unrest in Glasgow in January 1919 when the city was encircled by tanks. Six months later, the same problems sparked off one of the most vicious race riots in British history – the attacks on the homes of black people in Cardiff. The police went on strike in 1918 and again in 1919, and the economy was paralysed for nine days in September 1919 when the railwaymen withdrew their labour.

Cabinet papers testify that throughout 1919 the government was obsessed by the potential danger represented by the working class. Above all, they feared the miners. They, with their families, made up 10 per cent of the population of Britain and 35 per cent of the population of Wales. The Welsh miners reached their numerical peak in 1920, when there were 271,000 of them in the south Wales coalfield. At the end of the war, their confidence was at its height; fired by the belief that they were part of an international fight for justice, they were convinced that they were in the van of the battle against capitalism. In their conference in January 1919, the Miners' Federation of Great Britain accepted the proposal of the South Wales Miners' Federation that wages should be increased and hours of work reduced; they also accepted the Welsh miners' proposal that the coal industry should be nationalized and made over to the joint management of the miners and the state. The government was unwilling to grant more than a third of the wage increase demanded by the Federation, and therefore the miners voted by six to one in favour of a strike. This was, perhaps, the gravest challenge faced by Lloyd George in the whole of his political career. There were no stocks of coal and the government's hopes for reconstruction would be ruined if there were no fuel for industry and transport. France, which was also making efforts to rebuild its economy, was greedy for coal, particularly Welsh steam coal, and was prepared to pay £6 a ton for it; this was five times the 1914 price and the boom led to an extraordinary bonanza for Cardiff shipping companies. A coal strike would cause considerable tribulation to the businessmen who formed the majority of the coalition MPs, but they considered it would be even more disastrous if the government yielded to the most militant of the trade unions. Lloyd George's response was to buy time. He did so by offering the miners a royal commission which would report swiftly on the matter of wages and hours, and would then give detailed consideration to the issue of nationalization. The miners agreed on condition that half the members of the commission should be their nominees.

Thus was set up the Royal Commission on Coal of 1919, a fateful milestone in the history of Wales's major industry. Judge John Sankey was chosen as the commission's chairman, and three industrialists, three coal-owners, three miners' leaders and three economists sympathetic to Labour were appointed to assist him. On 20 March, seventeen days after the commission had begun its work, the government received three reports on the subject of wages and hours of work. The report of the miners and the economists endorsed the Federation's demand, while that of the coal-owners rejected it; Sankey and the industrialists tried to steer a middle course by proposing a rise of two shillings a shift and a reduction of the hours of work from eight to seven hours a day. In addition, Sankey's report contained the following observation: 'Even upon the evidence already given, the present system of ownership and working stands condemned, and some other system must be substituted for it.' On 21 March, Bonar Law confirmed that the government was prepared to act upon Sankey's recommendations 'in the spirit and the letter'. By 15 April the miners had agreed by 693,684 votes to 76,992 to accept the Sankey proposals. With the threat of strike action withdrawn, coal stocks on the increase and demobilization proceeding apace, the government could breathe a sigh of relief.

The commission resumed its work on 23 April, this time to consider nationalization. The evidence which it collected received widespread attention; for example, the *Western Mail* – never a paper to favour the cause of the miners – published it virtually word for word. Smillie, the president of the Miners' Federation of Great Britain, was so skilful in his questioning of witnesses that the sessions of the commission appeared to be a public trial of capitalism. Sankey was horrified by the inhuman attitude of some of the owners and by the arrogance of landlords such as the duke of Northumberland and Baron Tredegar, men who had profited greatly from the royalties paid upon the coal mined beneath their estates. When the reports of the commissioners were submitted on 20 June, it was seen that there was unanimity over the need to nationalize the actual coal, but there were deep divisions over the issue of the nationalization of the collieries. This was recommended by Sankey, and he was supported by the three miners and the three economists, although they also pressed for a system which would give the workers a measure of control over the industry. Five of the other commissioners condemned any kind of nationalization of the collieries, while the sixth, Arthur Duckham, proposed a plan for uniting the pits in each district into one big company.

The commission's failure to offer a clear, united recommendation gave Lloyd George the excuse to reject the policy of nationalization. As the miners were under the impression that Bonar Law had, by his statement, committed the government to that policy, they were angered by Lloyd George's announcement on 19 August that the industry would not be nationalized. 'Why was the Commission set up?' demanded Vernon Hartshorn. 'Was it a huge game of bluff? . . . We have been deceived, betrayed, duped.' During the winter of 1919,

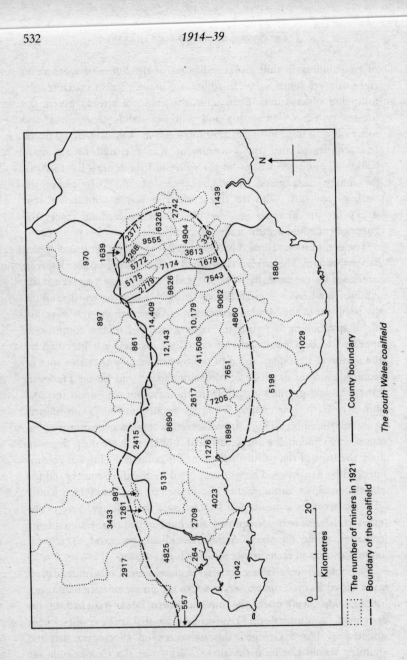

The number of miners in 1921 — County boundary

.... Boundary of the coalfield

The south Wales coalfield

Kilometres

0   20

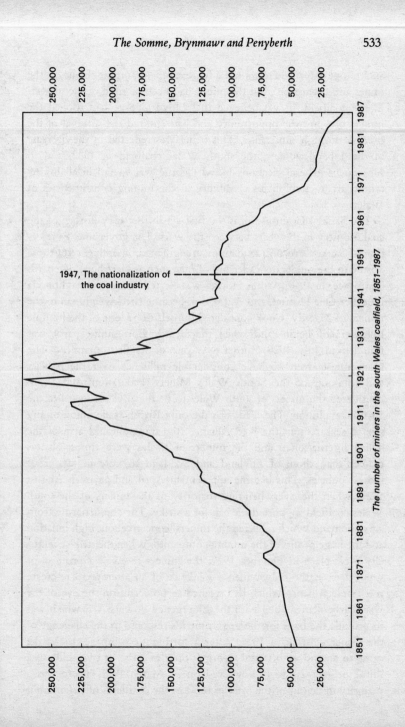

1947, The nationalization of the coal industry

The number of miners in the south Wales coalfield, 1851–1987

an attempt was made to mount a huge campaign on the theme of 'the mines and the nation', but the public had become tired of the subject. In the coalfield, it was believed that Lloyd George had robbed the miners of a historic opportunity and had ensured the survival of the owners through subterfuge. This belief was reflected in the decrease in the Liberal vote in the south Wales coalfield in 1922, and in subsequent general elections Lloyd George was to fail in all his attempts to re-establish his credibility in the mining constituencies of Wales.

The Sankey Commission is the first act in the sorry history of the coal industry in the years between the wars. The government's rejection of Sankey's recommendations strengthened the influence of those hostile to the moderate leadership of men such as Hartshorn, Richards and Brace. In 1919, Arthur Horner was elected agent of the Rhondda Number One District, and A. J. Cook became checkweighman to the miners of Maerdy. Cook considered himself to be 'one of the humble followers of Lenin' and when the British Communist party was founded in July 1920 Horner was one of its first members. The Communists were to have considerable influence over the policies and thinking of the South Wales Miners' Federation, and Lenin considered the miners of south Wales to be the advance guard of the British revolution. The 'Fed' was the only British trade union of any size to seek to join the Red Alliance (the trade-unionist arm of the Third International) and the miners of Wales were almost always readier than those of England and Scotland to vote in favour of radical policies. This became apparent in April and again in August 1920, when the overwhelming majority of the miners of the south Wales coalfield supported the call for a strike. The conflict arose from a pay demand which reflected the miners' concern about high inflation and the huge profits of the mining companies. When the strike eventually took place in October 1920, the miners received a promise of support from the railwaymen – evidence of an attempt to re-create the Triple Alliance which had seemed so powerful on the eve of the war. Parliament replied with the Emergency Powers Act, which was to provide the basis for the government's response to the challenge of the General Strike in 1926. After a fortnight's stoppage, the strike came to an end with Lloyd George's offer of a rise of two shillings a shift, the increase to be reviewed on 31 March 1921. There was a majority in favour of the offer in most of the coalfields of Britain, but the south Wales miners voted heavily against it, causing Hartshorn and Brace to distance themselves, temporarily at least, from the leadership of the 'Fed'.

The agreement of November 1920 marked the height of the coal industry's prosperity. At the end of 1920, Welsh miners could earn as much as £5 a week and the mining companies were receiving a profit of ten shillings and more from every ton of coal they sold. This prosperity was dependent upon the willingness of customers in mainland Europe to pay inflated prices. By the beginning of 1921, that willingness was rapidly ebbing away. With the pits of France, Belgium and Poland restored to production, with Germany offering coal as reparation to her old enemies and with the United States eager to sell coal to Europe, there was no longer any need to pay high prices for the produce of British pits. Between 1920 and 1921, there was a decrease of 33 per cent in the price of British coal, but in south Wales – the region which had profited most from the international boom – the decrease was 50 per cent.

The government still controlled the coal industry, but in these new circumstances it was anxious to rid itself of its responsibilities. In February 1921, it was announced that the industry would be decontrolled on 31 March, and on that day the pits were returned to the unfettered possession of the owners. They wanted wage scales to be decided region by region and were determined to scrap the state-wide agreements cherished by the miners. The new scales cut wages savagely. Throughout the kingdom, they represented an average reduction of about 35 per cent, but in south Wales the reduction was 40 per cent for skilled men and 50 per cent for labourers. The terms were rejected, and the lock-out of 1921 ensued. The Miners' Federation of Great Britain appealed to the dockers and the railwaymen; they agreed to withhold their labour from 15 April and thus there was every indication that the conflict would develop into a general strike. The government declared a State of Emergency; soldiers were sent to the coalfields and a rumour was spread that the miners were being financed by Russian gold. On 14 April, Frank Hodges, the Federation's secretary (and a native of the Ogwr valley), having given the impression that he was ready to compromise, Lloyd George seized the opportunity to create a split between the miners and the rest of the Triple Alliance (the dockers and railwaymen); as a result, J. H. Thomas, the railwaymen's secretary (and a native of Newport), announced that the rail strike was cancelled. That meant that the miners' battle would be a solitary one, and 14 April 1921 became known as 'Black Friday' – 'the heaviest blow,' according to the *Daily Herald*, 'to strike the Labour movement since time immemorial'. The pits were idle for three months. The resources of the Federation were exhausted and in spite of the help they received from other unions and from the *Daily Herald*'s appeal fund, by the end of June the miners had no choice but to yield.

The strike was not completely in vain, for as a result of it the government granted a subsidy to the industry which allowed the reductions to be modified to some extent. Nevertheless, the wage reductions were drastic and by January 1922 miners' wages were only half what they had been in March 1921. In less than a year, the miners had fallen from the top of the wage table almost to the bottom. They were without defences against the harshness of the private system. The opportunity was taken to dismiss many of the militant miners, and Cook, Horner and others of the leaders spent some time in prison. Faith in unionism was shaken. The South Wales Miners' Federation had 200,000 members in 1920; it had 87,000 two years later. When the Lloyd George government fell in 1922, the largest labour force within the working class had become embittered and alienated – and there was worse to come.

As a new and lamentable chapter opened in the history of the Welsh miners, another chapter – one which had been quite as bitter in its day – was drawing to a close. On 1 April 1920, Anglicanism ceased to be the official religion of Wales. The Welsh bishops ceased to be members of the House of Lords and every denomination in Wales was henceforth equal in the eyes of the law. This was the final victory of Welsh political Nonconformity, the high point of generations of campaigning. Yet, despite the longevity of the battle, there was hardly any sense of triumph, and today few of the inhabitants of Wales are aware that theirs is the only country in Britain that has no official religion. With secularism rapidly gaining ground, there was little reason to take pride in sectarian bickering, bickering which was particularly meaningless to young men – Nonconformist and Anglican – who had suffered together in the trenches. Furthermore, by 1920 the substance of the Establishment had long been eroded; indeed, the bishop of Oxford had claimed in 1910 that the Church of England had already been disestablished everywhere except in the lunatic asylums.

Those who had been eager to see *yr Hen Estrones* (the Old Foreigner) brought down were disappointed by the Church Temporalities Act of 1919, an act which acknowledged that the economic situation after the war was very different from that which had existed when the disendowment legislation had been passed in 1914. It provided that the Church Commissioners should receive a million pounds from the Treasury. This was the 're-endowment' which caused such annoyance to Nonconformists such as Llewelyn Williams; it was, in his opinion, additional proof of the apostasy of Lloyd George. As a result of the act, disendowment was not so harmful financially as the supporters of the Church had feared. The Church was dispossessed of ancient endowments worth £48,000 a year. The bodies benefiting from disendowment were the county councils and the University of Wales, but the process was so complicated that it was not completed until 1947. By then, £2,466,617 had been transferred to the county councils and £989,196 to the University, and the money was used to promote a variety of cultural activities.

As the day of disestablishment drew near, Welsh Anglicans were oppressed by the feeling that disaster was impending. The bishop of Bangor, Watkin Williams, argued that no preparations should be made for the time when the Disestablishment Act would come into force, for the greater the confusion then, the stronger would be the grounds for demanding that the act be repealed. The bishops of St Asaph and St David's, A. G. Edwards and John Owen, were more circumspect. They saw no option but to acknowledge that disestablishment compelled them to create a Welsh province of the Anglican Communion under the leadership of its own archbishop. With the help of legal experts such as John Sankey, Owen and Edwards had by 1920 laid the foundations of the new province. A Representative Body was established to administer the property of the Church and a Governing Body to control its policy and doctrine.

In many ways, the disestablished Church was a microcosm of a self-governing Wales, and as was the case with every scheme for Welsh self-government it was a delicate matter to balance the interests of the populous areas of the south-east with those of the rest of the country. Furthermore, the Anglican Communion could be considered a microcosm of the British Empire; as the countries which made up the Empire became self-governing, so also did the Anglicans of five continents gain their independence. By the 1980s, the Anglican

Communion had twenty-three provinces and, as far as the antiquity of its origins is concerned, the Welsh province was the oldest of them. It was this development, above all, which stilled what had been the greatest fear of the Anglicans of Wales – that independence would divorce them from the main stream of Anglicanism. The Welsh bishops were released from their vow of obedience to the archbishop of Canterbury. Thus ended a chapter which had begun with the consecration of Urban as bishop of Llandaf in 1107 – if not with Augustine's visit to the borders of Wales in 602. A. G. Edwards was consecrated archbishop of Wales in St Asaph on 1 June 1920; it could thus be claimed that the dream of Giraldus Cambrensis had been fulfilled, although the fulfilment of that dream had been brought about, not by the Church, but by its enemies.

The Anglicans of Wales responded to the challenge of disestablishment with energy, dignity and courage. In order that the new province should be placed on a sound financial footing, a million-pound appeal was launched and by 1923 £676,000 had been collected. Strenuous efforts were made to equalize clerical salaries: there was a sharp reduction in the income of bishops and attempts were made to ensure that every parish clergyman was paid at least £250 a year. As disestablishment had put an end to lay patronage, a new and ingenious system for appointing to benefices was adopted. At last, a solution was found to the problem of the excessive size of the dioceses of Llandaf and St David's – the one containing more than half the population of Wales, the other extending over more than half the surface area of Wales. Monmouthshire was taken from Llandaf in 1921 when the diocese of Monmouth was created; two years later, the counties of Radnor and Brecon, together with the old commote of Gower, were taken from St David's to become the diocese of Swansea and Brecon.

In 1924, when the first handbook of the Church in Wales was published, Archbishop Edwards was able to take pride in the progress of his Church, and he was prepared to admit that the experience of disestablishment had not been as bad as he had feared. In the following decade, when the Church of England was in difficulties over the Prayer Book and over tithes, some of its members began to argue that it also should be disestablished, and Wales was cited as an example and an inspiration. This is one of a number of ironies connected with the disestablishment of the Church in Wales. Another was the fact that by the second quarter of the twentieth century, commitment to Anglicanism – measured by the numbers attending Easter Communion – was stronger in Wales than it was in England. By then, Anglicanism was the largest denomination in Wales, for the parish churches proved to be more successful than the chapels in wrestling with the challenge of secularism. In spite of disestablishment, the Anglicans held to the principle that they had a responsibility to parishioners in their entirety, and they continued to insist that their Church was the Holy Catholic Church of Wales. Indeed, as they retained possession of the parish churches and the cathedrals, they continued to look like an Establishment – and, to a considerable extent, to be treated as one. Although the alliance between Anglicanism and the Conservative party had little meaning after 1920, the connection between them was to continue for decades. Indeed, in many rural districts of the west and north it did not entirely disappear until the upsurge in rural Toryism in the 1970s. Doubts about the Welshness of Anglicanism persisted, a subject on which W. J. Gruffydd wrote a number of scornful articles. In the half century before 1920, no bishop unable to speak Welsh was appointed in Wales, for the government was sensitive to what it considered to be the opinion of the Welsh people; after 1920, a number of non-Welsh-speaking bishops were elected, which perhaps suggests that self-government is a necessary precondition if the English-speakers of Wales are to enjoy full rights. Those bishops able to speak Welsh had frequently only a feeble commitment to the language, and there would not be until the 1970s a bishop who habitually used Welsh as the language of his home. Nevertheless, with Anglicanism in Wales no longer an adjunct of the Church of England, the opportunity existed for *yr Hen Estrones* to become *yr Hen Fam* (the Old Mother), and a time would come when men such as Aneirin Talfan Davies and T. I. Ellis would claim that the Anglican Church is the proper spiritual home for a patriotic Welshman.

The Church Establishment was one of the two pillars of the system which had aroused the hostility of Welsh radicals. The other was the landowning class, and by 1920 that also was on its way to extinction. There was a huge boom in land sales immediately after the war and many Welsh estates disappeared altogether. At least a quarter of the land of Wales is believed to have changed hands between 1918 and 1922, part of the 'Green Revolution' which took place in many

European countries during those years. Some landlords were forced to sell because of large death duties or heavy debt, but for most of them the motivation to surrender their patrimony was the desire to seize the opportunity to invest in something which would give a better return than land. Their willingness to sell should not be exaggerated: of the twenty principal landowning families in Wales, three were still living in their mansions in the late twentieth century, and another four were still the owners of large tracts of land. Welsh landlords were more ready to sell than were their English counterparts, mainly because the leadership of the landowning class had been much more decisively rejected in Wales than in England. Most of the farms sold were bought by their tenants. The statistics are unreliable, but it is likely that by 1922 35 per cent of the farmers of Wales were freeholders, compared with 10 per cent before the war. The contraction in the size of estates was to continue in ensuing decades, and by 1970 64 per cent of land in Wales was owned by the person cultivating it.

Thus the nineteenth-century Welsh radicals' dream of ridding the countryside of landlordism was fulfilled. Yet, while the burdens implicit in that system must be acknowledged, those resulting from the freehold system were almost as numerous. Between 1922 and 1931, there was a drop of 20 per cent and more in the price of land; this was a heavy blow to those who had bought their farms during the post-war boom. Henceforth, the real owners of a large number of Welsh farms were the banks, and freeholders soon came to realize that mortgage payments were a heavier and less flexible burden than rent. As farms for rent were becoming rarer – indeed, were disappearing altogether in many districts – it was increasingly difficult for someone without access to substantial capital to take up a career in farming. Furthermore, a freeholder anxious to treat his children equally was faced with a difficult problem when he came to bequeath his property. One solution was to sell the farm and divide the money between the children; this undermined the tradition, characteristic of many estates, whereby a family continued to work the same farm for generations. Another solution was for the farm to continue after the death of the parents in the joint possession of unmarried brothers and sisters; by the second quarter of the twentieth century, this was a common feature of the Welsh countryside and was an important feature in the demographic history of rural Wales.

A landowner, whem renting a farm, is chiefly interested in getting a viable tenant with experience of local farming conditions. The owner of a farm, when putting it on the market, is chiefly interested in getting the highest possible price; he is therefore prepared to sell to the highest bidder, local or not. Thus the growth in freeholding is one of the main reasons why an increasing number of Welsh farms have become the property of purchasers from beyond Offa's Dyke, a development which has completely anglicized many of the rural communities of Wales. With the break-up of estates, the efforts of landowners to reorganize and consolidate their holdings came to an end. By the late twentieth century, the consolidation of holdings depended upon the purchasing power of the wealthiest farmers, and as a result the number of farms in Wales has been halved in less than a generation. The rise of freeholding has had such unexpected consequences that it is hardly surprising that the last quarter of the twentieth century has witnessed an increasing interest in socialist answers to the problems of land tenure.

With the landowning class and the Church Establishment fading away together, the essentials of the programme of the Welsh radicals had been achieved. Yet one other matter had at intervals made its appearance on that programme. That was self-government for Wales. Between 1918 and 1922, attempts were made to bring this matter also to a successful conclusion. Those years saw the growth of a Welsh bureaucracy; in 1919, the Welsh Board of Health and the Welsh Department of the Ministry of Agriculture were created, continuing a process which had begun with the establishment of the Welsh Department of the Board of Education in 1907. There was support for the view that these developments should be crowned with a Secretary of State for Wales, following the precedent of the secretaryship created (or, rather, re-created) for Scotland in 1885. In 1919, the appointment of a Secretary of State for Wales was undoubtedly within Lloyd George's power, but he urged its advocates to campaign for a parliament rather than a secretaryship. As has been noted, it was widely believed that Home Rule All Round would be an essential part of the post-war order. In June 1919, the House of Commons agreed by 137 votes to thirty-four that devolution was necessary if Westminster were to deal successfully with the principal affairs of the kingdom and the Empire. At the same time, a conference was set up to consider the subject; it was chaired by the Speaker of the House of Commons, and thirty-two members of the legislature – four from Wales among them – were appointed to assist him. Their report, published in April 1920, put forward two plans, each supported by an equal number of the members of the conference. One plan proposed that there should be separate elected bodies for the English, the Welsh and the Scots, while the other proposed that the MPs of each of the three countries should meet occasionally as a 'Grand Council'. Both plans were supported by three of the Welsh members, for, although they stated that only a legislative body could 'satisfy the national aspirations ... of Wales', they believed that the 'Grand Council' was a step in the right direction and one which could be taken at once.

The report received little attention. The Speaker, discussing the conference in his memoirs, noted: 'All along, I felt [our discussions] were academic rather than practical, and that the driving force of necessity was absent.' He was perfectly correct, for interest in devolution among the members of the English official class proved to be short-lived. They soon came to consider that the successful stand made by the authorities against the working-class challenge in 1919 was proof that the British system of government was essentially sound, a view reinforced by the government's ability to defeat the General Strike in 1926. The new states of eastern Europe, which had come into existence as the result of the recognition of the principle of the political rights of nationalities, were faced by intractable problems, and thus considerable cynicism arose about the principle itself. Above all, the situation in Ireland had been transformed. In May 1921, the quasi-federal Stormont system came into force in six of the island's northern counties; seven months later, the British parliament ratified the agreement through which the Irish Free State came into being, a state with a far greater degree of independence than had been proposed in the Home Rule Bills of Gladstone and Asquith. Thus there was no purpose in proposing Home Rule All Round as a means of curbing Irish ambitions. Consequently, the English official class saw no point in tampering with the British system of government, and thus no legislation resulted from the report of the Speaker's Conference.

Welsh patriots hoped that Lloyd George would somehow be able to present them with a parliament, but he did no more than make an occasional encouraging comment. Although there was a consensus in favour of self-government in Wales, it had little weight, for the subject was not considered a priority by any organization enjoying political influence. The Liberal party's interest in a parliament for Wales was waning, particularly when it became apparent that such a parliament would not have a majority of Liberal members; indeed, by 1926 Watkin Davies, the Liberal editor of *The Welsh Outlook*, was giving thanks that Westminster was a bulwark between the 'real' Welsh and the extremism of the 'Bolsheviks of the South'. The Labour party seemed more enthusiastic, and in consequence its ranks were joined by veteran home rulers such as E. T. John and Beriah Gwynfe Evans. Yet the socialists of Wales did not include men like Maclean in Scotland and Connolly in Ireland, who considered the freedom of their nation as part of a coherent strategy in the struggle against capitalism and imperialism. Many Labour supporters regarded Welsh nationalism as a remnant of the old radicalism – something to be used to attract the Welsh to socialism and then put aside. This was certainly the attitude of Arthur Henderson; despite his description of a self-governing Wales as a 'modern utopia', he was stubbornly opposed to any plan which would give the Labour party's organization a Welsh dimension.

While Labour appeared likely to win a majority in Wales and unlikely to win one in Britain, the party favoured Welsh self-government; once Labour's prospects in Westminster began to improve, its enthusiasm cooled. To those who had been trained in the Central Labour College – an increasingly influential group within the party in the 1920s – any attempt to emphasize the separateness of Wales was considered to be a threat to the unity of the proletariat; as their education had lacked any Welsh dimension, they believed that the experience of the English working class represented the universal. As the ILP tradition (which had in many ways been a revolt of the 'regions' against London) withered as a formative element in the Labour party, the party's ethos became increasingly centralist, a tendency strengthened by Sidney and Beatrice Webb's enthusiasm for planning and, later, by Herbert Morrison's faith in the corporate system. As a result of these developments, the Labour party lost interest in the issue of Welsh self-government. Indeed, it could be argued that the party's historical role was to consolidate the process of integrating the Welsh into the British system.

Thus it is frequently suggested that the year 1922, when Labour won half the seats in Wales, marks the end of the period in which specifically Welsh subjects were central to the political process.

According to Kenneth O. Morgan, the period between 1868 and 1922 'possesses a unity of its own. It covers the entire cycle of Welsh political nationalism as a major force in British public life'; after 1922, Morgan claims, the matters with which that nationalism was chiefly concerned became marginal to the interests of the majority of the people of Wales. In the three decades preceding 1922 there had been a marked growth in the constitutional recognition of the Welsh nation, but in the three decades after 1922 there was hardly any increase in that recognition. Yet, as Michael Hechter notes, 'The apparent vacillation in the strength of Welsh . . . nationalism is puzzling.' 'How,' he asks, 'can a social movement, such as nationalism, "die" [after 1922] and then suddenly "reappear" forty years later?'

Hechter suggests that Welsh nationalism did not die during those forty years but rather was deprived of a means of expression. After 1922, the Welsh vote was divided between the Labour party and the Liberal party; with the former acting as the voice of industrial Wales and the latter as the voice of rural Wales, the nation lacked a political organization able to speak for Wales as a whole. That duality came to an end in the 1960s, when the Labour party came to represent almost every corner of Wales – and that was the very time when Welsh nationalism 'reappeared'. The decreasing importance of the 'Welsh Question' can also be attributed to some extent to events in Ireland. Since 1868, the more patriotic among the Welsh MPs had looked to the six dozen and more Irish National Party MPs for support – and generally they had received it. When the representatives of Irish nationalism turned their backs on the British parliament, that support ended and parliament ceased to be a place where the political rights of a Celtic nation were frequently discussed. For a generation and more, the Welsh had followed in the footsteps of the Irish, but in the wake of the Easter Rising of 1916 the nationalism of Ireland took on a character which did not appeal to more than a tiny minority among the Welsh. That minority hoped that the Irish – as the only self-governing Celtic nation – would give practical help to Welsh nationalism, but the Free State proved exceptionally introverted – an embarrassment, indeed, rather than an inspiration to the supporters of Home Rule. Furthermore, the departure of the Irish from Westminster gave a big boost to the Conservative party (the party least in favour of self-government for Wales), for it meant that henceforward no anti-Tory government would be kept in office by the votes of the Irish Nationalists, as had been the case in 1892 and 1910.

Yet, although nothing approaching a Welsh parliament was established, the distinctive character of Welsh politics endured, for Welsh voting patterns strongly reflected what Hechter called 'peripheral sectionalism'. In the 1920s, there were three parties struggling for power in Britain; this was a situation with which the British electoral system, which did not acknowledge the principle of proportional representation, was ill-qualified to deal. According to David Butler, the period between the wars was a time of 'confusion between two periods of the effective operation of the two-party system'. The situation was totally different in Wales; what occurred there was that the Labour party won from the Liberal party the vast majority of the parliamentary seats. In England, the Conservative party won the largest number of seats in each of the seven general elections held between 1918 and 1935, but in Wales in all those elections it won fewer seats than either of the two other major parties. The tenacity of Welsh Liberalism was astonishing: in 1935, the Liberal party polled only 6 per cent of the English vote, but 18 per cent of the electors of Wales remained faithful to it. Support for the Labour party in Wales could be as much as 50 per cent higher than it was in England; the difference can be attributed mainly to class allegiance, but there was undoubtedly an ethnic dimension to the Welsh people's attachment to Labour.

This attachment became obvious in the general election which followed Lloyd George's resignation in 1922. The Labour party polled 41 per cent of the Welsh vote compared with 31 per cent in 1918. It won every one of the fifteen seats in the mining valleys of the south – the beginning of a complete electoral supremacy over those seats which would continue unbroken until the present day. One of the victors was Ramsay MacDonald, the candidate in Aberafan; he was chosen to lead the Parliamentary Labour Party, a powerful group with 142 members. Labour was also successful in Swansea East, Wrexham and Caernarfonshire, while General Owen Thomas retained Anglesey which he had won as an Independent Labour candidate in 1918. The Conservatives won the three Cardiff constituencies together with Barry, Newport and Monmouth. The remaining eleven seats went to one or the other of the two Liberal factions. Only one of those seats (Swansea West) was in any sense urban; it appeared therefore that the appeal of Liberalism was increasingly becoming restricted to the rural parts of Wales.

In Wales, the most prominent feature of the general election of 1922 was the advance of Labour, but in Britain as a whole it ushered in a period of Tory dominance. The Conservative party had not won an election since 1900, but in the half century after 1922 Conservative governments, or governments dominated by Conservatives, were to be in power for thirty-five years. But although the Tories in 1922 won a majority of seventy-seven over all the other parties combined, there was another general election within a year. It was caused by the desire of Baldwin, the Prime Minister, to obtain a mandate for the imposition of tariffs. Tariffs were put forward as an answer to Britain's economic problems, although it is likely that Baldwin's real motive was to strengthen the unity of the Conservative party and, in so doing, to destroy Lloyd George's hopes of creating a 'Centre party'. Indeed, it has frequently been claimed that one of the chief features of British politics in the decade after 1922 was the manoeuvring aimed at preventing Lloyd George from regaining power – an obsession with MacDonald as well as with Baldwin. Faced with the threat to Free Trade, the two wings of the Liberals agreed to unite under Asquith's leadership. Following the general election of 1923, Wales was represented by twenty Labour MPs (if George M. Ll. Davies, the Christian Pacifist member for the University, is included), twelve Liberals and four Conservatives. The new parliament contained 258 Conservatives, 191 Labour members and 158 Liberals but, as Baldwin had failed to obtain his mandate, Asquith decided that it would be proper to give the Labour party an opportunity to form a government.

It was in this manner that the first Labour government came into being. It was a moderate government, in accordance with Ramsay MacDonald's wish to prove that Labour was basically respectable. During its nine-month existence, it had important achievements in the fields of housing, education and international peace, but as it was totally dependent on Liberal votes it could not introduce any legislation which savoured of socialism. Lloyd George soon came to the conclusion that there would be no future for his kind of radicalism if Labour were to succeed. He, therefore, was chiefly responsible for engineering the fall of the government. It fell in an atmosphere of confusion and bitterness in October 1924. In the general election which followed, the Zinoviev Letter was used to insinuate that a vote for Labour would promote the international schemes of the

Bolsheviks. Yet, in that general election, it was the Liberals who suffered most. They were blamed by the right for permitting the formation of a Labour government, and by the left for overthrowing it. The Liberal share of the British vote fell from 30 per cent in 1923 to 18 per cent in 1924, and the number of their successful candidates decreased from 158 to forty. The Labour party's vote increased; nevertheless, it won only 151 seats, mainly because the other two parties were unwilling for the anti-Labour vote to be split. In 1924, there was not a single constituency in the south Wales coalfield in which a Liberal stood against a Tory; in the coalfield, the anti-Labour vote went almost without distinction to a Conservative or a Liberal, a development highly damaging to the survival of a distinct Liberal image. The Labour party kept its grip on sixteen seats in Wales; the Liberals won eleven and the Tories nine – their best performance since 1895. In Westminster, the Conservatives had a majority of more than two hundred, and this time Baldwin was content to continue in office for the full five years before calling an election.

The results of the elections of 1922, 1923 and 1924 have been discussed in some detail, for these contests were central to the switch in party allegiance. Furthermore, in those three elections Wales as a political issue was increasingly eliminated from the agenda. After the general election of 1924, the editor of *The Welsh Outlook* declared that he could not remember an election in which so little attention had been paid to specifically Welsh questions. Yet by 1924 there were in Wales people eager to make their nationality the focus of Welsh politics. One of them was H. R. Jones, a commercial traveller from the slate-quarrying district, who was fascinated by the Irish national struggle. It was he, in Caernarfon in September 1924, who formed Byddin Ymreolwyr Cymru (the Army of Welsh Home Rulers). Another was Saunders Lewis, one of the sons of the Welsh diaspora of Merseyside, a lecturer in Welsh and a man who was heavily influenced by the Irish literary revival and by writers of the French 'reaction'. He was the most prominent member of Y Mudiad Cymreig (The Welsh Movement), a society established in Penarth in January 1924. Three members of each of these groups came together at Pwllheli on 5 August 1925, during the National Eisteddfod; in that meeting, Plaid Genedlaethol Cymru (the National Party of Wales) was founded.

The need for a Welsh party had been a subject of discussion for a generation; David Davies, the member for Montgomeryshire, had argued the case eloquently in the years immediately after the war. Davies and his like, however, were mainly concerned to make the Welsh Parliamentary Party more effective. The strategy and the aims of the new party were very different. It insisted that its members should cut all links with other British parties, and also with Westminster. It was agreed that the party's principal aim was the achievement of a Welsh-speaking Wales, and that Welsh should be the only medium of party activity. These were Saunders Lewis's ideas, and he insisted that they should be accepted before the meeting at Pwllheli. Implicit in them was a condemnation of Welsh national-ism as it had hitherto existed, a nationalism characterized by inter-party conferences, an obsession with Westminster and a willingness to accept a subservient position for the Welsh language. It was therefore hardly surprising that the new party failed to attract to its ranks any politician of experience. Indeed, in its early years it had only a handful of supporters; it published a monthly paper, *Y Ddraig Goch* (The Red Dragon), it held an annual summer school and H. R. Jones, its full-time secretary, established a few branches, but it did little more than that. Yet its members believed that the establishment of the party was an achievement in itself; merely by existing, the party was a declara-tion of the distinctiveness of Wales.

To the majority of the Welsh, 1925 was not the first year of the struggle for liberation but rather the first year of a distressing period in their history, for in 1925 the levels of unemployment in industrial Wales began to climb to dizzy heights. Despite the savage cuts in miners' wages in 1921, the pits of the south Wales coalfield were still able in the early 1920s to employ a vast workforce: there were 256,000 men working in them in 1923. There was a long miners' strike in the United States in 1922, and in 1923–4 the German coal industry was disrupted by the French seizure of the Ruhr valley. As a result, there was a huge international demand for the produce of the south Wales coalfield. In 1923, the percentage out of work in Wales was lower than it was in any other part of the United Kingdom. In that year, seventy-eight million tons of coal were exported from Britain, the highest figure ever. The number of people living in the mining valleys was still increasing: the population of the Rhondda reached its highest point in 1924, when the valley had 167,900 inhabit-ants. In 1925, however, the factors which had been responsible for this prosperity ceased to be operative, and this was reflected in rising unemployment among the miners. In April 1924, only 1.8 per cent of the miners of Wales were out of work; the percentage rose to 12.5 in January 1925 and to 28.5 in August, proof that a dire crisis had struck the chief sector of the Welsh economy.

The long depression which began in 1925 is the central happening in the history of twentieth-century Wales. It was responsible for halting and reversing the industrial growth which had been in full flood for a century and a half. In its wake, there was a vast efflux of people from Wales; every census, from 1801 until 1921, had recorded a growth in the country's population, but Wales had fewer inhabitants in 1931 than it had in 1921. Despite this demographic haemorrhage, the level of unemployment continued to rise. It reached its peak in August 1932, when 42.8 per cent of insured males of Wales were out of work. Every one of the developed western nations experienced depression in the years between the wars, but the experience of Wales was exceptional in severity and length. In most of those nations, the crisis was over by the mid-1930s, but as late as 1939 there were still more than a hundred thousand Welshmen out of work. With their economy collapsing, the Welsh people's faith in their society, their institutions and their future was gravely undermined, and a store of bitter memories accumulated among them which would not fade for generations.

The severity of the depression in Wales is attributable above all to the dependence of the Welsh economy on the coal industry, a striking example of the peril of having too many eggs in one basket. The root of the trouble lay in the fact that the south Wales coalfield had been developed, to a unique extent, to serve overseas markets. In 1920, when south Wales produced 20 per cent of Britain's coal, the ports of the Severn Sea handled 62 per cent of the kingdom's coal exports. In the 1920s and 1930s, the British domestic market remained comparatively stable; this is the reason for the prosperity (and the conservatism) of such coalfields as that of Nottinghamshire. But the overseas markets collapsed. In the century before 1914, world-wide demand for coal increased at a rate of 4 per cent a year; in the inter-war years, the yearly increase was only 0.3 per cent. This contrast is partly explained by the development of more efficient methods of fuel consumption, but the main reason was the increasing use of other sources of energy, particularly oil. By 1939, the navies of almost every country had changed from coal to oil, and half the world's merchant ships also depended on oil. Although the railways remained, on the whole, faithful to coal, they were no longer so central to transport because of the increasing role of the bus, the car and the lorry. There was little decline in the demand for anthracite coal, for that had a specialist market. It was the demand for steam coal, the foundation upon which the prodigious growth of the south Wales coalfield had been built, which slumped. The areas producing steam coal – the valleys of the Rhondda, the Cynon and the Rhymni in particular – had been the ones which had grown most rapidly in the decades before 1914; henceforth, the economy of those valleys would suffer almost total collapse. During the summer of 1927, when unemployment stood at 10 per cent in Ammanford, in the anthracite area, it was 40 per cent in Ferndale, in the area of steam-coal production.

Although the world-wide demand for coal remained virtually static in the inter-war years, there was an increase of 28 per cent in the coal available for sale. As the greater part of this increase occurred in countries where the industry was better placed financially than it was in Wales, it was inevitable that the south Wales coalfield's international markets should shrink. The amount of coal exported from the ports of the Severn Sea fell from 35.76 million tons in 1923 to 16.36 million tons in 1936; during that period the labour force in the south Wales pits fell by 126,497. Much of the trade with France and Italy – Wales's best customers – was lost, partly because Germany supplied them with coal as part of the reparations imposed under the terms of the Treaty of Versailles. There was heavy investment in the coalfields of Belgium and Poland, and those countries captured a significant number of Wales's former customers. Spain – formerly heavily dependent on Wales for coal – developed its own resources, while important markets in North and South America were lost to the United States. The rich mines of the United States could be worked cheaply, and the coal industries of most of the countries of the European mainland received substantial subsidies.

By the 1920s, the coal industry in Britain was reaping the fruits of having been a pioneer; in many mines, the best seams had been exhausted and a large number of companies were burdened with redundant investment. In Belgium and Poland, the mines were re-equipped following wartime destruction, and mainland coal companies were more willing than those of Britain to mechanize. The weaknesses of the British coal industry were at their worst in the south Wales coalfield. It was there that owners received the highest profits in time of prosperity, and the greatest losses when there was a slump; in 1924, productivity was 8 per cent a head lower than it was in the kingdom as a whole, while production costs per ton were 15 per cent higher; in that year, 5.4 per cent of south Wales coal was cut by machine, compared with 46.4 per cent in Scotland; in Wales, the royalties were heavier, the leases more complex and more of the accidents were fatal. Above all, it was in south Wales that the relationship between employer and employed was at its most bitter.

In April 1925, when the coal industry in Britain was already in difficulties, it received a further blow – this time from the government. In the Budget of that month, Winston Churchill, the Chancellor of the Exchequer, announced that Britain was returning to the Gold Standard; this meant that the value of the pound in relation to the dollar would be the same as it had been before the war. The distinguished economist J. M. Keynes claimed that as a result overseas customers would have to pay 10 per cent more for British goods; if those goods were to continue to be saleable it would be necessary to cut their production costs, mainly by means of wage reductions. The government, eager to strengthen the position of the City of London in the world of international finance and to return to pre-war 'normality', ignored Keynes's warnings. Keynes probably exaggerated in naming a figure of 10 per cent, but there is no doubt that the problems of the coal industry were worsened by the revaluation of the pound. By June 1925, almost all the coalfields in Britain were working at a loss. The employers announced that they would cease at the end of July 1925 to pay the wage scales agreed upon in the prosperous days of 1924 and they demanded that the seven-hour day, which had been won in 1919, should be given up. That announcement was the first step in the chain of events which led to the General Strike of 1926 and to the prolonged suffering of the miners in that year.

At the same time, another conflict was afoot in the western part of the coalfield. The anthracite area had been developed by a number of small coal-owners, but after the war most of the pits came into the possession of two combines, United Anthracite and Amalgamated Anthracite, an expensive process which created problems of over-capitalization. As the new owners wanted unrestricted control, and as the workers were determined to retain possession of the traditional rights of the anthracite miners, conflict was unavoidable. The most important of those traditional rights was the seniority rule which laid down that the last man to be employed was the first to lose his job. The refusal of the manager of the Number One Pit, Ammanford, to observe the rule was the main cause of the strike which spread through the anthracite coalfield in midsummer 1925. There was a great deal of violence during the strike – fierce fighting in Glynneath, for example, and a bloody battle in Ammanford, and the deputy chief constable of Carmarthenshire came within an inch of being beaten to death. Ammanford was controlled by the strike committee for ten days and after the disturbances ended 198 miners were prosecuted and fifty-eight of them imprisoned. The strike lasted from the beginning of July until 24 August, and the agreement which ended it preserved the seniority rule. The vast majority of the anthracite miners were Welsh speakers, and loyalty to the chapel was still strong among them. They had been less militant than their fellows in the steam-coal districts, but they were greatly radicalized by the troubles of 1925.

During those troubles, there were dramatic developments in the coalfield as a whole. As the employers' offer had been rejected, it was expected that pits throughout the kingdom would be idle from 31 July 1925. Six days before that date, the seamen and the railway workers agreed not to carry coal. Some form of general strike was therefore in prospect. Then, on the evening of 31 July, Baldwin offered an inquiry into the coal industry; while it was in progress – and it was estimated that it would take nine months – he promised a subsidy to the industry in order to avoid wage reductions. Baldwin's proposals could be represented as a victory for the miners, although they were in fact no more than a truce. To the *Daily Herald*, 31 July 1925 was 'Red Friday', sweet revenge for 'Black Friday'. From the point of view of the government, there was virtue in delay. 'The majority of the Cabinet,' Hankey, its secretary, informed the king, 'regard the present moment as badly chosen for the fight, though the conditions would be more favourable nine months hence.'

Those nine months were used to plan the response to a general strike on the basis of the Emergency Powers Act of 1920. It was foreseen that governmental authority might be put at risk, and therefore the kingdom was divided into regions – counter-revolutionary devolution, as it were. In an emergency, south Wales was to be administered from Dominions House, Cardiff, and the north from Liverpool. The government's efforts were facilitated by the rapid spread of cars and lorries, which were less likely than trains to be affected by a strike. The authorities gave their blessing to the Organization for the Maintenance of Supplies, a private body which considered resistance to strikers to be a patriotic act. Baldwin, a man who always sought to avoid conflict, was annoyed by the uncompromising attitude of the coal-owners. They were led by Evan Williams of Pontarddulais, the president of the Mining Association of Great Britain – 'an insignificant little man' according to Thomas Jones of Rhymni, who as deputy secretary to the cabinet was a powerful force behind the scenes. The miners' leader was A. J. Cook of the Rhondda, who had been elected secretary of the Miners' Federation of Great Britain in 1924. Cook was completely uncompromising and he was an agitator of genius. It was he who coined the slogan: 'Not a Minute on the Day, Not a Penny off the Pay'. Cook was the man 'the British middle class loved to hate', although his rhetoric also alarmed such people as R. H. Tawney, one of the most sincere of the supporters of the miners.

A distinguished Liberal, Sir Herbert Samuel, was appointed to chair the inquiry, and he was assisted by an economist, a banker and an industrialist. The commissioners' report, together with two huge volumes of evidence, was published in April 1926. It argued that much could be done to increase the efficiency of the industry and to improve the miners' conditions of work; it condemned the attempt of the owners to place the entire burden of the coal industry's problems on the labour force and rejected their suggestion that the hours of work should be extended. Nevertheless, as the commissioners saw no virtue in either subsidies or nationalization, they recommended that wages should be reduced. There were intensive discussions at the end of April, but the government was unwilling to impose restrictions on the coal-owners. They offered a reduction of 13 per cent in wages together with an addition of an hour to the working day; the terms were rejected and the miners were locked out on 30 April 1926. The Trades Union Congress had undertaken to assist the miners, but it was the government, by bringing discussions to an abrupt end on 2 May, which made a general strike inevitable.

The strike lasted from 3 to 12 May – the 'Nine Days' which are so remarkable a chapter in the history of trade-unionism in Britain. The

Trades Union Congress acknowledged that the south Wales coalfield, where almost every group of workers joined the strike, was one of the most 'solid' regions in the kingdom. The strikers there were almost entirely non-violent and there was hardly any governmental interference. Most members of the local authorities in the mining valleys were in total sympathy with the miners and there was cooperation between them and the Strike Committees and Action Councils. In the coastal towns, the strike was not quite so effective: production continued in the Spillers flour mill in Cardiff, for example, and the *Western Mail*, which was vicious in its condemnation of the strikers, appeared on every one of the 'Nine Days'. The strike had little effect in the rural areas, where many farmers were contemptuous of the miners' stand. In the north-east, with its 17,829 miners, there was considerable sympathy for their cause, particularly among railwaymen. The railwaymen were also in the van in Gwynedd, where the port of Holyhead was closed because they withheld their labour. The quarrymen had not been asked to strike, but there was great enthusiasm for the miners' cause among the printers of Caernarfon and Bangor. On 12 May, the Trades Union Council, believing that new proposals drafted by Samuel gave grounds for hope, declared the General Strike at an end. They were eager to do so, for the implications of the strike had terrified them. As Aneurin Bevan put it, 'They had forged a revolutionary weapon without having a revolutionary intent.' Many unionists were angered by the TUC's willingness to end the strike without ensuring victory; large numbers of them were unwilling to return to work and there were frequent accusations of treachery.

The leaders of the Miners' Federation of Great Britain saw no virtue in Samuel's proposals; the pits therefore remained idle, and the idleness continued for many months. Despite the drama of the 'Nine Days', it was the miners' stand after the General Strike came to an end which was the real battle of 1926. In that battle, there were many elements which were to manifest themselves in the miners' strike of 1984–5 – the prominent role played by women, for example, and the deprivation suffered by single men and the unique role played by the miners of south Wales. However, there was one fundamental difference – the scale of the two confrontations. Wales had 236,000 miners in 1926 and only 22,700 in 1984.

When the General Strike was over, Baldwin tried to present himself as an impartial arbitrator. However, as parliament renewed the Special Powers Act and repealed the Seven Hour Day Act of 1919, the coal-owners could feel confident that the government was on their side; as a result, they needed to do nothing but wait until the miners were forced to surrender. In July, significant numbers of the miners in the English midlands returned to work. At the beginning of October, George Spencer, the secretary of the Nottinghamshire miners, ar-ranged for the majority of the miners in that county to abandon their strike; a month later, Spencer established a breakaway union, much to the concern of the Miners' Federation of Great Britain. The situation was very different in the south Wales coalfield: there, as late as 11 November, no more than 3 per cent of the labour force was working. But, although the solidarity of the south Wales miners was a remark-able phenomenon, considerable pressure was needed to keep the ranks intact. Between July and November 1926, there were eighteen serious confrontations in the south Wales coalfield in addition to a host of minor skirmishes, all of them arising from police attempts to safeguard strike-breakers. Activists at Ystradgynlais called themselves Scotch Cattle and there was extensive fighting in the upper Afan valley at the beginning of October.

By 19 November, when 35 per cent of the miners of Britain were back at work, the proportion in south Wales was 14 per cent. It was a proposal made on that day by the south Wales miners which brought the struggle to an end. The principle of having the same wage scales for the kingdom as a whole had to be abandoned. The miners of south Wales were forced to work an eight-hour day, for which they received little more than ten shillings. Henceforth, they would be working for about half the pay they had been receiving for a seven-hour day in 1921.

Severe deprivation had forced the miners to accept such harsh terms. None of them had any money to fall back upon; indeed, many were still burdened by debts arising from the lock-out of 1921. In 1926, the miners of south Wales lost a total of £15,000,000 in wages – about £750,000,000 at present-day values. Their standard of living was meagre when they were at work, but between May and December 1926 they were obliged to survive on less than a third of the money they would have received had they been working. In the eyes of the authorities, they were refusing employment, and thus they received neither unemployment benefit nor assistance from the Poor

Law Guardians. The guardians could relieve wives and children; the rates to be paid were laid down in a circular from Neville Chamberlain, the Minister of Health – a maximum of twelve shillings a week for a wife and four shillings for a child. In addition, children received free school dinners at the expense of the Local Education Authority. The four shillings was supposed to be reduced to take account of the free dinners, but when the Pontypridd Guardians sought to do so they were confronted by thirty thousand protesters. Chamberlain believed that many of the Boards of Guardians were too lavish; in July 1926 the Board of Guardians (Default) Act was passed, empowering the Minister of Health to suspend boards and appoint commissioners in their place. A large proportion of the receipts of the Poor Law Unions came from rates levied on the industries within their boundaries; as no rates were levied on an idle colliery, the receipts of the coalfield unions shrank dramatically at the very time when their financial needs were greatest. They had to resort to loans: by the end of 1926, the Bedwellte Union, which consisted of six urban districts in western Monmouthshire, had debts of £976,520. The Bedwellte Board of Guardians was suspended in February 1927. The commissioners made harsh cuts, and as a result Chamberlain became an object of hatred in the south Wales coalfield.

In 1926, a family with two children received, at most, one pound a week from the guardians, but a single man did not get a penny from any public body. Other means of assistance had therefore to be found to save the mining communities from starvation. The South Wales Miners' Federation contributed £330,000 to the maintenance of the miners and substantial donations came from workers in the Soviet Union; male-voice choirs went on fund-raising journeys and extensive help was given by those inhabitants of the coalfield who were still in work. Most of the money collected was spent on the soup kitchens, institutions which were of vital importance in the dreary months of 1926. The food they provided was not the only contribution of the soup kitchens: the joint effort they entailed was central to the maintenance of the morale of the community, as were other kinds of communal activity – the jazz bands, for example, and the shoe-repairing centres. But these efforts only scratched the surface of need. By the beginning of the winter of 1926, every mining family was weighed down by debt; many of the children of the coalfield had no shoes and were carried to school on their fathers' backs; the wives, who gave all the available protein to their children and their husbands, were fainting from lack of nourishment; infant mortality was rising rapidly. Under such circumstances, there was no choice but to yield.

The events of 1926 cast a long shadow over the economy and the society of Wales. The coal industry was much weakened. Britain was obliged to import coal, thus strengthening the economies of its chief competitors. As the miners would henceforth be working an extra hour a day, it was possible to reduce the labour force while maintaining the same level of production. The numbers employed were further reduced by the necessity of closing pits which had been rendered unworkable by the long shutdown. In 1927, there were 194,000 miners in the south Wales coalfield compared with 218,000 a year earlier. The employers were able to pick and choose among the workers, and they took the opportunity to refuse employment to the militant elements; as a result, a high proportion of the political activists were out of work. For many of them, the lesson of 1926 was the need for uncompromising resistance to capitalism. During that year, there was a doubling in the membership of the Communist party, the only party to back the miners unreservedly. Arthur Horner, the most prominent of the Welsh Communists, clung to the syndicalist creed that the working class would achieve its freedom through industrial action, although the experiences of 1926 convinced him of the need for a centralized union for all the miners of Britain.

For most of the miners' leaders, however, the experiences of 1926 confirmed their doubts about syndicalism and strengthened their belief in the parliamentary path. Oliver Harris, the treasurer of the South Wales Miners' Federation, declared that it had been a serious mistake to allow the confrontation to continue for so long. James Griffiths, the agent of the anthracite miners, argued that there were better methods of obtaining justice than industrial conflict. After 1926, control of the unions came increasingly into the hands of moderate, circumspect leaders – men who were highly suspicious of the strike as a weapon. Between 1919 and 1925, an average of twenty-eight million working days was lost annually in Britain through strikes; the corresponding figure for the period 1927 to 1929 was three million. At the same time, there was a substantial decline in union membership: the number of unionists in Britain fell to less than five million in 1927, a year in which union rights were curtailed by the Trade Union Act, a spiteful measure passed by the Tory government. There was a

dramatic fall in the membership of the South Wales Miners' Federation – from 124,000 in 1924 to 73,000 in 1927. As its income was
shrinking, the 'Fed' ceased to finance the Central Labour College,
gave up publishing its magazine and reduced the wages of its officials.
Worse than the fall in membership was the existence in the south
Wales coalfield of another union, and one which was determined to
challenge the 'Fed'. The South Wales Miners' Industrial Union was
established in the new Taff-Merthyr colliery near Bedlinog in
December 1926, in the wake of the success of George Spencer's union
in Nottinghamshire. By April 1927, it had twenty-seven lodges and
was employing four full-time officials. The new union was favoured
by the coal-owners, and it was widely believed that they financed it –
although, as the union's archives have disappeared, this is difficult to
prove. It attracted to its ranks men who were tired of the 'Bolshevism'
of Cook and his kind, but in the eyes of the devotees of the 'Fed' it
was a union of blacklegs, a weapon of the owners and a threat to
working-class solidarity.

Despite the blows suffered by the miners, they were still the most
numerous workforce in Wales, a sufficient reason for discussing their
adversity in some detail. In considering the increasing difficulties
facing the Welsh economy, however, it must be borne in mind that
other sectors of the economy were also in trouble. As a result of the
depression in the coal trade, the labour force of the port of Cardiff
decreased by 25 per cent between 1923 and 1930, and the demand for
railway workers shrank as the amount of coal carried to the docks
declined. The fall in the purchasing power of the inhabitants of the
mining valleys was a severe blow to the woollen mills of the Teifi
valley and to holiday resorts such as the western seaside towns and the
spas of mid-Wales. 'After 1926,' it was said, 'Llanwrtyd was never the
same.' But these were small losses in employment compared with the
contraction in the iron and steel industry. Cyfarthfa closed in 1921,
Blaenafon in 1922, Ebbw Vale in 1929 and the greater part of Dowlais
in 1930; by 1930, the iron industry had almost completely disappeared
from northern Glamorgan and Monmouthshire. In the north-eastern
part of the south Wales coalfield – the birthplace of the Industrial
Revolution – the combination of pit and foundry closures led to
appalling levels of unemployment: in Brynmawr, in the furthest
corner of Breconshire, unemployment among insured males was as
high as 90 per cent. In the western part of the coalfield, however, the

steel industry enjoyed considerable prosperity; the area had fifteen steelworks in the 1920s, mainly supplying the tinplate industry. The demand for tinplate remained relatively stable throughout the decade, although the price of a box of plates declined sharply – from 59s. 10d. in 1920 to 18s. 2d. in 1928.

The slate industry also had a period of prosperity, particularly in the years immediately following the war. As a result of the building boom, the number of quarrymen in Gwynedd rose from 6,604 in 1919 to 9,525 in 1922. Thereafter, the industry was hit by competition from overseas slate and cheap tiles. Wages declined; although unemployment rates were never as high in the quarries as they were in the collieries, the quarrymen's wages – about 8s. 6d. a day in 1929 – were lower than those of the miners. But they were generous compared with those of farm labourers, who were lucky, by 1929, if they received £1 10s. a week. This was probably all their employers could afford, for the prices of agricultural produce halved between 1920 and 1929.

With depression affecting almost every part of the economy, it is not surprising that the 1920s are considered to be a time of tribulation in the history of Wales. This was not the entire story, for there were those in Wales for whom the decade was one of prosperity. Although unemployment reached distressing heights, there were more people in work than were out of work, and as prices fell the purchasing power of those with a stable income rose year by year. School teachers could afford holidays abroad, and there was much indulgence in the new entertainments of the age. A great deal was achieved in the field of social reform, for the governments of the 1920s were not as reactionary as is sometimes believed. Indeed, if statistics are judiciously selected, the period can be portrayed as an 'Age of Improvement', although the improvement was less apparent in Wales than in other, more favoured, parts of the kingdom. The mortality rate fell sharply, proof of the growing success of the fight against fatal diseases; although tuberculosis continued to be a cruel foe, the number who died from it declined by 25 per cent between 1920 and 1930. There was a particularly striking decrease in infant mortality. In 1911, the death rate among infants was 135 in every 1,000 births; in 1930, the figure was sixty-seven in every 1,000. Side by side with that improvement – and, to some extent, as a result of it – was the reduction in the size of families, one of the most important social developments of the twentieth century. The tendency to have fewer children was already apparent among middle-class families in the later decades of the nineteenth century. By the 1920s, the working class was following their example, although the exact mechanics of the process are unclear. In 1921, twenty-five children were born for every 1,000 of the inhabitants of Wales; in 1931, the rate was 16.7 per 1,000, and by then a family of a dozen and more was increasingly uncommon. This change had far-reaching effects: as the resources and time of the parents were divided among fewer children, the standard of child care rose – this was one of the reasons for the fall in the infant mortality rate; as homes were no longer awash with children, they could be arranged more comfortably and sedately – a factor of importance in the *embourgeoisement* of the working class. Above all, smaller families meant a new freedom for women. The number of women exhausted by carrying and rearing children declined rapidly; the reduction in the proportion of a woman's life spent in rearing a family meant that many women were free of child care by the time they reached early middle age, a change which had profound social implications.

The 1920s were a particularly notable period in the history of the rights of women. Women were appointed to the bench of magistrates for the first time in 1920 and were first called to the bar in 1922; they received the vote on equal terms with men in 1928, and Margaret Bondfield became the first woman member of the cabinet in 1929. In 1923, adultery by a husband was adjudged to be as culpable as adultery by a wife; in 1924 the rights of a mother over her child were acknowledged to be equal to those of a father, and in 1926 it was confirmed that a woman had the same rights to property as a man. The status of women was also advanced by the demise of the fussy, pampered image of femininity which had been promoted in the Victorian era. That image had received a heavy blow during the First World War; it was further dented by the permissiveness prevalent in some circles in the 1920s, and by Freud's claim that everyone experienced sexual passion. Clothes were the most obvious symbol of changing mores: by 1924, skirts ended above the knee, a startling change in view of the fact that showing the ankle was considered improper ten years earlier.

Yet too much should not be claimed; despite their prominence in English novels, the bright young things were not numerous in the Wales of the 1920s. The new freedom only benefited Welshwomen from wealthy and progressive backgrounds, for the Welsh, industrial and rural, were socially very conservative. Most members of the Welsh middle class were very prim and proper, as is demonstrated by the reluctance of many husbands to permit their wives to meet the talented musician Morfydd Llwyn Owen, who as the wife of Freud's biographer, Ernest Jones, was considered to be besmirched by the filth emanating from Vienna. Furthermore, movements such as the Women's Institute – which originated in Llanfairpwll in 1915 and which spread rapidly in the 1920s – and successful magazines such as *Woman*, emphasized that women should devote their main energies to the home. Above all, despite the improvement in the legal status of women, there was no corresponding improvement in their economic status. Their earnings were about half those of men and they had far less opportunity to gain promotion. In the Wales of the 1920s, there was virtually no increase in the proportion of women at work. Many employers – education authorities, for example – dismissed women when they married, a practice endorsed by most of the trade unions. Nevertheless, there was a revolution in progress: by the end of the 1920s, respectable females were dancing the Charleston and the Black Bottom in many a Palais de Danse, and in 1929 Amy Johnson brought off her greatest exploit – flying solo from England to Australia – a flight which made her a heroine and an inspiration to a host of women, Welsh women among them.

Adventure and technology, and mass interest in them, were one of the leading features of the 1920s. Although flying was within the reach of only a handful of the people of Wales, the greater part of the population was eager to read of the achievements of Johnson, Lindbergh and the rest. Other versions of the internal combustion engine were more accessible. Motor-cars had been seen on the streets of the larger towns since about 1890, and a car was driven for the first time through the village of Llanwenog in southern Cardiganshire in 1903. Up until the First World War, however, the car was the plaything of the rich. After the war, cars began to be manufactured for the mass market; an Austin Seven cost £225 in 1922, and £118 in 1932, a price which many members of the middle class were able to afford. By 1927, one in twenty of the families of Wales owned a car. Motor-bicycles were considerably cheaper, and until 1928 there were more motor-bicycles than cars in Wales. But the essence of the transport revolution of the 1920s was not the car or the motor-bicycle;

its essence was the bus. The bus was within the reach of almost everyone. In the 1920s, a network of bus services was created throughout Wales, services which were far more flexible than those provided by the railways. The coming of the bus was a major boost to labour mobility; henceforth it would be possible, even in railway-less districts, to accept a job a considerable distance from home. Furthermore, it was the buses, above all, which undermined the age-long isolation of the countryside; after the 1920s, it is doubtful whether Wales had any rural districts in the traditional sense. Side by side with the development of the bus services was the growing number of charabanc excursions which enabled tourists to reach the most distant places. The coming of the internal combustion engine did not merely facilitate the transport of people: the lorry and the van were quite as significant as the bus and the car. Thousands of cart drivers lost their jobs in the 1920s, as vans carried goods to every corner of the land. As lorries were able to carry bricks and tiles to the most remote locations, evidence of local styles of architecture vanished. 'By 1930,' wrote Peter Smith, 'the last vestiges of real regional architecture . . . had finally been destroyed.'

Concurrent with the revolution in transport was the revolution in energy. In 1885, Cardiff became the first town in Wales to have electricity, the supply being provided by a private company licensed by the local council. By the First World War, a number of towns had followed Cardiff's example and there were plans to produce hydro-electricity in the mountains of Snowdonia. Until 1914, electricity was used mainly to light streets and drive trolley buses, although industrial-ists were increasingly appreciative of its advantages. There were only 3,726 consumers of electricity in Cardiff in 1914, for very few private houses were connected to the supply. The industry expanded rapidly after the war: by the mid-1920s, there were dozens of electricity companies in Wales and their standards varied greatly. In 1926, the government stepped into the field by setting up the Central Electricity Board, a body which was given the responsibility of creating a grid to coordinate the service. When the grid was completed in 1933, about half the houses in Wales had electricity. They were almost all in urban areas; electricity from the grid was exceptional in the countryside before the middle of the twentieth century, although a number of villages had their own schemes, some of which were disturbingly primitive. In the 1920s, only the wealthy could take advantage of the service; to them, electrical implements were a great convenience, particularly in view of the increasing reluctance of girls to enter domestic service. Great as was the importance of electricity in the domestic sphere, its advent was even more significant in the sphere of industry. With the completion of the grid, production processes were freed from dependence on steam power. Consequently, it was no longer necessary to locate industry in the coalfields. Industrialists hastened to build factories in the lush surroundings of southern England, a development which hindered efforts to revive the Welsh economy.

Of all the novelties of the 1920s, the one to receive the warmest welcome was the film. Although moving pictures had been shown in public since 1894, the explosive growth of the cinema belongs to the years immediately after the First World War. By the mid-1920s, more than half the population of Britain went to the 'pictures' at least once a week. The new entertainment was an important factor in lessening the appeal of the public house – for the price of a pint of beer, it was possible to watch three hours of films. The vast majority of the films came from the United States, and they were silent until 1927, when talkies were first introduced. The popularity of the cinema was a cause of concern to the moralists and the highbrow, as numerous comments in the Welsh denominational press bear witness. Much of what was shown had little to recommend it; it is unlikely that there was much substance to *We're All Gamblers* and *Eager Lips* – the entertainment provided at the Palladium in Aberystwyth in January 1927. But although most films offered little beyond romantic escapism, there was something quite virtuous about the values they upheld, and the best films – Charlie Chaplin's, for example – were splendid works of art.

The popularity of the cinema meant that the entire population of the kingdom was drawn into the same pattern of entertainment, for the same films were shown in Caernarfon as in Ipswich or Dundee. The growing appeal of London newspapers, which, with the advent of the van, had become available almost everywhere in Wales, encouraged a similar tendency. In the 1920s, there was a revolution in the format of popular papers and at the end of the decade a fierce fight took place between them, with gifts being offered to new readers. As with the cinema, this was a field in which the Welsh language could not compete, and it is likely that it was in the 1920s that most Welsh speakers became more accustomed to read English than Welsh.

There was a possibility that they would also become more accustomed to hearing English, for it was in that decade that broadcasting was born. However, as broadcasting was a state monopoly, Welsh people concerned about their language could press for a Welsh broadcasting service, an option which was not open to them in the case of films or the press. Broadcasting in Britain was begun in 1920 by the companies manufacturing 'wireless telephones'. Confronted by the danger of chaos on the sound waves – a danger which was already a reality in the United States – the government granted a licence to the British Broadcasting Company in 1922 to broadcast from eight radio stations. One of these was at Cardiff, where the station began its work on 13 February 1923. In the beginning, broadcasts were listened to in halls or vestries, although more ardent spirits assembled their own 'crystal sets'. Box radios soon developed; by the beginning of the 1930s, the cheapest of these could be bought for a few pounds and in addition the licence cost ten shillings. As costs were relatively high, the wireless was out of the reach of a large number of the people of Wales: about one family in eight had a set in 1927, a proportion which had risen to five in every eight by 1939. John Reith, the head of the British Broadcasting Company (and from 1927 to 1938 the Director-General of the British Broadcasting Corporation) was the architect of the new service. A son of the manse and a man of strong convictions, he believed that the BBC's role was to enlighten the people, to elevate their taste and to uphold public morality. Reith's goal was a 'national' service within the reach of the entire population; although he was a patriotic Scot, implicit in his plans was the spreading of the accent, values and attitudes of the London upper-middle class to every corner of the kingdom.

It is difficult now to appreciate the thrill of hearing for the first time the sounds coming out of the ether and the huge enjoyment of the early radio listeners as new worlds opened up before them. In 1923, the service was obtainable only in the Cardiff area and in those parts of the north-east which were within the range of the Manchester transmitter. Broadcasting from Swansea began in 1924, and the following year a transmitter was built in Daventry which was powerful enough to reach most of the homes of the kingdom. Daventry transmitted the 'national' service. Cardiff produced much of its own material; initially, the Swansea studio was responsible for a considerable amount of the broadcasts of the Swansea transmitter, but by 1929

Swansea's transmissions were virtually identical to those of Cardiff. Listeners in the Cardiff area heard an occasional song in Welsh and sometimes a talk in the language, but the only Welsh-language material which was heard regularly in the rest of the country was a programme broadcast, from 1927 onwards, by Radio Éireann. The BBC had no intention of providing a special service for Wales; Cardiff was the headquarters of the West Region (the 'kingdom of King Arthur' as one of the corporation's officials once injudiciously called it) and initially its broadcasting staff included no natives of Wales. The Englishness of the BBC caused concern to devotees of the Welsh language. It gave rise to protests by Cylch Dewi (the Circle of St David), a patriotic group in Cardiff led by the University of Wales and by the Union of Welsh Societies. E. R. Appleton, the head of the Cardiff station, responded by declaring that it was natural to restrict broadcasting to the official language, and that it would be wrong to yield to extremists who were trying to force Welsh on the listeners. This was a battle which would become more intense in subsequent years; it was among the most important battles in the history of the language.

Protests over the policy of the BBC were one aspect of an increasing concern about the Welsh language. It was spoken by 977,366 of the inhabitants of Wales in 1921 and by 922,092 in 1931, and during the decade the number of Welsh monoglots fell from 155,989 to 97,932. The decline in the percentage able to speak Welsh was slight (from 37.1 to 36.8), partly because the census of 1921 had been held in the summer and did not therefore reflect fully the strength of the language in the holiday resorts. Yet the decline of Welsh was obvious, especially in the industrial areas: in the Rhondda in 1921 only 27 per cent of the children under five spoke the language, although 64 per cent of those over sixty-five had a knowledge of it. It was anxiety about the Welshness of the younger generation which inspired Ifan ab Owen Edwards in 1922 to establish Urdd Gobaith Cymru (the Welsh League of Youth), a movement which had fifty thousand members by 1934. The Urdd, with its camps, its sports, its magazines and its sections for different age groups, is the most obvious evidence that there was between the wars a hunger and thirst for Welshness.

A youth movement alone, however, was not enough; the Welsh language needed a proper place in the educational system. This was the theme of *Welsh in Education and Life*, a report published by the

Board of Education in 1927. To a large extent, it was the work of
W. J. Gruffydd, the Professor of Welsh at Cardiff, and it was characterized by an 'almost religious fervour'. Welsh had been recognized as a
school subject in 1889; thereafter, stalwart efforts were made to win a
larger place for the language in the educational system, particularly
under the leadership of Owen M. Edwards, the Chief Inspector of
Schools for Wales from 1909 until 1920. Nevertheless, the policies of
the authorities were undefined, the training of the teachers was
inadequate and the amount and variety of Welsh-language teaching
material were insufficient. The 1927 report aimed at remedying these
failings. Schemes for the teaching of Welsh were recommended, varying according to the linguistic character of the district, and the report
contained a host of suggestions for making the teaching more effective.
The recommendations directed at the Board of Education were carried
out but the local authorities were reluctant to act, partly because of
the fears of many Welsh parents that emphasis on Welsh would make
it difficult for their children to learn English. By the 1930s, however,
Welsh had become the chief medium of instruction in the elementary
schools of the Welsh-speaking areas, at least in the north and in Cardiganshire. Success was more limited in areas which were linguistically
mixed, and there was hardly any advance in the largely anglicized areas,
while the secondary schools continued to be fortresses of Englishness.

The 1927 report made little mention of the official status of Welsh,
for hardly anyone, apart from the members of the new Welsh
Nationalist Party, had any conception of Welsh language sovereignty.
Indeed, in the 1920s, Welsh speakers were still people 'under the
hatches', a people being imbued with self-contempt. That decade,
however, saw the emergence of a new phenomenon – middle-class
Welsh speakers confident in their Welshness. This happened
principally in Cardiff, with W. J. Gruffydd in the van. (Gruffydd and
his associates could often be extremely remote from the experiences
of the majority of the Welsh people. '1926 will be a black year for
Wales,' wrote Gruffydd, just after the failure of the General Strike;
'we had hardly accustomed ourselves to the loss of Principal Rees
when we heard of the death of Principal J. H. Davies.') Gruffydd,
with his quarterly, *Y Llenor* (The Man of Letters), was chiefly
responsible for the fact that the 1920s were years of considerable
achievement in Welsh literature. *Y Llenor* was launched in 1922; it
published the poems of R. Williams Parry, the essays of Saunders

Lewis and R. T. Jenkins, the short stories of Kate Roberts and the reviews of G. J. Williams – in addition to the editor's own pithy comments. Furthermore, hardly a year went by without the appearance of a substantial work on some aspect of the Welsh language and its literature – G. J. Williams's exciting researches on Iolo Morganwg, for example, and Henry Lewis's editions of the prose works of the Middle Ages, and that influential and controversial book *Orgraff yr Iaith Gymraeg* (The Orthography of the Welsh Language, 1928).

While the Welsh-language literary tradition was going from strength to strength, a school of Anglo-Welsh writers arose, although its full flowering did not occur until the following decade. Rhys Davies published his first novel in 1927, and a string of volumes by Caradoc Evans appeared in the 1920s. Caradoc was 'the father of the Anglo-Welsh'; with him, as Gwyn Jones put it, 'the war-horn was blown, the gauntlet thrown down, the gates of the temple shattered . . . The Anglo-Welsh had arrived . . . with the maximum of offence and the maximum of effect.' Caradoc was a bitter man, soured by his experiences as a child in Rhydlewis, Cardiganshire, and as an assistant in drapery shops in Carmarthen and London. He believed that prejudice, philistinism and sexual guilt were the foundations of the 'Welsh way of life'. He said so without any attempt at self-restraint, to the great entertainment of English readers and to the great fury of the Welsh. He delighted in being the chief bogeyman of his people; to him may be attributed the unwillingness of the Welsh-speaking Welsh, for a generation and more, to warm to Anglo-Welsh literature. He published his first book, *My People*, in 1915, 'a book,' to quote Gwyn Jones again, 'which for Welshmen added a final horror to war as surely as *My Neighbours* in 1919 and *Taffy* in 1923 robbed them of the peace that should have followed'.

What infuriated Caradoc more than anything was Nonconformity and the chapel tradition. By the 1920s, there was a growing tendency to dwell on the shortcomings of that tradition. Indeed, although it was only Caradoc who took the matter to extremes, finding fault with the religion of the Welsh of previous generations was one of the favourite diversions of the Welsh-speaking intellectuals of the decade. W. J. Gruffydd was in the lead yet again. He, like most of his fellow intellectuals, professed a liberal theology. That could be unmindful of older, orthodox beliefs, a fact which gave rise to much perplexity, particularly among the Calvinistic Methodists with their High Calvinist Confession of Faith. Thomas Nevin Williams (Tom Nefyn) was convicted of heresy in 1928, and his case caused a great deal of heart-searching within the denomination. As R. Tudur Jones has demonstrated, the 1920s was a period of intensive self-examination among the religious leaders of Wales, a time when many of them were 'struggling desperately for a clearer vision'. They knew that religion was no longer as central an element in the life of the Welsh people as it had been. Although there was little decline in the membership of the main denominations during the decade, there was a substantial decline in the size of congregations and in the numbers attending Sunday school, and a noticeable contraction in the group classed as 'hearers'. As the disestablishment campaign had come to an end, and as the Liberal party was in decline, political Nonconformity was left directionless, and it was frequently asserted that the 'Nonconformist Conscience' had been banished from public life. Many were drawn to socialism; some of them considered socialism to be a totally materialistic creed which denied the need for a personal God. By the 1920s, there were, even among prominent Welsh-speakers, those who were prepared to acknowledge, at least in private, that they were agnostics. The attitude the denominations had taken to the war had undermined the credibility of the moral directives of religious bodies. New recreations were attracting many who had previously been content with the activities organized under the aegis of the chapel, recreations which were threatening that object of veneration, the Welsh Sabbath.

Religious leaders made heroic efforts to resist the tide; indeed, it is unlikely that there has ever been in Wales more talented and dedicated ministers than those who laboured in the vineyard between the wars. *Y Geiriadur Beiblaidd* (The Biblical Dictionary) was published between 1924 and 1926, a monument to Welsh scriptural scholarship. There were ministers who sought to make amends for the clerical recruiters by involving themselves in the League of Nations Union or the peace movement. Others were active in ecumenical ventures, supporting Urdd y Deyrnas (the Order of the Kingdom) and its periodical, *Yr Efrydydd* (The Student). The Social Gospel won numerous advocates, and many were drawn to the activities of the Welsh School for Social Service and to those of the Christian Order in Politics, Economics and Citizenship (COPEC) – 'the most important religious movement since the Methodist Revival', according to *The Welsh Outlook*. These developments were not universally welcomed. In some circles, there was a strong desire to return to the old orthodoxy. Sabbath-breaking golfers were attacked at Aberdyfi in 1927 and many chapels yearned to return to the evangelical tradition; there were also signs of neo-Calvinism, a development promoted by the works of Karl Barth, a hero in some theological circles in Wales by the end of the decade. Despite the vitality of the churches, their efforts were hindered by lack of money, particularly in the coalfield; by 1930 the severity of the depression caused many congregations to be unable to afford to maintain a minister.

Financial problems also hindered the development of education. Because of the expense involved, some of the recommendations of the Fisher Act were not carried out, and the Burnham Scale caused numerous difficulties in the rural counties; many children were deprived of secondary education by the lack of maintenance grants, and the authorities were slow to tackle the problem of dilapidated school buildings. Nevertheless, the 1920s were an important period in the history of education in Wales. In 1926, the Haddow Report recommended that every child should attend a secondary school. This involved the abandonment of the notion which had been a ruling principle in educational policy throughout the years – that the greater part of the population should not be provided with anything beyond elementary schooling.

Although the recommendations of the Haddow Report were not fully carried out until after the Second World War, the years following the First World War saw a striking growth in numbers attending secondary schools in Wales – from 24,000 in 1918 to 40,000 in 1930. For a generation and more, the Welsh people had looked upon education as a way of enabling their children to escape from the restraints of the working class; that escape route was embraced with increasing enthusiasm as the depression deepened. A career in teaching had a particular appeal and by the end of the 1920s Wales was over-producing teachers on a vast scale. In 1928, nine out of every ten of the students trained in Bangor Normal College were obliged to seek work east of Offa's Dyke and the resulting braindrain proved injurious to Wales. The desire for teaching posts in Wales was so strong that candidates were willing to pay for them. 'There are a number of councillors,' W. J. Gruffydd asserted in 1933, 'who are living lavishly on the money they have received for their votes.' Despite such failings, education in Wales in the 1920s had substantial virtues. Considerations of class were not as dominant as they were in England. The private sector was insignificant in Wales. Of Welsh secondary school pupils, 63 per cent were not obliged to pay fees; the figure was 43 per cent in England. Of the students attending the University of Wales, 87 per cent had been educated in state elementary schools; the corresponding figure in English universities was 38 per cent. Despite its virtues, the Welsh system was under continuing pressure to conform to that of England. English preconceptions hindered plans to establish 'comprehensive' secondary schools in the rural areas of Wales and every attempt to create a National Education Council for Wales ended in failure.

Despite severe financial difficulties, the 1920s was a decade of considerable progress at the university level. The University of Wales had 2,500 students by the end of the decade, double the number it had had in 1913, and nine out of every ten were Welsh. A commission on the University was set up in 1916 under the chairmanship of Viscount Haldane. The commission approved of the federal system but argued in favour of greater freedom for individual colleges. It endorsed the plan to establish a University College at Swansea, a plan successfully carried out in 1920. There was more difficulty over the commission's recommendations concerning medical education, and the Welsh School of Medicine did not receive its charter until 1931. The University of Wales Press and the Board of Celtic Studies, institutions which were to be central to the growth of Welsh scholarship, also sprang from the Haldane Commission's recommendations. The 1920s were particularly exciting at Aberystwyth. Mainly through the generosity of the Davies family of Llandinam and Gregynog, chairs were created for T. Gwynn Jones, T. H. Parry-Williams, A. E. Zimmern and H. J. Fleure, as well as the post of Music Director in Wales for Walford Davies. With the help of Lawrence Philipps (Baron Milford), the Welsh Plant Breeding Station was established, the only scholarly institution in Wales to win world-wide recognition. It was headed by that man of genius, R. G. Stapledon, a scholar with a burning desire to transform the grasses of Wales and of the world. In 1924, A. W. Ashby came to Aberystwyth, and in 1929 the college appointed him Professor of Agricultural Economics; he also had a burning desire – to analyse the rural economy and to help Welsh farmers to make the most of their circumstances.

This research in agriculture, and in other fields, is proof of a desire among academics to have a close relationship with the society around them. That wish had found expression since 1910 through the colleges' tutorial classes, which after the war were organized under the University Extension Board. The University became aware of its responsibilities in this field at a time when adult education was becoming a controversial subject. The supporters of the Central Labour College maintained that traditional education was one of the weapons of the governing class, and that the class struggle presupposed an intellectual struggle. Throughout the 1920s, there was conflict between the supporters of this Marxist argument and those who sought to provide a more conventional education through the Extra-Mural Departments of the University and the Workers' Education Association. The Marxists were so eloquent that they convinced many people that adult education was inherently subversive, an idea which the *Western Mail* spread with avidity. The Central Labour College closed in 1929 because of the difficulties facing its patrons – the South Wales Miners' Federation and the National Union of Railwaymen – but part of its work continued through the Communist party and the miners' libraries. At the same time, the WEA went from strength to strength. Thomas Jones of Rhymni considered its work to be a powerful bulwark against Bolshevism. In 1927, Jones was instrumental in establishing Coleg Harlech, with the aim of building upon the work of the WEA; it was popularly known as 'the college of the second chance', although it is doubtful whether the 350 and more students who studied there between 1927 and 1939 had ever been offered a first chance.

Tom Jones succeeded in combining his efforts to lead the progressives of Wales along constructive paths with his post as deputy secretary to the cabinet. That post gave him considerable influence, particularly during Baldwin's second administration (1924–9). To those on the left, it was a despicably reactionary administration. Yet, despite its behaviour in 1926, its treatment of bodies such as the Bedwellte Board of Guardians and its decision in 1927 to curb the trade unions, the government of 1924–9 was not wholly unconstructive. Neville Chamberlain, the Minister of Health, was responsible for more than twenty parliamentary measures which were among the most important foundations of the welfare state. Pensions for widows and orphans were introduced in 1925, and in 1929 the Poor Law system was dismantled by giving responsibility for the needy to the Public Assistance Committees of the county councils and county borough councils.

Nevertheless, as its term was drawing to a close, Baldwin's government looked increasingly uninspiring. In the election campaign of 1929, the Conservatives put forward no new policies; in particular, they gave the impression that they were indifferent to the chief problem of the age – the million and more who were unemployed. In the campaign, the Labour party put forward an exalted argument for the morality of socialism, but it had little to say about what it would do if it were not granted full power. The marvel of the election was the Liberal campaign. David Lloyd George became leader of the party on the resignation of Asquith in 1926 and under his direction an exciting series of policies was formulated, much to the distress of the faint-hearted among the Liberals. In their bold manifesto, *We Can Conquer Unemployment*, the Liberals offered salvation through expenditure on public works – roads, houses, electricity, telephones, railways – financed by loans. The programme was proof that Lloyd George was one of the few politicians who had understood the significance of the ideas which John Maynard Keynes was developing, ideas which were given a theoretical basis in Keynes's book *A General Theory of Employment, Interest and Money* (1936). With the assistance of Lloyd George's political fund, the Liberals fought over five hundred seats, among them every seat in Wales with the exception of Bedwellte. With the Conservatives fielding thirty-six candidates, the Liberals thirty-five, Labour thirty-four, the Communists three and Plaid Genedlaethol Cymru one, Wales was awash with aspiring M Ps. The general election of 1929 was the second in the history of Wales in which no member was returned unopposed (the election of January 1910 was the first), and the first in which women and men had the same voting rights; indeed, as a result of the act of 1928, women constituted the majority of the voters in every constituency in Wales outside the coalfield.

The result of the general election of 1929 was a disappointment to Lloyd George. Although the Liberals received almost a quarter of the British vote, they won less than a tenth of the seats in the House of Commons. The new House contained 288 Labour M Ps, 260 Conservatives and fifty-nine Liberals; as Baldwin could not contemplate a coalition with Lloyd George, Labour had an opportunity to form a government for a second time. In Wales, it was the Conservatives who suffered from the weaknesses of the electoral system: they received almost a quarter of the votes cast, but their candidate in Monmouth was the only one elected. Ten Liberals were elected, among them Lloyd George, his son, his daughter and his son's brother-in-law. Megan Lloyd George, the MP for Anglesey, was the first woman to represent a Welsh constituency; since 1929, three others have been elected, a record which is among the worst in Europe. The Labour party won twenty-five Welsh seats, among them all the coalfield seats, all the seats in the southern ports and also the partly industrialized seats of Carmarthen, Brecon and Radnor, and Wrexham. Ramsay MacDonald abandoned Aberafan for a more tractable constituency in County Durham. Among the new Labour members was Aneurin Bevan, a thirty-one-year-old miner from Tredegar, the most brilliant product of the Welsh Labour movement. Support for the Communists was weak, other than in Rhondda East, where Arthur Horner polled 15 per cent of the vote. Support for Plaid Genedlaethol Cymru was even weaker, with its candidate at Caernarfon, Lewis Valentine, receiving a mere 609 votes.

The history of the second Labour government is controversial and woeful. Some of its achievements were striking: there was substance to its foreign and colonial policies; it was responsible for relaxing the strictness of the rules relating to unemployment benefit; it restricted the miners' hours of work to seven and a half a day; it launched a slum-clearance programme; it prepared schemes for paying guaranteed prices for agricultural produce. But it failed in its attempts to tackle the problem of unemployment. The Labour party believed that socialism was the answer, but as it lacked a parliamentary majority it did not attempt to implement socialist policies, much to the bitterness of those who belonged to the ILP tradition. J. H. Thomas, the minister responsible for employment, proved a failure, and his deputy, Oswald Mosley, was unable to persuade the party to adopt policies similar to those advocated by Lloyd George. During the government's term of office, the number of insured workers unemployed in Britain rose from 1,250,000 to 2,725,000. By 1931, even the privileged regions of south-east England were suffering, as unemployment became rampant throughout the capitalist world.

The economic crisis of the 1930s had its origins in the New York crash of October 1929, a disaster which exposed the inequities of the international financial system. It was the export industries – agriculture, coal, iron and steel, cotton, shipbuilding – which suffered worst. In Wales, where the inhabitants of the industrial areas were already experiencing structural unemployment, the strike brought cyclical unemployment as an additional burden. When the Labour government was formed in June 1929, unemployment among Welsh male insured workers stood at 19 per cent; when the government fell in August 1931, it was 35 per cent.

It was the cost of maintaining the unemployed which led to the government's fall. During the summer of 1931, when the economies of Austria and Germany were tottering, two reports were published which suggested that Britain's financial state was precarious in the extreme. With investors rushing to withdraw their money from London, it was argued that the only salvation lay in the curtailment of government spending, in particular its spending on the maintenance of the unemployed. The cabinet was divided on the issue, with ten members opposing cuts in benefit and eleven supporting them. MacDonald, the Prime Minister, offered the resignation of his government, but he was persuaded to continue in office as the head of a cabinet containing four members of the Labour party, four Conservatives and two Liberals. The new government was endorsed enthusiastically by the entire Conservative party, and rather more guardedly by the Liberals. (Lloyd George was seriously ill in August 1931 and therefore had no part in its establishment.) Only about fifteen Labour MPs followed MacDonald. The rest regrouped in opposition under the leadership of Arthur Henderson. Thus was the National government created – the result of MacDonald's patriotism according to the right; the result of his treachery, according to the left.

The new government immediately proceeded to cut unemployment benefit. The maximum weekly payment to a man with a wife and two children was reduced from 30s. to 27s. 3d.; in addition, payments to wives based upon the contributions they had made prior to marriage were abolished, a decision which affected 134,000 of the women of Britain. But to the unemployed, the most offensive blow was the new rule relating to means testing, a rule which meant that the assets of a claimant who had been out of work for more than six months were closely examined; it also meant that the income of any relation living under the same roof as the claimant – his son, his daughter, or a parent on a pension – was taken into account in determining his level of benefit. Thus, hundreds of thousands of skilled and respectable workers came face to face with attitudes and treatment characteristic of the old Poor Law. It was this humiliation, above all, which made the 1930s such a distressful period for the unemployed.

Despite the National government's curtailment of employment benefit and its reduction of the wages of everyone working in the public sector, the pound continued to fall. At the end of September 1931, Britain abandoned the Gold Standard; thus was sacrificed the very thing which the destruction of the Labour government was intended to save. As the vast majority of the supporters of the National government were Conservatives, they were in a position to demand a general election. With the Labour party reeling from shock, the Conservatives could hope for a great victory, one which would allow them to introduce duties on imports, the Tories' favourite answer to the problems of the economy. This emphasis upon protection caused a dilemma for the Liberals, the traditional guardians of Free Trade. By the general election of October 1931, they had split into three factions: the followers of John Simon, who were Conservatives to all intents and purposes; the followers of Herbert Samuel, who were prepared to support the National government as long as it adhered to Free Trade; and the followers of Lloyd George, who considered the election a dirty Tory trick. In the election, the supporters of the National government won 554 seats: the Conservatives, 472; the followers of MacDonald (National Labour), thirteen; the Simonites (National Liberal), thirty-five; the Samuelites, thirty-three. Of the opposition parties, Labour won fifty-two seats (including those of the ILP) and the Lloyd George Liberals four. With such a majority, the members of the National government could feel that they had a complete mandate and that socialism in Britain had been utterly defeated. Such a view was mistaken; although the number of Labour MPs decreased from 288 to fifty-two, the decline in the proportion voting for the party – from 37 per cent in 1929 to 31 per cent in 1931 – was by no means as steep. As the Labour party, even in the excruciating circumstances of 1931, had retained the support of a third of the British voters, its supporters were not without hope for the future. The real victim of the events of 1931 was the Liberal party: its various factions received the support of about 10 per cent of British voters, and every sign suggested that the party was facing rapid extinction.

The results in Wales were very different. There, the successful candidates consisted of sixteen Labour MPs (including one member of the ILP), eleven Liberals (four National Liberals, five Samuelites

and four Lloyd George Liberals), six Conservatives and one member
of the National Labour party. Despite the decrease in the number of
Labour representatives, there was an increase in the proportion of the
electorate voting for the party. Labour won all the coalfield constituencies; indeed, following the general election of 1931, the block of
sixteen seats stretching from Llanelli to Pontypool was by far the
largest of the party's strongholds. Yet, although almost a third of the
Labour representatives in the House of Commons between 1931 and
1935 represented Welsh constituencies, the leadership of the party
during that period included hardly any Welsh MPs. This can largely
be attributed to the fact that a safe seat in the coalfield was usually a
reward for lengthy service to trade-unionism – to the South Wales
Miners' Federation almost without exception. For men such as George
Daggar, the MP for Abertyleri, election to parliament was not the
first step in a career at Westminster but rather an episode in a career
of service to one's locality and its people.

There was an urgent need for such service, for the early years of
the National government were a distressing period for the industrial
communities of Wales. During the government's first year of office,
unemployment spiralled out of control. As has already been noted, it
reached its zenith in August 1932, when 42.8 per cent of insured
Welsh males were unemployed. In that month, there were fourteen
districts in Wales where over half the insured males were without
work. In proportional terms, unemployment was at its highest at
Brymbo, near Wrexham; the steelworks there closed in 1930 and 90
per cent of the insured workforce of 2,530 was on the dole. In terms
of numbers, however, the hardest-hit community was that of Merthyr
Tydfil, with its 13,000 unemployed. As unemployment was increasing
throughout the kingdom, the government could take the view that
the crisis was the consequence of the world-wide slump and that
matters would improve when trade revived. There was substance to
their optimism. Unemployment in Britain as a whole rose to 26.9 per
cent among insured males in September 1932; it fell rapidly in the
mid-1930s, and by 1936 male unemployment in south-east England
was only 6.2 per cent. Indeed, in Britain as a whole, the experience of
depression was by no means as severe as it was in the United States
and in Germany. In the one country the depression led to Franklin
Roosevelt's 'New Deal', and in the other to the rise of Nazism,
while Britain made do with governments led in turn by Baldwin

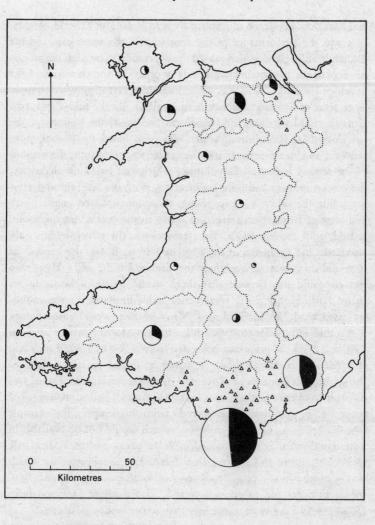

and MacDonald – 'zero multiplied by zero', to quote Oswald Mosley.

It was the performance of the economy in the south-east and the midlands of England which caused the depression to be a less nightmarish experience in Britain than it was in others of the countries of the developed world. There was no comparable revival in Wales, nor in large areas of Scotland and northern England. By the mid-1930s, two Britains could be discerned: the north and west, the regions of the first Industrial Revolution, which had been based upon coal, iron, railways and steam power; and the centre and the south, the regions of the second Industrial Revolution, which was based on electricity, the motor industry and light engineering. With the one region declining while the other was prospering, those unemployed in the north and west of Britain were urged to move to the centre and the south; indeed, until the late 1930s, 'transference' was the government's only answer to the problems of the depressed areas. But as the growth of new industry was slower than the decline of the old, those who moved could not be sure that there would be work available for them. Furthermore, there were considerable limitations upon mobility, particularly for married men. Many of them were house-owners; it was thus impossible to leave a place such as Maerdy, where between 1920 and 1935 the price of a house fell from £350 to £50; if they had children in secondary school, it would be foolish to move them to the suburbs of London or Coventry, where secondary education was difficult to obtain; in their own localities, families had some degree of protection against destitution – credit from shopkeepers, for example (the Co-op, in particular) – assistance which would not be available in a strange district. Some remained in Wales because of their allegiance to Welsh culture and because they feared the Cambrophobia which was common in the prosperous areas of south-eastern England. 'No, they won't get me to go to England,' said a native of Ferndale in 1938. 'I would prefer to starve here than starve among strangers.'

Despite these factors, there was a huge outflow from Wales in the wake of the depression. Between 1921 and 1925, the population of Wales rose from 2,656,474 to 2,736,800; by mid-1939 it had fallen to 2,487,000, a decrease of 249,800 in fourteen years. As the Welsh population experienced a natural growth of 140,171 during those years, the net loss through emigration was 389,971. In the 1930s, there was a decrease in the population of every Welsh county except Flintshire. (Flintshire was saved from the fate of the others by Deeside's varied industrial base and by the prosperity of the seaside resorts.) In some of the mining valleys, the exodus was immense: 50,000 people moved from the Rhondda and 27,000 from Merthyr and, as a disproportionate number of the migrants were young adults, such a haemorrhage had a marked impact upon the age structure of the population.

Some of the migrants went to America – thirteen thousand Welsh people settled in the United States in the 1920s – and others were attracted to the countries of the Empire – South Africa, Rhodesia and Australia in particular. But the vast majority moved to England. The census of 1951 (there was no census in 1941) recorded that 649,275 people born in Wales were living in England. As has been seen, north-western England was the chief resort of nineteenth-century migrants from Wales; in the twentieth century, however, south-eastern England proved more of an attraction, partly because of the sluggishness of the Merseyside economy and partly because the bulk of the migrants came from the industrialized regions of the south rather than from the rural areas of the north. A total of 190,722 people born in Wales had settled in south-eastern England by 1951, a year in which there were more Welsh-born in Middlesex than in Lancashire, and more in Slough than in Birkenhead. It was claimed that the Rhondda accent was prevalent in Slough, the home of more than five thousand Welsh people, and the Oxford Welsh came to be a term for people very different from the members of Cymdeithas Dafydd ap Gwilym.

The twentieth-century migrants were not as eager as their predecessors to create microcosms of Wales; the Welsh activities characteristic of nineteenth-century Merseyside were not therefore replicated in such places as Dagenham or Coventry. The contrast is largely explained by the fact that most of the inter-war migrants came from the more anglicized areas of the coalfield. Those areas had a tradition of militancy, and the trade-unionism of south-eastern England was to be greatly indebted to members of the Welsh diaspora. In the 1930s, the Welsh represented one in five of those who migrated there, and the influx imposed heavy burdens on its local authorities. Indeed, the government was roused to tackle the problems of the depressed areas by fear of congestion in south-eastern England as much as by concern over the distress of the unemployed.

Despite the scale of the diaspora, the fate of hundreds of thousands of Welsh people in the 1930s was to stay at home in idleness. In 1938,

62 per cent of the unemployed of the Rhondda had been out of work for three years or more, and life on the dole was the reality for vast numbers of the people of Wales. The experience stimulated in some of them a burning desire to transform society. Yet many of those without work, particularly the long-term idle, sank into fatalism and despondency. Rising late, loitering on street corners, scratching for coal on the tips, grasping the opportunity for an occasional visit to the cinema – these were the experiences of perhaps the majority of unemployed men. The experience of their wives was worse, burdened as they were with the task of feeding the family and maintaining their self-respect on the dole money. It was argued that unemployment benefit was enough to keep a family in food, but there is evidence from the mid-1920s onwards that the health of many of the inhabitants of the coalfield was deteriorating. A report in 1928 asserted that the mothers of young children were suffering 'to an unusual extent from languor and anaemia', and it was revealed in 1935 that 14.6 per cent of the children of the Rhondda were suffering from malnutrition. In the Rhondda there was an increase of 30 per cent in the proportion dying from tuberculosis between 1932 and 1937, a period when there was a marked decline in the incidence of the disease in Britain as a whole. Cases of mental illness also increased, for in losing his work a man was deprived not only of his income but also of the social context of his life; indeed, with the work ethic so strong in the coalfield, he could come to feel that his existence lacked any purpose.

Despite the adversity, the fabric of society in the depressed areas did not collapse. There was very little vandalism or lawlessness. The family unit, although buffeted by the means test, remained strong. The working-class organizations of the coalfield proved tenacious: there were over a hundred institutes there in the 1930s, and the minds of many of the unemployed were sharpened in the institute libraries. The WEA grew rapidly: under the leadership of John Davies (formerly of *Llais Llafur*), the South Wales District was holding eight thousand classes a year by 1938. In spite of its weakness, the South Wales Miners' Federation sought to serve the unemployed, and thousands of them continued to pay their membership fees. In some areas – in Maerdy ('Little Moscow') in particular, but not there only – the Communist party offered its members a firm framework of discipline and provided bold leadership in many local campaigns. The party was mainly responsible for establishing the National

Unemployed Workers' Movement, the body which organized the hunger marches and was responsible for many protests against the means test.

Religious leaders also 'shared the anguish of their age', to quote R. Tudur Jones: Alban Davies became one of the most prominent spokesmen for the unemployed of the Rhondda, and clergymen of all denominations served on welfare committees. The Salvation Army was prominent in providing soup kitchens and the Quakers were active in Bryn-mawr and at Maes-yr-haf in the Rhondda, a settlement with which the saintly George M. Ll. Davies was closely involved. Centres like Maes-yr-haf sought to train the unemployed in new skills, a task also undertaken by the clubs organized by the National Council for Social Service. Sterling work was done by teachers, who were perhaps more aware than any other professional group of the distress of their neighbours; they raised funds to buy shoes for their pupils, organized groups under the aegis of the Urdd, the Scouts and the Guides, and took children to summer camps by the thousand. (It was after one such trip to Torquay that a girl from Penydarren prayed: 'Thy will be done in Merthyr as it is in Devon'.) The local authorities of the depressed areas faced severe challenges. All in all, they reacted constructively, seeking to maintain and improve their services, particularly in the fields of health and education; most of the schools of the coalfield supplied school meals and almost every child had free milk, and the education committees were skilful in battling against the government's attempt in 1932 drastically to increase the fees paid by secondary school pupils.

Yet, although the resolute reaction of the coalfield community should be recognized, it cannot be denied that the depression did much to undermine that community. Symptomatic of the decay was the inability of the Welsh rugby team between the wars to repeat the feats it had achieved earlier in the century, and the failure of the male-voice choirs of the eastern part of the coalfield to continue in the ascendant in the competitions at the National Eisteddfod. Although the membership of the South Wales Miners' Federation had risen to 112,743 by 1936, its power was only a shadow of what it had been in 1919. Despite their tireless efforts, the Communists were not always a constructive force; because of their insidious zealotry, the Labour party kept them at arm's length, and their convoluted policies frequently led to confusion and bitterness. The depression was a particular blow to the chapels. Their debts increased greatly and by 1938 half the Independent chapels of the coalfield were pastorless, although ministers had accepted a sharp reduction in their salaries. The culture of the chapel, which had been central to the coalfield communities, was being pushed to the margins of life.

Hand in hand with the decline in religion was the decline in the Welsh language. In the 1930s, Welsh declined rapidly in most of the eastern communities of the coalfield; after all, what was the point of passing the language on to children who would have no future except in places like Luton or Dagenham? – a consideration not unlike that which had caused multitudes of Irish to abandon their mother tongue a century earlier. Welsh held its own in the anthracite areas, partly for geographical reasons but partly also because of the relative prosperity of the western part of the coalfield.

Despite their resoluteness, the local authorities faced almost insurmountable problems, particularly as their income contracted. The rateable value of the collieries of the Rhondda decreased from £241,000 in 1925 to £24,000 in 1935, and the councils of the Rhondda and its neighbours were obliged to make large increases in the rates they levied; the ratepayers of Merthyr were paying 27s. 6d. in the £1 in 1934, a burden which added to the reluctance of industrialists to establish factories in the borough. As the councils of the coalfield were in such straits, they were unable to take advantage of the government's readiness to promote housing improvements. Between the wars, on average only thirty council houses a year were built in Merthyr and little was done to improve the housing stock. The situation was similar in the rest of the coalfield and consequently the succeeding generation inherited dire problems.

The difficulties of the local authorities were exacerbated by their obligations in the field of public assistance. It has already been noted that the Local Government Act of 1929 had transferred to the Public Assistance Committees of the counties and the county boroughs the duty of providing for the needy. Thus those who had exhausted their right to insurance had to rely upon income from the local rates. It was a matter of taxing the unemployed to maintain the unemployed, especially in places such as the Merthyr County Borough, where 55 per cent of the rates were paid by occupiers of private dwellings. Of every 27s. 6d. raised in rates at Merthyr in 1934, 15s. 5d. was paid in relief, mainly to the 13,048 inhabitants of the borough who were on the dole. The Ministry of Health complained that Merthyr was too generous in its payments; the same complaint was made against the County Borough of Swansea and the counties of Monmouth and Glamorgan, and the Public Assistance Committees of Rotherham and County Durham were suspended in 1932 because of their alleged extravagance. The Ministry's officials felt that they had authentic grounds for complaint, for the authorities in the depressed areas were prepared to ignore the means test. In the areas where the rules were scrupulously observed, only a third of those claiming the dole received the maximum permitted sum; the proportion in Merthyr was 98 per cent. Indeed, to be unemployed in the south Wales coalfield was probably a better fate than to be unemployed in the more prosperous areas of the kingdom. A Royal Commission on Merthyr Tydfil was appointed in 1935; its report provides a full picture of the financial problems of a community overwhelmed by unemployment. The commissioners recommended that Merthyr should lose its status as a county borough, but, as the county of Glamorgan was not anxious to shoulder the responsibility, the recommendation was not carried out.

Benefit for the unemployed was reorganized through the Unemployment Act of 1934 which aimed at creating a uniform system unaffected by local political pressures. The act led to the establishment of a statutory commission – the Unemployed Assistance Board – which was to be responsible for the able-bodied needy throughout the kingdom. The board was to have its own officials, wholly independent of the local Public Assistance Committees, which henceforth would be concerned only with the old and the infirm. The chief purpose of the act was to reduce expenditure on the unemployed. It was vigorously opposed in the House of Commons, particularly by Aneurin Bevan, who was incensed by its miserly and anti-democratic implications. It was also opposed in the coalfield; indeed, it was the cause of the largest protests ever seen in the history of Wales. On 3 February 1935, sixty thousand people took part in a march in the Rhondda, fifty thousand in the Cynon valley and twenty thousand in Pontypool; it is probably not an exaggeration to claim that three hundred thousand of the people of Wales took to the streets on that day. On the following day, the Assistance Board's offices at Merthyr were ransacked by an army of women and there was violence at Abertyleri and at Blaenau. Then, on 5 February, the government yielded: it refrained from carrying out the measure until November

1936, and even after that the board was obliged to tolerate a host of anomalies in the payments it administered.

The Unemployment Act of 1934 was an admission that a rapid end to long-term unemployment was unlikely. By 1934, with prosperity returning to the south-east and the midlands of England, the contrast between the flourishing regions and the depressed regions was increasingly obvious. But as the depressed regions were fairly remote from the centre and as their representatives included very few supporters of the National government, the tendency in the corridors of power in Whitehall and Westminster was to ignore them. Following the hunger marches and some forceful articles in *The Times*, the cabinet came to the conclusion that some show of interest should be made, and in March 1934 a report was commissioned on the condition of four of the worst-hit areas. In the report on south Wales, the work of Sir Wyndham Portal, it was stated that the western districts of the coalfield were fairly prosperous. Portal therefore restricted his comments to the region to the east of Port Talbot, together with Pembroke Dock, a town ravaged by unemployment following the closure of the Admiralty Dock in 1926. Although he recommended some schemes which the government could finance, Portal believed that it would be folly to insist that industrialists should establish factories in the depressed areas. Even if prosperity returned to the industries of the coalfield, the region would still have a surplus of 39,000 adult males; Portal's main recommendation was that they, or at least the youngest of them, should be transferred to the south-east or the midlands of England.

Following the publication of the reports of Portal and his colleagues, two commissioners were appointed – one for Scotland and one for England and Wales; their functions were described as 'the initiation, organization, prosecution and assistance of measures designed to facilitate the economic development and social improvement' of the depressed areas (or rather the 'special areas', as the House of Lords insisted upon calling them). Malcolm Stewart, the commissioner for England and Wales, took up his duties in January 1935, but, as the two commissioners had no more than two million pounds to spend, and as their field of activity was rigidly limited, he came to feel increasingly frustrated. He brought forward numerous schemes, including a plan for a bridge over the Severn estuary, and he sought to persuade English companies to build factories in the coalfield. His appointment was a 'fleabite', according to the *Western Mail*. When he resigned in August 1936, Stewart declared that he saw little purpose to his office 'unless it is endowed with authority to take independent action'.

By 1936, however, it was possible to discern some more hopeful signs. With the support of Baldwin, the Prime Minister, the Richard Thomas steel company began building a steel-mill at Ebbw Vale – the clearest example in the 1930s of social factors being taken into account in determining the location of industry. The South Wales Trading Estate Company was established to prepare factory sites and the Nuffield Foundation made substantial grants to promote employment schemes. King Edward VIII visited the south Wales coalfield in November 1936 and in Blaenafon he made his famous remark: 'Something must be done.' Hilary Marquand published his influential book, *South Wales Needs a Plan*, offering two plans – a blue one for the Conservatives and a red one for the Labour party. Nevertheless, at the end of 1936, when unemployment among insured males in Britain as a whole was 12.9 per cent, the equivalent figure in Wales was 28.1 per cent. There were areas such as Brynmawr, Ferndale and Blaenau where over half the workforce was still on the dole. The upsurge in the trade cycle, low interest rates, duties on imports and the boom in the building industry – the keys to the revival of the economy in the prosperous parts of England – had made very little impact upon the structural unemployment of the coalfield.

A more constructive step was taken in 1937. That was the Special Areas Amendment Act, which provided direct assistance for companies creating jobs in areas of high unemployment. The act of 1937 marks the beginning of regional economic policy in Britain, a policy to which Wales was to be much indebted. The act proved particularly advantageous to the trading estate established at Treforest near Pontypridd in 1936, an estate which was employing 2,383 people by 1939. According to the economic historian C. J. Thomas, the Commission for Special Areas was directly responsible for creating about five thousand jobs in Wales, a wholly inadequate contribution in view of the fact that 214,088 insured Welsh workers were unemployed when the commission was established. Other jobs were created as a result of the government's rearmament programme: a huge shell-producing factory was established at Bridgend and employment in the steel industry increased because of the demand for 'Anderson' shelters. There was a marked revival in the Welsh economy in 1937, with the percentage of unemployed insured males falling to 20.6 by September. It rose again in the depressed circumstances of 1938 but there was a considerable improvement in 1939. In the last month of peace – August 1939 – 15.2 per cent of the insured males of Wales were unemployed, the lowest percentage since April 1927. Nevertheless, the figure represented almost a hundred thousand people; it is difficult therefore to argue that the Welsh economy had revived by the late 1930s, particularly in view of the fact that Wales had lost at least 25,000 people a year through migration in the course of the decade.

The depression of the 1930s was not only a blow to the industrial areas. During the years 1929–33, when the depression was at its worst, it was the market in primary products which suffered most severely. There was therefore a slump in agriculture; indeed, the inability of basically agricultural countries to buy industrial goods was the key to many of the problems of the industrialized world. The grain farmers of eastern England were paralysed by a 47 per cent fall in the price of wheat, but the difficulties which confronted the producers of wool, mutton, beef, butter and cheese – the staples of Welsh agriculture – were almost as severe. In consequence, deprivation among the rural population of Wales was as bad as anything experienced by the depressed industrial areas. Clement Davies, the MP for Montgomeryshire, was astounded, while visiting the Urdd Eisteddfod in Machynlleth in 1932, by his discovery that it was the children from the rural areas, rather than those from the coalfield, who looked pale and underfed. Professor Ashby noted small farmers in the Tywi valley whose income was lower than that paid by the Public Assistance Committees. By 1933, the minimum wage of a farm labourer in the mid-Wales counties had fallen to £1 17s. a week, and there were many who received less than that, for employers in rural Wales were reluctant to obey the rules. Between 1930 and 1939, there was a decrease of 17,779 – 33 per cent – in the number of farm labourers in Wales and the ranks of rural craftsmen also contracted. As the countryside had suffered depopulation for at least three generations, the structure of its population was lopsided. In Cardiganshire, for example, the marriage rate was only 65 per cent of that of Monmouthshire. In the Welsh rural counties the population was markedly older than it was in Britain as a whole. This had an obvious effect upon vital statistics: in every year between 1930 and 1939 the death rate in the counties of Anglesey, Caernarfon, Meirionnydd and Cardigan exceeded the birth rate – a factor of importance when considering the fortunes of the Welsh language in that period.

The government proved readier to react positively to the problems of agriculture than to the crisis of heavy industry, largely because so many Conservatives had interests in farming. Since 1846, Britain had sacrificed agriculture to Free Trade, but in 1932 the National government seized the opportunity to impose quotas on food imports and to tax some of them. This was followed in 1934 by deficiency payments, particularly for fatstock. At the same time, marketing boards were established for a number of products: the early potato industry in Pembrokeshire benefited from the Potato Board, and the Bacon Board enjoyed a measure of success. The most important of the new boards, however, was the Milk Marketing Board, which was launched in October 1933. By 1939, 19,944 of the farmers of Wales were selling milk to the board. For the first time ever, at least half the farmers of Wales had a secure market and a regular monthly income, a development which transformed their attitudes and their prospects. Then, through legislation passed in 1937 and 1939, grants were offered for spreading lime and basic slag, and subsidies were given for reseeding grazing land. Thus, by the late 1930s it was possible to discern the beginnings of the grant system which was to be the salvation of Welsh agriculture.

Despite these developments, the 1930s were woeful years for the inhabitants of rural Wales. Many of the problems sprang from the weakness of the administrative system in the countryside, particularly from the unwillingness of local authorities to fulfil their duties in the fields of health, housing and welfare. The per capita expenditure of the rural counties on health was less than half that of the industrial counties. The countryside lacked the services of full-time medical officers of health and of trained midwives; the efforts of the rural authorities to disinfect contaminated houses were grossly inadequate and they were tardy in providing meals and free milk for school-children. In spite of depopulation, there was an appalling shortage of adequate housing. The rural district councils did little to take advantage of the housing grants offered by the government; the local councils of Meirionnydd, for example, did not build a single house under the Addison Act, although local officials had frequently stressed that a large number of the county's houses were unfit for human habitation. In parts of Pembrokeshire and Anglesey, the rate of overcrowding was four times that of Glamorgan, and in 1939 the living conditions in one of the villages of Anglesey were declared to be 'worse than [those of] the native quarter of Shanghai'. The deficiencies in housing, services and nourishment were reflected in the poor health of the rural population. For decades, Cardiganshire had been near the top of the list in terms of deaths of mothers in giving birth, stuttering, rotten teeth, ear defects, blindness, imbecility and madness. On the eve of the First World War, *The Welsh Outlook* wrote of 'this shockingly backward county', but things were little better on the eve of the Second World War.

Despite the severe problems of the coalfield, tuberculosis was less than half as lethal there as it was in the rural areas of Caernarfonshire. The negligence of the rural authorities was the chief theme of a forceful report on the anti-tuberculosis service in Wales published in 1939. 'Gentlemen,' said Clement Davies, the main author of the report, to the members of the Caernarfonshire County Council, 'are you not ashamed of yourselves?' It was acknowledged that the structure of administration in rural Wales was inadequate and that the income of the authorities was insufficient, but it was claimed that much of the blame should be attributed to the niggardly and reactionary attitudes of the councillors. W. J. Gruffydd suggested that all councillors should be swept away, and it was urged in parliament that rural Wales should be designated a 'Special Area' in order to ensure that its social services were brought up to the level of those in other parts of the kingdom.

Yet, despite the intense deprivation of rural Wales, it was the suffering of industrial Wales that engaged the attention of writers, in both Welsh and English. In Welsh, there are the stories of Kate Roberts, with their perceptive, understated description of that suffering, and the poems of Gwenallt, imbued with his hatred of industrial capitalism. In English, there is a substantial body of writing; indeed, it could be claimed that it was the depression that gave birth to the Anglo-Welsh school of writers. The experiences of the 1930s in the coalfield were so intense as to create a deep desire to describe them to the world. The distress was at its worst in the eastern, most anglicized part of the coalfield. By the 1930s, that region had 'a reservoir of Anglo-Welshness', to quote Gwyn Jones. Idris Davies, the poet of the depression, was a native of Rhymni. The adjoining valley, the

Sirhywi, was the home of Gwyn Jones, the author of *Times Like These*, a novel offering a highly authentic portrait of life in the coalfield. Jack Jones, who composed many a saga of the valleys, was born in Merthyr; B. L. Coombes, the chronicler of the miners' day, was a native of Herefordshire who had settled in Resolfen. The Rhondda produced Rhys Davies, the most prolific of the Anglo-Welsh writers, Lewis Jones, the author of two documentary novels on the class struggle, and Gwyn Thomas, the caustic and witty story-teller. They were all sons of the working class and the anguish of their people was part of their inheritance and their mission. Their work had a warm welcome in London literary circles, where writing of a left-wing nature was very acceptable in the 1930s. Yet, ironically, it was a native of St David's, with only a passing experience of the industrial valleys, who created the best-known portrait of a coalfield community. Richard Llewellyn's *How Green Was My Valley* appeared in 1939; 150,000 copies of the book were sold within a few months and Llewellyn's clichés about the Welsh miner and his society spread to the ends of the earth. Ironically also, a wholly unpolitical figure from a fairly middle-class background proved to be the greatest English writer to emerge in Wales in the 1930s. The first volume of Dylan Thomas's poetry appeared in 1934, and it soon became obvious that Swansea had nurtured a poet of genius.

In the late 1930s, two magazines were launched to promote Anglo-Welsh literature – *Wales* in 1937 and *The Welsh Review* in 1939. By then the radio was also developing into an effective medium for the work of Welsh writers, especially after the Welsh region of the BBC received its own wavelength in 1937. The region proved to be as much a patron of Anglo-Welsh as it was of Welsh authors, although the great majority of those who had agitated for its establishment were Welsh-speakers. The discontent felt in the 1920s over the lack of Welsh on the radio has already been noted. The protests increased in the early 1930s: in 1931, ten of the thirteen county councils of Wales passed resolutions calling for a full national service, and in 1933 the University of Wales established a consultative committee on broadcasting. A national service for Scotland was created in 1932, but no similar arrangements were made for Wales; scarcity of wavelengths was the BBC's explanation, but much was also made of the scattered nature of the Welsh population and the mountainous character of the country. Plaid Genedlaethol Cymru launched a campaign to withhold the licence fee and its president, Saunders Lewis, proved skilful in answering the arguments of the corporation. Dr E. G. Bowen, a physics research student at Swansea, offered evidence that the wavelength problem could be overcome, and it was widely suggested that the BBC was intentionally anti-Welsh. John Reith was deeply offended. 'Welsh nationalists,' he stated in his autobiography, 'were impervious to reason or fact where broadcasting was concerned.'

There were new initiatives in the mid-1930s. The corporation appointed a Director of Regional Relations in 1934, and in 1935 the Bangor studio began producing programmes under the inspired leadership of Sam Jones. The increase in Welsh-language material broadcast by the West Region annoyed listeners in south-west England, and by 1935 they were volubly demanding the dismantling of the 'kingdom of King Arthur'. In April 1935, John Reith agreed that separation was inevitable and the Ullswater Committee recognized in 1936 that the 'kingdom' was a 'mutually uncomfortable partnership'. The Welsh Region of the BBC began broadcasting on a separate wavelength on 4 July 1937; although there was considerable criticism of the programmes, a vital battle had been won. It was a battle which would have to be fought again, a generation later, following the introduction of television.

The Welsh Region of the BBC was the only Welsh national institution to come into existence in the 1930s; indeed, the region was the only concession of substance to national feeling won between 1920, when the Church of England in Wales was disestablished, and 1948, when the Council of Wales was created. That period was more barren from the national point of view than any other since the Welsh revival of the later decades of the nineteenth century. Yet there existed during those years a nationalist party which professed a more intense and dedicated nationalism than anything that had ever been seen before in Wales. It has to be acknowledged that in the 1920s and 1930s Plaid Genedlaethol Cymru had little impact upon formal politics. It established a number of branches, particularly after the appointment of its energetic general secretary, J. E. Jones, in 1930, and it showed – on the matter of broadcasting, for example – an ability to be an effective pressure group. But its rare forays into the electoral field brought no success. As Hywel Davies argues, Plaid Genedlaethol Cymru was during the inter-war years a social and an educational movement rather than a political party.

To Saunders Lewis, its president from 1926 to 1939, the chief aim of the party was to 'take away from the Welsh their sense of inferiority . . . to remove from our beloved country the mark and the shame of conquest'. To that end, Lewis created a body of doctrine which served to place Welshness in a new context. He believed that it was necessary for the Welsh to conceive of themselves as members of one of the founder nations of European civilization – a rather exotic concept for them, for the context of the Welsh national revival had been almost exclusively British and imperial. He considered that the purpose of politics was the defence of civilization. 'Civilization,' he wrote, 'is more than an abstraction. It must have a local habitation and a name. Here its name is Wales.' Civilization is threatened when the people are without property, without tradition and without responsibility, and are therefore a prey to corrupt influences, economic and political. Lewis yearned above all for a social order which would ensure the well-being of Welsh-speaking communities. He believed that such communities had been at their most vital in the Middle Ages, before they were threatened by the advent of the centralized state and the capitalist system. Although he bitterly condemned capitalism, Lewis saw no virtue in socialism, a creed which aimed, he believed, at centralizing power and wealth in the hands of the state. As an alternative, he favoured what he called *perchentyaeth* – a policy of 'distributing property among the mass of the members of the nation'.

His fellow-nationalists did not accept every one of Lewis's ideas. As most of them came from a Nonconformist background, only a handful warmed to his religious views – he was received into the Roman Catholic Church in 1932. His policy of boycotting the House of Commons was rejected in 1930, and in 1938, following criticism from party members of socialist tendencies, it was agreed that *perchentyaeth* was not a fundamental tenet of Plaid Genedlaethol Cymru. Lewis's elitist views, together with his condescending attitude towards aspects of the Nonconformist, radical and pacifist traditions of Wales, attracted criticism, and the readiness of some prominent party members to see virtue in Mussolini and Franco was deeply offensive to left-wing Nationalists. D. J. Davies, a colourful figure from the anthracite coalfield, won support for his argument that much greater efforts should be made to campaign among the English-speaking communities of Wales. Davies stressed the need for emphasizing the territorial integrity of Wales; he praised warmly the achievements of the Scandinavian countries, and he and his wife – the Irishwoman Noëlle Ffrench – were active in considering the economic implications of self-government. Indeed, in many ways, the ideas which were to be central to Welsh Nationalist activity after the Second World War sprang from Davies rather than from Lewis.

Yet because of Lewis's brilliance and charismatic appeal, his image was firmly imprinted upon Plaid Genedlaethol Cymru in the 1930s. At the beginning of the decade, it was a very small group with an annual income of less than a thousand pounds and an active membership of no more than a few score. Although Lewis had not expected rapid success, he became increasingly frustrated as his party continued to be marginal to Welsh politics. 'The whole tone of Welsh Nationalism,' he wrote in 1932, 'is not challenging enough, not revolutionary enough.' In the mid-1930s, all the energies of the party were channelled into the battle against the government's intention of establishing in the Llŷn peninsula a centre for training pilots in bombing techniques. There were pacifist, cultural and environmental aspects to the protest against the 'Bombing School', but Lewis insisted upon making it primarily a nationalist question. To him, the point at issue was that the English government was intent upon turning one of the 'essential homes of Welsh culture, idiom and literature' into a place for promoting a barbaric method of warfare. The government had intended to establish 'bombing schools' in Northumberland and in Dorset, but it had yielded to the protests of naturalists and historians. Baldwin, the Prime Minister, refused to accept a deputation of Welsh protesters, although they had obtained the support of organizations representing over half a million of the people of Wales. The building of the 'Bombing School' at Penyberth near Pwllheli began exactly four hundred years after the passage of the Act of 'Union'. In the early morning of 8 September 1936, it was set on fire and responsibility for the act was accepted by Saunders Lewis, Lewis Valentine and D. J. Williams. In the trial at Caernarfon on 13 October, Lewis and Valentine each made passionate addresses to the jury. The jury failed to agree on a verdict and the case was taken to the Old Bailey in London, where the 'Three' were sentenced to nine months' imprisonment. They were released on 27 August 1937 and were acclaimed by fifteen thousand of their compatriots at the pavilion at Caernarfon on 11 September.

The 'Fire in Llŷn' is a central happening in the recent history of the Welsh-speaking community. (It had little impact upon English-speakers.) To quote Dafydd Glyn Jones, the fire was 'the first time in five centuries that Wales had struck back at England with a measure of violence . . . To the Welsh people, who had long ceased to believe that they had it in them, it was a profound shock.' There was a change in the nature of Welsh poetry after 1936. R. Williams Parry's consciousness was seared by the fire, and henceforth there were to be hardly any Welsh-language writers who delighted in the ties which bound Wales to England. Although the fire was the only example of violence against the 'Bombing School', it created a tradition of unconstitutional action to which subsequent generations of nationalists would appeal. In 1936 and 1937, there was some evidence that Penyberth and its aftermath would cause nationalism to become a mass movement in Wales. Many were angered by the judge's scornful treatment of the Welsh language, by the decision to move the case to London and by the decision of University College, Swansea, to dismiss Saunders Lewis from his post in the college's Department of Welsh before he had been found guilty. The ecstatic welcome given to the 'Three' – not only in Caernarfon, but also in places such as Maesteg – proves that their action had aroused deep feelings in Wales. But attempts to build upon the enthusiasm were not successful. In the main, nationalism attracted the young and they lacked the resources and the qualities expected of community leaders. Many of the members of Plaid Genedlaethol Cymru were sympathetic to socialism and were critical of the right-wing leanings of the leadership. In 1939, having become convinced that Wales would not accept the leadership of a Roman Catholic, Saunders Lewis resigned the presidency. By the end of the 1930s, the upsurge in nationalism had shot its bolt. Indeed, with Europe again at war, there were fears that the experience of another world war would extinguish not only Plaid Genedlaethol Cymru but also the identity of Wales itself. Yet by 1945 the party was stronger than it had been in 1939 – a fact which may above all be attributed to Penyberth.

The 'Bombing School' campaign is proof that some at least of the people of Wales were raising their heads after the trauma of the early 1930s. This was not only true of the Nationalists. As the black clouds began to scatter, confidence returned to the labour movement. Vigour returned to the South Wales Miners' Federation, an organization

which had languished since the events of 1926. It was reformed from
its foundations in 1934, when a new structure was created which
enabled its leaders to be more answerable to the membership. The
chief aim of the reformed 'Fed' was the destruction of its rival, the
Industrial Union. The first victory came at the Emlyn Colliery in
Pen-y-groes. There, under the leadership of Arthur Horner, the
Industrial Union came to an end in April 1934. The campaign was
then focused upon the Taff-Merthyr pit near Bedlinog, a recently
established colliery whose owners had from the beginning favoured
the Industrial Union. In October 1934, 250 members of the 'Fed'
employed at Taff-Merthyr were dismissed and unemployed miners –
'blacklegs' according to 'Fed' loyalists – were recruited to replace
them. In the bitter disputes which followed, the local Communists
were particularly active and the women of the district vigorously
tormented the 'blacklegs'. Two hundred constables were deployed to
defend them and the police were involved in many a confrontation in
Bedlinog during the autumn and winter of 1934. But the boldest of
the protests was that at Nine Mile Point colliery at Cwmfelin-fach
near Blackwood. In October 1935, the miners of the colliery, inspired
by the example of a protest in Hungary, staged a stay-down strike
which lasted for more than a week. James Griffiths, the president of the
'Fed' from 1934 to 1936, wrote a dramatic description of its final
outcome. His successor, Arthur Horner, succeeded in obtaining the
dissolution of the Industrial Union, and by 1939 the coal-owners no
longer had the power to insist that membership of a union of their
choice was a condition of employment.

Confidence also returned to the Labour party. In the general election of 1935 it won 154 seats, proof that the party was recovering its
strength after the thrashing it had received in 1931. In Wales, the
constituencies of Wrexham and Carmarthen were recaptured and
Brecon and Radnor was regained in a by-election in 1939. At the
same time, the party was consolidating its hold upon the local authorities of the coalfield; indeed, many of those authorities consisted almost
entirely of Labour councillors, although the party faced considerable
competition from the Communists in such places as the Rhondda. To
some prominent Labour politicians – Aneurin Bevan in particular –
this split in the ranks of the left was a cause for concern. Bevan was
prominent in the efforts to create a 'United Front' and a 'Popular
Front', efforts which led to his suspension from the Labour party in

1939. It was the growth of Fascism which lay at the root of the calls for unity. Fascism won a few footholds in Wales, and in 1933 Bevan sought to establish a working-class militia to oppose it. Oswald Mosley held occasional meetings in Wales, but he abandoned his attempts following a mass protest against him at Tonypandy in June 1936.

Concern over British Fascism was a secondary matter compared with the passions aroused by the challenge of Fascism in mainland Europe. The Spanish Civil War, the rehearsal for the Second World War, began in 1936. It stirred deep feelings in Wales. There were 174 Welshmen among the two thousand British subjects who fought from the Spanish Republic against Franco. They included 122 miners for the south Wales coalfield – the biggest single group among the British volunteers – but natives of rural Wales, the northern coalfield and the southern ports also served in the International Brigade. Some volunteers came from the ranks of the Labour party, but the vast majority were Communists. Of the Welsh volunteers, thirty-three were killed and a plaque to their memory was unveiled in the Miners' Library at Swansea in 1976. Many in Wales were active in assisting refugees from Spain, children from the Basque country in particular, and David John Jones, who carried provisions to Bilbao, won fame as *Jones El Patatero*. On the other hand, it was a leading Welsh landowner, the earl of Plymouth of St Fagan's Castle, who chaired the Non-Intervention Committee, the body which administered the policy which led to the demise of the Spanish Republic.

The growth of Fascism caused a dilemma for the advocates of peace, a vocal and dedicated group. To some among them, Fascism was an aspect of man's bellicosity, and the answer was to adopt absolute pacifism. In 1933, the Baptist Union of Wales adopted the pacifist viewpoint and that viewpoint was an important factor in the protest at Penyberth. In 1936 the Peace Pledge Union was founded, and the union received an avowal from thousands of Welshmen that they wholly rejected war. During the National Eisteddfod of 1937, an organization for Welsh-speaking pacifists was established. With George M. Ll. Davies as president and Gwynfor Evans as secretary, Cymdeithas Heddychwyr Cymru undertook energetic campaigns and published a total of thirty-one pamphlets. Those who embraced absolute pacifism were, however, a small minority. The majority of the advocates of peace sought joint security through the League of Nations, a policy which permitted the use of armed force in order to resist the activities of aggressive states. Enthusiasm for the League was one of the most prominent features of Welsh life in the 1920s and 1930s. The Welsh Council of the League of Nations Union came into being in 1922, with Gwilym Davies as secretary and David Davies of Llandinam as patron. Gwilym Davies initiated the Goodwill Message of the children of Wales; he organized a visit by Welsh women to Washington and sought to make Geneva, the headquarters of the League, a place of pilgrimage. There was an element of spiritual chauvinism in the Welsh enthusiasm for the League. 'Wales,' wrote Gwilym Davies in 1922, 'will be the bulwark against the next war,' and it was claimed in 1926 that it was by leading the world on the matter of the League that Wales would become a nation in the full sense. The readiness of 63 per cent of the adults of Wales to participate in the peace ballot held by the League of Nations Union in 1935 is proof of Welsh interest in its activities. (The figure for Britain as a whole was 38 per cent.)

With Fascism in the ascendant in Italy, Germany and Spain, the principle of joint security became increasingly irrelevant. By 1938 – the year in which the Temple of Peace was opened at Cardiff – the League of Nations had languished almost unto death. It was therefore argued that the democratic states should hasten to rearm. Disarmament had been central to the aspirations of the supporters of the League, precisely the people to whom Fascism was most abhorrent. In 1938, the Welsh MPs voted by twenty to thirteen against the Munich Agreement, which was endorsed by the House of Commons by 366 votes to 144. 'End Fascism and War' was the slogan of the left – but what if the one could not be ended without recourse to the other? This was the dilemma which faced men such as Aneurin Bevan, a passionate opponent of Fascism who was at the same time deeply hostile to the government's rearmament programme. That programme was rapidly stepped up in 1938–9 and military conscription was introduced at the end of April 1939, six months after Hitler had seized the remnants of Czechoslovakia. Five months later, the Second World War began.

CHAPTER TEN

Wales since 1939: Cardiff, Margam and Tryweryn

At least thirty million people died as a result of the Second World War, three times the number killed in the First World War. The greater part of the losses occurred among the civilians of eastern Europe and the soldiers of the Soviet Union. For the Welsh, the second war was less lethal than the first, as memorials to the dead of the two wars amply testify. Between 1914 and 1918, 750,000 members of the British armed forces were killed, 40,000 of them Welsh; between 1939 and 1945, the equivalent figures were 300,000 and 15,000. In addition, 60,000 Britons were killed in air raids compared with 1,117 in the First World War. Losses among the civilian population are proof of the fact that the second war was a 'total war' to a far greater extent than the first. 'It is not only the soldiers who are fighting,' declared Churchill in 1940, 'but the entire population – men, women and children . . . The front is everywhere.' It was often more dangerous to be at home than in the armed forces. 'Where is your husband?' a Swansea woman was asked at the height of the bombing there in February 1940. 'He is in the army, the coward,' she replied. As all the inhabitants of Britain were being drawn into the struggle, the authorities became aware that it was necessary to ensure their cooperation. As Angus Calder argues, between 1939 and 1945 the people of Britain were participants in their own history to a greater degree than ever before. Yet, despite the intensity of the experiences of the second war, it is the first which is still referred to as the 'Great War'. That was a more harrowing experience, for it destroyed the optimism which had been fostered by a long period of peace and progress. The Second World War came at the end of the 'low dishonest decade', as Auden put it, and its outbreak was not a surprise to anyone.

Public opinion in Britain and in Wales was more united in favour of the second war than of the first. Apart from Mosley's supporters –

who hardly existed in Wales – the war received the enthusiastic support of those on the right, who believed that what was at stake was the independence and greatness of Britain. They were probably correct, for A. J. P. Taylor claimed that the second war, like the first, was essentially a struggle for mastery between the great powers; the crusade against Nazism, he argued, was a 'top-dressing'. Nevertheless, Taylor acknowledged that that crusade meant that Britain and its allies were, between 1939 and 1945, engaged in that rare phenomenon, a just war. That was the belief of the upholders of Labour and Liberal traditions, and there was among them little of the hesitancy which characterized their predecessors during the First World War.

On the extreme left, matters were more complex. Until June 1941, when Germany attacked the Soviet Union, the Communist party adhered to Moscow's view that the war was yet another imperialist conflict, although not all Communists agreed, as the predicament of Arthur Horner testifies. After June 1941, the Communists did their utmost to support the war effort. Men like Horner strove to ensure the highest level of production in factories and pits, and condemned any suggestion of unofficial strikes. Thus a vacuum was created on the left, a vacuum which the Trotskyists, who continued to believe in the theory of an imperialist war, sought to fill. They had little success, although their leader, Jock Haston, received a not wholly trifling vote in the by-election at Neath in 1945 – the first time that a Trotskyist had contested a British parliamentary election.

Opposition from the left was therefore far less vocal in the second war than in the first. But in the Second World War, there was political opposition of a wholly new kind. It came from Plaid Genedlaethol Cymru. That party considered that the war was a conflict between groups of great powers and its leaders argued that Wales had the right, as had the other small nations of Europe, to choose not to have a part in it. Of course, they did not believe that the right would be respected. As A. O. H. Jarman put it: 'Neutrality was a state of mind . . . the maintenance of the right of the Welsh nation to decide its own attitude towards the war.' Implicit in neutrality was the denial 'of the right of any other country, such as England, to force the Welsh to serve in their armed forces'. The aim of the leaders of the party was to set 'a new loyalty in place of the old loyalty to the British State'. It was a challenging – indeed a revolutionary – policy, particularly in view of the smallness of the party.

Saunders Lewis, the architect of the policy, hoped that a substantial number of Welshmen would refuse to be conscripted on the grounds that they were Welsh. He was disappointed by the response. To most of those members of the party who refused to be conscripted, their political beliefs were only meaningful in the context of their moral and religious convictions. It was on the basis of those convictions that a proportion of them were released from service in the armed forces, for the tribunals of Wales claimed that the law did not recognize conscientious objection on political grounds. Nevertheless, about two dozen members of Plaid Genedlaethol Cymru made their politics the only ground for their objection, and twelve of them received prison sentences. Saunders Lewis considered their stand to be highly significant. It proved that the 'assimilation of Wales by England was being withstood, even under the most extreme pressures'. 'The only proof that the Welsh nation exists,' he argued, 'is that there are some who act as if it did exist.' Throughout the war, Lewis sought to uphold a neutral viewpoint, particularly through his column 'Cwrs y Byd' in *Y Faner*, an attempt to offer an interpretation of events uncoloured by the propaganda of either side. Yet not all members of Plaid Genedlaethol Cymru agreed with him: Ambrose Bebb considered Germany's total defeat to be essential, and some of the most dedicated of the party's members served in Britain's armed forces.

In denying that political beliefs were acceptable grounds for exemption, the tribunals in Wales were probably mistaken, for the Military Conscription Act of 1939 recognized wide categories of objection. In the second war, the authorities were far more considerate towards conscientious objectors than they had been in the first. Between 1939 and 1945, the tribunals of Britain dealt with 59,192 objectors, 3 per cent of whom received prison sentences; between 1916 and 1918 the equivalent figures were 16,500 and 30 per cent. Once again, there were more Welshmen, in proportional terms, than there were Englishmen and Scotsmen who refused to be conscripted, a fact which can largely be attributed to the strength of Christian pacifism in Wales. Throughout the war, Cymdeithas Heddychwyr Cymru continued its programme of publishing; George M. Ll. Davies persevered with his fervent campaign and in 1942 the Union of Welsh Independents voted for immediate peace negotiations. Yet those supporting Davies and his associates were a small minority, for the great pacifist upsurge of the 1930s ebbed very rapidly. In 1940–41, when there was a real danger that Britain would be invaded, pacifists suffered a degree of victimization. Some local authorities, Cardiff and Swansea among them, refused to employ workers unwilling to sign a statement that they 'whole-heartedly supported the war', and Iorwerth Peate was dismissed by the National Museum, an act which led to widespread and effective protests.

One of the most important factors which had fostered the peace movement of the 1930s was the belief that methods of warfare had become wholly barbaric. The fact that it was possible to bomb civilians from the air was the main reason for that belief. Official opinion held that six hundred thousand inhabitants of the cities of Britain would be killed by bombs during the first two months of a war against Germany. Thus there was a craving to flee from the cities; the statistics of the railway companies show that 150,000 people migrated to Wales during the Munich Crisis of 1938. The authorities believed that millions would flee in panic if war were declared. Apprehension concerning the chaos which might result was the chief motive for the plan to move four million children and mothers from the most vulnerable cities. The evacuation was one of the most remarkable features of the war. The government's scheme was far from implemented in its entirety. Of the evacuees that Wales was to receive, only a third actually arrived there. Most of Wales was denoted a 'reception area'; as there was no intention of moving anyone from Wales, all the evacuees billeted in Welsh homes came from England. (This was in marked contrast with the situation in Scotland, a country which received no English evacuees.) A substantial proportion of them came from the impoverished areas of Merseyside, and many middle-class families were astounded by the abysmal deprivation of the children of the slums.

In addition to the official evacuation, many people made their own arrangements. The offspring of London milk retailers were sent to the homes of their ancestors in Cardiganshire, and the children of the Welsh of Dagenham and Slough returned to the valleys of the coalfield; wealthy exiles from south-east England settled into hotels on the Welsh coast with the intention of sitting out the war drinking gin, reading novels and playing cards. Indeed, the unofficial evacuation was probably greater than the official one. Between 1939 and 1941, 1.75 million people moved from southern and eastern to northern and western Britain, about the same number as had moved in the other direction over the previous fifteen years. Wales received at least two hundred thousand immigrants in the first two years of the war, and by 1941 its population was almost back to the level it had been in 1921.

Wales's appeal was based upon the assumption that it was too far to the west to suffer from German bombing raids. The assumption proved to be unfounded. Cardiff suffered its first raid in June 1940 and during the following fifteen months thirty thousand buildings in the city were damaged, Llandaf Cathedral among them. In the same period there were several attacks upon Pembroke Dock, and the countryside did not escape unscathed as German airmen seized the opportunity to lighten their loads; in Denbighshire, for example, bombs fell on such places as Llandegla, Llansannan, Gwytherin and Nantglyn.

But it was Swansea which suffered most severely. Between 1940 and 1943, there were forty-four raids on the town. A total of 369 people were killed, including the 230 who died in the three-night blitz of 19, 20 and 21 February 1941. The entire town centre was destroyed and extensive damage was inflicted upon other quarters such as Bryn Hyfryd, Townhill and Manselton. With 'Swansea aflame', children were evacuated; in March 1941 the town, together with other towns in the western parts of Britain, was declared to be an evacuation area. There were further raids on Swansea, including a ferocious one in February 1942 when thirty-four people were killed. With that raid, the bombing came to an end; neither Swansea, nor any other town in Wales, suffered from the attacks of the V1s and the V2s which caused so much distress to the inhabitants of London towards the end of the war.

The danger from the air was one of the most important factors in determining the wartime environment. The black-out, in force from the first day, did more than anything to change the quality of life. With the shelters, the barrage balloons and the piles of sand-bags, the appearance of the towns was transformed. The government's propaganda machine ensured that only the most heartening news was made public; the BBC was insistent that there was no despondency in Swansea, even among those who had lost close relations. With the imposition of censorship, rumours were rife. According to hearsay, soldiers had to be sent to keep order in Swansea, and panzers had landed and captured Oystermouth Castle. Such stories were numerous in the dire days of 1940, when invasion was daily expected. All road signs were removed, maps were burned and bell-ringing was forbidden. May 1940 saw the establishment of the Local Defence Volunteers, an organization which rapidly recruited members: two hundred joined at Llandudno on the first day. This was the Home Guard, frequently represented as the 'People's Army', although it was often the means of giving a little authority to the most blinkered members of the old military and landed classes. It became the subject of many legends, especially in mid-Wales, where the 'Mountain Home Guard' had the task of preventing German parachutists from landing in the vast emptinesses between Tregaron and Llanwrtyd. Among the functions of the 'Home Guard' was rooting-out the 'Fifth Column', which was believed to be numerous and active. Fear of the internal enemy caused the government to intern Germans and Italians living in Britain, many of the Bracchis, Sidolis and Antoniazzis of the south Wales coalfield among them. The same fear also led to a great propaganda campaign in 1940 against the spread of defeatist rumours and remarks.

The chief purpose of the government's propaganda machine was to disseminate the notion that Britain was totally united. The Second World War, like the First, did much to strengthen Britishness. At the same time, it seemed to be a death blow to Welshness. W. J. Gruffydd, one of the staunchest supporters of Britain's stand, believed that 'England could win the war and Wales could lose it . . . The impact of [this war] on the future of Wales and the Welsh language,' he stated, 'will be inexpressibly greater than [the impact of the last war].' The cause of his greatest concern was the coming of the evacuees. 'In the villages of Arfon,' he wrote in *Y Llenor* in autumn 1939, 'there are now almost as many English children as there are Welsh children.' The evacuees did not prove as great a threat to the Welsh language as was feared, partly because their numbers were far fewer than had been intended. In those districts where the young natives were monoglot Welsh, the incomers were quickly assimilated linguistically. Some of them settled permanently in their places of evacuation, making substantial contributions to the local community. Many became members of Urdd Gobaith Cymru, a movement which flourished during the war, partly because the Board of Education insisted that every teenage child should join a youth club or a cadet force. But in those districts where the Welsh language was not wholly secure, the presence of the evacuees tipped the balance in favour of

English. That was the case at Aberystwyth, a consideration which led Ifan ab Owen Edwards to establish a private Welsh-medium school under the auspices of the Urdd, the first school since the time of Carnhuanawc to be designated a Welsh school. It was the starting-point of the Welsh schools movement which was to flourish greatly after the war. Yet, as it was a private school which catered for less than 10 per cent of the children of Aberystwyth, it would probably be more accurate to consider the Llanelli Welsh School, established by the Carmarthen County Council in 1947, as the true starting-point of the movement.

The evacuees were not the only cause of concern to Welsh patriots. The War Office coveted thousands of hectares of the land of Wales. From the first day of the war, the broadcasts of the BBC in Britain were limited to a unified Home Service, thus bringing the programmes of the Welsh region to an end. As Welsh speakers flooded into the army and into factories in England, there was a desire to provide for their cultural and spiritual well-being. The Committee for the Defence of the Culture of Wales was established in December 1939 and renamed Undeb Cymru Fydd (the New Wales Union) in August 1941. Most of its members were supporters of Plaid Genedlaethol Cymru, who felt that wartime circumstances obliged them to work through non-party organizations. The movement's first campaign was that against the War Office's plan to requisition Mynydd Epynt. It was a failure. By June 1940, the four hundred people who lived in the mountain's seven valleys had been dispersed; their homes were destroyed and sixteen thousand hectares of Breconshire became a vast firing range. As a result of the War Office's act, the boundary of Welsh-speaking Wales was moved fifteen kilometres westwards. Undeb Cymru Fydd took part in further battles against the army's demand for land; in some cases they were won, but by 1945 two hundred thousand hectares of Welsh land – 10 per cent of the surface of the country – was held by the War Office. Campaigns over broadcasting were more successful. Five minutes a day of 'official announcements' in Welsh were broadcast from London; broadcasting in the language was increased to three and a half hours a week in 1940, a year in which the National Eisteddfod was a radio event. Yet, despite constant pressure and the dedicated efforts of Welsh broadcasters, provision remained meagre until July 1945, when the Welsh region was re-established. English-language broadcasting from Wales flourished: programmes such as *Welsh Rarebit* and *Home Fires Burning* were popular throughout the kingdom, and *ITMA*, the best-known of wartime programmes, was produced in the safety of Bangor. The BBC sought to contact Welsh soldiers across the world; for example, it sent the script of a weekly programme to be included in *Seren y Dwyrain* (The Star of the East), the Welsh newspaper published in Cairo. This was also one of the chief spheres of activity for Undeb Cymru Fydd with its journal *Cofion Cymru* (Greetings from Wales), a publication with a circulation of 26,000. In addition, the union sought to keep in contact with people from Wales who worked in English factories. In December 1941, conscription of women was introduced; of the states involved in the Second World War, Britain was the only one to adopt such legislation. The purpose was to make use of what was called 'surplus unskilled women', a numerous class in the depressed areas of the kingdom. Welsh women were sent under some degree of compulsion to work in the factories of the midlands of England, a policy which attracted considered opposition particularly from Plaid Genedlaethol Cymru.

Yet, with the war transforming the economy, Wales was ceasing to be a land of depression. In some ways, the war was a blessing, for it led to the disappearance of the unemployment which had so long been the scourge of the Welsh. At the beginning of 1944, there were 7,302 unemployed males in Wales compared with 145,867 at the beginning of 1939. By 1944, 55 per cent of the workforce was serving the war machine – 22 per cent in the armed forces and 33 per cent in civilian employment associated with the war. The remaining 45 per cent were therefore responsible for carrying out the work undertaken by virtually the entire workforce in peace time. The demands of war did not, of course, offer a permanent solution to the unemployment problem in Wales. Nevertheless, the war did lead to a mitigation of that problem, partly because it resulted in a substantial contraction in the size of the Welsh workforce. In addition to the fifteen thousand killed in the fighting, a significant number of Welsh people found employment in England during the war, and many of them settled there permanently, as did some of those demobilized after the war. Wales had an insured male workforce of 602,000 in 1939; it had fallen to 547,000 in 1946. This decrease partly explains why Wales did not suffer from high levels of unemployment after the war had come to an end.

It was not the only explanation, for the war was responsible for more constructive developments in the field of employment in Wales. Between 1939 and 1945, the Welsh economy began to extricate itself in earnest from its overdependence upon heavy industry. In that period, the proportion of the Welsh workforce employed in general manufacturing rose from 10 to 20 per cent; in addition, the proportion employed by local and central government rose from 5 to 10 per cent. The aluminium industry came to the Tawe valley and the car-component industry to Llanelli, while the oil refinery capacity at Llandarcy was vastly expanded. By 1941, 37,000 people worked at Bridgend, in a complex of armament factories which represented the world's largest arsenal. Armament factories were also established at Hirwaun, Pen-bre and Glascoed, and a huge aircraft works was built at Broughton in Flintshire. The war industries introduced Welsh workers to new skills, a key contribution to the success of the efforts to diversify the Welsh economy after 1945.

During the war, there was a vast expansion in the opportunities for women to obtain employment, opportunities which had been rare in industrial Wales. In Britain in 1939 thirty-nine women were employed for every 100 men; the ratio in industrial south Wales was sixteen to 100. In that year, 94,000 Welsh women were in employment, a figure which was to rise to 204,000 by 1945. In Bridgend, women were the great majority of the labour force and they were transported there from all the valleys of Glamorgan. Ex-schoolmistresses were welcomed back to work; women were recruited by the tens of thousands to the ATS, the WRENS, the WAAFS and the Land Army, and heroic work was undertaken by the members of the Women's Voluntary Service. As in the First World War, it was assumed that most married women would give up their employment when the war ended. A substantial proportion of them did so, but in 1945 the urge to return them to the kitchen was less pressing than it had been in 1918; indeed, the employment of women would be a leading phenomenon of the second half of the twentieth century, particularly in Wales.

While opportunities for female employment were expanding, the numbers working in the macho industries which had previously dominated the Welsh economy were rapidly shrinking. Between 1939 and 1946, the workforce in the tinplate industry decreased from 23,000 to 12,600, and during the same period there was a decline of 75 per cent in the number of apprentices in the quarries of Gwynedd. So great was the contraction in the labour force of the coal industry that it represented a threat to the war effort. In 1939, thirty-five million tons of coal were mined in south Wales; during the war, the total declined by at least two million tons a year. In view of the experiences of the miners in the two previous decades, it is hardly surprising that many of them seized the opportunity to escape to the army or to other forms of employment. As a result, there were not enough miners by 1943 to meet the demand for coal. To fill the gap, one in ten of those conscripted at eighteen was sent to the pits; the scheme was devised by the Minister of Labour, Ernest Bevin, and the 'Bevin Boys' were scorned by the old hands of the coalfield.

As there was a demand for their labour, the miners regained their bargaining power. They used it. Between 1939 and 1945, they were responsible for over half the days lost through strikes. As in the First World War, they were ferociously condemned by the press, and there were Conservatives who suggested that the strike leaders should be shot. There were 524 stoppages in the south Wales coal industry in the period 1939–44; many of them were small-scale affairs, but in March 1944 a hundred thousand Welsh miners went on strike. The cause of the dispute was the Porter Award, which sought to abolish wage differentials between the skilled and the unskilled. In the agreement which ended the dispute, the miners won a minimum wage which put them almost at the top of the table of working-class wages. In 1942, the coal industry was placed under the control of the Ministry of Fuel and Power; ironically, in view of the events of 1916–22, the minister was Gwilym Lloyd George. The miners believed that this was the first step towards abolishing capitalist ownership of the mines. They were not alone in their belief, for an opinion poll in 1942 showed that 70 per cent of those questioned favoured state ownership of the mines. In order to enable the miners to bargain effectively with the state and the owners, the campaign to consolidate the unity of the miners of Britain was intensified, a campaign which Arthur Horner had been promoting for twenty years. On 1 January 1945, the National Union of Mineworkers was established and the South Wales Miners' Federation became the South Wales District of the centralized union. The south Wales miners voted by eight to one in favour of the change, although there were those in Wales who mourned the disappearance of the 'Fed'.

It was not only the miners who experienced an improvement in their wages during the war. Between 1939 and 1943, there was an increase of 42 per cent in the cost of living; on average, the increase in basic wages was 35 per cent, but with overtime the increase could be 75 per cent or more. The rise in family earnings could be even greater: with full employment for men and a vast expansion in the employment opportunities for women, there was a rapid growth in income, especially among those who had previously relied on the dole. But if people had more money, there were fewer goods to buy. This was especially true of the south Wales coalfield; the amount of goods received by each region was based upon the amount sold there before the war, a period when the purchasing power of the inhabitants of the coalfield had been very low. As a result, there was little that could be done with the extra money except to save it; this explains the popularity of Defence Bonds and National Savings Certificates. For the first time ever, working-class families had a little put by. It was not only wages which improved, but working conditions as well. Implicit in full employment is the need to conciliate the workforce. At the prompting of Ernest Bevin, the leading employers provided a variety of services – welfare officers, for example, and nurseries and canteens and rest rooms. The government had its own welfare schemes: it distributed milk, cod liver oil and orange juice to schoolchildren and the needs of the disabled were at last addressed. Indeed, despite the strain and the scarcities of the war, the bulk of the population was healthier in 1945 than in 1939.

One reason for the improvement was the efficiency of the rationing system. Rationing was much fairer in the Second World War than it had been in the First, although the wealthy were able to eat lavishly during both. By 1942, points were necessary when buying all ordinary foods apart from bread and potatoes. In the following year, when rationing was at its height, an adult was allowed each week a pound of meat, four ounces of bacon, two ounces of butter, an ounce of sweets and 0.6 of an egg. Yet, in spite of the stringency, the nutritional value of the food eaten by the greater part of the population was higher during the war than it had been in the 1930s.

As in all wars, the scarcity of food was a stimulus to agriculture. The re-established County Committees set ploughing targets for farmers. Arable land in Wales increased from 215,000 hectares in 1939 to 500,000 in 1944, a year in which the proportion of the country's land under the plough was greater than it had been during the heyday of nineteenth-century High Farming. Priority was given to wheat and potatoes. Wales had 53,000 hectares under wheat in 1943, ten times as much as in 1939; there was a great vogue for potato growing and it was claimed that enough of the bracken-covered land of Montgomeryshire was cleared for the crop to feed the entire population of Manchester. The rapid increase in arable land created a demand for machinery and for additional agricultural workers. The number of tractors on the farms of Wales rose from 1,932 in 1938 to 13,652 in 1946; in addition, a variety of machines could be hired from the County Committees. The day of mechanized farming was dawning in Wales. There was virtually no increase in the number of agricultural workers, but their ranks were temporarily supplemented by the Land Army, conscientious objectors and prisoners-of-war. As with the miners, the war increased the bargaining powers of farm labourers; their minimum weekly wage was £3 5s. a week in 1943 compared with £1 14s. in 1939. The rise in farmers' receipts was far greater. Official statistics indicate that the net income of British farmers increased by 207 per cent between 1938 and 1942, but as many farmers were involved with the black market such statistics probably understate the increase. Indeed, it has been claimed that the farmers of Wales bought their holdings with the profits of the First World War and modernized them with the profits of the Second.

The revival of the Welsh economy, rural and industrial, was a consequence of the collectivism which resulted from the war. As in the First World War, there was a determination to hold on to the advances that had come in the wake of that collectivism. There was reason to believe that the Conservative party, as well as the Labour party, would support a legislative programme to that end. After all, Churchill had at one time been among the most progressive of the Liberals and substantial numbers of the younger Tories were prepared to accept the social changes which had accompanied the war. It was the Conservative, R. A. Butler, who was responsible for the Education Act of 1944 and it was the Conservative government which was in office from May to July 1945 – Churchill's caretaker administration – which introduced family allowances, among the most significant acknowledgements of the role of the government in the field of welfare.

Nevertheless, it was generally assumed that the creation of a just society after the war was more of a priority for the Labour party than for the Conservatives. That assumption was strengthened by the discussion of the Beveridge Report, a document published in December 1942. It concerned the establishment and financing of a welfare state, and so great was the interest in the report that sales of versions of it totalled 635,000 copies. It was enthusiastically accepted by the Labour party, but the attitude of Churchill and his fellow-Conservatives was at best lukewarm. In the parliamentary debate on the report, James Griffiths, MP for Llanelli, proposed an amendment expressing warm approval of Beveridge's plans; it was defeated by 325 votes to 119, a fact which caused Griffiths to declare that the Labour party would be certain of victory when a general election was eventually held. There were other factors encouraging a movement to the left. The experience of war promoted an egalitarian consciousness as the entire population experienced raids and privation. Army education officers – men who were almost always of left-wing sympathies – influenced large numbers of the members of the armed forces. With the Soviet army fighting the battles which were to win the war, there was a revival in the appeal of the Communist party. The heroism of the people of the Soviet Union, it was claimed, resulted from the fact that they were the owners of their country. A great ceremony was held in Cardiff in February 1943 to celebrate the twenty-fifth anniversary of the Red Army; throughout Britain, mayors stood for the *Internationale*, and the praises of Stalin were sung by the most capitalistic of the Conservatives. In Wales, there were many who believed that Timoshenko, a leading Soviet general, was Thomas Jenkins, the descendant of a Welsh immigrant. The membership of the Communist party trebled in 1941 and the party enjoyed considerable popularity for the rest of the war; in 1945 its leader, Harry Pollitt, came within 972 votes of winning the constituency of Rhondda East.

Above all, the appeal of the left was fostered by the determination that there should be no return to the poverty of the 1930s. That determination was at its strongest in Wales. It was vividly expressed in Aneurin Bevan's book, *Why Not Trust the Tories?* (1944); the book was a plea to learn from the events which had followed the First World War and a declaration of the need for a socialist strategy. As he was convinced of the virtues of central planning, Bevan saw no necessity for that strategy to have a Welsh dimension. In his speech on 17 October 1944, he mocked the notion that Wales had problems unique to itself. The occasion was the first 'Welsh Day' in the history of the British parliament; that, and a feeble statute concerning the Welsh language passed in 1942, were the only concessions made to Welsh nationality during the war. Very different views were held by other Labour MPs, particularly James Griffiths. He was a prominent member of the Welsh Council for Reconstruction; the council published a report in 1944 which called for the recognition of Wales as a planning unit and for huge investment to revive the Welsh economy. James Griffiths was an ardent advocate of a secretaryship of state for Wales, an appointment supported by a number of Labour candidates in the general election of 1945. Some of them also pressed for a Broadcasting Corporation for Wales, for a south–north highway and for a measure of self-government.

Despite the growing tendency for public opinion to favour the Labour party, there was evidence in the later years of the war of a lack of confidence in all the main parties. To some extent that was the result of the 'party truce' – an agreement between the parties supporting the coalition that in a by-election they would not oppose the candidate of the party previously holding the seat. In England, this made possible the remarkable rise of the Common Wealth party, a group of idealistic socialists which won a large vote and three parliamentary seats between 1943 and 1945. In Scotland, the truce favoured the National party; the Motherwell constituency was captured by the party's president, Robert McIntyre, in a by-election in 1945. To some extent, that also happened in Wales. In April 1945, in the by-election in the Caernarfon Boroughs which followed the resignation of Lloyd George, 25 per cent of the vote went to Plaid Genedlaethol Cymru – or Plaid Cymru as it was beginning to call itself; three weeks later, it won 16 per cent of the vote in the Neath by-election.

But the most famous of the wartime by-elections was the contest for the University seat two years earlier, when W. J. Gruffydd stood as a Liberal and Saunders Lewis as a Nationalist. Gruffydd was the standard bearer of the members of the Welsh Establishment, who were appalled at the notion that Lewis might represent the University. As Gruffydd was the leading figure among Welsh-speaking intellectuals, he was the most likely to attract votes which might otherwise have gone to Lewis. Despite his brilliance, Gruffydd was a wayward character. In 1937 he had been the deputy vice-president of Plaid

Cymru and thus his candidature could be portrayed as apostasy. Nevertheless, he had for a decade and more been expressing his doubts about Lewis's ideas; although he did not bind himself to accept the Liberal whip, he was a liberal by temperament and conviction. The election split the Welsh-speaking intelligentsia, causing grave harm to *Y Llenor*, a journal which was to suffer from the dissension until its demise in 1955. Lewis's electoral letter is a document of importance, and the list of those who supported and opposed him is fascinating. Gruffydd won 52.3 per cent of the vote and Lewis 22.5 per cent; the remaining 25.2 per cent was shared between the three other candidates. Until university representation came to an end in 1950, Gruffydd was an interesting figure in the House of Commons; Lewis was embittered by the experience and almost twenty years were to go by before he again intervened in Welsh politics. The by-election was a significant stimulus to the Nationalists; as the fervour of Gruffydd's supporters testifies, Plaid Cymru was taken seriously as an electoral force. It was the first time for that to happen, and it led to considerable growth in the party's membership in the last years of the war.

The upsurge in the support for the smaller parties ebbed after the coalition government came to an end in May 1945. As they remembered the fate of the Liberals after the First World War, the Labour party was wholly opposed to a continuance of the coalition, although an opinion poll in 1944 suggested that this was the preferred option of the voters. The end of the war in Europe was celebrated on 8 May 1945; although fighting continued in the Far East, a general election was held on 5 July. In order to have time to collect the voting papers of members of the armed forces from all corners of the world, the results were not announced until 26 July. Stalin could not understand how Churchill lost the election despite the fact that the ballot boxes had been in the hands of the government for three weeks. But lose he did, to the astonishment of almost everyone. The number of Labour MPs increased from 166 to 393, and the number of Conservatives declined from 397 to 213. As the Labour party under Attlee had an absolute majority of 146, this was the victory for which its members had been longing since the days of Keir Hardie. It has been claimed that the general election of 1945 was the most emphatic verdict in favour of radical change ever delivered by the British electorate. Yet Labour's majority would have been far less but for the British voting system. Labour had 11,995,000 votes and the Conservatives 9,988,000, but if the votes for the parties advocating socialism are compared with those for the parties not advocating it, it will be seen that they were roughly equal – about 12.5 million votes to each group.

But if there were doubts about the British mandate, there were none about the Welsh mandate. The Labour party won twenty-five of the thirty-six seats of Wales, twenty-one of them with absolute majorities; in seven constituencies, the Labour candidate obtained over 80 per cent of the votes cast. Yet as the Labour party already had a tight grip upon the seats of the south Wales coalfield, the increase in its vote in Wales was not as great as it was in other parts of the kingdom; the swing to Labour was 12 per cent in Wales compared with 23 per cent in Birmingham. As the Conservative party won less than a quarter of the votes of the Welsh, they – together with the inhabitants of London's East End – were the most anti-Tory of the peoples of Britain. The Conservatives won three seats, Caernarfon Boroughs, Lloyd George's former constituency among them. In addition, Henry Morris-Jones, the National Liberal at Denbigh, and Gwilym Lloyd George, who was elected as a Liberal in Pembrokeshire, were Conservatives to all intents and purposes. Of the twelve Liberals elected in 1945, seven represented Welsh constituencies. They included Clement Davies, the member for Montgomeryshire and leader of the party from 1945 to 1956, and Rhys Hopkin Morris, the member for Carmarthen. Apart from Mile End in London, Carmarthen was the only constituency lost by the Labour party in 1945. Seven seats were fought by Plaid Cymru, a striking advance over the one it had fought in 1935. All its candidates, with the exception of Gwenan Jones, who stood for the University seat, lost their deposits; it is worth noting that the party's vote in the anglicized industrial constituencies of the south (6.4 per cent) was marginally higher than its vote in the Welsh-speaking rural constituencies of the north (6.2 per cent).

The new government faced awesome problems. Chief among them was the fact that Britain was bankrupt. During the war, Britain had sold overseas investments worth £1,000 million, and its debt had risen from £760 million to £3,355 million. In 1945, when the United States brought its Lend-Lease arrangements to an abrupt end, Britain's foreign expenditure was £2,000 million and its foreign earnings were

£350 million. The balance of payments, the scarcity of dollars and the value of the pound caused constant concern to Attlee's government. Because of the financial crisis, bread was rationed in 1946 and potatoes in 1947, and so great was the reduction in the clothes ration that it was less in 1948 than it had been during the war. The years 1945–51 were the 'age of austerity'; in consequence, it was possible to associate the Labour party with dreary minginess, an association which the Conservatives were eager to emphasize.

The collapse of optimism concerning international cooperation also caused difficulties for the government. In 1945, it was hoped that the Allies, following their defeat of Nazism, would co-exist happily; by 1948, however, the Cold War was a reality and the rearmament which came in its wake hindered the Labour party's plans and threatened its unity. In addition, there were serious imperial crises, particularly in India and Palestine. In Britain itself, the most urgent problem was housing, the subject raised most often by far during the election campaign. As the building industry had been inactive for six years and as over a hundred thousand buildings had been destroyed in air raids, the authorities were faced with serious problems as millions of men and women were demobilized. On top of all the government's difficulties, there were suggestions that even the forces of nature were arrayed against it. Between January and March 1947, when coal stocks were at their lowest, there occurred the worst snow-storms of the century; with industry lacking power, production ceased over large parts of the kingdom; almost every rural community in Wales was cut off for weeks and the needs of upland towns such as Brynmawr were supplied from the air; people shivered in their homes, while on the hills half the sheep died. The snow was followed by floods in the spring and a prolonged drought in the summer, causing further falls in agricultural production; by the end of 1947, the government was seeking to feed the population on snoek, a singularly tasteless fish from the coasts of Angola.

There had never before been a Labour government with an absolute majority; thus 1945 represented the culmination of hopes that had been dammed up for many decades. However much the government achieved, it could hardly fulfil those hopes in their entirety. To the more committed of its supporters, its task was to be the begetter of the socialist revolution. That was what its opponents expected also. It can hardly be claimed that it did usher in the revolution. There was no determined attack upon class divisions, and no basic shift in the distribution of income and property occurred; the royal family, the peerage and the public schools survived unscathed, and workers in 1951 had no more control over their lives than they had had in 1945; a secret decision by Attlee and his close colleagues committed Britain to an independent programme of nuclear weapons, and there was frequently an imperialistic flavour to the government's foreign and colonial policies. The Conservative government elected in 1951 was content to accept most of the changes of the previous six years, a suggestion that there was little that was revolutionary in those changes. Indeed, the activities of the Attlee government were to provide the basis for a British consensus which would last until it was successfully challenged by Thatcherism in 1979.

But in view of the difficulties facing the Attlee government, it is not its shortcomings which are striking but its achievements. In Wales, its greatest accomplishment was the maintenance of full employment. At the beginning of 1946, with demobilization in full swing, unemployment among the insured Welsh population rose to 7.5 per cent among men and to 17 per cent among women, causing a parliamentary deputation to express fears that the distress of the 1930s was returning. By the end of the 1940s, however, unemployment among the Welsh of both sexes had stabilized around 3 per cent. This improvement was not wholly the consequence of the government's efforts. As has been seen, the war led to a substantial decrease in the Welsh labour force; the scale of destruction in the Second World War was far greater than in the First, and therefore there were many more scarcities to be offset in 1945 than there had been in 1918; as Germany in 1945 was in ruins, there was no competition from its exports. In consequence, there was a vast demand for the raw materials and the finished goods produced in Britain, a fact which was central to the prosperity of the Welsh economy.

Yet the government's contribution to full employment should not be underrated. As J. M. Keynes's theories had been accepted, the Budget and the Bank Rate were used to maintain employment. The Labour government was determined to build upon the tentative efforts of the 1930s to create regional policies. The Royal Commission on the Distribution of the Industrial Population completed its work in 1942, and its report stressed that over-expansion in one part of the kingdom created almost as many problems as did depression in other parts. One of the last achievements of Churchill's coalition government was the passage of the Distribution of Industry Act, an important milestone in the development of regional policy. All the industrial districts of the south, along with the Wrexham region, were designated as Development Areas and were given concessions such as the authority to offer low rents and rates to industrialists who established factories within their boundaries. As building materials were exceptionally scarce, a licence had to be obtained to buy them; in granting licences, the Board of Trade gave priority to the needs of the Development Areas. Furthermore, under the Town and Country Planning Act of 1947, certificates were needed before factories could be built; in granting them, precedence was given to the Development Areas. Of those, south Wales was the nearest to the prosperous areas of south-east England and thus industrialists were eager to establish themselves there. Their plans were assisted by the existence of the vast armament factories; by 1950, three thousand people were employed in the old arsenal at Bridgend, and the changeover to civilian production was also successful at Hirwaun near Merthyr and at Marchwiail near Wrexham. Between 1945 and 1949, 179 factories were established in industrial south Wales, 112 of them with the direct assistance of the government. In 1952, 8,584 of the inhabitants of the Rhondda were employed in manufacturing, with women representing almost half the holders of the new factory jobs. At the same time, there was rapid growth in the service industries, although the proportion employed in them in Wales was lower than it was in Britain as a whole.

As the nightmare of the 1930s seemed to have been wholly dispelled, it is hardly surprising that many commentators suggested that Wales was experiencing a second Industrial Revolution. To the Labour government, planning was the key to the reconstruction of the economy. The central feature of its strategy was state control over the 'commanding heights of the economy' through nationalizing the chief industries and services. In 1946, acts were passed to nationalize the Bank of England, civil aviation, the cable and wireless service and the coal industry; in 1947, the railways, road haulage and electricity production came into state ownership; in 1948, the gas industry and the hospitals were nationalized; in 1949, the House of Commons passed a bill to nationalize the iron and steel industry. This extensive legislation met with little opposition; the measures relating to road haulage and to iron and steel were the only ones which aroused the ire of the Conservatives. They were ready to allow the state to relieve private capitalism of responsibility for enfeebled industries, particularly if the shareholders received generous compensation. And the compensation was generous – startlingly so in the case of the coal industry. Furthermore, the system created to administer the nationalized industries was acceptably conservative. Workers' ownership and workers' control had been advocated since the beginning of the century, but few detailed plans had been prepared on the subject since the discussions at the time of the Sankey Commission of 1919. The leaders of the trade unions considered that their task was to defend employees against employers and therefore they showed little enthusiasm over securing a central role for the workers in a nationalized system. The Labour party had been committed to 'common ownership of the means of production, distribution and exchange' since 1918; yet, when the party came to power in 1945 it had no clear ideas as to how it would fulfil its commitment. Emanuel Shinwell, the Minister of Fuel and Power, claimed that the only document on the nationalization of coal he found in the archives of his party was a pamphlet in Welsh by James Griffiths (*Glo*, 1945). In consequence, Herbert Morrison, the chairman of the Nationalization Committee, had a free hand to organize the state-owned industries in accordance with his belief in public corporations. Boards were established which were administered by officials and experts; they were not answerable to any democratic body and the employees had virtually no voice in their decisions. There was considerable criticism of this corporativism. It was claimed that nationalization had led only to superficial changes, for all that had happened was that an irresponsible board of private capitalists had been replaced by an unaccountable board of public bureaucrats.

Despite the criticism, the sight of the fall of one after another of the giants of private capitalism was an exciting experience for the socialists of Wales. The greatest victory was the nationalization of the coal industry, the culmination of half a century of struggle. The pits were transferred to public ownership on New Year's Day 1947, an occasion for celebration throughout the coalfield. The newly nationalized industry was in an appalling state. In the south Wales coalfield, there were 135 pits employing more than 250 men. The vast majority of them were nineteenth-century creations; only eleven had been sunk in the previous twenty-five years. Most of the easily workable seams had been exhausted, and pits in which modern machinery could be used were rare. Only 36 per cent of the coal was excavated by machine and only 64 per cent was mechanically transported. Per capita output was only 60 per cent of what it had been in 1880. In accordance with the cartel system, the market had been shared without distinction between efficient and inefficient pits, a system which discouraged the owners from investing in improvements. The market had contracted greatly. In 1947, only 736,000 tons of coal were exported from the port of Cardiff compared with 25,000,000 tons in 1913. As the number working in the pits of Wales had halved since the 1920s, the labour force inherited by the Coal Board was rapidly ageing.

Yet despite a multitude of problems, nationalization offered a new beginning. There were some signs of hope. The miners were eager to ensure the success of the new order, and the Coal Board was intent upon a massive investment in modernization; demand for coal was buoyant, a fact which allowed the board to be confident in planning for the future. The intention was to maintain a labour force of about a hundred thousand, an intention realized until the market for coal contracted in the mid-1950s. Stability of employment in the coal industry was one of the chief reasons for the low level of unemployment in Wales in the decade following the war. Of the investments of the Coal Board, 21 per cent were earmarked for the south Wales coalfield, although the coalfield only had 16 per cent of the industry's employees. In 1948, 22.5 million tons of saleable coal were mined; plans were prepared to raise production to 32 million tons by 1956, largely through mechanization and the sinking of new pits. Implicit in the board's policy was the closure of the bulk of the older pits; thirty-four of them were closed between 1947 and 1950, a foretaste of a process which was to result in most of the mining valleys being bereft of working pits by the 1980s. Almost from the beginning, the closures were the subject of protests, such as the strike by fifteen thousand miners in 1951 against the threat to the Wern Tarw pit near Pen-coed. There were complaints that the same men were in control after nationalization as under the private system. The first director of the South Western Division (the south Wales coalfield together with the coalfields of Somerset and the Forest of Dean) was the army officer and polo player from Berkshire, Sir Alfred Godwin-Austen, and throughout the coalfield most of the local managers were previous officials of the Powell Duffryn and Ocean companies. But despite much grumbling, the Coal Board was a symbol of victory and the old warriors were distressed to hear the young taking its name in vain.

While the coal industry was being transformed, basic changes were also occurring in Wales's second industry – iron and steel. That was nationalized also, although its nationalization proved short-lived. But although the Conservatives returned the bulk of the industry to private ownership in 1952, Richard Thomas and Baldwin, the second largest of the steel companies of Wales, remained in public ownership; furthermore, as the Iron and Steel Board was given wide powers, the private companies were also heavily dependent upon the state. The steel industry of Wales was revolutionized in the decade following the war. In 1945, when every sector of it, apart from Ebbw Vale, was grossly old-fashioned, it seemed that it would languish unto extinction. Ten years later, Wales was responsible for over a quarter of the steel produced in Britain; the output of the Welsh steelworks rose from 2.65 million tons of crude steel in 1946 to 4.6 million in 1955 – a great stimulus to the coal industry, for by the 1950s the furnaces were receiving at least a third of the coal mined in the coalfields of the south and the north.

This transformation was the result of a vast investment. Huge sums were spent on modernization by John Summers at Shotton, Richard Thomas and Baldwin at Ebbw Vale, and Guest, Keen and Nettlefold at Cardiff. The most exciting development, however, was at Margam; there the largest steelworks in Britain was opened in 1951, the venture of the Steel Company of Wales, a joint creation of the leading companies. A tinplate works linked with Margam was opened at Trostre near Llanelli in 1953 and another at Felindre near Swansea in 1956. The small tinplate works which bestrewed the valleys of the western part of the coalfield were considered to be redundant and most of them were closed within a decade of the opening of Trostre. During the heyday of the iron industry in the nineteenth century much of the demand for the products of the furnaces of Wales came from overseas, but in the years after 1945 only a quarter of the production of the Welsh steelworks was exported. Their chief customers were in England – among car factories and food-processing companies in particular. Thus the rebirth of the ferrous industries of Wales did not reconnect the country with the western sea-routes but rather linked it firmly with the economy of the midlands of England.

As the chief industry of Wales had been nationalized and as its second industry was heavily dependent upon the government, the private sector of the Welsh economy was contracting significantly. Coal and steel were only one facet of increasing state control. In addition to the services nationalized by the Labour government, there was also a substantial growth in the numbers employed in public services such as education and local government. Furthermore, the employees of many private companies owed their jobs to government initiative, and some of those companies – British Petroleum at Llandarcy, for example – were partly state-owned. It seemed as if native Welsh capitalism, which had been so vigorous in the days of D. A. Thomas and W. T. Lewis, was vanishing. In 1950, it was estimated that 40 per cent of the Welsh labour force was working for state bodies and that as much as 60 per cent was employed by industries and services which were directly controlled by government decisions. As these percentages were far higher than those for the kingdom in general, it could be considered that the Welsh economy by the mid twentieth century was the most socialistic economy in Britain.

The same tendency could be seen in farming, traditionally the most self-reliant of callings. During the First and Second World Wars the government had undertaken wide responsibilities in relation to agriculture. Those responsibilities had been abandoned soon after the First World War and the farmers were defenceless until the early 1930s, when their distress obliged the government to change its policies. Things were different after the Second World War. In 1947, Tom Williams, the Minister of Agriculture, introduced a comprehensive measure which guaranteed a market and stable prices for most of the products of the farms of Britain. The Agriculture Act of 1947 was the starting-point of the array of deficiency payments, grants, subsidies and improvement schemes which were to revolutionize Welsh agriculture in the subsequent decades. Henceforth, the farmer would be almost as dependent upon government decisions as were workers in nationalized industries; it was not the weather but rather the Annual Price Review which determined his success or failure.

The Labour government received little thanks from the farmers for ensuring a prosperous future for them. Indeed, outside the coalfields, the nationalization programme aroused little enthusiasm either. But one of the achievements of the post-war Labour government won resounding appreciation. That was the creation of the welfare state. The achievement was not as much of a novelty as is sometimes thought. From the 1830s onwards, almost all governments had introduced welfare legislation; Lloyd George's activities between 1908 and 1911 were of central importance, and major advances were made during the two world wars; there was substance to the efforts of the inter-war governments and, had a Conservative government been elected in 1945, it would undoubtedly have created some form of welfare state. The welfare measures of the Labour government were carried through by two MPs from Wales – Aneurin Bevan, the Minister of Health, and James Griffiths, the Minister of National Insurance; as they were building upon the work of Lloyd George, the belief arose that concern for social justice was a particular trait of the Welsh.

The most prominent feature of the legislation which gave rise to the welfare state was its inclusiveness – precisely the feature which would probably have been absent if the Conservatives had been in office. The first step was the National Insurance Act of 1946 which obliged all workers – whatever their status or income – to insure themselves against ill-health and unemployment. In drafting the Insurance Act, and also the Industrial Injuries Act (1948), Griffiths drew upon the extensive experience of compensation cases he had obtained when working for the South Wales Miners' Federation. The intention was to abjure everything which savoured of the old Poor Law and of the means tests of the 1930s, but it was recognized that full employment was a prerequisite for the effective working of the new system. It was acknowledged that some might fall through the safety net; to provide for them, the National Assistance Board was established in 1948, a body which, it was believed, would deal with the needs of only a tiny proportion of the population.

The National Insurance Act came into force on 5 July 1948. On the same day the National Health Service began. Aneurin Bevan, the architect of the service, claimed that he was inspired by the Tredegar Medical Aid Society, which provided free medical treatment for its entire membership. His intention, asserted Bevan, was to extend the privileges of that society to all the inhabitants of the kingdom. Doctors feared that as a result they would become state employees, an appalling prospect in the opinion of the leaders of the British Medical Association. As had been the case with Lloyd George in 1911, Bevan was obliged to compromise with the Medical Association, in particular by allowing National Health doctors to treat private patients. Despite the compromise, Bevan fulfilled the essentials of his vision, and his scheme for nationalizing hospitals was especially bold. In 1948, the hospitals of Wales were in a dire condition: the bodies which ran them were close to bankruptcy; of the 141 hospitals in the southern counties, only three had adequate laboratories; of the twenty-one institutions housing the permanently infirm, all were old workhouses. At the time of the establishment of the welfare state, there were no resources to remedy the situation, but in subsequent decades there was heavy expenditure on new hospitals.

The Health Service received a warmer welcome in Wales than in almost any other part of the kingdom. Welsh doctors were less critical of Bevan's schemes than were their counterparts in England, and the Welsh almost in their entirety joined the service without delay. Far more use of it was made than the government had expected, and it was soon realized that the money earmarked for it was grossly inadequate. There was a huge demand for false teeth and spectacles, particularly among Welsh working-class women; for them, with their long-term deprivation, the service was truly revolutionary. As past neglect was greater in Wales, as heavy industries – with their frequent accidents – were more important to the country's economy, and as the population tended to be older, it is hardly surprising that the people of Wales made greater use of the social services than did the inhabitants of Britain as a whole. In 1952, expenditure on those services was 33 per cent higher in Wales than it was in the kingdom in general.

In planning the administration of the National Health Service, Bevan had to be content with a tripartite system – the caring services under the local authorities, the hospitals under regional boards and the doctors answerable to medical councils. Wales was given its own Regional Hospitals Board; that board and the Wales Gas Board were the only nationalized boards which recognized the unity of Wales. As has been seen, the south Wales coalfield was part of the South Western Region, while the coalfield of the north was included in the North Western Region. Despite James Griffiths' protests, responsibility for electricity in Wales was divided between the South Wales Electricity Board (SWEB) and the Merseyside and North Wales Electricity Board (MANWEB). Road transport in Wales became part of the

Western Region of the British Transport Authority, and Welsh railways became largely the responsibility of the Western Region of British Railways. (The Western Region was based upon the territory of the Great Western Railway Company, a company whose domain had been much increased following the great amalgamations in 1923, when the GWR absorbed most of the railways of Wales.)

This unwillingness to recognize the unity of Wales was wholly consistent with the convictions of the Labour government. Attlee believed that the problems of the 'regions' would be solved by integrated central planning, a belief also held by Morrison, the architect of the nationalization policy, and by Cripps, the President of the Board of Trade. Morgan Phillips, a native of the Rhymni valley and the general secretary of the Labour party, was suspicious of anything which could be considered a concession to Welsh sentiment. Above all, Aneurin Bevan, the most influential of the Welsh MPs, believed that any form of devolution would draw Wales away from the main stream of British politics; that, he believed, would be detrimental to the interests of Wales and harmful to the prospects of its representatives at Westminster. Peter Stead has argued that, in the 1940s, it was Bevan specifically who frustrated any significant advance in the recognition of Wales; furthermore, he maintains that in subsequent decades every scheme for devolution would have to wrestle with Bevan's notion of political priorities.

But Welsh sentiment could not be ignored entirely. Among Labour and Liberal MPs there was considerable support for the appointment of a Secretary of State for Wales. The issue was raised with the government in 1946 by a deputation led by D. R. Grenfell, member for Gower, and W. H. Mainwaring, member for Rhondda East; they were supported by James Griffiths, but the view of Morrison and Cripps prevailed. Nevertheless, it was felt that the government should not appear to be too inflexible, and therefore a few concessions were made. An annual White Paper on Welsh affairs was published from 1946 onwards, an attempt to draw together the activities of a number of government departments. The Welsh Regional Council of Labour was established in 1947; although it was intended to be wholly under the control of the party at the centre, it was eventually to develop a degree of independence. Then, in 1948, the Council of Wales was founded, a body of twenty-seven nominated members who were given the task of advising the government on matters relating to

Wales; it was granted no powers, a fact which caused increasing frustration to Huw T. Edwards, the secretary of the Transport and General Workers' Union in the north and the chairman of the Council of Wales from 1948 to 1958.

The members of Plaid Cymru made much of the Labour government's reluctance to give its policy a Welsh dimension, in particular in view of the promise made by some Labour candidates in 1945. Plaid Cymru also attacked the imposition of military conscription in peace time and the War Office's designs upon Welsh land – the subject of protests in the Preseli Mountains in 1946, in Tregaron in 1947 and in Trawsfynydd in 1951. As the party continued to be on the margin of Welsh politics, its leaders saw advantage in supporting an inter-party movement to promote the demand for self-government on the pattern of the Covenant Movement in Scotland. In 1950, the Parliament for Wales Campaign was initiated under the auspices of Undeb Cymru Fydd, a campaign which was to absorb the energies of Plaid Cymru members, and others, until 1956. Some left-wing members of the party felt the need to follow a bolder path. They believed that Plaid Cymru's emphasis upon the Welsh language and upon the interests of the rural areas prevented it from gaining support in the industrial south-east; they also argued that the pacificism of Gwynfor Evans, the leader since 1945, hindered the adoption of a militant stance. After a stormy conference in 1949, about fifty members left the party and founded the Welsh Republican Movement. The movement's paper, *The Welsh Republican* (thirty-seven issues, 1950–57), gave voice to a new form of nationalism – socialist, secular, anti-royalist and disrespectful, with English as its medium. The movement broke up in the mid-1950s, but over the following decades many of its characteristics were adopted by Plaid Cymru – the key, perhaps, to the party's increasing acceptability in the eyes of the voters.

Plaid Cymru's criticism of the Labour government was almost inaudible compared with the attacks of the Conservative media. After five years of 'socialist experiment', the Tories were convinced that the public was weary of the Labour party and they looked forward eagerly to the general election of 1950. As has already been noted, that was the first democratic general election in British history. As the Representation of the People Act of 1948 had abolished the business vote along with the university seats, the goal of one adult, one vote had been achieved. Although the University of Wales seat vanished, Wales continued to have thirty-six MPs, for the Flintshire constituency was divided into two. In 1950, the Labour party received 58 per cent of the votes cast in Wales, only marginally less than in 1945. The majorities of every one of its sixteen candidates in the seats of the south Wales coalfield exceeded twenty thousand votes; in Llanelli, James Griffiths obtained a majority of 31,626. In the rest of the kingdom, the verdict was more ambiguous; although the votes cast for the Labour party exceeded those for the Conservatives and their allies by more than three quarters of a million, the party's majority in the House of Commons was only five. The election was disastrous for the Liberal party. Of its 475 candidates, only a hundred saved their deposits; nine Liberals were elected, five of them representing Welsh constituencies.

As its command of the House of Commons was fragile, the government called another election in October 1951. Once again Labour won the largest vote; indeed, the 13,948,883 votes it received is the best performance by any party in the entire history of British elections. Nevertheless, the Conservatives, who received the support of 13,718,199 electors, won the election: they obtained 321 seats in the House of Commons compared with 295 for Labour. The Conservatives' success can largely be explained by the decision of the Liberals to nominate a mere 109 candidates. By 1951, the Liberal party image was increasingly blurred. Its leader, Clement Davies, gave the impression that his party was part of an anti-socialist front, and he was prepared to consider an invitation to join Churchill's new government. As 96.8 per cent of the voters of Britain had chosen one or another of the two main parties, it seemed as if there was little future for the Liberals. In Wales, the Labour party retained its 58 per cent of the vote; although it lost Conwy and Barry to the Conservatives, it maintained its hold upon twenty-seven seats through winning Meirionnydd and Anglesey from the Liberals. Its success in those constituencies was proof of the increasing appeal of the Labour party to the inhabitants of rural Wales; there were class aspects to that appeal, but the attraction of Labour may be attributed in part to the ability of candidates such as Cledwyn Hughes (Anglesey) to identify themselves with the cultural and radical traditions of the Welsh people. Of the six seats won by the Liberals, three were in Wales; with the Conservatives holding six Welsh seats, the Liberal party was the third of the parties of Wales, an astounding change in view of the fact that the party had, a few decades earlier, held the vast majority of the Welsh constituencies.

The general election of 1951 opened a period of Conservative dominance which was to last until 1964. As has already been suggested, the Tories did not make any determined efforts to undo what had been achieved by the Labour governments of 1945 to 1951. So great were the similarities between the fiscal policy of the Labour Chancellor, Gaitskell, and his Conservative successor, Butler, that the term Butskellism was coined to describe it. The Conservatives were fortunate to win when they did. As the economy strengthened, the privations of the 1940s abated; the rationing of petrol and sweets ceased in 1953, and in 1956 rationing of all kinds came to an end. The Conservative party could therefore be portrayed as the initiator of an age of affluence. The affluence was not without its problems. The governments of the 1950s were plagued with financial difficulties, and they reacted by curbing and stimulating the economy in turn – the so-called Stop–Go policy. As they had accepted Keynes's teachings, the Tories were eager to maintain full employment. In July 1955, only 1.4 per cent of the insured workforce of Wales was unemployed, the lowest recorded figure. Full employment was largely a consequence of the demand for coal and steel and of the general prosperity of the British economy, for in the early 1950s new developments in the Welsh economy were few. Graham Humphrys claims that those prosperous years offered a golden opportunity to strengthen the foundations of that economy. By and large, the opportunity was lost; as the government was permitting unrestricted expansion in midland and south-eastern England, industrialists were increasingly reluctant to establish factories in Wales.

The situation deteriorated in 1957. There was a recession in the British economy, and by the beginning of 1959 unemployment in Wales had risen to 4.7 per cent. Between 1957 and 1958, British coal stocks doubled to twenty million tons, and the challenge represented by the supply of cheap oil from the Near East began to make itself felt. The National Coal Board closed fifty of the pits of the south Wales coalfield between 1957 and 1964, a period when the number of miners in the coalfield declined from 104,600 to 76,500. The closure of the smaller tinplate works was accelerated and between 1955 and 1959 the industry shed 9,000 employees. The greatest increase in unemployment, however, occurred in the north-west. The numbers employed in the slate quarries of Caernarfonshire contracted from 3,607 in 1951 to 1,650 in 1961, and in 1958 9.2 per cent of the country's workforce was unemployed; in Anglesey in that year the figure was 12.5 per cent, largely because of the decline in the demand for farm workers caused by the increase in mechanized agriculture.

The economic recession of the late 1950s was a considerable blow to the Conservative government. There was also concern that Britain's economic growth was lagging behind that of others of the countries of western Europe. In consequence, the merits of planning were rediscovered and the government became more positive in its support for regional economic policies. Between 1958 and 1964, there was a second wave of vigorous state intervention in the Welsh economy; annual investment rose to £260 million, 25 per cent higher than in Britain as a whole. Prestcold came to Swansea, Rover to Cardiff, Fisher/Ludlow to Llanelli, Hoover to Merthyr and Revlon to Maesteg. In the north-west, Hotpoint came to Llandudno, and Ferodo and Bernard Wardle to Caernarfon; in 1958, a decision was made to establish a nuclear power station at Trawsfynydd, and another at Yr Wylfa was begun in 1964. Many of the industries established in Wales were capital- rather than labour-intensive, especially the developments at Milford Haven, where use was at last made of one of the world's greatest natural harbours. In 1960, the Esso Company built an oil refinery near Milford, and its example was followed by almost all the chief oil companies over the following decade. In 1974, Milford's trade totalled 58,554,000 tons, almost three times the combined trade of all the other ports of Wales. Despite the huge investment, the oil companies of the Haven employed fewer than two thousand workers. Once again, the most exciting developments in the Welsh economy took place in the steel industry. In 1962, the great venture of Richard Thomas and Baldwin at Llanwern was opened – a steel-mill with the capacity to produce two million tons of steel a year. At the same time, Britain's largest blast furnace was built at Shotton and there were also major investments at Margam and at Ebbw Vale.

As a result of these developments, unemployment in Wales in the first half of the 1960s was held at 2 to 3 per cent. It rose to 4 per cent in the later years of the decade, causing concern to the Labour government elected in 1964. Much of the increase can be attributed to further contraction in employment in the coal industry. During the

Labour governments of 1964–70, forty of the pits of the coalfield of the south and four of the six pits of the coalfield of the north were closed. Of the twenty-five pits in the Rhondda in 1947, only one – that of Maerdy – was left in 1969. The number of miners in Wales decreased from 82,000 to 40,000, and for the first time since 1881 the census recorded in 1971 that there were more people in Wales working on the land than in the pits. A person dying in old age in the 1960s would have lived through the entire cycle of the coal industry's domination of the Welsh economy. The closures prompted few protests; if there were alternative employment available locally, it would seem that the miners of Wales turned their backs on the pits without regret – this, at least, is what was suggested by the songs of Max Boyce, the folk poet of these changes.

The Labour government of 1964–70 was confident that it could promote substantial and continuous economic growth and believed that its policies would usher in a new world of technological efficiency. But the fiscal problems it faced were dire and its course was marked by lurchings from crisis to crisis. Despite its problems, it struggled to maintain full employment; in the second half of the 1960s, there was a third wave of public investment in the Welsh economy. Almost all the industrial districts of Wales were designated Development Areas and were granted substantial concessions. There was considerable investment in the steel industry, the whole of which, after re-nationalization in 1967, was in the hands of the state. With the assistance of the government, the Ford Company was attracted to Swansea, while across the bay the petro-chemical industry at Baglan was vastly expanded. Employment in administration increased with the locating of the Licensing Centre at Swansea and the Passport Office at Newport, and in 1968 one of the most renowned of state enterprises – the Royal Mint – moved to Llantrisant. A variety of factories came to the north-east, and the Rio Tinto Company established an aluminium works in Anglesey in 1970; in the 1960s, the population of Flintshire rose by 17.1 per cent and that of Anglesey by 15.6 per cent, increases which were far greater than those in the rest of the counties of Wales. In that decade Wales as a whole experienced population growth: in 1961, the country had 2,644,000 inhabitants, 12,000 fewer than in 1921; it had 2,731,000 inhabitants in 1971. This increase of 3.3 per cent was highly significant when considered in the context of the demographic history of Wales since the First World War; it was proof that the economy had strengthened sufficiently to allow the country to retain a significant proportion of its natural population growth.

The changes of the quarter of a century following the Second World War transformed the economy and society of Wales. With the emphasis on steel for the motor industry, car components factories and oil refineries, coal was wholly displaced from its leading position by enterprises relating to motor transport. Although attempts to attract industries to the valleys of the coalfield had some degree of success, it was the coastal strip south of the coalfield which received the greatest investment. The concentration between Llanelli and Port Talbot was especially striking, and Graham Humphrys asserted that Swansea had become the centre of an urban agglomeration containing over three hundred thousand inhabitants. By 1970, there was a chain of industries from Llanelli to Newport which was linked with an arc of factories along the northern edge of the Vale of Glamorgan. The essential element in this development was the M4 motorway, which was built in sections from the early 1960s onwards. The Severn Bridge was opened in September 1966, and by the 1970s the journey by car from Swansea to London took less than three hours. There were not dissimilar developments in the north-east as increasing sections of the A55 became dual carriageways.

Because of the emphasis upon developments to the south of the coalfield, the Welsh labour force was becoming increasingly mobile. By the 1960s, there was a daily outflow of ten thousand commuters from the Rhondda, and the valley was coming to be described as a dormitory area. Many workers chose to move closer to their place of work. Between 1951 and 1971, there was a substantial decline in the population of the coal valleys – a fall of 20 per cent in the Rhondda, for example, and of 16 per cent in Abertyleri. In 1945, work began on the new town of Cwmbrân, situated on lowlands eight kilometres from Newport; by 1971, Cwmbrân, with a population of 31,670, had outstripped in size all the towns of northern Monmouthshire. Commuting weakened the close community spirit characteristic of the coalfield. The values of the Welsh working class were not as dominant in the newly industrialized areas as they were in the coalfield; as the economic foundations of the traditional Welsh working class were eroded, that class became less confident in its politics and its culture.

As heavy industry retreated from the coalfield, there was an opportunity to cleanse and beautify the industrial valleys. By the late 1960s, the river Taf was fairly free from pollution; nature trails were created, industrial archaeology won popularity and the industrial south-east began to be promoted as a tourist area. Yet the Aber-fan tragedy proved that death was still lurking there. On 21 October 1966, part of the village of Aber-fan, including its primary school, was buried under the waste of a coal tip. A total of 144 people were killed, 111 children among them – the most heart-rending tragedy in the history of modern Wales.

In the heyday of coal, one of the chief features of the industrial society of the south was the scarcity of employment for women. Gwyn A. Williams has claimed that Wales's experience of industrialization caused the word 'work' to be 'reconstructed on masculine principles'. This all changed in the decades after the Second World War. Although there was a decline in employment among women in the years immediately after the war, the industrialists who established factories in Wales discovered a reservoir of women eager to work and ready to accept wages which would be scorned by men. Between 1951 and 1971, there was a 49 per cent increase in the female workforce in Wales, a period when the male workforce decreased by 6 per cent. As heavy industries gave way to factory work and to employment in the service industries, it was possible to foresee the day when half the workforce of Wales would be female; indeed, by 1977 that day had already dawned in Treorci, the capital of Rhondda Fawr.

While industrial Wales was being transformed, there were even greater changes in train in rural Wales. There is substance to the claim that Welsh rural communities experienced greater changes in the thirty years following the Second World War than they had in the previous three hundred years. The key to change was mechanization. By the 1960s, every farm of any size had its tractor, its bailer, its spreader and its milking-machine. This caused a rapid decrease in the number of farm labourers, by far the largest workforce in the country a century earlier. There were 33,385 farm labourers in Wales in 1951 and only 11,275 in 1971. To the poet R. S. Thomas there was something paradoxical about 'Cynddylan on his tractor'; by 1971 there were more tractors than there were Cynddylans to drive them. With mechanization, a farmer could farm a larger area of land, and such was the cost of the machines that he was obliged to maximize his income. As a result, farm amalgamation proceeded apace. In 1945,

Wales had about forty thousand farms in the full sense; by 1971, it had hardly twenty thousand. Of the employed population of Wales, 8.2 per cent worked in agriculture in 1951, a percentage which had fallen to 4.5 by 1971.

Despite the decrease in the agricultural workforce, there was a marked increase in agricultural production. Agriculture was the miracle industry of post-war Britain. Of the food consumed in Britain in 1939, a third was produced by its farmers; they were producing over half by 1970. Between 1950 and 1970, the number of sheep in Wales increased from 3.8 million to 6 million, and the number of milking cows from 369,000 to 528,000. In 1950, the Milk Marketing Board bought a total of 820 million litres of milk from its thirty thousand Welsh suppliers; in 1970, there were only fifteen thousand suppliers but they produced 1,270 million litres. The standard of the milk was higher too, for all the herds of Wales were free from bovine tuberculosis by 1958. Between 1950 and 1970, there was a decrease of 45 per cent in the number of hectares planted with grain in Wales, but there was an increase of 16 per cent in the tonnage of grain harvested. This productivity depended upon large subsidies, a matter of concern to politicians as surpluses accumulated. By the 1980s, it was felt that the productivity of agriculture should be restrained. In 1984, strict quotas were imposed upon milk producers, a severe blow to the prosperity of many rural districts, particularly in the south-west. The efficiency of farmers was proof of their understanding of the business world and of agricultural science; by 1970, the image of the Welsh farmer as a dim-witted and homespun peasant was stone-dead – assuming that there had ever been any substance to the image.

The amalgamation of holdings was assisted by the fact that by 1970 two thirds of the farmers of Wales were freeholders. Thus amalgamation could proceed unhindered, for henceforth landed proprietors with the power to control it were few; the attempt by the Labour government of 1966–70 to fill the gap with its proposed Rural Development Board for Wales proved a failure. In the main, the process was not a matter of uniting two small farms to create one viable holding, but rather the expansion of farms that were already substantial in size. As a result, a class of kulaks emerged, thus undermining the homogeneity which had once been a feature of Welsh smallholder society. Because of mechanization and amalgamation, a large proportion of the housing stock of the countryside was released for purposes other than agriculture; some of the houses were bought as second homes, a development which was to lead to bitter protest in the 1970s and 1980s.

As a result of the prosperity of agriculture, there was a rapid increase in the price of land; in 1970, land in the Tywi valley cost £2,500 a hectare. Yet compared with the price of land in England, Welsh land appeared to be cheap; it was therefore attractive to those English people who had an urge to farm. Many of them were inspired by the self-sufficiency movement – the craving to go back to the land which enjoyed such a vogue in the 1960s. English colonization of the Welsh countryside was on a scale sufficient to change the ethnic character of many communities. The opportunity to farm was not the only factor attracting English people to the rural areas of Wales. There was considerable contraction in the indigenous members of the secondary rural population – those who provided services for the primary population; by 1970, the craftsmen and businessmen of the rural areas of Wales were incomers as often as not. In addition, there was a huge increase in the number of adventitious rural dwellers – those who had no economic role in the countryside but who lived there from choice.

The motor-car, of course, was the key to the growth of this class. On the edge of all the towns of rural Wales, a process of suburbanization was in train – at Abergwili, near Carmarthen, for example, and at Bow Street, near Aberystwyth; at the same time, many urban workers chose to settle in remoter rural areas. Furthermore, along the coasts of Wales – in Anglesey and in the seaside resorts of the northeast in particular – there was extensive house-building in places popular among those seeking to retire to quiet and beautiful places. 'We are fortunate in our neighbours,' said a woman from Liverpool who had settled in Llanfair Mathafarn Eithaf; 'they are nearly all from Merseyside.' Where the survival of Welsh-speaking communities was concerned, this was by far the most injurious development of the decades after the Second World War. Most of the towns of Wales had been centres of anglicization from their inception. By the mid twentieth century, the Welsh language was in retreat in the rural areas of eastern Wales, but in the west there were extensive districts which were entirely Welsh in speech. By the 1970s, these were nearly all being eroded, and it was the awareness of this fact, above all, which gave a sense of urgency to the campaigns of those committed to the language. In the early 1980s, with forty thousand English people migrating to Wales each year, the fear arose that Welsh-speaking rural communities would be utterly swamped.

Despite the increasing appeal of the Welsh countryside to migrants from beyond Offa's Dyke, rural depopulation remained a matter of concern. Between 1951 and 1971, there was a substantial decrease in the population of most of the rural districts of Wales – as much as 22 per cent in the Tregaron Rural District, for example, and of 18 per cent in that of Penllyn. Such decreases are largely explained by the distorted age structure of the rural Welsh population – the result of a century and more of emigration; in 1951, 18 per cent of the population of Cardiganshire were pensioners compared with 12 per cent in Cardiff. The government commissioned a number of reports on the problems of rural Wales. In 1953, the Council of Wales called for an investment of £60 million to strengthen the foundations of the Welsh rural economy, and a report of 1964 on mid-Wales also stressed the need for extensive expenditure. According to the Labour government of 1964–6, the answer was the establishment of a new town in mid-Wales. A linear town was planned which would stretch from Llanidloes to Newtown and which would house sixty thousand people. The plan was abandoned in 1967; instead, the Development Board for Rural Wales set about doubling the population of Newtown.

As the industries of Wales, and therefore the Welsh themselves, were becoming increasingly concentrated along the southern rim of the country and, to a lesser extent, in the north-east, the lop-sided distribution of the population became even more marked. The geographical centre of Wales lies in the upper Tywi valley, but by 1971 the centre of its population lay in the Cynon valley. A traveller making the 280 kilometre journey from Holyhead to Mountain Ash would have crossed the region inhabited by half the population of Wales; he would cross the region inhabited by the other half by making the thirty-two kilometre journey from Mountain Ash to Cardiff. On the journey, he could not but be conscious of the great emptinesses of mid-Wales – the 'Green Desert', as Harri Webb described it. That part of Wales, with its low population and its fragile economy, was very vulnerable. Its railways did not pay their way and most of them were closed following the Beeching Report of

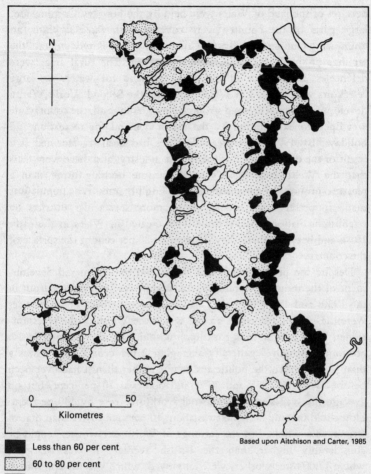

N

Based upon Aitchison and Carter, 1985

■ Less than 60 per cent

░ 60 to 80 per cent

□ Over 80 per cent

The percentage of the population born in Wales, according to the census of 1981

1963; by the mid-1960s, Wales had fewer kilometres of rail than it had had a century earlier. There was some expenditure on roads, but investment in roads in rural Wales did not compare with that which transformed the economy of some of the poorest regions of southern Italy. The government's policy of increasing timber production represented a threat to the traditional rural economy. By 1970, 130,000 hectares of the land of Wales were held by the Forestry Commission; large parts of the country were covered with *Picea sitchensis*, an uninspiring conifer from British Columbia, and in Rhydcymerau 'the saplings of the Third War' were flourishing. The rural areas were defenceless in the face of the urban demand for water: six large reservoirs were created in Wales following the Second World War, a development which aroused strong feelings. Above all, the countryside was open to exploitation by the urban demand for recreation and holidays. By 1970, large areas of Wales had been transformed as a result of the development of the tourist industry, and there were fears that the Welsh countryside would become nothing more than a pleasure-ground for the inhabitants of English cities. An attempt was made to preserve the beauty of the more spectacular districts by establishing national parks; three were created in Wales in the early 1950s and between them they represented 20 per cent of the surface of the country.

Despite the problems of rural Wales and the chequered development of the industrial economy, the Welsh were more prosperous in the 1950s and 1960s than they had ever been before. Those decades were the 'age of affluence', an age which the Welsh of the recession-ridden 1980s were to look back upon with nostalgia. Although British economic growth – generally averaging 2 per cent a year – was a disappointment to the politicians, it was higher than it had ever been before. Between 1955 and 1970, inflation was 70 per cent, but on average the wages of the industrial workforce rose by 140 per cent. Household income in Wales was about 10 per cent lower than that of Britain as a whole, but the earnings of Welsh steelworkers could be considerably higher than the British average; it was Margam, where 17,000 steelworkers were employed, which was the epitome of the new world of affluence. There was considerable erosion in the income differentials between the middle and working classes, and many mocking references were made to the extravagant spending of the young men of the furnaces. Nevertheless, the prosperity of working-class families depended heavily upon overtime earnings, and the fact that a job was available for the wife as well as the husband was central to their standard of living.

The new prosperity was expressed in expenditure on goods of all kinds. There were 110,000 licensed cars in Wales in 1951 and 606,000 in 1971; in relation to income, the cost of cars and petrol was falling continuously, causing a revolution in mobility. There were over 300,000 private telephones in Wales in 1971 compared with less than 50,000 in 1951. By 1971, the majority of Welsh households had a washing-machine and a refrigerator, and a quarter of them were warmed by central-heating. During the 1950s, the Electricity Boards were busily working on plans to supply electricity to the inhabitants of rural areas. The work had been largely completed by the mid-1960s, and country-dwellers could therefore share in the luxuries of the age. Foreign travel came within the reach of the bulk of the population, and some fifty thousand Welsh people sunbathed on the beaches of Spain in 1970. Foreign travel fostered an interest in food other than the usual British stodge; the pioneers were the Indian and Chinese restaurateurs and they provided a foretaste of an exotic abundance.

Above all, there was television. There was a set in 60 per cent of the homes of Wales in 1960, a percentage which was to rise to 92 by 1969. At first, the sole channel was that of the BBC, but from 1955 onwards the services of the commercial companies spread across the kingdom. Wales was made part of the territory of Television Wales and the West (TWW) – 'the kingdom of King Arthur' once again – although viewers in the north-east could receive the programmes of Granada from Manchester. With its lively advertisements, commercial television was a central factor in the consumerism which became increasingly dominant from the 1960s onwards. With every living-room (or 'lounge' – one of the significant words of the 1960s) a picture-house, there was little reason to go to the cinema; there were 350 cinemas in Wales in 1950 and only 100 in 1975. A host of social activities waned in the wake of the popularity of the box – whist drives, drama groups, local *eisteddfodau* and male-voice choirs. Yet it is possible to romanticize what was killed by the coming of television, and it would appear that social activities revived after the first wave of enthusiasm had passed.

Efforts to improve and augment the housing stock were central to the rise in living standards. To Aneurin Bevan, the minister responsible for housing in the Attlee government, this was a wholly crucial matter. Because of the scarcity of building materials, that government's record was poor, and many Welsh people – the inhabitants of Tin-Town, Pontypridd, for example – were obliged to live in pre-fabs for a decade and more. Between 1945 and 1951, an average of

8,250 houses were built each year in Wales, 87 per cent of them council houses. The Conservative government which came to power in 1951 promised that 300,000 houses a year would be built and, under the energetic direction of Harold Macmillan, it kept its promise. Between 1951 and 1964, an average of 13,500 houses was completed each year in Wales, 63 per cent of them council houses. This percentage was markedly higher than it was in the kingdom in general; the chief reason for that was the reluctance of speculators to venture their money in the valleys of the coalfield. The valleys had had a high level of owner-occupation, but as 165,000 council houses were built in Wales in the twenty years following the end of the Second World War, the council estate had become the habitat of a quarter of the Welsh people by the end of the 1960s.

In addition, grants were given to renovate and modernize existing housing. Between 1951 and 1971, 220,000 of the houses of Wales were improved through providing their inhabitants with services such as hot water, baths and lavatories. Advances in the rural areas were especially striking. In the 1960s, there seemed to be a cement-mixer outside every farmhouse. Mud walls were demolished and old chimneys were closed up; indoor water-closets were installed, for the 'elsan culture' so scornfully mentioned by R. S. Thomas proved to be short-lived. There were great changes in the towns also. In Caernarfon, many of the buildings within the town walls were cleared; half of Cardiff's Butetown vanished and Merthyr's China was totally demolished. In the process of getting rid of sub-standard buildings, many attractive features were lost, a fact which helped to foster the conservation movement of subsequent decades. By the 1960s, there was one subject relating to housing which caused increasing concern. That was the leasehold issue. Most of the houses of the industrial south-east had been built on the basis of ninety-nine-year leases, and a similar system existed in seaside resorts such as Llandudno and Aberystwyth. As Wales had experienced rapid urbanization in the 1850s and 1860s, leases which were due to expire ninety-nine years later were a matter of anxiety. A Leasehold Reform Act was passed in 1967, but it proved to be an inadequate solution to the problem.

Education was also central to aspirations for a richer and more civilized society. Ever since the age of Rousseau, social reformers had considered the education of the young to be the key to a world of contentment and fulfilment. This was another field where the record of the Labour government of 1945–51 was criticized. As a major education act had been passed in 1944, Attlee and his fellow ministers saw. no need for further legislation on the subject. As most of the members of that government were products either of the public schools or of the elementary schools, they were curiously ill-informed about one of the chief sections of the educational system – secondary schools maintained by public funds. The 1944 act was put into effect. The school-leaving age was raised to fifteen in 1947, and efforts were made to ensure that every child would attend a secondary school and attend without paying fees. Implicit in the legislation was the abandonment of the distinctive features of the Welsh educational system, in particular those inherited from the Welsh Intermediate Education Act of 1889. The Central Welsh Board – the CWB – was abolished in 1949 and its functions were transferred to the Welsh Joint Education Committee. As the Education Act of 1944 had acknowledged the importance of parental wishes (specifically in the sphere of religious education), it opened the way to the establishment of a network of Welsh-medium schools, a development which will need further discussion.

The Education Act of 1944 took it for granted that only a minority could benefit from an academic education. The 11+ examination was therefore retained and 'modern' schools were built for those unsuccessful in the examination, despite the opposition of such experienced educationalists as W. G. Cove, the MP for Aberafan. 'Modern' schools were less prominent in Wales than in England, largely because of the legacy of the Intermediate Act of 1889. In 1950, 20 per cent of those attending secondary schools in England went to schools of a 'grammar' type; the figure was 50 per cent in Wales. In rural areas, it could be substantially higher; in Tregaron in 1947, two thirds of those sitting the 11+ examination were successful. The examination came under increasing criticism; by the 1960s, there were even Conservatives – Edward Boyle, for example, the Minister of Education from 1962 to 1964 – who supported its abolition. It was argued that the examination was particularly harmful to the prospects of working-class children; nevertheless, the least socialist regions of Wales were the first to abandon it. After the war, bilateral or comprehensive schools were established in many of the rural areas of Wales, and Anglesey, in 1957, was the first Local Education Authority in the kingdom to abolish the 11+ examination. In 1965, the Labour government instructed education authorities to prepare plans to ensure that pupils in secondary education attended comprehensive schools; at that time, 8 per cent of the secondary pupils of England attended such schools compared with 20 per cent in Wales. The Welsh percentage had risen to 75 when Labour returned to power in 1974. The new Labour government insisted that the grammar/modern division should be abolished, and, by the end of the 1970s, the 11+ examination had disappeared from the whole of Wales apart from parts of Carmarthenshire. As a result of the reorganization, famous institutions such as Lewis Pengam, Grove Park Wrexham and Friars Bangor ceased to be grammar schools, much to the distress of traditionalists. A number of huge schools containing two thousand pupils and more were created; they were defended on the ground that they could offer a wider choice of subjects, but they were attacked also because their size, it was argued, rendered them amorphous and impersonal.

Before the implementation of the Education Act of 1944, the children who failed the 11+ stayed on in the junior school, at least in those areas where senior schools had not been established. The reorganization was a lengthy process, and the departure of the last teenager from a junior school did not occur until 1968. That year therefore denotes the final abandonment of the notion that the less fortunate sections of society need no schooling beyond the elementary level. The school-leaving age was raised to sixteen in 1969; even after that, the years in the primary school constituted the greater part of the educational experience of the majority of the Welsh people. Primary education was transformed in the quarter of a century following the Second World War. By the 1960s, pupils did not sit quietly at their desks; instead, they 'received a variety of experiences' which 'satisfied their curiosity on the basis of groups dealing with different aspects of the same activity' – to quote the Gittins Report (1967). 'Conventional timetabling' was abandoned; the task of the teacher was not to 'prepare lessons [but rather] ... to organize learning opportunites.' Henceforth, children in infants' schools did not learn psalms by heart; rather did they make pretty things from the inner rolls of toilet paper. Large sums were spent on buildings; by the mid-1960s, the elsan had disappeared even from the most remote schools of Cardiganshire. In the wake of rural depopulation, there was a marked fall in the number of pupils attending rural schools. In 1921, there were 3,319 children between five and nine years of age in the rural districts of Cardiganshire; the number had fallen to 2,155 by 1971. The Gittins Report urged the establishment of 'district schools', each having at least sixty pupils – a plan which, if carried out, would have halved the number of rural schools. There was a hostile reaction to the programme of closures, for it was believed that a community lacking a school was doomed; nevertheless, it was difficult to refute the argument that children attending a school containing less than a dozen pupils were disadvantaged.

The developments in primary and secondary education were accompanied by vast changes in higher education. Between 1951 and 1971, the cost of maintaining the University of Wales rose from £1 million to £16 million, and during the same period the number of its students rose from 4,863 to 14,915. The most rapid growth occurred in the second half of the 1960s, in response to the Robbins Report (1963), which recommended an increase of 170 per cent in the number of undergraduates in the United Kingdom. The enthusiasm of the state proved short-lived. In the 1970s, the cost of maintaining the universities came to be considered excessive, and from the late 1970s onwards the public money they received was reduced, a policy which led to a crisis in the academic world. New universities were established in England, Scotland and Northern Ireland, but in Wales no university institutions were created *de novo*. However, the College of Advanced Technology at Cardiff became part of the University of Wales in 1964 and it was followed by St David's College, Lampeter, in 1972. As a result of expansion, the number of subjects taught in the University increased greatly, and there was also a vast increase in the scholarly productions of its academic staff. The expansion whetted the appetite of the senates of the individual colleges for the status of independent universities. In 1960, a commission was established to consider the future of the University. While it sat, Alwyn D. Rees, head of the Extramural Department at Aberystwyth, led a skilful campaign to persuade the graduates of the University to testify in favour of its continuance. The report of the commission was published in 1964; fourteen of its members – most of whom were English – were defederalists; the other twelve – all of whom were Welsh – were federalists. Following a debate on the report in the court of the University, the federal system was confirmed by 103 votes to thirty-three.

From the point of view of the Welsh character of the University, the threat to its unity was a minor factor compared with the change in its ethnic composition. In 1951, 84 per cent of the students were natives of Wales; of the rest, 13 per cent came from other parts of Britain and 3 per cent from overseas; in 1971, the percentages were 37, 59 and 4. If it is accepted that Wales is a nation in the same sense as the other nations of Europe, its university by the late twentieth century was unique, for there was no other nation in which the native population was in the minority in every constituent part of its university system. For generations, it had been a matter of pride that a fairly high percentage of the young people of Wales received a university education; it could be argued that the expansion of the University of Wales was a contribution to the attempt to ensure that a similar proportion of the young people of England enjoyed that privilege. Yet it has to be acknowledged that the decline in the percentage of students from Wales in the University of Wales was partly the result of the increasing tendency of Welsh students to attend universities in England, a tendency greatly promoted by the UCCA system introduced in 1963. The anglicization of the University was the subject of much protest, part of the unrest on Welsh-language issues which was a prominent feature of the 1960s.

That decade was a troubled period in universities throughout the western world as the 'youth revolt' gathered steam. The troubles were an aspect of one of the most striking developments of the 1960s – the growth of a youth sub-culture. As the young had a greater purchasing power than ever before, and, as the values of society were changing so rapidly, a chasm opened between the younger and the older generations. Because of the 'baby boom' of the late 1940s, there were more teenagers in Wales in the 1960s than in any other decade since the war. In 1960, the poet Anthony Conran wrote: 'A Welshman at twenty/ Is either an awkward edition of fifty/ Or else he's gone English,' a comment which was to be wholly misleading ten years later. The most obvious expression of the youth culture was popular music. Bill Haley and his Comets performed in Cardiff in 1957; they were condemned by the city fathers, who were appalled to hear that the audience had danced in the theatre aisles. In Welsh, there was Parti Sgiffl Llandygái, which astounded those who believed that hymns, *cerdd dant* (singing to the harp) and the sweet melodies of Jac a Wil represented the sum total of Welsh music. In the early 1960s, Ffred Ffransis – later to be the most dedicated of Welsh-language activists – was an eager member of the Flintshire branch of the Elvis Presley Fan Club. His fellow activist, Dafydd Iwan, began playing the guitar in 1962; from 1965 onwards, his regular appearances on the television programme *Y Dydd* launched the career of the central figure in Welsh pop and folk music. In 1964, the Welsh language had its first rock group – Y Blew – four student intellectuals from Aberystwyth. Dafydd Iwan and Y Blew gave rise to a host of imitators and folk and rock enjoyed a great vogue. The pub was an essential part of these developments. Many of the performers were children of the manse, and others of them had teetotal parents. As Dafydd Iwan notes in his autobiography, going to a public house was an 'act which challenged the system'. In the mid-1960s, Welsh-language entertainment moved, overnight almost, from the chapel vestry into (or perhaps back to) the pub, and once again there was evidence of the innate beeriness of the Welsh.

The youth culture was associated with the 'new morality'. The 1960s were the first decade of the 'permissive society', a decade in which Victorian morality collapsed with remarkable suddenness. The *Lady Chatterley* case was heard in 1959 and it opened the way for publications such as John Rowlands's *Ienctid yw 'Mhechod*, the first novel in Welsh to offer a detailed description of the sexual act. Betting-shops were legalized in 1960 and an act permitting abortion was passed in 1967; in the same year, male homosexual activity was decriminalized largely as the result of the tireless efforts of Leo Abse, the MP for Pontypool; censorship in the theatre was abolished in 1968 and the law relating to divorce was reformed in 1969. The breakdown of marriage became common: the number of the inhabitants of Wales who had experienced divorce rose from 12,000 in 1961 to 24,000 in 1971 and to 72,000 in 1981. In the 1950s, contraceptive devices were bought through ambiguous advertisements in the press. By the late 1960s, they were on sale in machines in public lavatories or were given away free by clinics; in addition, at least 10 per cent of the women of Wales were taking the contraceptive pill.

It is difficult to measure the degree to which these developments resulted in an increase in sexual intercourse outside marriage, but it was widely believed that a sexual revolution was occurring. Yet too much should not be claimed. A study of communities around Swansea published in 1965 showed that the family unit remained wholly central; the social attitudes of most of the Welsh people continued to be conservative and the feminist movement had hardly struck roots in the Wales of the 1960s. It is easier to measure the decline in another aspect of traditional morality – the observance of the Sabbath. Following a referendum in 1961, public houses opened on Sundays in five of the counties and in all the county boroughs of Wales; as a result, 72 per cent of the Welsh people lived in 'wet' areas. There were further referenda in 1968, 1975, 1982 and 1989; by 1989, Dwyfor, with no more than 1 per cent of the population of Wales, was the only remaining 'dry' district.

All this suggests that the Welsh were rapidly abandoning their allegiance to religion. Indeed, religious decline is one of the most striking aspects of the history of Wales in the period after the Second World War; by the last quarter of the twentieth century, with only 13 per cent of the inhabitants of Wales regularly attending a place of worship, it was difficult to claim that the Welsh were a Christian nation, an astonishing change in view of their much vaunted devotion to religious observance at the beginning of the twentieth century. Because of the shortcomings of the statistics, the decline in attendance cannot be chronicled in detail, but there was probably a halving in the number of those regularly attending the services of the denominations belonging to the Nonconformist tradition between the 1950s and the 1970s. In terms of language, those were the most Welsh of the denominations and they undoubtedly suffered in the wake of the decline in the numbers of Welsh-speakers; nevertheless, English-language chapels in Wales often suffered an even greater decline. Anglicanism was boosted by immigration, particularly in the northeast and the rural areas of the west; there was, however, a 25 per cent decrease in the number of Easter communicants in the Church in Wales between the 1950s and the 1970s. The Catholic Church continued to grow, although the rate of growth had declined by the late 1960s; the emergence of Catholicism as the strongest denomination in many parts of Wales came as a shock to many.

Up until the 1960s, organized religion held its own fairly well among members of the middle class, particularly those who were Welsh-speaking. It had numerous adherents also among the working class in the older industrial areas, but it was very weak in the newly urbanized districts, although some exotic sects found footholds there. By the 1970s, however, the majority of the middle class had ceased to attend a place of worship and a new phenomenon had arisen – Welsh people, wholly conscious of their Welshness, who were professed non-believers. Yet fervent opposition to religion, such as may be found in Roman Catholic countries, was rare in Wales. Although civil marriages increased by 15 per cent between 1951 and 1971, the majority still got married in a place of worship. In many districts, the minister retained his position as the leader of local society, and the heads of theological colleges continued to be among the most distinguished of Welsh intellectuals, as the careers of R. Tudur Jones and Pennar Davies testify. The Welsh did not revolt against Christianity; rather did they slip from its grasp, and the empty chapels were a cause of sadness and regret even to those who never darkened their doors. By the 1960s, it was obvious that there were far more chapels than were needed and many of them were converted into houses, shops or garages. (The man who converted Penuel in the Cynon valley into a house was so pleased with his bargain that he carved the word 'spent' beneath the name of the chapel.) With the chapels under threat, they came to be appreciated as architecture, and a team of scholars set about recording them. The marked decline in the number of worshippers led to an increasing interest in church unity; in 1962, David James, a London Welsh millionaire, offered a large sum of money to the denominations on condition that they abandoned their divisions. The upholders of the fundamentalist standpoint maintained that the traditional denominations had wandered into a slough of heterodoxy and they began to establish separate evangelical congregations. To believe, argued R. Tudur Jones, was the only option that remained, for the twentieth century had forced 'Christians of the evangelical tradition in Wales to abandon their confidence in their political power, in the eloquence of their preaching, in the distinction of their philosophy and in the effectiveness of their organization'.

One of the chief reasons for the decline in the appeal of the chapels was the growth of other diversions. Indeed, attendance at Sunday school declined in exact inverse proportion to the rise in car ownership. In the second half of the twentieth century, the Welsh showed an increasing interest in open-air activities. They began climbing their own mountains; young people from Wales went on skiing holidays in their thousands, and new sports such as surfboarding and hang-gliding came into vogue. Cricket, a game previously considered to be incorrigibly English, enjoyed growing esteem; Australia was beaten by Glamorgan in 1964 and 1968 and the standard of local teams such as

Gowerton was high. Despite the publicity given to rugby, association football was the most popular game among the Welsh throughout the years; some Welsh teams – Swansea and Wrexham in particular – enjoyed periods of success, but it was the English teams which attracted the loyalty of Welsh devotees, particularly in the north, where there was a fanatical allegiance to the giants of Merseyside. Nevertheless, rugby attracted many followers outside its traditional heartlands, and there was pride throughout Wales in the marvellous achievements of the national team. Growth in the awareness of Cardiff as the capital of Wales may be partly attributed to the trek from all parts of the country to attend international matches at Cardiff Arms Park. There was much building in the park in the 1960s and it emerged renamed the Welsh National Stadium in 1970. In Cardiff Arms Park, as Trevor Fishlock put it, 'Englishmen are sacrificed on a Saturday afternoon,' an apt comment, for in the fifteen years between 1964 and 1979 the English team failed to gain a single victory there; during that period, the Welsh won the Triple Crown seven times and there was much acclamation for such players as Gareth Edwards and Barry John, the architects of that glory.

The passion for rugby was such as to cause a redefinition of the characteristics of the Welsh. They were no longer conceived of as puritan chapel-goers but rather as muscular boozers who were doubtful whether there was life beyond the dead-ball line. The portrait was misleading, of course, but it reflected the difficulty of forming any definition of Welshness which would be relevant to the nation in its entirety. A definition based upon linguistic considerations had long become untenable, although there were those who sang the praises of Wenglish, a vernacular which has been the object of far greater prejudice than anything suffered by Welsh.

Nevertheless, the Welsh language continued to be a central element in Welsh national identity, despite the decrease in the numbers who spoke it. In 1931, 909,261 of the inhabitants of Wales claimed to speak Welsh; the number declined to 714,686 in 1951, 656,002 in 1961, 542,425 in 1971 and 508,207 in 1981; the proportion of the people of Wales claiming a knowledge of the language also fell – from 36.8 per cent in 1931, to 28.9 per cent in 1951, to 26 per cent in 1961, to 20.9 per cent in 1971 and to 18.9 per cent in 1981. During those years monolingualism in Welsh among adults disappeared; the 1960s was probably the decade which saw the passing of the last adult with no English at his – or more probably her – command. Between 1931 and 1951, there was a 20 per cent decrease in the number of Welsh-speakers, evidence of the damage inflicted upon the language by the depression and the war. The decrease in Glamorgan was as high as 35 per cent, and by 1951 the language was faltering in such places as Treorci and Aberdare, towns in which it had once been widely spoken. In the 1950s – a fairly prosperous decade in Wales – the decline was only 8 per cent, but in the 1960s it increased to 17 per cent. The increase can in part be attributed to the fact that the census of 1971 inquired about the ability of Welsh-speakers to read and write the language; many of those who had some command of Welsh were reluctant to acknowledge that they were illiterate in it, and they therefore chose to declare that they were monoglot English-speakers. Indeed, there is some evidence that the official nature of the census has always discouraged less fluent Welsh speakers from recording their knowledge of the language: a survey in 1979 suggested that about 28 per cent of the adults in Wales had some command of it.

To Welsh-language enthusiasts, education was the key weapon in the battle to safeguard and foster the language. As has been seen, a Welsh-medium primary school was established at Llanelli by the Carmarthenshire Education Committee in 1947. About a dozen others were opened between 1947 and 1951; by 1970, forty-one had come into existence, among them Ysgol Dewi Sant in Cardiff, at one time the largest primary school in Wales. In addition, there were a few dozen schools containing Welsh units – the pattern of development increasingly favoured by the Labour party, despite the opposition of educationalists and parents. In the early years, the Welsh schools tended to have a rather bourgeois intake, but as they expanded this became far less pronounced. The prospects of the Welsh language in the urban areas were transformed by the advent of the Welsh schools. Previously, it was difficult for Welsh-speaking parents in English-speaking districts to ensure that their children had a command of the language, and there were examples of distinguished Welsh writers whose children were unable to read their works. Henceforth, it was possible to raise a generation of Welsh-speaking city dwellers, a development with wide-reaching social implications. In some areas, there was a striking increase in the proportion of Welsh-speaking

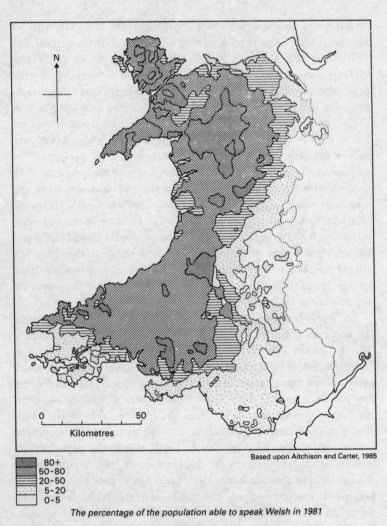

Based upon Aitchison and Carter, 1985

▨	80+
▧	50-80
▨	20-50
⠿	5-20
	0-5

The percentage of the population able to speak Welsh in 1981

children; of the children aged between three and fifteen in Cardiff, 4.03 per cent had a knowledge of Welsh in 1971 and 7.19 per cent in 1981 – an increase which if sustained would ensure that the majority of the children of the city were Welsh-speaking by 2021. The 'official' Welsh schools were established at precisely the time when the 'natural'

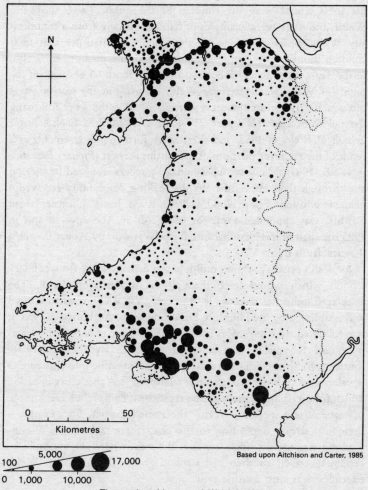

Based upon Aitchison and Carter, 1985

100 5,000 17,000
0 1,000 10,000

The number able to speak Welsh in 1981

Welsh schools were facing a serious threat; by 1970, as the result of English immigration into the Welsh-speaking areas of the west and the north, most 'natural' Welsh schools were facing major linguistic problems. There were parishes in which Welsh was spoken by three quarters of the population, but where three quarters of the pupils in the local school were the children of the quarter who spoke no Welsh, and there were examples of families moving from a tradition- ally Welsh-speaking area to an anglicized area in order that their children should receive an education through the medium of Welsh. In the years immediately following the war, about 65 per cent of the pupils of Wales were receiving Welsh lessons, but the teaching was often ineffective; more resources were allocated to the work following the publication of the report *The Place of Welsh and English in the Schools of Wales* in 1953, and there were further improvements as a result of the recommendations of the Gittins Report (*Primary Education in Wales*, 1967). Many second-language teachers laboured heroically, and through their efforts the Welsh-speaking community received a valuable infusion of new blood; in 1980, R. M. Jones, a 'learner' from Cardiff, was appointed professor of Welsh at Aberystwyth and in 1985 the chair at the National Eisteddfod was won by Robat Powel, a 'learner' from Ebbw Vale.

As Welsh primary schools multiplied, a demand arose for secondary schools which would teach through the medium of Welsh. The anglicized industrial counties led the way. Ysgol Gyfun Glan Clwyd was established by the Flintshire Local Education Authority in 1956; it was followed by Ysgol Maes Garmon in the same county in 1961 and by Ysgol Rhydfelen in Glamorgan in 1962. By the mid-1980s, fourteen Welsh-medium secondary schools had come into existence, a development which was greatly facilitated by the reorganization which followed in the wake of the creation of comprehensive schools. In some Welsh-speaking areas – the Preseli district, for example – there was strong opposition to the plans for establishing a Welsh- medium secondary school; it was in the areas where parents could be certain that their children had a sound grasp of English that Welsh education was most warmly welcomed.

There were also efforts to expand Welsh-medium teaching in the University of Wales. In 1950, on the initiative of Gwynfor Evans, the University set up a committee to consider the creation of a Welsh- medium college. The members of the committee had little sympathy for the notion, but in 1955 the University announced that expansion of provision for teaching through the medium of Welsh would be commensurate with the increase in the number of pupils who had received a Welsh-language education. Lecturers with particular responsibility for lecturing through the medium of Welsh were appointed, a scheme which from the mid-1960s onwards was confined to the colleges at Bangor and Aberystwyth. By the 1980s, they amounted to about two dozen, almost all of them teaching in Arts departments. Although the provision was not extensive, there were by that time graduates, in subjects other than Welsh itself, who had followed university courses through the medium of Welsh, and that experience spread more widely from 1980 onwards by means of the Welsh-medium External Degree offered by Aberystwyth. There was a demand for institutions within the colleges where Welsh-speakers would be in the majority; after bitter disputes, Neuadd Pantycelyn at Aberystwyth became a Welsh hall of residence in 1974, as did Neuadd John Morris-Jones in Bangor in the following year – successfully, on the whole. There were also developments in other sectors of advanced education, with the Normal College, Bangor, in particular, offering a variety of courses through the medium of Welsh.

With so much campaigning in favour of Welsh in education, it is surprising that until the 1960s there were few efforts to win official status for the language. In the mid-1950s, virtually the only examples of visible, official Welsh were the few bilingual signs erected on county boundaries. ('Why,' asked an English visitor, 'have you knighted your counties?') From 1952 until 1960, the Beasley family of Llangennech fought to obtain a Welsh rate demand from the Llanelli Rural District Council, but their fight was a lonely one. It was not considered odd that bodies such as the Welsh Books Committee of the Cardiganshire County Council held its meetings entirely in English, and hardly anyone filled in a cheque in Welsh. There was a great change in the 1960s, a development largely to be attributed to the activities of Cymdeithas yr Iaith Gymraeg (the Welsh Language Society – of the second creation), a movement established during the Plaid Cymru summer school at Pontarddulais in 1962. The society sprang from the frustrations felt by younger party members in the face of the slow and uncertain growth of Plaid Cymru; the catalyst, however, was the radio lecture given by Saunders Lewis on 13 February 1962. In his lecture, Lewis called on his listeners 'to make it impossible to conduct local or central government business without the Welsh language'. 'This is not,' he stated, 'a haphazard policy for isolated individuals . . . It is a policy for a movement, a movement rooted in those areas where Welsh is an everyday spoken language.' The movement he had in mind was Plaid Cymru, but the party refused the role on the grounds that it could not, as Gwynfor Evans put it, 'combine an effective fight for the Welsh language with being a political party'. The society's first protest occurred at Aberystwyth on 2 February 1963; on that day, in an attempt to force the authorities to issue Welsh summonses, the public buildings of the town were placarded and traffic was stopped on Trefechan Bridge. Members of the society went on to campaign for Welsh in the Post Office, on car licences, on birth certificates and on signposts, activities which led to a host of court cases, and the experience of imprisonment became commonplace among the younger generation of Welsh-language activists.

There was some movement on the part of the authorities. The ambiguity in the status of Welsh was highlighted by a case at Ammanford in 1961 concerning nomination papers. The incident was largely responsible for the government's decision in 1963 to establish a committee to consider the legal status of the language. The committee's report, published in 1965, recommended that Welsh be given 'equal validity' – 'that anything done in Welsh in Wales should have the same legal force as it would in English'. A diluted version of this principle was incorporated into the Welsh Language Act of 1967. As protest had nurtured a thirst for Welshness, the measure was considered inadequate, and demands soon arose for further legislation to strengthen the rights of Welsh-speakers. In the late 1960s, the campaigns of Cymdeithas yr Iaith Gymraeg became increasingly militant – the Welsh version, perhaps, of the unrest prevalent in those years among young people throughout the western world. The campaigns touched a raw nerve in the life of Wales. Officials reacted with confused anger and grudging concessions. Member of the older generation of Welsh-speakers were obliged to reconsider their allegiance to the language, and their perplexity was intensified by Alwyn D. Rees's provocative articles in the monthly journal *Barn*. Some Welsh magistrates showed sympathy for law-breaking; indeed, it could almost be claimed that they approved of it, particularly in a celebrated case in 1970 involving Dafydd Iwan. The protest movement inspired an array of other activities – the Welsh pop scene, for example, and the efforts to establish bookshops, publishing houses, record companies and housing associations operating through the medium of Welsh.

In the 1970s, Cymdeithas yr Iaith Gymraeg concentrated its attention upon television. Ever since the coming of television to Wales in the early 1950s, supporters of the Welsh language had been aware of the challenge it represented. There was a little television in Welsh almost from the beginning, largely because of the efforts of Alun Oldfield-Davies and Hywel Davies, and the promptings of the Broadcasting Council for Wales, a body which came into existence in 1953. Following the publication of the Pilkington Report (1962), BBC Wales was established and was given the responsibility of preparing twelve hours of television programmes a week, about half of them in the Welsh language. Welsh-language programmes were also broadcast by TWW and Granada, but large areas of the west and north were beyond the reach of the transmitters of the two companies. Television Wales (West and North), a company established by a group of Welsh patriots led by Haydn Williams, the director of education of Flintshire, began broadcasting to those areas in 1962. As its territory was thinly populated and its resources inadequate to fulfil the duties imposed upon it, the company came to an end in 1963 after broadcasting for ten months. It was taken over by TWW, which was then obliged to broadcast five and a half hours of Welsh-language programmes a week. In 1968, that obligation was inherited by Harlech Television (HTV), the company which replaced TWW when licences were redistributed. Welsh language programmes tended to be broadcast at inconvenient times, for showing them at peak hours annoyed those unable to understand them. To avoid broadcasts unintelligible to them, many viewers in the south-east forsook all programmes produced in Wales by ensuring that their sets received the Bristol service. Thus, while the scarcity of programmes in their language was anglicizing the Welsh-speakers, the fact that such programmes existed at all was causing English-speakers to turn their backs upon everything emanating from Wales. Demands arose for a separate channel for Welsh programmes, a solution advocated by a national conference convened by the lord mayor of Cardiff in 1973 and recommended in the report of the Crawford Commission in 1974, a report accepted by the Labour government. Preparatory work on the new channel was undertaken, and the plans were endorsed by the Conservatives in their manifesto for the general election of 1979.

Publications in Welsh were also considered central by devotees of the Welsh language. In the 1940s, when only a few dozen new books were published annually, there were fears that the appetite for Welsh books would decline to extinction. Through the efforts of Alun R.

Edwards, the county librarian, the Cardiganshire Education Committee began publishing Welsh books for children in 1950, an enterprise which received the support of other counties in the following years. In 1954, under the patronage of the Welsh Joint Education Committee, the Welsh Books Scheme was set up to prepare material for schools. In 1956, the government gave a subsidy of £1,000 towards publishing Welsh books for adults, a sum which rose to £3,000 in 1960. Then, in 1961, the Welsh Books Council was established, an institution which had an annual income of £300,000 by 1988. The council's grants and the labours of authors led to a marked increase in the number of Welsh books published – from 239 in 1973 to 488 in 1988. From 1977 onwards, after a decade of struggle, the noble old weekly *Y Faner* was saved by subsidy, a condition which most Welsh periodicals soon came to share. The Welsh Arts Council was established in 1967, an important milestone in the history of culture in Wales. By 1985, the council was receiving an annual grant of £7 million; specifically Welsh-language activities received only a small part of the grant, but by the last quarter of the twentieth century Welsh drama, the National *Eisteddfod* and bodies such as the Welsh Academy (founded in 1959) were heavily dependent upon the patronage of the British state. It almost seemed as if that state was experiencing a fit of remorse and was paying compensation for the defeat of Llywelyn, the Act of 'Union', the English bishops, the 'Treachery of the Blue Books' and the 'Welsh Note'. It has already been suggested that by the 1950s the Welsh economy was the most socialistic in Britain. A decade or two later, Welsh culture, in particular its Welsh-language aspects, was equally socialistic.

Because of the sponsorship available, the third quarter of the twentieth century was, according to John Rowlands, 'a period of unparalleled opportunity and encouragement for the Welsh writer'. As a result of the number of publications made possible by grants, the literary output of that period is particularly difficult to assess. The works of greatest distinction were those produced by writers who had already won recognition before the war. Kate Roberts resumed her calling in her fifties and eleven of her works were published between 1949 and 1981. Saunders Lewis wrote seventeen plays between 1948 and 1978, and his enthralling novel *Merch Gwern Hywel* appeared in 1964. Gwenallt produced volumes of poetry in 1951, 1959 and 1969; R. Williams Parry's *Gerddi'r Gaeaf* appeared in 1952 and D. J. Williams's splendid chronicles were published in 1953 and 1959. Three volumes of the work of T. H. Parry-Williams appeared between 1949 and 1966, and readers were able to savour the charms of R. T. Jenkins's autobiography in 1968. As T. Rowland Hughes had from 1943 to 1947 delighted readers of Welsh with his annual novels, writers in subsequent years were able to build upon his achievement. This was done by Islwyn Ffowc Elis with his *Cysgod y Cryman* (1953); it was that novel (together with the radio serial *Gari Tryfan*) which convinced the adolescents of the 1950s that there was something for them in Welsh. From the late 1950s onwards, there was a substantial increase in the number of Welsh novels published. Some of them were remarkable works – Caradog Prichard's *Un Nos Ola Leuad*, in particular. The historical novel proved highly popular, with Marion Eames excelling in a talented company.

As ever, there was a considerable market for Welsh poetry. Between 1957 and 1960, volumes of poetry represented 15 per cent of the sales of Welsh books for adults. The most outstanding work published since the war was undoubtedly Waldo Williams's *Dail Pren* (1956), the only volume by that remarkable genius. By the 1970s, virtually the entire generation of poets who had won renown before the war had died; as Welsh writers could no longer draw upon the resources of a monolingual society, it was feared that it would have no successor. The fear proved baseless, as the work of middle-aged and young poets testifies; Gwyn Thomas can perhaps be cited as the most notable example of the former and Siôn Eirian of the latter. Some poets were eager to experiment – Euros Bowen, for example, and Bobi Jones. Yet despite enthusiasm for symbolism, *vers libre* and concrete poetry, there was a strong desire to hold on to Welsh traditional metres: in the 1970s, *cynghanedd* – the peculiarly Welsh poetic system of alliteration and consonance – experienced a marked revival, a revival nurtured from 1976 onwards by Cymdeithas Cerdd Dafod, and its journal, *Barddas*. Subsidies enabled the work of many folk poets to be published, and the patronizing treatment that they had once received came to be a matter of regret.

Because of the grants, it was possible to publish many works of reminiscence, 'as if,' as John Rowlands put it, 'the last generation of Welsh monoglots were making haste to record a civilization at death's door'. Although the older generation remained productive, the determination of members of the younger generation to apply

themselves to literature, and the fact that state patronage permitted
the publication of their work, were among the main features of
Welsh literary life in the 1960s and 1970s. Some younger writers felt
frustrated by the nature of their medium; they had no experience of a
monolingual society; there was much opposition to work which
reflected the debased language used by many Welsh-speakers; it was
difficult to write a novel with an urban setting without concentrating
on the Welsh-speaking bourgeoisie. There was also uncertainty about
the purpose of writing. Was a Welsh writer 'doing his own thing' or
was he writing 'good bad literature' in order to 'save the language'?
Yet, despite the problems of the medium, there was no sign of a
desire to abandon it. Indeed, to judge by the statements of some
Welsh authors writing in English – R. S. Thomas, Emyr Humphreys
and Harri Webb, in particular – it might be considered that they,
despite their hundreds of millions of potential readers, were envious
of those of their compatriots who wrote in Welsh.

Grants were also important to Anglo-Welsh literature. By the
1970s, about seventy English books of a literary nature were published
annually in Wales, and every one of them received a measure of
assistance from the bodies established to promote Welsh books. There
were subsidies for Anglo-Welsh periodicals, especially *The Anglo-
Welsh Review* (which had begun as *Dock Leaves* in 1949), *Poetry Wales*
(established in Merthyr in 1965) and *Planet* (1970–80, 1985–). The era
when the production of such periodicals involved their editors in
financial sacrifice – the experience of Gwyn Jones and Keidrych Rhys
– had come to an end. Nevertheless, assistance for English books by
Welsh writers was far less extensive than it was for Welsh books. As
the great world of the English language was open to Anglo-Welsh
writers, it was felt that they needed less succouring. But as an
autonomous market for English books did not exist in Wales, such
writers had to win recognition in London before any attention was
paid to them. This was precisely the experience of R. S. Thomas, the
leading Anglo-Welsh poet by the 1960s. Until the 1970s, Thomas's
main theme was Wales – rural Wales in particular – and his sensitive,
ironic poems were entrancing. He inherited his position of pre-
eminence from a poet a year younger than he – a very different
Thomas. Dylan Thomas had not reached his fortieth birthday when
he died in 1953; his private life was capricious and disreputable and it
is difficult to separate his achievement from the legends which

gathered around him. Yet that achievement was magnificent. His *Collected Poems* (1952) proved that he was one of the great English poets of the century. His 'drama for voices', *Under Milk Wood*, appeared in 1954 – the best-known literary work ever to be produced by a Welsh writer. In considering the Anglo-Welsh poets, another name can be placed alongside those of the two Thomases. The name is that of David Jones, who although a native of Kent was keenly aware of his Anglo-Welshness. His poems are saturated with his feeling for Wales; although they can be difficult to appreciate fully, there is an increasing readiness to consider them among the greatest works of the century.

The interests of this trio of poets were very different from those which had engaged the generation of Anglo-Welsh writers who came to prominence in the 1930s. Some of the best work of those writers appeared in the decades after the war – the novels of Glyn Jones, Gwyn Jones and Jack Jones, for example, and the collection of the verse of Idris Davies. The most productive writer of those decades was Gwyn Thomas, who through his tragi-comic works produced a passionate commentary on the anguish of the coalfield communities. The rich vein mined by Richard Llewellyn – the emotional historical novel on the industrial south – was reworked, particularly by Alexander Cordell. There were many admirers of the five novels of Raymond Williams, a thinker whose theories of culture have been influential in Welsh intellectual circles. The significance of the growth of Anglo-Welsh literature has been examined, particularly by Glyn Jones in his valuable book *The Dragon Has Two Tongues* (1968); it was claimed that Anglo-Welsh literature has deep roots, a thesis that Raymond Garlick has tirelessly advocated. Efforts were made, as Roland Mathias put it, 'to heal the breach that had existed between Welsh and Anglo-Welsh authors since the original "treason" of Caradoc Evans'. Some of the leading English writers of Wales produced polished translations spanning all the centuries of Welsh literature; a considerable body of studies on the work of Welsh writers was published, in particular through the series *Writers of Wales*, launched in 1970; the breach was finally healed in 1968 with the founding of the English section of the Welsh Academy. In these developments, the key figure was Meic Stephens, the literature director of the Welsh Arts Council; it was his desire to portray the literary output of Wales in its entirety – whatever its medium – which led to

the production of *The Companion to the Literature of Wales* (1986).
There was an increasing convergence between the themes which were
of interest to Anglo-Welsh writers and the themes of interest to those
writing in Welsh. This is apparent in the work of Emyr Humphreys,
by the 1960s the most prominent of Wales's English-language novel-
ists. The nature of Welshness and of the values associated with
Nonconformity are the matters which are of greatest concern to him.
Harri Webb, an Anglo-Welsh poet whose work was warmly appreciated by Welsh-speakers, is an ardent nationalist who has gained a firm
command of the Welsh language. Yet too much should not be
claimed. By the last quarter of the twentieth century there were
writers living in Wales who had virtually no association with Welshness, and only a small proportion of the people of Wales came into
contact with the literature of Wales – be it in Welsh or in English.

There were striking developments in other branches of the arts in
the second half of the twentieth century, and with them also the
patronage of the state was of central importance. Without that patronage, the live theatre could well have become extinct in Wales. In the
1930s, the country had almost five hundred amateur dramatic societies
performing plays in Welsh, and a host of others performing in English.
Their numbers contracted greatly during the war, and the coming of
television led to the demise of most of those which remained. As
television drama was so expensive, little was produced in Wales. As
with literature, a new chapter opened with the establishment of the
Welsh Arts Council in 1967. The great debate of the 1960s was that
over a national theatre – a necessity to those concerned above all with
high standards, an irrelevance to those who sought to ensure that the
professional theatre should be brought to the people in their local
communities. After much discussion, the scheme for a national theatre
collapsed in the early 1970s. A network of theatres was created, a
venture made possible by state grants and by college patronage; by
the mid-1970s, there were eight new theatres in Wales and a further
three had been refurbished. At the same time, resources were made
available to establish companies of professionals – a word used to
excess in the 1960s and 1970s. The structure was crowned by the
Welsh Theatre Company and Cwmni Theatr Cymru, although both
eventually collapsed. Some believed that in the 1960s plans for theatri-
cal provision in Wales went seriously awry. Nevertheless, from that
decade onwards, a greater number than ever before of the people of

Wales had an opportunity to see drama of distinction skilfully performed. The craft of the playwright flourished. In Welsh, the finest works were those of Saunders Lewis and John Gwilym Jones, but good plays were also written by others, particularly Gwenlyn Parry and Huw Lloyd Edwards. In English, there were several able Welsh dramatists, Gwyn Thomas, Alun Owen and Alun Richards among them. The craft of the actor also flourished, with actors from Wales taking their place among the international stars.

The Welsh were even more prominent in the field of opera. Indeed, it was in that field, above all, that Wales won an international reputation in the second half of the twentieth century, a fact to be attributed to the brilliance of Welsh singers and to the achievements of the National Opera Company. The company was established in 1946, largely through the dogged efforts of Idloes Owen of Merthyr. With only a part-time chorus and a borrowed orchestra, it rapidly won a high reputation; by the 1970s, when it had a professional chorus and a permanent orchestra, it was considered to be among the world's finest opera companies. Opera is expensive, and the fact that the company absorbed up to a quarter of the funds made available to the arts in Wales was a matter of controversy.

Nevertheless, there was patronage for other forms of music. Assistance was given to the Welsh Youth Orchestra, established in 1946. Some of the world's most famous orchestras performed in Wales, and for the first time a considerable audience for symphonic music developed. As a result, there were increasing demands for a national orchestra and a purpose-built concert hall – demands largely satisfied by the expansion of the BBC Welsh Symphony Orchestra to 78 instrumentalists and the opening of St David's Hall in Cardiff in 1982. Composers of distinction arose, as did able instrumentalists, particularly on the harp. Music festivals multiplied and praiseworthy efforts were made by the Society for the Promotion of Welsh Music. There was a decline in the tradition of choral singing and some male-voice choirs contracted in size; the quality of their singing improved, however, partly because of the stimulus of the Llangollen International Eisteddfod launched in 1947. *Cerdd dant* experienced a renaissance; there was exciting experimentation, particularly by Cor Neuadd Pantycelyn, much to the surprise of many of those who attended the annual *Cerdd dant* festival. Nor should performers of pop music be overlooked; although Dafydd Iwan acknowledged that his skill on the guitar was not outstanding, there were others – Meic Stevens, for example – who were masters of the instrument.

There is less to be said about the visual arts. Nevertheless, with educational advance and with patronage for artists and galleries, the third quarter of the twentieth century was a promising period in their history also. By the 1970s, Wales had about fifteen public galleries; in addition, there were about twenty private galleries, although a number of them proved to be short-lived. Some members of the Welsh middle class could afford to buy pictures by contemporary artists and for the first time there were artists able to live in Wales and survive on their earnings. After much uncertainty, the status of the art colleges of Cardiff and Newport was enhanced, a development which provided a livelihood for a number of able artists. A desire to give prominence to the avant-garde made itself felt among them, and as a result the '1956 Group', the organization which has taken upon itself the function of representing modern art in Wales, was founded. With the assistance of the Arts Council, various groups of artists have had the opportunity to pursue their interests – from Op to Funk, from Pop to Hard Edge. Many of the followers of these fashions merely happened to live in Wales, but the country itself has provided inspiration for a number of artists, native and immigrant. The Welsh landscape is the subject of Kyffin Williams's craggy pictures and of the more tender paintings of John Elwyn; Wales and its people attracted Graham Sutherland and John Piper from England, Joseph Herman from Poland and Friedrich Könekamp from Germany. Ceri Richards (1903–71), one of the most distinguished painters of his age, was keenly aware of his Welsh origins. In addition to his gifts as a writer, David Jones was a brilliant artist; his chief themes were the traditions of Wales and he has been hailed as 'the most Welsh painter ever'.

There was also an attempt to emphasize the Welsh dimension in the field of architecture. The Welsh School of Architecture won an increasing reputation, and under its able director, Dewi-Prys Thomas, a generation of young architects was taught to feel a responsibility towards the environment and society of Wales. Because of the depression of the 1920s and 1930s, Wales had little experience of the first wave of modern architecture. The most remarkable buildings erected in Wales between the wars were the creation of the anti-modernist Clough Williams-Ellis – the splendid fantasy at Port Meirion. With the reconstruction of the Welsh economy after the war, a number of striking industrial buildings were erected, including the Semtex Factory at Brynmawr, 'the first really modern work of architecture in Wales'. Buildings of distinction were, however, more frequently commissioned by public institutions than by commercial companies. The expansion of higher education provided architects with numerous opportunities, as the Great Hall, Aberystwyth, the University Hospital at Cardiff and some of the buildings at Coleg Harlech testify. The Great Hall was designed by the Percy Thomas Partnership, the company which dominated architecture in post-war Wales; Percy Thomas (1883–1969) was the first Welsh architect to win an international reputation. The history of Welsh housing was studied, and, in the light of the knowledge acquired, attempts were made to design council estates which would blend with the landscape, a field pioneered by Alwyn Lloyd (1881–1960). Yet too much should not be claimed. Much of what was built was wholly uninspired – the dreadful rebuilding at Swansea in particular. Although Wales was largely saved from the most unfortunate of the architects' innovations – the tower blocks of flats – many soulless estates were built; a number of them won praise from the experts, although several proved to be socially disastrous – the Pen-rhys estate between Rhondda Fawr and Rhondda Fach in particular.

Of all the intellectual fields in which the Welsh were involved in the decades after the war, the most productive were undoubtedly those relating to the nation itself. There were remarkable advances in the understanding of the nature of the Welsh literary tradition. In 1945, Thomas Parry published his *Hanes Llenyddiaeth Gymraeg* (A History of Welsh Literature), a polished attempt to trace Welsh literature from its beginnings to 1900. His *Gwaith Dafydd ap Gwilym*, a study which provided a firm foundation for further research on the greatest of the poets of Wales, came from the press in 1952. Ifor Williams's researches on the *Cynfeirdd* and the *Mabinogi* were even more exciting; his works, from *Canu Llywarch Hen* (1935) to *Canu Taliesin* (1960), are the greatest contribution to Welsh scholarship ever made by a single individual. With the staff of Departments of Welsh expanding, and with grants to research students increasing, it became possible at last to fulfil the ambition cherished by Welsh patriots since the Renaissance – to reveal to the world the riches of the manuscripts. By the 1980s, the bulk of Welsh medieval poetry was accessible, in either print or typescript, and the *Gogynfeirdd* have become the object of a scholarly blitz. Learned efforts were made to interpret the literature of the Renaissance, the Methodist Revival and the eisteddfod. The linguistic studies pioneered by John Morris-Jones provided the basis for further work, particularly by scholars associated with University College, Swansea. The chief contribution in this field is *Geiriadur Prifysgol Cymru* (A Dictionary of the Welsh Language; thirty-eight parts since 1950); it is a magnificent achievement, particularly in view of the small number working on it and the massiveness of the task. Fascinating work has been done on the dialects of Wales, particularly at the museum at St Ffagans, the splendid centre for Welsh folk studies established in 1946.

In the first half of the twentieth century, the scholars of the literature and language of Wales were far more productive than its historians – a fact which can largely be attributed to the tardiness of the University in recognizing the importance of the nation's history. The situation improved vastly from mid-century onwards, and the 1960s and 1970s were an exciting period for the historians of Wales. *Y Bywgraffiadur Cymreig* appeared in 1953 (the English version, *The Dictionary of Welsh Biography*, was published in 1959); although it lays excessive emphasis on religious figures – it is 'black with *parchs*' as Dylan Thomas said of the beer-tent – it immediately became an essential manual for the Welsh historian. As in every country, there was a revolution in archaeology. Understanding of prehistoric Wales was transformed; important work was done on the Roman period, and there were valuable studies – especially by V. E. Nash-Williams and Leslie Alcock – on the difficult centuries following the collapse of the Roman Empire. J. E. Lloyd's masterly work on medieval Wales inspired further studies, particularly by Beverley Smith and Dafydd Jenkins, and there were heroic attempts to wrestle with the problems of the Later Middle Ages. In that field, the contributions of T. Jones Pierce and Rees Davies were especially perceptive, and Glanmor Williams produced a masterpiece on the history of the Church. Glanmor Williams was the central figure in this renaissance in Welsh history. He was chiefly responsible for founding the *Welsh History Review* (1960); he was an ardent supporter of every venture in local history; he laboured to ensure the success of the Oxford series on the history of Wales and he was an inspiration and a stimulus to an entire generation of younger colleagues.

The early centuries had always attracted historians, but no scholarly account of the experience of the Welsh in the centuries following the Middle Ages was available until 1950. That year saw the publication of David Williams's *A History of Modern Wales*, a comprehensive and singularly judicious discussion of the history of Wales since 1485. David Williams, as Gwyn A. Williams put it, 'was the father of us all', and in his masterpiece, *The Rebecca Riots* (1955), he set a standard which his 'children' would be delighted to attain. Valuable studies of Early Modern Wales were published – on politics by A. H. Dodd, on culture by Geraint H. Jenkins and Prys Morgan and on the ruling class by Penry Williams, J. Gwynfor Jones and others – but it was the more recent history of Wales that attracted the attention of most of the new generation of historians. On religious history, R. T. Jenkins created an exciting and polished body of work, and his achievement was built upon, in their different ways, by Ieuan Gwynedd Jones and R. Tudur Jones. Kenneth O. Morgan worked a rich vein with his *Wales in British Politics* (1963), and he went on to show his skill time and time again with a series of works on Welsh political history. Historians were slow to get to grips with the history of the south Wales coalfield – a matter of surprise in view of the fact that the industrialization of the north had been the subject of a major study by A. H. Dodd as early as 1933. In the 1960s and 1970s, however, works on the industrial south poured from the presses. Some of them had a missionary air, for among the historians of the south-east there were those who believed that Welsh historiography has been excessively concerned with rural Wales. Their criticism was sometimes over-done, but in its essentials it had solid substance. It is strange that the interpreters of the experience of the Welsh have been so tardy in acknowledging that the central fact of their modern history is the creation of the community of the south Wales coalfield and in recognizing the unique nature of the working-class struggles of that community. The desire to stress the one and to analyse the other inspired the founders of the Welsh Labour History Society (1971), a society which won a widespread and immediate welcome. This new 'school' of Welsh historians included Marxists and feminists, and Welsh historiography benefited greatly from their vision. Efforts were made to save the libraries of the Miners' Institutes and to collect material relating to the history of the coalfield, a campaign launched at Swansea in 1969.

The desire to safeguard evidence of the history of the labour movement was motivated in part by the realization that by the 1960s
traditional Welsh coalfield society was declining rapidly. Yet labour
in its political aspect was at its height during that decade. In the
general elections of the 1950s (1950, 1951, 1955 and 1959) the proportion of Welsh voters supporting the Labour party remained stable at
around 56 to 57 per cent; it was 58 per cent in 1964 and it rose to 61
per cent in the general election of 1966 – the highest percentage so
far. In that year, Labour won thirty-two of the thirty-six constituencies of Wales, twenty-seven of them with absolute majorities. Conwy,
Monmouth and Cardiff North were captured from the Conservatives,
and in Cardiganshire, a seat which had been held by the Liberals since
1880, the Labour candidate, Elystan Morgan (who had once been a
leading figure in Plaid Cymru), won a dramatic victory. In 1966, it
was possible (by using the ferry from Ynyslas to Aberdyfi) to travel
from Holyhead to Chepstow and from Pembroke to Connah's Quay
without leaving a Labour constituency.

Yet, although the Labour party wholly dominated the politics of
Wales in the mid-1960s, weaknesses could be discerned beneath the
surface. The vivacity which had once characterized Welsh socialism
was in decline. Aneurin Bevan had died in 1960, and thereafter there
was no truly charismatic figure in the Labour party in Wales – nor in
Britain generally. Despite the sweeping victories of Labour candidates
in 1966, they were unable to identify with the working-class members
of their electorate to the same extent as their predecessors had done a
generation earlier. The number of MPs who had risen through the
National Union of Mineworkers was falling rapidly and by 1974
none was left. A process of *embourgeoisement* was taking place. In
1966, about half the Welsh Labour MPs came from the ranks of
professional men – solicitors and lecturers in the main; the proportion
had risen to three quarters in the 1970s – 'able young men,' according
to an old miner, 'but they haven't been in the oven'. In the industrial
areas, the Labour party's control over local government was so
complete that on many councils it had virtually no opposition. This
could provide a platform for a constructive local politician – Llewellyn
Heycock in Glamorgan, for example – but it could also lead to the
absolute power which permits nepotism and sometimes corruption, as
was seen in Swansea and elsewhere. In the constituencies where the
Labour party was virtually in complete control, there was very little

campaigning or political education. In large parts of the coalfield, the party could appear to be a monolithic structure existing solely to perpetuate the authority of the *apparatchik*.

Other areas were more lively. As the Labour party had, since the war, made great strides outside its stronghold in the coalfield, there was substance to the claim that the party was the party of Wales. The more of the constituencies of Wales it won, the more Welsh interests it was expected to represent. Nevertheless, its leaders were suspicious of anything which could be interpreted as a concession to nationalism. The five Labour MPs active in the Parliament for Wales campaign were considered to be fellow travellers of Plaid Cymru and were severely rebuked. The most prominent of them was S. O. Davies, the member for Merthyr Tydfil. He brought his Parliament for Wales Bill before parliament in 1955 but it received little support. Neither did Goronwy Roberts in 1956, when he presented to the House of Commons a petition in favour of a Welsh parliament bearing the names of 240,000 signatories.

Yet within the Labour party there were influential voices in favour of some step towards devolution, in particular in view of the readiness of the Conservative government to make occasional gestures in that direction. When Churchill returned to power in 1951, his government created the office of Minister for Welsh Affairs as an adjunct of the office of Home Secretary. The title was transferred to the Minister of Housing and Local Government in 1957, and a Minister of State – Baron Brecon – was appointed to assist him. The publication of *The Digest of Welsh Statistics* began in 1954, Cardiff was recognized as the capital of Wales in 1955, the Welsh Grand Committee was established in 1960 and a small office to superintend the economy was set up in Cardiff in 1963. By then, the Labour party had gone further by committing itself to the appointment of a Secretary of State for Wales with a seat in the cabinet. It was the reports of the Council for Wales, inspired by the fervour of Huw T. Edwards, which had placed the question of the secretaryship on the political agenda, but the commitment was made because James Griffiths warmly endorsed the notion and wore down Aneurin Bevan with his arguments. Bevan abandoned his opposition and the pledge to appoint a Secretary of State was incorporated in the Labour party's manifesto for the general election of 1959.

The Labour party's readiness to advocate a substantial measure of administrative devolution arose in part from the realization that Plaid Cymru was winning a degree of support. The party had only four candidates in the general election of 1951; the number rose to eleven in 1955 and to twenty in 1959. In 1959, Plaid Cymru polled a total of 77,571 votes and its candidates obtained quite respectable results in some of the constituencies of the industrialized south-east, where an indigenous nationalism, different in its emphasis from that of the Welsh-speaking districts of the north and west, was striking roots. By the late 1950s, Huw T. Edwards, once a stern critic of the party, came to the conclusion that it had a promising future; in 1958, he resigned from the chairmanship of the Council of Wales in a protest against what he called Whitehallism, and from 1959 to 1965 he was a member of Plaid Cymru.

The increase in the vote for Plaid Cymru can be attributed in part to a scarcity of Liberal candidates, but it was also an expression of discontent with some of the policies and attitudes of the Labour party. Furthermore, there was an awareness that the Welsh, although more prosperous than ever before, were considerably poorer than were the inhabitants of the richer areas of England. As the people of some of the smaller states of Europe came to enjoy a higher standard of living than that of the British, the appeal of belonging to the centralized British state was eroded. According to many academic commentators, this awareness of 'unequal development' is the key to the recent growth in nationalism among peoples like the Welsh. The mystique of belonging to the world's greatest empire faded as the process of decolonization accelerated and as states smaller in population and resources than Wales came into existence. By the end of the 1950s, the Conservatives had won three general elections in succession; doubts arose whether the Labour party could ever return to power in Britain, and thus there were those who saw virtue in a Welsh parliament, a body which would be certain to have a left-wing majority. The arguments of Plaid Cymru were fostered by the Tryweryn case: in 1957, parliament passed a bill permitting the Liverpool Corporation to drown the Tryweryn valley in Meirionnydd, although almost all the Welsh MPs voted against it. Liverpool's ability to ignore the virtually unanimous opinion of the representatives of the Welsh people confirmed one of the central tenets of Plaid Cymru – that the national Welsh community, under the existing order, was wholly powerless. The perseverance and prudent leadership of Gwynfor Evans won considerable admiration, even among those who had little sympathy for his aims. Above all, the decrease in the number of Welsh-speakers and the decline in the values considered to be central to Welshness fostered the feeling that uncompromising nationalism alone could save the nation from extinction.

Despite the growth in the support for Plaid Cymru, the party was still a long way from winning a seat. As a result, its members felt considerable frustration as their party remained marginal in Welsh politics. A few patriots were prepared to use violence. On three occasions in 1962–3, installations at Tryweryn were attacked, and in 1963 the 'Free Wales Army' began a recruiting drive. As has already been noted, the frustrations felt by nationalists were partly responsible for the readiness of some of them to undertake direct action on the language issue in the wake of Saunders Lewis's radio lecture. In his lecture, Lewis referred scathingly to the readiness of Plaid Cymru to 'waste money on purposeless parliamentary elections', an opinion voiced by other party members, particularly after the general election of 1964, which proved that support for the party was ebbing.

That election brought the Labour party back to power after thirteen years in the wilderness. The new government hastened to fulfil its promise regarding a secretaryship of state for Wales, an office to which James Griffiths was appointed on 17 October 1964. The secretaryship could have been created without establishing a Welsh Office; indeed, leading civil servants and a number of Labour MPs would have preferred a guard-dog secretary without specific duties and without a staff or a department. Griffiths insisted upon a measure of real authority and he threatened to resign unless he had his way. On 19 November 1964, Harold Wilson, the Prime Minister, announced that housing, local government and roads would be administered by the Welsh Office. The Conservative government of 1970–74 added primary and secondary education and industry and employment and the Labour government of 1974–9 added agriculture and fisheries, higher education (apart from the University) and assistance to urban areas. In addition, the government of 1974–9 greatly strengthened the economic role of the secretary by giving him authority over the Welsh Development Agency, the Development Board for Rural Wales and the Welsh Land Authority. By 1984, the Welsh Office employed 2,206 civil servants and from its splendid headquarters in Cathays Park it administered an annual expenditure of £2,585,000,000. The office worked within a highly centralized framework. The priorities of the government – a government which frequently was not the chosen government of the people of Wales – determined its policies; as a result, its influence was limited to the ability to adapt directives from London and to do so mainly in areas which were not of particular interest to Whitehall.

Although the Welsh Office was not an independent body in any sense, its existence strengthened the concept of the territorial unity of Wales and created the need for other organizations reflecting that unity. Some of those were quasi-governmental – for example, the Councils for the Arts (1967), for Sport (1972) and for Consumers (1975). But non-governmental organizations could not ignore the new situation created by the establishment of the Welsh Office. A very significant step was taken in 1973 with the creation of TUC Wales, the result of the efforts of Dai Francis, the secretary of the NUM in south Wales. The political parties felt the need to strengthen their organization in Wales. The Welsh Liberal party was established in 1966 and the Conservatives of Wales began to hold an annual conference in 1972; in 1975, the Welsh Regional Council of Labour was reorganized under the title The Labour Party – Wales. Recognition of the unity of Wales created a need for information and news concerning the nation in its entirety. The publishing of statistics relating to the economy and society of Wales increased greatly – a major bonus for historians. There was a marked increase in the attention given to Welsh news on television, and radio provision was strengthened, particularly with the establishment of Radio Wales and Radio Cymru in 1977 and their major expansion in 1979.

As with the Welsh Office, the headquarters of the media were located in Cardiff. By the late 1960s, Cardiff was becoming a meaningful capital city. It is probably in that decade that the Welsh cast aside the leadership of the London Welsh, a significant change in view of the longevity of that leadership. As Gwyn A. Williams put it, Cardiff became a 'subordinate metropolis', a development which occurred side by side with the de-industrialization of the city. As it became the centre of Welsh bureaucracy it became more Welsh in language, and by the 1980s children could be heard playing in Welsh on the streets of its more prosperous suburbs. Henceforth, it was Cardiff which attracted the young people of Welsh-speaking Wales, particularly those intent upon a career in the media – a development which gave rise to that interesting phenomenon, the *Cypy*, the Welsh-speaking Yuppy.

While a system of Welsh administration was striking roots, there were dramatic developments in the political field. Plaid Cymru had been disappointed with its results in the general election held on 31 March 1966, but fifteen weeks later, on 14 July, it had an astonishing victory. In the by-election at Carmarthen which followed the death of Lady Megan Lloyd George, Gwynfor Evans had a majority of 2,436 over the Labour candidate, Gwilym Prys Davies. After the long years in the wilderness, Evans's success caused rejoicing among members of Plaid Cymru, but it also gave pleasure to many outside its ranks. The confidence which came in the wake of victory goes far to explain the liveliness of many aspects of Welsh nationalist activity in the late 1960s, in particular the increasing boldness of Welsh-language activists. It was possible to argue that Gwynfor Evans was a unique figure and that Carmarthen was an eccentric constituency. But as Plaid Cymru, in the by-election in Rhondda West in 1967 and in that in Caerffili in 1968, won a higher proportion of the vote than it had won in Carmarthen, it was difficult to sustain that argument. As the party was able to demonstrate its appeal in anglicized industrial districts as well as in Welsh-speaking rural districts, it is not surprising that James Griffiths expressed fears that it might displace the Labour party as the leading party of Wales. As parallel, but more striking, political shifts were occurring in Scotland, the need to satisfy (or undermine) the national movements in Wales and Scotland became a matter of importance in British politics.

There were within the Labour party elements who wished the political system in Wales to be more answerable to the electorate. With the growth in the support for Plaid Cymru, they could argue that it was only through moving in that direction that the Labour party could retain its hold upon the majority of the seats of Wales. Gwilym Prys Davies had published a pamphlet in 1963 calling for an elected assembly for Wales, a notion which greatly appealed to James Griffiths, particularly in the context of the reorganization of local government. For a generation and more, there had been support for the belief that most of the counties and many of the rural and urban districts of Wales were too small to fulfil their functions adequately, a view supported by the report of the Commission on Local Government in Wales in 1963.

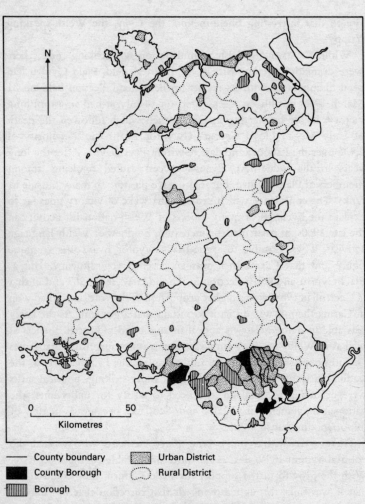

Local government in Wales before 1974

In 1967, a plan was drawn up which combined the need for reorganization with the desire for an executive body for the whole of Wales. Cledwyn Hughes, James Griffiths's successor, who had also been inspired by Gwilym Prys Davies's vision, presented the plan to the cabinet; it failed to find endorsement there largely because of the

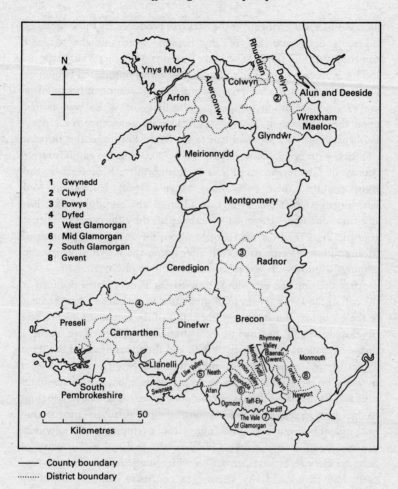

1 Gwynedd
2 Clwyd
3 Powys
4 Dyfed
5 West Glamorgan
6 Mid Glamorgan
7 South Glamorgan
8 Gwent

—— County boundary
········ District boundary

Local government in Wales after 1974

opposition of the Secretary of State for Scotland and the hostility of those Welsh Labour MPs who were against anything which could be interpreted as a concession to nationalism. This was the central paradox of the nationalist upsurge of the 1960s. The subject of self-government would probably have never reached the political agenda but for the successes of Plaid Cymru; yet the backlash produced by those successes led to a deep suspicion of any policies which sought to react constructively to them. The devolutionists lost a crucial battle in 1967. Cledwyn Hughes had to be content with a nominated Economic Council, and, when a bill reorganizing local government became law in 1973, no institution recognizing the unity of Wales was grafted upon the new system. That system came into existence on 1 April 1974; previously, Wales had had four county boroughs and thirteen counties, with populations varying from 750,000 in the administrative county of Glamorgan to 18,250 in Radnorshire; henceforth it had eight counties, their populations varying from 531,800 in Mid Glamorgan to 99,200 in Powys. In addition, the boroughs and urban and rural districts – 164 in all – were replaced by thirty-seven district councils. As a result of the reorganization, the anomalous position of Monmouthshire came to an end: after losing the Rhymni valley and gaining Brynmawr, it was reborn as the county of Gwent.

After the upsurge of 1966–8, support for Plaid Cymru declined at the end of the 1960s. That can be attributed in part to an improvement in the economy, but it was also the result of the fear that violence was developing under the mantle of nationalism. There were about a dozen explosions in Wales in 1968–9, and the shenanigans of the 'Free Wales Army' received wide publicity in a lengthy court case at Swansea in 1969. Cymdeithas yr Iaith Gymraeg became increasingly militant; its members displayed considerable self-discipline in adhering to their non-violent policy, but some of their campaigns – the painting out of monolingual English signs, for example – were widely unpopular. In 1968, Cledwyn Hughes was replaced as Secretary of State by George Thomas, an action which suggested that the government had abandoned any attempt to conciliate nationalist opinion. Thomas's attempts to persuade non-Welsh-speakers that the Welsh language represented a threat to them were among his more publicized activities, and his period as Secretary of State was marked by 'awful provincial shabbiness', to quote the journal *Planet*. The heir to the throne was invested with the Principality of Wales in 1969, an occasion which gave Thomas and some of his fellow Labour MPs an opportunity to fawn upon the royal family and to lambast the nationalists. Before the ceremony at Caernarfon, Prince Charles spent a term at the University College of Wales, where he gained some knowledge of the Welsh language. He proved to be an amiable and intelligent young man, and as all the resources of the media were in his favour the investiture won extensive support among the Welsh. As the ceremony commemorated the Conquest, Plaid Cymru refused to be involved with it; Cymdeithas yr Iaith Gymraeg was openly hostile and there were violent protests by an organization which called itself Mudiad Amddiffyn Cymru (the Movement for the Defence of Wales). On the morning of the ceremony, two young men were killed at Abergele, apparently while they were preparing to attack the royal train. Their deaths were a wholly wretched happening, although there were in Wales those prepared to find significance in the fact that two Welshmen, five and three quarter centuries after the Glyn Dŵr Rising, had 'died for Wales'.

Although these occurrences impeded the growth of nationalism, the Labour government included among its members men who were reluctant to abandon the notion that the Welsh administrative system should be more answerable to the people of Wales. The ablest of them was Elystan Morgan, the member for Cardiganshire. It was his efforts, above all, which led to the government's decision in October 1968 to establish a royal commission on the constitution; the subject was open-ended, but it was recognized that devolution for Scotland and Wales would be the main field of investigation.

The general election of 1970 returned an ambiguous verdict on the nationalist upsurge of the 1960s. The vote for Plaid Cymru rose from the 61,071 it obtained in 1966 to 175,016, but the Labour candidate succeeded in capturing Carmarthen with a majority of 3,017. The general election was won by the Conservatives. With the Labour party in opposition, it seemed likely that it would receive the protest vote of the Welsh electors, a belief which proved unfounded when the Plaid Cymru candidate, Emrys Roberts, polled 37 per cent of the vote in the Merthyr by-election in 1972. The chief priority of Edward Heath, the Prime Minister from 1970 to 1974, was to ensure the entry of the United Kingdom into the European Economic Community, an aim achieved in 1972. As a result, a new context was created for discussions concerning the political future of Wales. To many Welsh patriots, there was no virtue in a system which centralized power in the hands of bureaucrats in Brussels, but to others the link with Europe offered exciting possibilities. Within the Labour party there were deep suspicions of the European Community, and after the party returned to power a referendum on British membership was held in 1975. Every one of the eight counties of Wales recorded a majority in favour of continued membership, the affirmative percentages varying from 74.3 in Powys to 56.9 in Mid Glamorgan.

Largely because of the generosity of its Common Agricultural Policy, the Common Market proved to be a blessing to Welsh agriculture, at least in the short term; as a result, the farmers of Wales were increasingly prepared to support the Conservative party, the architects of 'the entry into Europe'. Other sectors of the Welsh economy were less prosperous. Unemployment in Wales rose to 5.4 per cent in 1972; although it declined in the following two years, it leapt to 7 per cent in 1975 in the wake of the international recession caused by the huge increase in the price of oil in 1974. By the beginning of the 1970s, it was clear that the world-wide demand for steel was declining and that Welsh steel was being priced out of the market by the produce of the more efficient mills of the United States, Germany and Japan. In 1972, plans to reduce the labour force of the industry were published and it was suggested that 6,000 jobs would vanish at Shotton, 4,500 at Ebbw Vale and 4,100 at Cardiff. The number of miners continued to fall: there were 36,000 in the south Wales coalfield in 1972 compared with 80,000 a decade earlier. In the early 1970s, unrest spread among them as severe inflation reduced the value of their earnings. In December 1971, the miners of Britain, with those of south Wales in the van, agreed by 145,000 votes to 102,000 to go on strike.

The strike began on 9 January 1972. It was the first time since 1926 that the miners of the kingdom had jointly withdrawn their labour. With the electricity supply under threat, the government declared a 'state of emergency' and the working week was reduced to three days. The strike was highly significant: it provided the context for the creation of TUC Wales and it fostered a new interest in syndicalist ideas. As a result of the agreement which brought the strike to an end, the miners rose to the top of the table of working-class wage-earners. Within twenty months, however, they had slipped back to the eighteenth position; in November 1973, there was another vote in favour of a strike, a decision supported by 93 per cent of the miners of south Wales. Edward Heath insisted upon making the miners' challenge the issue of a general election. In the poll on 28 February

1974, the Conservative party received 308,000 more votes than Labour, but 301 seats in the House of Commons were won by the Labour party compared with 296 by the Conservatives. With the Labour party again in power, an agreement with the miners was rapidly reached. Thus, the National Union of Mineworkers could claim that it had brought down a Tory government, a notion which seized the imagination of its leaders.

Despite the Labour party's success in the general election of February 1974, its hold upon the electors of Wales was weakening. It obtained only 47 per cent of the Welsh vote, the first time since the war for its proportion to fall below 50 per cent. This can partly be attributed to the revival of the Liberal party, which nominated thirty-one candidates in Wales compared with nineteen in 1970. Of the thirty-one, twenty-five succeeded in retaining their deposits, and in Cardiganshire Elystan Morgan was defeated by the Liberal candidate, Geraint Howells. But the surprise of the election was the success of Plaid Cymru: although its total vote was less than it had been in 1970, it won the constituencies of Caernarfon and Meirionnydd, and Gwynfor Evans came within three votes of recapturing Carmarthen. As the position of the Labour government was so precarious, another general election was held in October 1974. On that occasion, Gwynfor Evans was successful; the members for Caernarfon and Meirionnydd retained their seats, and in Scotland eleven members of the National Party (the SNP) were elected. The electoral pattern in the new parliament was as follows: Labour, 319; Conservatives, 276; the Welsh and Scottish Nationalists, fourteen; Liberals, thirteen; various parties in Northern Ireland, twelve. Although the Labour party had a majority of forty-three over the Conservatives, it had a majority of only four over all the other parties together; by the end of 1976, following Labour losses in by-elections, that majority had dwindled to nothing. A pact with the Liberals was formed in 1977; Labour also wanted the support of the Nationalist MPs, and thus devolution became an issue which the government of 1974–9 was obliged to address.

The devolutionists were heartened by the report of the Royal Commission on the Constitution (the Kilbrandon Report), published in 1973. Every one of the thirteen commissioners agreed that the current situation was unsatisfactory; two of them advocated a system of regional councils for the kingdom in its entirety, while two others wanted the Welsh and Scottish Offices to have greater powers. The rest recommended an elected assembly for Wales, and six of them – the two Welsh members among them – wanted that assembly to have legislative powers. The Labour party had been in favour of an elected assembly since 1966, and it offered further details of its policy in 1970 when it emphasized that in its view the proposed assembly should mainly be involved with local government and with nominated bodies. Pressure from Plaid Cymru increased following the party's successes in local elections in 1976; it won a majority on the Merthyr Council, became the largest party on the Rhymney Valley Council and had numerous victories in Gwynedd. The growth of the SNP represented an even greater threat to the Labour party. In October 1974, the SNP polled 30 per cent of the Scottish vote and was second to Labour in thirty-five constituencies. It won sweeping victories in the local elections of 1976 and it was widely believed that Scotland was moving rapidly towards independence and towards taking possession of the bulk of the earnings from North Sea oil, revenues which were central to the aspirations of the British government.

In framing its devolution policy, the Labour party's main stimulus was concern about events in Scotland. The Scotland and Wales Bill was placed before parliament in November 1976, and it was probably the developments in Scotland which led the government to offer to Wales a more far-reaching scheme than had been approved in 1970 by the Labour party in Wales. The Scottish Assembly was to have legislative powers, but these were not to be granted to the Welsh Assembly; nevertheless, the Welsh Assembly was to have substantial administrative authority, including supervision of an annual expenditure approaching £1,500,000,000. Although all the Labour candidates in the general election of October 1974 supported their party's manifesto – a manifesto which included a commitment to devolution – there was increasing unease among them as the government set about fulfilling that commitment. The anti-devolutionists believed a referendum might offer an escape route – a notion first ventilated by Labour's Caerffili constituency party in 1975. In the hope of obtaining a parliamentary majority for its bill, the government agreed on 10 February 1977 to hold a consultative referendum. The concession proved fruitless. On 22 February, with discussions collapsing under a welter of amendments, there was an attempt to curtail them through the guillotine, but the motion was defeated by 312 to 283.

The issue was readdressed in November 1977, and this time Wales had a bill to itself. After twenty-nine days of discussion and a host of amendments, the Wales Act received the royal assent on 31 July 1978. The most important amendment was the one which laid down that 40 per cent of the electorate had to vote in favour of carrying out the measure before it became law, an amendment which meant that the referendum was mandatory rather than consultative. The members of the Wales for the Assembly Campaign realized that they were faced with a difficult task, but they were heartened by an opinion poll in May 1978 which showed that about 41 per cent of the Welsh electorate supported the proposed assembly; although the same proportion were opposed to it, there were enough 'don't knows' to turn the balance in favour of the affirmative camp. If the referendum had been held at the end of the summer of 1978 and if the members of the government had campaigned vigorously in favour of its policy, that might have happened. But it did not. The vote was postponed until St David's Day 1979, and in the three months leading up to it Britain suffered some of the worst industrial unrest in its history. With rubbish not cleared, corpses not buried and patients not treated, the debate over devolution appeared highly irrelevant. Only two members of the cabinet – Michael Foot and John Morris – showed any enthusiasm for devolution; the Prime Minister, James Callaghan, made a speech or two, but little attempt was made to stress that the assembly was official government policy. As the Wales Act had many weaknesses, the advocates of an affirmative vote tended to base their arguments on the general principle of devolution, a situation which allowed their opponents to make much of the shortcomings of the proposed assembly.

The advocates of a negative vote consisted of highly disparate groups. They included virtually all the Conservatives; although Edward Heath's attitude was ambiguous, Margaret Thatcher, his successor as leader of the party, was wholly contemptuous of the plans for Wales. In many rural areas – the Montgomery constituency, for example – the Campaign against the Assembly was the local Tory party under a different label. Throughout the discussions on the Devolution Bill, the Conservatives worked hand in hand with a group of Labour MPs, most of whom belonged to the left wing of the party. They included Neil Kinnock, the most eloquent of the six Welsh Labour MPs actively seeking a negative vote. Kinnock's attitude was based upon Aneurin Bevan's credo that the promotion of 'regional' allegiances was a blow to the unity of the British working class, and that the creation of an assembly for Wales would make it difficult for Welsh MPs to be in the main stream of British political life. He and his associates concentrated on four themes: the cost of the assembly, the over-government implicit in it, the threat to the unity of Britain, and the belief that it might endanger the interests of non-Welsh speakers.

This last issue was given marked prominence, particularly by Leo Abse, the MP for Pontypool. Nevertheless, some of the anti-devolutionists argued that the Welsh-speaking Welsh would suffer at the hands of an assembly which would inevitably be dominated by the representatives of the populous English-speaking areas of the south-east. To the extent that they paid any attention to Wales, almost all the London newspapers advocated a negative vote. The most widely bought of Welsh-based newspapers, the *South Wales Echo*, was strongly opposed to devolution, but its stable-mate, the *Western Mail*, gave the proposed assembly detailed and sympathetic treatment. It was the only daily newspaper to do so, a marked contrast with Scotland, where several daily newspapers advocated devolution. The Wales Act had authorized the proposed assembly to review the framework of local government in Wales, a clause included in the hope of attracting the support of those who disapproved of the new counties created in 1974. By 1979, however, those counties had won a degree of acceptance, and their councillors and officials were opposed to any suggestions of further reorganization. In consequence, all the county councils in Wales, apart from Gwynedd, called for a negative vote, and the National Association of Local Government Officers made highly vocal criticisms of devolution.

With Labour councillors in almost all areas of Wales calling for a negative vote and with the local organization of Labour devolutionists in many districts so weak as to be hardly discernible, much of the canvassing in favour of the assembly was carried out by members of Plaid Cymru; thus, the public obtained the impression that the scheme of devolution on offer was that of the nationalists. Plaid Cymru saw little virtue in the Wales Act, but, as the party's leaders had endorsed it as a step towards full self-government, the opponents of the assembly could portray it as a slippery slope towards the break-up of the United Kingdom. Phil Williams, a former vice-president of Plaid

Cymru, argued that the entire scheme was a plot to discredit the nationalists, but his was a lonely voice as members of Plaid Cymru trudged from door to door – as often as not to distribute the propaganda of the Labour party.

On St David's Day 1979, the government's devolution policy was rejected more decisively than even the most pessimistic of the devolutionists could have imagined. A total of 58.3 per cent of the electors of Wales cast their votes in the referendum, 243,048 of them in favour of the assembly and 956,330 against. There was a negative majority in every one of the eight counties, varying from 33.1 per cent in Gwynedd to 75.8 per cent in Gwent. As the assembly had received the support of only one in four of those who had voted, John Morris, the Secretary of State, was obliged to acknowledge the immensity of the defeat. 'When you see an elephant on your doorstep,' he said, 'you know that it's there.'

A host of hopes were trampled underfoot by the elephant. It was claimed that the strategy of twenty years – indeed, the strategy of Welsh patriots since the era of Cymru Fydd – had come to naught. Gwyn A. Williams went further, stating that the Welsh had written '*finis* to nearly two hundred years of Welsh history'. There were those who went further still, arguing that the vote of 1979 was not a vicissitude in that history but rather its quietus. It was interpreted as a defeat for Welshness, as a declaration that the notion of Welsh nationality was unacceptable to the majority of the inhabitants of Wales. 'Let us not deceive ourselves,' wrote Hywel Teifi Edwards; 'the campaign of the negativists was essentially a campaign against the identity of the Welsh.' Political commentators claimed that a process of acculturation was in train, and that not only the political values but also the cultural and social values of England were taking possession of the Welsh.

It can be argued that these interpretations went too far. It is generally recognized that a referendum is a reactionary instrument which invites a response supportive of the existing order. The vote was held at the worst possible time for the devolutionists. In the face of the severe economic problems of the winter of 1978–9, perhaps the greatest weakness in the efforts of the supporters of the assembly was their failure to convince the public that devolution had a bearing upon a more prosperous future for Wales. It could be argued that what was rejected in 1979 was not the concept of devolution but rather the version of it contained in the Wales Act; in early February 1979, an opinion poll showed that 45 per cent of the people of Wales favoured some form of devolution, but the proposed assembly was the choice they favoured least. John Osmond argued that the identity of Wales was not a factor in the vote: according to an opinion poll held in 1979, 57 per cent of the electors of Wales considered themselves to be Welsh, 34 per cent British and 8 per cent English, but of the 'Welsh identifiers' only a minority voted for the assembly. Osmond argued that, had the assembly been established, it would have hindered attempts to create a more radical consensus in favour of self-government; the result of the referendum should therefore be welcomed.

While the devolutionists of the left found comfort in arguments such as these, it was the unionists of the right who profited from the vote of St David's Day, 1979. The Conservative party was the only party (apart from the National Front) which offered uncompromising opposition to the Wales Act; after a century of being considered unacceptable by the people of Wales, it was a pleasant experience for the party to find that the majority of the Welsh electorate agreed with it. With their confidence and credibility rapidly increasing, the Tories of Wales looked forward eagerly to the forthcoming general election. That was held in May 1979, as a direct result of the referendum. The 40 per cent rule had robbed Scotland of the assembly which had, by a hair's breadth, received the support of the majority of those Scots who had voted. In their frustration, the Scottish Nationalist MPs turned against the government, providing the Conservatives with a golden opportunity to encompass its fall. In the vote of confidence on 28 March 1979, the three Plaid Cymru MPs voted with the government. They had made such skilful use of the Labour party's eagerness to ensure their support that the Queen's Speech in November 1978 was studded with concessions to them. They feared that the fall of the government might threaten one of the most important of those concessions – the promise to pay compensation to quarrymen suffering from silicosis. But there was a more fundamental reason for the readiness of the Plaid Cymru MPs to vote for the continuance of the Labour government: to be part of the stratagems of the Tories was unacceptable to them and to the bulk of their supporters.

The results of the general election of 1979 proved that the optimism of the Conservatives had sound foundations. They won eleven of the seats of Wales, the highest number since 1874. Their victory in Brecon and Radnor was not unexpected, but their success in

Montgomeryshire came as a shock, for the constituency had been represented since 1880 by an unbroken succession of Liberal MPs. The result in Anglesey, where a Conservative had last been elected in 1784, was even more startling: there, Elystan Morgan, the Labour candidate, was defeated by Keith Best, a young barrister from Brighton. Henceforth it was possible to travel from Holyhead to Chepstow without leaving a Conservative constituency.

But although the Tory upsurge was remarkable, too much was probably made of it. In 1979, the Conservatives polled 35 per cent of the Welsh vote, only 2 per cent more than in 1959. In terms of the number of seats they won, the electoral system almost always gave an unfair reflection of the support the Conservatives received from the voters of Wales; all that happened in 1979 was that their proportion of the seats was, for once, broadly similar to their proportion of the votes. Yet, with four parties in the field, the ability of the Tories to win the support of over one in three of the voters of Wales attracted considerable attention. It was attributed in part to a change in the nature of the electorate, particularly in places like Anglesey, a constituency which had received a considerable number of incomers, many of whom leaned to Conservatism. The farmers of Wales were becoming increasingly Conservative and it is likely that some Welsh Liberals, on discovering that their party supported dangerously radical ideas such as devolution, changed from being conservative to being Conservative. Throughout the years, the essence of the Conservatism of rural Wales had been the traditional Toryism of the old squires; in 1979, there was something different on offer – the populism of Margaret Thatcher, something far more to the taste of the lower middle class of the Welsh countryside.

These factors (together with a misleading BBC opinion poll) caused the Conservative share of the vote in Carmarthen to increase from 6 to 23 per cent, enabling the Labour candidate to capture the seat from Gwynfor Evans. Plaid Cymru strengthened its hold upon Meirionnydd and Caernarfon, but so great was the contraction in its vote in the south-east that it seemed as if its support was being restricted to the Welsh-speaking areas. The Labour party also retreated to its traditional strongholds; it won twenty-one seats, its worst record since 1935. At Westminster, Margaret Thatcher had a majority of forty-three, and the bulk of the newly elected Conservatives were eager to support her efforts to introduce a new kind of Toryism.

The consequences of the votes of March and May 1979 rapidly became apparent. On the morrow of the referendum it was announced that two thousand jobs would disappear in the Welsh steel industry. The rise in unemployment following the new government's adoption of monetarist policies was so great as to cause that new body, the House of Commons Committee on Welsh Affairs, to express concern in 1980 that lack of work, particularly among the young, would lead to 'serious social disorder'. The referendum brought perplexity and anguish to the nationalists. Some of them saw salvation in Marxism, and the Welsh Socialist Republican Movement was founded in 1980. Socialism also appealed to mainstream nationalists, and in 1981 Plaid Cymru declared that its fundamental aims included the establishment of a Welsh 'decentralist socialist state'. To the members of Adfer – a movement which considered the Welsh-speaking areas to be the only true Wales – the result of the referendum served to confirm their belief that there was little substance to Welshness outside those areas. As the path of constitutional development had been blocked, there were fears that there would be a resort to unconstitutional methods. A holiday home was burned on 12 December 1979 and thirty others were set on fire before the end of the winter; a bombing campaign began in March 1980 and during that year rumours arose concerning a movement bearing the name WAWR (dawn) – the Workers' Army of the Welsh Republic.

Believing that Welsh nationalism was 'in a paralysis of helplessness', the Home Secretary announced in September 1979 that the government would not honour its pledge to establish a Welsh television channel. Vigorous campaigning and severe prison sentences had been needed in order to secure that pledge, and its casual abandonment caused widespread anger. By the beginning of 1980, two thousand members of Plaid Cymru had vowed to go to prison rather than pay for a television licence. In the spring, Gwynfor Evans announced that he would fast unto death if a Welsh channel were not established. He appointed 6 October 1980 as the first day of his fast, and early in September he addressed thousands of his compatriots in meetings at which passions ran high. The government yielded on 17 September – too early according to Gwynfor Evans, who was convinced that a few more weeks of agitation would have placed Plaid Cymru in 'an impregnable position'. The Welsh Fourth Channel (S4C) was launched on 2 November 1982. Welsh speakers were delighted to have the world brought to them through the medium of their mother tongue, and other countries were eager to buy some of the channel's best programmes. There were lengthy discussions of the viewing figures; some of the most popular programmes attracted up to 200,000 viewers, a tiny number compared with those viewing British network channels but one that represented 30 per cent of the potential viewers, a proportion of which any television company could be proud. With the coming of S4C, there was a considerable increase in the number working in the media in Wales, and in Cardiff in particular the culture of the *Cypy* flourished mightily.

The slogan of those involved in the Welsh-language media was *'rhoi'r iaith ar waith'* (putting the language to work), a rather ironic slogan, for in the early 1980s the making of Welsh programmes was virtually the only kind of employment which was expanding. Between 1980 and 1982, there was a decrease of 106,000 in the numbers employed in Wales. The most severe cuts occurred in the steel industry. Steel-making came to an end in Shotton, Ebbw Vale and Cardiff; in 1983, the British Steel Corporation had only 19,199 employees in Wales compared with 65,981 in 1973. With its furnaces using less fuel, there was less demand for coal and the number of miners in Wales decreased from 34,000 in 1973 to 25,000 in 1983. There were contractions in the workforce in other parts of the economy also, and the number of employees in the social services declined in the wake of the cuts in grants to local authorities. Between 1974 and 1979, unemployment hovered around 7 to 8 per cent; it rose to 12.8 per cent in 1980 and to 16 per cent in 1983. Over the following four years it oscillated between 15 and 19 per cent; in 1986, with 173,000 of the insured workers of Wales unemployed, there seemed to be substance to the claim that the nightmare of the 1930s was returning. There were some signs of hope – the coming of the Ford Company to Bridgend, for example, and the substantial investment by Japanese concerns. There was heavy expenditure on work creation schemes, particularly for the young, and the living conditions of the unemployed were by no means as distressing as they had been in the 1930s. Yet it was difficult in the late 1980s to be optimistic about the future of the Welsh economy.

Although the Conservatives lost much of their support in the early 1980s, that did not benefit the Labour party. Under the leadership of Michael Foot, the MP for Ebbw Vale, the party went through a bitter phase of internecine struggle. In 1981, some members of Labour's right wing left the party and founded the Social Democratic party (the SDP). The SDP allied with the Liberals and, because of the unpopularity of the Conservative and Labour parties, a large proportion of the electorate expressed its readiness to support the Alliance – as many as 50 per cent according to an opinion poll in November 1981. Then, from April to June 1982, the Falklands (Malvinas) War was fought, a war which re-established the popularity of the Conservatives and which cost the lives of 950 men, thirty-two members of the Welsh Guards among them. A year later, with the 'Falklands factor' still powerful, and with inflation only a quarter of what it had been four years earlier, the Conservative government felt confident that it would be re-elected. In the general election of June 1983, the Tories won a majority of 188 over Labour; they polled 42.4 per cent of the vote compared with 27.6 for Labour and 25.4 for the Alliance. As the Labour party had made a shambles of the election, it needed a scapegoat; Michael Foot agreed to give up the leadership and in October 1983 Neil Kinnock was elected to succeed him. Kinnock was the fifth Welsh MP to lead the Labour party, but the first to have deep roots in the socialist tradition of the south Wales coalfield.

In the general election of 1983, the voters of Wales were more ready than those in any other part of the kingdom to abandon the Labour party. The Labour share of the Welsh vote was 38 per cent, less than it had been in any general election since 1918. The percentages won by the Conservatives (31) and by Plaid Cymru (8) were lower than in previous elections because the Alliance polled 23 per cent of the votes. The Conservatives benefited from the redistribution of seats, a redistribution which reflected the fact that the population of the old industrial areas was falling and that of the suburbs and the seaside towns was rising. The number of constituencies in Wales was increased from thirty-six to thirty-eight; twenty of them were won by the Labour party, fourteen by the Conservatives, two by Plaid Cymru and two by the Liberals. The Liberals recaptured Montgomery and retained Cardiganshire (enlarged and renamed Ceredigion and Pembroke North). These were the Alliance's only successes in Wales; although three Welsh Labour MPs had joined the SDP, that party failed to win a single seat in Wales. Gwynfor Evans slipped to third place in Carmarthen, but the two Plaid Cymru MPs in Gwynedd were re-elected. The result in Caernarfon was especially noteworthy – 53 per cent of the vote went to Dafydd Wigley, the president of the party since Gwynfor Evans's retirement in 1981. On the basis of the 1983 results, it was claimed that there were three political regions in Wales: 'British Wales' – the eastern constituencies and the southern coastal areas, a region in which Conservatism was strong; 'Welsh Wales' – the southern coalfields, Labour's stronghold; and *y Gymru Gymraeg* (Welsh-speaking Wales) – Gwynedd and most of Dyfed, a region where four parties were struggling for supremacy.

The essentials of this tripartite division were confirmed by the results of the general election of June 1987. The Labour party increased its proportion of the poll to 45 per cent mainly through piling up votes in 'Welsh Wales'. It captured four seats from the Conservative party, but the Conservatives continued to be the leading party in 'British Wales'. The Liberals retained possession of Brecon and Radnor, a seat they had captured in a by-election in 1985; nevertheless, the Alliance was disappointed by its overall performance and was severely harmed by the quarrels which followed. Plaid Cymru had a high vote in *y Gymru Gymraeg* – its members were overjoyed by the party's victory in Anglesey – but elsewhere its support was minimal. With the Labour party once again well in the lead, it could be claimed that the Tory upsurge of 1979 and 1983 was a flash in the pan. Nevertheless, although the Conservative party won six fewer Welsh seats than it had in 1983, its share of the vote declined by a mere 1.5 per cent. Furthermore, it remained the strongest party in those parts of Wales which were increasing in population and prosperity.

As the Conservatives in 1983 were securely in power for another term, they were eager to continue with their policies of strengthening private capitalism and of restricting the role of the state. Central to the government's strategy was the privatization of some nationalized enterprises while ensuring that the rest were managed in accordance with the rules of the market. It had launched these policies in 1980 following huge losses in the steel industry. Ian MacGregor, a Scot who had had a successful career in the United States, was appointed chairman of the British Steel Corporation; his task was to make the industry more efficient, and between 1980 and 1985 the number of the corporation's employees was reduced by 112,000. In 1983, MacGregor was appointed chairman of the National Coal Board. It was announced in the following year that twenty pits would close, and there were fears that twenty thousand jobs would disappear. The south Wales coalfield, which was making a loss of £2,500,000 a week, was particularly vulnerable. Since nationalization in 1947, over two hundred of its pits had been closed and 95,000 jobs had been lost. As the only source of employment vanished, many districts of the coalfield were in a lamentable condition and there were frequent appeals for militant action to save coalfield communities; in 1981, and again in 1982, the majority of the south Wales miners were prepared to strike against the policy of pit closures.

Nevertheless, in March 1984, when Arthur Scargill, the leader of the National Union of Mineworkers, called upon all the members of the Union to withdraw their labour, he received support from only ten of the twenty-eight pits in south Wales. But the strike went ahead; of all the pits of Wales, only Point of Ayr in the upper corner of Clwyd was still producing coal by the end of the spring of 1984. To Scargill, the strike was a battle for the survival of mining communities, but he was also inspired by the hope that the miners could bring down a Conservative government as they had done in 1974. To MacGregor, it was a battle concerning the right of the Coal Board to manage the industry, but he in turn was inspired by the hope of weakening the miners' union. Thus, on the one side and the other, the strike was essentially a political contest. Basic services such as electricity were not disrupted; there were considerable stocks of coal and a substantial amount was imported – evidence of the reluctance of dockers and railwaymen to give their full support to the miners. In consequence, although some members of the cabinet sought a compromise, Thatcher and MacGregor could afford to wait until the miners lost heart. The strike dragged on for almost a year – a period of bitter picketing, protests and severe poverty.

There was a unique character to the strike in the south Wales coalfield. There, only 6 per cent of the miners abandoned the struggle, and at Maerdy, the only pit in the Rhondda, there was not a single strike-breaker. At times, the strike appeared to be a Wales-wide crusade: the miners were assisted by the quarrymen of Gwynedd and the farmers of Ceredigion, and the nationalists – particularly Dafydd Elis Thomas, the president of Plaid Cymru since 1983 – were among the staunchest of their supporters. Throughout the years, the women of the coalfield had played a central role in every industrial dispute, but there had been nothing hitherto to compare with their role in 1984–5; it seemed as if a basic shift was occurring in the consciousness of the women of Wales, a development which had already become apparent in their willingness to assume leadership in the anti-nuclear movement. During the strike, the Welsh leaders on both sides kept the British leaders at arm's length. Emlyn Williams, the president of the south Wales miners, was deeply suspicious of the tactics and personality of Scargill, and Philip Weekes, the director of the Coal Board in south Wales, believed that MacGregor's behaviour was disastrous. 'It's a pity,' said Weekes, 'that he didn't stay in America.' The movement which brought the strike to an end originated in the south Wales coalfield; that coalfield also provided the most remarkable image of the long struggle – the miners of Maerdy on 5 March 1985 marching in procession to their doomed pit with their banners flying and their band playing before the break of day. Despite the suffering and the solidarity, the strike furthered the very process it was intended to avert. Within eighteen months of its end, twelve of the pits of the south Wales coalfield, Maerdy among them, had been closed; by October 1986 there were only sixteen pits and 13,000 miners in south Wales, figures which were to drop to seven and 4,000 by the end of the decade.

At the end of the 1980s, with more Welshmen working in banks than in pits, one of the most remarkable chapters in the history of the Welsh had closed. By then, there was unmistakable evidence that other chapters in that history had also come to an end. With up to half of them supporting parties of the centre and the right, it was no longer possible to portray the Welsh as a people especially loyal to radicalism and socialism. With only one in eight of them attending a place of worship, they could not be lauded as a people who showed marked respect for spiritual values. There seemed every sign that the age of full employment had come to an end and that agriculture was in crisis. With the University in severe difficulties and with secondary education facing increasing criticism, confidence in the future of the educational institutions of Wales, institutions which had once been regarded with such pride, was gravely weakened. The assumption that the nation was moving step by step towards self-government had been undermined. As the national language of Wales was under siege in its former strongholds and as the communities of its industrial valleys were languishing, there was cause for concern regarding the future of its culture, in both its Welsh and its Anglo-Welsh aspects. In many localities, the influx of newcomers was so great that the bulk of their inhabitants had no consciousness of any kind of Welshness. Did these developments mean that the Welsh nation itself was facing extinction? This was the fear that caused Welsh patriots in the late 1980s to feel a shiver of hopelessness.

Yet the prediction that Wales and its attributes are coming to an end is by no means new. Tacitus, in about AD 100, mentions the extermination of the Ordovices; the entry for 682 in *Brut y Tywysogyon* states that the Brythons had lost the crown of the kingdom; another entry in 823 asserts that the English had taken possession of much of the country; Rhygyfarch, in about 1094, lamented as he contemplated the imminent extinction of his people; it was noted in 1247 that Wales had been 'pulled down to nothing', and in 1282 it was claimed that the whole of Wales had been 'thrown to the ground'; the scholars of the Renaissance feared that the identity of the Welsh would soon disappear; William Richards asserted in 1682 that the Welsh language was on the verge of death; Thomas Jones in 1688 expressed his concern that the Welsh would be deleted from history; many of the Welsh leaders of the nineteenth century believed that Welshness would not survive the century; a commentator in *The Welsh Outlook* in 1916 forecast that the Welsh language would be extinct by 1950. Yet the Welsh survived all the crises of their history, remaking their nation time and time again. As Wales seems to experience recurrent death and rebirth, it would almost seem as if the history of the nation is an endless journey back and fore between the mortuary and the delivery room. Thus, those who proclaim its funeral are singularly unwise, for tenacity is the hallmark of this ancient nation.

Once again, in the closing years of the twentieth century, there are signs of rebirth: the resolution and the successes of the language movement; the institutional growth which has resulted from the establishment of the Welsh Office; the increasing awareness of the significance of the working-class struggles of the Welsh; the new spirit arising among the women of Wales; the reawakening in Scotland and the liveliness of Catalonia and others of the non-historic nations of Europe; the growth in intellectual ideas supportive of the identity of those nations. These are the factors which permit the patriot and historian Robin Okey to declare boldly that 'time is on our side'. 'When *was* Wales?' asks the most provocative of our historians. This book was written in the faith and confidence that the nation in its fullness is yet to be.

Index